PENGUIN BOOKS

THE PENGUIN STEPHEN LEACOCK

Stephen Leacock was born in Hampshire in 1869. When he was six years old his family emigrated to Canada, where the eleven children, of whom Stephen was the third, were brought up in isolation and poverty as their father tried unsuccessfully to make a living as a farmer. However, a legacy left to their mother paid for the education of the three eldest sons at Upper Canada College, Toronto. Stephen Leacock then qualified as a teacher and for eight years held a post at his former school. In 1900 he married Beatrix Hamilton, who bore him one son. In 1901 he was appointed lecturer at McGill University, Montreal, and from 1908 until his retirement in 1936 he was head of the Department of Economics and Political Science there. His first writing dealt with economics and Canadian history, but in 1910 the publication of *Literary Lapses* showed that his real genius was as a humorist. He continued to write in this genre for the rest of his life, and his quick sense of the ridiculous found expression in over thirty books, of which the best known are *Sunshine Sketches of a Little Town* (1912) and *Arcadian Adventures with the Idle Rich* (1914). He also lectured widely and with great success both in Canada and abroad.

Stephen Leacock died in 1944.

14th April 1985.

To dear Anne,

With love & Best Wishes

for your Birthday

Suzanne & Brody

THE PENGUIN
STEPHEN LEACOCK

Selected and Introduced by
ROBERTSON DAVIES

PENGUIN BOOKS

Penguin Books Ltd, Harmondsworth, Middlesex, England
Viking Penguin Inc., 40 West 23rd Street, New York, New York 10010, U.S.A.
Penguin Books Australia Ltd, Ringwood, Victoria, Australia
Penguin Books Canada Ltd, 2801 John Street, Markham, Ontario, Canada L3R 1B4
Penguin Books (N.Z.) Ltd, 182–190 Wairau Road, Auckland 10, New Zealand

First published 1981
Reprinted 1982, 1985

Typeset, printed and bound in Great Britain by
Hazell Watson & Viney Limited,
Member of the BPCC Group,
Aylesbury, Bucks
Set in VIP Times

Table of Contents

Introduction

As I introduce Stephen Leacock to you it is important for me to remember that he was a Victorian. Important for me, because during my childhood and early life he was a vivid presence in Canada, whose books were still appearing, to be snatched at once by an addicted audience, so that he does not appear to me to be remote. Important for you, because unless you were at least eighteen in 1944, when he died, he must seem a figure belonging to the past. As he tells us in the autobiographical fragment which is included in this collection, he was born in 1869, which was exactly the middle year of Queen Victoria's reign. Must we regard him therefore as a mid-Victorian? Not quite, but we must understand that his world is not quite our world, and that even though he did not begin to regard himself as a writer until 1910, when he was forty-one, some of his important ideas about life had been acquired many years earlier. This must make a difference to the way in which a new, young generation of readers approaches him.

He grew up in a happier time, when people were not so nervous about enjoying themselves as they seem to be today. I don't believe that it was really a simpler time, and as you read *The Boy I Left Behind Me* you will find that he knew what hard luck was and had to struggle to make his way in the world. Two things were against him; poverty, of which he had an extensive experience, and his temperament, which made it hard for him to work in a subordinate position, and to take seriously things which he thought foolish. When at last he became a professor at McGill, and was undisputed king in his lectureroom, he felt himself free, and when in middle age he became one of the most popular comic writers in the English-speaking world, he found himself at last on Easy Street.

At one time and another I have written a good deal about Leacock, and I believe I was the first to press the point that as a comic writer he was not necessarily a man of continuously sunny, carefree temperament. He had plenty of hard luck, and the loss of his adored wife was a blow from which he never fully recovered; furthermore, his somewhat imperious temper made it hard for him to endure contradiction and reverses. He had, in fact, the temperament of a humorist, and they are by no means unfailingly sunny people. A favourite story, which he told again and again, was of the man who went to his doctor complaining of melancholia. 'My dear sir,' said the medical man, 'you need taking out of yourself. You must go to the theatre, and see the wonderful new clown, Grimaldi. His jokes and his antics, his infectious high spirits, will lift you right out of yourself.' 'Doctor,' said the man in the patient's chair. '*I* am Grimaldi!'

Out of my great sorrows I write my little songs, said Heine. I do not think we are far amiss in supposing that Leacock wrote some of his funny pieces (which is what he called them) out of his sadness and frustration. Also, it must be said, out of his quick temper.

How did he write them? As a literary artist Leacock was formed in part by the publishing conditions of his time. He wrote during an era when magazines were numerous; many of them were devoted solely to humour, and virtually all of them included some humorous writing in every issue. The men who now write funny scripts for television comedians wrote for the magazines then, and in terms of the times, their work was well paid. The leaders in this field – and Leacock was perhaps at the top of the list – gathered their year's work together and published a collection from time to time, usually offered for sale before Christmas.

Leacock seems to have liked this manner of working, for he made few attempts to write at length. *Sunshine Sketches of a Little Town* (1912) was his only attempt at anything resembling a novel, and fine as it is, he never tried again. As a writer he was a man for the hundred yard dash, not a marathoner. He seized upon a single comic idea, exploited it in a few hundred words, and sometimes the result, as in *My Financial Career* or *A, B and C*, is perfection in its kind. Writing, as he liked to say, is simple; you just jot down amusing ideas as they occur to you. And then he would add – the jotting presents no problem; it is the occurring that is difficult.

If this occurring was difficult for Leacock, he never let it show. It is the ease, the charm, the geniality of his work that wins us, and preserves his writing when virtually everything else that used to appear in those comic magazines has disappeared. Why is this so?

Undoubtedly because he was something that the ordinary breed of comic writers is not, which is to say a man whose observation of the world was wide-ranging, possessed of an extensive education, classically based. He made fun of the classics (the ancient classics, that is to say, for his reading in English was spotty and uncritical) but he never forgot them, and his sense of a large world in which the minds and passions of men are unchanging but ever-renewing, is classical. *The Spiritual*

Outlook of Mr Doomer, for instance, was hilarious when it appeared in 1915, and it is still funny; but if it could be translated into Latin and whisked back in a Time Machine to the Rome of the Caesars, I think those ancient Romans would think it yet another funny thing that happened on the way to the Forum. Leacock's mind was not solely of the world of *Puck*, or *Judge*, or *Punch*; its roots went deeper.

There is no parade of learning in his work, however. He wrote before the time when the universities had taken their icy grip on writing of all sorts, and it was a time when jeering at universities was popular. No revealing study of Leacock can neglect the language in which he wrote. It seems to be the language of common speech, for it moves easily and frightens nobody. But if you analyse it – and the best way is by trying to re-write some of his things in language of your own – you will discover what a subtle and powerful instrument it is. Here is the simplicity of art, not the simplicity of someone who knows no complexity. The complexity of Leacock is in his point of view, not in his mode of expression.

His point of view – this is where we must move carefully, because without being a disagreeable or bitter man, Leacock was by temperament a satirist and an ironist, and satire and irony are edged tools; like the surgeon's knife they must cut deep, and cut out, but they must not kill. As a public lecturer Leacock gave the impression of a man delighting in his own fun. A lady who once said to him, 'You certainly seem to enjoy your own jokes,' received the unexpected but unquestionably true answer, 'Madam, they are as new to me as they are to you.' But what has been preserved for us in print, although we may enjoy it simply as fun of a high order, often has a hint of criticism in it, of a way of looking at society that is not likely to make society pleased with itself. The *Sunshine Sketches* are a case in point; they are very funny, but is there a character in them with whom you would willingly associate yourself? This is not the humour of Dickens, whom Leacock so greatly admired; it is the humour of the classical mind, when the classical mind takes a humorous course. It is an observing, cool, apparently easy-going mind, but it is a mind that misses nothing, and is deluded by nothing. It is very much an adult mind.

What did Leacock think of himself? People who knew him told me he was somewhat vain, but what appears to be vanity to ungifted observers may sometimes be the exasperation of a quicker, more inclusive, stronger intellect. Would he have been surprised to learn that yet another collection of his work was appearing now? I do not think so. Read that final passage in *Three Score and Ten*, in which he speaks of 'something done that may give one hope to say, *non omnis moriar*

(I shall not altogether die).' I think Leacock knew how good he was, and how high his head was raised above the other popular humorists of his time. He knew he had something to say to you, dear reader, and he knew that humour, which foolish people value so lightly, is precious stuff.

That is why you hold this book in your hand. *Non omnis moriar*. No indeed, dear Professor Leacock.

5 February 1981　　　　　　　　　　　　　ROBERTSON DAVIES

One
My Financial Career

When I go into a bank I get rattled. The clerks rattle me; the wickets rattle me; the sight of the money rattles me; everything rattles me.

The moment I cross the threshold of a bank and attempt to transact business there, I become an irresponsible idiot.

I knew this beforehand, but my salary had been raised to fifty dollars a month and I felt that the bank was the only place for it.

So I shambled in and looked timidly round at the clerks. I had an idea that a person about to open an account must needs consult the manager.

I went up to a wicket marked 'Accountant'. The accountant was a tall, cool devil. The very sight of him rattled me. My voice was sepulchral.

'Can I see the manager?' I said, and added solemnly, 'alone.' I don't know why I said 'alone.'

'Certainly,' said the accountant, and fetched him.

The manager was a grave, calm man. I held my fifty-six dollars clutched in a crumpled ball in my pocket. 'Are you the manager?' I said. God knows I didn't doubt it.

'Yes,' he said.

'Can I see you,' I asked, 'alone?' I didn't want to say 'alone' again, but without it the thing seemed self-evident.

The manager looked at me in some alarm. He felt that I had an awful secret to reveal.

'Come in here,' he said, and led the way to a private room. He turned the key in the lock.

'We are safe from interruption here,' he said: 'sit down.'

We both sat down and looked at each other. I found no voice to speak.

'You are one of Pinkerton's men, I presume,' he said.

He had gathered from my mysterious manner that I was a detective. I knew what he was thinking, and it made me worse.

'No, not from Pinkerton's,' I said, seeming to imply that I came from a rival agency.

'To tell the truth,' I went on, as if I had been prompted to lie about it, 'I am not a detective at all. I have come to open an account. I intend to keep all my money in this bank.'

11

The manager looked relieved but still serious: he concluded now that I was a son of Baron Rothschild or a young Gould.

'A large account, I suppose,' he said.

'Fairly large,' I whispered. 'I propose to deposit fifty-six dollars now and fifty dollars a month regularly.'

The manager got up and opened the door. He called to the accountant.

'Mr Montgomery,' he said unkindly loud, 'this gentleman is opening an account, he will deposit fifty-six dollars. Good morning.'

I rose.

A big iron door stood open at the side of the room.

'Good morning,' I said, and stepped into the safe.

'Come out,' said the manager coldly, and showed me the other way.

I went up to the accountant's wicket and poked the ball of money at him with a quick convulsive movement as if I were doing a conjuring trick.

My face was ghastly pale.

'Here,' I said, 'deposit it.' The tone of the words seemed to mean, 'Let us do this painful thing while the fit is on us.'

He took the money and gave it to another clerk.

He made me write the sum on a slip and sign my name in a book. I no longer knew what I was doing. The bank swam before my eyes.

'Is it deposited?' I asked in a hollow, vibrating voice.

'It is,' said the accountant.

'Then I want to draw a cheque.'

My idea was to draw out six dollars of it for present use. Someone gave me a cheque-book through a wicket and someone else began telling me how to write it out. The people in the bank had the impression that I was an invalid millionaire. I wrote something on the cheque and thrust it in at the clerk. He looked at it.

'What! are you drawing it all out again?' he asked in surprise. Then I realized that I had written fifty-six instead of six. I was too far gone to reason now. I had a feeling it was impossible to explain the thing. All the clerks had stopped writing to look at me.

Reckless with misery, I made a plunge.

'Yes, the whole thing.'

'You withdraw your money from the bank?'

'Every cent of it.'

'Are you not going to deposit any more?' said the clerk, astonished.

'Never.'

An idiot hope struck me that they might think something had insulted me while I was writing the cheque and that I had changed my mind. I made a wretched attempt to look like a man with a fearfully quick temper.

The clerk prepared to pay the money.

'How will you have it?' he said.

'What?'

'How will you have it?'

'Oh' – I caught his meaning and answered without even trying to think – 'in fifties.'

He gave me a fifty-dollar bill.

'And the six?' he asked dryly.

'In sixes,' I said.

He gave it me and I rushed out.

As the big door swung behind me I caught the echo of a roar of laughter that went up to the ceiling of the bank. Since then I bank no more. I keep my money in cash in my trousers pocket and my savings in silver dollars in a sock.

Boarding-house Geometry

DEFINITIONS AND AXIOMS

All boarding-houses are the same boarding-house.

Boarders in the same boarding-house and on the same flat are equal to one another.

A single room is that which has no parts and no magnitude.

The landlady of a boarding-house is a parallelogram – that is, an oblong angular figure, which cannot be described, but which is equal to anything.

A wrangle is the disinclination for each other of two boarders that meet together but are not in the same line.

All the other rooms being taken, a single room is said to be a double room.

POSTULATES AND PROPOSITIONS

A pie may be produced any number of times.

The landlady can be reduced to her lowest terms by a series of propositions.

A bee line may be made from any boarding-house to any other boarding-house.

The clothes of a boarding-house bed, though produced ever so far both ways, will not meet.

Any two meals at a boarding-house are together less than two square meals.

If from the opposite ends of a boarding-house a line be drawn passing through all rooms in turn, then the stovepipe which warms the boarders will lie within that line.

On the same bill and on the same side of it there should not be two charges for the same thing.

If there be two boarders on the same flat, and the amount of side of the one be equal to the amount of side of the other, each to each, and the wrangle between one boarder and the landlady be equal to the wrangle between the landlady and the other, then shall the weekly bills of the two boarders be equal also, each to each.

For if not, let one bill be the greater.

Then the other bill is less than it might have been – which is absurd.

The Awful Fate of Melpomenus Jones

Some people – not you nor I, because we are so awfully self-possessed – but some people, find great difficulty in saying good-bye when making a call or spending the evening. As the moment draws near when the visitor feels that he is fairly entitled to go away he rises and says abruptly, 'Well, I think I . . .' Then the people say, 'Oh, must you go now? Surely it's early yet!' and a pitiful struggle ensues.

I think the saddest case of this kind of thing that I ever knew was that of my poor friend Melpomenus Jones, a curate – such a dear young man, and only twenty-three! He simply couldn't get away from people. He was too modest to tell a lie, and too religious to wish to appear rude. Now it happened that he went to call on some friends of his on the very first afternoon of his summer vacation. The next six weeks were entirely his own – absolutely nothing to do. He chatted awhile, drank two cups of tea, then braced himself for the effort and said suddenly:

'Well, I think I . . .'

But the lady of the house said, 'Oh, no! Mr Jones, can't you really stay a little longer?'

Jones was always truthful. 'Oh, yes,' he said, 'of course, I – er – can stay.'

'Then please don't go.'

He stayed. He drank eleven cups of tea. Night was falling. He rose again.

'Well now,' he said shyly, 'I think I really . . .'

'You must go?' said the lady politely. 'I thought perhaps you could have stayed to dinner . . .'

'Oh well, so I could, you know,' Jones said, 'if . . .'

'Then please stay, I'm sure my husband will be delighted.'

'All right,' he said feebly, 'I'll stay,' and he sank back into his chair, just full of tea, and miserable.

Papa came home. They had dinner. All through the meal Jones sat planning to leave at eight-thirty. All the family wondered whether Mr Jones was stupid and sulky, or only stupid.

After dinner mamma undertook to 'draw him out,' and showed him photographs. She showed him all the family museum, several gross of them – photos of papa's uncle and his wife, and mamma's brother and his little boy, an awfully interesting photo of papa's uncle's friend in his Bengal uniform, an awfully well-taken photo of papa's grandfather's partner's dog, and an awfully wicked one of papa as the devil for a fancy-dress ball.

At eight-thirty Jones had examined seventy-one photographs. There were about sixty-nine more that he hadn't. Jones rose.

'I must say good night now,' he pleaded.

'Say good night!' they said, 'why it's only half-past eight! Have you anything to do?'

'Nothing,' he admitted, and muttered something about staying six weeks, and then laughed miserably.

Just then it turned out that the favourite child of the family, such a dear little romp, had hidden Mr Jones's hat; so papa said that he must stay, and invited him to a pipe and a chat. Papa had the pipe and gave Jones the chat, and still he stayed. Every moment he meant to take the plunge, but couldn't. Then papa began to get very tired of Jones, and fidgeted and finally said, with jocular irony, that Jones had better stay all night, they could give him a shake-down. Jones mistook his meaning and thanked him with tears in his eyes, and papa put Jones to bed in the spare room and cursed him heartily.

After breakfast next day, papa went off to his work in the city, and left Jones playing with the baby, broken-hearted. His nerve was utterly gone.

He was meaning to leave all day, but the thing had got on his mind and he simply couldn't. When papa came home in the evening he was surprised and chagrined to find Jones still there. He thought to jockey him out with a jest, and said he thought he'd have to charge him for his board, he! he! The unhappy young man stared wildly for a moment, then wrung papa's hand, paid him a month's board in advance, and broke down and sobbed like a child.

In the days that followed he was moody and unapproachable. He lived, of course, entirely in the drawing-room, and the lack of air and exercise began to tell sadly on his health. He passed his time in drinking tea and looking at the photographs. He would stand for hours gazing at the photographs of papa's uncle's friend in his Bengal uniform – talking to it, sometimes swearing bitterly at it. His mind was visibly failing.

At length the crash came. They carried him upstairs in a raging delirium of fever. The illness that followed was terrible. He recognized no one, not even papa's uncle's friend in his Bengal uniform. At times he would start up from his bed and shriek, 'Well, I think I . . .' and then fall back upon the pillow with a horrible laugh. Then, again, he would leap up and cry, 'Another cup of tea and more photographs! More photographs! Har! Har!'

At length after a month of agony, on the last day of his vacation, he passed away. They say that when the last moment came, he sat up in bed with a beautiful smile of confidence playing upon his face, and said, 'Well – the angels are calling me; I'm afraid I really must go now. Good afternoon.'

And the rushing of his spirit from its prison-house was as rapid as a hunted cat passing over a garden fence.

A, B, and C

THE HUMAN ELEMENT IN MATHEMATICS

The student of arithmetic who has mastered the first four rules of his art, and successfully striven with money sums and fractions, finds himself confronted by an unbroken expanse of questions known as problems. These are short stories of adventure and industry with the end omitted, and, though betraying a strong family resemblance, are not without a certain element of romance.

The characters in the plot of a problem are three people called A, B, and C. The form of the question is generally of this sort:

'A, B, and C do a certain piece of work. A can do as much work in one hour as B in two, or C in four. Find how long they work at it.'

Or thus:

'A, B, and C are employed to dig a ditch. A can dig as much in one hour as B can dig in two, and B can dig twice as fast as C. Find how long, etc. etc.'

Or after this wise:

'A lays a wager that he can walk faster than B or C. A can walk half as fast again as B, and C is only an indifferent walker. Find how far, and so forth.'

The occupations of A, B, and C are many and varied. In the older arithmetics they contented themselves with doing 'a certain piece of work.' This statement of the case, however, was found too sly and mysterious, or possibly lacking in romantic charm. It became the fashion to define the job more clearly and to set them at walking matches, ditch-digging, regattas, and piling cord-wood. At times they became commercial and entered into partnership, having with their old mystery a 'certain' capital. Above all they revel in motion. When they tire of walking matches, A rides on horseback, or borrows a bicycle and competes with his weaker-minded associates on foot. Now they race on locomotives; now they row; or again they become historical and engage stagecoaches; or at times they are aquatic and swim. If their occupation is actual work they prefer to pump water into cisterns, two of which leak through holes in the bottom and one of which is water-tight. A, of course, has the good one; he also takes the bicycle, and the best locomotive, and the right of swimming with the current. Whatever they do they put money on it, being all three sports. A always wins.

In the early chapters of arithmetic, their identity is concealed under the names John, William and Henry, and they wrangle over the division of marbles. In algebra they are often called X, Y, Z. But these are only their Christian names, and they are really the same people.

Now to one who has followed the history of these men through countless pages of problems, watched them in their leisure hours dallying with cord-wood, and seen their panting sides heave in the full frenzy of filling a cistern with a leak in it, they become something more than mere symbols. They appear as creatures of flesh and blood, living men with their own passions, ambitions, and aspirations like the rest of us. Let us view them in turn. A is a full-blooded blustering fellow, of energetic temperament, hot-headed and strongwilled. It is he who proposes everything, challenges B to work, makes the bets, and bends the others to his will. He is a man of great physical strength and phenomenal endurance. He has been known to walk forty-eight hours at a stretch, and to pump ninety-six. His life is arduous and full of peril. A mistake in the working of a sum may keep him digging a fortnight without sleep. A repeating decimal in the answer might kill him.

B is a quiet, easy-going fellow, afraid of A and bullied by him, but very gentle and brotherly to little C, the weakling. He is quite in A's power, having lost all his money in bets.

Poor C is an undersized, frail man, with a plaintive face. Constant walking, digging, and pumping has broken his health and ruined his nervous system. His joyless life has driven him to drink and smoke more than is good for him, and his hand often shakes as he digs ditches. He has not the strength to work as the others can; in fact, as Hamlin Smith has said, 'A can do more work in one hour than C in four.'

The first time that ever I saw these men was one evening after a regatta. They had all been rowing in it, and it had transpired that A could row as much in one hour as B in two, or C in four, B and C had come in dead fagged and C was coughing badly. 'Never mind, old fellow,' I heard B say, 'I'll fix you up on the sofa and get you some hot tea.' Just then A came blustering in and shouted, 'I say, you fellows, Hamlin Smith has shown me three cisterns in his garden and he says we can pump them until tomorrow night. I bet I can beat you both. Come on. You can pump in your rowing things, you know. Your cistern leaks a little, I think, C.' I heard B growl that it was a dirty shame and that C was used up now, but they went, and presently I could tell from the sound of the water that A was pumping four times as fast as C.

For years after that I used to see them constantly about town and always busy. I never heard of any of them eating or sleeping. Then, owing to a long absence from home, I lost sight of them. On my return I was surprised to no longer find A, B and C at their accustomed tasks; on inquiry I heard that work in this line was now done by M, N and O, and that some people were employing for algebraical jobs four foreigners called Alpha, Beta, Gamma, and Delta.

Now it chanced one day that I stumbled upon old D, in the little garden in front of his cottage, hoeing in the sun. D is an aged labouring man who used occasionally to be called in to help A, B and C. 'Did I know 'em, sir?' he answered, 'why, I knowed 'em ever since they was little fellows in brackets. Master A, he were a fine lad, sir, though I always said, give me Master B for kind-heartedness-like. Many's the job as we've been on together, sir, though I never did no racing nor aught of

that, but just the plain labour, as you might say. I'm getting a bit too old
and stiff for it nowadays, sir – just scratch about in the garden here and
grow a bit of a logarithm, or raise a common denominator or two. But
Mr Euclid he use me still for them propositions, he do.'

From the garrulous old man I learned the melancholy end of my former
acquaintances. Soon after I left town, he told me, C had been taken ill.
It seems that A and B had been rowing on the river for a wager, and C
had been running on the bank and then sat in a draught. Of course the
bank had refused the draught and C was taken ill. A and B came home
and found C lying helpless in bed. A shook him roughly and said, 'Get up,
C, we're going to pile wood.' C looked so worn and pitiful that B said,
'Look here, A, I won't stand this, he isn't fit to pile wood tonight.' C
smiled feebly and said, 'Perhaps I might pile a little if I sat up in bed.'
Then B, thoroughly alarmed, said, 'See here, A, I'm going to fetch a
doctor; he's dying.' A flared up and answered, 'You've no money to fetch
a doctor.' 'I'll reduce him to his lowest terms,' B said firmly, 'that'll fetch
him.' C's life might even then have been saved but they made a mistake
about the medicine. It stood at the head of the bed on a bracket, and the
nurse accidentally removed it from the bracket without changing the
sign. After the fatal blunder C seems to have sunk rapidly. On the
evening of the next day, as the shadows deepened in the little room, it
was clear to all that the end was near. I think that even A was affected at
the last as he stood with bowed head, aimlessly offering to bet with the
doctor on C's laboured breathing. 'A,' whispered C, 'I think I'm going
fast.' 'How fast do you think you'll go, old man?' murmured A. 'I don't
know,' said C, 'But I'm going at any rate.' – the end came soon after that.
C rallied for a moment and asked for a certain piece of work that he had
left downstairs. A put it in his arms and he expired. As his soul sped
heavenward, A watched its flight with melancholy admiration. B burst
into a passionate flood of tears and sobbed, 'Put away his little cistern
and the rowing clothes he used to wear, I feel as if I could hardly ever dig
again.' – The funeral was plain and unostentatious. It differed in nothing
from the ordinary, except that out of deference to sporting men and
mathematicians, A engaged two hearses. Both vehicles started at the
same time, B driving the one which bore the sable parallelopiped
containing the last remains of his ill-fated friend. A on the box of the
empty hearse generously consented to a handicap of a hundred yards,
but arrived first at the cemetery by driving four times as fast as B. (Find
the distance to the cemetery.) As the sarcophagus was lowered, the grave
was surrounded by the broken figures of the first book of Euclid. – It was
noticed that after the death of C, A became a changed man. He lost
interest in racing with B, and dug but languidly. He finally gave up his

work and settled down to live on the interest of his bets. – B never recovered from the shock of C's death; his grief preyed upon his intellect and it became deranged. He grew moody and spoke only in monosyllables. His disease became rapidly aggravated, and he presently spoke only in words whose spelling was regular and which presented no difficulty to the beginner. Realizing his precarious condition he voluntarily submitted to be incarcerated in an asylum, where he abjured mathematics and devoted himself to writing the History of the Swiss Family Robinson in words of one syllable.

Two

Gertrude the Governess: or Simple Seventeen

Synopsis of Previous Chapters:
There are no Previous Chapters.

It was a wild and stormy night on the West Coast of Scotland. This, however, is immaterial to the present story, as the scene is not laid in the West of Scotland. For the matter of that the weather was just as bad on the East Coast of Ireland.

But the scene of this narrative is laid in the South of England and takes place in and around Knotacentinum Towers (pronounced as if written Nosham Taws), the seat of Lord Knotacent (pronounced as if written Nosh).

But it is not necessary to pronounce either of these names in reading them.

Nosham Taws was a typical English home. The main part of the house was an Elizabethan structure of warm red brick, while the elder portion, of which the Earl was inordinately proud, still showed the outlines of a Norman Keep, to which had been added a Lancastrian Jail and a Plantagenet Orphan Asylum. From the house in all directions stretched magnificent woodland and park with oaks and elms of immemorial antiquity, while nearer the house stood raspberry bushes and geranium plants which had been set out by the Crusaders.

About the grand old mansion the air was loud with the chirping of thrushes, the cawing of partridges and the clear sweet note of the rook, while deer, antelope, and other quadrupeds strutted about the lawn so tame as to eat off the sun-dial. In fact, the place was a regular menagerie.

From the house downwards through the park stretched a beautiful broad avenue laid out by Henry VII.

Lord Nosh stood upon the hearthrug of the library. Trained diplomat and statesman as he was, his stern aristocratic face was upside down with fury.

'Boy,' he said, 'you shall marry this girl or I disinherit you. You are no son of mine.'

Young Lord Ronald, erect before him, flung back a glance as defiant as his own.

21

'I defy you,' he said. 'Henceforth you are no father of mine. I will get another. I will marry none but a woman I can love. This girl that we have never seen –'

'Fool,' said the Earl, 'would you throw aside our estate and name of a thousand years? The girl, I am told, is beautiful; her aunt is willing; they are French; pah! they understand such things in France.'

'But your reason –'

'I give no reason,' said the Earl. 'Listen, Ronald, I give you one month. For that time you remain here. If at the end of it you refuse me, I cut you off with a shilling.'

Lord Ronald said nothing; he flung himself from the room, flung himself upon his horse and rode madly off in all directions.

As the door of the library closed upon Ronald the Earl sank into a chair. His face changed. It was no longer that of the haughty nobleman, but of the hunted criminal. 'He must marry the girl,' he muttered. 'Soon she will know all. Tutchemoff has escaped from Siberia. He knows and will tell. The whole of the mines pass to her, this property with it, and I – but enough.' He rose, walked to the sideboard, drained a dipper full of gin and bitters, and became again a high-bred English gentleman.

It was at this moment that a high dogcart, driven by a groom in the livery of Earl Nosh, might have been seen entering the avenue of Nosham Taws. Beside him sat a young girl, scarce more than a child, in fact not nearly so big as the groom.

The apple-pie hat which she wore, surmounted with black willow plumes, concealed from view a face so face-like in its appearance as to be positively facial.

It was – need we say it – Gertrude the Governess, who was this day to enter upon her duties at Nosham Taws.

At the same time that the dogcart entered the avenue at one end there might have been seen riding down it from the other a tall young man, whose long, aristocratic face proclaimed his birth and who was mounted upon a horse with a face even longer than his own.

And who is this tall young man who draws nearer to Gertrude with every revolution of the horse? Ah, who, indeed? Ah, who, who? I wonder if any of my readers could guess that this was none other than Lord Ronald.

The two were destined to meet. Nearer and nearer they came. And then still nearer. Then for one brief moment they met. As they passed, Gertrude raised her head and directed towards the young nobleman two eyes so eye-like in their expression as to be absolutely circular, while Lord Ronald directed towards the occupant of the dogcart a gaze so gaze-like that nothing but a gazelle, or a gas-pipe, could have emulated its intensity.

Was this the dawn of love? Wait and see. Do not spoil the story.

Let us speak of Gertrude. Gertrude DeMongmorenci McFiggin had known neither father nor mother. They had both died years before she was born. Of her mother she knew nothing, save that she was French, was extremely beautiful, and that all her ancestors and even her business acquaintances had perished in the Revolution.

Yet Gertrude cherished the memory of her parents. On her breast the girl wore a locket in which was enshrined a miniature of her mother, while down her neck inside at the back hung a daguerreotype of her father. She carried a portrait of her grandmother up her sleeve and had pictures of her cousins tucked inside her boot, while beneath her – but enough, quite enough.

Of her father Gertrude knew even less. That he was a high-born English gentleman who had lived as a wanderer in many lands, this was all she knew. His only legacy to Gertrude had been a Russian grammar, a Roumanian phrase-book, a theodolite, and a work on mining engineering.

From her earliest infancy Gertrude had been brought up by her aunt. Her aunt had carefully instructed her in Christian principles. She had also taught her Mohammedanism to make sure.

When Gertrude was seventeen her aunt had died of hydrophobia.

The circumstances were mysterious. There had called upon her that day a strange bearded man in the costume of the Russians. After he had left, Gertrude had found her aunt in a syncope from which she passed into an apostrophe and never recovered.

To avoid scandal it was called hydrophobia. Gertrude was thus thrown upon the world. What to do? That was the problem that confronted her.

It was while musing one day upon her fate that Gertrude's eye was struck with an advertisement.

'Wanted a governess; must possess a knowledge of French, Italian, Russian, and Roumanian, Music, and Mining Engineering. Salary £1, 4 shillings and 4 pence half-penny per annum. Apply between half-past eleven and twenty-five minutes to twelve at No. 4l A Decimal Six, Belgravia Terrace. The Countess of Nosh.'

Gertrude was a girl of great natural quickness of apprehension, and she had not pondered over this announcement more than half an hour before she was struck with the extraordinary coincidence between the list of items desired and the things that she herself knew.

She duly presented herself at Belgravia Terrace before the Countess, who advanced to meet her with a charm which at once placed the girl at her ease.

'You are proficient in French?' she asked.

'*Oh, oui*,' said Gertrude modestly.

'And Italian?' continued the Countess.

'*Oh, si,*' said Gertrude.

'And German?' said the Countess in delight.

'*Ah, ja,*' said Gertrude.

'And Russian?'

'*Yaw.*'

'And Roumanian?'

'*Jep.*'

Amazed at the girl's extraordinary proficiency in modern languages, the Countess looked at her narrowly. Where had she seen those lineaments before? She passed her hand over her brow in thought, and spit on the floor, but no, the face baffled her.

'Enough,' she said, 'I engage you on the spot; tomorrow you go down to Nosham Taws and begin teaching the children. I must add that in addition you will be expected to aid the Earl with his Russian correspondence. He has large mining interests at Tschminsk.'

Tschminsk! why did the simple word reverberate upon Gertrude's ears? Why? Because it was the name written in her father's hand on the title page of his book on mining. What mystery was here?

It was on the following day that Gertrude had driven up the avenue.

She descended from the dogcart, passed through a phalanx of liveried servants drawn up seven-deep, to each of whom she gave a sovereign as she passed and entered Nosham Taws.

'Welcome,' said the Countess, as she aided Gertrude to carry her trunk upstairs.

The girl presently descended and was ushered into the library, where she was presented to the Earl. As soon as the Earl's eye fell upon the face of the new governess he started visibly. Where had he seen those lineaments? Where was it? At the races? or the theatre? on a bus? No. Some subtler thread of memory was stirring in his mind. He strode hastily to the sideboard, drained a dipper and a half of brandy, and became again the perfect English gentleman.

While Gertrude has gone to the nursery to make the acquaintance of the two tiny golden-haired children who are to be her charges, let us say something here of the Earl and his son.

Lord Nosh was the perfect type of the English nobleman and statesman. The years that he had spent in the diplomatic service at Constantinople, St Petersburg, and Salt Lake City had given to him a peculiar finesse and noblesse, while his long residence at St Helena, Pitcairn Island, and Hamilton, Ontario, had rendered him impervious to external impressions. As deputy paymaster of the militia of the country he had seen something of the sterner side of the military life, while his hereditary office of Groom of the Sunday Breeches had brought him into direct contact with Royalty itself. His passion for outdoor sports endeared him to his tenants. A keen sportsman, he excelled in foxhunting, doghunting, pig-killing, bat-catching and the pastimes of his class.

In this latter respect Lord Ronald took after his father. From the start the lad had shown the greatest promise. At Eton he had made a splendid showing at battledore and shuttlecock, and at Cambridge had been first in his class at needlework. Already his name was whispered in connection with the All England ping-pong championship, a triumph which would undoubtedly carry with it a seat in Parliament.

Thus was Gertrude the Governess installed at Nosham Taws.

The days and the weeks sped past.

The simple charm of the beautiful orphan girl attracted all hearts. Her two little pupils became her slaves. 'Me loves oo,' the little Rasehellfrida would say, leaning her golden head in Gertrude's lap. Even the servants loved her. The head gardener would bring a bouquet of beautiful roses to her room before she was up, the second gardener a bunch of early cauliflowers, the third a spray of late asparagus, and even the tenth and eleventh a sprig of mangel-wurzel or an armful of hay. Her room was full of gardeners all the time, while at evening the aged butler, touched at the friendless girl's loneliness, would tap softly at her door to bring her a rye whisky and seltzer or a box of Pittsburg Stogies. Even the dumb creatures seemed to admire her in their own dumb way. The dumb rooks settled on her shoulder and every dumb dog around the place followed her.

And Ronald! ah, Ronald! Yes, indeed! They had met. They had spoken.

'What a dull morning,' Gertrude had said. '*Quel triste matin! Was für ein allerverdamnter Tag!*'

'Beastly,' Ronald had answered.

'Beastly!!' The word rang in Gertrude's ears all day.

After that they were constantly together. They played tennis and ping-pong in the day, and in the evening, in accordance with the stiff routine of the place, they sat down with the Earl and Countess to twenty-five-cent poker, and later still they sat together on the verandah and watched the moon sweeping in great circles around the horizon.

It was not long before Gertrude realized that Lord Ronald felt towards her a warmer feeling than that of mere ping-pong. At times in her presence he would fall, especially after dinner, into a fit of profound subtraction.

Once at night, when Gertrude withdrew to her chamber and before seeking her pillow, prepared to retire as a preliminary to disrobing – in other words, before going to bed, she flung wide the casement (opened the window) and perceived (saw) the face of Lord Ronald. He was sitting on a thorn bush beneath her, and his upturned face wore an expression of agonized pallor.

Meantime the days passed. Life at the Taws moved in the ordinary routine of a great English household. At 7 a gong sounded for rising, at 8 a horn blew for breakfast, at 8.30 a whistle sounded for prayers, at 1 a flag was run up at half-mast for lunch, at 4 a gun was fired for afternoon tea, at 9 a first bell sounded for dressing, at 9.15 a second bell for going on dressing, while at 9.30 a rocket was sent up to indicate that dinner was ready. At midnight dinner was over, and at 1 a.m. the tolling of a bell summoned the domestics to evening prayers.

Meanwhile the month allotted by the Earl to Lord Ronald was passing away. It was already July 15, then within a day or two it was July 17, and, almost immediately afterwards, July 18.

At times the Earl, in passing Ronald in the hall, would say sternly, 'Remember, boy, your consent, or I disinherit you.'

And what were the Earl's thoughts of Gertrude? Here was the one drop of bitterness in the girl's cup of happiness. For some reason that she could not divine the Earl showed signs of marked antipathy.

Once as she passed the door of the library he threw a bootjack at her. On another occasion at lunch alone with her he struck her savagely across the face with a sausage.

It was her duty to translate to the Earl his Russian correspondence. She sought in it in vain for the mystery. One day a Russian telegram was handed to the Earl. Gertrude translated it to him aloud.

'Tutchemoff went to the woman. She is dead.'

On hearing this the Earl became livid with fury, in fact this was the day that he struck her with the sausage.

Then one day while the Earl was absent on a bat hunt, Gertrude, who was turning over his correspondence, with that sweet feminine instinct of interest that rose superior to ill-treatment, suddenly found the key to the mystery.

Lord Nosh was not the rightful owner of the Taws. His distant cousin of the older line, the true heir, had died in a Russian prison to which the machinations of the Earl, while Ambassador at Tschminsk, had consigned him. The daughter of this cousin was the true owner of Nosham Taws.

The family story, save only that the documents before her withheld the name of the rightful heir, lay bare to Gertrude's eye.

Strange is the heart of a woman. Did Gertrude turn from the Earl with spurning? No. Her own sad fate had taught her sympathy.

Yet still the mystery remained! Why did the Earl start perceptibly each time that he looked into her face? Sometimes he started as much as four centimetres, so that one could distinctly see him do it. On such occasions he would hastily drain a dipper of rum and vichy water and become again the correct English gentleman.

The denouement came swiftly. Gertrude never forgot it.

It was the night of the great ball at Nosham Taws. The whole neighbourhood was invited. How Gertrude's heart had beat with anticipation, and with what trepidation she had overhauled her scant wardrobe in order to appear not unworthy in Lord Ronald's eyes. Her resources were poor indeed, yet the inborn genius for dress that she inherited from her French mother stood her in good stead. She twined a single rose in her hair and contrived herself a dress out of a few old newspapers and the inside of an umbrella that would have graced a court. Round her waist she bound a single braid of bagstring, while a piece of old lace that had been her mother's was suspended to her ear by a thread.

Gertrude was the cynosure of all eyes. Floating to the strains of the music she presented a picture of bright girlish innocence that no one could see undisenraptured.

The ball was at its height. It was away up!

Ronald stood with Gertrude in the shrubbery. They looked into one another's eyes.

'Gertrude,' he said, 'I love you.'

Simple words, and yet they thrilled every fibre in the girl's costume.

'Ronald!' she said, and cast herself about his neck.

At this moment the Earl appeared standing beside them in the moonlight. His stern face was distorted with indignation.

'So!' he said, turning to Ronald, 'it appears that you have chosen!'

'I have,' said Ronald with hauteur.

'You prefer to marry this penniless girl rather than the heiress I have selected for you.'

Gertrude looked from father to son in amazement.

'Yes,' said Ronald.

'Be it so,' said the Earl draining a dipper of gin which he carried, and resuming his calm. 'Then I disinherit you. Leave this place, and never return to it.'

'Come, Gertrude,' said Ronald tenderly, 'let us flee together.'

Gertrude stood before them. The rose had fallen from her head. The lace had fallen from her ear and the bagstring had come undone from her waist. Her newspapers were crumpled beyond recognition. But dishevelled and illegible as she was, she was still mistress of herself.

'Never,' she said firmly. 'Ronald, you shall never make this sacrifice for me.' Then to the Earl, in tones of ice, 'There is a pride, sir, as great even as yours. The daughter of Metschnikoff McFiggin need crave a boon from no one.'

With that she hauled from her bosom the daguerreotype of her father and pressed it to her lips.

The Earl started as if shot. 'That name!' he cried, 'that face! that photograph! stop!'

There! There is no need to finish; my readers have long since divined it. Gertrude was the heiress.

The lovers fell into one another's arms. The Earl's proud face relaxed. 'God bless you,' he said. The Countess and the guests came pouring out upon the lawn. The breaking day illuminated a scene of gay congratulations.

Gertrude and Ronald were wed. Their happiness was complete. Need we say more? Yes, only this. The Earl was killed in the hunting-field a few days after. The Countess was struck by lightning. The two children fell down a well. Thus the happiness of Gertrude and Ronald was complete.

Guido the Gimlet of Ghent:
A Romance of Chivalry

It was in the flood-tide of chivalry. Knighthood was in the pod.

The sun was slowly setting in the east, rising and falling occasionally as it subsided, and illuminating with its dying beams the towers of the grim castle of Buggensberg.

Isolde the Slender stood upon an embattled turret of the castle. Her arms were outstretched to the empty air, and her face, upturned as if in colloquy with heaven, was distraught with yearning.

Anon she murmured, 'Guido' – and bewhiles a deep sigh rent her breast.

Sylph-like and ethereal in her beauty, she scarcely seemed to breathe.

In fact she hardly did.

Willowy and slender in form, she was as graceful as a meridian of longitude. Her body seemed almost too frail for motion, while her features were of a mould so delicate as to preclude all thought of intellectual operation.

She was begirt with a flowing kirtle of deep blue, bebound with a belt bebuckled with a silvern clasp, while about her waist a stomacher of point lace ended in the ruffled farthingale at her throat. On her head she bore a sugar-loaf hat shaped like an extinguisher and pointing backward at an angle of 45 degrees.

'Guido,' she murmured, 'Guido.'

And erstwhile she would wring her hands as one distraught and mutter, 'He cometh not.'

The sun sank and night fell, enwrapping in shadow the frowning castle of Buggensberg, and the ancient city of Ghent at its foot. And as the darkness gathered, the windows of the castle shone out with fiery red, for it was Yuletide, and it was wassail all in the Great Hall of the castle, and this night the Margrave of Buggensberg made him a feast, and celebrated the betrothal of Isolde, his daughter, with Tancred the Tenspot.

And to the feast he had bidden all his liege lords and vassals – Hubert the Husky, Edward the Earwig, Rollo the Rumbottle, and many others.

In the meantime the Lady Isolde stood upon the battlements and mourned for the absent Guido.

The love of Guido and Isolde was of that pure and almost divine type, found only in the middle ages.

They had never seen one another. Guido had never seen Isolde, Isolde had never seen Guido. They had never heard one another speak. They had never been together. They did not know one another.

Yet they loved.

Their love had sprung into being suddenly and romantically, with all the mystic charm which is love's greatest happiness.

Years before, Guido had seen the name of Isolde the Slender painted on a fence.

He had turned pale, fallen into a swoon and started at once for Jerusalem.

On the very same day Isolde in passing through the streets of Ghent had seen the coat of arms of Guido hanging on a clothes line.

She had fallen back into the arms of her tire-women more dead than alive.

Since that day they had loved.

Isolde would wander forth from the castle at earliest morn, with the name of Guido on her lips. She told his name to the trees. She whispered it to the flowers. She breathed it to the birds. Quite of lot of them knew it. At times she would ride her palfrey along the sands of the sea and call 'Guido' to the waves! At other times she would tell it to the grass or even to a stick of cordwood or a ton of coal.

Guido and Isolde, though they had never met, cherished each the features of the other. Beneath his coat of mail Guido carried a miniature of Isolde, carven on ivory. He had found it at the bottom of the castle crag, between the castle and the old town of Ghent at its foot.

How did he know that it was Isolde?

There was no need for him to ask.

His *heart* had spoken.

The eye of love cannot be deceived.

And Isolde? She, too, cherished beneath her stomacher a miniature of Guido the Gimlet. She had it of a travelling chapman in whose pack she had discovered it, and had paid its price in pearls. How had she known that he it was, that is, that it was he? Because of the Coat of Arms emblazoned beneath the miniature. The same heraldic design that had first shaken her to the heart. Sleeping or waking it was ever before her eyes: A lion, proper, quartered in a field of gules, and a dog, improper, three-quarters in a field of buckwheat.

And if the love of Isolde burned thus purely for Guido, the love of Guido burned for Isolde with a flame no less pure.

No sooner had love entered Guido's heart than he had determined to do some great feat of emprise or adventure, some high achievement of derring-do which should make him worthy to woo her.

He placed himself under a vow that he would eat nothing, save only food, and drink nothing, save only liquor, till such season as he should have performed his feat.

For this cause he had at once set out for Jerusalem to kill a Saracen for her. He killed one, quite a large one. Still under his vow, he set out again at once to the very confines of Pannonia determined to kill a Turk for her. From Pannonia he passed into the Highlands of Britain, where he killed her a Caledonian.

Every year and every month Guido performed for Isolde some new achievement of emprise.

And in the meantime Isolde waited.

It was not that suitors were lacking. Isolde the Slender had suitors in plenty ready to do her lightest hest.

Feats of arms were done daily for her sake. To win her love suitors were willing to vow themselves to perdition. For Isolde's sake, Otto the Otter had cast himself into the sea, Conrad the Coconut had hurled himself from the highest battlement of the castle head first into the mud. Hugo the Hopeless had hanged himself by the waistband to a hickory tree and had refused all efforts to dislodge him. For her sake Sickfried the Susceptible had swallowed sulphuric acid.

But Isolde the Slender was heedless of the court thus paid to her.

In vain her stepmother, Agatha the Angular, urged her to marry. In vain her father, the Margrave of Buggensberg, commanded her to choose the one or the other of the suitors.

Her heart remained unswervingly true to the Gimlet.

From time to time love tokens passed between the lovers. From Jerusalem Guido had sent to her a stick with a notch in it to signify his undying constancy. From Pannonia he sent a piece of board, and from Venetia about two feet of scantling. All these Isolde treasured. At night they lay beneath her pillow.

Then, after years of wandering, Guido had determined to crown his love with a final achievement for Isolde's sake.

It was his design to return to Ghent, to scale by night the castle cliff and to prove his love for Isolde by killing her father for her, casting her stepmother from the battlements, burning the castle, and carrying her away.

This design he was now hastening to put into execution. Attended by fifty trusty followers under the lead of Carlo the Corkscrew and Beowulf the Bradawl, he had made his way to Ghent. Under cover of night they had reached the foot of the castle cliff; and now, on their hands and knees in single file, they were crawling round and round the spiral path that led up to the gate of the fortress. At six of the clock they had spiralled once. At seven of the clock they had reappeared at the second round, and as the feast in the hall reached its height, they reappeared on the fourth lap.

Guido the Gimlet was in the lead. His coat of mail was hidden beneath a parti-coloured cloak and he bore in his hand a horn.

By arrangement he was to penetrate into the castle by the postern gate in disguise, steal from the Margrave by artifice the key of the great door, and then by a blast of his horn summon his followers to the assault. Alas! there was need for haste, for at this very Yuletide, on this very night, the Margrave, wearied of Isolde's resistance, had determined to bestow her hand upon Tancred the Tenspot.

It was wassail all in the great hall. The huge Margrave, seated at the head of the board, drained flagon after flagon of wine, and pledged deep the health of Tancred the Tenspot, who sat plumed and armoured beside him.

Great was the merriment of the Margrave, for beside him, crouched upon the floor, was a new jester, whom the seneschal had just admitted by the postern gate, and the novelty of whose jests made the huge sides of the Margrave shake and shake again.

'Odds Bodikins!' he roared, 'but the tale is as rare as it is new! and so the wagoner said to the Pilgrim that sith he had asked him to put him off the wagon at that town, put him off he must, albeit it was but the small of the night – by St Pancras! whence hath the fellow so novel a tale? –

nay, tell it me but once more, haply I may remember it' – and the Baron fell back in a perfect paroxysm of merriment.

As he fell back, Guido – for the disguised jester was none other than he, that is, than him – sprang forward and seized from the girdle of the Margrave the key of the great door that dangled at his waist.

Then, casting aside the jester's cloak and cap, he rose to his full height, standing in his coat of mail.

In one hand he brandished the double-headed mace of the Crusader, and in the other a horn.

The guests sprang to their feet, their hands upon their daggers.

'Guido the Gimlet!' they cried.

'Hold,' said Guido, 'I have you in my power!!'

Then placing the horn to his lips and drawing a deep breath, he blew with his utmost force.

And then again he blew – blew like anything.

Not a sound came.

The horn wouldn't blow!

'Seize him!' cried the Baron.

'Stop,' said Guido, 'I claim the laws of chivalry. I am here to seek the Lady Isolde, betrothed by you to Tancred. Let me fight Tancred in single combat, man to man.'

A shout of approbation gave consent.

The combat that followed was terrific.

First Guido, raising his mace high in the air with both hands, brought it down with terrible force on Tancred's mailed head. Then Guido stood still, and Tancred raising his mace in the air brought it down upon Guido's head. Then Tancred stood still and turned his back, and Guido, swinging his mace sideways, gave him a terrific blow from behind, mid way, right centre. Tancred returned the blow. Then Tancred knelt down on his hands and knees and Guido brought the mace down on his back. It was a sheer contest of skill and agility. For a time the issue was doubtful. Then Tancred's armour began to bend, his blows weakened, he fell prone. Guido pressed his advantage and hammered him out as flat as a sardine can. Then placing his foot on Tancred's chest, he lowered his vizor and looked around about him.

At this second there was a resounding shriek.

Isolde the Slender, alarmed by the sounds of the blows, precipitated herself into the room.

For a moment the lovers looked into each other's faces.

Then with their countenances distraught with agony they fell swooning in different directions.

There had been a mistake!

Guido was not Guido, and Isolde was not Isolde. They were wrong about the miniatures. Each of them was a picture of somebody else.

Torrents of remorse flooded over the lovers' hearts.

Isolde thought of the unhappy Tancred, hammered out as flat as a picture-card and hopelessly spoilt; of Conrad the Coconut head first in the mud, and Sickfried the Susceptible coiled up with agonies of sulphuric acid.

Guido thought of the dead Saracens and the slaughtered Turks.

And all for nothing!

The guerdon of their love had proved vain. Each of them was not what the other had thought. So it is ever with the loves of this world, and herein is the medieval allegory of this tale.

The hearts of the two lovers broke together.

They expired.

Meantime Carlo the Corkscrew and Beowulf the Bradawl, and their forty followers, were hustling down the spirals as fast as they could crawl, hind end uppermost.

Hannah of the Highlands:
or The Laird of Loch Aucherlocherty

> *Sair maun ye greet, but hoot awa!*
> *There's muckle yet, love isna' a' –*
> *Nae more ye'll see, howe'er ye whine*
> *The bonnie breeks of Auld Lang Syne!*

The simple words rang out fresh and sweet upon the morning air.

It was Hannah of the Highlands. She was gathering lobsters in the burn that ran through the Glen.

The scene about her was typically Highland. Wild hills rose on both sides of the burn to a height of seventy-five feet, covered with a dense Highland forest that stretched a hundred yards in either direction. At the foot of the burn a beautiful Scotch loch lay in the hollow of the hills. Beyond it again, through the gap of the hills, was the sea. Through the Glen, and close beside the burn where Hannah stood, wound the road that rose again to follow the cliffs along the shore.

The tourists in the Highlands will find no more beautiful spot than the Glen of Aucherlocherty.

Nor is there any spot which can more justly claim to be historic ground.

It was here in the Glen that Bonnie Prince Charlie had lain and hidden after the defeat of Culloden. Almost in the same spot the great boulder still stands behind which the Bruce had lain hidden after Bannockburn; while behind a number of lesser stones the Covenanters had concealed themselves during the height of the Stuart persecution.

Through the Glen Montrose had passed on his fateful ride to Killiecrankie; while at the lower end of it the rock was still pointed out behind which William Wallace had paused to change his breeches while flying from the wrath of Rob Roy.

Grim memories such as these gave character to the spot.

Indeed, most of the great events of Scotch history had taken place in the Glen, while the little loch had been the scene of some of the most stirring naval combats in the history of the Grampian Hills.

But there was little in the scene which lay so peaceful on this April morning to recall the sanguinary history of the Glen. Its sides at present were covered with a thick growth of gorse, elderberry, egg-plants, and ghillie flower, while the woods about it were loud with the voice of the throstle, the linnet, the magpie, the jackdaw, and other song-birds of the Highlands.

It was a gloriously beautiful Scotch morning. The rain fell softly and quietly, bringing dampness and moisture, and almost a sense of wetness to the soft moss underfoot. Grey mists flew hither and thither, carrying with them an invigorating rawness that had almost a feeling of dampness.

It is the memory of such a morning that draws a tear from the eye of Scotchmen after years of exile. The Scotch heart, reader, can be moved to its depths by the sight of a raindrop or the sound of a wet rag.

And meantime Hannah, the beautiful Highland girl, was singing. The fresh young voice rose high above the rain. Even the birds seemed to pause to listen, and as they listened to the simple words of the Gaelic folk song, fell off the bough with a thud on the grass.

The Highland girl made a beautiful picture as she stood.

Her bare feet were in the burn, the rippling water of which laved her ankles. The lobsters played about her feet, or clung affectionately to her toes, as if loath to leave the water and be gathered in the folds of her blue apron.

It was a scene to charm the heart of a Burne-Jones, or an Alma Tadema, or of anybody fond of lobsters.

The girl's golden hair flowed widely behind her, gathered in a single braid with a piece of stovepipe wire.

'Will you sell me one of your lobsters?'

Hannah looked up. There, standing in the burn a few yards above her, was the vision of a young man.

The beautiful Highland girl gazed at him fascinated.

He seemed a higher order of being.

He carried a fishing-rod and basket in his hand. He was dressed in a salmon-fishing costume of an English gentleman. Salmon-fishing boots reached to his thighs, while above them he wore a fishing-jacket fastened loosely with a fishing-belt about his waist. He wore a small fishing-cap on his head.

There were no fish in his basket.

He drew near to the Highland girl.

Hannah knew as she looked at him that it must be Ian McWhinus, the new laird.

At sight she loved him.

'Ye're sair welcome,' she said, as she handed to the young man the finest of her lobsters.

He put it in his basket.

Then he felt in the pocket of his jacket and brought out a sixpenny piece.

'You must let me pay for it,' he said.

Hannah took the sixpence and held it a moment, flushing with true Highland pride.

'I'll no be selling the fush for money,' she said.

Something in the girl's speech went straight to the young man's heart. He handed her half a crown. Whistling lightly, he strode off up the side of the burn. Hannah stood gazing after him spell bound. She was aroused from her reverie by an angry voice calling her name.

'Hannah, Hannah,' cried the voice, 'come away ben; are ye daft, lass, that ye stand there keeking at a McWhinus?'

Then Hannah realized what she had done.

She had spoken with a McWhinus, a thing that no McShamus had done for a hundred and fifty years. For nearly two centuries the McShamuses and the McWhinuses, albeit both dwellers in the Glen, had been torn asunder by one of those painful divisions by which the life of the Scotch people is broken into fragments.

It had arisen out of a point of spiritual belief.

It had been six generations agone at a Highland banquet, in the days when the unrestrained temper of the time gave way to wild orgies, during which the theological discussions raged with unrestrained fury. Shamus McShamus, an embittered Calvinist, half crazed perhaps with liquor, had maintained that damnation could be achieved only by faith. Whimper

McWhinus had held that damnation could be achieved also by good works. Inflamed with drink, McShamus had struck McWhinus across the temple with an oatcake and killed him. McShamus had been brought to trial. Although defended by some of the most skilled lawyers of Aucherlocherty, he had been acquitted. On the very night of his acquittal, Whangus McWhinus, the son of the murdered man, had lain in wait for Shamus McShamus, in the hollow of the Glen road where it rises to the cliff, and had shot him through the bagpipes. Since then the feud had raged with unquenched bitterness for a century and a half.

With each generation the difference between the two families became more acute. They differed on every possible point. They wore different tartans, sat under different ministers, drank different brands of whisky, and upheld different doctrines in regard to eternal punishment.

To add to the feud the McWhinuses had grown rich, while the McShamuses had become poor.

At least once in every generation a McWhinus or a McShamus had been shot, and always at the turn of the Glen road where it rose to the edge of the cliff. Finally, two generations gone, the McWhinuses had been raised to sudden wealth by the discovery of a coal mine on their land. To show their contempt for the McShamuses they had left the Glen to live in America. The McShamuses, to show their contempt for the McWhinuses, had remained in the Glen. The feud was kept alive in their memory.

And now the descendant of the McWhinuses had come back, and bought out the property of the Laird of Aucherlocherty beside the Glen. Ian McWhinus knew nothing of the feud. Reared in another atmosphere, the traditions of Scotland had no meaning for him. He had entirely degenerated. To him the tartan had become only a piece of coloured cloth. He wore a kilt as a masquerade costume for a Hallowe'en dance, and when it rained he put on a raincoat. He was no longer Scotch. More than that, he had married a beautiful American wife, a talcum-powder blonde with a dough face and the exquisite rotundity of the packing-house district of the Middle-West. Ian McWhinus was her slave. For her sake he had bought the lobster from Hannah. For her sake, too, he had scrutinized closely the beautiful Highland girl, for his wife was anxious to bring back a Scotch housemaid with her to Chicago.

And meantime Hannah, with the rapture of a new love in her heart, followed her father, Oyster McOyster McShamus, to the cottage. Oyster McOyster, even in advancing age, was a fine specimen of Scotch manhood. Ninety-seven years of age, he was approaching the time when many of his countrymen begin to show the ravages of time. But he bore himself straight as a lath, while his tall stature and his native Highland costume accentuated the fine outline of his form. This costume consisted of a black velvet beetle-shell jacket, which extended from the shoulder halfway down the back, and was continued in a short kilt of the tartan of the McShamuses, which extended from the waist halfway to the thigh. The costume reappeared again after an interval in the form of rolled golf stockings, which extended halfway up to the knee, while on his feet a pair of half-shoes were buckled halfway up with a Highland clasp. On his head halfway between the ear and the upper superficies of the skull he wore half a Scotch cap, from which a tall rhinoceros feather extended halfway into the air.

A pair of bagpipes were beneath his arm, from which, as he walked, he blew those deep and plaintive sounds which have done much to imprint upon the characters of those who hear them a melancholy and resigned despair.

At the door of the cottage he turned and faced his daughter.

'What said Ian McWhinus to you i' the burnside?' he said fiercely.

' 'Twas nae muckle,' said Hannah, and she added, for the truth was ever more to her than her father's wrath, 'he gi'ed me a saxpence for a fush.'

'Siller!' shrieked the Highlander. 'Siller from a McWhinus!'

Hannah handed him the sixpence. Oyster McOyster dashed it fiercely on the ground, then picking it up he dashed it with full force against the wall of the cottage. Then, seizing it again he dashed it angrily into the pocket of his kilt.

They entered the cottage.

Hannah had never seen her father's face so dour as it looked that night.

Their home seemed changed.

Hannah and her mother and father sat down that night in silence to their simple meal of oatmeal porridge and Scotch whisky. In the evening the mother sat to her spinning. Busily she plied her work, for it was a task of love. Her eldest born, Jamie, was away at college at Edinburgh, preparing for the ministry. His graduation day was approaching, and Jamie's mother was spinning him a pair of breeches against the day. The breeches were to be a surprise. Already they were shaping that way. Oyster McShamus sat reading the Old Testament in silence, while Hannah looked into the peat fire and thought of the beautiful young Laird. Only once the Highlander spoke.

'The McWhinus is back,' he said, and his glance turned towards the old flint-lock musket on the wall. That night Hannah dreamed of the feud, of the Glen and the burn, of love, of lobsters, and of the Laird of Loch Aucherlocherty. And when she rose in the morning there was a wistful look in her eyes, and there came no song from her throat.

The days passed.

Each day the beautiful Highland girl saw the young Laird, though her father knew it not.

In the mornings she would see him as he came fishing to the burn. At times he wore his fishing-suit, at other times he had on a knickerbocker suit of shepherd's plaid with a domino pattern *négligé* shirt. For his sake the beautiful Highland girl made herself more beautiful still. Each morning she would twine a Scotch thistle in her hair, and pin a spray of burdock at her heart.

And at times he spoke to her. How Hannah treasured his words. Once, catching sight of her father in the distance, he had asked her who was the old sardine in the petticoats, and the girl had answered gladly that it was her father for, as a fisherman's daughter, she was proud to have her father mistaken for a sardine.

At another time he had asked her if she was handy about the work of the house. How Hannah's heart had beat at the question. She made up her mind to spin him a pair of breeches like the ones now finished for her brother Jamie.

And every evening as the sun set Hannah would watch in secret from the window of the cottage waiting for the young Laird to come past in his motor car, down the Glen road to the sea. Always he would slacken the car at the sharp turn at the top of the cliff. For six generations no McWhinus had passed that spot after nightfall with his life. But Ian McWhinus knew nothing of the feud.

At times Oyster McOyster would see him pass, and standing at the roadside would call down Gaelic curses on his head.

Once, when her father was from home, Hannah had stood on the roadside, and Ian had stopped the machine and had taken her with him in the car for a ride. Hannah, her heart beating with delight, had listened to him as he explained how the car was worked. Had her father known that she had sat thus beside a McWhinus, he would have slain her where she sat.

The tragedy of Hannah's love ran swiftly to its close.

Each day she met the young Laird at the burn.

Each day she gave him the finest of her lobsters. She wore a new thistle every day.

And every night, in secret as her mother slept, she span a new concentric section of his breeches.

And the young Laird, when he went home, said to the talcum blonde, that the Highland fisher-girl was not half such a damn fool as she seemed.

Then came the fateful afternoon.

He stood beside her at the burn.

'Hannah,' he said, as he bent towards her, 'I want to take you to America.'

Hannah had fallen fainting in his arms.

Ian propped her against a tree, and went home.

An hour later, when Hannah entered her home, her father was standing behind the fireplace. He was staring fixedly into the fire, with the flint-lock musket in his hands. There was the old dour look of the feud upon his face, and there were muttered curses on his lips. His wife Ellen clung to his arm and vainly sought to quiet him.

'Curse him,' he muttered, 'I'll e'en kill him the night as he passes in his deil machine.'

Then Hannah knew that Oyster McShamus had seen her with Ian beside the burn. She turned and fled from the house. Straight up the road she ran towards the manor house of Aucherlocherty to warn Ian. To save him from her father's wrath, that was her one thought. Night gathered about the Highland girl as she ran. The rain clouds and the gathering storm hung low with fitful lightning overhead. She still ran on. About her was the rolling of the thunder and the angry roaring of the swollen burn. Then the storm broke upon the darkness with all the fury of the Highland gale. The sky was rent with the fierce play of the elements. Yet on Hannah ran. Again and again the lightning hit her, but she ran on still. She fell over the stones, tripped and stumbled in the ruts, butted into the hedges, cannoned off against the stone walls. But she never stopped. She went quicker and quicker. The storm was awful. Lightning, fire, flame, and thunder were all about her. Trees were falling, hurdles were flying, birds were being struck by lightning. Dogs, sheep, and even cattle were hurled through the air.

She reached the manor house, and stood a moment at the door. The storm had lulled, the rain ceased, and for a brief moment there was quiet. The light was streaming from the windows of the house. Hannah paused. Suddenly her heart misgave her. Her quick ear had caught the sound of a woman's voice within. She approached the window and looked in. Then, as if rooted to the spot, the Highland girl gazed and listened at the pane.

Ian lay upon a sofa. The *négligé* dressing-gown that he wore enhanced the pallid beauty of his face. Beside him sat the talcum-powder blonde. She was feeding him with chocolates. Hannah understood. Ian had trifled with her love. He had bought her lobsters to win her heart, only to cast it aside.

Hannah turned from the window. She plucked the thistle from her throat and flung it on the ground. Then, as she turned her eye, she caught sight of the motor standing in the shed.

'The deil machine!' she muttered, while the wild light of Highland frenzy gathered in her eye; then, as she rushed to it and tore the tarpaulin from off it, 'Ye'll no be wanting of a mark the night, Oyster McShamus,' she cried.

A moment later, the motor, with Hannah at the wheel, was thundering down the road to the Glen. The power was on to the full, and the demented girl clung tight to the steering-gear as the machine rocked and thundered down the descent. The storm was raging again, and the thunder mingled with the roar of the machine as it coursed madly towards the sea. The great eye of the motor blazed in front. The lurid light of it flashed a second on the trees and the burn as it passed, and flashed blinding on the eyes of Oyster as he stood erect on the cliff-side below, musket in hand, and faced the blazing apparition that charged upon him with the old Highland blood surging in his veins.

It was all over in a moment – a blinding flash of lightning, the report of a musket, a great peal of thunder, and the motor bearing the devoted girl hurled headlong over the cliff.

They found her there in the morning. She lay on her side motionless, half buried in the sand, upturned towards the blue Highland sky, serene now after the passing of the storm. Quiet and still she lay. The sea birds seemed to pause in their flight to look down on her. The little group of Scotch people that had gathered stood and gazed at her with reverential awe. They made no attempt to put her together. It would have been useless. Her gasoline tubes were twisted and bent, her tank burst, her sprockets broken from their sides, and her steering-gear an utter wreck. The motor would never run again.

After a time they roused themselves from their grief and looked for Hannah. They found her. She lay among the sand and seaweed, her fair hair soaked in gasoline. Then they looked about for Oyster McShamus. Him, too, they found, lying half buried in the grass and soaked in whisky. Then they looked about for Ellen. They found her lying across the door of the cottage half buried in Jamie's breeches.

Then they gathered them up. Life was not extinct. They chafed their hands. They rubbed their feet. They put hot bricks upon their stomachs. They poured hot whisky down their throats. That brought them to.

Of course.

It always does.

They all lived.

But the feud was done for. That was the end of it. Hannah had put it to the bad.

Three
Homer and Humbug

The following discussion is of course only of interest to scholars. But as the public schools returns show that in the United States there are now over a million coloured scholars alone, the appeal is wide enough.

I do not mind confessing that for a long time past I have been very sceptical about the classics. I was myself trained as a classical scholar. It seemed the only thing to do with me. I acquired such a singular facility in handling Latin and Greek that I could take a page of either of them, distinguish which it was by merely glancing at it, and with the help of a dictionary and a pair of compasses whip off a translation of it in less than three hours.

But I never got any pleasure from it. I lied about it. At first, perhaps, I lied through vanity. Any coloured scholar will understand the feeling. Later on I lied through habit; later still because after all the classics were all that I had, and so I valued them. I have seen thus a deceived dog value a pup with a broken leg and a pauper child nurse a dead doll with the sawdust out of it. So I nursed my dead Homer and my broken Demosthenes, though I knew in my heart that there was more sawdust in the stomach of one modern author than in the whole lot of them. Observe, I am which it is that has it full of it.

So, as I say, I began to lie about the classics. I said to people who knew no Greek that there was a sublimity, a majesty about Homer which they could never hope to grasp. I said it was like the sound of the sea beating against the granite cliffs of the Ionian Esophagus, or words to that effect. As for the truth of it, I might as well have said that it was like the sound of a rum distillery running a nightshift on half-time. At any rate this is what I said about Homer, and when I spoke of Pindar – the dainty grace of his strophes – and Aristophanes – the delicious sallies of his wit, sally after sally, each sally explained in a note calling it a sally – I managed to suffuse my face with an animation which made it almost beautiful.

I admitted, of course, that Virgil, in spite of his genius, had a hardness and a cold glitter which resembled rather the brilliance of a cut diamond

41

than the soft grace of a flower. Certainly, I admitted this: the mere admission of it would knock the breath out of anyone who was arguing.

From such talks my friends went away sad. The conclusion was too cruel. It had all the cold logic of a Syllogism (like that almost brutal form of argument so much admired in the Paraphernalia of Socrates.) For if:

> Virgil and Homer and Pindar had all this
>   grace, and pith and these sallies, –
> And if I read Virgil and Homer and Pindar,
> And if they only read Mrs Wharton and
>   Mrs Humphry Ward,
> Then where were they?

So continued lying brought its own reward in the sense of superiority, and I lied more.

When I reflect that I have openly expressed regret, as a personal matter, even in the presence of women, for the missing books of Tacitus, and the entire loss of the Abracadabra of Polyphemus of Syracuse, I can find no words in which to beg for pardon. In reality I was just as much worried over the loss of the ichthyosaurus. More, indeed: I'd like to have seen it; but if the books Tacitus lost were like those he didn't, I wouldn't.

I believe all scholars lie like this. An ancient friend of mine, a clergyman, tells me that in Hesiod he finds a peculiar grace that he doesn't find elsewhere. He's a liar. That's all. Another man, in politics and in the legislature, tells me that every night before going to bed he reads over a page or two of Thucydides to keep his mind fresh. Either he never goes to bed or he's a liar. Doubly so: no one could read Greek at that frantic rate: and anyway his mind isn't fresh. How could it be? he's in the legislature. I don't object to this man talking freely of the classics, but he ought to keep it for the voters. My own opinion is that before he goes to bed he takes whisky: why call it Thucydides?

I know there are solid arguments advanced in favour of the classics. I often hear them from my colleagues. My friend the professor of Greek tells me that he truly believes the classics have made him what he is. This is a very grave statement, if well founded. Indeed, I have heard the same argument from a great many Latin and Greek scholars. They all claim, with some heat, that Latin and Greek have practically made them what they are. This damaging charge against the classics should not be too readily accepted. In my opinion some of these men would have been what they are, no matter what they were.

Be this as it may, I for my part bitterly regret the lies I have told about my appreciation of Latin and Greek literature. I am anxious to do what I can to set things right. I am therefore engaged on, indeed have nearly completed, a work which will enable all readers to judge the matter for themselves. What I have done is a translation of all the great classics, not in the usual literal way but on a design that brings them into harmony with modern life. I will explain what I mean in a minute.

The translation is intended to be within reach of everybody. It is so designed that the entire set of volumes can go on a shelf twenty-seven feet long, or even longer. The first edition will be an édition de luxe, bound in vellum or perhaps in buckskin, and sold at five hundred dollars. It will be limited to five hundred copies, and, of course, sold only to the feeble-minded. The next edition will be the Literary Edition, sold to artists, authors, actors and contractors. After that will come the Boarding House Edition, bound in board and paid for in the same way.

My plan is so to transpose the classical writers as to give, not the literal translation word for word, but what is really the modern equivalent. Let me give an odd sample or two to show what I mean. Take the passage in the *First Book of Homer* that describes Ajax the Greek dashing into the battle in front of Troy. Here is the way it runs (as nearly as I remember) in the usual word-for-word translation of the classroom, as done by the very best professor, his spectacles glittering the literary rapture of it.

Then he too Ajax on the one hand leaped (or possibly jumped) into the fight wearing on the other hand yes certainly a steel corslet (or possibly a bronze under-tunic) and on his head of course yes without doubt he had a helmet with a tossing plume taken from the mane (or perhaps extracted from the tail) of some horse which once fed along the banks of the Scamander (and it sees the herd and raises its head and paws the ground) and in his hand a shield worth a hundred oxen and on his knees too especially in particular greaves made by some cunning artificer (or perhaps blacksmith) and he blows the fire and it is hot. Thus Ajax leapt (or, better, was propelled from behind) into the fight.

Now, that's grand stuff. There is no doubt of it. There's a wonderful movement and force to it. You can almost see it move, it goes so fast. But the modern reader can't get it. It won't mean to him what it meant to the early Greek. The setting, the costume, the scene has all got to be changed in order to let the reader have a real equivalent to judge just how good the Greek verse is. In my translation I alter it just a little, not much, but just enough to give the passage a form that reproduces the proper literary values of the verses, without losing anything of the majesty. It describes, I may say, the Directors of the American Industrial Stocks rushing into the Balkan War cloud:

> Then there came rushing to the shock of war
> Mr McNicoll of the C.P.R.
> He wore suspenders and about his throat

High rose the collar of a sealskin coat,
He had on gaiters and he wore a tie,
He had his trousers buttoned good and high,
About his waist a woollen undervest
Bought from a sad-eyed farmer of the West,
(And every time he clips a sheep he sees
Some bloated plutocrat who ought to freeze),
Thus in the Stock Exchange he burst to view,
Leaped to the post, and shouted, 'Ninety-two,'

There! That's Homer, the real thing! Just as it sounded to the rude crowd of Greek peasants who sat in a ring and guffawed at the rhymes and watched the minstrel stamp it out into 'feet' as he recited it!

Or let me take another example from the so-called *Catalogue of the Ships* that fills up nearly an entire book of Homer. This famous passage names all the ships, one by one, and names the chiefs who sailed on them and names the particular town or hill or valley that they came from. It has been much admired. It has that same majesty of style that has been brought to an even loftier pitch in the *New York Business Directory* and the *City Telephone Book*. It runs along, as I recall it, something like this:

And first indeed Oh yes was the ship of Homistogetes the Spartan, long and swift, having both its masts covered with cowhide and two rows of oars. And he, Homistogetes, was born of Hermogenes and Ophthalmia and was at home in Syncope beside the fast flowing Paresis. And after him came the ship of Preposterus the Eurasian, son of Oasis and Hysteria

– and so on endlessly.

Instead of this I substitute, with the permission of the New York Central Railway, the official catalogue of their locomotives taken almost word for word from the list compiled by their superintendent of works. I admit that he wrote in hot weather. Part of it runs:

Out in the yard and steaming in the sun
Stands locomotive engine number forty-one.
Seated beside the windows of the cab
Are Pat McGaw and Peter James McNab.
Pat comes from Troy and Peter from Cohoes,
And when they pull the throttle off she goes,
And as she vanishes there comes to view
Steam locomotive engine number forty-two.
Observe her mighty wheels, her easy roll,
With William J. Macarthy in control.
They say her engineer some time ago
Lived in a farm outside of Buffalo,
Whereas his fireman Henry Edward Foy

Attended school in Springfield, Illinois.
Thus does the race of man decay or rot:
Some men can hold their jobs and some can not.

Please observe that if Homer had actually written that last line it would have been quoted for a thousand years as one of the deepest sayings ever said. Orators would have rounded out their speeches with the majestic phrase, quoted in sonorous and unintelligible Greek verse, 'some men can hold their jobs and some can not'; essayists would have begun their most scholarly dissertations with the words, 'It has been finely said by Homer that (in Greek) "some men can hold their jobs": and the clergy in mid-pathos of a funeral sermon would have raised their eyes aloft and echoed, 'Some men can not!'

This is what I should like to do. I'd like to take a large stone and write on it in very plain writing: 'The classics are only primitive literature. They belong to the same class as primitive machinery and primitive music and primitive medicine,' and then throw it through the windows of a University and hide behind a fence to see the professors buzz!

Four
The Spiritual Outlook of Mr Doomer

One generally saw old Mr Doomer looking gloomily out of the windows of the library of the club. If not there, he was to be found staring sadly into the embers of a dying fire in a deserted sitting-room.

His gloom always appeared out of place as he was one of the richest of the members.

But the cause of it, – as I came to know, – was that he was perpetually concerned with thinking about the next world. In fact he spent his whole time brooding over it.

I discovered this accidentally by happening to speak to him of the recent death of Podge, one of our fellow members.

'Very sad,' I said, 'Podge's death.'

'Ah,' returned Mr Doomer, 'very shocking. He was quite unprepared to die.'

'Do you think so?' I said, 'I'm awfully sorry to hear it.'

'Quite unprepared,' he answered. 'I had reason to know it as one of his executors, – everything is confusion, – nothing signed, – no proper power of attorney, – codicils drawn up in blank and never witnessed, – in short, sir, no sense apparently of the nearness of his death and of his duty to be prepared.'

'I suppose,' I said, 'poor Podge didn't realise that he was going to die.'

'Ah, that's just it,' resumed Mr Doomer with something like sternness, 'a man *ought* to realise it. Every man ought to feel that at any moment, – one can't tell when, – day or night, – he may be called upon to meet his,' – Mr Doomer paused here as if seeking a phrase – 'to meet his Financial Obligations, face to face. At any time, sir, he may be hurried before the Judge, – or rather his estate may be, – before the Judge of the probate court. It is a solemn thought, sir. And yet when I come here I see about me men laughing, talking, and playing billiards, as if there would never be a day when their estate would pass into the hands of their administrators and an account must be given of every cent.'

'But after all,' I said, trying to fall in with his mood, 'death and dissolution must come to all of us.'

'That's just it,' he said solemnly. 'They've dissolved the tobacco people, and they've dissolved the oil people and you can't tell whose turn it may be next.'

Mr Doomer was silent a moment and then resumed, speaking in a tone of humility that was almost reverential.

'And yet there is a certain preparedness for death, a certain fitness to die that we ought all to aim at. Any man can at least think solemnly of the Inheritance Tax, and reflect whether by a contract *inter vivos* drawn in blank he may not obtain redemption; any man if he thinks death is near may at least divest himself of his purely speculative securities and trust himself entirely to those gold bearing bonds of the great industrial corporations whose value will not readily diminish or pass away.' Mr Doomer was speaking with something like religious rapture.

'And yet what does one see?' he continued. 'Men affected with fatal illness and men stricken in years occupied still with idle talk and amusements instead of reading the financial newspapers, – and at the last carried away with scarcely time perhaps to send for their brokers when it is already too late.'

'It is very sad,' I said.

'Very,' he repeated, 'and saddest of all, perhaps, is the sense of the irrevocability of death and the changes that must come after it.'

We were silent a moment.

'You think of these things a great deal, Mr Doomer?' I said.

'I do,' he answered. 'It may be that it is something in my temperament, I suppose one would call it a sort of spiritual mindedness. But I think of it all constantly. Often as I stand here beside the window and see these cars go by' – he indicated a passing street car – 'I cannot but realise that the time will come when I am no longer a managing director and wonder whether they will keep on trying to hold the dividend down by improving the rolling stock or will declare profits to inflate the securities. These mysteries beyond the grave fascinate me, sir. Death is a mysterious thing. Who for example will take my seat on the Exchange? What will happen to my majority control of the power company? I shudder to think of the changes that may happen after death in the assessment of my real estate.'

'Yes,' I said, 'it is all beyond our control, isn't it?'

'Quite,' answered Mr Doomer; 'especially of late years one feels that, all said and done, we are in the hands of a Higher Power, and that the State Legislature is after all supreme. It gives one a sense of smallness. It makes one feel that in these days of drastic legislation with all one's efforts the individual is lost and absorbed in the controlling power of the state legislature. Consider the words that are used in the text of the Income Tax Case, Folio Two, or the text of the Trans-Missouri Freight Decision, and think of the revelation they contain.'

I left Mr Doomer still standing beside the window, musing on the vanity of life and on things, such as the future control of freight rates, that lay beyond the grave.

I noticed as I left him how broken and aged he had come to look. It seemed as if the chafings of the spirit were wearing the body that harboured it.

*   *   *

It was about a month later that I learned of Mr Doomer's death.

Dr Slyder told me of it in the club one afternoon, over two cocktails in the sitting-room.

'A beautiful bedside,' he said, 'one of the most edifying that I have ever attended. I knew that Doomer was failing and of course the time came when I had to tell him.

' "Mr Doomer," I said, "all that I, all that any medical can do for you is done; you are going to die. I have to warn you that it is time for other ministrations than mine."

' "Very good," he said faintly but firmly, "send for my broker."

'They sent out and fetched Jarvis, – you know him I think, – most sympathetic man and yet most business-like – he does all the firm's business with the dying, – and we two sat beside Doomer holding him up while he signed stock transfers and blank certificates.

'Once he paused and turned his eyes on Jarvis. "Read me from the text of the State Inheritance Tax Statute," he said. Jarvis took the book and read aloud very quietly and simply the part at the beginning – "Whenever and wheresoever it shall appear," down to the words, "shall be no longer a subject of judgement or appeal but shall remain in perpetual possession."

'Doomer listened with his eyes closed. The reading seemed to bring him great comfort. When Jarvis ended he said with a sigh, "That covers it. I'll put my faith in that." After that he was silent a moment and then said: "I wish I had already crossed the river and be safe on the other side." We knew what he meant. He had always planned to move over to New Jersey. The inheritance tax is so much more liberal.

'Presently it was all done.

' "There," I said, "it is finished now."

' "No," he answered, "there is still one thing. Doctor, you've been very good to me. I should like to pay your account now without it being a charge on the estate. I will pay it as" – he paused for a moment and a fit of coughing seized him, but by an effort of will he found the power to say – "cash."

'I took the account from my pocket (I had it with me, fearing the worst), and we laid his cheque-book before him on the bed. Jarvis thinking him too faint to write tried to guide his hand as he filled in the sum. But he shook his head.

' "The room is getting dim," he said. "I can see nothing but the figures."

' "Never mind," said Jarvis, – much moved, "that's enough."

' "Is it four hundred and thirty?" he asked faintly.

' "Yes," I said, and I could feel the tears rising in my eyes, "and fifty cents."

'After signing the cheque his mind wandered for a moment and he fell to talking, with his eyes closed, of the new federal banking law, and of the prospect of the reserve associations being able to maintain an adequate gold supply.

'Just at the last he rallied.

' "I want," he said in quite a firm voice, "to do something for both of you before I die."

' "Yes, yes," we said.

' "You are both interested, are you not," he murmured, "in City Traction?"

' "Yes, yes," we said. We knew of course that he was the managing director.

'He looked at us faintly and tried to speak.

' "Give him a cordial," said Jarvis. But he found his voice.

' "The value of that stock," he said, "is going to take a sudden –"

'His voice grew faint.

' "Yes, yes," I whispered, bending over him (there were tears in both our eyes), "tell me is it going up, or going down?"

' "It is going" – he murmured, – then his eyes closed – "it is going –"

' "Yes, yes," I said, "which?"

' "It is going" – he repeated feebly and then, quite suddenly he fell back on the pillows and his soul passed. And we never knew which way it was going. It was very sad. Later on, of course, after he was dead, we knew, as everybody knew, that it went down.'

Five
Arcadian Adventures with the Idle Rich

VI. THE RIVAL CHURCHES OF ST ASAPH AND ST OSOPH

The church of St Asaph, more properly called St Asaph's in the Fields, stands among the elm-trees of Plutoria Avenue opposite the university, its tall spire pointing to the blue sky. Its rector is fond of saying that it seems to him to point, as it were, a warning against the sins of a commercial age. More particularly does he say this in his Lenten services at noonday, when the business men sit in front of him in rows, their bald heads uncovered and their faces stamped with contrition as they think of mergers that they should have made, and real estate that they failed to buy for lack of faith.

The ground on which St Asaph's stands is worth seven dollars and a half a foot. The mortgagees, as they kneel in prayer in their long frock-coats, feel that they have built upon a rock. It is a beautifully appointed church. There are windows, with priceless stained glass, that were imported from Normandy, the rector himself swearing out the invoices to save the congregation the grievous burden of the customs duty. There is a pipe organ in the transept that cost ten thousand dollars to install. The debenture-holders, as they join in the morning anthem, love to hear the dulcet notes of the great organ, and to reflect that it is as good as new. Just behind the church is St Asaph's Sunday School, with a ten-thousand dollar mortgage of its own. And below that again, on the side street, is the building of the Young Men's Guild, with a bowling-alley and a swimming-bath deep enough to drown two young men at a time, and a billiard-room with seven tables. It is the rector's boast that with a Guild House such as that there is no need for any young man of the congregation to frequent a saloon. Nor is there.

And on Sunday mornings, when the great organ plays, and the mortgagees and the bond-holders and the debenture-holders and the Sunday School teachers and the billiard markers all lift up their voices together, there is emitted from St Asaph's a volume of praise that is practically as fine and effective as paid professional work.

St Asaph's is episcopal. As a consequence it has in it and about it all those things which go to make up the episcopal church – brass tablets let into its walls, blackbirds singing in its elm-trees, parishioners who dine at eight o'clock, and a rector who wears a little crucifix and dances the tango.

On the other hand, there stands upon the same street, not a hundred yards away, the rival church of St Osoph – presbyterian down to its very foundations in bed-rock, thirty feet below the level of the avenue. It has a short, squat tower and a low roof, and its narrow windows are glazed with frosted glass. It has dark spruce trees instead of elms, crows instead of blackbirds, and a gloomy minister with a shovel hat who lectures on philosophy on week-days at the university. He loves to think that his congregation are made of the lowly and the meek in spirit, and to reflect that, lowly and meek as they are, there are men among them that could buy out half the congregation of St Asaph's.

St Osoph's is only presbyterian in a special sense. It is, in fact, too presbyterian to be any longer connected with any other body whatsoever. It seceded some forty years ago from the original body to which it belonged, and later on, with three other churches, it seceded from the group of seceding congregations. Still later it fell into a difference with the three other churches on the question of eternal punishment, the word 'eternal' not appearing to the elders of St Osoph's to designate a sufficiently long period. The dispute ended in a secession which left the church of St Osoph practically isolated in a world of sin whose approaching fate it neither denied nor deplored.

In one respect the rival churches of Plutoria Avenue had had a similar history. Each of them had moved up by successive stages from the lower and poorer parts of the city. Forty years ago St Asaph's had been nothing more than a little frame church with a tin spire, away in the west of the slums, and St Osoph's a square, diminutive building away in the east. But the site of St Asaph's had been bought by a brewing company, and the trustees, shrewd men of business, themselves rising into wealth, had rebuilt it right in the track of the advancing tide of a real-estate boom. The elders of St Osoph's, quiet men, but illumined by an inner light, had followed suit and moved their church right against the side of an expanding distillery. Thus both the churches, as decade followed decade, made their way up the slope of the city, till St Asaph's was presently gloriously expropriated by the street railway company, and planted its spire in triumph on Plutoria Avenue itself. But St Osoph's followed. With each change of site it moved nearer and nearer to St Asaph's. Its elders were shrewd men. With each move of their church they took careful thought in the rebuilding. In the manufacturing district it was built with sixteen windows on each side, and was converted at a huge profit into a bicycle factory. On the residential street it was made long and deep and was sold to a moving picture company without the alteration of so much as a pew. As a last step a syndicate, formed among the members of the congregation themselves, bought ground on Plutoria Avenue, and sublet it to themselves as a site for the church, at a nominal interest of five per cent per annum, payable nominally every three months and secured by a nominal mortgage.

As the two churches moved, their congregations, or at least all that was best of them – such members as were sharing in the rising fortunes of the city – moved also, and now for some six or seven years the two churches and the two congregations had confronted one another among the elm-trees of the avenue opposite to the university.

But at this point the fortunes of the two churches had diverged. St Asaph's was a brilliant success; St Osoph's was a failure. Even its own trustees couldn't deny it. At a time when St Asaph's was not only paying its interest but showing a handsome surplus on everything it undertook, the church of St Osoph was moving steadily backwards.

There was no doubt, of course, as to the cause. Everybody knew it. It was simply a question of men, and, as everybody said, one had only to compare the two men conducting the churches to see why one succeeded and the other failed.

The Reverend Edward Fareforth Furlong of St Asaph's was a man who threw his whole energy into his parish work. The subtleties of theological controversy he left to minds less active than his own. His creed was one of works rather than of words, and whatever he was doing he did it with his whole heart. Whether he was lunching at the Mausoleum Club with one of his churchwardens, or playing the flute – which he played as only the episcopal clergy can play it – accompanied on the harp by one of the fairest of the ladies of his choir, or whether he was dancing the new episcopal tango with the younger daughters of the elder parishioners, he threw himself into it with all his might. He could drink tea more gracefully and play tennis better than any clergyman on this side of the Atlantic. He could stand beside the white stone font of St Asaph's in his long white surplice holding a white-robed infant, worth half a million dollars, looking as beautifully innocent as the child itself, and drawing from every matron of the congregation with unmarried daughters the despairing cry, 'What a pity that he has no children of his own!'

Equally sound was his theology. No man was known to preach shorter sermons or to explain away the book of Genesis more agreeably than the rector of St Asaph's; and if he found it necessary to refer to the Deity he did so under the name of Jehovah or Jah, or even Yaweh, in a manner calculated not to hurt the sensitiveness of any of the parishioners. People who would shudder at brutal talk of the older fashion about the wrath of God listened with well-bred interest to a sermon on the personal characteristics of Jah. In the same way Mr Furlong always referred to the devil, not as Satan but as Sû or Swâ, which took all the sting out of him. Beelzebub he spoke of as Behel-Zawbab, which rendered him perfectly harmless. The Garden of Eden he spoke of as the Paradeisos, which explained it entirely; the flood as the Diluvium, which cleared it up completely; and Jonah he named, after the correct fashion, Joh Nah, which put the whole situation (his being swallowed by Baloo, or the Great Lizard) on a perfectly satisfactory footing. Hell itself was spoken of as She-ol, and it appeared that it was not a place of burning, but rather of what one might describe as moral torment. This settled She-ol once and for all: nobody minds moral torment. In short, there was nothing in the theological system of Mr Furlong that need have occasioned in any of his congregation a moment's discomfort.

There could be no greater contrast with Mr Fareforth Furlong than the minister of St Osoph's, the Reverend Dr McTeague, who was also honorary professor of philosophy at the university. The one was young, the other was old; the one could dance, the other could not; the one moved about at church picnics and lawn teas among a bevy of disciples in pink and blue sashes; the other moped around under the trees of the university campus, with blinking eyes that saw nothing and an abstracted mind that had spent fifty years in trying to reconcile Hegel with St Paul, and was still busy with it. Mr Furlong went forward with the times; Dr McTeague slid quietly backwards with the centuries.

Dr McTeague was a failure, and all his congregation knew it. 'He is not up to date,' they said. That was his crowning sin. 'He don't go forward any,' said the business members of the congregation. 'That old man believes just exactly the same sort of stuff now that he did forty years ago. What's more, he *preaches* it. You can't run a church that way, can you?'

His trustees had done their best to meet the difficulty. They had offered Dr McTeague a two-years vacation to go and see the Holy Land. He refused; he said he could picture it. They reduced his salary by fifty per cent; he never noticed it. They offered him an assistant; but he shook his head, saying that he did not know where he could find a man to do just the work that he was doing. Meantime he mooned about among the trees concocting a mixture of St Paul with Hegel, three parts to one, for his Sunday sermon, and one part to three for his Monday lecture.

No doubt it was his dual function that was to blame for his failure. And this, perhaps, was the fault of Dr Boomer, the president of the university. Dr Boomer, like all university presidents of today, belonged to the presbyterian church; or rather, to state it more correctly, he included presbyterianism within himself. He was, of course, a member of the board of management of St Osoph's, and it was he who had urged, very strongly, the appointment of Dr McTeague, then senior professor of philosophy, as minister.

'A saintly man,' he said, 'the very man for the post. If you should ask me whether he is entirely at home as a professor of philosophy on our staff at the university, I should be compelled to say no. We are forced to admit that as a lecturer he does not meet our views. He appears to find it difficult to keep religion out of his teaching. In fact, his lectures are suffused with a rather dangerous attempt at moral teaching which is apt to contaminate our students. But in the Church I should imagine that would be, if anything, an advantage. Indeed, if you were to come to me and say, "Boomer, we wish to appoint Dr McTeague as our minister," I should say, quite frankly, "Take him."'

So Dr McTeague had been appointed. Then, to the surprise of everybody, he refused to give up his lectures in philosophy. He said he felt a call to give them. The salary, he said, was of no consequence. He wrote to Mr Furlong senior (the father of the episcopal rector, and honorary treasurer of the Plutoria University), and stated that he proposed to give his lectures for nothing. The trustees of the college protested; they urged that the case might set a dangerous precedent which other professors might follow. While fully admitting that Dr McTeague's lectures were well worth giving for nothing, they begged him to reconsider his offer. But he refused; and from that day on, in spite of all offers that he should retire on double his salary, that he should visit the Holy Land, or Syria, or Armenia, where the dreadful massacres of Christians were taking place, Dr McTeague clung to his post with a tenacity worthy of the best traditions of Scotland. His only internal perplexity was that he didn't see how, when the time came for him to die, twenty or thirty years hence, they would ever be able to replace him.

Such was the situation of the two churches on a certain beautiful morning in June, when an unforeseen event altered entirely the current of their fortunes.

* * *

'No, thank you, Juliana,' said the young rector to his sister across the breakfast table – and there was something as near to bitterness in his look as his saintly, smooth-shaven face was capable of reflecting – 'no, thank you, no more porridge. Prunes? no, no, thank you; I don't think I care for any. And, by the way,' he added, 'don't bother to keep any lunch for me. I have a great deal of business – that is, work in the parish

– to see to, and I must just find time to get a bite of something to eat when and where I can.'

In his own mind he was resolving that the place should be the Mausoleum Club, and the time just as soon as the head waiter would serve him.

After which the Rev. Edward Fareforth Furlong bowed his head for a moment in a short, silent blessing, the one prescribed by the episcopal church in America for a breakfast of porridge and prunes.

It was their first breakfast together, and it spoke volumes to the rector. He knew what it implied. It stood for his elder sister Juliana's views on the need of personal sacrifice as a means of grace. The rector sighed as he rose. He had never missed his younger sister Philippa, now married and departed, so keenly. Philippa had had opinions of her own on bacon and eggs and on lamb chops with watercress as a means of stimulating the soul. But Juliana was different. The rector understood now exactly why it was that his father had exclaimed, on the news of Philippa's engagement, without a second's hesitation, 'Then of course Juliana must live with you! Nonsense, my dear boy, nonsense! It's my duty to spare her to you. After all, I can always eat at the club; they can give me a bite of something or other, surely. To a man of my age, Edward, food is really of no consequence. No, no; Juliana must move into the rectory at once.'

The rector's elder sister rose. She looked tall and sallow and forbidding in the plain black dress that contrasted sadly with the charming clerical costumes of white and pink and the broad episcopal hats with flowers in them that Philippa used to wear for morning work in the parish.

'For what time shall I order dinner?' she asked. 'You and Philippa used to have it at half-past seven, did you not? Don't you think that rather too late?'

'A trifle, perhaps,' said the rector uneasily. He didn't dare to explain to Juliana that it was impossible to get home any earlier from the kind of *thé dansant* that everybody was giving just now. 'But don't trouble about dinner. I may be working very late. If I need anything to eat I shall get a biscuit and some tea at the Guild Rooms, or –'

He didn't finish the sentence, but in his mind he added, 'or else a really first-class dinner at the Mausoleum Club, or at the Newberrys' or the Rasselyer-Browns' – anywhere except here.'

'If you are going, then,' said Juliana, 'may I have the key of the church?'

A look of pain passed over the rector's face. He knew perfectly well what Juliana wanted the key for. She meant to go into the church and pray in it.

The rector of St Asaph's was, he trusted, as broadminded a man as an

Anglican clergyman ought to be. He had no objection to any reasonable use of his church – for a thanksgiving festival or for musical recitals, for example – but when it came to opening up the church and using it to pray in, the thing was going a little too far. What was more, he had an idea from the look on Juliana's face that she meant to pray for *him*. This, for a clergyman, was hard to bear. Philippa, like the good girl that she was, had prayed only for herself, and then only at the proper times and places, and in a proper praying costume. The rector began to realise what difficulties it might make for a clergyman to have a religious sister as his house-mate.

But he was never a man for unseemly argument. 'It is hanging in my study,' he said.

And with that the Rev. Fareforth Furlong passed into the hall, took up the simple silk hat, the stick and gloves of the working clergyman, and walked out on to the avenue to begin his day's work in the parish.

The rector's parish, viewed in its earthly aspect, was a singularly beautiful place. For it extended all along Plutoria Avenue, where the street is widest and the elm-trees are at their leafiest and the motors at their very drowsiest. It lay up and down the shaded side-streets of the residential district, darkened with great chestnuts and hushed in a stillness that was almost religion itself. There was not a house in the parish assessed at less than twenty-five thousand, and in the very heart of it the Mausoleum Club, with its smooth white stone and its Grecian architecture, carried one back to the ancient world and made one think of Athens and of Paul preaching on Mars Hill. It was, all considered, a splendid thing to fight sin in such a parish and to keep it out of it. For kept out it was. One might look the length and breadth of the broad avenue and see no sign of sin all along it. There was certainly none in the smooth faces of the chauffeurs trundling their drowsy motors; no sign of it in the expensive children paraded by imported nursemaids in the chequered light of the shaded street; least of all was there any sign of it in the Stock Exchange members of the congregation, as they walked along side by side to their lunch at the Mausoleum Club, their silk hats nodding together in earnest colloquy on Shares Preferred and Profits Undivided. So might have walked, so must have walked, the very Fathers of the Church themselves.

Whatever sin there was in the city was shoved sideways into the roaring streets of commerce, where the elevated railway ran, and below that again into the slums. Here there must have been any quantity of sin. The rector of St Asaph's was certain of it. Many of the richer of his parishioners had been down in parties late at night to look at it, and the ladies of his congregation were joined together into all sorts of guilds and societies and bands of endeavour for stamping it out and driving it under or putting it into jail till it surrendered.

But the slums lay outside the rector's parish. He had no right to interfere. They were under the charge of a special mission, or auxiliary, a remnant of the St Asaph's of the past, placed under the care of a divinity student, at four hundred dollars per annum. His charge included all the slums and three police-courts and two music-halls and the city jail. One Sunday afternoon in every three months the rector and several ladies went down and sang hymns for him in his mission-house. But his work was really very easy. A funeral, for example, at the mission, was a simple affair, meaning nothing more than the preparation of a plain coffin and a glassless hearse, and the distribution of a few artificial everlasting flowers to women crying in their aprons; a thing easily done: whereas in St Asaph's parish, where all the really important souls were, a funeral was a large event, requiring taste and tact, and a nice shading of delicacy in distinguishing mourners from beneficiaries, and private grief from business representation at the ceremony. A funeral with a plain coffin and a hearse was as nothing beside an interment with a casket smothered in hot-house syringas, borne in a coach, and followed by special reporters from the financial papers.

* * *

It appeared to the rector afterwards as almost a shocking coincidence that the first person whom he met upon the avenue should have been the Rev. Dr McTeague himself. Mr Furlong gave him the form of amiable 'good morning' that the episcopal church always extends to those in error. But he did not hear it. The minister's head was bent low, his eyes gazed into vacancy, and from the movements of his lips and from the fact that he carried a leather case of notes, he was plainly on his way to his philosophical lecture. But the rector had no time to muse upon the abstracted appearance of his rival. For, as always happened to him, he was no sooner upon the street than his parish work of the day began. In fact, he had hardly taken a dozen steps after passing Dr McTeague when he was brought up standing by two beautiful parishioners with pink parasols.

'Oh, Mr Furlong,' exclaimed one of them, 'so fortunate to happen to catch you; we were just going into the rectory to consult you. Should the girls – for the lawn tea for the Guild on Friday, you know – wear white dresses with light blue sashes all the same, or do you think we might allow them to wear any coloured sashes that they like? What do you think?'

This was an important problem. In fact, there was a piece of parish work here that it took the Reverend Fareforth half an hour to attend to, standing the while in earnest colloquy with the two ladies under the shadow of the elm-trees. But a clergyman must never be grudging of his time.

'Good-bye, then,' they said at last. 'Are you coming to the Browning Club this morning? Oh, so sorry! but we shall see you at the musicale this afternoon, shall we not?'

'Oh, I trust so,' said the rector.

'How dreadfully hard he works,' said the ladies to one another as they moved away.

Thus slowly and with many interruptions the rector made his progress along the avenue. At times he stopped to permit a pink-cheeked infant in a perambulator to beat him with a rattle while he inquired its age of an episcopal nurse, gay with flowing ribbons. He lifted his hat to the bright parasols of his parishioners passing in glistening motors, bowed to episcopalians, nodded amiably to presbyterians, and even acknowledged with his lifted hand the passing of persons of graver forms of error.

Thus he took his way along the avenue and down a side street towards the business district of the city, until just at the edge of it, where the trees were about to stop and the shops were about to begin, he found himself at the door of the Hymnal Supply Corporation, Limited. The premises as seen from the outside combined the idea of an office with an ecclesiastical appearance. The door was as that of a chancel or vestry; there was a large plate-glass window filled with Bibles and Testaments, all spread open and showing every variety of language in their pages. These were marked, 'Arabic,' 'Syriac,' 'Coptic,' 'Ojibway,' 'Irish,' and so forth. On the window in small white lettering were the words, 'Hymnal Supply Corporation' and below that 'Hosanna Pipe and Steam Organ Incorporated,' and still lower the legend, 'Bible Society of the Good Shepherd, Limited.'

There was no doubt of the sacred character of the place.

Here laboured Mr Furlong senior, the father of the Rev. Edward Fareforth. He was a man of many activities, president and managing director of the companies just mentioned, trustee and secretary of St Asaph's, honorary treasurer of the university, etc.; and each of his occupations and offices was marked by something of a supramundane character, something higher than ordinary business. His different official positions naturally overlapped and brought him into contact with himself from a variety of angles. Thus he sold himself hymn-books at a price per thousand, made as a business favour to himself, negotiated with himself the purchase of the ten-thousand-dollar organ (making a price on it to himself that he begged himself to regard as confidential), and, as treasurer of the college, he sent himself an informal note of enquiry asking if he knew of any sound investment for the annual deficit of the college funds, a matter of some sixty thousand dollars a year, which needed very careful handling. Any man – and there are many such – who has been concerned with business dealings of this sort with himself realises that they are more satisfactory than any other kind.

To what better person then could the rector of St Asaph's bring the quarterly accounts and statements of his church than to Mr Furlong senior?

The outer door was opened to the rector by a sanctified boy with such a face as is only found in the choirs of the episcopal church. In an outer office through which the rector passed were two sacred stenographers, with hair as golden as the daffodils of Sheba, copying confidential letters on absolutely noiseless typewriters. They were making offers of Bibles in half-car-load lots at two and a half per cent Reduction, offering to reduce St Mark by two cents on condition of immediate export, and to lay down St John F.O.B. San Francisco for seven cents, while regretting that they could deliver fifteen thousand Rock of Ages in Missouri on no other terms than cash.

The sacred character of their work lent them a preoccupation beautiful to behold.

In the room beyond them was a white-haired confidential clerk, venerable as the Song of Solomon, and by him Mr Fareforth Furlong was duly shown into the office of his father.

'Good morning, Edward,' said Mr Furlong senior, as he shook hands. 'I was expecting you. And while I think of it, I have just had a letter from Philippa. She and Tom will be home in two or three weeks. She writes from Egypt. She wishes me to tell you, as no doubt you have already anticipated, that she thinks she can hardly continue to be a member of the congregation when they come back. No doubt you felt this yourself?'

'Oh, entirely,' said the rector. 'Surely in matters of belief a wife must follow her husband.'

'Exactly; especially as Tom's uncles occupy the position they do with regard to –' Mr Furlong jerked his head backwards and pointed with his thumb over his shoulder in a way that his son knew was meant to indicate St Osoph's church.

The Overend brothers, who were Tom's uncles (his name being Tom Overend), were, as everybody knew, among the principal supporters of St Osoph's. Not that they were, by origin, presbyterians. But they were self-made men, which put them once and for all out of sympathy with such a place as St Asaph's. 'We made ourselves,' the two brothers used to repeat, in defiance of the catechism of the Anglican church. They never wearied of explaining how Mr Dick, the senior brother, had worked overtime by day to send Mr George, the junior brother, to school by night, and how Mr George had then worked overtime by night to send Mr Dick to school by day. Thus they had come up the business ladder hand over hand, landing later on in life on the platform of success like two corpulent acrobats, panting with the strain of it. 'For years,' Mr George would explain, 'we had father and mother to keep as well; then they died, and Dick and me saw daylight.' By which he meant no harm at all, but only stated a fact, and concealed the virtue of it.

And being self-made men, they made it a point to do what they could to lessen the importance of such an institution as St Asaph's church. By the same contrariety of nature the two Overend brothers (their business name was Overend Brothers, Limited) were supporters of the dissentient Young Men's Guild, and the second or rival University Settlement, and of anything or everything that showed a likelihood of making trouble. On this principle they were warm supporters and friends of the Rev. Dr McTeague. The minister had even gone so far as to present to the brothers a copy of his philosophical work, 'McTeague's Exposition of the Kantian Hypothesis,' and the two brothers had read it through in the office, devoting each of them a whole morning to it. Mr Dick, the senior brother, had said that he had never seen anything like it, and Mr George, the junior, had declared that a man who could write that was capable of anything.

On the whole it was evident that the relations between the Overend family and the presbyterian religion were too intimate to allow Mrs Tom Overend, formerly Miss Philippa Furlong, to sit anywhere else of a Sunday than under Dr McTeague.

'Philippa writes,' continued Mr Furlong, 'that under the circumstances she and Tom would like to do something for your church. She would like – yes, I have the letter here – to give you, as a surprise, of course, either a new font or a carved pulpit; or perhaps a cheque. She wishes me on no account to mention it to you directly, but to ascertain indirectly from you what would be the better surprise.'

'Oh, a cheque, I think,' said the rector; 'one can do so much more with it, after all.'

'Precisely,' said his father; he was well aware of many things that can be done with a cheque that cannot possibly be done with a font.

'That's settled then,' resumed Mr Furlong; 'and now I suppose you want me to run my eye over your quarterly statements, do you not, before we send them in to the trustees? That is what you've come for, is it not?'

'Yes,' said the rector, drawing a bundle of blue and white papers from his pocket. 'I have everything with me. Our showing is, I believe, excellent, though I fear I fail to present it as clearly as it might be done.'

Mr Furlong senior spread the papers on the table before him and adjusted his spectacles to a more convenient angle. He smiled indulgently as he looked at the documents before him.

'I am afraid you would never make an accountant, Edward,' he said.

'I fear not,' said the rector.

'Your items,' said his father, 'are entered wrongly. Here, for example, in the general statement, you put down Distribution of Coals to the Poor to your credit. In the same way, Bibles and Prizes to the Sunday School you again mark to your credit. Why? Don't you see, my boy, that these things are debits? When you give out Bibles or distribute fuel to the poor you give out something for which you get no return. It is a debit. On the other hand, such items as Church Offertory, Scholars' Pennies, etc., are pure profit. Surely the principle is clear.'

'I think I see it better now,' said the Rev. Edward.

'Perfectly plain, isn't it?' his father went on. 'And here again, Paupers' Burial Fund, a loss; enter it as such. Christmas Gift to Verger and Sexton, an absolute loss – you get nothing in return. Widow's Mite, Fines inflicted in Sunday School, etc., these are profit; write them down as such. By this method, you see, in ordinary business we can tell exactly where we stand: anything which we give out without return or reward we count as a debit; all that we take from others without giving in return we count as so much to our credit.'

'Ah, yes,' murmured the rector. 'I begin to understand.'

'Very good. But after all, Edward, I mustn't quarrel with the mere form of your accounts; the statement is really a splendid showing. I see that not only is our mortgage and debenture interest all paid to date, but that a number of our enterprises are making a handsome return. I notice, for example, that the Girls' Friendly Society of the church not only pays for itself, but that you are able to take something out of its funds and transfer it to the Men's Book Club. Excellent! And I observe that you have been able to take a large portion of the Soup Kitchen Fund and put it into the Rector's Picnic Account. Very good indeed. In this respect your figures are a model for church accounts anywhere.'

Mr Furlong continued his scrutiny of the accounts. 'Excellent,' he murmured, 'and on the whole an annual surplus, I see, of several thousands. But stop a bit,' he continued, checking himself; 'what's this? Are you aware, Edward, that you are losing money on your Foreign Missions Account?'

'I feared as much,' said Edward.

'It's incontestable. Look at the figures for yourself: missionary's salary so much, clothes and books to converts so much, voluntary and other offerings of converts so much – why, you're losing on it, Edward!' exclaimed Mr Furlong, and he shook his head dubiously at the accounts before him.

'I thought,' protested his son, 'that in view of the character of the work itself –'

'Quite so,' answered his father, 'quite so. I fully admit the force of that. I am only asking you, is it worth it? Mind you, I am not speaking now as a Christian, but as a business man. Is it worth it?'

'I thought that perhaps, in view of the fact of our large surplus in other directions –'

'Exactly,' said his father, 'a heavy surplus. It is precisely on that point that I wished to speak to you this morning. You have at present a large annual surplus, and there is every prospect under Providence – in fact, I think in any case – of it continuing for years to come. If I may speak very frankly I should say that as long as our reverend friend Dr McTeague continues in his charge of St Osoph's – and I trust that he may be spared for many years to come – you are likely to enjoy the present prosperity of your church. Very good. The question arises, what disposition are we to make of our accumulating funds?'

'Yes,' said the rector, hesitating.

'I am speaking to you now,' said his father, 'not as the secretary of your church, but as president of the Hymnal Supply Company which I represent here. Now please understand, Edward, I don't want in any way to force or control your judgement. I merely wish to show you certain – shall I say certain opportunities that present themselves for the disposal of our funds? The matter can be taken up later, formally, by yourself and the trustees of the church. As a matter of fact, I have already written to myself as secretary in the matter, and I have received what I consider a quite encouraging answer. Let me explain what I propose.'

Mr Furlong senior rose, and opened the door of the office.

'Everett,' he said to the ancient clerk, 'kindly give me a Bible.'

It was given to him. Mr Furlong stood with the Bible poised in his hand.

'Now we,' he went on, 'I mean the Hymnal Supply Corporation, have an idea for bringing out an entirely new Bible.'

A look of dismay appeared on the saintly face of the rector.

'A new Bible!' he gasped.

'Precisely!' said his father, 'a new Bible! This one – and we find it every day in our business – is all wrong.'

'All wrong!' said the rector, with horror in his face.

'My dear boy,' exclaimed his father, 'pray, pray, do not misunderstand me. Don't imagine for a moment that I mean wrong in a religious sense. Such a thought could never, I hope, enter my mind. All that I mean is that this Bible is badly made up.'

'Badly made up!' repeated his son, as mystified as ever.

'I see that you do not understand me. What I mean is this. Let me try to make myself quite clear. For the market of today this Bible' – and he poised it again on his hand, as if to test its weight, 'is too heavy. The people of to-day want something lighter, something easier to get hold of. Now if –'

But what Mr Furlong was about to say was lost forever to the world.

For just at this juncture something occurred calculated to divert not only Mr Furlong's sentence, but the fortunes and the surplus of St Asaph's itself. At the very moment when Mr Furlong was speaking a newspaper delivery man in the street outside handed to the sanctified boy the office copy of the noonday paper. And the boy had no sooner looked at its headlines than he said, 'How dreadful!' Being sanctified, he had no stronger form of speech than that. But he handed the paper forthwith to one of the stenographers with hair like the daffodils of Sheba, and when she looked at it she exclaimed, 'How awful!' And she knocked at once at the door of the ancient clerk and gave the paper to him; and when he looked at it and saw the headline the ancient clerk murmured, 'Ah!' in the gentle tone in which very old people greet the news of catastrophe or sudden death.

But in turn he opened Mr Furlong's door and put down the paper, laying his finger on the column for a moment without a word.

Mr Furlong stopped short in his sentence. 'Dear me!' he said, as his eyes caught the item of news. 'How very dreadful!'

'What is it?' said the rector.

'Dr McTeague,' answered his father. 'He has been stricken with paralysis.'

'How shocking!' said the rector, aghast. 'But when? I saw him only this morning.'

'It has just happened,' said his father, following down the column of the newspaper as he spoke, 'this morning, at the university, in his class-room, at a lecture. Dear me, how dreadful! I must go and see the president at once.'

Mr Furlong was about to reach for his hat and stick when at that moment the aged clerk knocked at the door.

'Dr Boomer,' he announced in a tone of solemnity suited to the occasion.

Dr Boomer entered, shook hands in silence and sat down.

'You have heard our sad news, I suppose?' he said. He used the word 'our' as between the university president and his honorary treasurer.

'How did it happen?' asked Mr Furlong.

'Most distressing,' said the president. 'Dr McTeague, it seems, had just entered his ten o'clock class (the hour was about ten-twenty) and was about to open his lecture, when one of his students rose in his seat and asked a question. It is a practice,' continued Dr Boomer, 'which, I need hardly say, we do not encourage; the young man, I believe, was a newcomer in the philosophy class. At any rate, he asked Dr McTeague, quite suddenly, it appears, how he could reconcile his theory of transcendental immaterialism with a scheme of rigid moral determinism. Dr McTeague stared for a moment, his mouth, so the class assert, painfully open. The student repeated the question, and poor McTeague fell forward over his desk, paralysed.'

'Is he dead?' gasped Mr Furlong.

'No,' said the president. 'But we expect his death at any moment. Dr Slyder, I may say, is with him now and is doing all he can.'

'In any case, I suppose, he could hardly recover enough to continue his college duties,' said the young rector.

'Out of the question,' said the president. 'I should not like to state that of itself mere paralysis need incapacitate a professor. Dr Thrum, our professor of the theory of music, is, as you know, paralysed in his ears, and Mr Slant, our professor of optics, is paralysed in his right eye. But this is a case of paralysis of the brain. I fear it is incompatible with professorial work.'

'Then, I suppose,' said Mr Furlong senior, 'we shall have to think of the question of a successor.'

They had both *been* thinking of it for at least three minutes.

'We must,' said the president. 'For the moment I feel too stunned by the sad news to act. I have merely telegraphed to two or three leading colleges for a *locum tenens* and sent out a few advertisements announcing the chair as vacant. But it will be difficult to replace McTeague. He was a man,' added Dr Boomer, rehearsing in advance, unconsciously, no doubt, his forthcoming oration over Dr McTeague's death, 'of a singular grasp, a breadth of culture, and he was able, as few men are, to instil what I might call a spirit of religion into his teaching. His lectures, indeed, were suffused with moral instruction, and exercised over his students an influence second only to that of the pulpit itself.'

He paused.

'Ah yes, the pulpit,' said Mr Furlong; 'there indeed you will miss him.'

'That,' said Dr Boomer very reverently, 'is our real loss, deep, irreparable. I suppose, indeed I am certain, we shall never again see such a man in the pulpit of St Osoph's. Which reminds me,' he added more briskly, 'I must ask the newspaper people to let it be known that there will be service as usual the day after tomorrow, and that Dr McTeague's death will, of course, make no difference – that is to say – I must see the newspaper people at once.'

* * *

That afternoon all the newspaper editors in the city were busy getting their obituary notices ready for the demise of Dr McTeague.

'The death of Dr McTeague,' wrote the editor of the *Commercial and Financial Undertone*, a paper which had almost openly advocated the minister's dismissal for five years back, 'comes upon us as an irreparable loss. His place will be difficult, nay, impossible to fill. Whether as a philosopher or a divine he cannot be replaced.'

'We have no hesitation in saying,' so wrote the editor of the *Plutorian Times*, a three-cent point of view of men and things, 'that the loss of Dr McTeague will be just as much felt in Europe as in America. To Germany the news that the hand that penned "McTeague's Shorter Exposition of the Kantian Hypothesis" has ceased to write will come with the shock of poignant anguish; while to France –'

The editor left the article unfinished at that point. After all, he was a ready writer, and he reflected that there would be time enough before actually going to press to consider from what particular angle the blow of McTeague's death would strike down the people of France.

So ran in speech and in writing, during two or three days, the requiem of Dr McTeague.

Altogether there were more kind things said of him in the three days during which he was taken for dead than in thirty years of his life – which seemed a pity.

And after it all, at the close of the third day, Dr McTeague feebly opened his eyes.

But when he opened them the world had already passed on and left him behind.

VII. THE MINISTRATIONS OF THE REVEREND UTTERMUST DUMFARTHING

'Well then, gentlemen, I think we have all agreed upon our man?'

Mr Dick Overend looked around the table as he spoke at the managing trustees of St Osoph's church. They were assembled in an upper committee room of the Mausoleum Club. Their official place of meeting was in a board-room off the vestry of the church. But they had felt a draught in it, some four years ago, which had wafted them over to the club as their place of assembly. In the club there were no draughts.

Mr Dick Overend sat at the head of the table, his brother George beside him, and Dr Boomer at the foot. Beside them were Mr Boulder, Mr Skinyer (of Skinyer and Beatem) and the rest of the trustees.

'You are agreed, then, on the Reverend Uttermust Dumfarthing?'

'Quite agreed,' murmured several trustees together.

'A most remarkable man,' said Dr Boomer. 'I heard him preach in his present church. He gave utterance to thoughts that I have myself been thinking for years. I never listened to anything so sound or so scholarly.'

'I heard him the night he preached in New York,' said Mr Boulder. 'He preached a sermon to the poor. He told them they were no good. I never heard, outside of a Scotch pulpit, such splendid invective.'

'Is he Scotch?' said one of the trustees.

'Of Scotch parentage,' said the university president. 'I believe he is one of the Dumfarthings of Demferline, Dumfries.'

Everybody said 'Oh,' and there was a pause.

'Is he married?' asked one of the trustees.

'I understand,' answered Dr Boomer, 'that he is a widower with one child, a little girl.'

'Does he make any conditions?'

'None whatever,' said the chairman, consulting a letter before him, 'except that he is to have absolute control, and in regard to salary. These two points settled, he says, he places himself entirely in our hands.'

'And the salary?' asked someone.

'Ten thousand dollars,' said the chairman, 'payable quarterly in advance.'

A chorus of approval went round the table. 'Good,' 'Excellent,' 'A first-class man,' muttered the trustees; 'Just what we want.'

'I am sure, gentlemen,' said Mr Dick Overend, voicing the sentiments of everybody, 'we do *not* want a cheap man. Several of the candidates whose names have been under consideration here have been in many respects – in point of religious qualification, let us say – most desirable men. The name of Dr McSkwirt, for example, has been mentioned with great favour by several of the trustees. But he's a cheap man. I feel we don't want him.'

'What is Dr Dumfarthing getting where he is?' asked Mr Boulder.

'Nine thousand nine hundred,' said the chairman.

'And Dr McSkwirt?'

'Fourteen hundred dollars.'

'Well, that settles it!' exclaimed everybody with a burst of enlightenment.

And so it was settled.

In fact, nothing could have been plainer.

'I suppose,' said Mr George Overend as they were about to rise, 'that we are quite justified in taking it for granted that Dr McTeague will never be able to resume work?'

'Oh, absolutely for granted,' said Dr Boomer. 'Poor McTeague! I hear from Slyder that he was making desperate efforts this morning to sit up in bed. His nurse with difficulty prevented him.'

'Is his power of speech gone?' asked Mr Boulder.

'Practically so; in any case, Dr Slyder insists on his not using it. In fact, poor McTeague's mind is a wreck. His nurse was telling me that this morning he was reaching out his hand for the newspaper, and seemed to want to read one of the editorials. It was quite pathetic,' concluded Dr Boomer, shaking his head.

So the whole matter was settled, and next day all the town knew that St Osoph's church had extended a call to the Reverend Uttermust Dumfarthing, and that he had accepted it.

* * *

Within a few weeks of this date the Reverend Uttermust Dumfarthing moved into the manse of St Osoph's and assumed his charge. And forthwith he became the sole topic of conversation on Plutoria Avenue. 'Have you seen the new minister of St Osoph's?' everybody asked. 'Have you been to hear Dr Dumfarthing?' 'Were you at St Osoph's church on Sunday morning? Ah, you really should go; most striking sermon I ever listened to.'

The effect of him was absolute and instantaneous; there was no doubt of it.

'My dear,' said Mrs Buncomhearst to one of her friends, in describing how she had met him, 'I never saw a more striking man. Such power in his face! Mr Boulder introduced him to me on the avenue, and he hardly seemed to see me at all, simply scowled! I was never so favourably impressed with any man.'

On his very first Sunday he preached to his congregation on eternal punishment, leaning forward in his black gown and shaking his fist at them. Dr McTeague had never shaken his fist in thirty years, and as for the Reverend Fareforth Furlong, he was incapable of it.

But the Reverend Uttermust Dumfarthing told his congregation that he was convinced that at least seventy per cent of them were destined for eternal punishment; and he didn't call it by that name, but labelled it simply and forcibly 'Hell'. The word had not been heard in any church in the better part of the city for a generation. The congregation was so swelled next Sunday that the minister raised the percentage to eight-five, and everybody went away delighted. Young and old flocked to St Osoph's. Before a month had passed the congregation at the evening service at St

Asaph's church was so slender that the offertory, as Mr Furlong senior himself calculated, was scarcely sufficient to pay the overhead charge of collecting it.

The presence of so many young men sitting in serried files close to the front was the only feature of his congregation that extorted from the Reverend Dr Dumfarthing something like approval.

'It is joy to me to see,' he remarked to several of his trustees, 'that there are in the city so many godly young men, whatever the elders may be.'

But there may have been a secondary cause at work, for among the godly young men of Plutoria Avenue the topic of conversation had not been, 'Have you heard the new presbyterian minister?' but, 'Have you seen his daughter? You *haven't?* Well, say!'

For it turned out that the 'child' of Dr Uttermust Dumfarthing, so-called by the trustees, was the kind of child that wears a little round hat, straight from Paris, with an upright feather in it, and a silk dress in four sections, and shoes with high heels that would have broken the heart of John Calvin. Moreover, she had the distinction of being the only person on Plutoria Avenue who was not one whit afraid of the Reverend Uttermust Dumfarthing. She even amused herself, in violation of all rules, by attending evening service at St Asaph's, where she sat listening to the Reverend Edward, and feeling that she had never heard anything so sensible in her life.

'I'm simply dying to meet your brother,' she said to Mrs Tom Overend, otherwise Philippa; 'he's such a complete contrast with father' (she knew no higher form of praise). 'Father's sermons are always so frightfully full of religion.'

And Philippa promised that meet him she should.

But whatever may have been the effect of the presence of Catherine Dumfarthing, there is no doubt the greater part of the changed situation was due to Dr Dumfarthing himself.

Everything he did was calculated to please. He preached sermons to the rich and told them they were mere cobwebs, and they liked it; he preached a special sermon to the poor and warned them to be mighty careful; he gave a series of weekly talks to working men, and knocked them sideways; and in the Sunday School he gave the children so fierce a talk on charity and the need of giving freely and quickly that such a stream of pennies and nickels poured into Catherine Dumfarthing's Sunday School Fund as hadn't been seen in the church in fifty years.

Nor was Dr Dumfarthing different in his private walk of life. He was heard to speak openly of the Overend brothers as 'men of wrath', and they were so pleased that they repeated it to half the town. It was the best business advertisement they had had for years.

Dr Boomer was captivated with the man. 'True scholarship,' he murmured, as Dr Dumfarthing poured undiluted Greek and Hebrew from the pulpit, scorning to translate a word of it. Under Dr Boomer's charge the minister was taken over the length and breadth of Plutoria University, and reviled it from the foundations up.

'Our library,' said the president, 'two hundred thousand volumes!'

'Aye,' said the minister, 'a powerful heap of rubbish, I'll be bound!'

'The photograph of our last year's graduating class,' said the president.

'A poor lot, to judge by the faces of them,' said the minister.

'This, Dr Dumfarthing, is our new radiographic laboratory; Mr Spiff, our demonstrator, is preparing slides which, I believe, actually show the movements of the atom itself, do they not, Mr Spiff?'

'Ah,' said the minister, piercing Mr Spiff from beneath his dark brows, 'it will not avail you, young man.'

Dr Boomer was delighted. 'Poor McTeague,' he said – 'and by the way, Boyster, I hear that McTeague is trying to walk again; a great error, it shouldn't be allowed! – poor McTeague knew nothing of science.'

The students themselves shared in the enthusiasm especially after Dr Dumfarthing had given them a Sunday afternoon talk in which he showed that their studies were absolutely futile. As soon as they knew this they went to work with a vigour that put new life into the college.

* * *

Meantime the handsome face of the Reverend Edward Fareforth Furlong began to wear a sad and weary look that had never been seen on it before. He watched his congregation drifting from St Asaph's to St Osoph's and was powerless to prevent it. His sadness reached its climax one bright afternoon in the late summer, when he noticed that even his episcopal blackbirds were leaving his elms and moving westward to the spruce trees of the manse.

He stood looking at them with melancholy on his face.

'Why, Edward,' cried his sister Philippa, as her motor stopped beside him, 'how doleful you look! Get into the car and come out into the country for a ride. Let the parish teas look after themselves for today.'

Tom, Philippa's husband, was driving his own car – he was rich enough to be able to – and seated with Philippa in the car was an unknown person, as prettily dressed as Philippa herself. To the rector she was presently introduced as Miss Catherine Something – he didn't hear the rest of it. Nor did he need to. It was quite plain that her surname, whatever it was, was a very temporary and transitory affair.

So they sped rapidly out of the city and away out into the country, mile after mile, through cool, crisp air, and among woods with the touch of autumn bright already upon them, and with blue sky and great still clouds white overhead. And the afternoon was so beautiful and so bright that as they went along there was no talk about religion at all; nor was there any mention of Mothers' Auxiliaries, or Girls' Friendly Societies, nor any discussion of the poor. It was too glorious a day. But they spoke instead of the new dances, and whether they had come to stay, and of such sensible topics as that. Then presently, as they went on still further, Philippa leaned forward and talked to Tom over his shoulder and reminded him that this was the very road to Castel Casteggio, and asked him if he remembered coming up it with her to join the Newberrys ever so long ago. Whatever it was that Tom answered it is not recorded, but it is certain that it took so long in the saying that the Reverend Edward talked in tête-à-tête with Catherine for fifteen measured miles, and was unaware that it was more than five minutes. Among other things he said, and she agreed – or she said and he agreed – that for the new dances it was necessary to have always one and the same partner, and to keep that partner all the time. And somehow simple sentiments of that sort, when said direct into a pair of listening blue eyes behind a purple motor veil, acquire an infinite significance.

Then, not much after that, say three or four minutes, they were all of a sudden back in town again, running along Plutoria Avenue, and to the rector's surprise the motor was stopping outside the manse, and Catherine was saying, 'Oh thank you ever so much, Philippa; it was just heavenly!' which showed that the afternoon had had its religious features after all.

'What?' said the rector's sister, as they moved off again, 'didn't you know? That's Catherine Dumfarthing!'

*   *   *

When the Reverend Fareforth Furlong arrived home at the rectory he spent an hour or so in the deepest of deep thought in an armchair in his study. Nor was it any ordinary parish problem that he was revolving in his mind. He was trying to think out some means by which his sister Juliana might be induced to commit the sin of calling on the daughter of a presbyterian minister.

The thing had to be represented as in some fashion or other an act of self-denial, a form of mortification of the flesh. Otherwise he knew Juliana would never do it. But to call on Miss Catherine Dumfarthing seemed to him such an altogether delightful and unspeakably blissful process that he hardly knew how to approach the topic. So when Juliana presently came home the rector could find no better way of introducing the subject than by putting it on the ground of Philippa's marriage to Miss Dumfarthing's father's trustee's nephew.

'Juliana,' he said, 'don't you think that perhaps, on account of Philippa and Tom, you ought – or at least it might be best – for you to call on Miss Dumfarthing?'

Juliana turned to her brother as she laid aside her bonnet and her black gloves.

'I've just been there this afternoon,' she said.

There was something as near to a blush on her face as her brother had ever seen.

'But she was not there!' he said.

'No,' answered Juliana, 'but Dr Dumfarthing was. I stayed and talked some time with him, waiting for her.'

The rector gave a sort of whistle, or rather that blowing out of air which is the episcopal symbol for it.

'Didn't you find him pretty solemn?' he said.

'Solemn!' answered his sister. 'Surely, Edward, a man in such a calling as his ought to be solemn.'

'I don't mean that exactly,' said the rector; 'I mean – er – hard, bitter, so to speak.'

'Edward!' exclaimed Juliana, 'how can you speak so? Dr Dumfarthing hard! Dr Dumfarthing bitter! Why, Edward, the man is gentleness and kindness itself. I don't think I ever met anyone so full of sympathy, of compassion with suffering.'

Juliana's face had flushed. It was quite plain that she saw things in the Reverend Uttermust Dumfarthing – as some one woman does in every man – that no one else could see.

The Reverend Edward was abashed. 'I wasn't thinking of his character,' he said. 'I was thinking rather of his doctrines. Wait till you have heard him preach.'

Juliana flushed more deeply still. 'I heard him last Sunday evening,' she said.

The rector was silent, and his sister, as if impelled to speak, went on.

'And I don't see, Edward, how anyone could think him a hard or bigoted man in his creed. He walked home with me to the gate just now, and he was speaking of all the sin in the world, and of how few, how very few people, can be saved, and how many will have to be burned as worthless; and he spoke so beautifully. He regrets it, Edward, regrets it deeply. It is a real grief to him.'

On which Juliana, half in anger, withdrew, and her brother the rector sat back in his chair with smiles rippling all over his saintly face. For he had been wondering whether it would be possible, even remotely possible, to get his sister to invite the Dumfarthings to high tea at the rectory some day at six o'clock (evening dinner was out of the question), and now he knew within himself that the thing was as good as done.

* * *

While such things as these were happening and about to happen, there were many others of the congregation of St Asaph's beside the rector to whom the growing situation gave cause for serious perplexities. Indeed, all who were interested in the church, the trustees and the mortgagees and the underlying debenture-holders, were feeling anxious. For some of them underlay the Sunday School, whose scholars' offerings had declined forty per cent, and others underlay the new organ, not yet paid for, while others were lying deeper still beneath the ground site of the church with seven dollars and a half a square foot resting on them.

'I don't like it,' said Mr Lucullus Fyshe to Mr Newberry (they were both prominent members of the congregation). 'I don't like the look of things. I took up a block of Furlong's bonds on his Guild building from what seemed at the time the best of motives. The interest appeared absolutely certain. Now it's a month overdue on the last quarter. I feel alarmed.'

'Neither do I like it,' said Mr Newberry, shaking his head; 'and I'm sorry for Fareforth Furlong. An excellent fellow, Fyshe, excellent. I keep wondering, Sunday after Sunday, if there isn't something I can do to help him out. One might do something further perhaps in the way of new buildings or alterations. I have, in fact, offered – by myself, I mean, and without other aid – to dynamite out the front of his church, underpin it, and put him in a Norman gateway; either that, or blast out the back of it where the choir sit, just as he likes. I was thinking about it last Sunday as they were singing the anthem, and realising what a lot one might do there with a few sticks of dynamite.'

'I doubt it,' said Mr Fyshe. 'In fact, Newberry, to speak very frankly, I begin to ask myself, is Furlong the man for the post?'

'Oh, surely,' said Mr Newberry in protest.

'Personally a charming fellow,' went on Mr Fyshe; 'but is he, all said and done, quite the man to conduct a church? In the *first* place, he is *not* a business man.'

'No,' said Mr Newberry reluctantly, 'that I admit.'

'Very good. And, *secondly*, even in the matter of his religion itself, one always feels as if he were too little fixed, too unstable. He simply moves with the times. That, at least, is what people are beginning to say of him, that he is perpetually moving with the times. It doesn't do, Newberry, it doesn't do.'

Whereupon Mr Newberry went away troubled and wrote to Fareforth

Furlong a confidential letter with a signed cheque in it for the amount of Mr Fyshe's interest, and with such further offerings of dynamite, of underpinning and blasting, as his conscience prompted.

When the rector received and read the note and saw the figures of the cheque, there arose such a thankfulness in his spirit as he hadn't felt for months, and he may well have murmured, for the repose of Mr Newberry's soul, a prayer not found in the rubric of King James.

All the more cause had he to feel light at heart, for as it chanced it was on that same evening that the Dumfarthings, father and daughter, were to take tea at the rectory. Indeed, a few minutes before six o'clock they might have been seen making their way from the manse to the rectory.

On their way along the avenue the minister took occasion to reprove his daughter for the worldliness of her hat (it was a little trifle from New York that she had bought out of the Sunday School money – a temporary loan); and a little further on he spoke to her severely about the parasol she carried; and further yet about the strange fashion, specially condemned by the Old Testament, in which she wore her hair. So Catherine knew in her heart from this that she must be looking her very prettiest, and went into the rectory radiant.

The tea was, of course, an awkward meal at the best. There was an initial difficulty about grace, not easily surmounted. And when the Reverend Dr Dumfarthing sternly refused tea as a pernicious drink weakening to the system, the Anglican rector was too ignorant of the presbyterian system to know enough to give him Scotch whisky.

But there were bright spots in the meal as well. The rector was even able to ask Catherine, sideways as a personal question, if she played tennis; and she was able to whisper behind her hand, 'Not allowed,' and to make a face in the direction of her father, who was absorbed for the moment in a theological question with Juliana. Indeed, before the conversation became general again the rector had contrived to make a rapid arrangement with Catherine whereby she was to come with him to the Newberrys' tennis-court the day following and learn the game, with or without permission.

So the tea was perhaps a success in its way. And it is noteworthy that Juliana spent the days that followed it in reading Calvin's *Institutes* (specially loaned to her) and *Dumfarthing on the Certainty of Damnation* (a gift), and in praying for her mother – a task practically without hope. During which same time the rector, in white flannels, and Catherine, in a white duck skirt and blouse, were flying about on the green grass of the Newberrys' court, and calling 'love,' 'love all' to one another so gaily and so brazenly that even Mr Newberry felt that there must be something in it.

But all these things came merely as interludes in the moving currents of greater events; for as the summer faded into autumn and autumn into winter, the anxieties of the trustees of St Asaph's began to call for action of some sort.

* * *

'Edward,' said the rector's father on the occasion of their next quarterly discussion, 'I cannot conceal from you that the position of things is very serious. Your statements show a falling off in every direction. Your interest is everywhere in arrears; your current account overdrawn to the limit. At this rate, you know, the end is inevitable. Your debenture and bond-holders will decide to foreclose; and if they do, you know, there is no power that can stop them. Even with your limited knowledge of business you are probably aware that there is no higher power that can influence or control the holder of a first mortgage.'

'I fear so,' said the Reverend Edward very sadly.

'Do you not think perhaps that some of the shortcoming lies with yourself?' continued Mr Furlong. 'Is it not possible that as a preacher you fail somewhat, do not, as it were, deal sufficiently with fundamental things as others do? You leave untouched the truly vital issues, such things as the Creation, death, and, if I may refer to it, the life beyond the grave.'

As a result of which the Reverend Edward preached a series of special sermons on the Creation, for which he made a special and arduous preparation in the library of Plutoria University. He said that it had taken a million, possibly a hundred million, years of quite difficult work to accomplish, and that though when we looked at it all was darkness still we could not be far astray if we accepted and held fast to the teachings of Sir Charles Lyall. The book of Genesis, he said, was not to be taken as meaning a day when it said a day, but rather something other than a mere day; and the word 'light' meant not exactly light, but possibly some sort of phosphorescence, and that the use of the word 'darkness' was to be understood not as meaning darkness, but to be taken as simply indicating obscurity. And when he had quite finished, the congregation declared the whole sermon to be mere milk and water. It insulted their intelligence, they said. After which, a week later, the Reverend Dr Dumfarthing took up the same subject, and with the aid of seven plain texts pulverised the rector into fragments.

One notable result of the controversy was that Juliana Furlong refused henceforth to attend her brother's church, and sat, even at morning service, under the minister of St Osoph's.

'The sermon was, I fear, a mistake,' said Mr Furlong senior; 'perhaps you had better not dwell too much on such topics. We must look for aid in another direction. In fact, Edward, I may mention to you in confidence that certain of your trustees are already devising ways and means that may help us out of our dilemma.'

Indeed, although the Reverend Edward did not know it, a certain idea, or plan, was already germinating in the minds of the most influential supporters of St Asaph's.

Such was the situation of the rival churches of St Asaph and St Osoph as the autumn slowly faded into winter: during which time the elm-trees on Plutoria Avenue shivered and dropped their leaves and the chauffeurs of the motors first turned blue in their faces and then, when the great snows came, were suddenly converted into liveried coachmen with tall bearskins and whiskers like Russian horse-guards, changing back again to blue-nosed chauffeurs the very moment of a thaw. During this time also the congregation of the Reverend Fareforth Furlong was diminishing month by month, and that of the Reverend Uttermust Dumfarthing was so numerous that it filled up the aisles at the back of the church. Here the worshippers stood and froze, for the minister had abandoned the use of steam heat in St Osoph's on the ground that he could find no warrant for it.

During this same period also other momentous things were happening, such as that Juliana Furlong was reading, under the immediate guidance of Dr Dumfarthing, the *History of the Progress of Disruption in the Churches of Scotland* in ten volumes; such also as that Catherine Dumfarthing was wearing a green and gold winter suit with Russian furs and a Balkan hat and a Circassian feather which cut a wide swath of destruction among the young men on Plutoria Avenue every afternoon as she passed. Moreover, by the strangest of coincidences, she scarcely ever seemed to come along the snow-covered avenue without meeting the Reverend Edward – a fact which elicited new exclamations of surprise from them every day; and by an equally strange coincidence they generally seemed, although coming in different directions, to be bound for the same place, towards which they wandered together with such slow steps and in such oblivion of the passers-by that even children on the avenue knew by instinct whither they were wandering.

It was noted also that the broken figure of Dr McTeague had reappeared upon the street, leaning heavily upon a stick and greeting those he met with such a meek and willing affability, as if in apology for his stroke of paralysis, that all who talked with him agreed that McTeague's mind was a wreck.

'He stood and spoke to me about the children for at least a quarter of an hour,' related one of his former parishioners, 'asking after them by name, and whether they were going to school yet and a lot of questions like that. He never used to speak of such things. Poor old McTeague, I'm afraid he is getting soft in the head.'

'I know,' said the person addressed. 'His mind is no good. He stepped in the other day to say how sorry he was to hear about my brother's illness. I could see from the way he spoke that his brain is getting feeble. He's losing his grip. He was speaking of how kind people had been to him after his accident, and there were tears in his eyes. I think he's getting batty.'

Nor were even these things the most momentous happenings of the period, for as winter slowly changed to early spring it became known that something of great portent was under way. It was rumoured that the trustees of St Asaph's church were putting their heads together. This was striking news. The last time that the head of Mr Lucullus Fyshe, for example, had been placed side by side with that of Mr Newberry there had resulted a merger of four soda-water companies, bringing what was called industrial peace over an area as big as Texas and raising the price of soda by three peaceful cents per bottle. And the last time that Mr Furlong senior's head had been laid side by side with those of Mr Rasselyer-Brown and Mr Skinyer they had practically saved the country from the horrors of a coal famine by the simple process of raising the price of nut coal seventy-five cents a ton and thus guaranteeing its abundance.

Naturally, therefore, when it became known that such redoubtable heads as those of the trustees and the underlying mortgagees of St Asaph's were being put together, it was fully expected that some important development would follow.

It was never accurately known from which of the assembled heads first proceeded the great idea which was presently to solve the difficulties of the church. It may well have come from that of Mr Lucullus Fyshe. Certainly a head which had brought peace out of civil war in the hardware business by amalgamating ten rival stores, and which had saved the very lives of five hundred employees by reducing their wages fourteen per cent, was capable of it.

At any rate, it was Mr Fyshe who first gave the idea a definite utterance.

'It's the only thing, Furlong,' he said across the lunch table at the Mausoleum Club. 'It's the one solution. The two churches can't live under the present conditions of competition. We have here practically the same situation as we had with the rum distilleries – the output is too large for the demand. One or both of the two concerns must go under. It's their turn just now, but these fellows are business men enough to know that it may be ours tomorrow. We'll offer them a business solution. We'll propose a merger.'

'I've been thinking of it,' said Mr Furlong senior. 'I suppose it's feasible?'

'Feasible!' exclaimed Mr Fyshe. 'Why, look what's being done every day everywhere, from the Standard Oil Company downwards.'

'You would hardly, I think,' said Mr Furlong, with a quiet smile, 'compare the Standard Oil Company to a church?'

'Well, no, I suppose not,' said Mr Fyshe, and he too smiled – in fact he almost laughed. The notion was too ridiculous. One could hardly compare a church to a thing of the magnitude and importance of the Standard Oil Company.

'But on a lesser scale,' continued Mr Fyshe, 'it's the same sort of thing. As for the difficulties of it, I needn't remind you of the much greater difficulties we had to grapple with in the rum merger. There, you remember, a number of the men held out as a matter of principle. It was not mere business with them. Church union is different. In fact, it is one of the ideas of the day, and everyone admits that what is needed is the application of the ordinary business principles of harmonious combination, with a proper – er – restriction of output and general economy of operation.'

'Very good,' said Mr Furlong. 'I'm sure if you're willing to try, the rest of us are.'

'All right,' said Mr Fyshe. 'I thought of setting Skinyer, of Skinyer and Beatem, to work on the form of the organisation. As you know, he is not only a deeply religious man but he has already handled the Tin Pot Combination and the United Hardware and the Associated Tanneries. He ought to find this quite simple.'

* * *

Within a day or two Mr Skinyer had already commenced his labours. 'I must first,' he said, 'get an accurate idea of the existing legal organisation of the two churches.'

For which purpose he presently approached the rector of St Asaph's.

'I just want to ask you, Mr Furlong,' said the lawyer, 'a question or two as to the exact constitution, the form, so to speak, of your church. What is it? Is it a single corporate body?'

'I suppose,' said the rector thoughtfully, 'one would define it as an indivisible spiritual unit manifesting itself on earth.'

'Quite so,' interrupted Mr Skinyer, 'but I don't mean what is it in the religious sense: I mean, in the real sense.'

'I fail to understand,' said Mr Furlong.

'Let me put it very clearly, said the lawyer. 'Where does it get its authority?'

'From above,' said the rector reverently.

'Precisely,' said Mr Skinyer, 'no doubt. But I mean its authority in the *exact* sense of the term.'

'It was enjoined on St Peter –' began the rector, but Mr Skinyer interrupted him.

'That I am aware of,' he said, 'but what I mean is, where does your church get its power, for example, to hold property, to collect debts, to use distraint against the property of others, to foreclose its mortgages and to cause judgement to be executed against those who fail to pay their debts to it? You will say at once that it has these powers direct from Heaven. No doubt that is true, and no religious person would deny it. But we lawyers are compelled to take a narrower, a less elevating point of view. Are these powers conferred on you by the state legislature or by some higher authority?'

'Oh, by a Higher Authority, I hope,' said the rector very fervently. Whereupon Mr Skinyer left him without further questioning, the rector's brain being evidently unfit for the subject of corporation law.

On the other hand, he got satisfaction from the Reverend Dr Dumfarthing at once.

'The church of St Osoph,' said the minister, 'is a perpetual trust holding property as such under a general law of the state and able as such to be made the object of suit or distraint. I speak with some assurance, as I had occasion to enquire into the matter at the time when I was looking for guidance in regard to the call I had received to come here.'

* * *

'It's a quite simple matter,' Mr Skinyer presently reported to Mr Fyshe. 'One of the churches is a perpetual trust, the other practically a state corporation. Each has full control over its property, provided nothing is done by either to infringe the purity of its doctrine.'

'Just what does that mean?' asked Mr Fyshe.

'It must maintain its doctrine absolutely pure. Otherwise, if certain of its trustees remain pure and the rest do not, those who stay pure are entitled to take the whole of the property. This, I believe, happens every day in Scotland, where of course there is great eagerness to remain pure in doctrine.'

'And what do you define as *pure* doctrine?' asked Mr Fyshe.

'If the trustees are in dispute,' said Mr Skinyer, 'the courts decide; but any doctrine is held to be a pure doctrine if *all* the trustees regard it as a pure doctrine.'

'I see,' said Mr Fyshe thoughtfully, 'it's the same thing as what we called "permissible policy" on the directors in the Tin Pot Combination.'

'Exactly,' assented Mr Skinyer, 'and it means that for the merger we need nothing – I state it very frankly – except general consent.'

* * *

The preliminary stages of the making of the merger followed along familiar business lines. The trustees of St Asaph's went through the process known as 'approaching' the trustees of St Osoph's. First of all, for example, Mr Lucullus Fyshe invited Mr Asmodeus Boulder of St Osoph's to lunch with him at the Mausoleum Club; the cost of the lunch, as is usual in such cases, was charged to the General Expense account of the church. Of course nothing whatever was said during the lunch about the churches or their finances or anything concerning them. Such discussion would have been a gross business impropriety. A few days later the two brothers Overend dined with Mr Furlong senior, the dinner being charged directly to the Contingencies of St Asaph's. After which Mr Skinyer and his partner, Mr Beatem, went to the spring races together on the Profit and Loss account of St Osoph's, and Philippa Overend and Catherine Dumfarthing were taken (by the Unforeseen Disbursements Account) to the grand opera, followed by a midnight supper.

All of these things constituted what was called the promotion of the merger, and were almost exactly identical with the successive stages of the making of the Amalgamated Distilleries and the Associated Tin Pot Corporation; which was considered a most hopeful sign.

* * *

'Do you think they'll go into it?' asked Mr Newberry of Mr Furlong senior anxiously. 'After all, what inducement have they?'

'Every inducement,' said Mr Furlong. 'All said and done, they've only one large asset – Dr Dumfarthing. We're really offering to buy up Dr Dumfarthing by pooling our assets with theirs.'

'And what does Dr Dumfarthing himself say to it?'

'Ah, there I am not so sure,' said Mr Furlong; 'that may be a difficulty. So far there hasn't been a word from him, and his trustees are absolutely silent about his views. However, we shall soon know all about it. Skinyer is asking us all to come together one evening next week to draw up the articles of agreement.'

'Has he got the financial basis arranged, then?'

'I believe so,' said Mr Furlong. 'His idea is to form a new corporation to be known as the United Church Limited or by some similar name. All the present mortgagees will be converted into unified bond-holders, the pew rents will be capitalised into preferred stock, and the common stock, drawing its dividend from the offertory, will be distributed among all members in standing. Skinyer says that it is really an ideal form of church union, one that he thinks is likely to be widely adopted. It has the advantages of removing all questions of religion, which he says are practically the only remaining obstacle to a union of all the churches. In fact, it puts the churches once and for all on a business basis.'

'But what about the question of doctrine, of belief?' asked Mr Newberry.

'Skinyer says he can settle it,' answered Mr Furlong.

* * *

About a week after the above conversation the united trustees of St Asaph's and St Osoph's were gathered about a huge egg-shaped table in the board-room of the Mausoleum Club. They were seated in intermingled fashion, after the precedent of the recent Tin Pot Amalgamation, and were smoking huge black cigars specially kept by the club for the promotion of companies, and chargeable to expenses of organisation at fifty cents a cigar. There was an air of deep peace brooding over the assembly, as among men who have accomplished a difficult and meritorious task.

'Well, then,' said Mr Skinyer, who was in the chair with a pile of documents in front of him, 'I think that our general basis of financial union may be viewed as settled.'

A murmur of assent went round the meeting.

'The terms are set forth in the memorandum before us which you have already signed. Only one point – a minor one – remains to be considered. I refer to the doctrines or the religious belief of the new amalgamation.'

'Is it necessary to go into that?' asked Mr Boulder.

'Not entirely, perhaps,' said Mr Skinyer. 'Still, there have been, as you all know, certain points – I won't say of disagreement, but let us say of friendly argument – between the members of the different churches. Such things, for example,' here he consulted his papers, 'as the theory of the Creation, the salvation of the soul, and so forth, have been mentioned in this connection. I have a memorandum of them here, though the points escape me for the moment. These, you may say, are not matters of first importance, especially as compared with the intricate financial questions which we have already settled in a satisfactory manner. Still, I think it might be well if I were permitted, with your unanimous approval, to jot down a memorandum or two to be afterwards embodied in our articles.'

There was a general murmur of approval.

'Very good,' said Mr Skinyer, settling himself back in his chair. 'Now, first, in regard to the Creation,' here he looked all round the meeting in a way to command attention. 'Is it your wish that we should leave that merely to a gentleman's agreement or do you want an explicit clause?'

'I think it might be well,' said Mr George Overend, 'to leave no doubt about the theory of the Creation.'

'Good,' said Mr Skinyer. 'I am going to put it down then something after this fashion: "On and after, let us say, August lst proximo, the process of the Creation shall be held, and is hereby held, to be such and such only as is acceptable to a majority of the holders of common and preferred stock, voting pro rata." Is that agreed?'

'Carried,' cried several at once.

'Carried,' repeated Mr Skinyer. 'Now let us pass on' – here he consulted his notes – 'to item two, eternal punishment. I have made a memorandum as follows: "Should any doubts arise, on or after August lst proximo, as to the existence of eternal punishment, they shall be settled absolutely and finally by a pro rata vote of all the holders of common and preferred stock." Is that agreed?'

'One moment!' said Mr Fyshe. 'Do you think that quite fair to the bond-holders? After all, as the virtual holders of the property, they are the persons most interested. I should like to amend your clause and make it read – I am not phrasing it exactly but merely giving the sense of it – that eternal punishment should be reserved for the mortgagees and bond-holders.'

At this there was an outbreak of mingled approval and dissent, several persons speaking at once. In the opinion of some, the stock-holders of the company, especially the preferred stock-holders, had as good a right to eternal punishment as the bond-holders. Presently Mr Skinyer, who had been busily writing notes, held up his hand for silence.

'Gentlemen,' he said, 'will you accept this as a compromise? We will keep the original clause but merely add to it the words, "But no form of eternal punishment shall be declared valid if displeasing to a three-fifths majority of the holders of bonds." '

'Carried, carried,' cried everybody.

'To which I think we need only add,' said Mr Skinyer, 'a clause to the effect that all other points of doctrine, belief, or religious principle may be freely altered, amended, reversed, or entirely abolished at any general annual meeting.'

There was a renewed chorus of, 'Carried, carried,' and the trustees rose from the table shaking hands with one another, and lighting fresh cigars as they passed out of the club into the night air.

'The only thing that I don't understand,' said Mr Newberry to Dr Boomer as they went out from the club arm in arm (for they might now walk in that fashion with the same propriety as two of the principals in a distillery merger), 'the only thing that I don't understand is why the Reverend Dr Dumfarthing should be willing to consent to the amalgamation.'

'Do you really not know?' said Dr Boomer.

'No.'

'You have heard nothing?'

'Not a word,' said Mr Newberry.

'Ah,' rejoined the president, 'I see that our men have kept it very quiet – naturally so, in view of the circumstances. The truth is that the Reverend Dr Dumfarthing is leaving us.'

'Leaving St Osoph's!' exclaimed Mr Newberry in utter astonishment.

'To our great regret. He has had a call, a most inviting field of work, he says, a splendid opportunity. They offered him ten thousand one hundred; we were only giving him ten thousand here, though of course that feature of the situation would not weigh at all with a man like Dumfarthing.'

'Oh no, of course not,' said Mr Newberry.

'As soon as we heard of the call we offered him ten thousand three hundred – not that that would make any difference to a man of his character. Indeed, Dumfarthing was still waiting and looking for guidance when they offered him eleven thousand. We couldn't meet it. It was beyond us, though we had the consolation of knowing that with such a man as Dumfarthing the money made no difference.'

'And he has accepted the call?'

'Yes. He accepted it today. He sent word to Mr Dick Overend, our chairman, that he would remain in his manse, looking for light, until 2.30, after which, if we had not communicated with him by that hour, he would cease to look for it.'

'Dear me,' said Mr Newberry, deep in reflection; 'so that when your trustees came to the meeting –'

'Exactly,' said Dr Boomer – and something like a smile passed across his features for a moment. 'Dr Dumfarthing had already sent away his telegram of acceptance.'

'Why, then,' said Mr Newberry, 'at the time of our discussion tonight you were in the position of having no minister.'

'Not at all. We had already appointed a successor.'

'A successor?'

'Certainly. It will be in tomorrow morning's papers. The fact is that we have decided to ask Dr McTeague to resume his charge.'

'Dr McTeague!' repeated Mr Newberry in amazement. 'But surely his mind is understood to be –'

'Oh, not at all,' interrupted Dr Boomer. 'His mind appears, if anything, to be clearer and stronger than ever. Dr Slyder tells us that paralysis of the brain very frequently has this effect; it soothes the brain, clears it, as it were, so that very often intellectual problems which occasioned the greatest perplexity before present no difficulty whatever afterwards. Dr McTeague, I believe, finds no trouble now in reconciling St Paul's dialectic with Hegel as he used to. He says that so far as he can see they both mean the same.'

'Well, well,' said Mr Newberry. 'And will Dr McTeague also resume his philosophical lectures at the university?'

'We think it wiser not,' said the president. 'While we feel that Dr McTeague's mind is in admirable condition for clerical work, we fear that professorial duties might strain it. In order to get the full value of his remarkable intelligence we propose to elect him to the governing body of the university. There his brain will be safe from any shock. As a professor there would always be the fear that one of his students might raise a question in his class. This of course is not a difficulty that arises in the pulpit or among the governors of the university.'

'Of course not,' said Mr Newberry.

* * *

Thus was constituted the famous union or merger of the churches of St Asaph and St Osoph, viewed by many of those who made it as the beginning of a new era in the history of the modern Church. There is no doubt that it has been in every way an eminent success.

Rivalry, competition, and controversies over points of dogma have become unknown on Plutoria Avenue. The parishioners of the two churches may now attend either of them just as they like. As the trustees are fond of explaining, it doesn't make the slightest difference. The entire receipts of the churches, being now pooled, are divided without reference to individual attendance. At each half-year there is issued a printed statement which is addressed to the shareholders of the United Churches, Limited, and is hardly to be distinguished in style or material from the annual and semi-annual reports of the Tin Pot Amalgamation and the United Hardware and other quasi-religious bodies of the sort. 'Your directors,' the last of these documents states, 'are happy to inform you that, in spite of the prevailing industrial depression, the gross receipts of the corporation have shown such an increase as to justify the distribution of a stock dividend of special Offertory Stock Cumulative, which will be offered at par to all holders of common or preferred shares. You will also be gratified to learn that the directors have voted unanimously in favour of a special presentation to the Reverend Dr Uttermust Dumfarthing on the occasion of his approaching marriage. It was earnestly debated whether this gift should take the form, as at first proposed, of a cash presentation, or, as afterwards suggested, of a written testimonial in the form of an address. The latter course was finally adopted as being more fitting to the circumstances, and the address has accordingly been prepared, setting forth to the Reverend Dr Dumfarthing, in old English lettering and wording, the opinion which is held of him by his former parishioners.'

The 'approaching marriage' referred of course to Dr Dumfarthing's betrothal to Juliana Furlong. It was not known that he had ever exactly proposed to her. But it was understood that before giving up his charge he drew her attention, in very severe terms, to the fact that, as his daughter was now leaving him, he must either have someone else to look after his manse or else be compelled to incur the expense of a paid housekeeper. This latter alternative, he said, was not one that he cared to contemplate. He also reminded her that she was at a time of life when she could hardly expect to pick and choose, and that her spiritual condition was one of, at least, great uncertainty. These combined statements are held, under the law of Scotland at any rate, to be equivalent to an offer of marriage.

Catherine Dumfarthing did not join her father in his new manse. She first remained behind him, as the guest of Philippa Overend, for a few weeks while she was occupied in packing up her things. After that she stayed for another two or three weeks to unpack them. This had been rendered necessary by a conversation held with the Reverend Edward Fareforth in a shaded corner of the Overends' garden. After which, in due course of time, Catherine and Edward were married, the ceremony being performed by the Reverend Dr McTeague, whose eyes filled with philosophical tears as he gave them his blessing.

So the two churches of St Asaph and St Osoph stand side by side united and at peace. Their bells call softly back and forward to one another on Sunday mornings, and such is the harmony between them that even the episcopal blackbirds in the elm-trees of St Asaph's and the presbyterian crows in the spruce-trees of St Osoph's are known to exchange perches on alternate Sundays.

VIII. THE GREAT FIGHT FOR CLEAN GOVERNMENT

'As to the government of this city,' said Mr Newberry, leaning back in a leather arm-chair at the Mausoleum Club and lighting a second cigar, 'it's rotten, that's all.'

'Absolutely rotten,' assented Mr Dick Overend, ringing the bell for a whisky and soda.

'Corrupt,' said Mr Newberry, between two puffs of his cigar.

'Full of graft,' said Mr Overend, flicking his ash into the grate.

'Crooked aldermen,' said Mr Newberry.

'A bum city solicitor,' said Mr Overend, 'and an infernal grafter for treasurer.'

'Yes,' assented Mr Newberry, and then, leaning forward in his chair and looking carefully about the corridors of the club, he spoke behind his hand and said, 'And the mayor's the biggest grafter of the lot. And what's more,' he added, sinking his voice to a whisper, 'the time has come to speak out about it fearlessly.'

Mr Overend nodded. 'It's a tyranny,' he said.

'Worse than Russia,' rejoined Mr Newberry.

* * *

They had been sitting in a quiet corner of the club – it was a Sunday evening – and had fallen into talking, first of all, of the present rottenness of the federal politics of the United States, not argumentatively or with any heat, but with the reflective sadness that steals over an elderly man when he sits in the leather arm-chair of a comfortable club smoking a good cigar and musing on the decadence of the present day. The rottenness of the federal government didn't anger them. It merely grieved them.

They could remember, both of them, how different everything was when they were young men just entering on life. When Mr Newberry and Mr Dick Overend were young, men went into Congress from pure patriotism; there was no such thing as graft or crookedness, as they both admitted, in those days; and as for the United States Senate – here their voices were almost hushed in awe – why, when they were young the United States Senate –

But no, neither of them could find a phrase big enough for their meaning.

They merely repeated, 'As for the United States Senate –' and then shook their heads and took a long drink of whisky and soda.

Thus, very naturally, speaking of the rottenness of the federal government had led them to talk of the rottenness of the state legislature. How different from the state legislatures that they remembered as young men! Not merely different in the matter of graft, but different, so Mr Newberry said, in the calibre of the men. He recalled how he had been taken as a boy of twelve by his father to hear a debate. He would never forget it. Giants, he said, that was what they were! In fact, the thing was more like a Witenagemot than a legislature. He said he distinctly recalled a man, whose name he didn't recollect, speaking on a question – he didn't just remember what, either for or against he couldn't just recall which; but it thrilled him. He would never forget it. It stayed in his memory as if it were yesterday.

But as for the present legislature – here Mr Dick Overend sadly nodded assent in advance to what he knew was coming – as for the present legislature – well – Mr Newberry had had, he said, occasion to visit the state capital a week before in connection with a railway bill that he was trying to – that is, that he was anxious to – in short, in connection with a railway bill, and when he looked about him at the men in the legislature, positively he felt ashamed; he could put it no other way than that – ashamed.

After which, from speaking of the crookedness of the state government, Mr Newberry and Mr Dick Overend were led to talk of the crookedness of the city government. And they both agreed, as above, that things were worse than in Russia. What secretly irritated them both most was that they had lived and done business under this infernal corruption for thirty or forty years and hadn't noticed it. They had been too busy.

The fact was that their conversation reflected not so much their own original ideas as a general wave of feeling that was passing over the whole community.

There had come a moment – quite suddenly, it seemed – when it occurred to everybody at the same time that the whole government of the city was rotten. The word is a strong one. But it is the one that was used. Look at the aldermen, they said – rotten! Look at the city solicitor – rotten! And as for the mayor himself – phew!

The thing came like a wave. Everybody felt it at once. People wondered how any sane, intelligent community could tolerate the presence of a set of corrupt scoundrels like the twenty aldermen of the city. Their names, it was said, were simply a byword throughout the United States for rank criminal corruption. This was said so widely that everybody started hunting through the daily papers to try to find out who in blazes were aldermen, anyhow. Twenty names are hard to remember, and as a matter of fact till the moment when this wave of feeling struck the city, nobody knew or cared who were aldermen, anyway.

To tell the truth, the aldermen had been much the same persons for about fifteen or twenty years. Some were in the produce business, others were butchers, two were grocers, and all of them wore blue checkered waistcoats and red ties and got up at seven in the morning to attend the vegetable and other markets. Nobody had ever really thought about them – that is to say, nobody on Plutoria Avenue. Sometimes one saw a picture in the paper and wondered for a moment who the person was; but on looking more closely and noticing what was written under it, one said, 'Oh, I see, an alderman,' and turned to something else.

'Whose funeral is that?' a man would sometimes ask on Plutoria Avenue. 'Oh, just one of the city aldermen,' a passer-by would answer hurriedly. 'Oh, I see. I beg your pardon; I thought it might be somebody important.' At which both laughed.

* * *

It was not just clear how and where this movement of indignation had started. People said that it was part of a new wave of public morality that was sweeping over the entire United States. Certainly it was being remarked in almost every section of the country. Chicago newspapers were attributing its origin to the new vigour and the fresh ideals of the Middle West. In Boston it was said to be due to a revival of the grand old New England spirit. In Philadelphia they called it the spirit of William Penn. In the south it was said to be the reassertion of southern chivalry making itself felt against the greed and selfishness of the north, while in the north they recognised it at once as a protest against the sluggishness and ignorance of the south. In the west they spoke of it as a revolt against the spirit of the east, and in the east they called it a denunciation of the lawlessness of the west. But everywhere they hailed it as a new sign of the glorious unity of the country.

If therefore Mr Newberry and Mr Overend were found to be discussing the corrupt state of their city they only shared in the national sentiments of the moment. In fact, in the same city hundreds of other citizens, as disinterested as themselves, were waking up to the realisation of what was going on. As soon as people began to look into the condition of things in the city they were horrified at what they found. It was discovered, for example, that Alderman Schwefeldampf was an under-taker! Think of it! In a city with a hundred and fifty deaths a week, and sometimes even better, an undertaker sat on the council! A city that was about to expropriate land and to spend four hundred thousand dollars for a new cemetery had an undertaker on the expropriation committee itself! And worse than that. Alderman Undercutt was a butcher. In a city that consumed a thousand tons of meat every week! And Alderman O'Hooligan – it leaked out – was an Irishman! Imagine it! An alderman sitting on the police committee of the council in a city where thirty-eight and a half out of every hundred policemen were Irish, either by birth or parentage! The thing was monstrous.

So when Mr Newberry said, 'It's worse than Russia!' he meant it, every word.

* * *

Now just as Mr Newberry and Mr Dick Overend were finishing their discussion, the huge, bulky form of Mayor McGrath came ponderously past them as they sat. He looked at them sideways out of his eyes – he had eyes like plums in a mottled face – and, being a born politician, he knew by the very look of them that they were talking of something that they had no business to be talking about. But, being a politician, he merely said, 'Good evening, gentlemen,' without a sign of disturbance.

'Good evening, Mr Mayor,' said Mr Newberry, rubbing his hands feebly together and speaking in an ingratiating tone. There is no more pitiable spectacle than an honest man caught in the act of speaking boldly and fearlessly of the evil-doer.

'Good evening, Mr Mayor,' echoed Mr Dick Overend, also rubbing his hands; 'warm evening, is it not?'

The mayor gave no other answer than that deep guttural grunt which is technically known in municipal interviews as refusing to commit oneself.

'Did he hear?' whispered Mr Newberry, as the mayor passed out of the club.

'I don't care if he did,' whispered Mr Dick Overend.

Half an hour later Mayor McGrath entered the premises of the Thomas Jefferson Club, which were situated in the rear end of a saloon and pool room far down in the town.

'Boys,' he said to Alderman O'Hooligan and Alderman Gorfinke, who were playing freeze-out poker in a corner behind the pool tables, 'you want to let the boys know to keep pretty dark and go easy. There's a lot of talk I don't like about the elections going round the town. Let the boys know that just for a while the darker they keep the better.'

Whereupon the word was passed from the Thomas Jefferson Club to the George Washington Club and thence to the Eureka Club (Coloured) and to the Kossuth Club (Hungarian), and to various other centres of civic patriotism in the lower parts of the city. And forthwith such a darkness began to spread over them that not even honest Diogenes with his lantern could have penetrated their doings.

'If them stiffs wants to make trouble,' said the president of the George Washington Club to Mayor McGrath a day or two later, 'they won't never know what they've bumped up against.'

'Well,' said the heavy mayor, speaking slowly and cautiously and eyeing his henchman with quiet scrutiny, 'you want to go pretty easy now, I tell you.'

The look which the mayor directed at his satellite was much the same glance that Morgan the buccaneer might have given to one of his lieutenants before throwing him overboard.

* * *

Meantime the wave of civic enthusiasm as reflected in the conversations of Plutoria Avenue grew stronger with every day.

'The thing is a scandal,' said Mr Lucullus Fyshe. 'Why, these fellows down at the City Hall are simply a pack of rogues. I had occasion to do some business there the other day (it was connected with the assessment of our soda factories), and do you know, I actually found that these fellows *take money!*'

'I say!' said Mr Peter Spillikins, to whom he spoke. 'I say! You don't say!'

'It's a fact,' repeated Mr Fyshe. 'They take money. I took the assistant treasurer aside and I said, "I want such and such done," and I slipped a fifty-dollar bill into his hand. And the fellow took it, took it like a shot.'

'He took it?' gasped Mr Spillikins.

'He did,' said Mr Fyshe. 'There ought to be a criminal law for that sort of thing.'

'I say!' exclaimed Mr Spillikins; 'they ought to go to jail for a thing like that.'

'And the infernal insolence of them,' Mr Fyshe continued. 'I went down the next day to see the deputy assistant (about a thing connected with the same matter), and told him what I wanted and passed a fifty-dollar bill across the counter, and the fellow fairly threw it back at me, in a perfect rage. He refused it!'

'He refused it?' gasped Mr Spillikins. 'I say!'

Conversations such as this filled up the leisure and divided the business time of all the best people in the city.

In the general gloomy outlook, however, one bright spot was observable. The 'wave' had evidently come just at the opportune moment. For not only were civic elections pending, but just at this juncture four or five questions of supreme importance would have to be settled by the incoming council. There was, for instance, the question of the expropriation of the Traction Company – a matter involving many millions; there was the decision as to the renewal of the franchise of the Citizens' Light Company – a vital question; there was also the four-hundred-thousand-dollar purchase of the land for the new addition to the cemetery, a matter that must be settled. And it was felt, especially on Plutoria Avenue, to be a splendid thing that the city was waking up, in the moral sense, at the very time when these things were under discussion. All the shareholders of the Traction Company and the Citizens' Light – and they included the very best, the most highminded, people in the city – felt that what was needed now was a great moral effort, to enable them to lift the city up and carry it with them; or, if not all of it, at any rate as much of it as they could.

'It's a splendid movement,' said Mr Fyshe (he was a leading shareholder and director of the Citizens' Light), 'a splendid thing to think that we shan't have to deal for our new franchise with a set of corrupt rapscallions like these present aldermen. Do you know, Furlong, that when we approached them first with a proposition for a renewal for a hundred and fifty years they held us up! Said it was too long.

Imagine that! A hundred and fifty years (only a century and a half) too long for the franchise! They expect us to install all our poles, string our wires, set up our transformers in their streets and then perhaps at the end of a hundred years find ourselves compelled to sell out at a beggarly valuation. Of course we knew what they wanted. They meant us to hand them over fifty dollars each to stuff into their rascally pockets.'

'Outrageous!' said Mr Furlong.

'And the same thing with the cemetery land deal,' went on Mr Lucullus Fyshe. 'Do you realise that if the movement hadn't come along and checked them, those scoundrels would have given that rogue Schwefeldampf four hundred thousand dollars for his fifty acres! Just think of it!'

'I don't know,' said Mr Furlong with a thoughtful look upon his face, 'that four hundred thousand dollars is an excessive price, in and of itself, for that amount of land.'

'Certainly not,' said Mr Fyshe very quietly and decidedly, looking at Mr Furlong in a searching way as he spoke. 'It is *not* a high price. It seems to me, speaking purely as an outsider, a very fair, reasonable price for fifty acres of suburban land, if it were the right land. If, for example, it were a case of making an offer for that very fine stretch of land, about twenty acres, is it not? which I believe your Corporation owns on the *other* side of the cemetery, I should say four hundred thousand is a most modest price.'

Mr Furlong nodded his head reflectively. 'You had thought, had you not, of offering it to the city?' said Mr Fyshe.

'We did,' said Mr Furlong, 'at a more or less nominal sum – four hundred thousand or whatever it might be. We felt that for such a purpose, almost sacred as it were, one would want as little bargaining as possible.'

'Oh, none at all,' assented Mr Fyshe.

'Our feeling was,' went on Mr Furlong, 'that if the city wanted our land for the cemetery extension it might have it at its own figure – four hundred thousand, half a million, in fact at absolutely any price from four hundred thousand up that they cared to put on it. We didn't regard it as a commercial transaction at all. Our reward lay merely in the fact of selling it to them.'

'Exactly,' said Mr Fyshe; 'and of course your land was more desirable from every point of view. Schwefeldampf's ground is encumbered with a growth of cypress and evergreens and weeping willows which make it quite unsuitable for an up-to-date cemetery; whereas yours, as I remember it, is bright and open, a loose sandy soil with no trees and very little grass to overcome.'

'Yes,' said Mr Furlong. 'We thought, too, that our ground, having the tanneries and the chemical factory along the further side of it, was an ideal place for – for –' He paused, seeking a mode of expressing his thought.

'For the dead,' said Mr Fyshe with becoming reverence. And after this conversation Mr Fyshe and Mr Furlong senior understood one another absolutely in regard to the new movement.

It was astonishing, in fact, how rapidly the light spread. 'Is Rasselyer-Brown with us?' asked someone of Mr Fyshe a few day later.

'Heart and soul,' answered Mr Fyshe. 'He's very bitter over the way these rascals have been plundering the city's coal supply. He says that the city has been buying coal wholesale at the pit-mouth at three-fifty – utterly worthless stuff, he tells me. He has heard it said that every one of these scoundrels has been paid from twenty-five to fifty dollars a winter to connive at it.'

'Dear me!' said the listener.

'Abominable, is it not?' said Mr Fyshe. 'But, as I said to Rasselyer-Brown, what can one do if the citizens themselves take no interest in these things? "Take your own case," I said to him; "how is it that you, a coal man, are not helping the city in this matter? Why don't you supply the city?" He shook his head. "I wouldn't do it at three-fifty," he said. "No," I answered, "but will you at five?" He looked at me for a moment and then he said, "Fyshe, I'll do it; at five, or at anything over that they like to name. If we get a new council in, they may name their own figure." "Good," I said. "I hope all the other business men will be animated with the same spirit." '

* * *

Thus it was that the light broke and spread and illuminated in all directions. People began to realise the needs of the city as they never had before. Mr Boulder, who owned among other things a stone quarry and an asphalt company, felt that the paving of the streets was a disgrace. Mr Skinyer, of Skinyer and Beatem, shook his head and said that the whole legal department of the city needed reorganisation. It needed, he said, new blood. But he added, always in a despairing tone, how could one expect to run a department with the head of it drawing only six thousand dollars? The thing was impossible. If, he argued, they could superannuate the present chief solicitor and get a man, a *good* man (Mr Skinyer laid emphasis on this) at say fifteen thousand, there might be some hope.

'Of course,' said Mr Skinyer to Mr Newberry in discussing the topic, 'one would need to give him a proper staff of assistants so as to take off his hands all the *routine* work – the mere appearance in court, the preparation of briefs, the office consultations, the tax revision and expropriation departments, and the purely legal work. In that case he would have his hands free to devote himself entirely to those things which – in fact, to turn his attention in whatever direction he might feel it was advisable to turn it.'

* * *

Within a week or two the public movement had found definite expression and embodied itself in the Clean Government Association. This was organised by a group of leading and disinterested citizens who held their first meeting in the largest upstairs room of the Mausoleum Club. Mr Lucullus Fyshe, Mr Boulder, and others keenly interested in obtaining simple justice for the stock-holders of the Traction and the Citizens' Light were prominent from the start. Mr Rasselyer-Brown, Mr Furlong senior, and others were there, not from special interest in the light or traction questions, but, as they said themselves, from pure civic spirit. Dr Boomer was there to represent the university, with three of his most presentable professors, cultivated men who were able to sit in a first-class club and drink whisky and soda and talk as well as any business man present. Mr Skinyer, Mr Beatem, and others represented the bar. Dr McTeague, blinking in the blue tobacco smoke, was there to stand for the church. There were all-round enthusiasts as well, such as Mr Newberry and the Overend brothers and Mr Peter Spillikins.

'Isn't it fine,' whispered Mr Spillikins to Mr Newberry, 'to see a set of men like these all going into a thing like this, not thinking of their own interests a bit?'

* * *

Mr Fyshe, as chairman, addressed the meeting. He told them they were there to initiate a great, free, voluntary movement of the people. It had been thought wise, he said, to hold it with closed doors and to keep it out of the newspapers. This would guarantee the League against the old underhand control by a clique that had hitherto disgraced every part of the administration of the city. He wanted, he said, to see everything done henceforth in broad daylight, and for this purpose he had summoned them at night to discuss ways and means of action. After they were once fully assured exactly what they wanted to do and how they meant to do it, the League, he said, would invite the fullest and freest advice from all classes in the city. There were none, he said, amid great applause, that were so lowly that they would not be invited, once the platform of the League was settled, to advise and co-operate. All might help, even the poorest. Subscription lists would be prepared which would allow any sum at all, from one to five dollars, to be given to the treasurer. The League was to be democratic or nothing. The poorest might contribute as little as one dollar; even the richest would not be allowed to give more than five. Moreover, he gave notice that he intended to propose that no actual official of the League should be allowed under its bye-laws to give anything. He himself – if they did him the honour to make him president, as he had heard it hinted was their intention – would be the first to bow to this rule. He would efface himself. He would obliterate himself, content in the interests of all to give nothing. He was able to announce similar pledges from his friends, Mr Boulder, Mr Furlong, Dr Boomer, and a number of others.

Quite a storm of applause greeted these remarks by Mr Fyshe, who flushed with pride as he heard it.

'Now, gentlemen,' he went on, 'this meeting is open for discussion. Remember, it is quite informal; anyone may speak. I as chairman make no claim to control or monopolise the discussion. Let everyone understand –'

'Well then, Mr Chairman –' began Mr Dick Overend.

'One minute, Mr Overend,' said Mr Fyshe. 'I want everyone to understand that he may speak as freely –'

'May I say then –' began Mr Newberry.

'Pardon me, Mr Newberry,' said Mr Fyshe, 'I was wishing first to explain that not only may *all* participate but that we *invite* –'

'In that case –' began Mr Newberry.

'Before you speak,' interrupted Mr Fyshe, 'let me add one word. We must make our discussion as brief and to the point as possible. I have a great number of things which I wish to say to the meeting, and it might be well if all of you would speak as briefly and as little as possible. Has anybody anything to say?'

'Well,' said Mr Newberry, 'what about organisation and officers?'

'We have thought of it,' said Mr Fyshe. 'We were anxious above all things to avoid the objectionable and corrupt methods of a "slate" and a prepared list of officers, which have disgraced every part of our city politics until the present time. Mr Boulder, Mr Furlong, and Mr Skinyer and myself have therefore prepared a short list of offices and officers which we wish to submit to your fullest, freest consideration. It runs thus: Hon. President, Mr L. Fyshe; Hon. Vice-President, Mr A. Boulder; Hon. Secretary, Mr Furlong; Hon. Treasurer, Mr O. Skinyer; et cetera, et cetera – I needn't read it all. You'll see it posted in the hall later. Is that carried? Carried! Very good,' said Mr Fyshe.

There was a moment's pause while Mr Furlong and Mr Skinyer moved into seats beside Mr Fyshe, and while Mr Furlong drew from his pocket and arranged the bundle of minutes of the meeting which he had brought with him. As he himself said, he was too neat and methodical a writer to trust to jotting them down on the spot.

'Don't you think,' said Mr Newberry '– I speak as a practical man – that we ought to do something to get the newspapers with us?'

'Most important,' assented several members.

'What do you think, Dr Boomer?' asked Mr Fyshe of the university president. 'Will the newspapers be with us?'

Dr Boomer shook his head doubtfully. 'It's an important matter,' he said. 'There is no doubt that we need more than anything the support of a clean, wholesome, unbiased press that can't be bribed and is not subject to money influence. I think on the whole our best plan would be to buy up one of the city newspapers.'

'Might it not be better simply to buy up the editorial staff?' said Mr Dick Overend.

'We might do that,' admitted Dr Boomer. 'There is no doubt that the corruption of the press is one of the worst factors that we have to oppose. But whether we can best fight it by buying the paper or buying the staff is hard to say.'

'Suppose we leave it to a committee with full power to act,' said Mr Fyshe. 'Let us direct them to take whatever steps may in their opinion be best calculated to elevate the tone of the press, the treasurer being authorised to second them in every way. I for one am heartily sick of old underhand connections between city politics and the city papers. If we can do anything to alter and elevate it, it will be a fine work, gentlemen, well worth whatever it costs us.'

* * *

Thus after an hour or two of such discussion the Clean Government League found itself organised and equipped, with a treasury and a programme and a platform. The latter was very simple. As Mr Fyshe and Mr Boulder said, there was no need to drag in specific questions or try to define the action to be taken towards this or that particular detail, such as the hundred-and-fifty-year franchise, beforehand. The platform was simply expressed as Honesty, Purity, Integrity. This, as Mr Fyshe said, made a straight, flat, clean issue between the League and all who opposed it.

This first meeting was of course confidential. But all that it did was presently done over again, with wonderful freshness and spontaneity, at a large public meeting open to all citizens. There was a splendid impromptu air about everything. For instance, when somebody away back in the hall said, 'I move that Mr Lucullus Fyshe be president of the

League,' Mr Fyshe lifted his hand in unavailing protest, as if this were the newest idea he had ever heard in his life.

After all of which the Clean Government League set itself to fight the Cohorts of Darkness. It was not just known where these were, but it was understood that they were there all right, somewhere. In the platform speeches of the epoch they figured as working underground, working in the dark, working behind the scenes, and so forth. But the strange thing was that nobody could state with any exactitude just who or what it was that the League was fighting. It stood for 'honesty, purity, and integrity.' That was all you could say about it.

Take, for example, the case of the press. At the inception of the League it had been supposed that such was the venality and corruption of the city newspapers that it would be necessary to buy one of them. But the words 'clean government' had been no sooner uttered than it turned out that every one of the papers in the city was in favour of it – in fact, they had been working for it for years.

They vied with one another now in giving publicity to the idea. The *Plutorian Times* printed a dotted coupon on the corner of its front sheet with the words, 'Are you in favour of Clean Government? If so, send us ten cents with this coupon and your name and address.' The *Plutorian Citizen and Home Advocate* went even further. It printed a coupon which said, 'Are you out for a Clean City? If so, send us twenty-five cents to this office. We pledge ourselves to use it.'

The newspapers did more than this. They printed from day to day such pictures as the portrait of Mr Fyshe with the legend below, 'Mr Lucullus Fyshe, who says that government ought to be by the people, from the people, for the people, and to the people'; and the next day another labelled, 'Mr P. Spillikins, who says that all men are born free and equal'; and the next day a picture with the words, 'Tract of ground offered for cemetery by Mr Furlong, showing rear of tanneries, with head of Mr Furlong inserted.'

It was of course plain enough that certain of the aldermen of the old council were to be reckoned as part of the Cohort of Darkness. That at least was clear. 'We want no more men in control of the stamp of Alderman Gorfinkel and Alderman Schwefeldampf,' so said practically every paper in the city. 'The public sense revolts at these men. They are vultures who have feasted too long on the prostrate corpses of our citizens.' And so on.

The only trouble was to discover who or what had ever supported Alderman Gorfinkel and Alderman Schwefeldampf. The very organisations that might have seemed to be behind them were evidently more eager for clean government than the League itself.

'The Thomas Jefferson Club out for Clean Government,' so ran the newspaper headings of one day; and of the next,

'Will help to clean up City Government. Eureka Club (Coloured) endorses the League; is done with Darkness,' and the day after that,

'Sons of Hungary Share in Good Work: Kossuth Club will vote with the League.'

So strong, indeed, was the feeling against the iniquitous aldermen that the public demand arose to be done with a council of aldermen altogether, and to substitute government by a board. The newspapers contained editorials on the topic each day, and it was understood that one of the first efforts of the League would be directed towards getting the necessary sanction of the legislature in this direction. To help to enlighten the public on what such government meant, Professor Proaser of the university (he was one of the three already referred to) gave a public lecture on the growth of Council Government. He traced it from the Amphictionic Council of Greece as far down as the Oligarchical Council of Venice; it was thought that had the evening been longer he would have traced it clean down to modern times.

But most amazing of all was the announcement that was presently made, and endorsed by Mr Lucullus Fyshe in an official interview, that Mayor McGrath himself would favour Clean Government, and would become the official nominee of the League itself.

This certainly was strange. But it would perhaps have been less mystifying to the public at large had they been able to listen to certain of the intimate conversations of Mr Fyshe and Mr Boulder.

'You say, then,' said Mr Boulder, 'to let McGrath's name stand?'

'We can't do without him,' said Mr Fyshe; 'he has seven of the wards in the hollow of his hand. If we take his offer he absolutely pledges us every one of them.'

'Can you rely on his word?' said Mr Boulder.

'I think he means to play fair with us,' answered Mr Fyshe. 'I put it to him as a matter of honour, between man and man, a week ago. Since then I have had him carefully dictaphoned, and I'm convinced he's playing straight.'

'How far will he go with us?' said Mr Boulder.

'He is willing to throw overboard Gorfinkel, Schwefeldampf, and Undercutt. He says he must find a place for O'Hooligan. The Irish, he says, don't care for clean government; they want Irish government.'

'I see,' said Mr Boulder very thoughtfully; 'and in regard to the renewal of the franchise and the expropriation, tell me just exactly what his conditions are.'

But Mr Fyshe's answer to this was said so discreetly and in such a low voice, that not even the birds listening in the elm-trees outside the Mausoleum Club could hear it. No wonder then that if even the birds failed to know everything about the Clean Government League, there were many things which such people as Mr Newberry and Mr Peter Spillikins never heard at all and never guessed.

* * *

Each week and every day brought fresh triumphs to the onward march of the movement.

'Yes, gentlemen,' said Mr Fyshe to the assembled committee of the Clean Government League a few days later, 'I am glad to be able to report our first victory. Mr Boulder and I have visited the state capital and we are able to tell you definitely that the legislature will consent to change our form of government so as to replace our council by a board.'

'Hear, hear!' cried all the committee men together.

'We saw the Governor,' said Mr Fyshe. 'Indeed, he was good enough to lunch with us at the Pocahontas Club. He tells us that what we are doing is being done in every city and town of the state. He says that the days of the old-fashioned city council are numbered. They are setting up boards everywhere.'

'Excellent!' said Mr Newberry.

'The Governor assures us that what we want will be done. The chairman of the Democratic State Committee (he was good enough to dine with us at the Buchanan Club) has given us the same assurance. So also has the chairman of the Republican State Committee, who was kind enough to be our guest in a box at the Lincoln theatre. It is most gratifying,' concluded Mr Fyshe, 'to feel that the legislature will give us such a hearty, such a thoroughly American support.'

'You are sure of this, are you?' questioned Mr Newberry. 'You have actually seen the members of the legislature?'

'It was not necessary,' said Mr Fyshe. 'The Governor and the different chairmen have them so well fixed – that is to say, they have such confidence in the Governor and their political organisers – that they will all be prepared to give us what I have described as a thoroughly American support.'

'You are quite sure,' persisted Mr Newberry, 'about the Governor and the others you mentioned?'

Mr Fyshe paused a moment, and then he said very quietly, 'We are quite sure,' and he exchanged a look with Mr Boulder that meant volumes to those who could read it.

* * *

'I hope you didn't mind my questioning you in that fashion,' said Mr Newberry, as he and Mr Fyshe strolled home from the club. 'The truth is, I didn't feel sure in my own mind just what was meant by a "board", and "getting them to give us government by a board." I know I'm speaking like an ignoramus. I've really not paid as much attention in the past to civic politics as I ought to have. But what is the difference between a council and a board?'

'The difference between a council and a board?' repeated Mr Fyshe.

'Yes,' said Mr Newberry, 'the difference between a council and a board.'

'Or call it,' said Mr Fyshe reflectively, 'the difference between a board and a council.'

'Precisely,' said Mr Newberry.

'It's not altogether easy to explain,' said Mr Fyshe. 'One chief difference is that in the case of a board, sometimes called a commission, the *salary* is higher. You see, the salary of an alderman or councillor in most cities is generally not more than fifteen hundred or two thousand dollars. The salary of a member of a board or commission is at least ten thousand. That gives you at once a very different class of men. As long as you only pay fifteen hundred you get your council filled up with men who will do any kind of crooked work for fifteen hundred dollars; and as soon as you pay ten thousand you get men with larger ideas.'

'I see,' said Mr Newberry.

'If you have a fifteen-hundred-dollar man,' Mr Fyshe went on, 'you can bribe him at any time with a fifty-dollar bill. On the other hand, your ten-thousand-dollar man has a wider outlook. If you offer him fifty dollars for his vote on the board, he'd probably laugh at you.'

'Ah, yes,' said Mr Newberry, 'I see the idea. A fifteen-hundred-dollar salary is so low that it will tempt a lot of men into office merely for what they can get out of it.'

'That's it, exactly,' answered Mr Fyshe.

* * *

From all sides support came to the new League. The women of the city – there were fifty thousand of them on the municipal voters' list – were not behind the men. Though not officials of the League, they rallied to its cause.

'Mr Fyshe,' said Mrs Buncomhearst, who called at the office of the president of the League with offers of support, 'tell me what we can do. I represent fifty thousand women voters of this city –'

(This was a favourite phrase of Mrs Buncomhearst's, though it had never been made quite clear how or why she represented them.)

'We want to help, we women. You know we've any amount of initiative, if you'll only tell us what to do. You know, Mr Fyshe, we've just as good executive ability as you men if you'll just tell us what to do. Couldn't we hold a meeting of our own, all our own, to help the League along?'

'An excellent idea,' said Mr Fyshe.

'And could you get three or four men to come and address it so as to stir us up?' asked Mrs Buncomhearst anxiously.

'Oh, certainly,' said Mr Fyshe.

So it was known after this that the women were working side by side with the men. The tea rooms of the Grand Palaver and the other hotels were filled with them every day, busy for the cause. One of them even invented a perfectly charming election scarf to be worn as a sort of badge to show one's allegiance; and its great merit was that it was so fashioned that it would go with anything.

'Yes,' said Mr Fyshe to his committee, 'one of the finest signs of our movement is that the women of the city are with us. Whatever we may think, gentlemen, of the question of woman's rights in general – and I think we know what we *do* think – there is no doubt that the influence of women makes for purity in civic politics. I am glad to inform the committee that Mrs Buncomhearst and her friends have organised all the working women of the city who have votes. They tell me that they have been able to do this at a cost as low as five dollars per woman. Some of the women – foreigners of the lower classes whose sense of political morality is as yet imperfectly developed – have been organised at a cost as low as one dollar per vote. But of course with our native American women, with a higher standard of education and morality, we can hardly expect to do it as low as that.'

* * *

Nor were the women the only element of support added to the League.

'Gentlemen,' reported Dr Boomer, the president of the university, at the next committee meeting, 'I am glad to say that the spirit which animates us has spread to the students of the university. They have organised entirely by themselves, and on their own account, a Students' Fair Play League, which has commenced its activities. I understand that they have already ducked Alderman Gorfinkel in a pond near the university. I believe they are looking for Alderman Schwefeldampf tonight. I understand they propose to throw him into the reservoir. The leader of them – a splendid set of young fellows – have given me a pledge that they will do nothing to bring discredit on the university.'

'I think I heard them on the street last night,' said Mr Newberry.

'I believe they had a procession,' said the president.

'Yes, I heard them; they were shouting, "Rah! rah! rah! clean government! Clean government! Rah! rah! rah!" It was really inspiring to hear them.'

'Yes,' said the president, 'they are banded together to put down all the hoodlumism and disturbance on the street that has hitherto disgraced our municipal elections. Last night, as a demonstration, they upset two street cars and a milk wagon.'

'I heard that two of them were arrested,' said Mr Dick Overend.

'Only by an error,' said the president. 'There was a mistake. It was not known that they were students. The two who were arrested were smashing the windows of the car, after it was upset, with their hockey sticks. A squad of police mistook them for rioters. As soon as they were taken to the police station the mistake was cleared up at once. The chief of police telephoned an apology to the university. I believe the Fair Play League is out again tonight looking for Alderman Schwefeldampf. But the leaders assure me there will be no breach of the peace whatever. As I say, I think their idea is to throw him into the reservoir.'

In the face of such efforts as these, opposition itself melted rapidly away. The *Plutorian Times* was soon able to announce that various undesirable candidates were abandoning the field. 'Alderman Gorfinkel,' it said, 'who, it will be recalled, was thrown into a pond last week by the students of the college, was still confined to his bed when interviewed by our representative. Mr Gorfinkel stated that he should not offer himself as a candidate in the approaching election. He was, he said, weary of civic honours. He had had enough. He felt it incumbent on him to step out and make way for others who deserved their turn as well as himself. In future he proposed to confine his whole attention to his Misfit Semi-Ready Establishment, which he was happy to state was offering as nobby a line of early fall suiting as was ever seen at the price.'

*   *   *

There is no need to recount here in detail the glorious triumph of the election day itself. It will always be remembered as the purest, cleanest election ever held in the precincts of the city. The citizens' organisation turned out in overwhelming force to guarantee that it should be so. Bands of Dr Boomer's students armed with baseball bats surrounded the polls to guarantee fair play. Any man wishing to cast an unclean vote was driven from the booth; all those attempting to introduce an element of brute force or rowdyism into the election were cracked over the head. In the lower part of the town scores of willing workers, recruited often from the humblest classes, kept order with pickaxes. In every part of the city, motor cars, supplied by all the leading business men, lawyers, and doctors, acted as patrols to see that no unfair use should be made of other vehicles in carrying voters to the polls.

It was a foregone victory from the first – overwhelming and complete. The Cohorts of Darkness were so completely routed that it was practically impossible to find them. As it fell dusk the streets were filled with roaring and surging crowds celebrating the great victory for Clean Government, while in front of every newspaper office huge lantern pictures of *Mayor McGrath, the Champion of Pure Government,* and *O. Skinyer, the People's Solicitor,* and the other nominees of the League, called forth cheer after cheer of frenzied enthusiasm.

* * *

They held that night in celebration a great reception at the Mausoleum Club on Plutoria Avenue, given at its own suggestion by the city. The city indeed insisted on it.

Nor was there ever witnessed even in that home of art and refinement a scene of greater charm. In the spacious corridors of the club a Hungarian band wafted Viennese music from Tyrolese flutes through the rubber-trees. There was champagne bubbling at a score of sideboards where noiseless waiters poured it into goblets as broad and flat as floating water-lily leaves. And through it all moved the shepherds and shepherd-esses of the beautiful Arcadia – the shepherds in their Tuxedo jackets with vast white shirt-fronts broad as the map of Africa, with spotless white waistcoats girdling their equators, wearing heavy gold watch-chains and little patent shoes blacker than sin itself; and the shepherdesses in foaming billows of silks of every colour of the kaleidoscope, their hair bound with glittering headbands or coiled with white feathers, the very symbol of municipal purity. One would search in vain the pages of pastoral literature to find the equal of it.

And as they talked the good news spread from group to group that it was already known that the new franchise of the Citizens' Light was to be made for two centuries so as to give the company a fair chance to see what it could do. At the word of it the grave faces of manly bond-holders flushed with pride, and the soft eyes of listening shareholders laughed back in joy. For they had no doubt or fear, now that clean government had come. They knew what the company could do.

Thus all night long, outside of the club, the soft note of the motor-horns arriving and departing wakened the sleeping leaves of the elm-trees with their message of good tidings. And all night long, within its lighted corridors, the bubbling champagne whispered to the listening rubber-trees of the new salvation of the city. So the night waxed and waned till the slow day broke, dimming with its cheap prosaic glare the shaded beauty of the artificial light; and the people of the city – the best of them – drove home to their well-earned sleep; and the others – in the lower parts of the city – rose to their daily toil.

Six
Are the Rich Happy?

Let me admit at the outset that I write this essay without adequate material. I have never known, I have never seen, any rich people. Very often I have thought that I had found them. But it turned out that it was not so. They were not rich at all. They were quite poor. They were hard up. They were pushed for money. They didn't know where to turn for ten thousand dollars.

In all the cases that I have examined this same error has crept in. I had often imagined, from the fact of people keeping fifteen servants, that they were rich. I had supposed that because a woman rode down-town in a limousine to buy a fifty-dollar hat, she must be well-to-do. Not at all. All these people turn out on examination to be not rich. They are cramped. They say it themselves. Pinched, I think, is the word they use. When I see a glittering group of eight people in a stage box at the opera, I know that they are all pinched. The fact that they ride home in a limousine has nothing to do with it.

A friend of mine who has ten thousand dollars a year told me the other day with a sigh that he found it quite impossible to keep up with the rich. On his income he couldn't do it. A family that I know who have twenty thousand a year have told me the same thing. They can't keep up with the rich. There is no use in trying. A man that I respect very much who has an income of fifty thousand dollars a year from his law practice has told me with the greatest frankness that he finds it absolutely impossible to keep up with the rich. He says it is better to face the brutal fact of being poor. He says he can only give me a plain meal, what he calls a home dinner – it takes three men and two women to serve it – and he begs me to put up with it.

As far as I remember, I have never met Mr Carnegie. But I know that if I did he would tell me that he found it quite impossible to keep up with Mr Rockefeller. No doubt Mr Rockefeller has the same feeling.

On the other hand there are and there must be rich people, somewhere. I run across traces of them all the time. The janitor in the building where I work has told me that he has a rich cousin in England who is in the South-Western Railway and gets ten pounds a week. He says that the railway wouldn't know what to do without him. In the same way the lady who washes at my house has a rich uncle. He lives in Winnipeg and owns his own house, clear, and has two girls at the high school.

But these are only reported cases of richness. I cannot vouch for them myself.

When I speak therefore of rich people and discuss whether they are happy, it is understood that I am merely drawing my conclusions from the people whom I see and know.

My judgement is that the rich undergo cruel trials and bitter tragedies of which the poor know nothing.

In the first place I find that the rich suffer perpetually from money troubles. The poor sit snugly at home while sterling exchange falls ten points in a day. Do they care? Not a bit. An adverse balance of trade washes over the nation like a flood. Who have to mop it up? The rich. Call money rushes up to a hundred per cent, and the poor can still sit and laugh at a ten cent moving picture show and forget it.

But the rich are troubled by money all the time.

I know a man, for example – his name is Spugg – whose private bank account was overdrawn last month twenty thousand dollars. He told me so at dinner at his club, with apologies for feeling out of sorts. He said it was bothering him. He said he thought it rather unfair of his bank to have called his attention to it. I could sympathise, in a sort of way, with his feelings. My own account was overdrawn twenty cents at the time, I knew that if the bank began calling in overdrafts it might be my turn next. Spugg said he supposed he'd have to telephone his secretary in the morning to sell some bonds and cover it. It seemed an awful thing to have to do. Poor people are never driven to this sort of thing. I have known cases of their having to sell a little furniture, perhaps, but imagine having to sell the very bonds out of one's desk. There's a bitterness about it that the poor can never know.

With this same man, Mr Spugg, I have often talked of the problem of wealth. He is a self-made man and he has told me again and again that the wealth he has accumulated is a mere burden to him. He says that he was much happier when he had only the plain, simple things of life. Often as I sit at dinner with him over a meal of nine courses, he tells me how much he would prefer a plain bit of boiled pork with a little mashed turnip. He says that if he had his way he would make his dinner out of a couple of sausages, fried with a bit of bread. I forget what it is that stands in his way. I have seen Spugg put aside his glass of champagne – or his glass after he had drunk his champagne – with an expression of something like contempt. He says that he remembers a running creek at the back of his father's farm where he used to lie at full length upon the grass and drink his fill. Champagne, he says, never tasted like that. I have suggested that he should lie on his stomach on the floor of the club and drink a saucerful of soda water. But he won't.

I know well that my friend Spugg would be glad to be rid of his wealth altogether, if such a thing were possible. Till I understood about these things, I always imagined that wealth could be given away. It appears that it cannot. It is a burden that one must carry. Wealth, if one has enough of it, becomes a form of social service. One regards it as a means of doing good to the world, of helping to brighten the lives of others – in a word, a solemn trust. Spugg has often talked with me so long and so late on this topic – the duty of brightening the lives of others – that the waiter who held blue flames for his cigarettes fell asleep against a door post, and the chauffeur outside froze to the seat of his motor.

Spugg's wealth, I say, he regards as a solemn trust. I have often asked him why he didn't give it, for example, to a college. But he tells me that unfortunately he is not a college man. I have called his attention to the need of further pensions for college professors; after all that Mr Carnegie and others have done, there are still thousands and thousands of old professors of thirty-five and even forty, working away day after day and getting nothing but what they earn themselves, and with no provision beyond the age of eighty-five. But Mr Spugg says that these men are the nation's heroes. Their work is its own reward.

But, after all, Mr Spugg's troubles – for he is a single man with no ties – are in a sense selfish. It is perhaps in the homes, or more properly in the residences, of the rich that the great silent tragedies are being enacted every day – tragedies of which the fortunate poor know and can know nothing.

I saw such a case only a few nights ago at the house of the Ashcroft-Fowlers, where I was dining. As we went in to dinner, Mrs Ashcroft-Fowler said in a quiet aside to her husband, 'Has Meadows spoken?' He shook his head rather gloomily and answered, 'No, he has said nothing yet.' I saw them exchange a glance of quiet sympathy and mutual help, like people in trouble, who love one another.

They were old friends and my heart beat for them. All through the dinner as Meadows – he was their butler – poured out the wine with each course, I could feel that some great trouble was impending over my friends.

After Mrs Ashcroft-Fowler had risen and left us, and we were alone over our port wine, I drew my chair near to Fowler's and I said, 'My dear Fowler, I'm an old friend and you'll excuse me if I seem to be taking a liberty. But I can see that you and your wife are in trouble.'

'Yes,' he said very sadly and quietly, 'we are.'

'Excuse me,' I said. 'Tell me – for it makes a thing easier if one talks about it – is it anything about Meadows?'

'Yes,' he said, 'it is about Meadows.'

There was silence for a moment, but I knew already what Fowler was going to say. I could feel it coming.

'Meadows,' he said presently, constraining himself to speak with as little emotion as possible, 'is leaving us.'

'Poor old chap!' I said, taking his hand.

'It's hard, isn't it?' he said. 'Franklin left last winter – no fault of ours; we did everything we could – and now Meadows.'

There was almost a sob in his voice.

'He hasn't spoken definitely as yet,' Fowler went on, 'but we know there's hardly any chance of his staying.'

'Does he give any reason?' I asked.

'Nothing specific,' said Fowler. 'It's just a sheer case of incompatibility. Meadows doesn't like us.'

He put his hand over his face and was silent.

I left very quietly a little later, without going up to the drawing-room. A few days afterwards I heard that Meadows had gone. The Ashcroft-Fowlers, I am told, are giving up in despair. They are going to take a little suite of ten rooms and four baths in the Grand Palaver Hotel, and rough it there for the winter.

Yet one must not draw a picture of the rich in colours altogether gloomy. There are cases among them of genuine, light-hearted happiness.

I have observed that this is especially the case among those of the rich who have the good fortune to get ruined, absolutely and completely ruined. They may do this on the Stock Exchange or by banking or in a dozen other ways. The business side of getting ruined is not difficult.

Once the rich are ruined, they are, as far as my observation goes, all right. They can then have anything they want.

I saw this point illustrated again just recently. I was walking with a friend of mine and a motor passed bearing a neatly dressed young man, chatting gaily with a pretty woman. My friend raised his hat and gave it a jaunty and cheery swing in the air as if to wave goodwill and happiness.

'Poor old Edward Overjoy!' he said, as the motor moved out of sight.

'What's wrong with him?' I asked.

'Hadn't you heard?' said my friend. 'He's ruined – absolutely cleaned out – not a cent left.'

'Dear me!' I said. 'That's awfully hard. I suppose he'll have to sell that beautiful motor?'

'Oh, no,' he said. 'He'll hardly do that. I don't think his wife would care to sell that.'

My friend was right. The Overjoys have not sold their motor. Neither have they sold their magnificent sandstone residence. They are too much attached to it, I believe, to sell it. Some people thought they would have given up their box at the opera. But it appears not. They are too musical to care to do that. Meantime it is a matter of general notoriety that the Overjoys are absolutely ruined; in fact, they haven't a single cent. You could buy Overjoy – so I am informed – for ten dollars.

But I observe that he still wears a seal-lined coat worth at least five hundred.

Seven
Sunshine Sketches of a Little Town

I. THE HOSTELRY OF MR SMITH

I don't know whether you know Mariposa. If not, it is of no consequence, for if you know Canada at all, you are probably well acquainted with a dozen towns just like it.

There it lies in the sunlight, sloping up from the little lake that spreads out at the foot of the hillside on which the town is built. There is a wharf beside the lake, and lying alongside of it a steamer that is tied to the wharf with two ropes of about the same size as they use on the *Lusitania.* The steamer goes nowhere in particular, for the lake is landlocked and there is no navigation for the *Mariposa Belle* except to 'run trips' on the first of July and the Queen's Birthday, and to take excursions of the Knights of Pythias and the Sons of Temperance to and from the Local Option Townships.

In point of geography the lake is called Lake Wissanotti and the river running out of it the Ossawippi, just as the main street of Mariposa is called Missinaba Street and the country Missinaba Country. But these names do not really matter. Nobody uses them. People simply speak of the 'lake' and the 'river' and the 'main street,' much in the same way as they always call the Continental Hotel, 'Peter Robinson's' and the Pharmaceutical Hall, 'Eliot's Drug Store.' But I suppose this is just the same in everyone else's town as in mine, so I need lay no stress on it.

The town, I say, has one broad street that runs up from the lake, commonly called the Main Street. There is no doubt about its width. When Mariposa was laid out there was none of that shortsightedness which is seen in the cramped dimensions of Wall Street and Piccadilly. Missinaba Street is so wide that if you were to roll Jeff Thorpe's barber shop over on its face it wouldn't reach half-way across. Up and down the Main Street are telegraph poles of cedar of colossal thickness, standing at a variety of angles and carrying rather more wires than are commonly seen at a transatlantic cable station.

On the Main Street itself are a number of buildings of extraordinary importance – Smith's Hotel and the Continental and the Mariposa

House, and the two banks (the Commercial and the Exchange), to say nothing of McCarthy's Block (erected in 1878), and Glover's Hardware Store with the Oddfellows' Hall above it. Then on the 'cross' street that intersects Missinaba Street at the main corner there is the Post Office and the Fire Hall and the Young Men's Christian Association and the office of the Mariposa *Newspacket* – in fact, to the eye of discernment a perfect jostle of public institutions comparable only to Threadneedle Street or Lower Broadway. On all the side streets there are maple trees and board sidewalks, trim gardens with upright calla lilies, houses with verandahs, which are here and there being replaced by residences with piazzas.

To the careless eye the scene on the Main Street of a summer afternoon is one of deep and unbroken peace. The empty street sleeps in the sunshine. There is a horse and buggy tied to the hitching post in front of Glover's hardware store. There is, usually and commonly, the burly figure of Mr Smith, proprietor of Smith's Hotel, standing in his chequered waistcoat on the steps of his hostelry, and perhaps, farther up the street, Lawyer Macartney going for his afternoon mail, or the Rev. Mr Drone, the Rural Dean of the Church of England church, going home to get his fishing rod after a Mothers' Auxiliary meeting.

But this quiet is mere appearance. In reality, and to those who know it, the place is a perfect hive of activity. Why, at Netley's butcher shop (established in 1882) there are no less than four men working on the sausage machines in the basement; at the *Newspacket* office there are as many more jobprinting; there is a long-distance telephone with four distracting girls on high stools wearing steel caps and talking incessantly; in the offices in McCarthy's block are dentists and lawyers, with their coats off, ready to work at any moment; and from the big planing factory down beside the lake where the railroad siding is, you may hear all through the hours of the summer afternoon the long-drawn music of the running saw.

Busy – well, I should think so! Ask any of its inhabitants if Mariposa isn't a busy, hustling, thriving town. Ask Mullins, the manager of the Exchange Bank, who comes hustling over to his office from the Mariposa House every day at 10.30 and has scarcely time all morning to go out and take a drink with the manager of the Commercial; or ask – well, for the matter of that, ask any of them if they ever knew a more rushing go-ahead town than Mariposa.

Of course if you come to the place fresh from New York, you are deceived. Your standard of vision is all astray. You do think the place is quiet. You do imagine that Mr Smith is asleep merely because he closes his eyes as he stands. But live in Mariposa for six months or a year and then you will begin to understand it better; the buildings get higher and higher; the Mariposa House grows more and more luxurious; McCarthy's block towers to the sky; the buses roar and hum to the station; the trains shriek; the traffic multiplies; the people move faster and faster; a dense crowd swirls to and fro in the post-office and the five and ten cent store – and amusements! well, now! lacrosse, baseball, excursions, dances, the Firemen's Ball every winter and the Catholic picnic every summer; and music – the town band in the park every Wednesday evening, and the Oddfellows' brass band on the street every other Friday; the Mariposa Quartette, the Salvation Army – why, after a few months' residence you begin to realize that the place is a mere mad round of gaiety.

In point of population, if one must come down to figures, the Canadian census puts the numbers every time at something round five thousand. But it is very generally understood in Mariposa that the census is largely the outcome of malicious jealousy. It is usual that after the census the editor of the Mariposa *Newspacket* makes a careful re-estimate (based on the data of relative non-payment of subscriptions), and brings the population up to 6,000. After that the Mariposa *Times-Herald* makes an estimate that runs the figures up to 6,500. Then Mr Gingham, the undertaker, who collects the vital statistics for the provincial government, makes an estimate from the number of what he calls the 'demised' as compared with the less interesting persons who are still alive, and brings the population to 7,000. After that somebody else works it out that it's 7,500; then the man behind the bar of the Mariposa offers to bet the whole room that there are 9,000 people in Mariposa. That settles it, and the population is well on the way to 10,000, when down swoops the federal census-taker on his next round and the town has to begin all over again.

Still, it is a thriving town and there is no doubt of it. Even the transcontinental railways, as any townsman will tell you, run through Mariposa. It is true that the trains mostly go through at night and don't stop. But in the wakeful silence of the summer night you may hear the long whistle of the through train for the west as it tears through Mariposa, rattling over the switches and past the semaphores and ending in a long, sullen roar as it takes the trestle bridge over the Ossawippi. Or, better still, on a winter evening about eight o'clock you will see the long row of the Pullmans and diners of the night express going north to the mining country, the windows flashing with brilliant light, and within them a vista of cut glass and snow-white table linen, smiling negroes and millionaires with napkins at their chins whirling past in the driving snowstorm.

I can tell you the people of Mariposa are proud of the trains, even if they don't stop! The joy of being on the main line lifts the Mariposa people above the level of their neighbours in such places as Tecumseh and Nichols Corners into the cosmopolitan atmosphere of through traffic and the larger life. Of course, they have their own train, too – the Mariposa Local, made up right there in the station yard, and running south to the city a hundred miles away. That, of course, is a real train, with a box stove on end in the passenger car, fed with cord-wood upside down, and with seventeen flat cars of pine lumber set between the passenger car and the locomotive so as to give the train its full impact when shunting.

Outside of Mariposa there are farms that begin well but get thinner and meaner as you go on, and end sooner or later in bush and swamp and the rock of the north country. And beyond that again, as the background of it all, though it's far away, you are somehow aware of the great pine woods of the lumber country reaching endlessly into the north.

Not that the little town is always gay or always bright in the sunshine. There never was such a place for changing its character with the season. Dark enough and dull it seems of a winter night, the wooden sidewalks creaking with the frost, and the lights burning dim behind the shop windows. In olden times the lights were coal-oil lamps; now, of course, they are, or are supposed to be, electricity – brought from the power house on the lower Ossawippi nineteen miles away. But, somehow, though it starts off as electricity from the Ossawippi rapids, by the time it gets to Mariposa and filters into the little bulbs behind the frosty windows of the shops, it has turned into coal-oil again, as yellow and bleared as ever.

After the winter, the snow melts and the ice goes out of the lakes, the sun shines high and the shanty-men come down from the lumber woods and lie round drunk on the sidewalk outside of Smith's Hotel – and that's spring time. Mariposa is then a fierce, dangerous lumber town, calculated to terrorize the soul of a newcomer who does not understand that this also is only an appearance and that presently the rough-looking shanty-men will change their clothes and turn back again into farmers.

Then the sun shines warmer and the maple trees come out and Lawyer Macartney puts on his tennis trousers, and that's summer time. The little town changes to a sort of summer resort. There are visitors up from the city. Every one of the seven cottages along the lake is full. The *Mariposa Belle* churns the waters of the Wissanotti into foam as she sails out from the wharf, in a cloud of flags, the band playing and the daughters and sisters of the Knights of Pythias dancing gaily on the deck.

That changes too. The days shorten. The visitors disappear. The golden rod beside the meadow droops and withers on its stem. The maples blaze in glory and die. The evening closes dark and chill, and in the gloom of the main corner of Mariposa the Salvation Army around a naphtha lamp lift up the confession of their sins – and that is autumn. Thus the year runs its round, moving and changing in Mariposa, much as it does in other places.

If, then, you feel that you know the town well enough to be admitted into the inner life and movement of it, walk this June afternoon half-way down the Main Street – or, if you like, half-way up from the wharf – to where Mr Smith is standing at the door of his hostelry. You will feel as you draw near that it is no ordinary man that you approach. It is not alone the huge bulk of Mr Smith (two hundred and eighty pounds as tested on Netley's scales). It is not merely his costume, though the chequered waistcoat of dark blue with a flowered pattern forms, with his shepherd's plaid trousers, his grey spats and patent-leather boots, a colour scheme of no mean order. Nor is it merely Mr Smith's finely mottled face. The face, no doubt, is a notable one – solemn, inexpressible, unreadable, the face of the heaven-born hotel keeper. It is more than that. It is the strange dominating personality of the man that somehow holds you captive. I know nothing in history to compare with the position of Mr Smith among those who drink over his bar, except, though in a lesser degree, the relation of the Emperor Napoleon to the Imperial Guard.

When you meet Mr Smith first you think he looks like an over-dressed pirate. Then you begin to think him a character. You wonder at his enormous bulk. Then the utter hopelessness of knowing what Smith is thinking by merely looking at his features gets on your mind and makes the Mona Lisa seem an open book and the ordinary human countenance as superficial as a puddle in the sunlight. After you have had a drink in Mr Smith's bar, and he has called you by your Christian name, you realise that you are dealing with one of the greatest minds in the hotel business.

Take, for instance, the big sign that sticks out into the street above Mr Smith's head as he stands. What is on it? Simply: 'JOS. SMITH, PROP.' Nothing more, and yet the thing was a flash of genius. Other men who had had the hotel before Mr Smith had called it by such feeble names as the Royal Hotel and the Queen's and the Alexandria. Every one of them failed. When Mr Smith took over the hotel he simply put up the sign with 'JOS. SMITH, PROP.', and then stood underneath in the sunshine as a living proof that a man who weighs nearly three hundred pounds is the natural king of the hotel business.

But on this particular afternoon, in spite of the sunshine and deep peace, there was something as near to profound concern and anxiety as the features of Mr Smith were ever known to express.

The moment was indeed an anxious one. Mr Smith was awaiting a telegram from his legal adviser who had that day journeyed to the county town to represent the proprietor's interest before the assembled Licence Commissioners. If you know anything of the hotel business at all, you will understand that as beside the decisions of the Licence Commissioners of Missinaba County, the opinions of the Lords of the Privy Council are mere trifles.

The matter in question was very grave. The Mariposa Court had just fined Mr Smith for the second time for selling liquors after hours. The commissioners, therefore, were entitled to cancel the licence.

Mr Smith knew his fault and acknowledged it. He had broken the law. How he had come to do so, it passed his imagination to recall. Crime always seems impossible in retrospect. By what sheer madness of the moment could he have shut up the bar on the night in question, and shut Judge Pepperleigh, the district judge of Missinaba County, outside of it? The more so inasmuch as the closing up of the bar under the rigid licence law of the province was a matter that the proprietor never trusted to any hands but his own. Punctually every night at 11 o'clock Mr Smith strolled from the desk of the 'rotunda' to the door of the bar. If it seemed properly full of people and all was bright and cheerful, then he closed it. If not, he kept it open a few minutes longer till he had enough people inside to warrant closing. But never, never unless he was assured that Pepperleigh, the judge of the court, and Macartney, the prosecuting attorney, were both safely in the bar, or the bar parlour, did the proprietor venture to close up. Yet on this fatal night Pepperleigh and Macartney had been shut out – actually left on the street without a drink, and compelled to hammer and beat at the street door of the bar to gain admittance.

This was the kind of thing not to be tolerated. Either a hotel must be run decently or quit. An information was laid next day, and Mr Smith convicted in four minutes, his lawyers practically refusing to plead. The Mariposa court, when the presiding judge was cold sober, and it had the force of public opinion behind it, was a terrible engine of retributive justice.

So no wonder that Mr Smith awaited with anxiety the message of his legal adviser.

He looked alternately up the street and down it again, hauled out his watch from the depths of his embroidered pocket, and examined the hour hand and the minute hand and the second hand with frowning scrutiny.

Then wearily, and as one mindful that a hotel man is ever the servant of the public, he turned back into the hotel.

'Billy,' he said to the desk clerk, 'if a wire comes bring it into the bar parlour.'

The voice of Mr Smith is of a deep guttural such as Plancon or Edouard de Reszke might have obtained had they had the advantages of the hotel business. And with that, Mr Smith, as was his custom in off moments, joined his guests in the back room. His appearance, to the untrained eye, was merely that of an extremely stout hotel-keeper walking from the 'rotunda' to the back bar. In reality, Mr Smith was on the eve of one of the most brilliant and daring strokes ever effected in the history of licensed liquor. When I say that it was out of the agitation of this situation that Smith's Ladies' and Gents' Café originated, anybody who knows Mariposa will understand the magnitude of the moment.

Mr Smith, then, moved slowly from the doorway of the hotel through the 'rotunda', or more simply the front room with the desk and the cigar case in it, and so to the bar and thence to the little room or back bar behind it. In this room, as I have said, the brightest minds of Mariposa might commonly be found in the quieter part of a summer afternoon.

Today there was a group of four who looked up as Mr Smith entered, somewhat sympathetically, and evidently aware of the perplexities of the moment.

Henry Mullins and George Duff, the two bank managers, were both present. Mullins is a rather short, rather round, smooth-shaven man of less than forty, wearing one of those round banking suits of pepper and salt, with a round banking hat of hard straw, and with the kind of gold tiepin and heavy watch-chain and seals necessary to inspire confidence in matters of foreign exchange. Duff is just as round and just as short, and equally smoothly shaven, while his seals and straw hat are calculated to prove that the Commercial is just as sound a bank as the Exchange. From the technical point of view of the banking business, neither of them had any objection to being in Smith's Hotel or to taking a drink as long as the other was present. This, of course, was one of the cardinal principles of Mariposa banking.

Then there was Mr Diston, the high-school teacher, commonly known as the 'one who drank'. None of the other teachers ever entered a hotel unless accompanied by a lady or protected by a child. But as Mr Diston was known to drink beer on occasions and to go in and out of the Mariposa House and Smith's Hotel, he was looked upon as a man whose life was a mere wreck. Whenever the School Board raised the salaries of the other teachers, fifty or sixty dollars per annum at one lift, it was well understood that public morality wouldn't permit of an increase for Mr Diston.

Still more noticeable, perhaps, was the quiet, sallow-looking man dressed in black, with black gloves and with black silk hat heavily craped and placed hollow-side-up on a chair. This was Mr Golgotha Gingham, the undertaker of Mariposa, and his dress was due to the fact that he had just come from what he called an 'interment'. Mr Gingham had the true spirit of his profession, and such words as 'funeral' or 'coffin' or 'hearse' never passed his lips. He spoke always of 'interments', of 'caskets', and 'coaches', using terms that were calculated rather to bring out the majesty and sublimity of death than to parade its horrors.

To be present at the hotel was in accord with Mr Gingham's general conception of his business. No man had ever grasped the true principles of undertaking more thoroughly than Mr Gingham. I have often heard him explain that to associate with the living, uninteresting though they appear, is the only way to secure the custom of the dead.

'Get to know people really well while they are alive,' said Mr Gingham: 'be friends with them, close friends, and then when they die you don't need to worry. You'll get the order every time.'

So naturally, as the moment was one of sympathy, it was Mr Gingham who spoke first.

'What'll you do, Josh,' he said, 'if the Commissioners go against you?'

'Boys,' said Mr Smith, 'I don't rightly know. If I have to quit, the next move is to the city. But I don't reckon that I will have to quit. I've got an idea that I think's good every time.'

'Could you run a hotel in the city?' asked Mullins.

'I could,' said Mr Smith, 'I'll tell you. There's big things doin' in the hotel business right now, big chances if you go into it right. Hotels in the city is branching out. Why, you take the dining-room side of it,' continued Mr Smith, looking round at the group, 'there's thousands in it. The old plan's all gone. Folks won't eat now in an ordinary dining-room with a high ceiling and windows. You have to get 'em down underground in a room with no windows and lots of sawdust round and waiters that can't speak English. I seen them places last time I was in the city. They call 'em Rats' Coolers. And for light meals they want a caff, a real French caff, and for folks that come in late another place that they call a Girl Room that don't shut up at all. If I go to the city that's the kind of place I mean to run. What's yours, Gol? It's on the house.'

And it was just at the moment when Mr Smith said this that Billy, the desk clerk, entered the room with the telegram in his hand.

But stop – it is impossible for you to understand the anxiety with which Mr Smith and his associates awaited the news from the Commissioners, without first realizing the astounding progress of Mr Smith in the three past years, and the pinnacle of public eminence to which he had attained.

Mr Smith had come down from the lumber country of the Spanish

River, where the divide is toward the Hudson Bay – 'back north' as they called it in Mariposa.

He had been, it was said, a cook in the lumber shanties. To this day Mr Smith can fry an egg on both sides with a lightness of touch that is the despair of his own 'help'.

After that, he had run a river driver's boarding-house.

After that, he had taken a food contract for a gang of railroad navvies on the transcontinental.

After that, of course, the whole world was open to him.

He came down to Mariposa and bought out the 'inside' of what had been the Royal Hotel.

Those who are educated understand that by the 'inside' of a hotel is meant everything except the four outer walls of it – the fittings, the furniture, the bar, Billy the desk-clerk, the three dining-room girls, and above all the licence granted by King Edward VII, and ratified further by King George, for the sale of intoxicating liquors.

Till then the Royal had been a mere nothing. As 'Smith's Hotel' it broke into a blaze of effulgence.

From the first, Mr Smith, as a proprietor, was a wild, rapturous success.

He had all the qualifications.

He weighed two hundred and eighty pounds.

He could haul two drunken men out of the bar each by the scruff of the neck without the faintest anger or excitement.

He carried money enough in his trousers pockets to start a bank, and spent it on anything, bet it on anything, and gave it away in handfuls.

He was never drunk, and, as a point of chivalry to his customers, never quite sober. Anybody was free of the hotel who cared to come in. Anybody who didn't like it could go out. Drinks of all kinds cost five cents, or six for a quarter. Meals and beds were practically free. Any person foolish enough to go to the desk and pay for them, Mr Smith charged according to the expression of their faces.

At first the loafers and the shanty-men settled down on the place in a shower. But that was not the 'trade' that Mr Smith wanted. He knew how to get rid of them. An army of charwomen, turned into the hotel, scrubbed it from top to bottom. A vacuum cleaner, the first seen in Mariposa, hissed and screamed in the corridors. Forty brass beds were imported from the city, not, of course, for the guests to sleep in, but to keep them out. A bartender with a starched coat and wicker sleeves was put behind the bar.

The loafers were put out of business. The place had become too 'high-toned' for them.

To get the high-class trade, Mr Smith set himself to dress the part. He wore wide-cut coats of filmy serge, light as gossamer; chequered waistcoats with a pattern for every day in the week; fedora hats light as autumn leaves; four-in-hand ties of saffron and myrtle green with a diamond pin the size of a hazel nut. On his fingers there were as many gems as would grace a native prince of India; across his waistcoat lay a gold watch-chain in huge square links and in his pocket a gold watch that weighed a pound and a half and marked minutes, seconds and quarter seconds. Just to look at Josh Smith's watch brought at least ten men to the bar every evening.

Every morning Mr Smith was shaved by Jefferson Thrope, across the way. All that art could do, all that Florida water could effect, was lavished on his person.

Mr Smith became a local character. Mariposa was at his feet. All the reputable business men drank at Mr Smith's bar, and in the little parlour behind it you might find at any time a group of the brightest intellects in the town.

Not but what there was opposition at first. The clergy, for example, who accepted the Mariposa House and the Continental as a necessary and useful evil, looked askance at the blazing lights and the surging crowd of Mr Smith's saloon. They preached against him. When the Rev. Dean Drone led off with a sermon on the text 'Lord be merciful even unto this publican Matthew Six,' it was generally understood as an invitation to strike Mr Smith dead. In the same way the sermon at the Presbyterian church the week after was on the text 'Lo, what now doeth Abiram in the land of Melchisideck Kings Eight and Nine?' and it was perfectly plain that what was meant was, 'Lo, what is Josh Smith doing in Mariposa?'

But this opposition had been countered by a wide and sagacious philanthropy. I think Mr Smith first got the idea of that on the night when the steam merry-go-round came to Mariposa. Just below the hostelry, on an empty lot, it whirled and whistled, steaming forth its tunes on the summer evening while the children crowded round it in hundreds. Down the street strolled Mr Smith, wearing a soft fedora to indicate that it was evening.

'What d'you charge for a ride, boss?' said Mr Smith.

'Two for a nickel,' said the man.

'Take that,' said Mr Smith, handing out a ten-dollar bill from a roll of money, 'and ride the little folks free all evening.'

That night the merry-go-round whirled madly till after midnight, freighted to capacity with Mariposa children, while up in Smith's Hotel parents, friends and admirers, as the news spread, were standing four deep along the bar. They sold forty dollars' worth of lager alone that night, and Mr Smith learned, if he had not already suspected it, the blessedness of giving.

The uses of philanthropy went further. Mr Smith subscribed to everything, joined everything, gave to everything. He became an Oddfellow, a Forester, a Knight of Pythias and a Workman. He gave a hundred dollars to the Mariposa Hospital and a hundred dollars to the Young Men's Christian Association.

He subscribed to the Ball Club, the Lacrosse Club, the Curling Club, to anything, in fact, and especially to all those things which needed premises to meet in and grew thirsty in their discussions.

As a consequence the Oddfellows held their annual banquet at Smith's Hotel and the Oyster Supper of the Knights of Pythias was celebrated in Mr Smith's dining-room.

Even more effective, perhaps, were Mr Smith's secret benefactions, the kind of giving done by stealth of which not a soul in town knew anything, often, for a week after it was done. It was in this way that Mr Smith put the new font in Dean Drone's church, and handed over a hundred dollars to Judge Pepperleigh for the unrestrained use of the Conservative Party.

So it came about that, little by little, the antagonism had died down. Smith's Hotel became an accepted institution in Mariposa. Even the temperance people were proud of Mr Smith as a sort of character who added distinction to the town. There were moments, in the earlier quiet of the morning, when Dean Drone would go so far as to step in the 'rotunda' and collect a subscription. As for the Salvation Army, they ran in and out all the time unreproved.

On only one point difficulty still remained. That was the closing of the bar. Mr Smith could never bring his mind to it – not as a matter of profit, but as a point of honour. It was too much for him to feel that Judge Pepperleigh might be out on the sidewalk thirsty at midnight, that the night hands of the *Times-Herald* on Wednesday might be compelled to go home dry. On this point Mr Smith's moral code was simplicity itself – do what is right and take the consequences. So the bar stayed open.

Every town, I suppose, has its meaner spirits. In every genial bosom some snake is warmed – or, as Mr Smith put it to Golgotha Gingham – 'There are some fellers even in this town skunks enough to inform.'

At first the Mariposa court quashed all indictments. The presiding judge, with his spectacles on and a pile of books in front of him, threatened the informer with the penitentiary. The whole bar of Mariposa was with Mr Smith. But by sheer iteration the informations had proved successful. Judge Pepperleigh learned that Mr Smith had subscribed a hundred dollars for the Liberal Party and at once fined him for keeping open after hours. That made one conviction. On the top of this had come the untoward incident just mentioned and that made two. Beyond that was the deluge. This then was the exact situation when Billy, the desk clerk, entered the back bar with the telegram in his hand.

'Here's your wire, sir,' he said.

'What does it say?' said Mr Smith.

He always dealt with written documents with a fine air of detachment. I don't suppose there were ten people in Mariposa who knew that Mr Smith couldn't read.

Billy opened the message and read, 'Commissioners give you three months to close down.'

'Let me read it,' said Mr Smith, 'that's right, three months to close down.'

There was dead silence when the message was read. Everybody waited for Mr Smith to speak. Mr Gingham instinctively assumed the professional air of hopeless melancholy.

As it was afterwards recorded, Mr Smith stood and 'studied' with the tray in his hand for at least four minutes. Then he spoke.

'Boys,' he said, 'I'll be darned if I'll close down till I'm ready to close down. I've got an idea. You wait and I'll show you.'

And beyond that, not another word did Mr Smith say on the subject.

But within forty-eight hours the whole town knew that something was doing. The hotel swarmed with carpenters, bricklayers and painters. There was an architect up from the city with a bundle of blueprints in his hand. There was an engineer taking the street level with a theodolite, and a gang of navvies with shovels digging like fury as if to dig out the back foundations of the hotel.

'That'll fool 'em,' said Mr Smith.

Half the town was gathered round the hotel crazy with excitement. But not a word would the proprietor say.

Great dray loads of square timber, and two-by-eight pine joists kept arriving from the planing mill. There was a pile of matched spruce sixteen feet high lying by the sidewalk.

Then the excavation deepened and the dirt flew, and the beams went up and the joists across, and all the day from dawn till dusk the hammers of the carpenters clattered away, working overtime at time and a half.

'It don't matter what it costs,' said Mr Smith; 'get it done.'

Rapidly the structure took form. It extended down the side street, joining the hotel at a right angle. Spacious and graceful it looked as it reared its uprights into the air.

Already you could see the place where the row of windows was to come, a veritable palace of glass, it must be, so wide and commodious were they. Below it, you could see the basement shaping itself, with a low ceiling like a vault and big beams running across, dressed, smoothed, and ready for staining. Already in the street there were seven crates of red and white awning.

And even then nobody knew what it was, and it was not till the seventeenth day that Mr Smith, in the privacy of the back bar, broke the silence and explained.

'I tell you, boys,' he says, 'it's a caff – like what they have in the city – a ladies' and gents' caff, and that underneath (what's yours, Mr Mullins?) is a Rats' Cooler. And when I get her started, I'll hire a French Chief to do the cooking, and for the winter I will put in a "girl room," like what they have in the city hotels. And I'll like to see who's going to close her up then.'

Within two more weeks the plan was in operation. Not only was the caff built but the very hotel was transformed. Awnings had broken out in a red and white cloud upon its face, its every window carried a box of hanging plants, and above in glory floated the Union Jack. The very stationery was changed. The place was now Smith's Summer Pavilion. It was advertised in the city as Smith's Tourists' Emporium, and Smith's Northern Health Resort. Mr Smith got the editor of the *Times-Herald* to write up a circular all about ozone and the Mariposa pine woods, with illustrations of the maskinonge (piscis mariposis) of Lake Wissanotti.

The Saturday after that circular hit the city in July, there were men with fishing rods and landing nets pouring in on every train, almost too fast to register. And if, in the face of that a few little drops of whisky were sold over the bar, who thought of it?

But the caff! that, of course, was the crowning glory of the thing, that and the Rats' Cooler below.

Light and cool, with swinging windows open to the air, tables with marble tops, palms, waiters in white coats – it was the standing marvel of Mariposa. Not a soul in the town except Mr Smith, who knew it by instinct, ever guessed that waiters and palms and marble tables can be rented over the long-distance telephone.

Mr Smith was as good as his word. He got a French Chief with an aristocratic saturnine countenance, and a moustache and imperial that recalled the late Napoleon III. No one knew where Mr Smith got him. Some people in the town said he was a French marquis. Others said he was a count and explained the difference.

No one in Mariposa had ever seen anything like the caff. All down the side of it were the grill fires, with great pewter dish covers that went up and down on a chain, and you could walk along the row and actually pick out your own cutlet and then see the French marquis throw it on to the broiling iron; you could watch a buckwheat pancake whirled into existence under your eyes and see fowls' legs devilled, peppered, grilled, and tormented till they lost all semblance of the original Mariposa chicken.

Mr Smith, of course, was in his glory.

'What have you got today, Alf?' he would say, as he strolled over to the marquis. The name of the Chief was, I believe, Alphonse, but 'Alf' was near enough for Mr Smith.

The marquis would extend to the proprietor the menu, 'Voilà, m'sieu, la carte du jour.'

Mr Smith, by the way, encouraged the use of the French language in the caff. He viewed it, of course, solely in its relation to the hotel business, and, I think, regarded it as a recent invention.

'It's comin' in all the time in the city,' he said, 'and y'ain't expected to understand it.'

Mr Smith would take the carte between his finger and thumb and stare at it. It was all covered with such devices as Potage à la Mariposa – Filet mignon à la proprietaire – Côtellette à la Smith, and so on.

But the greatest thing about the caff were the prices. Therein lay, as everybody saw at once, the hopeless simplicity of Mr Smith.

The prices stood fast at 25 cents a meal. You could come in and eat all they had in the caff for a quarter.

'No, sir,' Mr Smith said stoutly, 'I ain't going to try to raise no prices on the public. The hotel's always been a quarter and the caff's a quarter.'

Full? Full of people?

Well, I should think so! From the time the caff opened at ll till it closed at 8.30, you could hardly find a table. Tourists, visitors, travellers, and half the people of Mariposa crowded at the little tables; crockery rattling, glasses tinkling on trays, corks popping, the waiters in their white coats flying to and fro, Alphonse whirling the cutlets and pancakes into the air, and in and through it all, Mr Smith, in a white flannel suit and a broad crimson sash about his waist. Crowded and gay from morning to night, and even noisy in its hilarity.

Noisy, yes; but if you wanted deep quiet and cool, if you wanted to step from the glare of a Canadian August to the deep shadow of an enchanted glade – walk down below into the Rats' Cooler. There you had it; dark old beams (who could believe they were put there a month ago?), great casks set on end with legends such as Amontillado Fino done in gilt on a black ground, tall steins filled with German beer soft as moss, and a German waiter noiseless as moving foam. He who entered the Rats' Cooler at three of a summer afternoon was buried there for the day. Mr Golgotha Gingham spent anything from four to seven hours there of every day. In his mind the place had all the quiet charm of an interment, with none of its sorrows.

But at night, when Mr Smith and Billy, the desk clerk, opened the cash register and figured out the combined losses of the caff and the Rats' Cooler, Mr Smith would say:

'Billy, just wait till I get the licence renood, and I'll close up this damn caff so tight they'll never know what hit her. What did that lamb cost? Fifty cents a pound, was it? I figure it, Billy, that every one of them hogs eats about a dollar's worth a grub for every twenty-five cents they pay on it. As for Alf – by gosh, I'm through with him.'

But that, of course, was only a confidential matter as between Mr Smith and Billy.

I don't know at what precise period it was that the idea of a petition to the Licence Commissioners first got about the town. No one seemed to know just who suggested it. But certain it was that public opinion began to swing strongly towards the support of Mr Smith. I think it was perhaps on the day after the big fish dinner that Alphonse cooked for the Mariposa Canoe Club (at twenty cents a head) that the feeling began to find open expression. People said it was a shame that a man like Josh Smith should be run out of Mariposa by three Licence Commissioners. Who were the Licence Commissioners, anyway? Why, look at the licence system they had in Sweden; yes, and in Finland and in South America. Or, for the matter of that, look at the French and Italians, who drink all day and all night. Aren't they all right? Aren't they a musical people? Take Napoleon, and Victor Hugo; drunk half the time, and yet look what they did.

I quote these arguments not for their own sake, but merely to indicate the changing temper of public opinion in Mariposa. Men would sit in the caff at lunch perhaps for an hour and a half and talk about the licence question in general, and then go down into the Rats' Cooler and talk about it for two hours more.

It was amazing the way the light broke in in the case of particular individuals, often the most unlikely, and quelled their opposition.

Take, for example, the editor of the *Newspacket*. I suppose there wasn't a greater temperance advocate in town. Yet Alphonse queered him with an Omelette à la Licence in one meal.

Or take Pepperleigh himself, the judge of the Mariposa court. He was put to the bad with a game pie – pâté normand aux fines herbes – the real thing, as good as a trip to Paris in itself. After eating it, Pepperleigh had the common sense to realize that it was sheer madness to destroy a hotel that could cook a thing like that.

In the same way, the secretary of the School Board was silenced with a stuffed duck à la Ossawippi.

Three members of the town council were converted with a Dindon farci à la Josh Smith.

And then, finally, Mr Diston persuaded Dean Drone to come, and as soon as Mr Smith and Alphonse saw him they landed him with a fried flounder that even the apostles would have appreciated.

After that, everyone knew that the licence question was practically settled. The petition was all over the town. It was printed in duplicate at the *Newspacket* and you could see it lying on the counter of every shop in Mariposa. Some of the people signed it twenty or thirty times.

It was the right kind of document too. It began – 'Whereas in the bounty of providence the earth putteth forth her luscious fruits and her vineyards for the delight and enjoyment of mankind –' It made you thirsty just to read it. Any man who read that petition over was wild to get to the Rats' Cooler.

When it was all signed up they had nearly three thousand names on it.

Then Nivens, the lawyer, and Mr Gingham (as a provincial official) took it down to the county town, and by three o'clock that afternoon the news had gone out from the long-distance telephone office that Smith's licence was renewed for three years.

Rejoicings! Well, I should think so! Everybody was down wanting to shake hands with Mr Smith. They told him that he had done more to boom Mariposa than any ten men in town. Some of them said he ought to run for the town council, and others wanted to make him the Conservative candidate for the next Dominion election. The caff was a mere babel of voices, and even the Rats' Cooler was almost floated away from its moorings.

And in the middle of it all, Mr Smith found time to say to Billy, the desk clerk: 'Take the cash registers out of the caff and the Rats' Cooler and start counting up the books.'

And Billy said: 'Will I write the letters for the palms and the tables and the stuff to go back?'

And Mr Smith said: 'Get 'em written right away.'

So all evening the laughter and the chatter and the congratulations went on, and it wasn't till long after midnight that Mr Smith was able to join Billy in the private room behind the 'rotunda'. Even when he did, there was a quiet and a dignity about his manner that had never been there before. I think it must have been the new halo of the Conservative candidacy that already radiated from his brow. It was, I imagine, at this very moment that Mr Smith first realized that the hotel business formed the natural and proper threshold of the national legislature.

'Here's the account of the cash registers,' said Billy.

'Let me see it,' said Mr Smith. And he studied the figures without a word.

'And here's the letters about the palms, and here's Alphonse up to yesterday –'

And then an amazing thing happened.

'Billy,' said Mr Smith, 'tear 'em up. I ain't going to do it. It ain't right and I won't do it. They got me the licence for to keep the caff and I'm going to keep the caff. I don't need to close her. The bar's good for anything from forty to a hundred a day now, and the Rats' Cooler going good, and that caff will stay right here.'

And stay it did.

There it stands, mind you, to this day. You've only to step round the corner of Smith's Hotel on the side street and read the sign: LADIES' AND GENTS' CAFÉ, just as large and as imposing as ever.

Mr Smith said that he'd keep the caff, and when he said a thing he meant it!

Of course there were changes, small changes.

I don't say, mind you, that the fillet de beef that you get there now is perhaps quite up to the level of the filet de boeuf aux champignons of the days of glory.

No doubt the lamb chops in Smith's Caff are often very much the same, nowadays, as the lamb chops of the Mariposa House or the Continental.

Of course, things like Omelette aux Trufles practically died out when Alphonse went. And, naturally, the leaving of Alphonse was inevitable. No one knew just when he went, or why. But one morning he was gone. Mr Smith said that 'Alf had to go back to his folks in the old country.'

So, too, when Alf left, the use of the French language, as such, fell off tremendously in the caff. Even now they use it to some extent. You can still get fillet de beef, and saucission au juice, but Billy the desk clerk has considerable trouble with the spelling.

The Rats' Cooler, of course, closed down, or rather Mr Smith closed it for repairs, and there is every likelihood that it will hardly open for three years. But the caff is there. They don't use the grills, because there's no need to, with the hotel kitchen so handy.

The 'girl room', I may say, was never opened. Mr Smith promised it, it is true, for the winter, and still talks of it. But somehow there's been a sort of feeling against it. Everyone in town admits that every big hotel in the city has a 'girl room' and that it must be all right. Still, there's a certain – well, you know how sensitive opinion is in a place like Mariposa.

III. THE MARINE EXCURSIONS OF THE KNIGHTS OF PYTHIAS

Half-past six on a July morning! The *Mariposa Belle* is at the wharf, decked in flags, with steam up ready to start.

Excursion day!

Half-past six on a July morning, and Lake Wissanotti lying in the sun as calm as glass. The opal colours of the morning light are shot from the surface of the water.

Out on the lake the last thin threads of the mist are clearing away like flecks of cotton wool.

The long call of the loon echoes over the lake. The air is cool and fresh. There is in it all the new life of the land of the silent pine and the moving waters. Lake Wissanotti in the morning sunlight! Don't talk to me of the Italian lakes or the Tyrol or the Swiss Alps. Take them away. Move them somewhere else. I don't want them.

Excursion Day, at half-past six of a summer morning! With the boat all decked in flags and all the people in Mariposa on the wharf, and the band in peaked caps with big cornets tied to their bodies ready to play at any minute! I say! Don't tell me about the Carnival of Venice and the Delhi Durbar. Don't! I wouldn't look at them. I'd shut my eyes! For light and colour give me every time an excursion out of Mariposa down the lake to the Indian's Island out of sight in the morning mist. Talk of your Papal Zouaves and your Buckingham Palace Guard! I want to see the Mariposa band in uniform and the Mariposa Knights of Pythias with their aprons and their insignia and their picnic baskets and their five-cent cigars!

Half-past six in the morning, and all the crowd on the wharf and the boat due to leave in half an hour. Notice it! – in half an hour. Already she's whistled twice (at six, and at six-fifteen), and at any minute now, Christie Johnson will step into the pilot house and pull the string for the warning whistle that the boat will leave in half an hour. So keep ready. Don't think of running back to Smith's Hotel for the sandwiches. Don't be fool enough to try to go up to the Greek store, next to Netley's, and buy fruit. You'll be left behind for sure if you do. Never mind the sandwiches and the fruit! Anyways, here comes Mr Smith himself with a huge basket of provender that would feed a factory. There must be sandwiches in that. I think I can hear them clinking. And behind Mr Smith is the German waiter from the caff with another basket – indubitably lager beer; and behind him, the bartender of the hotel, carrying nothing, as far as one can see. But of course if you know Mariposa you will understand that why he looks so nonchalant and empty handed is because he has two bottles of rye whisky under his linen duster. You know, I think, the peculiar walk of a man with two bottles of whisky in the inside pockets of a linen coat. In Mariposa, you see, to bring beer to an excursion is quite in keeping with public opinion. But, whisky – well, one has to be a little careful.

Do I say that Mr Smith is here? Why, everybody's here. There's Hussell, the editor of the *Newspacket*, wearing a blue ribbon on his coat, for the Mariposa Knights of Pythias are, by their constitution, dedicated to temperance; and there's Henry Mullins, the manager of the Exchange Bank, also a Knight of Pythias, with a small flask of Pogram's Special in his hip pocket as a sort of amendment to the constitution. And there's Dean Drone, the Chaplain of the Order, with a fishing-rod (you never saw such green bass as lie among the rocks at Indian's Island), and with a trolling line in case of maskinonge, and a landing net in case of pickerel, and with his eldest daughter, Lilian Drone, in case of young men. There never was such a fisherman as the Rev. Rupert Drone.

*   *   *

Perhaps I ought to explain that when I speak of the excursion as being of the Knights of Pythias, the thing must not be understood in any narrow sense. In Mariposa practically everybody belongs to the Knights of Pythias just as they do to everything else. That's the great thing about the town and that's what makes it so different from the city. Everybody is in everything.

You should see them on the seventeenth of March, for example, when everybody wears a green ribbon and they're all laughing and glad – you know what the Celtic nature is – and talking about Home Rule.

On St Andrew's Day every man in town wears a thistle and shakes hands with everybody else, and you see the fine old Scotch honesty beaming out of their eyes. And on St George's Day! – well, there's no heartiness like the good old English spirit, after all; why shouldn't a man feel glad that he's an Englishman?

Then on the Fourth of July there are stars and stripes flying over half the stores in town, and suddenly all the men are seen to smoke cigars and to know all about Roosevelt and Bryan and the Philippine Islands. Then you learn for the first time that Jeff Thorpe's people came from Massachusetts and that his uncle fought at Bunker Hill (it must have been Bunker Hill – anyway Jefferson will swear it was in Dakota all right enough); and you find that George Duff has a married sister in Rochester and that her husband is all right; in fact, George was down there as recently as eight years ago. Oh, it's the most American town imaginable is Mariposa – on the Fourth of July.

But wait, just wait, if you feel anxious about the solidity of the British connection, till the twelfth of the month, when everybody is wearing an orange streamer in his coat and the Orangemen (every man in town) walk in the big procession. Allegiance! Well, perhaps you remember the address they gave to the Prince of Wales on the platform of the Mariposa station as he went through on his tour to the west. I think that pretty well settled that question.

So you will easily understand that of course everybody belongs to the Knights of Pythias and the Masons and Oddfellows, just as they all belong to the Snow Shoe Club and the Girls' Friendly Society.

And meanwhile the whistle of the steamer has blown again for a quarter to seven – loud and long this time, for anyone not here now is late for certain, unless he should happen to come down in the last fifteen minutes.

What a crowd upon the wharf and how they pile on to the steamer! It's a wonder that the boat can hold them all. But that's just the marvellous thing about the *Mariposa Belle*.

I don't know – I have never known – where the steamers like the *Mariposa Belle* come from. Whether they are built by Harland and Wolff of Belfast, or whether, on the other hand, they are not built by Harland and Wolff of Belfast, is more than one would like to say offhand.

The *Mariposa Belle* always seems to me to have some of those strange properties that distinguish Mariposa itself. I mean, her size seems to vary so. If you see her there in the winter, frozen in the ice beside the wharf with a snowdrift against the windows of the pilot house, she looks a pathetic little thing the size of a butternut. But in the summer time, especially after you've been in Mariposa for a month or two, and have paddled alongside of her in a canoe, she gets larger and taller, and with a great sweep of black sides, till you see no difference between the *Mariposa Belle* and the *Lusitania*. Each one is a big steamer and that's all you can say.

Nor do her measurements help you much. She draws about eighteen inches forward, and more than that – at least half an inch more, astern, and when she's loaded down with an excursion crowd she draws a good two inches more. And above the water – why, look at all the decks on her! There's the deck you walk on to, from the wharf, all shut in, with windows along it, and the after cabin with the long table, and above that the deck in front where the band stand round in a circle, and the pilot house is higher than that, and above the pilot house is the board with the gold name and the flag pole and the steel ropes and the flags; and fixed in somewhere on the different levels is the lunch counter where they sell the sandwiches, and the engine room, and down below the deck level, beneath the water line, is the place where the crew sleep. What with steps and stairs and passages and piles of cordwood for the engine – oh no, I guess Harland and Wolff didn't build her. They couldn't have.

Yet even with a huge boat like the *Mariposa Belle*, it would be impossible for her to carry all of the crowd that you see in the boat and on the wharf. In reality, the crowd is made up of two classes – all of the people in Mariposa who are going on the excursion and all those who are not. Some come for the one reason and some for the other.

The two tellers of the Exchange Bank are both there standing side by side. But one of them – the one with the cameo pin and the long face like a horse – is going, and the other – with the other cameo pin and the face like another horse – is not. In the same way, Hussell of the *Newspacket* is going, but his brother, beside him, isn't. Lilian Drone is going, but her sister can't; and so on all through the crowd.

* * *

And to think that things should look like that on the morning of a steamboat accident.

How strange life is!

To think of all these people so eager and anxious to catch the steamer, and some of them running to catch it, and so fearful that they might miss it – the morning of a steamboat accident. And the captain blowing his whistle, and warning them so severely that he would leave them behind – leave them out of the accident! And everybody crowding so eagerly to be in the accident.

Perhaps life is like that all through.

Strangest of all to think, in a case like this, of the people who were left behind, or in some way or other prevented from going, and always afterwards told of how they had escaped being on board the *Mariposa Belle* that day!

Some of the instances were certainly extraordinary.

Nivens, the lawyer, escaped from being there merely by the fact that he was away in the city.

Towers, the tailor, only escaped owing to the fact that, not intending to go on the excursion, he had stayed in bed till eight o'clock and so had not gone. He narrated afterwards that, waking up that morning at half-past five, he had thought of the excursion and for some unaccountable reason had felt glad that he was not going.

* * *

The case of Yodel, the auctioneer, was even more inscrutable. He had been to the Oddfellows' excursion on the train the week before and to the Conservative picnic the week before that, and had decided not to go on this trip. In fact, he had not the least intention of going. He narrated afterwards how the night before someone had stopped him on the corner of Nippewa and Tecumseh Streets (he indicated the very spot) and asked: 'Are you going to take in the excursion tomorrow?' and he had said, just as simply as he was talking when narrating it: 'No.' And ten minutes after that, at the corner of Dalhousie and Brock Streets (he offered to lead a party of verification to the precise place) somebody else had stopped him and asked: 'Well, are you going on the steamer trip to-morrow?' Again he had answered: 'No,' apparently almost in the same tone as before.

He said afterwards that when he heard the rumour of the accident it seemed like the finger of Providence, and he fell on his knees in thankfulness.

There was the similar case of Morison (I mean the one in Glover's hardware store that married one of the Thompsons). He said afterwards that he had read so much in the papers about accidents lately – mining accidents, and aeroplanes and gasoline – that he had grown nervous. The night before his wife had asked him at supper: 'Are you going on the excursion?' He had answered: 'No, I don't think I feel like it,' and had added: 'Perhaps your mother might like to go.' And the next evening just at dusk, when the news ran through the town, he said the first thought that flashed through his head was: 'Mrs Thompson's on that boat.'

He told this right as I say it – without the least doubt or confusion. He never for a moment imagined she was on the *Lusitania* or the *Olympic* or any other boat. He knew she was on this one. He said you could have knocked him down where he stood. But no one had. Not even when he got half-way down – on his knees, and it would have been easier still to knock him down or kick him. People do miss a lot of chances.

Still, as I say, neither Yodel nor Morison nor anyone thought about there being an accident until just after sundown when they –

Well, have you ever heard the long booming whistle of a steamboat two miles out on the lake in the dusk, and while you listen and count and wonder, seen the crimson rockets going up against the sky and then heard the fire bell ringing right there beside you in the town, and seen the people running to the town wharf?

That's what the people of Mariposa saw and felt that summer evening as they watched the Mackinaw lifeboat go plunging out into the lake with seven sweeps to a side and the foam clear to the gunwale with the lifting stroke of fourteen men!

But, dear me, I am afraid that this is no way to tell a story. I suppose the true art would have been to have said nothing about the accident till it happened. But when you write about Mariposa, or hear of it, if you know the place, it's all so vivid and real that a thing like the contrast

between the excursion crowd in the morning and the scene at night leaps
into your mind and you must think of it.

* * *

But never mind about the accident – let us turn back again to the
morning.

The boat was due to leave at seven. There was no doubt about the
hour – not only seven, but seven sharp. The notice in the *Newspacket*
said: 'The boat will leave sharp at seven'; and the advertising posters on
the telegraph poles on Missinaba Street that began 'Ho, for Indian's
Island!' ended up with the words: 'Boat leaves at seven sharp.' There was
a big notice on the wharf that said: 'Boat leaves sharp on time.'

So at seven, right on the hour, the whistle blew loud and long, and then
at seven-fifteen three short peremptory blasts, and at seven-thirty one
quick angry call – just one – and very soon after that they cast off the last
of the ropes and the *Mariposa Belle* sailed off in her cloud of flags, and
the band of the Knights of Pythias, timing it to a nicety, broke into the
'Maple Leaf for Ever!'

I suppose that all excursions when they start are much the same.
Anyway, on the *Mariposa Belle* everybody went running up and down all
over the boat with deck-chairs and camp stools and baskets, and found
places, splendid places, to sit, and then got scared that there might be
better ones and chased off again. People hunted for places out of the sun
and when they got them swore that they weren't going to freeze to please
anybody; and the people in the sun said that they hadn't paid fifty cents
to get covered with cinders, and there were still others who hadn't paid
fifty cents to get shaken to death with the propeller.

Still, it was all right presently. The people seemed to get sorted out
into the places on the boat where they belonged. The women, the older
ones, all gravitated into the cabin on the lower deck and by getting round
the table with needlework, and with all the windows shut, they soon had
it, as they said themselves, just like being at home.

All the young boys and the toughs and the men in the band got down
on the lower deck forward, where the boat was dirtiest and where the
anchor was the coils of rope. And upstairs on the after deck there were
Lilian Drone and Miss Lawson, the high-school teacher, with a book of
German poetry – Gothey I think it was – and the bank teller and the
younger men.

In the centre, standing beside the rail, were Dean Drone and Dr
Gallagher, looking through binocular glasses at the shore.

Up in front on the little deck forward of the pilot house was a group
of the older men, Mullins and Duff and Mr Smith in a deck chair, and
beside him Mr Golgotha Gingham, the undertaker of Mariposa, on a

stool. It was part of Mr Gingham's principles to take in an outing of this sort, a business matter, more or less – for you never know what may happen at these water parties. At any rate, he was there in a neat suit of black, not, of course, his heavier or professional suit, but a soft clinging effect as of burnt paper that combined gaiety and decorum to a nicety.

* * *

'Yes,' said Mr Gingham, waving his black glove in a general way towards the shore, 'I know the lake well, very well. I've been pretty much all over it in my time.'

'Canoeing?' asked somebody.

'No,' said Mr Gingham, 'not in a canoe.' There seemed a peculiar and quiet meaning in his tone.

'Sailing, I suppose,' said somebody else.

'No,' said Mr Gingham, 'I don't understand it.'

'I never knowed that you went on to the water at all, Gol,' said Mr Smith, breaking in.

'Ah, not now,' explained Mr Gingham; 'it was years ago, the first summer I came to Mariposa. I was on the water practically all day. Nothing like it to give a man an appetite and keep him in shape.'

'Was you camping?' asked Mr Smith.

'We camped at night,' assented the undertaker, 'but we put in practically the whole day on the water. You see we were after a party that had come up here from the city on his vacation and gone out in a sailing canoe. We were dragging. We were up every morning at sunrise, lit a fire on the beach and cooked breakfast, and then we'd light our pipes and be off with the net for a whole day. It's a great life,' concluded Mr Gingham wistfully.

'Did you get him?' asked two or three together.

There was a pause before Mr Gingham answered.

'We did,' he said – 'down in the reeds past Horseshoe Point. But it was no use. He turned blue on me right away.'

After which Mr Gingham fell into such a deep reverie that the boat had steamed another half-mile down the lake before anybody broke the silence again.

Talk of this sort – and after all what more suitable for a day on the water? – beguiled the way.

* * *

Down the lake, mile by mile over the calm water, steamed the *Mariposa Belle*. They passed Poplar Point where the high sand-banks are with all the swallows' nests in them, and Dean Drone and Dr Gallagher looked at them alternately through the binocular glasses, and it was wonderful how plainly one could see the swallows and the banks and the shrubs – just as plainly as with the naked eye. And a little further down they passed the Shingle Beach, and Dr Gallagher, who knew Canadian history, said to Dean Drone that it was strange to think that Champlain had landed there with his French explorers three hundred years ago; and Dean Drone, who didn't know Canadian history, said it was stranger still to think that the hand of the Almighty had piled up the hills and rocks long before that; and Dr Gallagher said it was wonderful how the French had found their way through such a pathless wilderness; and Dean Drone said that it was wonderful also to think that the Almighty had placed even the smallest shrub in its appointed place. Dr Gallagher said it filled him with admiration. Dean Drone said it filled him with awe. Dr Gallagher said he'd been full of it ever since he was a boy; and Dean Drone said so had he.

Then a little further, as the *Mariposa Belle* steamed on down the lake, they passed the Old Indian Portage where the great grey rocks are; and Dr Gallagher drew Dean Drone's attention to the place where the narrow canoe track wound up from the shore to the woods, and Dean Drone said he could see it perfectly well without the glasses.

Dr Gallagher said that it was just here that a party of five hundred French had made their way with all their baggage and accoutrements across the rocks of the divide and down to the Great Bay. And Dean Drone said that it reminded him of Xenophon leading his ten thousand Greeks over the hill passes of Armenia down to the sea. Dr Gallagher said that he had often wished he could have seen and spoken to Champlain, and Dean Drone said how much he regretted to have never known Xenophon. And then after that they fell to talking of relics and traces of the past, and Dr Gallagher said that if Dean Drone woud come round to his house some night he would show him some Indian arrow heads that he had dug up in his garden. And Dean Drone said that if Dr Gallagher would come round to the rectory any afternoon he would show him a map of Xerxes' invasion of Greece. Only he must come some time between the Infant Class and the Mothers' Auxiliary.

So presently they both knew that they were blocked out of one another's houses for some time to come, and Dr Gallagher walked forward and told Mr Smith, who had never studied Greek, about Champlain crossing the rock divide.

Mr Smith turned his head and looked at the divide for half a second and then said he had crossed a worse one up north back of the Wahnipitae and that the flies were Hades – and then went on playing freeze-out poker with the two juniors in Duff's bank.

So Dr Gallagher realized that that's always the way when you try to tell people things, and that as far as gratitude and appreciation goes one might as well never read books or travel anywhere or do anything.

In fact, it was at this very moment that he made up his mind to give the arrows to the Mariposa Mechanics' Institute – they afterwards became, as you know, the Gallagher Collection. But, for the time being, the doctor was sick of them and wandered off round the boat and watched Henry Mullins showing George Duff how to make a John Collins without lemons, and finally went and sat down among the Mariposa band and wished that he hadn't come.

So the boat steamed on and the sun rose higher and higher, and the freshness of the morning changed into the full glare of noon, and they went on to where the lake began to narrow in at its foot, just where the Indian's Island is – all grass and trees and with a log wharf running into the water. Below it the Lower Ossawippi runs out of the lake, and quite near are the rapids, and you can see down among the trees the red brick of the power house and hear the roar of the leaping water.

The Indian's Island itself is all covered with trees and tangled vines, and the water about it is so still that it's all reflected double and looks the same either way up. Then when the steamer's whistle blows as it comes into the wharf, you hear it echo among the trees of the island, and reverberate back from the shores of the lake.

The scene is all so quiet and still and unbroken that Miss Cleghorn – the sallow girl in the telephone exchange, that I spoke of – said she'd like to be buried there. But all the people were so busy getting their baskets and gathering up their things that no one had time to attend to it.

I mustn't even try to describe the landing and the boat crunching against the wooden wharf and all the people running to the same side of the deck and Christie Johnson calling out to the crowd to keep to the starboard and nobody being able to find it. Everyone who has been on a Mariposa excursion knows all about that.

Nor can I describe the day itself and the picnic under the trees. There were speeches afterwards, and Judge Pepperleigh gave such offence by bringing in Conservative politics that a man called Patriotus Canadiensis wrote and asked for some of the invaluable space of the Mariposa *Times-Herald* and exposed it.

I should say that there were races too, on the grass on the open side of the island, graded mostly according to ages – races for boys under thirteen and girls over nineteen and all that sort of thing. Sports are generally conducted on that plan in Mariposa. It is realized that a woman of sixty has an unfair advantage over a mere child.

Dean Drone managed the races and decided the ages and gave out the prizes; the Wesleyan minister helped, and he and the young student, who was relieving in the Presbyterian Church, held the string at the winning point.

They had to get mostly clergymen for the races because all the men had wandered off, somehow, to where they were drinking lager beer out of two kegs stuck on pine logs among the trees.

But if you've ever been on a Mariposa excursion you know all about these details anyway.

So the day wore on and presently the sun came through the trees on a slant and the steamer whistle blew with a great puff of white steam and all the people came straggling down to the wharf and pretty soon the *Mariposa Belle* had floated out on to the lake again and headed for the town, twenty miles away.

* * *

I suppose you have often noticed the contrast there is between an excursion on its way out in the morning and what it looks like on the way home.

In the morning everybody is so restless and animated and moves to and fro all over the boat and asks questions. But coming home, as the afternoon gets later and later and the sun sinks beyond the hills, all the people seem to get so still and quiet and drowsy.

So it was with the people on the *Mariposa Belle*. They sat there on the benches and the deck chairs in little clusters, and listened to the regular beat of the propeller and almost dozed off asleep as they sat. Then when the sun set and the dusk drew on, it grew dark on the deck and so still that you could hardly tell there was anyone on board.

And if you had looked at the steamer from the shore or from one of the islands, you'd have seen the row of lights from the cabin windows shining on the water and the red glare of the burning hemlock from the funnel, and you'd have heard the soft thud of the propeller miles away over the lake.

Now and then, too, you could have heard the singing on the steamer – the voices of the girls and the men blended into unison by the distance, rising and falling in long-drawn melody: '*O – Can-a-da – O – Can-a-da*.'

You may talk as you will about the intoning choirs of your European cathedrals, but the sound of 'O Can-a-da,' borne across the waters of a silent lake at evening, is good enough for those of us who know Mariposa.

I think that it was just as they were singing like this: '*O – Can-a-da*,' that word went round that the boat was sinking.

If you have ever been in any sudden emergency on the water, you will understand the strange psychology of it – the way in which what is happening seems to become known all in a moment without a word being said. The news is transmitted from one to the other by some mysterious process.

At any rate, on the *Mariposa Belle* first one and then the other heard that the steamer was sinking. As far as I could ever learn, the first of it was that George Duff, the bank manager, came very quietly to Dr Gallagher and asked him if he thought that the boat was sinking. The doctor said no, that he had thought so earlier in the day but that he didn't now think that she was.

After that Duff, according to his own account, had said to Macartney, the lawyer, that the boat was sinking, and Macartney said that he doubted it very much.

Then somebody came to Judge Pepperleigh and woke him up and said that there was six inches of water in the steamer and that she was sinking. And Pepperleigh said it was a perfect scandal and passed the news on to his wife and she said that they had no business to allow it and that if the steamer sank that was the last excursion she'd go on.

So the news went all round the boat and everywhere the people gathered in groups and talked about it in the angry and excited way that people have when a steamer is sinking on one of the lakes like Lake Wissanotti.

Dean Drone, of course, and some others were quieter about it, and said that one must make allowances and that naturally there were two sides to everything. But most of them wouldn't listen to reason at all. I think, perhaps, that some of them were frightened. You see the last time but one that the steamer had sunk, there had been a man drowned and it made them nervous.

What? Hadn't I explained about the depth of Lake Wissanotti? I had taken it for granted that you knew; and in any case parts of it are deep enough, though I don't suppose in this stretch of it, but from the big reed beds up to within a mile of the town wharf, you could find six feet of water in it if you tried. Oh, pshaw! I was not talking about a steamer sinking in the ocean and carrying down its screaming crowds of people into the hideous depths of green water. Oh, dear me, no! That kind of thing never happens on Lake Wissanotti.

But what does happen is that the *Mariposa Belle* sinks every now and then, and sticks there on the bottom till they get things straightened up.

On the lakes round Mariposa, if a person arrives late anywhere and explains that the steamer sank, everybody understands the situation.

You see when Harland and Wolff built the *Mariposa Belle*, they left some cracks in between the timbers that you fill up with cotton waste every Sunday. If this is not attended to, the boat sinks. In fact, it is part of the law of the province that all the steamers like the *Mariposa Belle* must be properly corked – I think that is the word – every season. There are inspectors who visit all the hotels in the province to see that it is done.

So you can imagine, now that I've explained it a little straighter, the indignation of the people when they knew that the boat had come uncorked and that they might be stuck out there on a shoal or a mudbank half the night.

I don't say either that there wasn't any danger; anyway, it doesn't feel very safe when you realize that the boat is settling down with every hundred yards that she goes, and you look over the side and see only the black water in the gathering night.

Safe! I'm not sure now that I come to think of it that it isn't worse than sinking in the Atlantic. After all, in the Atlantic there is wireless telegraphy, and a lot of trained sailors and stewards. But out on Lake Wissanotti – far out, so that you can only just see the lights of the town away off to the south – when the propeller comes to a stop – and you can hear the hiss of steam as they start to take out the engine fires to prevent an explosion – and when you turn from the red glare that comes from the furnace doors as they open them, to the black dark that is gathering over the lake – and there's a night wind beginning to run among the rushes – and you see the men going forward to the roof of the pilot house to send up the rockets to rouse the town – safe? Safe yourself, if you like; as for me, let me once get back into Mariposa again, under the night shadow of the maple trees, and this shall be the last, last time I'll go on Lake Wissanotti.

Safe! Of yes! Isn't it strange how safe other people's adventures seem after they happen? But you'd have been scared, too, if you'd been there just before the steamer sank, and seen them bringing up all the women on to the top deck.

I don't see how some of the people took it so calmly; how Mr Smith, for instance, could have gone on smoking and telling how he'd had a steamer 'sink on him' on Lake Nipissing and a still bigger one, a side-wheeler, sink on him in Lake Abbitibbi.

Then, quite suddenly, with a quiver, down she went. You could feel the boat sink, sink – down, down – would it never get to the bottom? The water came flush up to the lower deck, and then – thank heaven – the sinking stopped and there was the *Mariposa Belle* safe and tight on a reed bank.

Really, it made one positively laugh! It seemed so queer and, anyway, if a man has a sort of natural courage, danger makes him laugh. Danger? pshaw! fiddlesticks! everybody scouted the idea. Why, it is just the little things like this that give zest to a day on the water.

Within half a minute they were all running round looking for sandwiches and cracking jokes and talking of making coffee over the remains of the engine fires.

* * *

I don't need to tell at length how it all happened after that.

I suppose the people on the *Mariposa Belle* would have had to settle down there all night or till help came from the town, but some of the men who had gone forward and were peering out into the dark said that it couldn't be more than a mile across the water to Miller's Point. You could almost see it over there to the left – some of them, I think, said 'off on the port bow,' because you know when you get mixed up in these marine disasters you soon catch the atmosphere of the thing.

So pretty soon they had the davits swung out over the side and were lowering the old lifeboat from the top deck into the water.

There were men leaning out over the rail of the *Mariposa Belle* with lanterns that threw the light as they let her down, and the glare fell on the water and the reeds. But when they got the boat lowered, it looked such a frail, clumsy thing as one saw it from the rail above, that the cry was raised: 'Women and children first!' For what was the sense, if it should turn out that the boat wouldn't even hold women and children, of trying to jam a lot of heavy men into it?

So they put in mostly women and children and the boat pushed out into the darkness so freighted down it would hardly float.

In the bow of it was the Presbyterian student who was relieving the minister, and he called out that they were in the hands of Providence. But he was crouched and ready to spring out of them at the first moment.

So the boat went and was lost in the darkness except for the lantern in the bow that you could see bobbing on the water. Then presently it came back and they sent another load, till pretty soon the decks began to thin out and everybody got impatient to be gone.

It was about the time that the third boat-load put off that Mr Smith took a bet with Mullins for twenty-five dollars, that he'd be home in Mariposa before the people in the boats had walked round the shore.

No one knew just what he meant, but pretty soon they saw Mr Smith disappear down below into the lowest part of the steamer with a mallet in one hand a big bundle of marline in the other.

They might have wondered more about it, but it was just at this time that they heard the shouts from the rescue boat – the big Mackinaw lifeboat – that had put out from the town with fourteen men at the sweeps when they saw the first rockets go up.

I suppose there is always something inspiring about a rescue at sea, or on the water.

After all, the bravery of the lifeboat man is the true bravery – expended to save life, not to destroy it.

Certainly they told for months after of how the rescue boat came out to the *Mariposa Belle*.

I suppose that when they put her in the water the lifeboat touched it for the first time since the old Macdonald Government placed her on Lake Wissanotti.

Anyway, the water poured in at every seam. But not for a moment – even with two miles of water between them and the steamer – did the rowers pause for that.

By the time they were half-way there the water was almost up to the thwarts, but they drove her on. Panting and exhausted (for mind you, if you haven't been in a fool boat like that for years, rowing takes it out of you), the rowers stuck to their task. They threw the ballast over and chucked into the water the heavy cork jackets and lifebelts that encumbered their movements. There was no thought of turning back. They were nearer to the steamer than the shore.

'Hang to it, boys,' called the crowd from the steamer's deck, and hang they did.

They were almost exhausted when they got them; men leaning from the steamer threw them ropes and one by one every man was hauled aboard just as the lifeboat sank under their feet.

Saved! by Heaven, saved, by one of the smartest pieces of rescue work ever seen on the lake.

There's no use describing it; you need to see rescue work of this kind by lifeboats to understand it.

Nor were the lifeboat crew the only ones that distinguished themselves.

Boat after boat and canoe after canoe had put out from Mariposa to the help of the steamer. They got them all.

Pupkin, the other bank teller, with a face like a horse, who hadn't gone on the excursion – as soon as he knew that the boat was signalling for help and that Miss Lawson was sending up rockets – rushed for a row boat, grabbed an oar (two would have hampered him), and paddled madly out into the lake. He struck right out into the dark with the crazy skiff almost sinking beneath his feet. But they got him. They rescued him. They watched him, almost dead with exhaustion, make his way to the steamer, where he was hauled up with ropes. Saved! Saved!

* * *

They might have gone on that way half the night, picking up the rescuers, only, at the very moment when the tenth load of people left for the shore – just as suddenly and saucily as you please, up came the *Mariposa Belle* from the mud bottom and floated.

FLOATED?

Why, of course she did. If you take a hundred and fifty people off a steamer that has sunk and if you get a man as shrewd as Mr Smith to plug the timber seams with mallet and marline, and if you turn ten bandsmen of the Mariposa band on to your hand pump on the bow of the lower decks – float? why, what else can she do?

Then, if you stuff in hemlock into the embers of the fire that you were raking out, till it hums and crackles under the boiler, it won't be long before you hear the propeller thud-thudding at the stern again, and before the long roar of the steam whistle echoes over to the town.

And so the *Mariposa Belle*, with all steam up again and with the long train of sparks careering from the funnel, is heading for the town.

But no Christie Johnson at the wheel in the pilot house this time.

'Smith! Get Smith!' is the cry.

Can he take her in? Well, now! Ask a man who has had steamers sink on him in half the lakes from Temiscaming to the Bay, if he can take her in? Ask a man who has run a York boat down the rapids of the Moose when the ice is moving, if he can grip the steering wheel of the *Mariposa Belle* So there she steams safe and sound to the town wharf!

Look at the lights and the crowd! If only the federal census-taker could count us now! Hear them calling and shouting back and forward from the deck to the shore! Listen! There is the rattle of the shore ropes as they get them ready, and there's the Mariposa band – actually forming a circle on the upper deck just as she docks, and the leader with his baton – one – two – ready now –

'O CAN – A – DA!'

IX. THE MARIPOSA BANK MYSTERY

Suicide is a thing that ought not to be committed without very careful thought. It often involves serious consequences, and in some cases brings pain to others than oneself.

I don't say that there is no justification for it. There often is. Anybody who has listened to certain kinds of music, or read certain kinds of poetry, or heard certain kinds of performances upon the concertina, will admit that there are some lives which ought not to be continued, and that even suicide has its brighter aspects.

But to commit suicide on grounds of love is at the best a very dubious experiment. I know that in this I am expressing an opinion contrary to that of most true lovers who embrace suicide on the slightest provocation as the only honourable termination of an existence that never ought to have begun.

I quite admit that there is a glamour and a sensation about the thing which has its charm, and that there is nothing like it for causing a girl to realize the value of the heart that she has broken and which breathed forgiveness upon her at the very moment when it held in its hand the half-pint of prussic acid that was to terminate its beating for ever.

But apart from the general merits of the question, I suppose there are few people, outside of lovers, who know what it is to commit suicide four times in five weeks.

Yet this was what happened to Mr Pupkin, of the Exchange Bank of Mariposa.

Ever since he had known Zena Pepperleigh he had realized that his love for her was hopeless. She was too beautiful for him and too good for him; her father hated him and her mother despised him; his salary was too small and his own people were too rich.

If you add to all that that he came up to the judge's house one night and found a poet reciting verses to Zena, you will understand the suicide at once. It was one of those regular poets with a solemn jackass face, and lank parted hair and eyes like puddles of molasses. I don't know how he came there – up from the city, probably – but there he was on the Pepperleighs' verandah that August evening. He was reciting poetry – either Tennyson's or Shelley's, or his own, you couldn't tell – and about him sat Zena with her hands clasped and Nora Gallagher looking at the sky and Jocelyn Drone gazing into infinity, and a little tubby woman looking at the poet with her head falling over sideways – in fact, there was a whole group of them.

* * *

I don't know what it is about poets that draws women to them in this way. But everybody knows that a poet has only to sit and saw the air with his hands and recite verses in a deep stupid voice, and all the women are crazy over him. Men despise him and would kick him off the verandah if they dared, but the women simply rave over him.

So Pupkin sat there in the gloom and listened to this poet reciting Browning and he realized that everybody understood it but him. He could see Zena with her eyes fixed on the poet as if she were hanging on to every syllable (she was; she needed to), and he stood it just about fifteen minutes and then slid off the side of the verandah and disappeared without even saying good night.

He walked straight down Oneida Street and along the Main Street just as hard as he could go. There was only one purpose in his mind – suicide. He was heading straight for Jim Eliot's drug store on the main corner and his idea was to buy a drink of chloroform and drink it and die right there on the spot.

As Pupkin walked down the street, the whole thing was so vivid in his mind that he could picture it to the remotest detail. He could even see it all in type, in big headings in the newspapers of the following day:

APPALLING SUICIDE
PETER PUPKIN POISONED

He perhaps hoped that the thing might lead to some kind of public inquiry and that the question of Browning's poetry and whether it is altogether fair to allow of its general circulation would be fully ventilated in the newspapers.

Thinking all that, Pupkin came to the main corner.

On a warm August evening the drug store of Mariposa, as you know, is all a blaze of light. You can hear the hissing of the soda-water fountain half a block away, and inside the store there are ever so many people – boys and girls and old people too – drinking sarsaparilla and chocolate sundaes and lemon sours and foaming drinks that you take out of long straws. There is such a laughing and a talking as you never heard, and the girls are all in white and pink and cambridge blue, and the soda fountain is of white marble with silver taps, and it hisses and sputters, and Jim Eliot and his assistant wear white coats with red geraniums in them, and it's all just as gay as gay.

The foyer of the opera in Paris may be a fine sight, but I doubt if it can compare with the inside of Eliot's drug store in Mariposa – for real gaiety and joy of living.

This night the store was especially crowded because it was a Saturday and that meant early closing for all the hotels, except, of course, Smith's. So as the hotels were shut, the people were all in the drug store, drinking like fishes. It just shows the folly of Local Option and the Temperance Movement and all that. Why if you shut the hotels you simply drive the people to the soda fountains and there's more drinking than ever, and not only of the men, too, but the girls and young boys and children. I've seen little things of eight and nine that had to be lifted up on the high stools at Eliot's drug store, drinking great goblets of lemon soda, enough to burst them – brought there by their own fathers, and why? Simply because the hotel bars were shut.

What's the use of thinking you can stop people drinking merely by cutting off whisky and brandy? The only effect is to drive them to taking lemon sour and sarsaparilla and cherry pectoral and caroka cordial and things they wouldn't have touched before. So in the long run they drink more than ever. The point is that you can't prevent people having a good time, no matter how hard you try. If they can't have it with lager beer and brandy, they'll have it with plain soda and lemon pop, and so the whole gloomy scheme of the temperance people breaks down, anyway.

But I was only saying that Eliot's drug store in Mariposa on a Saturday night is the gayest and brightest spot in the world.

And just imagine what a fool of a place to commit suicide in!

Just imagine going up to the soda-water fountain and asking for five cents' worth of chloroform and soda! Well, you simply can't, that's all.

That's the way Pupkin found it. You see, as soon as he came in, somebody called out: 'Hello, Pete!' and one or two others called: 'Hullo, Pup!' and some said: 'How goes it?' and others: 'How are you toughing it?' and so on, because you see they had all been drinking more or less and naturally they felt jolly and glad-hearted.

So the upshot of it was that instead of taking chloroform, Pupkin stepped up to the counter of the fountain and he had a bromoseltzer with cherry soda, and after that he had one of those aerated seltzers, and then a couple of lemon seltzers and a bromophizzer.

I don't know if you know the mental effect of a bromoseltzer.

But it's a hard thing to commit suicide on.

You can't.

You feel so buoyant.

Anyway, what with the phizzing of the seltzer and the lights and the girls, Pupkin began to feel so fine that he didn't care a cuss for all the Brownings in the world, and as for the poet – oh, to blazes with him! What's poetry, anyway? – only rhymes.

So, would you believe it, in about ten minutes Peter Pupkin was off again, heading straight for the Pepperleighs' house, poet or no poet, and what was more to the point, he carried with him three great bricks of Eliot's ice-cream – in green, pink and brown layers. He struck the verandah just at the moment when Browning was getting too stale and dreary for words. His brain was all sizzling and jolly with the bromoseltzer, and when he fetched out the ice-cream bricks and Zena ran to get plates and spoons to eat it with, and Pupkin went with her to help fetch them and they picked out the spoons together, they were so laughing and happy that it was just a marvel. Girls, you know, need no bromoseltzer. They're full of it all the time.

And as for the poet – well, can you imagine how Pupkin felt when Zena told him that the poet was married, and that the tubby little woman with her head on sideways was his wife?

So they had the ice-cream, and the poet ate it in bucketfuls. Poets always do. They need it. And after it the poet recited some stanzas of his own and Pupkin saw that he had misjudged the man, because it was dandy poetry, the very best. That night Pupkin walked home on air and there was no thought of chloroform, and it turned out that he hadn't committed suicide, but like all lovers he had commuted it.

* * *

I don't need to describe in full the later suicides of Mr Pupkin, because they were all conducted on the same plan and rested on something the same reasons as above.

Sometimes he would go down at night to the offices of the bank below his bedroom and bring up his bank revolver in order to make an end of himself with it. This, too, he could see headed up in the newspapers as:

BRILLIANT BOY BANKER
BLOWS OUT BRAINS

But blowing your brains out is a noisy, rackety performance, and Pupkin soon found that only special kinds of brains are suited for it. So he always sneaked back again later in the night and put the revolver in its place, deciding to drown himself instead. Yet every time that he walked down to the Trestle Bridge over the Ossawippi he found it was quite unsuitable for drowning – too high, and the water too swift and black, and the rushes too gruesome – in fact, not at all the kind of place for a drowning.

Far better, he realized, to wait there on the railroad track and throw himself under the wheels of the express and be done with it. Yet, though Pupkin often waited in this way for the train, he was never able to pick out a pair of wheels that suited him. Anyhow, it's awfully hard to tell an express from a fast freight.

I wouldn't mention these attempts at suicide if one of them hadn't finally culminated in making Peter Pupkin a hero and solving for him the whole perplexed entanglement of his love affair with Zena Pepperleigh. Incidentally it threw him into the very centre of one of the most impenetrable bank mysteries that ever baffled the ingenuity of some of the finest legal talent that ever adorned one of the most enterprising communities in the country.

It happened one night, as I say, that Pupkin decided to go down into the office of the bank and get his revolver and see if it would blow his brains out. It was the night of the Firemen's Ball and Zena had danced four times with a visitor from the city, a man who was in the fourth year at the University and who knew everything. It was more than Peter Pupkin could bear. Mallory Tompkins was away that night, and when Pupkin came home he was all alone in the building, except for Gillis, the caretaker, who lived in the extension at the back.

He sat in his room for hours brooding. Two or three times he picked up a book – he remembered afterwards distinctly that it was Kant's

Critique of Pure Reason – and tried to read it, but it seemed meaningless and trivial. Then with a sudden access of resolution he started from his chair and made his way down the stairs and into the office room of the bank, meaning to get a revolver and kill himself on the spot and let them find his body lying on the floor.

It was then far on in the night and the empty building of the bank was as still as death. Pupkin could hear the stairs creak under his feet, and as he went he thought he heard another sound like the opening or closing of a door. But it sounded not like the sharp ordinary noise of a closing door but with a dull muffled noise as if someone had shut the iron door of a safe in a room under the ground. For a moment Pupkin stood and listened with his heart thumping against his ribs. Then he kicked his slippers from his feet and without a sound stole into the office on the ground floor and took the revolver from his teller's desk. As he gripped it, he listened to the sounds on the back-stairway and in the vaults below.

I should explain that in the Exchange Bank of Mariposa the offices are on the ground floor level with the street. Below this is another floor with low dark rooms paved with flagstones, with unused office desks and with piles of papers stored in boxes. On this floor are the vaults of the bank, and lying in them in the autumn – the grain season – there is anything from fifty to a hundred thousand dollars in currency tied in bundles. There is no other light down there than the dim reflection from the lights out on the street, that lies in patches on the stone floor.

I think as Peter Pupkin stood, revolver in hand, in the office of the bank, he had forgotten all about the maudlin purpose of his first coming. He had forgotten for the moment all about heroes and love affairs, and his whole mind was focused, sharp and alert, with the intensity of the night-time, on the sounds that he heard in the vault and on the back-stairway of the bank.

Straight away, Pupkin knew what it meant as plainly as if it were written in print. He had forgotten, I say, about being a hero and he only knew that there was sixty thousand dollars in the vault of the bank below, and that he was paid eight hundred dollars a year to look after it.

As Peter Pupkin stood there listening to the sounds in his stockinged feet, his face showed grey as ashes in the light that fell through the window from the street. His heart beat like a hammer against his ribs. But behind its beatings was the blood of four generations of Loyalists, and the robber who would take that sixty thousand dollars from the Mariposa bank must take it over the dead body of Peter Pupkin, teller.

* * *

Pupkin walked down the stairs to the lower room, the one below the ground with the bank vault in it, with as fine a step as any of his ancestors showed on parade. And if he had known it, as he came down the stairway in the front of the vault room, there was a man crouched in the shadow of the passageway by the stairs at the back. This man, too, held a revolver in his hand, and, criminal or not, his face was as resolute as Pupkin's own. As he heard the teller's step on the stair, he turned and waited in the shadow of the doorway without a sound.

There is no need really to mention all these details. They are only of interest as showing how sometimes a bank teller in a corded smoking jacket and stockinged feet may be turned into such a hero as even the Mariposa girls might dream about.

All of this must have happened at about three o'clock in the night. This much was established afterwards from the evidence of Gillis, the caretaker. When he first heard the sounds he had looked at his watch and noticed that it was half-past two; the watch he knew was three-quarters of an hour slow three days before and had been gaining since. The exact time at which Gillis heard footsteps in the bank and started downstairs, pistol in hand, became a nice point afterwards in the cross-examination.

But one must not anticipate. Pupkin reached the iron door of the bank safe, and knelt in front of it, feeling in the dark to find the fracture of the lock. As he knelt, he heard a sound behind him, and swung round on his knees and saw the bank robber in the half light of the passageway and the glitter of a pistol in his hand. The rest was over in an instant. Pupkin heard a voice that was his own, but that sounded strange and hollow, call out: 'Drop that, or I'll fire!' and then just as he raised his revolver there came a blinding flash of light before his eyes, and Peter Pupkin, junior teller of the bank, fell forward on the floor and knew no more.

* * *

At that point, of course, I ought to close down a chapter, or volume, or, at least, strike the reader over the head with a sandbag to force him to stop and think. In common fairness one ought to stop here and count a hundred or get up and walk round a block, or, at any rate, picture to oneself Peter Pupkin lying on the floor of the bank, motionless, his arms distended, the revolver still grasped in his hand. But I must go on.

By half-past seven on the following morning it was known all over Mariposa that Peter Pupkin, the junior teller of the Exchange, had been shot dead by a bank robber in the vault of the building. It was known also that Gillis, the caretaker, had been shot and killed at the foot of the stairs, and that the robber had made off with fifty thousand dollars in currency; that he had left a trail of blood on the sidewalk and that the men were out tracking him with bloodhounds in the great swamps to the north of the town.

This, I say, and it is important to note it, was what they knew at half-past seven. Of course as each hour went past they learned more and more. At eight o'clock it was known that Pupkin was not dead, but dangerously wounded in the lungs. At eight-thirty it was known that he was not shot in the lungs, but that the ball had traversed the pit of his stomach.

At nine o'clock it was learned that the pit of Pupkin's stomach was all right, but that the bullet had struck his right ear and carried it away. Finally it was learned that his ear had not exactly been carried away, that is, not precisely removed by the bullet, but that it had grazed Pupkin's head in such a way that it had stunned him, and if it had been an inch or two more to the left it might have reached his brain. This, of course, was just as good as being killed from the point of view of public interest.

Indeed, by nine o'clock Pupkin could be himself seen on the Main Street with a great bandage sideways on his head, pointing out the traces of the robber. Gillis, the caretaker, too, it was known by eight, had not been killed. He had been shot through the brain, but whether the injury was serious or not was only a matter of conjecture. In fact, by ten o'clock it was understood that the bullet from the robber's second shot had grazed the side of the caretaker's head, but as far as could be known his brain was just as before. I should add that the first report about the blood-stains and the swamp and the bloodhounds turned out to be inaccurate. The stains may have been blood, but as they led to the cellar way of Netley's store, they may have also been molasses, though it was argued, to be sure, that the robber might well have poured molasses over the bloodstains from sheer cunning.

It was remembered, too, that there were no bloodhounds in Mariposa, although, mind you, there are any amount of dogs there.

So you see that by ten o'clock in the morning the whole affair was settling into the impenetrable mystery which it ever since remained.

Not that there wasn't evidence enough. There was Pupkin's own story and Gillis's story, and the stories of all the people who had heard the shots and seen the robber (some said, the bunch of robbers) go running past (others said, walking past) in the night. Apparently the robber ran up and down half the streets of Mariposa before he vanished.

But the stories of Pupkin and Gillis were plain enough. Pupkin related that he heard sounds in the bank and came downstairs just in time to see the robber crouching in the passage way, and that the robber was a large, hulking, villainous-looking man, wearing a heavy coat. Gillis told exactly the same story, having heard the noises at the same time, except that he first described the robber as a small thin fellow (peculiarly villainous-looking however, even in the dark), wearing a short jacket; but on thinking it over, Gillis realized that he had been wrong about the size of the criminal, and that he was even bigger, if anything, than what Mr Pupkin thought. Gillis had fired at the robber; just at the same moment had Mr Pupkin.

Beyond that, all was mystery, absolute and impenetrable.

By eleven o'clock the detectives had come up from the city under orders from the head of the bank.

* * *

I wish you could have seen the two detectives as they moved to and fro in Mariposa – fine-looking, stern, impenetrable men that they were. They seemed to take in the whole town by instinct and so quietly. They found their way to Mr Smith's Hotel just as quietly as if it wasn't design at all and stood there at the bar, picking up scraps of conversation – you know the way detectives do it. Occasionally they allowed one or two bystanders – confederates, perhaps – to buy a drink for them, and you could see from the way they drank it that they were still listening for a clue. If there had been the faintest clue in Smith's Hotel or in the Mariposa House or in the Continental, those fellows would have been at it like a flash.

To see them moving round the town that day – silent, massive, imperturbable – gave one a great idea of their strange, dangerous calling. They went about the town all day and yet in such a quiet peculiar way that you couldn't have realized that they were working at all. They ate their dinner together at Smith's café and took an hour and half over it to throw people off the scent. Then when they got them off it, they sat and talked with Josh Smith in the back bar to keep them off. Mr Smith seemed to take to them right away. They were men of his own size, or near it, and anyway hotel men and detectives have a general affinity and share in the same impenetrable silence and in their confidential knowledge of the weaknesses of the public.

Mr Smith, too, was of great use to the detectives. 'Boys,' he said, 'I wouldn't ask too close as to what folks was out late at night: in this town it don't do.'

When those two great brains finally left for the city on the five-thirty, it was hard to realize that behind each grand, impossible face a perfect vortex of clues was seething.

But if the detectives were heroes, what was Pupkin? Imagine him with his bandage on his head standing in front of the bank and talking of the midnight robbery with that peculiar false modesty that only heroes are entitled to use.

I don't know whether you have ever been a hero, but for sheer exhilaration there is nothing like it. And for Mr Pupkin, who had gone through life thinking himself no good, to be suddenly exalted into the class of Napoleon Bonaparte and John Maynard and the Charge of the

Light Brigade – oh, it was wonderful. Because Pupkin was a brave man now and he knew it and acquired with it all the brave man's modesty. In fact, I believe he was heard to say that he had only done his duty, and that what he did was what any other man would have done: though when somebody else said: 'That's so, when you come to think of it,' Pupkin turned on him that quiet look of the wounded hero, bitterer than words.

And if Pupkin had known that all of the afternoon papers in the city reported him dead, he would have felt more luxurious still.

That afternoon the Mariposa court sat in enquiry – technically it was summoned in inquest on the dead robber – though they hadn't found the body – and it was wonderful to see them lining up the witnesses and holding cross-examinations. There is something in the cross-examination of great criminal lawyers like Nivens, of Mariposa, and in the counter-examinations of the presiding judges like Pepperleigh that thrills you to the core with the astuteness of it.

They had Henry Mullins, the manager, on the stand for an hour and a half, and the excitement was so breathless that you could have heard a pin drop. Nivens took him on first.

'What is your name?' he said.

'Henry Augustus Mullins.'

'What position do you hold?'

'I am manager of the Exchange Bank.'

'When were you born?'

'December 30, 1869.'

After that, Nivens stood looking quietly at Mullins. You could feel that he was thinking pretty deeply before he shot the next question at him.

'Where did you go to school?'

Mullins answered straight off: 'The high school down home,' and Nivens thought again for a while and then asked:

'How many boys were at the school?'

'About sixty.'

'How many masters?'

'About three.'

After that Nivens paused a long while and seemed to be digesting the evidence, but at last an idea seemed to strike him and he said:

'I understand you were not on the bank premises last night. Where were you?'

'Down the lake, duck shooting.'

You should have seen the excitement in the court when Mullins said this. The judge leaned forward in his chair and broke in at once.

'Did you get any, Harry?' he asked.

'Yes,' Mullins said, 'about six.'

'Where did you get them? What? In the wild rice marsh past the river? You don't say so! Did you get them on the sit or how?'

All of these questions were fired off at the witness from the court in a single breath. In fact, it was the knowledge that the first ducks of the season had been seen in the Ossawippi marsh that led to the termination of the proceedings before the afternoon was a quarter over. Mullins and George Duff and half the witnesses were off with shotguns as soon as the court was cleared.

* * *

I may as well state at once that the full story of the robbery of the bank at Mariposa never came to the light. A number of arrests – mostly vagrants and suspicious characters – were made, but the guilt of the robbery was never brought home to them. One man was arrested twenty miles away, at the other end of Missinaba County, who not only corresponded exactly with the description of the robber, but, in addition to this, had a wooden leg. Vagrants with one leg are always regarded with suspicion in places like Mariposa, and whenever a robbery or a murder happens they are arrested in batches.

It was never even known just how much money was stolen from the bank. Some people said ten thousand dollars, others more. The bank, no doubt for business motives, claimed that the contents of the safe were intact and that the robber had been foiled in his design.

But none of this matters to the exaltation of Mr Pupkin. Good fortune, like bad, never comes in small instalments. On that wonderful day, every good thing happened to Peter Pupkin at once. The morning saw him a hero. At the sitting of the court, the judge publicly told him that his conduct was fit to rank among the annals of the pioneers of Tecumseh Townships, and asked him to his house for supper. At five o'clock he received the telegram of promotion from the head office that raised his salary to a thousand dollars, and made him not only a hero but a marriageable man. At six o'clock he started up to the judge's house with his resolution nerved to the most momentous step of his life.

His mind was made up.

He would do a thing seldom if ever done in Mariposa. He would propose to Zena Pepperleigh. In Mariposa this kind of step, I say, is seldom taken. The course of love runs on and on through all its stages of tennis playing and dancing and sleigh riding, till by sheer notoriety of circumstance an understanding is reached. To propose straight out would be thought priggish and affected and is supposed to belong only to people in books.

But Pupkin felt that what ordinary people dare not do, heroes are allowed to attempt. He would propose to Zena, and more than that, he would tell her in a straight, manly way that he was rich and take the consequences.

And he did it.

That night on the piazza, where the hammock hangs in the shadow of the Virginia creeper, he did it. By sheer good luck the judge had gone indoors to the library, and by a piece of rare good fortune Mrs Pepperleigh had gone indoors to the sewing room, and by a happy trick of coincidence the servant was out and the dog was tied up – in fact, no such chain of circumstances was ever offered in favour of mortal man before.

What Zena said – beyond saying yes – I do not know. I am sure that when Pupkin told her of the money, she bore up as bravely as so fine a girl as Zena would, and when he spoke of diamonds she said she would wear them for his sake.

They were saying these things and other things – ever so many other things – when there was such a roar and a clatter up Oneida Street as you never heard, and there came bounding up to the house one of the most marvellous limousine touring cars that ever drew up at the home of a judge on a modest salary of three thousand dollars. When it stopped there sprang from it an excited man in a long sealskin coat – worn not for the luxury of it at all but from the sheer chilliness of the autumn evening. And it was, as of course you know, Pupkin's father. He had seen the news of his son's death in the evening paper in the city. They drove the car through, so the chauffeur said, in two hours and a quarter, and behind them there was to follow a special trainload of detectives and emergency men, but Pupkin senior had cancelled all that by telegram half-way up when he heard that Peter was still living.

For a moment as his eye rested on young Pupkin you would almost have imagined, had you not known that he came from the Maritime Provinces, that there were tears in them and that he was about to hug his son to his heart. But if he didn't hug Peter to his heart, he certainly did within a few moments clasp Zena to it, in that fine fatherly way in which they clasp pretty girls in the Maritime Provinces. The strangest thing is that Pupkin senior seemed to understand the whole situation without any explanations at all.

Judge Pepperleigh, I think, would have shaken both of Pupkin senior's arms off when he saw him; and when you heard them call one another 'Ned' and 'Philip' it made you feel that they were boys again attending classes together at the old law school in the city.

If Pupkin thought that his father wouldn't make a hit in Mariposa, it only showed his ignorance. Pupkin senior sat there on the judge's verandah smoking a corn-cob pipe as if he had never heard of Havana cigars in his life. In the three days that he spent in Mariposa that autumn, he went in and out of Jeff Thorpe's barber shop and Eliot's drug store, shot black ducks in the marsh and played poker every evening at a hundred matches for a cent as if he had never lived any other life in all his days. They had to send him telegrams enough to fill a satchel to make him come away.

So Pupkin and Zena in due course of time were married, and went to live in one of the enchanted houses on the hillside in the newer part of the town, where you may find them to this day.

You may see Pupkin there at any time cutting enchanted grass on a little lawn in as gaudy a blazer as ever.

But if you step up to speak to him or walk with him into the enchanted house, pray modulate your voice a little – musical though it is – for there is said to be an enchanted baby on the premises whose sleep must not lightly be disturbed.

XI. THE CANDIDACY OF MR SMITH

'Boys,' said Mr Smith to the two hostlers, stepping out on to the sidewalk in front of the hotel – 'hoist that there British Jack over the place and hoist her up good.'

Then he stood and watched the flag fluttering in the wind.

'Billy,' he said to the desk clerk, 'get a couple more and put them up on the roof of the caff behind the hotel. Wire down to the city and get a quotation on a hundred of them. Take them signs *American Drinks* out of the bar. Put up noo ones with *British Beer at all Hours*; clear out the rye whisky and order in Scotch and Irish, and then go up to the printing office and get me them placards.'

Then another thought struck Mr Smith.

'Say, Billy,' he said, 'wire to the city for fifty pictures of King George. Get 'em good, and get 'em coloured. It don't matter what they cost.'

'All right, sir,' said Billy.

'And Billy,' called Mr Smith, as still another thought struck him (indeed, the moment Mr Smith went into politics you could see these thoughts strike him like waves), 'get fifty pictures of his father, old King Albert.'

'All right, sir.'

'And say, I tell you, while you're at it, get some of the old queen, Victorina, if you can. Get 'em in mourning, with a harp and one of them lions and a three-pointed prong.'

* * *

It was on the morning after the Conservative Convention. Josh Smith had been chosen the candidate. And now the whole town was covered with flags and placards and there were bands in the streets every evening, and noise and music and excitement that went on from morning till night.

Election times are exciting enough even in the city. But there the excitement dies down in business hours. In Mariposa there aren't any business hours and the excitement goes on *all* the time.

Mr Smith had carried the Convention before him. There had been a feeble attempt to put up Nivens. But everybody knew that he was a lawyer and a college man and wouldn't have a chance by a man with a broader outlook like Josh Smith.

So the result was that Smith was the candidate and there were placards out all over the town with SMITH AND BRITISH ALLEGIANCE in big letters, and people were wearing badges with Mr Smith's face on one side and King George's on the other, and the fruit store next to the hotel had been cleaned out and turned into committee rooms with a gang of workers smoking cigars in it all day and half the night.

There were other placards, too, with BAGSHAW AND LIBERTY, BAGSHAW AND PROSPERITY, VOTE FOR THE OLD MISSINABA STANDARD BEARER, and up town beside the Mariposa House there were the Bagshaw committee rooms with a huge white streamer across the street, and with a gang of Bagshaw workers smoking their heads off.

But Mr Smith had an estimate made which showed that nearly two cigars to one were smoked in his committee rooms as compared with the Liberals. It was the first time in five elections that the Conservative had been able to make such a showing as that.

One might mention, too, that there were Drone placards out – five or six of them – little things about the size of a pocket handkerchief, with a statement that 'Mr Edward Drone solicits the votes of the electors of Missinaba County.' But you would never notice them. And when Drone tried to put up a streamer across the Main Street with DRONE AND HONESTY the wind carried it away into the lake.

The fight was really between Smith and Bagshaw, and everybody knew it from the start.

I wish that I were able to narrate all the phases and the turns of the great contest from the opening of the campaign till the final polling day. But it would take volumes.

First of all, of course, the trade question was hotly discussed in the two newspapers of Mariposa, and the *Newspacket* and the *Times-Herald* literally bristled with statistics. Then came interviews with the candidates and the expression of their convictions in regard to tariff questions.

'Mr Smith,' said the reporter of the Mariposa *Newspacket*, 'we'd like to get your views of the effect of the proposed reduction of the differential duties.'

'By gosh, Pete,' said Mr Smith, 'you can search me. Have a cigar.'

'What do you think, Mr Smith, would be the result of lowering the *ad valorem* British preference and admitting American goods at a reciprocal rate?'

'It's a corker, ain't it?' answered Mr Smith. 'What'll you take, lager or domestic?'

And in that short dialogue Mr Smith showed that he had instantaneously grasped the whole method of dealing with the press. The interview in the paper next day said that Mr Smith, while unwilling to state positively that the principle of tariff discrimination was at variance with sound fiscal science, was firmly of opinion that any reciprocal interchange of tariff preferences with the United States must inevitably lead to a serious per capita reduction of the national industry.

* * *

'Mr Smith,' said the chairman of a delegation of the manufacturers of Mariposa, 'what do you propose to do in regard to the tariff if you're elected?'

'Boys,' answered Mr Smith, 'I'll put her up so darned high they won't never get her down again.'

* * *

'Mr Smith,' said the chairman of another delegation, 'I'm an old free trader –'

'Put it there,' said Mr Smith, 'so'm I. There ain't nothing like it.

* * *

'What do you think about imperial defence?' asked another questioner.

'Which?' said Mr Smith

'Imperial defence.'

'Of what?'

'Of everything.'

'Who says it?' said Mr Smith.

'Everybody is talking of it.'

'What do the Conservative boys at Ottaway think about it?' answered Mr Smith.

'They're all for it.'

'Well, I'm fer it too,' said Mr Smith.

* * *

These little conversations represented only the first stage, the argumentative stage, of the great contest. It was during this period, for example, that the Mariposa *Newspacket* absolutely proved that the price of hogs in Mariposa was decimal six higher than the price of oranges in

Southern California and that the average decennial import of eggs into Missinaba County had increased four decimal six eight two in the last fifteen years more than the import of lemons in New Orleans.

Figures of this kind made the people think. Most certainly.

After all this came the organizing stage and after that the big public meetings and the rallies. Perhaps you have never seen a country being 'organized'. It is a wonderful sight. First of all the Bagshaw men drove through crosswise in top buggies and then drove through it again lengthwise. Whenever they met a farmer they went in and ate a meal with him, and after the meal they took him out to the buggy and gave him a drink. After that the man's vote was absolutely solid until it was tampered with by feeding a Conservative.

In fact, the only way to show a farmer that you are in earnest is to go in and eat a meal with him. If you can't eat it, he won't vote for you. That is the recognized political test. But, of course, just as soon as the Bagshaw men had begun to get the farming vote solidified, the Smith buggies came driving through in the other direction, eating meals and distributing cigars and turning all the farmers back into Conservatives.

Here and there you might see Edward Drone, the Independent candidate, wandering round from farm to farm in the dust of the political buggies. To each of the farmers he explained that he pledged himself to give no bribes, to spend no money and to offer no jobs, and each one of them gripped him warmly by the hand and showed him the way to the next farm.

After the organization of the county there came the period of the public meetings and the rallies and the joint debates between the candidates and their supporters.

I suppose there was no place in the whole Dominion where the trade question – the reciprocity question – was threshed out quite so thoroughly and in quite such a national patriotic spirit as in Mariposa. For a month, at least, people talked of nothing else. A man would stop another in the street and tell him that he had read last night that the average price of an egg in New York was decimal ought one more than the price of an egg in Mariposa, and the other man would stop the first one later in the day and tell him that the average price of a hog in Idaho was point six of a cent per pound less (or more – he couldn't remember which for the moment) than the average price of beef in Mariposa.

People lived on figures of this sort, and the man who could remember most of them stood out as a born leader.

But of course it was at the public meetings that these things were most fully discussed. It would take volumes to do full justice to all the meetings that they held in Missinaba County. But here and there single speeches stood out as masterpieces of convincing oratory. Take, for example, the speech of John Henry Bagshaw at the Tecumseh Corners School House. The Mariposa *Times-Herald* said next day that that speech would go down in history, and so it will – ever so far down.

Anyone who has heard Bagshaw knows what an impressive speaker he is, and on this night when he spoke with the quiet dignity of a man old in years and anxious only to serve his country, he almost surpassed himself. Near the end of his speech somebody dropped a pin, and the noise it made in falling fairly rattled the windows.

'I am an old man now, gentlemen,' Bagshaw said, 'and the time must soon come when I must not only leave politics but must take my way towards that goal from which no traveller returns.'

There was a deep hush when Bagshaw said this. It was understood to imply that he thought of going to the United States.

'Yes, gentlemen, I am an old man, and I wish, when my time comes to go, to depart leaving as little animosity behind me as possible. But before I *do* go, I want it pretty clearly understood that there are more darn scoundrels in the Conservative party than ought to be tolerated in any decent community. I bear,' he continued, 'malice towards none and I wish to speak with gentleness to all, but what I will say is that how any set of rational responsible men could nominate such a skunk as the Conservative candidate passes all bounds of my comprehension. Gentlemen, in the present campaign there is no room for vindictive abuse. Let us rise to a higher level than that. They tell me that my opponent, Smith, is a common saloon keeper. Let it pass. They tell me that he has stood convicted of horse stealing, that he is a notable perjurer, that he is known as the blackest-hearted liar in Missinaba Country. Let us not speak of it. Let no whisper of it pass our lips.

'No, gentlemen,' continued Bagshaw, pausing to take a drink of water, 'let us rather consider this question on the high plane of national welfare. Let us not think of our own particular interests but let us consider the good of the country at large. And to do this, let me present to you some facts in regard to the price of barley in Tecumseh Township.'

Then, amid a deep stillness, Bagshaw read off the list of prices of sixteen kinds of grain in sixteen different places during sixteen years.

'But let me turn,' Bagshaw went on to another phase of the national subject, 'and view for a moment the price of marsh hay in Missinaba County –'

When Bagshaw sat down that night it was felt that a Liberal vote in Tecumseh Township was a foregone conclusion. But here they hadn't reckoned on the political genius of Mr Smith. When he heard next day of the meeting, he summoned some of his leading speakers to him and he said:

'Boys, they're beating us on them statissicks. Ourn ain't good enough.'

Then he turned to Nivens and he said:

'What was them figures you had here the other night?'

Nivens took out a paper and began reading.

'Stop,' said Mr Smith, 'What was that figure for bacon?'

'Fourteen million dollars,' said Nivens.

'Not enough,' said Mr Smith, 'make it twenty. They'll stand for it, them farmers.'

Nivens changed it.

'And what was that for hay?'

'Two dollars a ton.'

'Shove it up to four,' said Mr Smith. 'And I tell you,' he added, 'if any of them farmers says the figures ain't correct, tell them to go to Washington and see for themselves; say that if any man wants the proof of your figures let him go over to England and ask – tell him to go straight to London and see it all for himself in the books.'

* * *

After this, there was no more trouble over statistics. I must say though that it is a wonderfully convincing thing to hear trade figures of this kind properly handled. Perhaps the best man on this sort of thing in the campaign was Mullins, the banker. A man of his profession simply has to have figures of trade and population and money at his fingers' ends and the effect of it in public speaking is wonderful.

No doubt you have listened to speakers of this kind, but I question whether you have ever heard anything more typical of the sort of effect that I allude to than Mullins's speech at the big rally at the Fourth Concession. Mullins himself, of course, knows the figures so well that he never bothers to write them into notes and the effect is very striking.

'Now, gentlemen,' he said very earnestly, 'how many of you know just to what extent the exports of this country have increased in the last ten years? How many could tell what per cent of increase there has been in one decade of our national importation?' – then Mullins paused and looked round. Not a man knew it.

'I don't recall,' he said, 'exactly the precise amount myself, – not at this moment – but it must be simply tremendous. Or take the question of population,' Mullins went on, warming up again as a born statistician always does at the proximity of figures, 'how many of you know, how many of you can state, what has been the decennial percentage increase in our leading cities –?'

There he paused, and would you believe it, not a man could state it.

'I don't recall the exact figures,' said Mullins, 'but I have them at home and they are positively colossal.'

But just in one phase of the public speaking, the candidacy of Mr Smith received a serious setback.

It had been arranged that Mr Smith should run on a platform of total prohibition. But they soon found that it was a mistake. They had imported a special speaker from the city, a grave man with a white tie, who put his whole heart into the work and would take nothing for it except his expenses and a sum of money for each speech. But beyond the money, I say, he would take nothing.

He spoke one night at the Tecumseh Corners social hall at the same time when the Liberal meeting was going on at the Tecumseh Corners school house.

'Gentlemen,' he said, as he paused half-way in his speech – 'while we are gathered here in earnest discussion, do you know what is happening over at the meeting place of our opponents? Do you know that seventeen bottles of rye whisky were sent out from the town this afternoon to that innocent and unsuspecting school house? Seventeen bottles of whisky hidden in between the blackboard and the wall, and every single man that attends that meeting – mark my words, every single man – will drink his fill of the abominable stuff at the expense of the Liberal candidate!'

Just as soon as the speaker said this, you could see the Smith men at the meeting look at one another in injured surprise, and before the speech was half over the hall was practically emptied.

After that the total prohibition plank was changed and the committee substituted a declaration in favour of such a form of restrictive licence as should promote temperance while encouraging the manufacture of spirituous liquors, and by a severe regulation of the liquor traffic should place intoxicants only in the hands of those fitted to use them.

* * *

Finally there came the great day itself, the Election Day that brought, as everybody knows, the crowning triumph of Mr Smith's career. There is no need to speak of it at any length, because it has become a matter of history.

In any case, everybody who has ever seen Mariposa knows just what Election Day is like. The shops, of course, are, as a matter of custom, all closed, and the bar rooms are all closed by law so that you have to go in by the back way. All the people are in their best clothes and at first they walk up and down the street in a solemn way just as they do on the twelfth of July and on St Patrick's Day, before the fun begins. Everybody keeps looking in at the different polling places to see if anybody else has voted yet, because, of course, nobody cares to vote first for fear of being fooled after all and voting on the wrong side.

Most of all did the supporters of Mr Smith, acting under his instructions, hang back from the poll in the early hours. To Mr Smith's mind voting was to be conducted on the same plan as bear-shooting.

'Hold back your votes, boys,' he said, 'and don't be too eager. Wait till when she begins to warm up and then let 'em have it good and hard.'

In each of the polling places in Mariposa there is a returning officer and with him are two scrutineers, and the electors, I say, peep in and out like mice looking into a trap. But if once the scrutineers get a man well into the polling booth, they push him in behind a little curtain and make him vote. The voting, of course, is by secret ballot, so that no one except the scrutineers and the returning officer and the two or three people who may be round the poll can possibly tell how a man has voted.

That's how it comes about that the first results are often so contradictory and conflicting. Sometimes the poll is badly arranged and the scrutineers are unable to see properly just how the ballots are being marked and they count up the Liberals and Conservatives in different ways. Often, too, a voter makes his mark so hurriedly and carelessly that they have to pick it out of the ballot box and look at it to see what it is.

I suppose that may have been why it was that in Mariposa the results came out at first in such a conflicting way. Perhaps that was how it was that the first reports showed that Edward Drone, the Independent candidate, was certain to win. You should have seen how the excitement grew upon the streets when the news was circulated. In the big rallies and meetings of the Liberals and Conservatives, everybody had pretty well forgotten all about Drone, and when the news got round at about four o'clock that the Drone vote was carrying the poll, the people were simply astounded. Not that they were not pleased. On the contrary. They were delighted. Everybody came up to Drone and shook hands and congratulated him and told him that they had known all along that what the country wanted was a straight, honest, non-partisan representation. The Conservatives said openly that they were sick of party, utterly done with it, and the Liberals said that they hated it. Already three or four of them had taken Drone aside and explained that what was needed in the town was a straight, clean, non-partisan post-office, built on a piece of ground of a strictly non-partisan character, and constructed under contracts that were not tainted and smirched with party affiliation. Two or three men were willing to show to Drone just where a piece of ground of this character could be bought. They told him too that in the matter of the postmastership itself they had nothing against Trelawney, the present postmaster, in any personal sense, and would say nothing against him except merely that he was utterly and hopelessly unfit for his job and that if Drone believed, as he had said he did, in a purified civil service, he ought to begin by purifying Trelawney.

Already Edward Drone was beginning to feel something of what is meant to hold office and there was creeping into his manner the quiet self-importance which is the first sign of conscious power.

In fact, in that brief half-hour of office, Drone had a chance to see something of what it meant. Henry McGinnis came to him and asked straight out for a job as federal census-taker on the ground that he was hard up and had been crippled with rheumatism all winter. Nelson Williamson asked for the post of wharf master on the plea that he had been laid up with sciatica all winter and was absolutely fit for nothing. Erasmus Archer asked him if he could get his boy Pete into one of the departments at Ottawa, and made a strong case of it by explaining that he had tried his cussedest to get Pete a job anywhere else and it was simply impossible. Not that Pete wasn't a willing boy, but he was slow – even his father admitted it – slow as the devil, blast him, and with no head for figures and unfortunately he'd never had the schooling to bring him on. But if Drone could get him in at Ottawa, his father truly believed it would be the very place for him. Surely in the Indian Department or in the Astronomical Branch or in the New Canadian Navy there must be any amount of opening for a boy like this? And to all of these requests Drone found himself explaining that he would take the matter under his very earnest consideration and that they must remember that he had to consult his colleagues and not merely follow the dictates of his own wishes. In fact, if he had ever in his life had any envy of Cabinet Ministers, he lost it in this hour.

But Drone's hour was short. Even before the poll had closed in Mariposa, the news came sweeping in, true or false, that Bagshaw was carrying the county. The Second Concession had gone for Bagshaw in a regular landslide – six votes to only two for Smith – and all down the township line road (where the hay farms are) Bagshaw was said to be carrying all before him.

Just as soon as that news went round the town, they launched the Mariposa band of the Knights of Pythias (every man in it is a Liberal) down the Main Street with big red banners in front of it with the motto BAGSHAW FOR EVER in letters a foot high. Such rejoicing and enthusiasm began to set in as you never saw. Everybody crowded round Bagshaw on the steps of the Mariposa House and shook his hand and said they were proud to see the day and that the Liberal party was the glory of the Dominion and that as for this idea of non-partisan politics the very thought of it made them sick. Right away in the committee rooms they began to organize the demonstration for the evening with lantern slides and speeches and they arranged for a huge bouquet to be presented to Bagshaw on the platform by four little girls (all Liberals) all dressed in white.

And it was just at this juncture, with one hour of voting left, that Mr Smith emerged from his committee rooms and turned his voters on the town, much as the Duke of Wellington sent the whole line to the charge at Waterloo. From every committee room and sub-committee room they poured out in flocks with blue badges fluttering on their coats.

'Get at it, boys,' said Mr Smith, 'vote and keep on voting till they make you quit.'

Then he turned to his campaign assistant. 'Billy,' he said, 'wire down to the city that I'm elected by an overwhelming majority and tell them to wire it right back. Send word by telephone to all the polling places in the county that the hull town has gone solid Conservative and tell them to send the same news back here. Get carpenters and tell them to run up a platform in front of the hotel; tell them to take the bar door clean off its hinges and be all ready the minute the poll quits.'

It was that last hour that did it. Just as soon as the big posters went up in the windows of the Mariposa *Newspacket* with the telegraphic dispatch that Josh Smith was reported in the city to be elected, and was followed by the messages from all over the county, the voters hesitated no longer. They had waited, most of them, all through the day, not wanting to make any error in their vote, but when they saw the Smith men crowding into the polls and heard the news from the outside, they went solid in one great stampede, and by the time the poll was declared closed at five o'clock there was no shadow of doubt that the county was saved and that Josh Smith was elected for Missinaba.

* * *

I wish you could have witnessed the scene in Mariposa that evening. It would have done your heart good – such joy, such public rejoicing as you never saw. It turned out that there wasn't really a Liberal in the whole town and that there never had been. They were all Conservatives and had been for years and years. Men who had voted, with pain and sorrow in their hearts, for the Liberal party for twenty years, came out that evening and owned up straight that they were Conservatives. They said they could stand the strain no longer and simply had to confess. Whatever the sacrifice might mean, they were prepared to make it.

Even Mr Golgotha Gingham, the undertaker, came out and admitted that in working for John Henry Bagshaw he'd been going straight against his conscience. He said that right from the first he had had his misgivings. He said it had haunted him. Often at night when he would be working away quietly, one of these sudden misgivings would overcome him so that he could hardly go on with his embalming. Why, it appeared that on the very first day when reciprocity was proposed, he had come home and said to Mrs Gingham that he thought it simply meant selling out the country. And the strange thing was that ever so many others had just the same misgivings. Trelawney admitted that he had said to Mrs Trelawney that it was madness, and Jeff Thrope, the barber, had, he admitted, gone home to his dinner, the first day reciprocity was talked of, and said to Mrs Thrope that it would simply kill business in the country and introduce a cheap, shoddy, American form of haircut that would render true loyalty impossible. To think that Mrs Gingham and Mrs Trelawney and Mrs Thrope had known all this for six months and kept quiet about it! Yet I think there were a good many Mrs Ginghams in the country. It is merely another proof that no woman is fit for politics.

*   *   *

The demonstration that night in Mariposa will never be forgotten. The excitement in the streets, the torchlights, the music of the band of the Knights of Pythias (an organization which is conservative in all but name), and above all the speeches and the patriotism.

They had put up a big platform in front of the hotel, and on it were Mr Smith and his chief workers, and behind them was a perfect forest of flags. They presented a huge bouquet of flowers to Mr Smith, handed to him by four little girls in white – the same four that I spoke of above, for it turned out that they were all Conservatives.

Then there were the speeches. Judge Pepperleigh spoke and said that there was no need to dwell on the victory that they had achieved, because it was history; there was no occasion to speak of what part he himself had played, within the limits of his official position, because what he had done was henceforth a matter of history; and Nivens, the lawyer, said that he would only say just a few words, because anything that he might have done was now history; later generations, he said, might read it but it was not for him to speak of it, because it belonged now to the history of the country. And, after them, others spoke in the same strain and all refused absolutely to dwell on the subject (for more than half an hour) on the ground that anything that they might have done was better left for future generations to investigate. And no doubt this was very true, as to some things, anyway.

Mr Smith, of course, said nothing. He didn't have to – not for four years – and he knew it.

Eight
Impressions of London

Before setting down my impressions of the great English metropolis – a phrase which I have thought out as a designation for London – I think it proper to offer an initial apology. I find that I receive impressions with great difficulty and have nothing of that easy facility in picking them up which is shown by British writers on America. I remember Hugh Walpole telling me that he could hardly walk down Broadway without getting at least three dollars' worth and on Fifth Avenue five dollars' worth; and I recollect that St John Ervine came up to my house in Montreal, drank a cup of tea, borrowed some tobacco, and got away with sixty dollars' worth of impressions of Canadian life and character.

For this kind of thing I have only a despairing admiration. I can get an impression if I am given time and can think about it beforehand. But it requires thought. This fact was all the more distressing to me, inasmuch as one of the leading editors of America had made me a proposal as honourable to him as it was lucrative to me that immediately on my arrival in London – or just before it – I should send him a thousand words on the genius of the English, and five hundred words on the spirit of London, and two hundred words of personal chat with Lord Northcliffe. This contract I was unable to fulfil except the personal chat with Lord Northcliffe, which proved an easy matter as he happened to be away in Australia.

But I have since pieced together my impressions as conscientiously as I could and I present them here. If they seem to be a little bit modelled on British impressions of America, I admit at once that the influence is there. We writers all act and react on one another; and when I see a good thing in another man's book I react on it at once.

London, the name of which is already known to millions of readers of this book, is beautifully situated on the river Thames, which here sweeps in a wide curve with much the same breadth and majesty as the St Jo River at South Bend, Indiana. London, like South Bend itself, is a city of clean streets and admirable sidewalks and has an excellent water supply. One is at once struck by the number of excellent and well-appointed motor-cars that one sees on every hand, the neatness of the shops, and the cleanliness and cheerfulness of the faces of the people. In short, as an

161

English writer said of Peterborough, Ontario, there is a distinct note of optimism in the air. I forget who it was who said this, but, at any rate, I have been in Peterborough myself and have seen it.

Contrary to my expectations and contrary to all our Transatlantic precedent, I was *not* met at the depot by one of the leading citizens, himself a member of the Municipal Council, driving his own motor-car. He did *not* tuck a fur rug about my knees, present me with a really excellent cigar, and proceed to drive me about the town so as to show me the leading points of interest – the municipal reservoir, the gasworks, and the municipal abattoir. In fact, he was not there. But I attribute his absence not to any lack of hospitality, but merely to a certain reserve in the English Character. They are as yet unused to the arrival of lecturers. When they get to be more accustomed to their coming, they will learn to take them straight to the municipal abattoir, just as we do.

For lack of better guidance, therefore, I had to form my impressions of London by myself. In the mere physical sense there is much to attract the eye. The city is able to boast of many handsome public buildings and offices which compare favourably with anything on the other side of the Atlantic. On the bank of the Thames itself rises the power house of the Westminster Electric Supply Corporation, a handsome modern edifice in the later Japanese style. Close by are the commodious premises of the Imperial Tobacco Company, while at no great distance the Chelsea Gas Works add a striking feature of rotundity. Passing northward, one observes Westminster Bridge, notable as a principal station of the Underground Railway. This station and the one next above it, the Charing Cross one, are connected by a wide thoroughfare called Whitehall. One of the best American drug stores is here situated. The upper end of Whitehall opens into the majestic and spacious Trafalgar Square. Here are grouped in imposing proximity the offices of the Canadian Pacific and other railways, the International Sleeping Car Company, the Montreal *Star*, and the Anglo-Dutch Bank. Two of the best American barber shops are conveniently grouped near the Square, while the existence of a tall stone monument in the middle of the Square itself enables the American visitor to find them without difficulty. Passing eastward towards the heart of the city, one notes on the left hand the imposing pile of St Paul's, an enormous church with a round dome on the top, suggesting strongly the first Church of Christ (Scientist) on Euclid Avenue, Cleveland. But, the English Churches not being labelled, the visitor is often at a loss to distinguish them.

A little further on one finds oneself in the heart of financial London. Here all the great financial institutions of America – The First National Bank of Milwaukee, The Planters' National Bank of St Louis, The

Montana Farmers Trust Co., and many others – have either their offices or their agents. The Bank of England, which acts as the London Agent of The Montana Farmers Trust Company, and the London County Bank, which represents The People's Deposit Co., of Yonkers, N.Y., are said to be in the neighbourhood.

This particular part of London is connected with the existence of that strange and mysterious thing called the 'City'. I am still unable to decide whether the City is a person, or a place, or a thing. But as a form of being I give it credit for being the most emotional, the most volatile, the most peculiar creature in the world. You read in the morning paper that the City is 'deeply depressed'. At noon it is reported that the City is 'buoyant', and by four o'clock that the City is 'wildly excited'.

I have tried in vain to find the causes of these peculiar changes of feeling. The ostensible reasons, as given in the newspaper, are so trivial as to be hardly worthy of belief. For example, here is the kind of news that comes out from the City: 'The news that a *modus vivendi* has been signed between the Sultan of Kowfat and the Shriek-ul-Islam has caused a sudden buoyancy in the City. Steel rails which had been depressed all the morning reacted immediately, while American mules rose up sharply to par.' . . .'Monsieur Poincaré, speaking at Bordeaux, said that henceforth France must seek to retain by all possible means the ping-pong championship of the world: values in the City collapsed at once.' . . . 'Despatches from Bombay say that the Shah of Persia yesterday handed a golden slipper to the Grand Vizier Feebli Pasha as a sign that he might go and chase himself. The news was at once followed by a drop in oil, and a rapid attempt to liquidate everything that is fluid.'

But these mysteries of the City I do not pretend to explain. I have passed through the place dozens of times and never noticed anything particular in the way of depression or buoyancy, or falling oil, or rising rails. But no doubt it is there.

A little beyond the City and further down the river the visitor finds this district of London terminating in the gloomy and forbidding Tower, the principal penitentiary of the City. Here Queen Victoria was imprisoned for many years.

Excellent gasoline can be had at the American Garage immediately north of the Tower, where motor repairs of all kinds are also carried on.

These, however, are but the superficial pictures of London, gathered by the eye of the tourist. A far deeper meaning is found in the examination of the great historic monuments of the City. The principal ones of these are the Tower of London (just mentioned), the British Museum, and Westminster Abbey. No visitor to London should fail to see these. Indeed, he ought to feel that his visit to England is wasted unless he has seen them. I speak strongly on the point because I feel strongly on it. To my mind there is something about the grim fascination of the historic Tower, the cloistered quiet of the Museum, and the majesty of the ancient Abbey which will make it the regret of my life that I didn't see any one of the three. I fully meant to, but I failed; and I can only hope that the circumstances of my failure may be helpful to other visitors.

The Tower of London I most certainly intended to inspect. Each day, after the fashion of every tourist, I wrote for myself a little list of things to do, and I always put the Tower of London on it. No doubt the reader knows the kind of little list that I mean. It runs:

1. Go to bank.
2. Buy a shirt.
3. National Gallery.
4. Razor blades.
5. Tower of London
6. Soap.

The itinerary, I regret to say, was never carried out in full. I was able at times both to go to the bank and buy a shirt in a single morning; at other times I was able to buy razor blades and almost to find the National Gallery. Meantime I was urged on all sides by my London acquaintances not to fail to see the Tower. 'There's a grim fascination about the place,' they said, 'you mustn't miss it.' I am quite certain that in due course of time I should have made my way to the Tower but for the fact that I made a fatal discovery. I found out that the London people who urged me to go and see the Tower had never seen it themselves. It appears they never go near it. One night at a dinner a man next to me said, 'Have you seen the Tower? You really ought to. There's a grim fascination about it.' I looked him in the face. 'Have you seen it yourself?' I asked. 'Oh, yes,' he answered. 'I've seen it.' 'When?' I asked. The man hesitated. 'When I was just a boy,' he said, 'my father took me there.' 'How long ago is that?' I inquired. 'About forty years ago,' he answered. 'I always mean to go again, but I don't somehow seem to get the time.'

After this I got to understand that when a Londoner says, 'Have you seen the Tower of London?' the answer is, 'No, and neither have you.'

Take the parallel case of the British Museum. Here is a place that is a veritable treasure house. A repository of some of the most priceless historical relics to be found upon the earth. It contains, for instance, the famous Papyrus Manuscript of Totmes II of the first Egyptian dynasty – a thing known to scholars all over the world as the oldest extant specimen of what can be called writing; indeed, one can here see the actual evolution (I am quoting from a work of reference, or at least from my recollection of it) from the ideographic cuneiform to the phonetic syllabic script. Every time I have read about that manuscript and have happened to be in Orillia (Ontario) or Schenectady (N.Y.), or any such place, I have felt that I would be willing to take a whole trip to England to have five minutes at the British Museum, just five, to look at that papyrus. Yet as soon as I got to London this changed. The railway stations of London have been so arranged that to get to any train for the north or west, the traveller must pass the British Museum. The first time I went by it in a taxi I felt quite a thrill. 'Inside those walls,' I thought to myself, 'is the manuscript of Totmes II.' The next time I actually stopped the taxi. 'Is that the British Museum?' I asked the driver. 'I think it is something of the sort, sir,' he said. I hesitated. 'Drive me,' I said, 'to where I can buy safety razor blades.'

After that I was able to drive past the Museum with the quiet assurance of a Londoner, and to take part in dinner-table discussions as to whether the British Museum or the Louvre contains the greatest treasures. It is quite easy, anyway. All you have to do is to remember that the Winged Victory of Samothrace is in the Louvre, and the Papyrus of Totmes II (or some such document) is in the Museum.

The Abbey, I admit, is indeed majestic. I did not intend to miss going into it. But I felt, as so many tourists have, that I wanted to enter it in the proper frame of mind. I never got into the frame of mind; at least, not when near the Abbey itself. I have been in exactly that frame of mind when on State Street, Chicago, or on King Street, Toronto, or anywhere three thousand miles away from the Abbey. But by bad luck I never struck both the frame of mind and the Abbey at the same time.

But the Londoners, after all, in not seeing their own wonders, are only like the rest of the world. The people who live in Buffalo never go to see the Niagara Falls; people in Cleveland don't know which is Mr Rockefeller's house; and people live and even die in New York without going up to the top of the Woolworth Building. And, anyway, the past is remote and the present is near. I know a cab driver in the city of Quebec whose business in life it is to drive people up to see the Plains of Abraham, but, unless they bother him to do it, he doesn't show them the spot where Wolfe fell. What he does point out with real zest is the place where the Mayor and the City Council sat on the wooden platform that they put up for the municipal celebration last summer.

No description of London would be complete without a reference, however brief, to the singular salubrity and charm of the London climate. This is seen at its best during the autumn and winter months. The climate of London, and indeed of England generally, is due to the influence of the Gulf Stream. The way it works is thus. The Gulf Stream, as it nears the shores of the British Isles and feels the propinquity of Ireland, rises into the air, turns into soup, and comes down on London. At times the soup is thin and is, in fact, little more than a mist; at other times it has the consistency of a thick Potage St Germain. London people are a little sensitive on the point and flatter their atmosphere by calling it a fog; but it is not; it is soup. The notion that no sunlight ever gets through and that in the London winter people never see the sun is, of course, a ridiculous error, circulated, no doubt, by the jealousy of foreign nations. I have myself seen the sun plainly visible in London, without the aid of glasses, on a November day in broad daylight; and again one night about four o'clock in the afternoon I saw the sun distinctly appear through the clouds. The whole subject of daylight in the London winter is, however, one which belongs rather to the technique of astronomy than to a book of description. In practice daylight is but little used. Electric lights are burned all the time in all houses, buildings, railway stations, and clubs. This practice, which is now universally observed, is called Daylight Saving.

But the distinction between day and night during the London winter is still quite obvious to anyone of an observant mind. It is indicated by various signs, such as the striking of clocks, the tolling of bells, the closing of saloons, and the raising of taxi rates. It is much less easy to distinguish the technical approach of night in the other cities of England that lie outside the confines, physical and intellectual, of London and live in a continuous gloom. In such places as the great manufacturing cities, Buggingham-under-Smoke or Gloomsbury-on-Ooze, night may be said to be perpetual.

* * *

I had written the whole of the above chapter and looked on it as finished when I realized that I had made a terrible omission. I neglected to say anything about the Mind of London. This is a thing that is always put into any book of discovery and observation, and I can only apologize for not having discussed it sooner. I am quite familiar with other people's chapters on 'The Mind of America' and 'The Chinese Mind,' and so forth. Indeed, so far as I know, it has turned out that almost everybody all over the world has a mind. Nobody nowadays travels, even in Central America or Tibet, without bringing back a chapter on 'The Mind of Costa Rica,' or on 'The Psychology of the Mongolian.' Even the gentler peoples, such as the Burmese, the Siamese, the Hawaiians, and the Russians, though they have no minds, are written up as souls.

It is quite obvious, then, that there is such a thing as the mind of

London; and it is all the more culpable in me to have neglected it, inasmuch as my editorial friend in New York had expressly mentioned it to me before I sailed. 'What,' said he, leaning far over his desk after his massive fashion and reaching out into the air, 'is in the *minds* of these people? Are they,' he added, half to himself, though I heard him, 'thinking? And, if they think, *what* do they think?'

I did, therefore, during my stay in London make an accurate study of the things that London seemed to be thinking about. As a comparative basis for this study I brought with me a carefully selected list of the things that New York was thinking about at the moment. These I selected from the current newspapers in the proportion to the amount of space allotted to each topic and the size of the heading that announced it. Having thus a working idea of what I may call 'the mind of New York,' I was able to collect and set beside it a list of similar topics taken from the London press to represent 'the mind of London.' The two placed side by side make an interesting piece of psychological analysis. They read as follows:

The Mind of New York	The Mind of London
(What is it thinking)	*(What is it thinking)*
1. Do chorus girls make good wives?	1. Do chorus girls marry well?
2. Is red hair a sign of temperament?	2. What is red hair a sign of?
3. Can a woman be in love with two men?	3. Can a man be in love with two women?
4. Is fat a sign of genius?	4. Is genius a sign of fat?

Looking over these lists, I think it is better to present them without comment. I feel sure that somewhere or other in them one should detect the heart-throbs, the pulsations of two great peoples. But I don't get it. In fact, the two lists look to me terribly like 'the mind of Costa Rica.'

The same editor also advised me to mingle, at his expense, in the brilliant intellectual life of England. 'There,' he said, 'is a coterie of men, probably the most brilliant group east of the Mississippi' (I think he said the Mississippi). 'You will find them,' he said to me, 'brilliant, witty, filled with repartee.' He suggested that I should send him back, as far as words could express it, some of this brilliance. I was very glad to be able to do this, although I fear that the results were not at all what he had anticipated. Still, I held conversations with these people, and I gave him in all truthfulness the result. Sir James Barrie said, 'This is really very exceptional weather for this time of year.' Cyril Maude said, 'And so a

Martini cocktail is merely gin with vermouth.' Ian Hay said, 'You'll find
the Underground ever so handy once you understand it.'

I have a lot more of these repartees that I could insert here if it was
necessary. But somehow I feel that it is not.

Oxford as I See It

My private station being that of a university professor, I was naturally
deeply interested in the system of education in England. I was therefore
led to make a special visit to Oxford and to submit the place to a
searching scrutiny. Arriving one afternoon at four o'clock, I stayed at
the Mitre Hotel and did not leave until eleven o'clock next morning. The
whole of this time, except for one hour spent in addressing the
undergraduates, was devoted to a close and eager study of the great
university. When I add to this that I had already visited Oxford in 1907
and spent a Sunday at All Souls with Colonel L. S. Amery, it will be seen
at once that my views on Oxford are based upon observations extending
over fourteen years.

At any rate, I can at least claim that my acquaintance with the British
university is just as good a basis for reflection and judgement as that of
the numerous English critics who come to our side of the water. I have
known a famous English author arrive at Harvard University in the
morning, have lunch with President Lowell, and then write a whole
chapter on the excellence of higher education in America. I have known
another one come to Harvard, have lunch with President Lowell, and do
an entire book on the decline of serious study in America. Or take the
case of my own university. I remember Mr Rudyard Kipling coming to
McGill and saying in his address to the undergraduates at 2.30 p.m., 'You
have here a great institution.' But how could he have gathered this
information? As far as I knew, he spent the entire morning with Sir
Andrew Macphail in his house beside the campus, smoking cigarettes.
When I add that he distinctly refused to visit the Palæontologic Museum,
that he saw nothing of our new hydraulic apparatus, or of our classes in
Domestic Science, his judgement that we had here a great institution
seems a little bit superficial. I can only put beside it, to redeem it in some
measure, the hasty and ill-formed judgement expressed by Lord Milner,
'McGill is a noble university'; and the rash and indiscreet expression of

the Prince of Wales, when we gave him an LL.D. degree, 'McGill has a glorious future.'

To my mind these unthinking judgements about our great college do harm, and I determined, therefore, that anything that I said about Oxford should be the result of the actual observation and real study based upon a *bona fide* residence in the Mitre Hotel.

On the strength of this basis of experience I am prepared to make the following positive and emphatic statements. Oxford is a notable university. It has a great past. It is at present the greatest university in the world; and it is quite possible that it has a great future. Oxford trains scholars of the real type better than any other place in the world. Its methods are antiquated. It despises science. Its lectures are rotten. It has professors who never teach and students who never learn. It has no order, no arrangement, no system. Its curriculum is unintelligible. It has no president. It has no state legislature to tell it how to teach, and yet – it gets there. Whether we like it or not, Oxford gives something to its students, a life and a mode of thought which in America as yet we can emulate but not equal.

If anybody doubts this let him go and take a room at the Mitre Hotel (ten and six for a wainscoted bedroom, period of Charles I) and study the place for himself.

These singular results achieved at Oxford are all the more surprising when one considers the distressing conditions under which the students work. The lack of an adequate building fund compels them to go on working in the same old buildings which they have had for centuries. The buildings of Brasenose had not been renewed since the year 1525. In New College and Magdalen the students are still housed in the old buildings erected in the sixteenth century. At Christ Church I was shown a kitchen which had been built at the expense of Cardinal Wolsey in 1527. Incredible though it may seem, they have no other place to cook in than this and are compelled to use it today. On the day when I saw this kitchen, four cooks were busy roasting an ox whole for the students' lunch: this, at least, is what I presumed they were doing from the size of the fireplace used; but it may not have been an ox, perhaps it was a cow. On a huge table, twelve feet by six and made of slabs of wood five inches thick, two other cooks were rolling out a game pie. I estimated it as measuring three feet across. In this rude way, unchanged since the time of Henry VIII, the unhappy Oxford students are fed. I could not help contrasting it with the cosy little boarding-houses on Cottage Grove Avenue where I used to eat when I was a student at Chicago, or the charming little basement dining-rooms of the students' boarding-houses in Toronto. But then, of course, Henry VIII never lived in Toronto.

The same lack of a building fund necessitates the Oxford students living in the identical old boarding-houses they had in the sixteenth and seventeenth centuries. Technically they are called 'quadrangles', 'closes', and 'rooms'; but I am so broken in to the usage of my student days that I can't help calling them boarding-houses. In many of these the old stairway has been worn down by the feet of ten generations of students; the windows have little latticed panes; there are old names carved here and there upon the stone, and a thick growth of ivy covers the walls. The boarding-house at St John's dates from 1509, the one at Christ Church from the same period. A few hundred thousand pounds would suffice to replace these old buildings with neat steel and brick structures like the normal school at Schenectady, N.Y., or the Peel Street High School at Montreal. But nothing is done. A movement was, indeed, attempted last autumn towards removing the ivy from the walls, but the result was unsatisfactory and they are putting it back. Anyone could have told them beforehand that the mere removal of the ivy would not brighten Oxford up, unless at the same time one cleared the stones of the old inscriptions, put in steel fire-escapes, and, in fact, brought the boarding-houses up to date.

But Henry VIII being dead, nothing was done. Yet, in spite of its dilapidated buildings and its lack of fire-escapes, ventilation, sanitation, and up-to-date kitchen facilities, I persist in my assertion that I believe that Oxford, in its way, is the greatest university in the world. I am aware that this is an extreme statement and needs explanation. Oxford is much smaller in numbers, for example, than the State University of Minnesota, and is much poorer. It has, or had till yesterday, fewer students than the University of Toronto. To mention Oxford beside the 26,000 students of Columbia University sounds ridiculous. In point of money, the $39,000,000 endowment of the University of Chicago, the $35,000,000 of Columbia, and the $43,000,000 of Harvard seem to leave Oxford nowhere. Yet the peculiar thing is that it is not nowhere. By some queer process of its own it seems to get there every time. It was therefore of the very greatest interest to me, as a profound scholar, to try to investigate just how this peculiar excellence of Oxford arises.

It has hardly been due to anything in the curriculum or programme of studies. Indeed, to anyone accustomed to the best models of a university curriculum as it flourishes in the United States and Canada, the programme of studies is frankly quite laughable. There is less Applied Science in the place than would be found with us in a theological college. Hardly a single professor at Oxford would recognise a dynamo if he met it in broad daylight. The Oxford student learns nothing of chemistry, physics, heat, plumbing, electric wiring, gasfitting, or the use of a blowtorch. Any American college student can run a motor-car, take a gasoline engine to pieces, fix a washer on a kitchen tap, mend a broken electric bell, and give an expert opinion on what has gone wrong with the furnace. It is these things, indeed, which stamp him as a college man and occasion a very pardonable pride in the minds of his parents. But in all these things the Oxford student is the merest amateur.

This is bad enough. But, after all, one might say, this is only the mechanical side of education. True; but one searches in vain in the Oxford curriculum for any adequate recognition of the higher and more cultured studies. Strange though it seems to us on this side of the Atlantic, there are no courses at Oxford in Housekeeping, or in Salesmanship, or in Advertising, or on Comparative Religion, or on the influence of the press. There are no lectures whatever on Human Behaviour, on Altruism, on Egotism, or on the Play of Wild Animals. Apparently, the Oxford student does not learn these things. This cuts him off from a great deal of the larger culture of our side of the Atlantic, 'What are you studying this year?' I once asked a fourth-year student at one of our great colleges. 'I am electing Salesmanship and Religion,' he answered. Here was a young man whose training was destined inevitably to turn him into a moral business man: either that or nothing. At Oxford, Salesmanship is not taught, and Religion takes the feeble form of the New Testament. The more one looks at these things the more amazing it becomes that Oxford can produce any results at all.

The effect of the comparison is heightened by the peculiar position occupied at Oxford by the professor's lectures. In the colleges of Canada and the United States the lectures are supposed to be a really necessary and useful part of the student's training. Again and again I have heard the graduates of my own college assert that they had got as much, or nearly as much, out of the lectures at college as out of athletics or the Greek Letter Society or the Banjo and Mandolin Club. In short, with us the lectures form a real part of the college life. At Oxford it is not so. The lectures, I understand, are given and may even be taken. But they are quite worthless and are not supposed to have anything much to do with the development of the student's mind. 'The lectures here,' said a Canadian student to me, 'are punk.' I appealed to another student to know if this was so. 'I don't know whether I'd call them exactly punk,' he answered, 'but they're certainly rotten.' Other judgements were that the lectures were of no importance; that nobody took them; that they don't matter; that you can take them if you like; that they do you no harm.

It appears, further, that the professors themselves are not keen on their lectures. If the lectures are called for they give them; if not, the professor's feelings are not hurt. He merely waits and rests his brain until in some later year the students call for his lectures. There are men at Oxford who have rested their brains this way for over thirty years: the accumulated brain power thus dammed up is said to be colossal.

I understand that the key to this mystery is found in the operations of the person called the tutor. It is from him, or rather with him, that the students learn all that they know: one and all are agreed on that. Yet it is a little odd to know just how he does it. 'We go over to his rooms,' said one student, 'and he just lights a pipe and talks to us.' 'We sit round with him,' said another, 'and he simply smokes and goes over our exercises with us.' From this and other evidence I gather that what an Oxford tutor does is to get a little group of students together and smoke at them. Men who have been systematically smoked at for four years turn into ripe scholars. If anybody doubts this, let him go to Oxford and he can see the thing actually in operation. A well-smoked man speaks and writes English with a grace that can be acquired in no other way.

In what was said above, I seem to have been directing criticism against the Oxford professors as such; but I have no intention of doing so. For the Oxford professor and his whole manner of being I have nothing but a profound respect. There is, indeed, the greatest difference between the modern up-to-date American idea of a professor and the English type. But even with us in older days, the bygone time when such people as Henry Wadsworth Longfellow were professors, one found the English idea: a professor was supposed to be a venerable kind of person, with snow-white whiskers reaching to his stomach. He was expected to moon around the campus oblivious of the world around him. If you nodded to him he failed to see you. Of money he knew nothing; of business far less. He was, as his trustees were proud to say of him, 'a child'.

On the other hand, he contained within him a reservoir of learning of such depth as to be practically bottomless. None of this learning was supposed to be of any material or commercial benefit to anybody. Its use was in saving the soul and enlarging the mind.

At the head of such a group of professors was one whose beard was even whiter and longer, whose absence of mind was even still greater, and whose knowledge of money, business, and practical affairs was below zero. Him they made the president.

All this is changed in America. A university professor is now a busy, hustling person, approximating as closely to a business man as he can do it. It is on the business man that he models himself. He has a little place that he calls his 'office', with a typewriter machine and a stenographer. Here he sits and dictates letters, beginning after the best business models, 'In *re* yours of the eighth ult., would say, etc. etc.' He writes these letters to students, to his fellow-professors, to the president – indeed, to any people who will let him write to them. The number of letters that he writes each month is duly counted and set to his credit. If he writes enough he will get a reputation as an 'executive', and big things may happen to him. He may even be asked to step out of the college and take a post as an 'executive' in a soap company or an advertising firm. The man, in short, is a 'hustler', and 'advertiser' whose highest aim is to be a 'live-wire'. If he is not, he will presently be dismissed, or, to use the business term, be 'let go', by a board of trustees who are themselves hustlers and live-wires. As to the professor's soul, he no longer needs to think of it, as it has been handed over along with all the others to a Board of Censors.

The American professor deals with his students according to his lights. It is his business to chase them along over a prescribed ground at a prescribed pace like a flock of sheep. They all go humping together over the hurdles with the professor chasing them with a set of 'tests' and 'recitations', 'marks' and 'attendances', the whole apparatus obviously copied from the time-clock of the business man's factory. This process is what is called 'showing results'. The pace set is necessarily that of the slowest, and thus results in what I have heard Mr Edward Beatty describe as the 'convoy system of education'.

In my own opinion, reached after fifty-two years of profound reflection, this system contains in itself the seeds of destruction. It puts a premium on dullness and a penalty on genius. It circumscribes that attitude of mind which is the real spirit of learning. If we persist in it we shall presently find that true learning will fly away from our universities and will take rest wherever some individual and inquiring mind can mark out its path for itself.

Now, the principal reason why I am led to admire Oxford is that the place is little touched as yet by the measuring of 'results' and by this passion for visible and provable 'efficiency'. The whole system at Oxford is such as to put a premium on genius and to let mediocrity and dullness go their way. On the dull student Oxford, after a proper lapse of time, confers a degree which means nothing more than that he lived and breathed at Oxford and kept out of jail. This for many students is as much as society can expect. But for the gifted student Oxford offers great opportunities. There is no question of his hanging back till the last sheep has jumped over the fence. He need wait for no one. He may move forward as fast as he likes, following the bent of his genius. If he has in him any ability beyond that of the common herd, his tutor, interested in his studies, will smoke at him until he kindles him into a flame. For the tutor's soul is not harassed by herding dull students, with dismissal hanging by a thread over his head in the class-room. The American professor has not time to be interested in a clever student. He has time to be interested in his 'department', his letter-writing, his executive work, and his organizing ability and his hope of promotion to a soap factory. But with that his mind is exhausted. The student of genius merely means to him a student who gives no trouble, who passes all his 'tests', and is present at all his 'recitations'. Such a student also, if he can be trained to be a hustler and an advertiser, will undoubtedly 'make good'. But beyond that the professor does not think of him. The everlasting principle of equality has inserted itself in a place where it has no right to be, and where inequality is the breath of life.

American or Canadian college trustees would be horrified at the notion of professors who apparently do no work, give few or no lectures, and draw their pay merely for existing. Yet these are really the only kind of professors worth having – I mean, men who can be trusted with a vague general mission in life, with a salary guaranteed at least till their death, and a sphere of duties entrusted solely to their own conscience and the promptings of their own desires. Such men are rare, but a single one of them, when found, is worth ten 'executives' and a dozen 'organizers'.

The excellence of Oxford, then, as I see it, lies in the peculiar vagueness of the organization of its work. It starts from the assumption that the professor is a really learned man whose sole interest lies in his own sphere; and that a student, or at least the only student with whom the university cares to reckon seriously, is a young man who desires to know. This is an ancient medieval attitude long since buried in more up-to-date places under successive strata of compulsory education, state teaching, the democratization of knowledge and the substitution of the shadow for the substance, and the casket for the gem. No doubt, in newer places, the thing has got to be so. Higher education in America flourishes chiefly as a qualification for entrance into a money-making profession, and not as a thing in itself. But in Oxford one can still see the surviving outline of a nobler type of structure and a higher inspiration.

I do not mean to say, however, that my judgement of Oxford is one undiluted stream of praise. In one respect at least I think that Oxford has fallen away from the high ideals of the Middle Ages. I refer to the fact that it admits women students to its studies. In the Middle Ages women were regarded with a peculiar chivalry long since lost. It was taken for granted that their brains were too delicately poised to allow them to learn anything. It was presumed that their minds were so exquisitely hung that intellectual effort might disturb them. The present age has gone to the other extreme; and this is seen nowhere more than in the crowding of women into colleges originally designed for men. Oxford, I regret to find, has not stood out against this change.

To a profound scholar like myself the presence of these young women, many of them most attractive, flittering up and down the streets of Oxford in their caps and gowns is very distressing.

Who is to blame for this and how they first got in I do not know. But I understand that they first of all built a private college of their own close to Oxford, and then edged themselves in foot by foot. If this is so, they only followed up the precedent of the recognized method in use in America. When an American college is established, the women go and build a college of their own overlooking the grounds. Then they put on becoming caps and gowns and stand and look over the fence at the college athletics. The male undergraduates, who were originally and by nature a hardy lot, were not easily disturbed. But inevitably some of the senior trustees fell in love with the first-year girls and became convinced that co-education was a noble cause. American statistics show that between 1880 and 1900 the number of trustees and senior professors who married girl undergraduates, or who wanted to do so, reached a percentage of – I forget the exact percentage; it was either a hundred or a little over.

I don't know just what happened at Oxford, but presumably something of the sort took place. In any case, the women are now all over the place. They attend the college lectures, they row in a boat, and they perambulate the High Street. They are even offering a serious competition against the men. Last year they carried off the ping-pong championship and took the chancellor's prize for needlework, while in music, cooking, and millinery the men are said to be nowhere.

There is no doubt that, unless Oxford puts the women out while there is yet time, they will overrun the whole university. What this means to the progress of learning few can tell, and those who know are afraid to say.

Cambridge University, I am glad to see, still sets its face sternly against this innovation. I am reluctant to count any superiority in the University of Cambridge. Having twice visited Oxford, having made the place a subject of profound study for many hours at a time, having twice addressed its undergraduates, and having stayed at the Mitre Hotel, I consider myself an Oxford man. But I must admit that Cambridge has chosen the wiser part.

Last autumn, while I was in London on my voyage of discovery, a vote was taken at Cambridge to see if the women who have already a private college close by should be admitted to the university. They were triumphantly shut out; and, as a fit and proper sign of enthusiasm, the undergraduates went over in a body and knocked down the gates of the women's college. I know that it is a terrible thing to say that anyone approved of this. All the London papers came out with headings that read, ARE OUR UNDERGRADUATES TURNING INTO BABOONS? and so on. The *Manchester Guardian* bordered its pages in black, and even the *Morning Post* was afraid to take bold ground in the matter. But I do know, also, that there was a great deal of secret chuckling and jubilation in the London clubs. Nothing was expressed openly. The men of England have been too terrorized by the women for that. But in safe corners of the club, out of ear-shot of the waiters and way from casual strangers, little groups of elderly men chuckled quietly together. 'Knocked down their gates, eh?' said the wicked old men to one another, and then whispered guiltily behind an uplifted hand, 'Serve 'em right.' Nobody dared to say anything outside. If they had, someone would have got up and asked a question in the House of Commons. When this is done all England falls flat upon its face.

But for my part, when I heard of the Cambridge vote I felt as Lord Chatham did when he said in parliament, 'Sir, I rejoice that America has resisted.' For I have long harboured views of my own upon the higher education of women. In these days, however, it requires no little hardihood to utter a single word of criticism against it. It is like throwing half a brick through the glass roof of a conservatory. It is bound to make trouble. Let me hasten, therefore, to say that I believe most heartily in the higher education of women; in fact, the higher the better. The only question to my mind is: What is 'high education', and how do you get it? With which goes the secondary inquiry: What is a woman, and is she just the same as a man? I know that it sounds a terrible thing to say in these days, but I don't believe she is.

Let me say, also, that when I speak of co-education I speak of what I know. I was co-educated myself some thirty-five years ago, at the very beginning of the thing. I learned my Greek alongside a bevy of beauty on the opposite benches that mashed up the irregular verbs for us very badly. Incidentally, those girls are all married long since, and all the Greek they know now you could put under a thimble. But of that presently.

I have had further experience as well. I spent three years in the graduate school of Chicago, where co-educational girls were as thick as autumn leaves – and some thicker. And as a college professor at McGill University, in Montreal, I have taught mingled classes of men and women for twenty years.

On the basis of which experience I say with assurance that the thing is a mistake and has nothing to recommend it but its relative cheapness. Let me emphasize this last point and have done with it. Co-education is, of course, a great economy. To teach ten men and ten women in a single class of twenty costs only half as much as to teach two classes. Where economy must rule, then, the thing has got to be. But where the discussion turns not on what is cheapest, but on what is best, then the case is entirely different.

The fundamental trouble is that men and women are different creatures, with different minds and different aptitudes and different paths in life. There is no need to raise here the question of which is superior and which is inferior (though I think, the Lord help me, I know the answer to that too). The point lies in the fact that they are different.

But the mad passion for equality has masked this obvious fact. When women began to demand, quite rightly, a share in higher education, they took for granted that they wanted the same curriculum as the men. They never stopped to ask whether their aptitudes were not in various directions higher and better than those of the men, and whether it might not be better for their sex to cultivate the things which were best suited to their minds. Let me be more explicit. In all that goes with physical and mathematical science, women, on the average, are far below the standard of men. There are, of course, exceptions. But they prove nothing. It is no use to quote to me the case of some brilliant girl who stood first in physics at Cornell. That's nothing. There is an elephant in the zoo that can count up to ten; yet I refuse to reckon myself his inferior.

Tabulated results spread over years, and the actual experience of those who teach, show that in the whole domain of mathematics and physics women are outclassed. At McGill the girls of our first year have wept over their failures in elementary physics these twenty-five years. It is time that someone dried their tears and took away the subject.

But, in any case, examination tests are never the whole story. To those who know, a written examination is far from being a true criterion of capacity. It demands too much of mere memory, imitativeness, and the insidious willingness to absorb other people's ideas. Parrots and crows would do admirably in examinations. Indeed, the colleges are full of them.

But take, on the other hand, all that goes with the aesthetic side of education, with imaginative literature and the cult of beauty. Here women are, or at least ought to be, the superiors of men. Women were in primitive times the first story-tellers. They are still so at the cradle side. The original college woman was the Witch, with her incantations and her prophecies and the glow of her bright imagination, and if brutal men of duller brains had not burned it out of her she would be incanting still. To my thinking, we need more witches in the colleges and less physics.

I have seen such young witches myself – if I may keep the word: I like it – in colleges such as Wellesley in Massachusetts and Bryn Mawr in Pennsylvania, where there isn't a man allowed within the three-mile limit. To my mind, they do infinitely better thus by themselves. They are freer, less restrained. They discuss things openly in their classes; they lift up their voices, and they speak; whereas a girl in such a place as McGill, with men all about her, sits for four years as silent as a frog full of shot.

But there is a deeper trouble still. The careers of the men and women who go to college together are necessarily different, and the preparation is all aimed at the man's career. The men are going to be lawyers, doctors, engineers, business men, and politicians. And the women are not.

There is no use pretending about it. It may sound an awful thing to say, but the women are going to be married. That is, and always has been, their career; and, what is more, they know it; and even at college, while they are studying algebra and political economy, they have their eye on it sideways all the time. The plain fact is that, after a girl has spent four years of her time and a great deal of her parents' money in equipping herself for a career that she is never going to have, the wretched creature goes and gets married, and in a few years has forgotten which is the hypotenuse of a right-angled triangle, and she doesn't care. She has much better things to think of.

At this point someone will shriek: 'But surely, even for marriage, isn't it right that a girl should have a college education?' To which I hasten to answer: most assuredly. I freely admit that a girl who knows algebra, or once knew it, is a far more charming companion and a nobler wife and mother than a girl who doesn't know x from y. But the point is this: Does the higher education that fits a man to be a lawyer also fit a person to be a wife and mother? Or, in other words, is a lawyer a wife and mother? I say he is not. Granted that a girl is to spend four years in time and four thousand dollars in money in going to college, why train her for a career that she is never going to adopt? Why not give her an education that will have a meaning and a harmony with the real life that she is to follow?

For example, suppose that during her four years every girl lucky enough to get a higher education spent at least six months of it in the training and discipline of a hospital as a nurse. There is more education and character-making in that than in a whole bucketful of algebra.

But no, the woman insists on snatching her share of an education designed by Erasmus or William of Wykeham or William of Occam for the creation of scholars and lawyers; and when later on in her home there is a sudden sickness or accident, and the life or death of those nearest to her hangs upon skill and knowledge and a trained fortitude in emergency, she must needs send in all haste for a hired woman to fill the place that she herself has never learned to occupy.

But I am not here trying to elaborate a whole curriculum. I am only trying to indicate that higher education for the man is one thing, for the woman another. Nor do I deny the fact that women have got to earn their living. Their higher education must enable them to do that. They cannot all marry on their graduation day. But that is no great matter. No scheme of education that anyone is likely to devise will fail in this respect.

The positions that they hold as teachers or civil servants they would fill all the better if their education were fitted to their wants.

Some few, a small minority, really and truly 'have a career' – husbandless and childless – in which the sacrifice is great and the honour to them, perhaps, all the higher. And others, no doubt, dream of a career in which a husband and a group of blossoming children are carried as an appendage to a busy life at the bar or on the platform. But all such are the mere minority, so small as to make no difference to the general argument.

But there – I have written quite enough to make plenty of trouble except, perhaps, at Cambridge University. So I return with relief to my general study of Oxford.

Viewing the situation as a whole, I am led, then, to the conclusion that there must be something in the life of Oxford itself that makes for higher learning. Smoked at by his tutor, fed in Henry VIII's kitchen, and sleeping in a tangle of ivy, the student evidently gets something not easily obtained in America. And the more I reflect on the matter the more I am convinced that it is the sleeping in the ivy that does it. How different it is from student life as I remember it!

When I was a student at the University of Toronto thirty years ago I lived, from start to finish, in seventeen different boarding-houses. As far as I am aware, these houses have not, or not yet, been marked with tablets. But they are still to be found in the vicinity of McCaul and Darcy and St Patrick Streets. Anyone who doubts the truth of what I have to say may go and look at them.

I was not alone in the nomadic life that I led. There were hundreds of us drifting about in this fashion from one melancholy habitation to another. We lived, as a rule, two or three in a house, sometimes alone. We dined in the basement. We always had beef, done up in some way after it was dead, and there were always soda biscuits on the table. They used to have a brand of soda biscuits in those days in the Toronto boarding-houses that I have not seen since. They were better than dog biscuits, but with not so much snap. My contemporaries will all remember them. A great many of the leading barristers and professional men of Toronto were fed on them.

In the life we led we had practically no opportunities for association on a large scale, no common rooms, no reading rooms, nothing. We never saw the magazines – personally I didn't even know the names of them. The only interchange of ideas we ever got was by going over to the Caer Howell Hotel of University Avenue and interchanging them there.

I mention these melancholy details not for their own sake, but merely to emphasize the point that when I speak of students' dormitories, and the larger life which they offer, I speak of what I know.

If we had had at Toronto, when I was a student, the kind of living-in system and common rooms that they have at Oxford, I don't think I would ever have graduated. I'd have been there still. The trouble is that the universities on our continent are only just waking up to the idea of what a university should mean. They were, very largely, instituted and organized with the idea that a university was a place where young men were sent to absorb the contents of books and to listen to lectures in the class-rooms. The student was pictured as a pallid creature, burning what was called the 'midnight oil', his wan face bent over his desk. If you wanted to do something for him, you gave him a book; if you wanted to do something really large on his behalf, you gave him a whole basketful of them. If you wanted to go still further and be a benefactor to the college at large, you endowed a competitive scholarship and set two or more pallid students working themselves to death to get it.

The real thing for the student is the life and environment that surrounds him. All that he really learns he learns, in a sense, by the active operation of his own intellect and not as the passive recipient of lectures. And for this active operation what he really needs most is the continued and intimate contact with his fellows. Students must live together and eat together, talk and smoke together. Experience shows that that is how their minds really grow. And they must live together in a rational and comfortable way. They must eat in a big dining-room or hall, with oak beams across the ceiling, and the stained glass in the windows, and with a shield or tablet here or there upon the wall, to remind them between times of the men who went before them and left a name worthy of the memory of the college. If a student is to get from his college what it ought to give him, rooms in college, with the life in common that they bring, are his absolute right. A university that fails to give it to him is cheating him.

If I were founding a university – and I say it with all the seriousness of which I am capable – I would found first a smoking room; then when I had a little more money in hand I would build rooms; then after that, or more probably with it, a decent reading room and a library. After that, if I still had money over that I couldn't use, I would hire a professor and get some textbooks.

This chapter has sounded in the most part like a continuous eulogy of Oxford with but little in favour of our American colleges. I turn therefore with pleasure to the more congenial task of showing what is wrong with Oxford and with the English university system generally, and the aspect in which our American universities far excel the British.

The point is that Henry VIII is dead. The English are so proud of what Henry VIII and the benefactors of earlier centuries did for their universities that they forget the present. There is little or nothing in England to compare with the magnificent generosity of individuals, provinces, and states which is building up the colleges of the United States and Canada. There used to be. But by some strange confusion of thought the English people admire the noble gifts of Cardinal Wolsey and Henry VIII and Queen Margaret, and do not realize that the Carnegies and Rockefellers and the William Macdonalds are the Cardinal Wolseys of today. The University of Chicago was founded upon oil. McGill University rests largely on a basis of tobacco. In America the world of commerce and business levies on itself a noble tribute in favour of the higher learning. In England, with a few conspicuous exceptions, such as that at Bristol, there is little of the sort. The feudal families are content with what their remote ancestors have done: they do not try to emulate it in any great degree.

In the long run this must count. Of all the various reforms that are talked of at Oxford, and of all the imitations of American methods that are suggested, the only one worth while, to my thinking, is to capture a few millionaires, give them honorary degrees at a million pounds sterling apiece, and tell them to imagine that they are Henry VIII. I give Oxford warning that if this is not done the place will not last another two centuries.

'We Have with Us Tonight'

Not only during my tour in England, but for many years past it has been my lot to speak and to lecture in all sorts of places, under all sorts of circumstances, and before all sorts of audiences. I say this, not in boastfulness, but in sorrow. Indeed, I only mention it to establish the fact that when I talk of lecturers and speakers I talk of what I know.

Few people realize how arduous and how disagreeable public lecturing is. The public sees the lecturer step out on to the platform in his little white waistcoat and his long-tailed coat and with a false air of a conjurer about him, and they think him happy. After about ten minutes of his talk they are tired of him. Most people tire of a lecture in ten minutes; clever people can do it in five. Sensible people never go to lectures at all. But the people who do go to a lecture and who get tired of it presently hold it as a sort of a grudge against the lecturer personally. In reality his sufferings are worse than theirs.

For my own part, I always try to appear as happy as possible while I am lecturing. I take this to be part of the trade of anybody labelled a humorist and paid as such. I have no sympathy whatever with the idea that a humorist ought to be a lugubrious person with a face stamped with melancholy. This is a cheap and elementary effect belonging to the level of a circus clown. The image of 'laughter shaking both his sides' is the truer picture of comedy. Therefore I say that I always try to appear cheerful at my lectures and even to laugh at my own jokes. But even this arouses a kind of resentment in some of the audience. 'Well, I will say,' said a stern-looking woman who spoke to me after one of my lectures, 'you certainly do seem to enjoy your own fun.' 'Madam,' I answered, 'if I didn't, who would?' But in reality the whole business of being a public lecturer is one long variation of boredom and fatigue. So I propose to set down here some of the many trials which the lecturer has to bear.

The first of the troubles which anyone who begins giving public lectures meets at the very outset is the fact that the audience won't come to hear him. This happens invariably and constantly, and not through any fault or shortcoming of the speaker.

I don't say that this happened very often to me in my tour in England. In nearly all cases I had crowded audiences: by dividing up the money that I received by the average number of people present to hear me I have calculated that they paid thirteen cents each. And my lectures are evidently worth thirteen cents. But at home in Canada I have very often tried the fatal experiment of lecturing for nothing, and in that case the audience simply won't come. A man will turn out at night when he knows he is going to hear a first-class thirteen-cent lecture; but when the thing is given for nothing, why go to it?

The city in which I live is overrun with little societies, clubs, and associations always wanting to be addressed. So at least it is in appearance. In reality the societies are composed of presidents, secretaries, and officials who want the conspicuousness of office, and a large list of other members who won't come to the meetings. For such an association the invited speaker who is to lecture for nothing prepares his lecture on 'Indo-Germanic Factors in the Current of History.' If he is a professor, he takes all the winter at it. You may drop in at his house at any time, and his wife will tell you that he is 'upstairs working on his lecture'. If he comes down at all, it is in carpet slippers and dressing-gown. His mental vision of his meeting is that of a huge gathering of keen people with Indo-Germanic faces, hanging upon every word.

Then comes the fated night. There are seventeen people present. The lecturer refuses to count them. He refers to them afterwards as 'about a hundred'. To this group he reads his paper on the Indo-Germanic Factor. It takes him two hours. When it is over the chairman invites discussion. There is *no* discussion. The audience is willing to let the Indo-Germanic factors go unchallenged. Then the chairman makes this speech. He says:

'I am very sorry indeed that we should have had such a very poor turn-out tonight. I am sure that the members who were not here have missed a real treat in the delightful paper that we have listened to. I want to assure the lecturer that if he comes to the Owls' Club again we can guarantee him next time a capacity audience. And will any members, please, who haven't paid their dollar this winter pay it either to me or to Mr Sibley as they pass out?'

I have heard this speech (in the years when I have had to listen to it) so many times that I know it by heart. I have made the acquaintance of the Owls' Club under so many names that I recognize it at once. I am aware that its members refuse to turn out in cold weather; that they do not turn out in wet weather; that when the weather is really fine it is impossible to get them together; that the slightest counter-attraction – a hockey match, a sacred concert – goes to their heads at once.

There was a time when I was the newly appointed occupant of a college chair and had to address the Owls' Club. It is a penalty that all new professors pay, and the Owls batten upon them like bats. It is one of the compensations of age that I am free of the Owls' Club for ever. But in the days when I still had to address them I used to take it out of the Owls in a speech delivered, in imagination only and not out loud, to the assembled meeting of the seventeen Owls, after the chairman had made his concluding remarks. It ran as follows:

'Gentlemen – if you are such, which I doubt. I realize that the paper which I have read on 'Was Hegel a deist?' has been an error. I spent all the winter on it, and now I realize that not one of you pups know who Hegel was or what a deist is. Never mind. It is over now, and I am glad. But just let me say this, only this, which won't keep you a minute. Your chairman has been good enough to say that if I come again you will get together a capacity audience to hear me. Let me tell you that if your society waits for its next meeting till I come to address you again, you will wait indeed. In fact, gentlemen – I say it very frankly – it will be in another world.'

But I pass over the audience. Suppose there is a real audience, and suppose them all duly gathered together. Then it becomes the business of that gloomy gentleman – facetiously referred to in the newspaper reports as the genial chairman – to put the lecturer to the bad. In nine cases out of ten he can do so. Some chairmen, indeed, develop a great gift for it. Here are one or two examples from my own experience:

'Gentlemen,' said the chairman of a society in a little village town in Western Ontario to which I had come as a paid (a very humbly paid) lecturer, 'we have with us tonight a gentleman' (here he made an attempt to read my name on a card, failed to read it, and put the card back in his pocket) 'a gentleman who is to lecture to us on' (here he looked at his card again), 'on Ancient – Ancient – I don't very well see what it is – Ancient – Britain? Thank you, on Ancient Britain. Now, this is the first of our series of lectures for this winter. The last series, as you all know, was not a success. In fact, we came out at the end of the year with a deficit. So this year we are starting a new line and trying the experiment of cheaper talent.'

Here the chairman gracefully waved his hand toward me, and there was a certain amount of applause. 'Before I sit down,' the chairman added, 'I'd like to say that I am sorry to see such a poor turn-out tonight and to ask any of the members who haven't paid their dollar to pay it either to me or to Mr Sibley as they pass out.'

Let anybody who knows the discomfiture of coming out before an audience on any terms judge how it feels to crawl out in front of them labelled 'cheaper talent'.

Another charming way in which the chairman endeavours to put both the speaker for the evening and the audience into an entirely good humour is by reading out letters of regret from persons unable to be present. This, of course, is only for grand occasions when the speaker has been invited to come under very special auspices. It was my fate, not long ago, to 'appear' (this is the correct word to use in this connection) in this capacity when I was going about Canada trying to raise some money for the relief of the Belgians. I travelled in great glory with a pass on the Canadian Pacific Railway (not since extended: officials of the road, kindly note this) and was most kindly entertained wherever I went.

It was, therefore, the business of the chairman at such meetings as these to try and put a special distinction or *cachet* on the gathering. This is how it was done:

'Ladies and gentlemen,' said the chairman, rising from his seat on the platform with a little bundle of papers in his hand, 'before I introduce the speaker of the evening I have one or two items that I want to read to you.' Here he rustled his papers, and there was a deep hush in the hall while he selected one. 'We had hoped to have with us tonight Sir Robert Borden, the Prime Minister of this Dominion. I have just received a telegram from Sir Robert in which he says that he will not be able to be here.' (*Great applause.*) The chairman put up his hand for silence, picked up another telegram, and continued: 'Our committee, ladies and gentlemen, telegraphed an invitation to Sir Wilfrid Laurier very cordially inviting him to be here tonight. I have here Sir Wilfrid's answer in which he says that he will not be able to be with us.' (*Renewed applause.*) The chairman again put up his hand for silence and went on, picking up one paper after another: 'The Minister of Finance regrets that he will be unable to come.' (*Applause*). 'Mr Rodolphe Lemieux' (*applause*) 'will not be here.' (*Great applause.*) 'The Mayor of Toronto' (*applause*) 'is detained on business.' (*Wild applause.*) 'The Anglican Bishop of the Diocese' (*applause*), 'the Principal of the University College, Toronto' (*great applause*), 'the Minister of Education' (*applause*) – 'none of these are coming.' There was a great clapping of hands and enthusiasm, after which the meeting was called to order with a very distinct and palpable feeling that it is one of the most distinguished audiences ever gathered in the hall.

Here is another experience of the same period while I was pursuing the same exalted purpose. I arrived in a little town in Eastern Ontario, and found to my horror that I was billed to 'appear' *in a church*. I was supposed to give readings from my works, and my books are supposed to be of a humorous character. A church hardly seemed the right place to get funny in. I explained my difficulty to the pastor of the church, a very solemn-looking man. He nodded his head, slowly and gravely, as he grasped my difficulty. 'I see,' he said, 'I see, but I think that I can introduce you to our people in such a way as to make that right.'

When the time came, he led me up on to the pulpit platform of the church, just beside and below the pulpit itself, with a reading desk and a big Bible and a shaded light beside it. It was a big church, and the audience, sitting in half darkness, as is customary during a sermon, reached away back into the gloom. The place was packed full and absolutely quiet. Then the chairman spoke.

'Dear friends,' he said, 'I want you to understand that it will be all right to laugh tonight. Let me hear you laugh heartily, laugh right out, just as much as ever you want to, because' (and here his voice assumed the deep, sepulchral tones of the preacher) 'when we think of the noble object for which the professor appears tonight we may be assured that the Lord will forgive anyone who will laugh at the professor.'

I am sorry to say, however, that none of the audience, even with the plenary absolution in advance, were inclined to take a chance on it.

I recall in this same connection the chairman of a meeting at a certain town in Vermont. He represents the type of chairman who turns up so late at the meeting that the committee have no time to explain to him properly what the meeting is about or who the speaker is. I noticed on this occasion that he introduced me very guardedly by name (from a little card) and said nothing about the Belgians, and nothing about my being (supposed to be) a humorist. This last was a great error. The audience, for want of guidance, remained very silent and decorous and well-behaved during my talk. Then, somehow, at the end, while someone was moving a vote of thanks, the chairman discovered his error. So he tried to make it good. Just as the audience were getting up to put on their wraps he rose, knocked on his desk, and said:

'Just a minute, please, ladies and gentlemen, just a minute. I have just found out – I should have known it sooner, but I was late in coming to this meeting – that the speaker who has just addressed you has done so in behalf of the Belgian Relief Fund. I understand that he is a well-known Canadian humorist (ha ha!), and I am sure that we have all been immensely amused (ha, ha!). He is giving his delightful talks (ha ha!), though I didn't know this till just this minute – for the Belgian Relief Fund, and he is giving his services for nothing. I am sure, when we realize this, we shall all feel that it has been well worth while to come. I am only sorry that we didn't have a better turn-out tonight. But I can assure the speaker that if he will come again we shall guarantee him a capacity audience. And I may say that if there are any members of this association who have not paid their dollar this season, they can give it either to myself or to Mr Sibley as they pass out.'

With the amount of accumulated experience that I had behind me I was naturally interested during my lectures in England in the chairmen who were to introduce me. I cannot help but feel that I have acquired a fine taste in chairmen. I know them just as other experts know old furniture and Pekinese dogs. The Witty Chairman, the Prosy Chairman, the Solemn Chairman – I know them all. As soon as I shake hands with the chairman in the committee room I can tell exactly how he will act.

There are certain types of chairmen who have so often been described and are so familiar that it is not worth while to linger on them. Everybody knows the chairman who says, 'Now, ladies and gentlemen, you have not come here to listen to *me*. So I will be very brief – in fact, I will confine my remarks to just one or two very short observations.' He then proceeds to make observations for twenty-five minutes. At the end of it he remarks, with charming simplicity, 'Now I know that you are all impatient to hear the lecturer –.'

And everybody knows also the chairman who comes to the meeting with a very imperfect knowledge as to who or what the lecturer is, and is driven to introduce him by saying:

'Our lecturer of the evening is widely recognized as one of the greatest authorities on – on – on his subject in the world today. He comes to us from – from a great distance, and I can assure him that it is a great pleasure to this audience to welcome a man who has done so much to – to – to advance the interests of – of – everything as he has.'

But this man, bad as he is, is not so bad as the chairman whose preparation for introducing the lecturer has obviously been made at the eleventh hour. Just such a chairman it was my fate to strike in the form of a local alderman, built like an ox, in one of those small manufacturing places in the north of England where they grow men of this type and elect them to office.

'I never saw the lecturer before,' he said, 'but I've read his book' (I have written nineteen books). 'The committee was good enough to send me over his book last night. I didn't read it all, but I took a look at the preface, and I can assure him he is very welcome. I understand he comes from a college –' Then he turned directly towards me and said in a loud voice, 'What was the name of that college over there you said you came from?'

'McGill,' I answered equally loudly.

'He comes from McGill,' the chairman boomed out. 'I never heard of McGill myself, but I can assure him he's welcome. He's going to lecture to us on – what did you say it was to be about?'

'It's a humorous lecture,' I said.

'Ay, it's to be a humorous lecture, ladies and gentlemen, and I'll venture to say it will be a rare treat. I'm only sorry I can't stay for it myself, as I have to get back to the Town Hall for a meeting. So without more ado I'll get off the platform and let the lecturer go on with his humour.'

A still more terrible type of chairman is the one whose mind is evidently preoccupied and disturbed with some local happening and who comes on to the platform with a face imprinted with distress. Before introducing the lecturer he refers in moving tones to the local sorrow, whatever it is. As a prelude to a humorous lecture this is not gay.

Such a chairman fell to my lot one night before a gloomy audience in a London suburb.

'As I look about this hall tonight,' he began in a doleful whine. 'I see many empty seats.' Here he stifled a sob. 'Nor am I surprised that a great many of our people should prefer tonight to stay quietly at home.'

I had no clue to what he meant. I merely gathered that some peculiar sorrow must have overwhelmed the town that day.

'To many it may seem hardly fitting that after the loss our town has sustained we should come out here to listen to a humorous lecture.'

'What's the trouble?' I whispered to a citizen sitting beside me on the platform.

'Our oldest resident,' he whispered back, 'he died this morning.'

'How old?'

'Ninety-four,' he whispered.

Meantime the chairman, with deep sobs in his voice, continued:

'We debated in our committee whether or not we should have the lecture. Had it been a lecture of another character our position would have been less difficult –'

By this time I began to feel like a criminal.

'The case would have been different had the lecture been one that contained information, or that was inspired by some serious purpose, or that could have been of any benefit. But this is not so. We understand that this lecture which Mr Leacock has already given, I believe, twenty or thirty times in England –'

Here he turned to me with a look of mild reproval while the silent audience, deeply moved, all looked at me as at a man who went round the country insulting the memory of the dead by giving a lecture thirty times.

'We understand, though this we shall have an opportunity of testing for ourselves presently, that Mr Leacock's lecture is not of a character which – has not, so to speak, the kind of value – in short, is not a lecture of that class.'

Here he paused and choked back a sob.

'Had our poor friend been spared to us for another six years he would have rounded out the century. But it was not to be. For two or three years past he has noted that somehow his strength was failing, that, for some reason or other, he was no longer what he had been. Last month he began to droop. Last week he began to sink. Speech left him last Tuesday. This morning he passed away, and he has gone now, we trust, in safety to where there are no lectures.'

The audience were now nearly in tears.

The chairman made a visible effort towards firmness and control.

'But yet,' he continued, 'our committee felt that, in another sense, it was our duty to go on with our arrangements. I think, ladies and gentlemen, that the war has taught us all that it is always our duty to "carry on," no matter how hard it may be, no matter with what reluctance we do it, and, whatever be the difficulties and the dangers, we must carry on to the end; for, after all, there is an end, and by resolution and patience we can reach it.

'I will, therefore, invite Mr Leacock to deliver to us his humorous lecture, the title of which I have forgotten, but I understand it to be the same lecture which he has already given thirty or forty times in England.'

But contrast with this melancholy man the pleasing and genial person who introduced me, all upside-down, to a metropolitan audience.

He was so brisk, so neat, so sure of himself that it didn't seem possible that he could make any kind of mistake. I thought it unnecessary to coach him. He seemed absolutely all right.

'It is a great pleasure,' he said, with a charming easy appearance of being entirely at home on the platform, 'to welcome here tonight, our distinguished Canadian fellow-citizen, Mr Learoyd.' He turned half-way towards me as he spoke with a sort of gesture of welcome, admirably executed. If only my name had been Learoyd instead of Leacock it would have been excellent.

'There are many of us,' he continued, 'who have awaited Mr Learoyd's coming with the most pleasant anticipations. We seemed from his books to know him already as an old friend. In fact, I think I do not exaggerate when I tell Mr Learoyd that his name in our city has long been a household word. I have very, very great pleasure, ladies and gentlemen, in introducing to you Mr Learoyd.'

As far as I know, the chairman never knew his error. At the close of my lecture he said that he was sure that the audience were 'deeply indebted to Mr Learoyd,' and then, with a few words of rapid, genial apology, buzzed off, like a humming-bird, to other avocations. But I have amply forgiven him. Anything for kindness and geniality; it makes the whole of life smooth. If that chairman ever comes to my home town he is hereby invited to lunch or dine with me, as Mr Learoyd or under any name that he selects.

Such a man is, after all, in strong contrast to the kind of chairman who has no native sense of the geniality that ought to accompany his office. There is, for example, a type of man who thinks that the fitting way to introduce a lecturer is to say a few words about the finances of the society to which he is to lecture (for money) and about the difficulty in getting members to turn out to hear lectures.

Everybody has heard such a speech a dozen times. But it is the paid lecturer sitting on the platform who best appreciates it. It runs like this:

'Now, ladies and gentlemen, before I invite the lecturer of the evening to address us there are a few words I would like to say. There are a good many of the members who are in arrears with their fees. I am aware that these are hard times and it is difficult to collect money, but at the same time the members ought to remember that the expenses of the society are very heavy. The fees that are asked by the lecturers, as I suppose you know, have advanced very greatly in the last few years. In fact, I may say that they are becoming almost prohibitive.'

This discourse is pleasant hearing for the lecturer. He can see the members who have not yet paid their annual dues eyeing him with hatred. The chairman goes on:

'Our finance committee were afraid at first that we could not afford to bring Mr Leacock to our society. But fortunately, through the personal generosity of two of our members, who subscribed ten pounds each out of their own pockets, we were able to raise the required sum.'

Applause; during which the lecturer sits looking and feeling like the embodiment of 'the required sum'.

'Now, ladies and gentlemen,' continues the chairman, 'what I feel is that when we have members in the society who are willing to make this sacrifice – because it is a sacrifice, ladies and gentlemen – we ought to support them in every way. The members ought to think it their duty to turn out to the lectures. I know that it is not an easy thing to do. On a cold night, like this evening, it is hard – I admit it is hard – to turn out from the comfort of one's own fireside and come and listen to a lecture. But I think that the members should look at it not as a matter of personal comfort, but as a matter of duty towards this society. We have managed to keep this society alive for fifteen years, and, though I don't say it in any spirit of boasting, it has not been an easy thing to do. It has required a good deal of pretty hard spadework by the committee. Well, ladies and gentlemen, I suppose you didn't come here to listen to me, and perhaps I have said enough about our difficulties and troubles. So without more ado' (this is always a favourite phrase with chairmen) 'I'll invite Mr Leacock to address the society – oh! just one word before I sit down: will all those who are leaving before the end of the lecture kindly go out through the side door and step as quietly as possible? Mr Leacock.'

Anybody who is in the lecture business knows that that introduction is far worse than being called Mr Learoyd.

When any lecturer goes across to England from this side of the water there is naturally a tendency upon the part of the chairman to play upon this fact. This is especially true in the case of a Canadian like myself. The chairman feels that the moment is fitting for one of those great imperial thoughts that bind the British Empire together. But sometimes the expression of the thought falls short of the full glory of the conception.

Witness this (word for word) introduction that was used against me by a clerical chairman in a quiet spot in the south of England.

'Not so long ago, ladies and gentlemen,' said the vicar, 'we used to send out to Canada various classes of our community to help build up that country. We sent out our labourers, we sent out scholars and professors. Indeed, we even sent out our criminals. And now,' with a wave of his hand towards me, 'they are coming back.'

There was no laughter. An English audience is nothing if not literal; and they are as polite as they are literal. They understood that I was a reformed criminal, and as such they gave me a hearty burst of applause.

But there is just one thing that I would like to chronicle here in favour of the chairman and in gratitude for his existence. Even at his worst he is far better than having no chairman at all. Over in England a great many societies and public bodies have adopted the plan of 'cutting out the chairman'. Wearying of his faults, they have forgotten the reasons for his existence and undertake to do without him.

The result is ghastly. The lecturer steps on to the platform alone and unaccompanied. There is a feeble ripple of applause; he makes his miserable bow and explains with as much enthusiasm as he can who he is. The atmosphere of the thing is so cold that an arctic expedition isn't in it with it. I found also the further difficulty that in the absence of the chairman very often the audience, or a large part of it, doesn't know who the lecturer is. On many occasions I received on appearing a wild burst of applause under the impression that I was somebody else. I have been mistaken in this way for M. Briand, then Prime Minister of France, for Charlie Chaplin, for Mrs Asquith – but stop, I may get into a libel suit. All I mean is that without a chairman 'we celebrities' get terribly mixed up together.

To one experience of my tour as a lecturer I shall always be able to look back with satisfaction. I nearly had the pleasure of killing a man with laughing. American lecturers have often dreamed of doing this. I nearly did it. The man in question was a comfortable, apoplectic-looking man with the kind of merry, rubicund face that is seen in countries where they don't have prohibition. He was seated near the back of the hall and was laughing uproariously. All of a sudden I realized that something was happening. The man had collapsed sideways on to the floor. A little group of men gathered about him; they lifted him up, and I could see them carrying him out a silent and inert mass. As in duty bound, I went right on with my lecture. But my heart beat high with satisfaction. I was sure that I had killed him. The reader may judge how high these hopes rose when, a moment or two later, a note was handed to the chairman, who then asked me to pause for a moment in my lecture and stood up and asked, 'Is there a doctor in the audience?' A doctor rose and silently went out. The lecture continued, but there was no more laughter: my aim had now become to kill another of them and they knew it. They were aware that if they started laughing they might die. In a few minutes a second note was handed to the chairman. He announced very gravely, 'A second doctor is wanted.' The lecture went on in deeper silence than ever. All the audience were waiting for a third announcement. It came. A new message was handed to the chairman. He rose and said, 'If Mr Murchison, the undertaker, is in the audience, will he kindly step outside?'

That man, I regret to say, got well. Disappointing though it is to read it, he recovered. I sent back next morning from London a telegram of inquiry (I did it, in reality, so as to have a proper proof of his death), and received the answer, 'Patient doing well; is sitting up in bed and reading Lord Haldane's *Relativity*: no danger of relapse.'

Nine

How to Introduce Two People to One Another

Nothing is more important in introducing two people to each other than to employ a fitting form of words. The more usually recognized forms are easily learned and committed to memory and may be utilized as occasion requires. I pass over such rudimentary formulas as 'Ed, shake hands with Jim Taylor,' or 'Boys, this is Pete, the new hand; Pete, get hold of the end of that cant-hook.' In fact, we are speaking only of polite society as graced by the fair sex, the only kind that we need care about.

THE THIRD AVENUE PROCEDURE

A very neat and convenient form is that in vogue in Third Avenue circles, New York, as, for instance, at a fifty-cents-a-head dance (ladies free) in the hall of the Royal Knights of Benevolence.

'Miss Summerside, meet Mr O'Hara,' after which Miss Summerside says very distinctly 'Mr O'Hara,' and Mr O'Hara says with equal clearness 'Miss Summerside.' In this circle a mark of exquisite breeding is found in the request to have the name repeated. 'I don't quite catch the name!' says Mr O'Hara critically; then he catches it and repeats it – 'Miss Summerside.'

'Catching the name' is a necessary part of this social encounter. If not caught the first time it must be put over again. The peculiar merit of this introduction is that it lets Miss Summerside understand clearly that Mr O'Hara never heard of her before. That helps to keep her in her place.

In superior circles, however, introduction becomes more elaborate, more flattering, more unctuous. It reaches its acme in what everyone recognizes at once as

THE CLERICAL METHOD

This is what would be instinctively used in Anglican circles – as, for example, by the Episcopal Bishop of Boof in introducing a Canon of the Church to one of the 'lady workers' of the congregation (meaning a lady too rich to work) who is expected to endow a crib in the Diocesan Home for Episcopal Cripples. A certain quantity of soul has to be infused into

193

this introduction. Anybody who has ever heard it can fill in the proper accentuation, which must be very rich and deep.

'Oh, Mrs Putitover, *may* I introduce my very dear old friend, Canon Cutitout? The Canon, Mrs Putitover, is one of my *dearest* friends. Mrs Putitover, my dear Canon, is quite one of our most enthusiastic workers.'

After which outburst of soul the Bishop is able to add, 'Will you excuse me, I'm afraid I simply *must* run.'

Personally, I have never known or met a Bishop in society in any other situation than just about to run. Where they run to, I do not know. But I think I understand what they run from.

THE LOUNGE ROOM OF THE CLUB

Equally high in the social scale but done quite differently is the Club Introduction. It is done by a club man who, for the life of him, can't remember the names of either of the two club men whom he is introducing, and who, each for the life of him, can't think of the name of the man they are being introduced by. It runs –

'Oh, I say, I beg your pardon – I thought, of course, you two fellows knew one another perfectly well – let me introduce – urr – wurr –'

Later on, after three whisky-and-sodas, each of the three finds out the names of the other two, surreptitiously from the hall porter. But it makes no difference. They forget them again anyway.

Now let us move up higher, in fact very high. Let us approach the real thing.

INTRODUCTION TO H.E. THE VICEROY OF INDIA, K.C.B., K.C.S.I., S.O.S.

The most exalted form of introduction is seen in the presentation of Mr Tomkins, American tourist, to H.E. the Viceroy of India. An aide-de-camp in uniform at the foot of a grand staircase shouts, 'Mr Tomkins!' An aide-de-camp at the top (one minute later) calls 'Mr Thompson'; another aide, four feet further on, calls 'Mr Torps.' Then a military secretary, standing close to His Excellency, takes Mr Tomkins by the neck and bends him down toward the floor and says very clearly and distinctly, 'Mr Torpentine.' Then he throws him out by the neck into the crowd beyond and calls for another. The thing is done. Mr Tomkins wipes the perspiration from his hair with his handkerchief and goes back at full speed to the Hoogli Hotel, Calcutta, eager for stationery to write at once to Ohio and say that he knows the Viceroy.

THE OFFICE INTRODUCTION, ONE-SIDED

This introduction comes into our office, slipping past whoever keeps the door with a packet of books under its arm. It says –

'Ledd me introduze myself. The book proposition vidge I am introduzing is one vidge ve are now pudding on the market . . .'

Then, of two things, one –

Either a crash of glass is heard as the speaker is hurled through the skylight, or he walks out twenty minutes later, bowing profusely as he goes, and leaving us gazing in remorse at a signed document entitling us to receive the *Masterpieces of American Poetry* in sixty volumes.

ON THE STAGE

Everything on the stage is done far better than in real life. This is true of introductions. There is a warmth, a soul, in the stage introduction not known in the chilly atmosphere of the everyday society. Let me quote as an example of a stage introduction the formula used, in the best melodramatic art, in the kitchen-living-room (stove right centre) of the New England farm.

'Neighbour Jephson's son, this is my little gal, as good and sweet a little gal, as mindful of her old father, as you'll find in all New England. Neighbour Jephson's son, she's been my all in all to me, this little gal, since I laid her mother in the ground five Christmases ago –' The speaker is slightly overcome and leans against a cardboard clock for strength: he recovers and goes on – 'Hope, this is Neighbour Jephson's son, new back from over the seas, as fine a lad, gal, if he's like the folk that went before him, as ever followed the sea. Hope, your hand. My boy, your hand. See to his comfort, Hope, while I go and read the Good Book a spell in the barnyard.'

THE INDIAN FORMULA

Many people, tired of the empty phrases of society, look back wistfully to the simple direct speech of savage life. Such persons will find useful the usual form of introduction (the shorter form) prevalent among our North American Indians (at least as gathered from the best literary model):

> Friends and comrades who are worthy,
> See and look with all your eyesight,
> Listen with your sense of hearing,
> Gather with your apprehension –

> Bow your heads, O trees, and hearken.
> Hush thy rustling, corn, and listen;
> Turn thine ear and give attention;
> Ripples of the running water,
> Pause a moment in your channels –
> Here I bring you, – Hiawatha.

The last line of this can be changed to suit the particular case. It can just as easily read, at the end, 'Here is Henry Edward Eastwood,' or, 'Here is Hal McGiverin, Junior,' or anything else. All names fit the sense. That, in fact, was the wonderful art of Longfellow – the sense being independent of the words.

THE PLATFORM INTRODUCTION

Here is a form of introduction cruelly familiar to those who know it. It us used by the sour-looking villain facetiously called in newspaper reports the 'genial chairman' of the meeting. While he is saying it the victim in his little chair on the platform is a target for the eyes of a thousand people who are wondering why he wears odd socks.

'The next speaker, ladies and gentlemen, is one who needs no introduction to this gathering. His name' (here the chairman consults a little card) 'is one that has become a household word. His achievements in' (here the chairman looks at his card again, studies it, turns it upside down and adds) 'in many directions are familiar to all of you.' There is a feeble attempt at applause and the chairman then lifts his hand and says in a plain business-like tone – 'Will those of the audience who are leaving kindly step as lightly as possible.' He is about to sit down, but then adds as a pleasant afterthought for the speaker to brood over – 'I may say, while I am on my feet, that next week our society is to have a *real* treat in hearing . . .' et cetera and so forth.

Ten

Oroastus – A Greek Tragedy

(AS PRESENTED IN OUR COLLEGES)

The Greek Drama, as everybody knows, possesses a majesty that we do not find elsewhere. It has a loftiness, a sublimity, to which no later theatre has obtained. Anybody who has seen the play of Alcestis put on by the Senior class of the Podunk High School will admit this at once.

The Greek Drama, unfortunately, is no longer exhibited to the ordinary theatre-going public.

It is too sublime for them. They are away beneath it. The attempt to put on one act of the Œdippus Polyphlogistus of Boanerges at the entertainment evening of the annual convention of the Rubber Men of America last January was voted down by a nine to one vote in favour of having Highland Dances of the Six Susquehanna Sisters.

Another difficulty is that a lot of the Greek Drama is lost. Some critics think that all the best of it is lost; others say, not all; others again claim that what we have, ought to make us feel that we have no right to complain over what is lost.

But though the Greek Drama is not presented in our commercial theatres, it still flourishes in our institutions of learning. One may yet see the stupendous tragedies of Sophocles and Euripides put on in the auditorium of the Jefferson High School or acted, under pressure, by the boys of St Peter's (Episcopal) Resident Academy, or presented in commencement week by the Fi Fi Omega (oil) Fraternity of the University of Atalanta.

The open season for the Greek Drama in the college is the month of February. This gives the students four months to learn the Greek lines, and is based on a piece-work rate of five words a day. After the play they have still time to get back to what is now called 'normalcy' before the end of the college session.

Let us therefore transport ourselves in fancy to the winter evening in a college town when the Greek play is to be put on by the senior class in classics. There is no unusual light or brilliance in the streets to announce this fact. On the contrary, the general appearance is as of gloom. Here and

197

there a glaring light against a boarding brazenly announces the vulgar fact that Harold Lloyd, or rather the shade of him, is revolving at the Colisseum. But of the fact that the shade of Sophocles is to be at the auditorium of the Faculty of Liberal Arts, there is no public indication. Nor is the location of Sophocles easy to find. Our first attempt to follow what seems to be the movement of the crowd leads us vainly towards the entrance of Third Street Skating Rink and then to the lighted portico of the Gayety Burlesque Theatre, Ladies Cordially Welcomed. No such lighted path leads to the august dead. Nor are the services of a taxi of any use to us. The driver has not heard of the performance, is not aware apparently of the existence of the college auditorium and can only suggest that Sophocles himself may be staying at the Jefferson. Most of the actors do.

But to anybody accustomed to colleges and their ways it is not difficult to find the auditorium. One has but to notice here and there among the elm trees of the side streets a few shivering figures moving in the same direction and wearing a costume half way between fashion and disreputability. These are college professors and they are going to the play. Let us follow them.

We do this and we easily find the auditorium, – in fact on a close inspection we can distinctly see light here and there in its windows and people going in. Entrance is effected in two ways, either by ticket, for those who have tickets, or without a ticket for those who haven't got a ticket. When we are well inside the place, we find a large placard, visible only to those who have got in, announcing the attraction:

There is quite a sprinkling of people already seated. There must be what is called 'easily three hundred'. But on such occasions nobody is mean enough to count the audience. We are shown to our seats by girl

---

A GREAT TRAGEDY

The Greek Play

OROASTUS

Put on in the original by the Senior Class

A MASTERPIECE OF SORROW

DON'T MISS IT

"ALL UP"

ushers in college gowns and bobbed hair, a touch of Old Greek life which goes to our heart.

If the senior class understood advertising as well as they know Greek, they would have put that placard near the railway station and had a band playing and one or two of the girls with bobbed hair selling tickets behind glass. Nor would it have been necessary to select the girls who know most Greek. But still, – we started by saying that the Greek drama was lofty: Let it remain so.

When we get to our seats we realize that we needn't have come for a long time yet. There is no evidence of anybody starting anything, Greek or otherwise. There is a subdued chatter among the audience and people straggling in, one, two, and even three at a time. We notice presently that all the audience in the hall except ourselves have got little books or pamphlets, – paper things that look like the uplift hymns at a Rotary Club six o'clock supper on the hymnal of a Chautauqua Society. We go back to the outer entrance and get one (fifty cents each) and find that this priceless thing is the book of the play with the Greek on one side and the English (it seems English) on the other. So now we can take our seats again and study the thing out. On the outside of the book of the play is an announcement for

KOLLEGE KLOTHES
Superb Suits, 13.50.
CLASSY OVERCOATS 9.50

– but we had always known that education was a struggle and we pass this by.

On the inside the thing begins in earnest.

It is still a little sprinkled with advertisements here and there, but we rightly gather that they are not essential to the tragedy. The book runs thus:

OROASTUS

KOLLEGE KLOTHES AND STUDENTS' BOOTS. A Greek Drama dating probably from the fifth century STUDENTS' SHIRTS before Christ. The play is generally attributed to Diplodocus, who lived probably at Megara but also perhaps KNIT TO FIT UNDERWEAR FOR COLLEGE MEN at Syracuse. His work ALL WOOL is generally esteemed on a par with that of his great contemporaries Iambilichus and Euarbilius. He is said on what seems credible ground to have died during the presentation of one of his own plays. But the place of his death

THIRD AVENUE AND JEFFERSON ST. THE HOME LUNCH
RESORT is unknown.

The entire works of Diplodocus with the single extant exception of
Oroastus are lost but they are none the less esteemed on that account. A
full account of his life was written by Polybius but is lost. (RAH! RAH!
JOIN THE MANDOLIN CLUB) A critique of his genius written by
Diogenes Laertius but attributed also to Pliny, has perished. The bust of
Diplodocus, said to be the work of Phidias Senior, was lost, either at sea
or on land. The bust now in the Louvre was executed one thousand six
hundred years after his supposed death, and may or may not show him
as he was. Internal evidence goes to show that Diplodocus was, internally,
very unhappy. TRY POSSUMS PILLS ONE A DAY From the play
before us many lines have unfortunately been lost. But the loss is in every
case indicated by asterisks in the text GET YOUR NECKTIES AT
APPLETONS.

The simple theme of sorrow, the rigour of fate, and the emptiness of
human desire dominate the play HAVE YOU JOINED THE BIBLE
CLASS? NOW IS THE TIME TO JOIN.

And at this point the solid Greek begins, pages and pages of it, and
facing it on the other side solid masses of English. And just as we begin
to try and study it out, – we ought really to have begun a month ago, –
we realize that the entertainment is beginning.

* * *

The huge white sheet that acts as a curtain slides sideways groaning on
a wire and behold the platform of the auditorium, converted into the
severe stage of the Greeks with white curtains at the sides and a bare
floor, and of stage properties no trace. No comfortable little red mica fire
burning at the side such as cheers the actors of a drawing-room play;
none of the green grass and the cardboard inn with the swinging sign that
stand for eighteenth century comedy; nothing of the sweep of rock and
the curtain of cloud that indicates that Forbes Robertson is about to be
Hamlet. Nothing, just nothing; boards, a little sawdust, room to come in
and out, and sorrow. That is all that the Greeks asked or wanted. How
infinitely superior to ourselves, who have so piled up the panoply of life
about us that our lightest acts and our deepest grief must alike be hanged
with priceless decorations. But the Greek Theatre like the four bare
walls of the Puritan House of Worship – but stop, the play has started.

A tall figure walks in, a player in a long draped sheet of white, a
bearded player, with a chaplet of leaves about his head . . . This must be
Oroastus, let me look, – yes, it's Oroastus, King of Thebes. What's he
saying? A sort of long-drawn howling '*Aie! Aie! Aie! Aie!*' My! My!
Oroastus must be in a terrible way –

Aie, aie, aie, aie.

This must be that note of sorrow that it spoke about; or else it is some of the internal melancholy of Diplodocus.

Oroastus, King of Thebes, walks out pretty well into the middle of the stage and stands their groaning, Aie, Aie, Aie . . .

So to get a clue to what is now going to happen we look at our book of the play to see that the next thing marked in the English text is: –

ENTRY OF THE CHORUS

Ah now! cheer up! that's something like, the chorus! Bring them right along in: No doubt they will be of that beautiful type of classic Greek girls. If there is one thing that we specialize on in the modern drama it is the chorus. Fetch the girls in by all means.

In they come. Help! What is this? Three old men – very aged, with cotton wool beards and long white robes like the one Oroastus wears.

No, there is no doubt about it, the Greek idea of a chorus is a matter on which we take issue at once. These three old men may think themselves terribly cute, but for us, quite frankly they are not in it. We knew before we came that the Greek tragedy was severe but this is a pitch of severity for which we were not prepared.

However, as these three saucy old men are on the stage, let's see what they're doing. Look, they all lift their arms up straight above their heads and they all begin to moan.

Aie, Aie, Aie-e.

In fact just like King Oroastus. They evidently have got the same internal trouble that he has.

Now they seem to be breaking into a kind of sustained talk in a sort of chant. It's impossible to know what they are saying because it's all in Greek, – or no, – of course we can follow it. We have the English in the book of the play; in fact you can see all the people in the audience turning the leaves of their little book and burying their heads in them up to their spectacles. At a Greek college play the audience don't look at the stage, they look at the little book.

This is what the three saucy old men are saying: –

O how unhappy is this (now standing before us) King!

O Fate! with what dark clouds art thou about to overwhelm (or perhaps to soak him).

O what grief is his: and how on the one hand shall he for his part escape it. Oh, woe! O anxiety, O grief, Oh woe!

In other words in the Greek play the business of the chorus is to come in and tell the audience what a classy spectacle it is going to be. Sorrow being the chief idea of Greek tragedy, the chorus have to inform the audience what they're going to get, and to get it good. It's a great idea in dramatic construction. It's just as if at the beginning of Hamlet the chorus stuck their heads over the battlements of Elsinore and said, in up-to-date English, 'Say, look at this young man! Isn't he going to get it in the neck. Eh what? Isn't he in for hard luck; just wait till his father's ghost gets a twist on him.'

So the chorus groan and the King keeps howling, Aie, aie, aie, and after they've done it long enough, the three chorus men walk out one behind the other like the figures on an Athenian frieze, and the King is left alone.

He speaks (and a footnote in the book says that this speech is one of the finest things in Greek tragedy):

What awful fate hangs over (or perhaps overhangs) me this unhappy king.

What sorrow now does the swift-moving hand (or perhaps the revolving finger) of doom make for me.

Where shall I turn? Whither shall I go? What is going to hit me next?

What would I not give, even if it were my palace itself to be let loose from this overwhelming anxiety (or perhaps this rather unusual situation).

Beside it my palace and my crown are nothing.

The King pauses and lifts his two hands straight up in the air and cries:

Oh, Zeus, what next?

And at this juncture the little book says:

ENTER A HERALD

and the audience look up from their books a minute to see this herald come in. In runs the herald. He is young and has no beard. He has a tunic and bare legs and on his feet are sandals with wings and on his head also are wings and he carries a wand. The wings on his feet are meant to show how fast he could go if he really had to, – like the bicycle that the telegraph messenger pushes along with him. The wand means that if he needed to he could fly.

The entrance of this Herald causes the only interruption from the audience that occurs during the play. There are cries from the gallery of 'Attaboy! Good work, Teddy!' The Herald is one of the most popular members of the Fi Fi Omega Society. Anybody looking at that Herald approves of him. He is the best stage effect of the lot. In fact there is more 'pep' about the Herald than in all the rest put together.

He confronts Oroastus and they hold a dialogue like this:

O King.

O Herald.

Aie.

Me, too.

Woe, woe! King.

I believe you.

Things are bad.

They are indeed. What misfortune brings you in this direction?

A grave one.

I guess it must be; but tell me that my ear may hear it.

Grievous are my tidings.

I am sure they are.

And hard for you to hear.

* * *

The slowness of the Herald in giving the bad news to the King is one of the striking things in the Greek drama. It is only equalled on the modern stage by the great detective revealing the mystery in the fifth act, or a lawyer explaining the terms of the secret will, or the dying criminal (shot, deservedly in a cellar) confessing the innocence of the heroine. In fact the Greek Herald was the man who started this kind of trouble. He was the first original exponent of the idea of not telling a good thing in a hurry.

He speaks again.

Things are not what they seem.

Oroastus groans, O: All the dialogue has by this time been knocked out of him. The Herald realizes that he can't get another rise out of him. So he gets down to facts.

Your palace, O King, has on the one hand been destroyed by fire and your crown which in and of itself for the most part signified your kingship, has on the other hand been stolen.

OROASTUS: Aie, Aie, Aie, my palace is destroyed and my crown is lost. Oh, woe, this is grief.

THE HERALD: It is. Good-bye. I have other tasks (or perhaps avocations).

The Herald says this and withdraws and as he goes out in come the three old chorus men again. That was the great thing about the Greek tragedy. It never stopped. It went right on. In the modern play when the Herald said 'Good-bye,' the curtain would fall on Act I. In the moving picture the scene would shift and show the palace being burnt. But the good old Greek tragedy went right on like sawing wood. This is called the unity of the drama, and so far nothing beats it.

The chorus of course have merely come in to have a good time by piling up the sorrow and gloating over Oroastus.

They line up and they chant out –

Oh! look at this – now standing before us King (or sometimes rendered this ordinary man). Sorrow has struck him.

His palace and his crown are destroyed.

But fate is not done with him yet.

All-compelling fate is getting ready another arrow (or, perhaps, is going to take another crack at him).

He has lost his palace.

But watch out.

There is more coming.

And at this the three miserable old brutes troop out again. Then the King says:

Oh, me, alas. My palace is gone and yet a further fate overhangs me. What is this hangover?

For so much indeed have I borne that to me now it seems that nothing further could overwhelm me even if it were the loss of my tender consort herself.–

And just as he says this the sign goes up again in the book.

THE HERALD ENTERS

The King speaks:

What now? And why have your feet brought you back?

It was evident that a favourite idea of the Greek tragedians that a man went where his feet took him. This was part of the general *necessity* or rigour of fate.

The Herald says: –

Terrible are the tidings.

What are they?

Something awful.

Tell me what they are.

How can I?

Go at it (or perhaps go to it).

Dark indeed is the news and terrible is the certainty.

What is it?

How can I say it. It is dark.

What is the dark stuff that you are giving to me. Does it perhaps concern my consort the fair-fingered Apologee?

It does.

How much?

Very much.

Tell me then the whole extent of the matter, concealing nothing.

I will.

Do.

With my lips I will say it.

Do so.

The King groans. The Herald knows that the time has come to let loose his information. He says, Listen then, oh King. Your queenly consort, the fair-fingered Apologee has gone to Hades.

THE KING: Too bad.

THE HERALD: Gloomy Pluto has carried her off.

THE KING: This is deplorable (or perhaps reprehensible).

THE HERALD: Good-bye. I have other avocations.

The Herald retires and the King has hardly had time to say Aie, before the chorus come trailing on again and take up their station. They chant out.

Look at this.

How's this for grief.

The royal consort has been carried off by the Gloomy Dis, he of the long ears, to his dark home. But sorrow is not yet done. There is a whole lot more coming. For such is the fate of Kings. Either they have a good time or they don't.

With this sentiment the chorus all troop off again. We gather from the little book, even if we didn't know it already that their last sentiment 'either they have a good time or they don't,' is considered one of the gems of the Greek drama. The commentator says that this shows us the profundity of the mind of Diplodocus: Some think that this places him above the lighter work of such men as Iambilichus or Euarbilius. Others again claim that this passage 'either they have a good time or they don't,' shows (internally of course) that the life of Diplodocus was not all sorrow. To write this Diplodocus must himself have had a good time some of the time. In fact these lines, we are given to understand, have occasioned one of those controversies which have made the Greek drama what it is.

King Oroastus being now left alone starts a new fit of sorrow, 'Aie, aie, aie,' – in fact just as we expected he would. By this time we have grasped the idea of the tragedy, the successive blows of sorrow that hit Oroastus one after the other. First the chorus say there'll be sorrow, then Oroastus says here comes a sorrow, and then the Herald comes in and says get ready now, stand by for a new sorrow, and lands it at him. There's a beautiful simplicity about it that you never see on the stage today. In fact this is that sublimity, that loftiness that only the Fi Fi Omega players can catch.

So the King groans:

Oh what an absolutely complete sorrow this is, this last one.

O Apologee!

O Hades!

For me, what now is left. My palace is destroyed and the fair-fingered Apologee has gone to Hades. What now is left to me but my old dog.

Old dog that I am myself on the one hand, my old dog on the other hand is all.

This passage 'old dog that I am myself' is indicated in the text as one of the high spots. In fact it is a joke. The text says so. From where we sit we can see the professor of Greek laughing at it. Indeed we could easily prove by looking up the large editions of the play that this is a joke. The commentator says.

The bitter jest of Oroastus in calling himself an old dog illustrates for us the delicious irony of the great tragedian. Certain commentators have claimed indeed that the passage is corrupt and that Oroastus called himself not an old dog but a hot dog. We prefer, however, the earlier reading which seems to us exquisite. Diplodocus undoubtedly felt that the weight of sorrow at this point had become more than Oroastus or even the spectators could bear. By making Oroastus call himself an old dog he removes exactly that much of it.

This contention seems pretty well sustained. In fact anybody accustomed to the modern stage will realize that we are here at the source of the alleviating joke, introduced at any moment of terrible tension. In the modern play a comic character is carried all through the piece in order to make these jokes. But the Greek tragedy was nothing if not simple, direct, and honest. The hero has to make his own jokes.

Still, we are keeping the Herald waiting. The time is ripe for him to come in again.

ENTER THE HERALD

In he comes just as before (the Greeks didn't believe in variety) and the King at once asks him the usual question about his feet.

For what purpose, Oh Herald, he enquires do your feet bring you this way again?

THE HERALD: A gloomy one.

Let me have it.

I will.

Do. For however dark it is I being now an old dog (or perhaps a hot dog) have no further consolation in life than my dog.

It is to be noticed that Diplodocus here uses the same joke twice. Anybody who deals in humour will warmly approve of this. To get the best out of a joke it must be used over and over again. In this matter the Greeks have nothing on us.

This time the Herald knows that Oroastus can't stand for much more. So he says. Old dog indeed? Did your lips lead you to say old dog?

They did indeed.

Are you perhaps under the impression, Oh King, that you still have an old dog?

Such is my impression.

In that case you never made a bigger mistake in your life.

Let me know it and if indeed I have made a mistake, let me hear it.

Hear it then. Your old dog is gone to Hades. Good-bye. I have other avocations. The Herald leaves and the King breaks out into lamentations.

Aie, aie, he says, my consort the fair-fingered Apologee and my old dog are in Hades. Why I am still left in the upper air (or perhaps in the air). Oh Whoa!

The King lifts his hands up in sorrow and a note in the book says: 'King Oroastus has now had nearly enough.' To this we quite agree. One might say, in fact, he had had plenty.

But the chorus are not done with him yet. On they come with the remorselessness of the Greek Drama.

They line up.

Look then at this standing before us King. What a load he has. But worse is yet coming. Keep your seats and watch him.

They go out in their usual undisturbed way, and Oroastus says; –

Oh, what a last final instalment (or hangover) of bitter grief is now mine. What now is left? Now that everything has gone to Hades of what use is life itself. O, day! Oh, sunshine! O, light! Let me withdraw myself, I before my time, to my tomb, to my mausoleum which I have had made by the skilled hands of artificers and there let me join hands with Death.

Oroastus has hardly said this when the Herald comes back. By this time everybody guesses the news that he brings. Under the circumstances not even a Greek Herald could string it out. The thing is too obvious.

The King says, – well there is no need to write it again, – the Herald's feet, that same stuff, but what he really means is, Are you back again? and the Herald says, 'Yes.' This is the first plain answer that the Herald has given all through the play.

Then Oroastus says: –

Is it dark stuff again?

And the Herald says:

The darkest?

At which the King gives a groan and says:

Then let me not hear it. For already to me thinking over pretty well everything the matter seems more or less what you would call played out (or possible worked to death). It is now in my mind hearing nothing further to repair to the mausoleum which I have long since caused to be built by skilled artificers and there lying down upon the stone to clasp the hand of Death.

THE HERALD: You can't.

THE KING: Why not? What is which? For your words convey nothing. Tell me what it is.

THE HERALD: I will.

THE KING: Do.

THE HERALD: All right. Get ready for something pretty tough. Are you all set?

THE KING: I am.

THE HERALD: Know then that your mausoleum no longer is. It was broken into by burglars and is unfit to use. Good-bye. I have other avocations.

OROASTUS: Aie, aie, aie . . .

Then they line up for a last crack at Oroastus.

Look at him!

Isn't he the unlucky bean (or perhaps turnip).

Did you ever hear of worse luck than his?

Can you beat it?

But such is life, Oroastus, and it is a necessity of the Gods that even Death is withheld from the sorrowful. Aie, aie, aie.

And with that the play gives every symptom of being over. The white sheet that acts as the curtain glides down and there is quite a burst of applause from the audience. The actors line up on the stage and all the Fi Fi Omega crowd in the gallery call out, 'Attaboy Oroastus! Good work Teddy!'

After which the audience doesn't break up as an ordinary theatre audience does, but coagulates itself into little knots and groups. It knows that presently coffee and sandwiches are going to be passed around and the Greek professor will stand in the middle of an admiring group while he explains to them that Oroastus is under the compulsion of ANANGKE.

But for us no cake nor coffee. Let us get back to the Jefferson Hotel Grill Room while the supper is still on and while we can still get places for the midnight vaudeville show with the Dances of the Susquehanna Sextette and the black-faced comedian with the saxophone. This Greek stuff is sublime, we admit it, and it is lofty, we know it; and it has a dignity that the Susquehanna Sextette has not.

But after seeing Greek tragedy once, we know our level. And henceforth we mean to stick to it.

Eleven
Further Progress in Specialization

In the old days of, say, twenty years ago, when a man got sick he went to a doctor. The doctor looked at him, examined him, told him what was wrong with him, and gave him some medicine and told him to go to bed. The patient went to bed, took the medicine, and either got better or didn't.

All of this was very primitive, and it is very gratifying to feel that we have got quite beyond it.

Now, of course, a consulting doctor first makes a diagnosis. The patient is then handed on to a 'heart-man' for a heart test, and to a 'nerve-man' for a nerve test. Then, if he has to be operated on, he is put to sleep by an anaesthetist, and operated on by an operating surgeon, and waked up by a resurrectionist.

All that is excellent – couldn't be better.

* * *

But just suppose that the other professions began to imitate it! And just suppose that the half professions that live in the reflection of the bigger ones start in on the same line!

We shall then witness little episodes in the routine of our lives such as that which follows:

'Dr Follicle will see you now,' said the young lady attendant.

The patient entered the inner sanctum of Dr Follicle, generally recognized as one of the greatest capillary experts in the profession. He carried after his name the degrees of Cap. D. from Harvard, Doc. Chev. from Paris, and was an Honorary Shampoo of half a dozen societies.

The expert ran his eye quickly over the face of the incoming patient. His trained gaze at once recognized a certain roughness in the skin, as if of a partial growth of hair just coming through the surface, which told the whole tale. He asked, however, a few questions as to personal history, parentage, profession, habits, whether sedentary or active, and so on, and then with a magnifying glass made a searching examination of the patient's face.

He shook his head.

'I think,' he said, 'there is no doubt about your trouble. You need a shave.'

The patient's face fell a little at the abrupt, firm announcement. He knew well that it was the expert's duty to state it to him flatly and fairly. He himself in his inner heart had known it before he had come in. But he had hoped against hope: perhaps he didn't need it after all, perhaps he could wait; later on, perhaps, he would accept it. Thus he had argued to himself, refusing, as we all refuse, to face the cruel and inevitable fact.

'Could it be postponed for a day or so more?' he asked. 'I have a good many things to do at the office.'

'My dear sir,' said the expert firmly, 'I have told you emphatically that you need a shave. You may postpone it if you wish, but if you do I refuse to be responsible.'

The patient sighed.

'All right,' he said, 'if I must, I must. After all, the sooner it's done, the sooner it's over. Go right ahead and shave me.'

The great expert smiled. 'My dear sir,' he said, 'I don't shave you myself. I am only a consulting hairologist. I make my diagnosis, and I pass you on to expert hands.'

He pushed a bell.

'Miss Smith,' he said to the entering secretary, 'please fill out a card for this gentleman for the Shaving Room. If Dr Scrape is operating get him to make the removal of the facial hair. Dr Clicker will then run the clippers over his neck. Perhaps he had better go right to the Soaping Room from here; have him sent down fully soaped to Dr Scrape.'

The young lady stepped close to the expert and said something in a lower tone, which the patient was not intended to hear.

'That's unfortunate,' murmured the specialist. 'It seems that we have no soapist available for at least an hour or so. Both our experts are busy – an emergency case that came in this morning, involving the complete removal of a full beard. Still, perhaps Dr Scrape can arrange something for you. And now,' he continued, looking over some notes in front of him, 'for the work around the ears. Have you any preference for anyone in particular? I mean any professional man of your own acquaintance whom you would like to call in?'

'Why, no,' said the patient, 'can't Dr What's-his-name do that too?'

'He could,' said the consultant, 'but only at a certain risk, which I hesitate to advise. Snipping the hair about and around the ears is recognized as a very delicate line of work, which is better confided to a specialist. In the old days in this line of work there were often some very distressing blunders and accidents due purely to lack of technique – severance of part of the ear, for example.'

'All right,' said the patient, 'I'll have a specialist.'

'Very good,' said the hairologist, 'now as to a shampoo – I think we had better wait till after the main work is over and then we will take special advice according to your condition. I am inclined to think that your constitution would stand an immediate shampoo. But I shouldn't care to advise it without a heart test. Very often a premature shampoo in cold weather will set up a nasal trouble of a very distressing character. We had better wait and see how we come along.'

'All right,' said the patient.

'And now,' added the expert more genially, 'at the end of all of it, shall we say – a shine?'

'Oh, yes, certainly.'

'A shine, very good, and a brush-up? To include the hat? Yes, excellent. Miss Smith, will you conduct this gentleman to the Soaping Room?'

The patient hummed and hawed a little. 'What about the fee?' he asked.

The consultant waved the question aside with dignity. 'Pray do not trouble about that,' he said, 'all that will be attended to in its place.'

And when the patient had passed through all the successive stages of the high-class expert work indicated, from the first soap to the last touch of powder, he came at the end, with a sigh of relief, to the special shoe-shining seat and the familiar coloured boy on his knees waiting to begin. Here, at last, he thought, is something that hasn't changed.

'Which foot?' asked the boy.

'How's that?' said the man. 'Oh, it doesn't matter – here, take the right.'

'You'll have to go to the other chair,' said the boy, rising up from his knees. 'I'm left-handed. I only do the left foot.'

Eddie the Bartender

A GHOST OF THE BYGONE PAST

There he stands – or rather, there he used to stand – in his wicker sleeves, behind the tall mahogany, his hand on the lever of the beer pump – Eddie the bartender.

Neat, grave, and courteous in the morning, was Eddie. 'What's yours, sir?'

Slightly subdued in the drowsier hours of the afternoon, but courteous still. 'What are you having, gentlemen?'

Cheerful, hospitable, and almost convivial in the evening. 'What is it this time, boys?'

All things to all men was Eddie, quiet with the quiet, affable with the affable, cheerful with the exhilarated and the gay; in himself nothing, a perfect reflection of his customer's own mind.

'Have one yourself, Ed,' said the customer.

'Thanks, I'll take a cigar.'

Eddie's waistcoat pockets, as day drew slowly on to evening, bristled with cigars like a fortress with cannon.

'Here, don't take a smoke, have a drink!' said the customer.

'Thanks, I'll take a lemon sour. Here's luck.'

Lemon sours, sarsparillas, and sickly beverages taken in little glassfuls, till the glassfuls ran into gallons – these were the price that Eddie paid for his abstemiousness.

'Don't you ever take anything, Ed?' asked the uninitiated.

'I never use it,' he answered.

But Eddie's principal office was that of a receptive listener, and, as such, always in agreement.

'Cold, ain't it?' said the customer.

'It sure is!' answered Eddie with a shiver.

'By Gosh, it's warm!' said another, ten minutes later.

'Certainly a hot day,' Ed murmured, quite faint with the heat.

Out of such gentle agreement is fabricated the structure of companionship.

'I'll bet you that John L. will lick Jim Corbett in one round!'

'I wouldn't be surprised,' says Eddie.

'I'll bet you that this young Jim Corbett will trim John L. in five minutes!'

'Yes, I guess he might easily enough,' says Eddie.

Out of this followed directly and naturally Eddie's function as arbitrator, umpire, and world's court.

'I'll leave it to Ed,' calls the customer. 'See here, Ed, didn't Maud S. hold the record at 2.35 before ever Jay Eye See ran at all? Ain't that so? I bet him a dollar and I says, "I'll leave it to Ed," says I.'

That was the kind of question that Eddie had to arbitrate – technical, recondite, controversial. The chief editor of the *Encyclopaedia Britannica* couldn't have touched it. And he had to do it with peace and goodwill on both sides, and make it end somehow with the interrogation, 'What are you having, gentlemen?'

But Eddie was not only by profession a conversationalist, a companion, and a convivialist, he was also in his degree a medical man, prescribing for his patients.

This was chiefly in the busy early morning, when the bar first opened up for the day.

Eddie's 'patients' lined up before him, asking for eye-openers, brain-clearers, head-removers.

Behind Eddie, on little shelves, was a regular pharmacopoeia; a phalanx of bottles – ticketed, labelled – some with marbles in the top stopper, some with little squirting tubes in the mouth. Out of these came bitters, sweets, flavours, peppers – things that would open the eyes, lift the hair, and renovate the whole man.

Eddie, shaking and mixing furiously, proceeded to open their eyes, clear up their brains, and remove their heads.

'I've got a head this morning, Ed. Fix me up something to take it away.'

'Sure,' said Eddie in return, 'I'll fix it for you.'

* * *

By 8 a.m. Eddie had them all straightened up and fixed. Some were even able to take a drink and start over.

This was in the early morning. But at other times, as, for example, quite late at night, Ed appeared in another role – that of the champion strong man. Who would suspect the muscles of steel concealed behind Eddie's wicker cuffs and his soft white shirt-sleeves? Who could expect anger from a countenance so undisturbed, a nature so unruffled, a mind so little given to argument?

But wait! Listen to that fierce quarrel punctuated with unpunctuatable language between two 'bums' out on the bar room floor. Lo! at the height of it Eddie clears the mahogany counter in a single leap, seizes the two 'bums' each by the collar, and with a short rush and a flying throw hurls them both out of the swinging doors bang on the sidewalk!

Anger? No, not that; inspired indignation is the proper phrase. Ed represented the insulted majesty of a peaceful public anxious only to be left alone.

'Don't make no trouble in here,' was Eddie's phrase. There must be 'no trouble' within the sacred precincts. Trouble was for the outside, for the sidewalk, for the open street, where 'trouble' could lie breathing heavily in the gutter till a 'cop' took it where it belonged.

Thus did Eddie, and his like, hurl 'trouble' out into the street, and with it, had they only known it, hurled away their profession and their livelihood.

This was their downfall.

Thus on the sunshine of Eddie's tranquil life descended, shadow by shadow, the eclipse of Prohibition.

Eddie watched its approach, nearer and nearer.

'What are you going to go at, Ed?' they asked.

'I've been thinking of going into chicken farming,' Eddie used to answer, as he swabbed off the bar. 'They say there's good money in chickens.'

Next week it was turkeys.

'A fellow was in here telling me about it,' Ed said. 'They say there's big money in turkeys.'

After that it was a farm in Vermont, and then it was a ranch out in Kansas. But it was always something agricultural, bucolic, quiet.

Meanwhile Eddie stayed right there, pumping up the flooding beer and swabbing off the foam from the mahogany, till the days, the hours, and the minutes ticked out his livelihood.

Like the boy on the burning deck, he never left.

Where is he now? Eddie and all the other Eddies, the thousands of them? I don't know. There are different theories about them. Some people say they turned into divinity students and that they are out as canvassers selling Bibles to farmers. You may still recognize them, it is claimed, by the gentle way in which they say, 'What's yours this morning?'

There is no doubt their tranquil existence, sheltered behind the tall mahogany, unfitted them for the rough and tumble of ordinary life.

Perhaps, under Prohibition, they took to drink. In the cities, even their habitat has gone. The corner saloon is now a soda fountain, where golden-headed blondes ladle out red and white sundaes and mushy chocolates, and smash eggs into orange phosphates.

But out in the solitude of the country you may still see, here and there, boarded up in oblivion and obliquity, the frame building that was once the 'tavern'. No doubt at night, if it's late enough and dark enough, ghostly voices still whisper in the empty bar-room, haunted by the spectres of the Eddies – 'What's yours, gentlemen?'

Twelve
The Dry Pickwick

ENGLAND'S GREATEST WRITER ADAPTED
TO AMERICA'S GREATEST LEGISLATION

Introduction

The demand from the American colleges for a revision of the works of Charles Dickens has now become so insistent that something must be done. 'How can we put before the eyes of our literature classes,' writes the president of the Mush Academy, 'such scenes as those of the Maypole Inn, or the taproom of the Ipswich White Horse?' 'Our girls,' writes Professor Lydia Leftover, 'are tough enough already. If they start to read the drinking episodes of the *Pickwick Papers*, we can't hold them.' 'We must have legislation in this matter,' declares a well-known Senator from a Middle West State. 'Our people are accustomed to lean on legislation. They can't progress without it. What we need is a State law to declare that Charles Dickens is not funny.'

'But would it not be the more moderate and sensible course,' so writes to me the president of a New England college, 'if we could obtain a revised edition of the works of Charles Dickens, so made as to retain all the charm of character and humour and to leave out those features of social life not in harmony with our environment?'

Exactly. But can it be done? Let us take some of the most famous and typical episodes of the Dickens books and imagine them undergoing such a revision.

All the world knows, at first hand or at second or third, the *Pickwick Papers*. All the world has read or heard of such unforgettable episodes as the Christmas visit of Mr Pickwick and his friends to the hospitable Manor Farm of Mr Wardle of Dingley Dell. What would revision leave of such a page of life?

Let us recall it as Dickens wrote it.

Here is the rubicund and jovial Mr Pickwick, together with his inimitable and immortal friends, setting out by coach to visit Dingley Dell. We recall the starting of the coach from the inn yard, the vast

215

hampers with mysterious bottles clinking within them; the cracking of the whips of the merry postillions; the pauses by the way for a change of horses at the wayside inns where Mr Pickwick and his friends descend from their perch to visit the bar. Here a rosy landlord behind the long mahogany dispenses sundry smoking punches and hot drinks redolent of gin and lemons. We recall the arrival at Dingley Dell with jolly old Wardle merrily greeting his friends; more punches; festivities within doors and festivities without; hot toddies, hot negus, sugar, lemons and spices – the very atmosphere of the West Indies wafted on the Christmas air of England; skating on the ice; whist, cards, and round games in the drawing-room; huge dinners and substantial suppers; the consumption of oysters by the barrel and spiced beef by the hundredweight; and through it all the soft aroma of hot punch, mulled ale, warmed claret and smoking gin and lemons; till at the end the merriment fades into somnolence and Mr Pickwick and his friends sink into innocent slumber, having broken enough laws – if the scene were in America – to have sent them all to the penitentiary for life.

Can such pictures be revised? We dare not read them as they stand. They would corrupt the young. Let us see what revision can do.

* * *

So here follows: –

THE REVISED OR DRY PICKWICK

The evening was that of the twenty-fourth of December. Mr Pickwick had retired early to his room in the inn and had betaken himself and his night-cap early to bed, in anticipation of an early start for Dingley Dell by the coach of the morrow. Mr Pickwick, we say, had retired early to bed, and reclined well propped up with pillows with a bedside book open on the coverlet before him as a scarcely necessary aid in the summons of slumber. Mr Pickwick's night-cap, in the corporeal or, so to speak, the flannel sense, was upon his head, while his night-cap in the metaphorical sense, stood beside the bed upon the settee in the form of a tall glass of smoking toddy, from which the great man punctuated his reading from time to time with little sips. If we had looked sideways over Mr Pickwick's shoulder at the book before him, we could have read its title as *The Eighteenth Amendment to the Constitution of the United States, together with the federal and state legislation for the enforcement thereof.* We would have observed, moreover, that as the great man read further and further into the volume before him his usual genial face took on a serious air which almost deepened into an expression of indignation. We should have heard Mr Pickwick from time to time give vent to such expressions

as 'Most extraordinary!' 'Not to be tolerated,' and various other ejacu-
lations of surprise, indignation and protest. Nay, we should have noted
that the repeated sips taken by Mr Pickwick from the tall flagon of punch
became more and more frequent and accentuated, as if assuming the
form of a personal assertion of independence against an unwarranted
intrusion upon the liberty of a Briton. Indeed we should have finally
noted that nothing but the emptying of the flagon and the simultaneous
expiration of Mr Pickwick's candle, as if blushing for shame to have
illuminated such a page, put an end to Mr Pickwick's reading. Indeed we
may well imagine that the brain of that august gentleman, usually so well
poised as to admit of a dreamless slumber, may for once have been
carried into a dreamland, haunted with the uncomfortable visions called
up by what he had read. Mr Pickwick indeed slept, but –

* * *

'Better get up,' growled a voice at Mr Pickwick's ear before he seemed
to have slept at all; 'only ten minutes to coach time.'

If that was the voice of Tracy Tupman, Mr Pickwick's friend and
contemporary, it was greatly changed; a surly voice with no good-
fellowship left in it; a mean voice – reflected Mr Pickwick, as he sadly
pulled on his clothes in the chill of a winter dawn – not like Tupman's at
all. No suggestion of a morning draught of gin and bitters, or of something
that might warm the system and set it all a-tune for Christmas Day! Not
even a 'Merry Christmas,' thought Mr Pickwick, as he dressed and
descended to the yard where the coach stood in readiness. Mr Pickwick's
friends were already gathered. They looked blue in the jowl and mournful
in the chops; a sour-looking hostler half-awake fussed about beside the
horses.

'Don't tip him,' whispered Mr Snodgrass to Mr Tupman.

'Tip him!' replied Tupman; 'a mean, disobliging fellow like that; not a
farthing.'

'Don't tip the postboys either,' added Snodgrass.

'Certainly not,' said Tupman; 'such a couple of lubberly stupid fellows
I never saw in my life.'

Mr Winkle, the fourth of the party, approached Mr Tupman. 'Have
you got the hooch?' he asked in a half-voice.

'For God's sake, Winkle, not so loud,' said Snodgrass. 'You can't tell
who is hearing. I'm told they've got spotters now in all these yards.
You're never safe.'

With a sigh Mr Pickwick ascended to the roof of the coach. 'I never
realized before,' he reflected, 'what dirty smelly things these coaches are,
intolerable.'

There were several other passengers on the Muggleton coach that morning. It had been Mr Pickwick's agreeable custom, hitherto, to invite conversation with his fellow-passengers, in whom he was accustomed to find a mine of interest and information. But the passengers of this morning – silent, muffled and mournful, their noses red with the cold, their hearts heavy with depression – inspired no such invitation to social intercourse. Mr Pickwick left them alone. 'They are a pack of bums,' he murmured, unconsciously making use of a word not known until fifty years after his own demise, 'not worth talking to.' And then, as it were, suddenly taken with surprise at his own lack of urbanity: 'I wish, Winkle,' he said behind his hand. 'I wish I could get a gin and bitters.'

'Shut up!' said Mr Winkle.

* * *

Mr Pickwick looked down from the coach roof at a mournful-looking man who was helping to adjust the luggage into the boot. 'Is everything there all right, Sam?' he inquired.

'Eh, what?' replied the man in a surly tone. 'I guess it is. Get down yourself and see, if you doubt it.'

'Surly fellow,' murmured Mr Pickwick to Mr Tupman, and he added with a sigh, 'How I ever could have thought that fellow Sam Weller obliging and amusing passes my belief.'

'Why not get rid of him?' said Mr Tupman in the same cautious whisper.

'Can't,' said Mr Pickwick, emphatically, 'he belongs to the union.'

* * *

At length, with no more delay than coaches usually take in starting at such a season of the year, the coach with a fierce cracking of the whips and with sundry snarls from the post-boys was off upon its way. 'Mean, nasty weather,' muttered Mr Snodgrass, shivering into the collar of his overcoat.

'What you can expect,' rejoined Mr Winkle in a tone of equal complaint, 'at this time of the year. It's, let me see, the twenty-fifth of December: always rotten weather then.'

'Dear me!' murmured Mr Pickwick, 'Christmas!' and he repeated as if lingering on the sound of a remembered melody, 'Christmas!'

'What's that?' said Mr Tupman.

'Nothing,' said Mr Pickwick.

* * *

It would be too painful to trace the slow progress of the coach along miry roads, down muddy lanes with ragged snow in the hedgerows and past gaunt trees shivering in the winter gloom. There was no gleam of sunlight. A chill east wind, flaked with sleet, blew in the faces of the travellers, while the sky darkened almost to the point of night. Conversation survived only in a few muttered imprecations at the weather, couched rather in the form of profane soliloquy than in that of mutual intercourse. Even the heart of the noble Mr Pickwick sank within him. 'I wish I had a drink,' he murmured from time to time. 'Winkle, don't you think we might take a sip out of the bottle?'

'Too dangerous,' replied Mr Winkle with a guarded look at the other passengers. 'One of those men,' he whispered behind his hand, 'is evidently a clergyman. You can't trust him. But wait awhile,' he added. 'There's an inn a little farther on, the Blue Boar. We can get in there and take a drink.'

'Ah, yes,' murmured Mr Pickwick, 'the Blue Boar!' and at the very name of that comfortable hostelry such a flood of recollections poured into his mind – memories of blazing fires and smoking viands, of hot punches and warm brandies, that for a moment the countenance of the great man resumed its usual aspect of serene good nature. 'The Blue Boar,' he kept repeating to himself, 'the Blue Boar,' and with his hat, face and spectacles well drawn within the folds of his collar and muffler, Mr Pickwick was able, in spite of all discomforts, to relapse into something like a doze, in which no doubt his mind passed once more in review those pleasant scenes and episodes which had made his name famous throughout the civilized world.

* * *

'Get down here for awhile if you want to. We're changing horses.' It was the voice of the guard which had rudely broken in on the somnolence of Mr Pickwick.

He sat forward with a start. 'Where are we?' he murmured, looking through the sleet at a large building, its main door boarded up, its windows for the most part shuttered and the swinging sign in front of it painted over with whitewash. 'Where are we?'

'The Blue Boar, coach-stop number six,' said the guard. 'Get down if you like. You have four minutes.'

Mr Pickwick looked in silent dismay at what had once been the spacious and hospitable hostelry of the Blue Boar. Where now was the genial landlord of the bygone days, and where the buxom landlady, bustling about the inn, with a swarm of pretty chambermaids busy at her bidding, with serving-men stirring up huge fires, dinners on vast trays moving to private dining-rooms, with activity, happiness, merriment everywhere, whither had it fled? This gloomy shuttered building with makeshift stables at the back, the bar boarded up, the licence painted out, the chimneys almost smokeless! Mr Pickwick sat motionless, scarce able to credit the transformation of the world he had once known.

'Get down, Pickwick, if you're coming,' called Tupman from the ground, and accompanied his words with sundry taps at his sidepockets and with sundry rapid and furtive gestures, apparently indicative of the general idea of drink. 'We may be able to get in,' continued Tupman, when Mr Pickwick had made his way to the ground, 'and we can perhaps get glasses and some soda water inside.'

The Pickwickians gathered in a little group in front of the closed-up door of the inn. They stood huddled together, their backs against the driving snow, while Mr Pickwick, as became the senior and the leader of the party, delivered with the head of his cane a series of firm, dignified and expressive knocks at the closed door. There was no response. 'Knock again,' said Mr Winkle. 'I understand that the landlady still lives here; if she once recognizes *us* she'll let us in in a moment.'

Mr Pickwick again delivered a series of firm raps upon the door in which the authority of command was delicately blended with plaintiveness of appeal. This time the response was not long in coming. An upper casement banged open. A fierce-looking virago, a shawl thrown about her head, leaned out of the window. 'If you loafers don't beat it out of there in five seconds,' she shouted, 'I'll put the sheriff after you.'

'My dear madam,' began Mr Pickwick in mild expostulation.

'You madam me, and I'll have you in the jug. You beat it,' cried the woman, and the window shut with a slam.

Aghast at what he heard, albeit couched in language he could not understand, Mr Pickwick turned to his followers.

'Can that be the same woman?' he asked.

'Certainly not,' said Mr Tupman.

'Certainly not,' repeated Mr Snodgrass and Mr Winkle. Yet they all knew that it was.

'It seems to me,' said Mr Snodgrass, whose mild poetic disposition was ever disposed to make the best of anything, 'that if we went around out of sight behind the stable we might take a drink out of the bottle. That's better than nothing.'

In accordance wth this excellent advice, the four Pickwickians, with much dodging and manoeuvring, retreated into a hidden angle behind the stable fence. Here Mr Winkle produced from the pocket of his greatcoat a bottle – alas! only a *pint* bottle – of a beverage which had already been referred to as hooch. 'There's no glass,' he said mournfully.

'That doesn't matter,' said Tupman.

'– and no soda or water.'

'It's of no consequence,' said Mr Pickwick majestically; 'drink it as it is. You, Winkle, drink first – I insist – you bought it.'

'I *think* it's all right,' said Mr Winkle, a little dubiously. 'I got it from a chemist in the Strand. He *said* it was all right. Try it yourself.'

'Drink first,' repeated Mr Pickwick sternly.

Thus adjured and with his eyes upon that Heaven to which he looked for protection, Mr Nathaniel Winkle took a long pull at the bottle, and then removed it from his lips with a deep 'Ah!' of satisfaction. 'It's all right,' he said.

The bottle passed from lip to lip. The four Pickwickians under its genial influence regained in some measure their wonted cheerfulness. Mr Tupman straightened up his coat collar and his shirt and adjusted his hat at a more becoming angle. Mr Pickwick beamed upon his companions with a kindly eye.

But alas! their little glow of happiness was as brief as it was welcome. One drink and one half-drink, even with the most honourable division done with the greatest sacrifice of self, exhausted the little bottle. In vain it was tilted to an angle of ninety degrees to the horizon. The little bottle was empty. Mr Pickwick gazed sadly at his followers, while a gust of wind and snow that rounded the corner of their little shelter, recalled them to an inclement world.

Mr Pickwick rebuttoned his coat about his neck. 'Come,' he said, 'let us get back to the coach. But I wish we had kept a drink for Wardle. Too bad.'

'Too bad,' re-echoed Mr Tupman, buttoning up his coat.

'Too bad,' echoed again Mr Snodgrass and Mr Winkle, buttoning up their coats.

Indeed the Pickwickians were just about to retrace their steps to the coach, filled with humanitarian sympathy for the fate of Mr Wardle, when there occurred one of those peculiar intrusions of fate into human affairs such as can only be attributed to a direct intervention of Providence.

Round the corner of the stable wall there approached, with sidelong steps and a stealthy backward glance, an individual whom even the charitable mind of Mr Pickwick could only classify as obviously one of the criminal class. The shabby habiliments, the tight scarf about the neck, the cap close down over the cropped head combined with the saturnine cast of an ill-shaven face and sunken eye to suggest an atmosphere of malevolence and crime.

'I seen yous,' snarled this ill-omened individual – 'I seen yous take that drink.'

Mr Winkle, as one acknowledged to be the most martial and combative of the Pickwickians, assumed an air of indignation and stepped forwards towards the newcomer as if fully prepared to take him by the scruff of the neck and hurl him over the adjacent fence. 'See here, fellow,' he began in a tone of mingled anger and contempt.

The 'fellow' backed towards the fence. 'Cut out that high hat stuff,' he sneered, and as he spoke he drew from his pocket an object which even the inexperienced eyes of Mr Winkle surmised to be a weapon of a mortal character. None of the Pickwickians, indeed, could from any freak of supernatural forecast have ever seen an automatic pistol, but there was something in the menacing clutch with which the villainous-looking scoundrel held the weapon which seemed to warn them of its power. Mr Winkle's naturally pale face grew a trifle paler, while even Mr Pickwick put up one hand as if to screen himself from an imaginary stream of bullets. 'My dear sir,' he protested.

The man put his weapon back in his pocket.

'I didn't come for no scrap,' he said. 'I seen yous take the drink and I seen yous finish the bottle. Now, then, do you want to buy some more? I've got it right here. How about it?'

'Ah,' said Mr Pickwick in a tone of enlightenment and relief, 'more liquor. You have some to sell? By all means, what is it – brandy?'

'It's the real thing,' said the man, pulling out a long black bottle from an inside pocket of his shabby coat. 'You don't get stuff like that every day.'

He held the bottle up in the dim daylight. It bore no label, the bottle itself looked greasy and no gleam of sunshine was reflected back from its contents.

'What is it?' again asked Mr Pickwick.

'The real thing,' repeated the man fiercely. 'Didn't I tell you it was the real stuff?'

'And how much,' asked Mr Winkle, whose martial air had entirely evaporated, 'do you ask for it?'

'For you gents,' said the ragged man, 'I'll make the price at five sovereigns!'

'Five sovereigns!' gasped all the Pickwickians.

'Five sovereigns,' replied the man, 'and you'd better hand it over quick or I'll report to the coachguard what I seen here, and you'll learn what the law is, if you don't know it already.'

'Give it to him, Tupman,' said Mr Pickwick, 'give it to him.' It was characteristic of that great and magnanimous man that the aspect of anger and quarrelling was overwhelmingly distasteful to him. Financial loss was easier to bear than a breach of those relations of goodwill and concord which alone hold humanity together.

Mr Tupman, as the treasurer of the party, counted five golden sovereigns into the hands of the ragged man. The black bottle was duly transferred to a capacious pocket of Mr Pickwick's coat. The ragged man, with a surly attempt at civility, based on the possibility of future business, took his departure.

'We might try a sip of it,' said Winkle suggestively.

'Let it be understood,' said Mr Pickwick, 'that there is to be no further mention of this bottle, until I myself produce it at the right time and place for the entertainment of our dear friend Wardle.'

* * *

With this understanding the four companions betook themselves sadly back to the coach, and were hustled up to the roof by the guard, already impatient at their long delay. There they resumed their melancholy journey, the wet sleet and the drizzling rain alternately in their face. The long day wore its gradual length away as the four Pickwickians were dragged over muddy roads, past mournful fields and leafless woods across the face of what had once been Merry England. Not till the daylight had almost faded did they find themselves, on reaching a turn in the road, in the familiar neighbourhood of the Manor Farm of Dingley Dell.

'There's Wardle,' cried Mr Pickwick, waking up to a new alacrity and making sundry attempts at waving signals with an umbrella. 'There's Wardle, waiting at the corner of the road.'

There, right enough, was the good old gentleman, his stout figure unmistakable, waiting at the corner of the road. Close by was a one-horse cart, evidently designed for the luggage, beside which stood a tall thin boy, whose elongated figure seemed to Mr Pickwick at once extremely strange and singularly familiar.

'You're late,' said Mr Wardle in a slightly testy tone. 'I've waited at this infernal corner the best part of an hour. What sort of journey did you have?'

'Abominable,' said Mr Pickwick.

'Always that way at this infernal time of the year,' said Wardle. 'Here, Joe, make haste with that luggage. Drive it on in the cart. We'll walk up.'

'Joe!' repeated Mr Pickwick with a glance of renewed wonder and partial recognition at the tall thin boy whose long legs seemed to have left his scanty trousers and his inadequate stockings far behind in their growth. 'Is that Joe? Why, Joe was –'

'Was the "Fat Boy",' interrupted Wardle. 'Exactly so. But when I had to cut his beer off he began to grow. Look at him!'

'Does he still sleep as much as ever?' asked Mr Tupman.

'Never!' said Mr Wardle.

The cart having set off at a jog-trot for the Manor Farm the five gentlemen, after sundry adjustments of mufflers, gaiters and gloves, disposed themselves to follow.

'And how are you, Wardle?' asked Mr Pickwick as they fell in side by side.

'Not so well,' said Mr Wardle.

'Too bad,' said Mr Pickwick.

'I find I don't digest as well as I used to.'

'Dear me!' said Mr Pickwick, who had passed more than half a century of life without being aware that he digested at all, and without connecting that interesting process with the anatomy of Wardle or of any other of his friends.

'No,' continued Wardle, 'I find that I have to keep away from starch. Proteids are all right for me, but I find that nitrogenous foods in small quantities are about all that I can take. You don't suffer from inflation at all, do you?'

'Good Lord, no!' said Mr Pickwick. He had no more idea of what inflation was than of the meaning of nitrogenous food. But the idea of itself was enough to make him aghast.

They walked along for some time in silence.

Presently Mr Wardle spoke again. 'I think that the lining of my oesophagus must be punctured here and there,' he said.

'Good heavens!' exclaimed Mr Pickwick.

'Either that or some sort of irritation in the alimentary canal. Ever have it?'

'My dear sir!' said Mr Pickwick.

'It's this damn bootleg stuff,' said Mr Wardle.

Mr Pickwick turned as he walked to take a closer look at his old and valued friend, whose whole manner and person seemed, as it were, transformed. He scrutinized closely the legs of Mr Wardle's boots, but was unable to see in those stout habiliments any suggested cause for the obvious alteration of mind and body which his friend had undergone. But when he raised his eyes from Wardle's boots to Wardle's face, he realized that the change was great. The jolly rubicund features had faded to a dull, almost yellow complexion. There were pouches beneath the eyes and heavy lines in the once smooth cheeks.

* * *

Musing thus on the obvious and distressing changes in his old friend, Mr Pickwick found himself arriving once more in sight of the Manor Farm, a prospect which even on such a gloomy day filled him with pleasant reminiscences. The house at any rate had not changed. Here was still the same warm red brick, the many gables and the smoking chimneys of that hospitable home. Around and beside it were the clustering evergreens and the tall elm trees which had witnessed the marksmanship of Mr Winkle in the slaughter of rooks. Mr Pickwick breathed a sigh of satisfaction at the familiar and pleasant prospect. Yet even here, in a nearer view, he could not but feel as if something of the charm of past years had vanished. The whole place seemed smaller, the house on a less generous scale, the grounds far more limited, and even the spruce trees fewer and the elms less venerable than at his previous visit.

In fact Dingley Dell seemed somehow oddly shrunken from what it had been. But Mr Pickwick, who contained within himself like all great intellects the attitude of the philosopher, resolutely put aside this feeling, as one always familiar in visits paid to scenes of former happiness.

Here at least as he entered the good old house was the same warm and hearty welcome as of yore. The old lady, Mr Wardle's mother, her deafness entirely laid aside, greeted Mr Pickwick and his younger companions with affectionate recognition: while the charming Emily Wardle and the dashing Arabella Allen appeared in a bevy of pretty girls for the special welcome and the complete distraction of the susceptible hearts of Messrs Snodgrass and Winkle. Here too, as essential members of the Christmas party, were the two young medical students, those queer combinations of rowdiness and good-humour, Mr Bob Sawyer and Mr Benjamin Allen, the brother of the fair Arabella.

Mr Wardle, also, as he re-entered his home and assumed his duties as host, seemed to recover in great measure his genial good-nature and high spirits.

'Now, then, mother,' he exclaimed, 'our friends I am sure are thirsty; before they go to their rooms let us see what we can offer them in the way of wine. Joe – where's that boy? – a couple of bottles of the red wine, the third bin in the cellar, and be smart about it.' The tall thin boy, whom the very word 'wine' seemed to galvanize out of his mournful passivity into something like energy, vanished in the direction of the cellar, while Mr Pickwick and his companions laid aside their outer wraps and felt themselves suddenly invaded with a glow of good-fellowship at the mere prospect of a 'drink'. Such is the magic of anticipation that the Pickwickians already felt their hearts warm and their pulses tingle at the very word.

'Now, then,' said the hospitable Wardle, 'bustle about, girls – glasses – a corkscrew – that's right – ah, here's Joe. Set it on the sideboard, Joe.'

The cork of the first bottle came out with a 'pop' that would have done credit to the oldest vintage of the Rhine, and Mr Wardle proceeded to fill the trayful of glasses with the rich red liquid.

'What is it?' asked Mr Pickwick, beaming through his spectacles at the fluid through which the light of the blazing fire upon the hearth reflected an iridescent crimson. 'What is it – Madeira?'

'No,' said Mr Wardle, 'it's a wine that we made here at home.'

'Ah,' said Mr Pickwick. Volumes could not have said more.

'It's made,' continued the hospitable old gentleman, passing round the glasses as he talked, 'from cranberries. I don't know whether one would exactly call it a claret –'

'No,' said Mr Pickwick, as he sipped the wine, 'hardly a claret.'

'No,' said Wardle, 'a little more of a Burgundy taste –'

'Yes,' said Mr Pickwick, 'a little more of a Burgundy taste.'

'Drink it,' said Mr Wardle.

'I am,' said Mr Pickwick, 'but I like to sip it rather slowly, to get the full pleasure of it.'

'You like it?' said Mr Wardle eagerly.

'It is excellent,' said Mr Pickwick.

'Then let me fill up your glass again,' said Wardle. 'Come along, there's lots more in the cellar. Here, Winkle, Tupman, your glasses.'

There was no gainsaying Mr Wardle's manner. It had in it something of a challenge which forbade the Pickwickians from expressing their private thoughts, if they had any, on the merits of Mr Wardle's wine. Even Mr Pickwick himself found the situation difficult. 'I think, perhaps,' he said as he stood with a second bumper of wine untasted in his hand, 'I will carry this up to my room and have the pleasure of drinking it as I dress for dinner.' Which no doubt he did, for at any rate the empty glass was found in due course in Mr Pickwick's bedroom. But whether or not certain splashes of red in the snow beneath Mr Pickwick's bedroom window may have been connected with the emptiness of the glass we are not at liberty to say.

* * *

Now just as the gentlemen were about to vanish upstairs to prepare for dinner the sprightly Emily pulled Mr Winkle aside. 'Wait till the old guys are out of the way,' she whispered. 'Arabella's got a flask of real old tranglefoot, and Bob Sawyer and Mr Allen are going to make cocktails. Come into our room and have some.'

'God bless my soul,' murmured Mr Winkle.

* * *

The assemblage of the party for dinner found much the same group gathered at the Manor Farm as on the occasion of Mr Pickwick's previous visit. Here among the first was the elderly clergyman whose charming poetic talent had afforded such pleasure to the company.

'I am glad to see you,' said Mr Pickwick heartily. 'I trust, sir, I see you well.'

'Not altogether,' said the old man. 'I am well enough except when it's humid, but I find that after a certain saturation of the air it affects me at once.'

'Indeed,' said Mr Pickwick.

'I imagine,' continued the clergyman, 'that it's my sebaceous glands? Don't you think so?'

'Possibly so,' said Mr Pickwick.

'Though it may be merely some form of subcutaneous irritation –'

'Quite likely,' said Mr Pickwick.

'You see,' continued the old gentleman, 'it's always possible that there's some kind of duodenal perforation –'

'Good heavens!' exclaimed Mr Pickwick.

The fortunate entry of Mr Wardle with a trayful of cocktails carried aloft by the Thin Boy interrupted this ultramedical conversation.

'These cocktails,' proclaimed Mr Wardle in the same tone of irritation and challenge with which he passed the wine, 'you may rely upon absolutely. There is no bootlegged stuff used in them.'

'Ah,' said Mr Pickwick, smiling, 'and what is the principal ingredient?'

'Harness oil,' said Mr Wardle. 'They were made here in the house by my old mother herself. Mother, your health!'

'Your health, madam,' echoed all the company, while the guests, with a resolution worthy of the sturdy race from which they sprang, drained the glasses with the unflinching courage of the Briton.

* * *

It would be as tedious as it would be needless to trace in detail the slow progress of the meal which followed. The oil cocktails indeed induced a temporary and hectic rise in spirits which lasted through the first of the many courses of that interminable meal. But the fires, thus falsely raised, died easily down.

Mr Pickwick found himself seated between the old lady, who entertained him with a sustained account of her rheumatism, and the ancient clergyman, who apparently found his sole intellectual diversion in the discussion of his glands.

Nor is it necessary to relate in detail the drear passage of the long evening in the drawing-room which followed upon the long dinner in the dining-room. Mr Pickwick found himself at the card table, with his friend Mr Tupman as his opponent and two elderly, angular and silent spinsters as their partners. Here Mr Pickwick slowly passed from dryness to desiccation; from desiccation to utter aridity such that the sand in the desert of Sahara was moistness itself in comparison. More than once he almost broke his fixed resolutions and dashed off to his room to fetch down the bottle of the 'real old stuff' which lay in the pocket of his greatcoat. But his firm resolve to share it with his host and to produce it as the final triumph of the evening kept him from so doing. His sufferings were all the more intense in that some instinct warned him that there was, as it were, 'something doing' among the younger people to which he was not a party. There were frequent absences from the card-room on the part of Winkle and Snodgrass and the two young medicos, closely coincident with similar absences of the lovely Emily and the dashing Arabella – absences from which the young people returned with laughing faces and sparkling eyes – in short, Mr Pickwick had that exasperating feeling that somebody somewhere was getting a drink and that he was not in on it. Only those who have felt this – and their numbers are many – can measure the full meaning of it.

The evening, however, like all things human, drew at length to its close. And as the guests rose from the card tables Mr Pickwick felt that the moment had at length arrived when he might disclose to the assembled company his carefully planned and welcome surprise.

Mr Pickwick signalled to the Thin Boy, who had remained in attendance in a corner of the room. 'Go up to my bedroom, Joe,' he said, 'and you'll see a bottle –'

'I seen it already,' said the Thin Boy.

'Very good,' said Mr Pickwick, 'fetch it here.'

'And now,' said Mr Pickwick, when the bottle was presently brought and placed with the cork removed beside him on the table, 'I have a toast to propose.' He knocked upon the table in order to call the attention of the company, some of whom were already leaving the room while others still stood about the table.

'The toast of Christmas!' said Mr Pickwick, holding aloft the bottle. At the sight of it and with the prospect of a real drink before them the company broke into loud applause.

'This bottle, my dear old friend,' continued Mr Pickwick, his face resuming as he spoke all of its old-time geniality and his gold spectacles irradiating the generosity of his heart, as he turned to Mr Wardle, '– this bottle I have bought specially for you. I could have wished that this bottle, like the fabled bottle of the Arabian nights (I think it was the Arabian nights; at any rate, certain nights) – that this bottle was everlasting and unemptiable. As it is, I fear I can only offer to each of us a mere pretence of a potation. But for you, my dear Wardle, I insist that there shall be a real bumper, a brimming bumper.'

Mr Pickwick suited the action to the word, and filling a glass to the brim, he handed it across the table to Mr Wardle.

'You, Wardle, shall set us a good example by first draining this glass in honour of the spirit of Christmas!'

The kindly face of Mr Wardle betrayed a noble struggle in which the desire for a drink, a real drink, struggled for mastery with more magnanimous feelings. He hesitated. He paused. The liquid in the glass might be dull in colour and lustreless to the eye, but the pungent aroma, or odour, with which it seemed to fill the room bore witness at least to the strength of it.

'Pickwick,' said Wardle, deeply moved, 'I can't. You are too kind,' and then suddenly: 'Damn it, I will.'

And as if anxious to leave no room for any weakening of his resolution, Mr Wardle lifted the glass and drained it to the bottom. Only when he had consumed the last drop did he set the glass down upon the table. He set it down, so it seemed to those about him, with a slow and heavy hand, and stood a moment, after his potation, as if pausing for speech.

'Pickwick,' he said at last, 'it's – you are –'

His utterance sounded suddenly thick. His eye seemed fixed in a strange way. He looked straight in front of him, not at his old friend, but as it were into nothingness.

'Pickwick,' he repeated, and then, in a loud voice like a cry of fear: 'Pickwick!'

Wardle's hands groped at the edge of the table. He swayed a moment, trying in vain to hold his balance, and then sank down in a heap against the edge of the table, unconscious, his breath coming in heavy gasps.

Mr Pickwick rushed to Wardle's side. The affrighted guests gathered about him in a group, vainly endeavouring to recall the good old man to consciousness.

Mr Pickwick alone retained some measure of decision. 'Sawyer,' he said, 'where's Sawyer? Sam, Joe – quick, go and find Mr Sawyer!'

'Here, sir,' said the voice of the young medico re-entering the room to which the tumult had recalled him.

He stepped up to Wardle's side and seized his wrist with one hand and with the other opened Mr Wardle's waistcoat to feel the beating of the heart.

Silence fell upon the room, broken only by the stertorous breathing of the old man lying against the table. The eyes of the guests were fixed upon young Bob Sawyer, who stood silent and intent, feeling for the beating of the flickering pulse, transformed in a moment by the instinct and inspiration of his profession from a roistering boy to a man of medicine.

Sawyer's eye fell upon the empty and reeking glass. 'What did he drink?' he asked.

'This,' said Mr Pickwick, silently passing the bottle to the young man. Bob Sawyer, with a shake of the head, released the wrist of Mr Wardle.

He poured a few spoonfuls of the liquid into the glass and with the utmost caution tasted it with the tip of his tongue.

'Good God!' he said.

'What is it,' said Mr Pickwick, 'raw alcohol?'

'With at least fifteen per cent of cyanide,' said Bob Sawyer.

'And that means?' Mr Pickwick asked with an agonized look at his old friend, whose breath had now grown faint and from whose face all vestige of colour was rapidly fading.

Bob Sawyer shook his head.

'It means death,' he said. 'He is dying now.'

Mr Pickwick threw his arms about the shoulders of his old friend. In an agony of remorse, he felt himself the destroyer of the man whom he had loved beyond all his friends. His own hand, his own act had brought about this terrible and overwhelming tragedy.

'Wardle, Wardle,' he cried in tones of despair, 'speak to me. Wake up! Wake up!'

* * *

Again and again, so it seemed at least to himself, he cried, 'Wake up, wake up!'

* * *

Then as he repeated the words yet again Mr Pickwick suddenly realized that not he but someone else was vociferating, 'Wake up, wake up!'

* * *

The voice echoed in his brain, driving out of it the last vestiges of sleep.

With a gasp of relief, as of one rescued from the terrors of a dreadful dream, Mr Pickwick slowly opened his eyes and assumed a sitting posture, his hands still grasping the coverlet of the bed.

'Wake up, Pickwick, wake up. Merry Christmas!'

There was no doubt of it now! It was the voice of Mr Tupman, or rather the combined voices of Mr Tupman, Mr Snodgrass and Mr Winkle, all fully dressed for the coaching journey and gathered in gay assemblage about the bed of their tardy leader.

It seemed too good to be true! Here was the cheerful face of Mr Tupman beaming with Christmas salutations as he pulled back the window curtains and let the sunlight flood into the room – here was Mr Snodgrass arrayed in the bright finery of a poet on a Christmas holiday, and here, most emphatical of all, was Mr Winkle proferring to Mr Pickwick a tall bubbling glass of brandy and soda that leaped and sparkled in the beams of sunlight as one of those early pick-me-ups or restoratives, so essential for the proper beginning of a proper Christmas.

'Bless my soul!' said Mr Pickwick, shaking off the remnants of his terrible dream. The great man leaped from his bed and assuming a dressing-gown rushed to the window and looked into the inn yard. There was the coach, gaily bedecked with sprigs of holly, in the very imminence of preparations for departure, the horses tossing at the bits, the postillions about to mount, the guard fingering his key bugle for a preparatory blast and Mr Sam Weller in his familiar wide-awake, his face illuminated with its familiar good-nature, gaily tossing minor articles of luggage in graceful spirals to the roof of the coach.

Mr Pickwick, with one last shuddering recollection of the world of the future, slipped back a hundred years into the Good Old Days of the past.

The Perfect Optimist

OR DAY-DREAMS IN A DENTAL CHAIR

Well, here we are again seated in the big red plush chair in for one of our jolly little mornings with our dentist. My! It certainly is cosy to settle back into this comfortable chair with a whole quiet morning in front of us – no work to do, no business to think of, just to lie in one of our comfortable day-dreams.

How pleasant it is in this chair, anyway, with the sunshine streaming in through the window upon us and illuminating every corner of the neat and immaculate little room in which we sit.

For immaculate neatness and cleanliness, I repeat, give me a little up-to-date dental room every time. Talk of your cosy libraries or your dens, they won't compare with this little nook. Here we are with everything we need around us, all within easy arm's-length reach. Here on this revolving tray are our pleasant little nippers, pincers and forceps, some so small and cute and others so big and strong that we feel a real confidence in them. They'd never let go of anything! Here is our dainty little electric buzzer with our revolving gimlets at the end; our little hammer on the left; our bradawl on the right – everything!

For the moment our dental friend is out of the room – telephoning, we imagine. The merry fellow is so popular with all his friends that they seem to ring him up every few minutes.

Little scraps of his conversation reach our ears as we lie half-buried in our white towel, in a sweet reverie of expectancy.

'Pretty bad in the night, was it, eh? Well, perhaps you'd better come along down and we'll make a boring through that bicuspid and see what's there!'

Full of ideas, he is, always like that – never discouraged, something new to suggest all the time. And then we hear him say: 'Well, let me see. I'm busy now for about a couple of hours –' Hurrah! That means us! We were so afraid he was going to say, 'I'll be through here in about five minutes.' But no, it's all right; we've got two long, dreamy hours in front of us.

He comes back into the room, and his cheery presence, as he searches among his instruments and gives a preliminary buzz to the buzzer, seems to make the sushine even brighter. How pleasant life seems – the dear old life; that is, the life we quitted ten minutes ago and to which, please Providence, we hope to return in two hours. We never felt till we sat here how full and pleasant life is. Think of it, the simple joy of being alive. That's all we ask – of going to work each day (without a toothache) and coming home each night to eat our dinner. If only people realized it – just to live in our world without a toothache . . .

So runs our pleasant reverie. But, meanwhile, our dental friend has taken up a little hammer and has tapped us, in his playful way, on the back teeth.

'Feel that?' he asks.

And he's right, the merry dog! We *do* feel it. He guessed it right away. We are hoping so much that he will hit us again.

Come on, let's have a little more fun like that. But no. He's laid aside his hammer and as nearly as we can see has rolled up his cuffs to the elbow and has started his good old electric buzzer into a roar.

Ah, ha! Now we are going to get something – this is going to be the big fun, the real thing. That's the greatest thing about our little dental mornings, there's always something new. Always as we sit we have a pleasant expectancy that our dental friend is planning a new one.

Now, then, let us sit back tight, while he drives at our jaw with the buzzer. Of all the exhilarating feelings of hand-to-hand conflict, of man against man, of mind matched against mind, and intelligence pitted against intelligence, I know of none more stimulating than when we brace ourselves for this conflict of man and machinery. He has on his side the power of electricity and the force of machinery.

But we are not without resource. We brace ourselves, laughingly, in our chair while he starts to bore. We need, in fact, our full strength; but, on the other hand, if he tries to keep up at this pace his hands will get tired. We realize, with a sense of amusement, that if his machine slips, he may get a nasty thump on the hand against our jawbone.

He slacks off for just a second – half withdraws his machine and says, 'Were you at the football match yesterday?' and then starts his instrument again at full roar.

'Were we at the football match yesterday?' How strange it sounds! 'Why, yes, of course we were!' In that far-away long-ago world where they play football and where there is no toothache – we were there only yesterday afternoon.

Yes, we remember, it was just towards the end of that game that we felt those twinges in one of the – what does he call it, the lower molars? Anyway, one of those twinges which started the exultant idea racing through our minds, 'Tomorrow we'll have to go to the dentist.'

* * *

A female voice speaking into the room has called him to the telephone, and again we are alone. What if he never comes back!

The awful thought leaps to our minds, what if he comes in and says, 'I'm sorry to say I have to take a train out of town at once.' How terrible!

Perhaps he'll come in and say, 'Excuse me, I have to let your work go; they've sent for me to go to China!'

* * *

But no, how lucky! Back he comes again. We've not lost him. And now what is he at? Stuffing cotton-wool up into our head, wool saturated with some kind of drugs, and pounding it in with a little hammer.

And then – all of a sudden, so it seems – he steps back and says, 'There, that will do nicely till Monday!' And we rise half-dazed from our chair to realize in our disappointment that it is over already. Somehow we had thought that our pleasant drowsy morning of pounding and boring and dreaming in the sunlight, while our dental friend mixed up something new, would last for ever. And now, all of a sudden, it is over.

Never mind! After all, he said Monday! It won't seem so long till then! And meantime we can think about it all day and look forward to it and imagine how it is going to feel. Oh! It won't be long.

And so we step out into the street – full of cotton-wool and drugs and electricity and reverie – like a person returning to a forgotten world and dazed to find it there.

Ho for Happiness

A PLEA FOR LIGHTER AND BRIGHTER LITERATURE

'Why is it,' said someone in conversation the other day, 'that all the really good short stories seem to contain so much sadness and suffering and to turn so much on crime and wickedness? Why can't they be happy all the time?'

No one present was able to answer the question. But I thought it over afterwards, and I think I see why it is so. A happy story, after all, would make pretty dull reading. It may be all right in real life to have everything come along just right, with happiness and good luck all the time, but in fiction it would never do.

Stop, let me illustrate the idea. Let us make up a story which is happy all the time and contrast it as it goes along with the way things happen in the really good stories.

* * *

Harold Herald never forgot the bright October morning when the mysterious letter, which was to alter his whole life, arrived at his downtown office.

His stenographer brought it in to him and laid it on his desk.

'A letter for you,' she said. Then she kissed him and went out again.

Harold sat for some time with the letter in front of him. Should he open it? After all, why not?

He opened the letter. Then the idea occurred to him to read it. 'I might as well,' he thought.

'Dear Mr Herald' (so ran the letter), 'if you will have the kindness to call at this office, we shall be happy to tell you something to your great advantage.'

The letter was signed John Scribman. The paper on which it was written bore the heading 'Scribman, Scribman & Company, Barristers, Solicitors, etc., No. 13 Yonge St'.

A few moments later saw Harold on his way to the lawyers' office. Never had the streets looked brighter and more cheerful than in this perfect October sunshine. In fact, they never had been.

Nor did Harold's heart misgive him and a sudden suspicion enter his mind as Mr Scribman, the senior partner, rose from his chair to greet him. Not at all. Mr Scribman was a pleasant, middle-aged man whose countenance behind his gold spectacles beamed with good-will and good-nature.

234

'Ah, Mr Harold Herald,' he said, 'or perhaps you will let me call you simply Harold. I didn't like to give you too much news in one short letter. The fact is that our firm has been entrusted to deliver you a legacy, or rather a gift . . . Stop, stop!' continued the lawyer, as Harold was about to interrupt with questions, '. . . our client's one request was that his name would not be divulged. He thought it would be so much nicer for you just to have the money and not know who gave it to you.'

Harold murmured his assent.

Mr Scribman pushed a bell.

'Mr Harold Herald's money, if you please,' he said.

A beautiful stenographer wearing an American Beauty rose at her waist entered the room carrying a silken bag.

'There is half a million dollars here in five-hundred-dollar bills,' said the lawyer. 'At least, we didn't count them, but that is what our client said. Did you take any?' he asked the stenographer.

'I took out a few last night to go to the theatre with,' admitted the girl with a pretty blush.

'Monkey!' said Mr Scribman. 'But that's all right. Don't bother with a receipt, Harold. Come along with me: my daughter is waiting for us down below in the car to take us to lunch.'

* * *

Harold thought he had never seen a more beautiful girl than Alicia Scribman. In fact he hadn't. The luxurious motor, the faultless chauffeur, the presence of the girl beside him and the bag of currency under the seat, the sunlit streets filled with happy people with the bright feeling of just going back to work, full of lunch – the sight of all this made Harold feel as if life were indeed a pleasant thing.

'After all,' he mused, 'how little is needed for our happiness! Half a million dollars, a motor-car, a beautiful girl, youth, health – surely one can be content with that . . .'

It was after lunch at the beautiful country home of the Scribmans that Harold found himself alone for a few minutes with Miss Scribman.

He rose, walked over to her and took her hand, kneeling on one knee and pulling up his pants so as not to make a crease in them.

'Alicia!' he said. 'Ever since I first saw you, I have loved you. I want to ask you if you will marry me?'

'Oh, Harold,' said Alicia, leaning forward and putting both her arms about his neck with one ear against the upper right-hand end of his cheekbone. 'Oh, Harold!'

'I can, as you know,' continued Harold, 'easily support you.'

'Oh, that's all right,' said Alicia. 'As a matter of fact, I have much more than that of my own, to be paid over to me when I marry.'

'Then you will marry me?' said Harold rapturously.

'Yes, indeed,' said Alicia, 'and it happens so fortunately just now, as papa himself is engaged to marry again and so I shall be glad to have a new home of my own. Papa is marrying a charming girl, but she is so much younger than he is that perhaps she would not want a grown-up step-daughter.'

* * *

Harold made his way back to the city in a tumult of happiness. Only for a moment was his delirium of joy brought to a temporary standstill.

As he returned to his own apartment, he suddenly remembered that he was engaged to be married to his cousin Winnie . . . The thing had been entirely washed out of his mind by the flood-tide of his joy.

He seized the telephone.

'Winnie,' he said, 'I am so terribly sorry. I want to ask you to release me from our engagement. I want to marry someone else.'

'That's all right, Hal!' came back Winnie's voice cheerfully. 'As a matter of fact, I want to do the same thing myself. I got engaged last week to the most charming man in the world, a little older, in fact quite a bit older than I am, but ever so nice. He is a wealthy lawyer and his name is Walter Scribman . . .'

* * *

The double wedding took place two weeks later, the church being smothered with chrysanthemums and the clergyman buried under Canadian currency. Harold and Alicia built a beautiful country home at the other side – the farthest-away side – of the city from the Scribmans'. A year or so after their marriage, they had a beautiful boy, and then another, then a couple of girls (twins), and then they lost count.

There. Pretty dull reading it makes. And yet, I don't know. There's something about it, too. In the real stories Mr Scribman would have been a crook, and Harold would have either murdered Winnie or been accused of it, and the stenographer with the rose would have stolen the money instead of just taking it, and it wouldn't have happened in bright, clear October weather but in dirty old November – oh no, let us have romance and happiness, after all. It may not be true, but it's better.

Thirteen
Our Summer Convention

Our summer convention, – the first annual convention of Peanut Men, – has just been concluded and has been such a success that I feel I'd like to set down a little account of it in print.

The way it began was that a few of us – all Peanut Men – got talking together about every other business except ours having conventions and ours not being represented in this way at all. Everybody knows there are now conventions of the electrical men and the shoemen and the pulp and paper men, and even of professors and psychologists and chiropodists. And as everybody knows too, these conventions are not merely for business and social purposes, but they are educative as well. People who go to a convention and listen to the papers that are read will learn things about their own business that they never would have thought of.

Anyway, we got together and formed an association and elected officers – a Grand Master of the Nuts, and a Grand Kernel, and seven Chief Shucks and a lot of lesser ones – and decided to hold a convention. We restricted the membership – because that is always found best in conventions – and made it open only to sellers, roasters, buyers, importers and consumers of peanuts. Others might come as friends, but they couldn't appear as Nuts. To make the thing social it was agreed that members might bring their wives, as many as they liked.

We thought first of New York or Chicago as the place for us, but they always seemed too crowded. Then we thought of Montreal and a whole lot of the members were all for it, partly because of the beautiful summer climate. But our final choice was Lake Owatawetness in the mountains.

It was a great sight the day we opened up the convention. We had flags across the street and big streamers with *Welcome to the Nuts* and things like that on them, and all the delegates rode in open hacks and pinned on each was a big badge with the words *I am a Complete Nut.* Underneath this motto was his name and his town and his height and weight and his religion and his age.

Well, we all went to the town hall and we had an address of welcome from the Grand Master. They said that it was one of the best addresses ever heard in the town hall, and lasted just over two hours. Personally I can't speak for it because I slipped out of the hall a little after it began. I had an idea that I would just ease off a little the first morning and wait till the afternoon to begin the real educative stuff in earnest. There were two other fellows who slipped out about the same time that I did, and so we went down to the lake and decided we'd hire a boat and go down the lake fishing so as to be ready for the solid work of the afternoon. One of the fellows was from Wichita, Kansas, and was a Presbyterian and weighed 168 pounds, and the other was from Owen Sound, Ontario, not classified, and weighed 178 pounds and was five feet nine and a half inches high.

We took some lunch with us so as not to need to get back till two, when the first big conference opened. We had a printed programme with us, and it showed that at the two o'clock session there was to be a paper read on *The Application of Thermodynamics to the Roasting of Peanuts*, and we all agreed that we wouldn't miss it for anything.

Well, we went clear down the lake to where we understood the best fishing was, and it was a longer row than we thought. We didn't really start fishing till noon – not counting one or two spots where we just fished for twenty minutes or so to see if any fish were there, but there weren't. After we got to the right place we didn't get a bite at all, which made us want to stay on a while, though it was getting near the time to go back, because it seemed a shame to quit before the fish began to bite, and we were just thinking of leaving when a Methodist from Oshkosh, Wisconsin, who was near by, caught a black bass, a real peach. There seemed to be a good many other boats coming down, too, and quite near us there was a Catholic delegate from Syracuse (five feet eight inches) who caught a catfish, and two Episcopalians (150 pounds each) from Burlington, Vermont, who seemed to be getting bites all the time.

So we decided to stay. We didn't get so many fish but we all agreed that an afternoon on the water for health's sake was a fine thing to put a man into shape for the convention work. We knew that in the evening Professor Pip of the State Agricultural College was to read a paper on *The Embryology of the Nut*, and we wanted to be right on deck for that.

Rowing back just before supper time some one of us happened to mention cards, just casually, and the delegate from Owen Sound, who was unclassified, asked me if I ever played poker. I told him that I *had* played it, once or twice, not so much for any money that might be on it, but just for the game itself, as you might say. The man from Wichita said that he had played it that way, too, and that if you took it like that it was a fine game: in fact for a quiet evening's amusement there was nothing like it. We all three agreed that if it hadn't been for wanting to hear Professor Pip's talk on the Embryology of the Peanut we could have had a quiet little game, a three-handed game, or, perhaps, get in one or two of the other boys after supper in one of the rooms.

Anyway, after supper we went upstairs and began throwing down hands just to see what would turn up while we were waiting for the lecture time, and first thing we knew we got seated round the table and started playing and it seemed a pity to quit and go to the lecture. For my part I didn't care so much, because I am not so much interested in the Embryology of the Nut as in the selling of it.

Later on I saw a delegate (from Saskatoon, Saskatchewan, a Universal Christian, six feet high) who said that he had spoken with a man who had heard the lecture and that it was fine. It appears there was only a small turn-out, smaller even than in the afternoon, but those who were there and stayed – some couldn't stay – said that it was all right. They said it was too long, – a lecture is apt to be too long, and that the professor spoke pretty low; in fact you couldn't exactly hear him, and that you couldn't understand the subject-matter, but the lecture itself was good. It was all right.

By the next morning we had the convention pretty well in full swing and you could see that the crowd were getting to know one another. This second morning was to be the big morning of the convention because the State Governor was to give us an address and everybody felt that it was a great honour to have him come. They had put up a sort of arch for him to drive under, with a motto *Welcome You Big Nut*. They say the Governor was awfully pleased with it and still more when they made him a Chief Grand Nut at the morning ceremony.

I didn't hear his address myself, not more than a few sentences. I couldn't stay. He had just begun a survey of the history of the development of the arable land of the state (he had it all in his hand and was reading it) when I had to go. I had said something to some of the boys the night before about golf – it appeared that the privileges of the Watawetness Golf Club had been extended to us – and I felt that I mustn't go back on it. It was disappointing, but there was no use worrying about it.

They said the Governor's address was great. It was too long, everybody admitted, and a few took exception to it because it was not exactly connected with the convention, and some criticized it because it was the same address that he had given to the Skiers and Snowshoemen Convention last February. But still it was good.

Playing golf cut me clean out of the afternoon session, too, as I didn't get back till it must have been started. In this session the programme was to divide the convention up into little groups for intensive study of the peanuts organized by Miss Mutt of the Botany Section, of the State Teachers' Association. Each study group was to take some topic under a special speaker and exhaust it. But quite a lot of the delegates had gone fishing, and some were playing pool and some were scattered round. It seems they couldn't make up the groups except just the speaker in each group and Miss Mutt herself, of course. So Miss Mutt gave them a talk on the Botany of Selling Peanuts. They said it was fine. It was too long, they thought, and would have been much better, ever so much better, if it had been shorter – quite short; but it was good.

That night was the big banquet. The Governor stayed over for it, and there was to be his speech and the Secretary of Agriculture and speeches from the Grand Master, and from Clergymen, and Teachers. In fact it looked pretty good, and from all I heard it was considered a big success. The only thing against it was that some of the delegates had brought in some stuff into the hotel (I don't know where they got it from), and a lot of them were slipping out of the banquet room and slipping up to the rooms where they had this stuff.

Some didn't come down. They said quite a lot didn't come down. I went up there for awhile, but I didn't stay long, or not so very long, and when I got back to the door of the banquet room, one of the guests, a minister, was talking on the moral aspect of Importing Peanuts. So I didn't stay, as I am more interested in the selling aspect.

The next morning I left early. There was to be another whole day and some mighty interesting papers to be read. But I felt I would be needed badly in my business at this time; in fact I felt pretty keen to get back to it. I saw many other delegates come away on the same train, a lot of them. They had taken off their badges, so I couldn't tell their names and their religions, but they all agreed that the convention had been a wonderful success and a great educative influence in our business.

At the Ladies' Culture Club

A LECTURE ON THE FOURTH DIMENSION

It has become a fixed understanding that with each approaching winter there begins the open season for the various Ladies' Culture Clubs. I suppose that this kind of club exists in everybody else's town just as it does in mine. We have one in my town that meets at eleven (every other Tuesday), has just a small cup of coffee and just a tiny sandwich, hears an hour's talk, usually on music or art, and then goes home.

Then there's one that meets at lunch, every second Thursday and every third Tuesday, quite informally, just eats a tiny beefsteak with a nice dish of apple pie after it and listens to a speech on national affairs, excluding of course all reference to political parties or politics, or public opinion, and all references to actual individuals or actual facts.

After that there's a club, mostly of older women, which meets at three (without refreshments till after) and discusses social problems such as how to keep younger women in hand. This club meets every first Monday in the month unless it falls at the beginning of a week.

But the club that has most interested me recently is the Ladies' Culture Club, because I had the honour of being invited to one of its meetings. The Club was founded two winters ago – as was explained to me over the ice-cream by the president – with the idea that it is a pity that women know so little of science and that nowadays science is really becoming a quite important thing, and when you think of radio and electrons and atoms and things like that one ought to know at least something about them for fear of your feeling ignorant.

So when the club was founded it was made absolutely and exclusively a women's club, men taking no part in it whatever, except that men are invited to be the speakers and to sit on the platform and to attend the meetings.

The day I was there the meeting was held in the ballroom of the new Grand Palaver Hotel, because that is a simple place suitable for science. There were no decorations except flowers, and no music except a Hungarian orchestra, which stopped the moment the lecture began. This is a rule of the club.

The attendance was so large that several of the ladies remarked with pride that it would hardly have been possible to get an equal number of men to come at three o'clock in the afternoon to listen to a lecture on Four-Dimensional Space.

The great mass of members were seated in chairs on the floor of the ballroom with a certain number of men here and there, among them; but they were a peculiar kind of men. The president and a group of ladies were on a raised platform, and they had in the middle of them Professor Droon who was to lecture on four-dimensional space. In front of him they had put a little table with a glass and water, enough water to last a camel for a four days' trip. Behind Professor Droon was a barricade of chairs and plants with spikes. He couldn't escape.

The president rose and made the regulation announcement that there were a good many members who had not yet paid their fees this season and it was desirable that they should do so owing to the high cost of bringing lecturers to the club.

She then picked up a piece of paper and read from it as follows:

'The Pythagorean philosophers as well as Philolaus and Hicetus of Syracuse conceived of space as immaterial. The Alexandrine geometers substituted a conception of rigid co-ordinates which has dominated all scientific thinking until our own day. I will now introduce Professor Droon, who will address the members on four-dimensional space if the ladies near the doorway will kindly occupy the chairs which are still empty at the front.'

Professor Droon, rising behind the water jug, requested the audience in a low voice to dismiss from their minds all preconceived notions of the spatial content of the universe. When they had done this, he asked them in a whisper to disregard the familiar postulate in regard to parallel lines. Indeed it would be far better, he murmured, if they dismissed all thought of lines as such and substituted the idea of motion through a series of loci conceived as instantaneous in time.

After this he drank half the water and started. In the address which followed and which lasted for one hour and forty minutes, it was clear that the audience were held in rapt attention. They never removed their eyes from the lecturer's face and remained soundless except that there was a certain amount of interested whispering each time he drank water.

When he mentioned that Euclid, the geometrician, was married four times there were distinct signs of amusement. There was a sigh of commiseration when he said that Archimedes was killed by a Roman soldier just as he was solving a problem in mechanics. And when he mentioned the name of Christopher Columbus there was obvious and general satisfaction.

In fact, the audience followed the lecture word for word. And when at length the professor asked in a whisper whether we could any longer maintain the conception of a discrete universe absolute in time and drank the rest of the water and sat down, the audience knew that it was the end of the lecture and there was a distinct wave of applause.

The comments of the audience as they flowed out of the hall showed how interested they had been. I heard one lady remark that Professor Droon had what she would call a sympathetic face; another said, yes, except that his ears stuck out too far.

Another said that she had heard that he was a very difficult man to live with; and another said that she imagined that all scientists must be because she had a friend who knew a lady who had lived in the same house all one winter with the Marconis and very often Marconi wouldn't eat. There was a good deal of comment on the way the professor's tie was up near his ear and a general feeling that he probably needed looking after.

There was a notice at the door where we went out which said that the next lecture would be by Professor Floyd of the college department of botany on the Morphology of Gymnasperms. They say there will be a big attendance again.

Fourteen
Old Junk and New Money

A LITTLE STUDY IN THE LATEST ANTIQUES

I went the other day into the beautiful home of my two good friends, the Hespeler-Hyphen-Jones, and I paused a moment, as my eye fell on the tall clock that stood in the hall.

'Ah,' said Hespeler-Hyphen-Jones, 'I see you are looking at the clock – a beautiful thing, isn't it, a genuine antique?'

'Does it go?' I asked.

'Good gracious, no!' exclaimed my two friends. 'But isn't it a beautiful thing!'

'Did it ever go?'

'I doubt it,' said Hespeler-Hyphen-Jones. 'The works, of course, are by Salvolatile – one of the really *great* clockmakers, you know. But I don't know whether the works ever went. That, I believe, is one way in which you can always tell a Salvolatile. If it's a genuine Salvolatile, it won't go.'

'In any case,' I said, 'it has no hands.'

'Oh dear, no,' said Mrs Jones. 'It never had, as far as we know. We picked it up in such a queer little shop in Amalfi and the man assured us that it never had had any hands. He guaranteed it. That's one of the things, you know, that you can tell by. Charles and I were terribly keen about clocks at that time and really studied them, and the books all agreed that no genuine Salvolatile has any hands.'

'And was the side broken, too, when you got it?' I asked.

'Ah, no,' said my friend. 'We had that done by an expert in New York after we got back. Isn't it exquisitely done? You see, he has made the break to look exactly as if someone has rolled the clock over and stamped on it. Every genuine Salvolatile is said to have been stamped upon like that.'

'Of course our break is only imitation, but it's extremely well done, isn't it? We go to Ferrugi's, that little place on Fourth Avenue, you know, for everything that we want broken. They have a splendid man there. He can break anything.'

'Really!' I said.

'Yes, and the day when we wanted the clock done Charles and I went down to see him do it. It was really quite wonderful, wasn't it, Charles?'

'Yes, indeed. The man laid the clock on the floor and turned it on its side and then stood looking at it intently, and walking round and round it and murmuring in Italian as if he were swearing at it. Then he jumped in the air and came down on it with both feet.'

'Did he?' I asked.

'Yes, and with such wonderful accuracy. Our friend Mr Appin-Hyphen-Smith – the great expert, you know – was looking at our clock last week and he said it was marvellous, hardly to be distinguished from a genuine *fractura.*'

'But he did say, didn't he, dear,' said Mrs Jones, 'that the better way is to throw a clock out of a fourth-story window? You see, that was the height of the Italian houses in the thirteenth century – is it the thirteenth century I mean, Charles?'

'Yes,' said Charles.

'Do you know, the other day I made the silliest mistake about a spoon. I thought it was a twelfth-century spoon and said so and in reality it was only eleven and a half. Wasn't it, Charles?'

'Yes,' said Charles.

'But do come into the drawing-room and have some tea. And, by the way, since you are interested in antiques, do look please at my teapot.'

'It looks an excellent teapot,' I said, feeling it with my hand, 'and it must have been very expensive, wasn't it?'

'Oh, not *that* one,' interposed Mr Hespeler-Hyphen-Jones. 'That is nothing. We got that here in New York at Hoffany's – to make tea in. It *is* made of solid silver, of course, and all that, but even Hoffany's admitted that it was made in America and was probably not more than a year or so old and had never been used by anybody else. In fact, they couldn't guarantee it in any way.'

'Oh, I see,' I said.

'But let me pour you out tea from it and then do look at the perfect darling beside it. Oh, don't touch it please, it won't stand up.'

'Won't stand up?' I said.

'No,' said Hespeler-Jones, 'that's one of the tests. We know from that that it is a genuine Swaatsmaacher. None of them stand up.'

'Where did you buy it,' I asked, 'here?'

'Oh, heavens, no, you couldn't buy a thing like that here! As a matter of fact, we picked it up in a little gin shop in Obehellandam in Holland. Do you know Obehellandam?'

'I don't,' I said.

'It's just the dearest little place, nothing but little, wee, smelly shops filled with most delightful things – all antique, everything broken. They guarantee that there is nothing in the shop that wasn't smashed at least a hundred years ago.'

'You don't use the teapot to make tea,' I said.

'Oh, no,' said Mrs Hespeler-Hyphen-Jones as she handed me a cup of tea from the New York teapot. 'I don't think you could. It leaks.'

'That again is a thing,' said her husband, 'that the experts always look for in a Swaatsmaacher. If it doesn't leak, it's probably just a faked-up thing not twenty years old.'

'Is it silver?' I asked.

'Ah, no. That's another test,' said Mrs Jones. 'The real Swaatsmaachers were always made of pewter bound with barrel iron off the gin barrels. They try to imitate it now by using silver, but they can't get it.'

'No, the silver won't take the tarnish,' interjected her husband. 'You see it's the same way with ever so many of the old things. They rust and rot in a way that you simply cannot imitate. I have an old drinking horn that I'll show you presently – ninth century, isn't it, dear? – that is all coated inside with the most beautiful green slime, absolutely impossible to reproduce.'

'Is it?'

'Yes, I took it to Squeeziou's, the Italian place in London – they are the great experts on horns, you know; they can tell exactly the century and the breed of cow – and they told me that they had tried in vain to reproduce that peculiar and beautiful rot. One of their head men said that he thought that this horn had probably been taken from a dead cow that had been buried for fifty years. That's what gives it its value, you know.'

'You didn't buy it in London, did you?' I asked.

'Oh, no,' answered Hespeler-Hyphen-Jones. 'London is perfectly impossible – just as hopeless as New York. You can't buy anything real there at all.'

'Then where do you get all your things?' I asked, as I looked round at the collection of junk in the room.

'Oh, we pick them up here and there,' said Mrs Jones. 'Just in any out-of-the-way corners. That little stool we found at the back of a cow stable in Loch Aberlocherty. They were actually using it for milking. And the two others – aren't they beautiful? though really it's quite wrong to have two chairs alike in the same room – came from the back of a tiny little whisky shop in Galway. Such a delight of an old Irishman sold them to us and he admitted that he himself had no idea how old they were. They might, he said, be fifteenth century, or they might not.

'But, oh, Charles,' my hostess interrupted herself to say, 'I've just had a letter from Jane (Jane is my sister, you know) that is terribly exciting. She's found a table at a tiny place in Brittany that she thinks would exactly do in our card room. She says that it is utterly unlike anything else in the room and has quite obviously no connection with cards. But let me read what she says – let me see, yes, here's where it begins:

' "... a perfectly sweet little table. It probably had four legs originally and even now has two which, I am told, is a great find, as most people have to be content with one. The man explained that it could either be leaned up against the wall or else suspended from the ceiling on a silver chain. One of the boards of the top is gone, but I am told that that is of no consequence, as all the best specimens of Brittany tables have at least one board out." '

'Doesn't that sound fascinating, Charles? Do send Jane a cable at once not to miss it.'

* * *

And when I took my leave a little later, I realized once and for all that the antique business is not for me.

How to Borrow Money

THE PROCESS IS QUITE EASY, PROVIDED YOU BORROW ENOUGH

Have you ever, my dear readers, had occasion to borrow money? Have you ever borrowed ten dollars under a rigorous promise of your word of honour as a Christian to pay it back on your next salary day? Have you ever borrowed as much as a million at a time?

If you have done these things, you cannot have failed to notice how much easier it is to borrow ten thousand dollars than ten, how much easier still to borrow a hundred thousand, and that when you come at last to raising an international loan of a hundred million the thing loses all difficulty.

Here below are the little things that take place on the occasion of an ascending series of loans.

TABLEAU NO. I

The scene in which Hardup Jones borrows ten dollars till the first of next month from his friend, Canny Smith

'Say, look here, old man, I was wondering whether perhaps you wouldn't mind letting me have ten dollars till the end of the month –'

'Ten dollars!!'

'Oh, I could give it back all right, for dead sure, just the minute I get my salary.'

'Ten dollars!!!'

'You see, I've got into an awful tangle – I owe seven and a half on my board, and she said yesterday she'd have to have it. I couldn't pay my laundry last week, so he said he wouldn't leave it, and I got this cursed suit on the instalment plan and they said they'd seize my trunk, and –'

'Say, but Gol darn it, I lent you five dollars, don't you remember, last November, and you swore you'd pay it back on the first and I never got it till away after New Year's –'

'I know, I know. But this is absolutely sure. So help me, I'll pay it right on the first, the minute I get my cheque.'

'Yes, but you won't –'

'No, I swear I will –'

And after about half an hour of expostulations and protests of this sort, having pledged his soul, his body, and his honour, the borrower at last gets his ten dollars.

TABLEAU NO. II

The scene in which Mr McDuff of the McDuff Hardware Store in Central City (pop. 3,862) borrows $1,000 from the local bank

The second degree in borrowing is represented by this scene in which Mr John McDuff, of McDuff Bros. Hardware Store (Everything in Hardware), calls on the local bank manager with a view to getting $1,000 to carry the business forward for one month till the farmers' spring payments begin to come in.

Mr McDuff is told by one of the (two) juniors in the bank to wait – the manager is engaged for the moment.

The manager in reality is in his inner office, sorting out trout flies. But he knows what McDuff wants and he means to make him wait for it and suffer for it.

When at last McDuff does get in, the manager is very cold and formal.

'Sit down, Mr McDuff,' he says.

When they go fishing together, the manager always calls McDuff 'John.' But this is different. McDuff is here to borrow money. And borrowing money in Central City is a criminal act.

'I came in about that loan,' says McDuff.

The manager looks into a ledger.

'You're overdrawn $17.00 right now,' he says.

'I know, but I'll be getting my accounts in any time after the first.'

Then follows a string of severe questions. What are McDuff's daily receipts? What is his overhead? What is his underfoot? Is he a church-goer? Does he believe in a future life?

And at last even when the manager finally consents to lend the thousand dollars (he always meant to do it), he begins tagging on conditions:

'You'll have to get your partner to sign.'

'All right.'

'And you'd better get your wife to sign.'

'All right.'

'And your mother, she might as well sign too –'

There are more signatures on a county bank note for one month than on a Locarno treaty.

And at last McDuff, of Everything in Hardware, having pledged his receipts, his premises, his credit, his honour, his wife, and his mother – gets away with the thousand dollars.

TABLEAU NO. III

How Mr P. Q. Pingpoint, of the great financial House of Pingpoint, Pingpong and Company, New York and London, borrows a million dollars before lunch

Here the scene is laid in a fitting setting. Mr Pingpoint is shown into the sumptuous head office of the president of the First National Bank.

'Ah, good morning,' says the president as he rises to greet Mr Pingpoint, 'I was expecting you. Our general manager told me that you were going to be good enough to call in. Won't you take this larger chair – you'll find it easier?'

'Ah, thank you. You're very comfortable here.'

'Yes, we rather think this a pleasant room. And our board-room, we think, is even better. Won't you let me show you our board-room?'

'Oh, thanks, I'm afraid I hardly have the time. I just came in for a minute to complete our loan of a million dollars.'

'Yes, our executive vice-president said that you are good enough to come to us. It is very kind of you, I'm sure.'

'Oh, not at all.'

'And you are quite sure that a million is all that you care to take? We shall be delighted, you know, if you will take a million and a half.'

'Oh, scarcely. A million, I think, will be ample just now; we can come back, of course, if we want more.'

'Oh, certainly, certainly.'

'And do you want us to give any security, or anything of that sort?'

'Oh no, quite unnecessary.'

'And is there anything you want me to sign while I am here?'

'Oh no, nothing, the clerks will attend to all that.'

'Well, thanks, then, I needn't keep you any longer.'

'But won't you let me drive you up-town? My car is just outside. Or, better still, if you are free, won't you come and eat some lunch with me at the club?'

'Well, thanks, yes, you're really extremely kind.'

And with this, quite painlessly and easily, the million dollars has changed hands.

But even that is not the last degree. Eclipsing that sort of thing, both in ease and in splendour, is the international loan, as seen in –

TABLEAU NO. IV

The scenes which accompany the flotation of an Anglo-French loan, in the American market, of a hundred million dollars, by the Right Hon. Samuel Rothstein of England and the Vicomte Baton Rouge de Chauve Souris of France

This occurrence is best followed as it appears in its triumphant progress in the American press.

NEW YORK, *Friday*. – An enthusiastic reception was given yesterday to the Right Hon. Mr Samuel Rothstein, of the British Cabinet, and to the Vicomte de Chauve Souris, French plenipotentiary, on their landing from the Stacquitania. It is understood that they will borrow $100,000,000. The distinguished visitors expect to stay only a few days.

NEW YORK, *Saturday*. – An elaborate reception was given last evening in the home of Mrs Bildermont to the Right Hon. Samuel Rothstein and the Baron de Chauve Souris. It is understood that they are borrowing a hundred million dollars.

NEW YORK, *Monday*. – The Baron de Chauve Souris and the Right Hon. Samuel Rothstein were notable figures in the Fifth Avenue church parade yesterday. It is understood that they will borrow a hundred million dollars.

NEW YORK, *Tuesday*. – The Baron de Chauve Souris and the Right Hon. Samuel Rothstein attended a baseball game at the Polo Grounds. It is understood that they will borrow a hundred million dollars.

NEW YORK, *Wednesday*. – At a ball given by Mr and Mrs Ashcoop-Vandermore for the distinguished English and French plenipotentiaries, Mr Samuel Rothstein and the Baron de Chauve Souris, it was definitely stated that the loan which they are financing will be limited to a hundred million dollars.

NEW YORK (WALL STREET), *Thursday*. – The loan of $100,000,000 was subscribed this morning at eleven o'clock in five minutes. The Right Hon. Mr Rothstein and the Baron Baton Rouge de Chauve Souris left America at twelve noon, taking the money with them. Both plenipotentiaries expressed their delight with America.

'It is,' said the Baron – 'how do you call it? – a cinch.'

EPILOGUE

And yet, six months later, what had happened? Who paid and who didn't?

Hardup Jones paid $5.40 within a month, $3.00 the next month and the remaining one dollar and sixty cents two weeks later.

McDuff Bros met their note and went fishing with the manager like old friends.

The Pingpoint Syndicate blew up and failed for ten million dollars.

And the international loan got mixed up with a lot of others, was funded, equated, spread out over fifty years, capitalized, funded again – in short, it passed beyond all recognition.

And, the moral is, when you borrow, borrow a whole lot.

Save Me from My Friends

THE REPORTER

He came up to me on the platform just after I had finished giving my address, his notebook open in his hand.

'Would you mind,' he said, 'just telling me the main points of your speech? I didn't get to hear it.'

'You weren't at the lecture?'

'No,' he answered, pausing to sharpen his pencil, 'I was at the hockey game.'

'Reporting it?'

'No, I don't report that sort of thing. I only do the lectures and the highbrow stuff. Say, it was a great game. What did you say the lecture was about?'

'It was called "The Triumphal Progress of Science".'

'On science, eh?' he said, writing rapidly as he spoke.

'Yes,' I answered, 'on science.'

He paused.

'How do you spell "triumphal",' he asked; 'is it a PH or an F?'

I told him.

'And now,' he went on, 'what was the principal idea, just the main thing, don't you know, of your address?'

'I was speaking of our advanced knowledge of radiating emanations and the light it throws on the theory of atomic structure.'

'Wait a minute,' he said, 'till I get that. Is it r–a–d–i–a–t–i–n–g? . . . the light it throws, eh? . . . good . . . I guess I got that.'

He prepared to shut his little book.

'Have you ever been here before?'

'No,' I said, 'it's my first time.'

'Are you staying in the new hotel?'

'Yes.'

'How do you like it?'

'It's very comfortable,' I said.

He reopened his book and scribbled fast.

'Did you see the big new abattoir they are putting in?'

'No,' I said, 'I didn't hear of it.'

'It's the third biggest north of Philadelphia. What do you think of it?'

'I didn't see it,' I said.

He wrote a little and then paused.

'What do you think,' he asked, 'of this big mix-up in the city council?'

'I didn't hear of it,' I said.

'Do you think that the aldermen are crooked?'

'I don't know anything about these aldermen,' I said.

'No,' he answered, 'perhaps not, but wouldn't you think it likely that they'd be crooked?'

'They often are crooked enough,' I admitted; 'in fact, very often a pack of bums.'

'Eh, what's that, a pack of bums? That's good, that's great' – he was all enthusiasm now – 'that's the kind of stuff, you know, that our paper likes to get. You see, so often you go and take a lecture and there's nothing said at all – nothing like that, don't you see? And there's no way to make anything out of it . . . But with this I can feature it up fine. "A pack of bums!" Good. Do you suppose they took a pretty big graft out of building the abattoir?'

'I'm afraid,' I said, 'that I don't know anything about it.'

'But say,' he pleaded, 'you'd think it likely that they did?'

'No, no,' I repeated, 'I don't know anything about it.'

'All right,' he said reluctantly, 'I guess I'll have to leave that out. Well, much obliged. I hope you come again. Good night.'

And the next morning as I was borne away from that city in the train I read his report in the paper, headed with appropriate capitals and sub-headings:

THINKS ALDERMEN PACK OF BUMS
Distinguished Lecturer Talks on Christian Science

'The distinguished visitor,' so ran his report, 'gave an interesting talk on Christian Science in the auditorium of the Y.M.C.A. before a capacity audience. He said that we were living in an age of radio and that in his opinion the aldermen of the city were a pack of bums. The lecturer discussed very fully the structure of anatomy which he said had emanated out of radio. He expressed his desire to hazard no opinion about the question of graft in regard to the new abattoir which he considers the finest that he has seen at any of his lectures. The address, which was freely punctuated with applause, was followed with keen attention, and the wish was freely expressed at the close that the lecturer might give it in other cities.'

There! That's the way he does it, as all of us who deal with him are only too well aware.

And am I resentful? I should say not. Didn't he say that there was a 'capacity audience' when really there were only sixty-eight people; didn't he 'punctuate the lecture with applause,' and animate it with 'keen attention'? What more can a lecturer want? And as to the aldermen and the graft and the heading, that's our fault, not his. We want that sort of thing in our morning paper, and he gives it to us.

And with it, as his own share, a broad and kindly human indifference that never means to offend.

Let him trudge off into the night with his little book and pencil and his uncomplaining industry and take my blessing with him.

The Old Men's Page

A BRAND-NEW FEATURE IN JOURNALISM

I observe that nowadays far too much of the space in the newspapers is given up to children and young people. Open almost any paper, published in any British or American city, and you may find a children's page and a girls' page and a women's page – special columns for tiny tots, poetry by highschool girls, notes for boy scouts, fashion notes for young women, and radio hints for young men.

This thing is going too far – unless the old men get a chance. What the newspapers need now is a special page for old men. I am certain that it would make an enormous hit at once.

Let me try to put together a few samples of what ought to go on such a page. My talented readers can carry it on for themselves.

NOTES FOR OLD MEN SCOUTS

A general field meeting of the (newly established) Old Men Scouts will be held next Saturday. The scouts will assemble at the edge of the pine woods about seven miles out of town. Every scout will tell his chauffeur to have the car ready for an early start, not later than 10.30. The scout will see that the chauffeur brings a full kit of cooking utensils and supplies. A good chauffeur can easily carry 150 pounds and the scout will see that he does it.

Each scout is to have a heavy greatcoat and a thick rug and folding camp-chair strapped together in a bundle and will see to it personally that these are loaded on the chauffeur.

Each scout, in advancing into the woods, will carry his own walking stick and will smoke his own cigar.

In passing through the woods, the scout is expected to recognize any trees that he knows, such as pine trees, lilac trees, rubber trees, and so forth. If in any doubt of the nature or species of a tree, the scout may tell the chauffeur to climb it and see what it is.

The scouts will also recognise and remark any species or genera of birds that are sitting on the path which are familiar to them, such as tame canaries, parrots, partridges, cooked snipe, and spring chicken.

Having arrived at an open glade, the scouts will sit about on their camp-chairs, avoiding the damp, while the chauffeurs kindle a fire and prepare lunch. During this time the Scout Master, and other scouts in order of seniority, may relate stories of woodcraft, or, if they can't think of any stories of woodcraft, they may tell any other kind that they know.

As exercise before lunch, the scouts may open the soda-water bottles.

After lunch, each scout will place his rug and cushion under a suitable tree and smoke a cigar while listening in silence for any especial calls and wood notes of birds, bees and insects, such as cicada, the rickshaw, the gin-ricki, and others that he has learned to know. Should he see any insect whose call is not familiar to him, he should crawl after it and listen to it, or if he prefers, tell his chauffeur to follow it up.

At five p.m. the scouts should reload the chauffeurs and themselves, and, when all are well loaded, drive to any country club for more stories of woodcraft.

* * *

Every old man – being really just a boy in a disguised form – is naturally interested in how to make things. One column in the old men's page therefore ought to contain something in the way of

HINTS ON MECHANICS

CARPENTRY FOR OLD MEN

How to Make a Rustic Table. – Get hold of any hard-working rustic and tell him to make a table.

How to Make a Camera Stand. – Put it right on the table. It will stand.

How to Tell the Time by the Sun. – First look at your watch and see what time it is. Then step out into the sunlight with your face towards the sun and hold the watch so that the hour hand points directly at the sun. This will be the time.

How to Make a Book-case. – Call up any wood factory on the telephone and tell them to cut you some plain boards, suitable for making a book-case. Ask them next where you can get nails. Then send your chauffeur to bring the boards and nails. Then advertise for a carpenter.

To stain your table, when it is complete, a good method is to upset soda water on it.

* * *

No column of the sort which I am here proposing would be complete unless it contained some sort of correspondence. And here the topic that is opportune and welcome to the old as well as the young is the eternal subject of love. But it must be treated in a way to suit it to those whose hearts have passed the first mad impulses of unrestrained youth.

PROBLEMS OF LOVE AND MARRIAGE

Mr Elder, Bachelor's Court, Lone Street.

I can quite understand your dilemma in regard to your cook. It is one that many a bachelor has had to face and to think out for himself, and I am sure that you will face it bravely and clearly.

You say that you do not know whether your cook loves you or not, and I gather that you do not give a hoot either way. But the point is that she has an excellent offer to be cook in an Old Man's Home and you are likely to lose her. Your problem is whether to let her go and try to get another, or to marry her, or to move into the Home where she is going to cook.

Mr Oldspark, Evergreen Alley, Blossom Street.

It is very difficult indeed to advise you, especially as you are at an age (you tell me you are only 61) when your heart is apt to run away with you. You say that three young girls all want to marry you. You have been letting one of them drive you out in her car and she has a certain right to think you have given her encouragement.

On the other hand, one of the others has taken you to the matinee. In the case of the third, though you do not know her so well, you were told by someone at the golf club that she had said that you were 'a perfect darling'.

You say that you are very fond of all three, but that you cannot tell whether what you feel is really love. It may be indigestion.

Mr O. O. Overslow, Linger Lodge.

Your case is one in which it is difficult for an outsider to give advice. You say that you have been paying attentions to a lady, of about your own age, for a little over thirty years. You have taken her to evening church service each third Sunday for some years back, and you have, for nearly ten years now, sent her an Easter card and an April-fool card. Her father, who is ninety-six, is distinctly favourable to your suit, but, as he has lost most of his faculties, he may not know one suit from another.

You rightly feel that you ought to be cautious and not act hastily. You have fifteen thousand a year of your own, but you hate to part with any of it.

Your problem is, should you propose to her, or wait a little? My advice is by all means wait – keep on waiting – wait till her father is dead, and her mother is dead, and you are half dead – and then propose to her and wonder why you have spent your life waiting.

Don't you remember – look back over thirty years and try to remember – that evening long ago when you stood with her on the bridge over the little river in the dusk of a summer evening, and so nearly, oh, so nearly, proposed to her? But you waited. You had only a thousand dollars a year then, so you waited.

And don't you remember, five years later on, that winter evening by the fireside when you were left alone with her for ten minutes, and again the words almost came to your lips. But you had only three thousand a year then, and you waited.

Oh, yes, my dear old friend, by all means keep on waiting. It is all that you are fit for.

J.J.X. – No, we don't lend money to old men through this column.

Fifteen
My Victorian Girlhood

BY LADY NEARLEIGH SLOPOVER

The life we led at Gloops – Gloops was my father's seat – had all the charm and quiet and order which went with life in my young days. My dear Papa (he was the eleventh Baron Gloops) was most strict in his household. As a nobleman of the old school, he believed fully in the maxim *noblesse oblige*. He always insisted on the servants assembling for prayers at eight every morning. Indeed his first question to his own man when he brought up his brandy and soda at ten was whether the servants had been at prayers at eight.

My dear Mama, too, always seemed to fulfil my idea of what a *grande dame* should be. She fully understood the routine of a great house like Gloops, and had a wonderful knowledge, not only of the kitchen, but of all sorts of draughts, simples and samples and the use of herbs. If any of the maids were ill, Mama never called a doctor but herself mixed up a draught from roots that would have the girl on her feet in half an hour.

Nor did she disdain to do things herself, especially in an emergency. Once when Papa was taken faint in the drawing-room, Mama herself rang the bell for an egg, told the butler to hand her a glass and a decanter and herself broke the egg into the glass with her own hands. Papa revived at the sight of her presence of mind and himself reached for the brandy.

To myself and my younger sister Lucy, Papa and Mama were ideal parents. Never a day passed but Papa would either come up to our nursery himself and chat with our governess Mademoiselle Fromage – she was one of the De Bries – or would at least send up his own man to ask how we were. Even as quite little girls Papa could tell us apart without difficulty.

Mama too was devoted to us, and would let us come down to her boudoir and see her all dressed to go out to dinner, or let us come and speak to her when she was ready to drive in the phaeton; and once when Lucy was ill Mama sent her own maid to sleep in Lucy's room, in spite of the infection.

Gloops was on the border of Lincolnshire. All of Papa's tenants and cottagers spoke with the beautiful old broad accent of the fen country and said 'yowp' for 'yes', and 'nowp' for 'no', and 'thowp' for 'thou', and 'sowp' for 'soup'. It seems so musical. It is a pity it is dying out.

Papa was a model landlord. The tenantry were never evicted unless they failed to pay their rent, and when the cottages fell down Papa had them propped up again. Once a year Papa gave a great ball for the tenantry on his estate, and our friends used to drive long distances to be there, and the great hall was cleared for dancing, for the gentry, and the tenantry danced in the great barn. Papa gave each of them a bun and an orange and a prayer book for each child. The working class was happier, I think, in those days.

Papa was not only democratic in that way with his tenantry but also with the people of the neighbourhood and of the village, though none of them were gentlemen. Quite often he would bring Dr McGregor, the doctor of the village, to dine at Gloops, I mean if no one else was there. Dr McGregor had taken a very high degree at Edinburgh, but was not a gentleman. He had travelled a great deal and had been decorated by the King of France for some wonderful medical work for the French armies in Algeria, so it was a pity that he wasn't a gentleman: especially as you couldn't tell that he wasn't if no one said so.

Isolated as Gloops was, many great people drove down from London to see us, on account of Papa's position in the Lords. Indeed the most wonderful thing about our life as children at Gloops was the visit every now and then of one of these great and distinguished people whose names are now history. How well one remembers them – such old-world manners and courtesy! I recall how Lucy and I were brought into the drawing-room to shake hands with dear old Lord Melrush, the Prime Minister – always so pleasant and jolly. I remember Mama said, 'These are my two little girls' – and Lord Melrush laughed and said, 'Well, thank God, they don't look like their father, eh?' Which was really quite clever of him, because we didn't. And I remember old Field-Marshal Lord Stickett, perhaps England's greatest strategist – they called him Wellington's right-hand man – he'd lost his left arm. I can still see him standing on the hearth-rug saying, 'Your two little girls, ma'am: well, I don't think much of them!' He was always like that, concise and abrupt.

I liked much better Admiral Rainbow, who had been one of Nelson's captains and had a black patch over his eye where someone hit him in the face at Trafalgar. I was quite a growing girl when he came, fourteen at least, and he said 'By Gad! Madam, shiver my spankers, but here's a gal for you! Look at the stern run under her counter!'

Another great thing in the life at Gloops was when I got old enough to dine with Mama and Papa and their guests. Such dinners were a wonderful education. I was taken into dinner once by Lord Glower, the great archaeologist. He hardly spoke. I asked him if he thought the Pyramids were built by the Hittites. He said he didn't know.

We used to dine in the old wainscoted dining-hall – it was a marvellous room, dating from Richard III, with the panels all worm-eaten almost to pieces. Papa was offered huge sums for them. It had some grand old paintings – one a Vandyke, so blackened you couldn't possibly tell what it was, especially as most of the paint had fallen off: Papa later on presented it to the Nation – the year the Prime Minister voted him the Garter – refusing any pay for it, though the Prime Minister made him accept a thousand guineas as a *solatium*. Papa fetched down another Vandyke from the storeroom.

By the time I was eighteen I think I may claim to have grown to be a very handsome girl and certainly, as everybody said, very artistocratic-looking. I was several times compared with the Princess Eulalie of Schlatz and once with the Grand Duchess Marianna Maria of Swig-Pisener. Dear old Dr Glowworm, our Vicar, who was so old that he remembered the French Revolution, said that if I had lived then, I would certainly have been guillotined, or at least shut up.

But presently there came into my life, a little earlier than that – I was eighteen – the greatest event of all, when I first met Alfred, my dear husband that was to be. It was at a great dinner party that Papa gave at Gloops, given for Sir John Overdraft, the head of the new bank that had just made Papa a director. Sir John was the head of the bank and had been knighted, but the strange thing was that he was really nobody. I mean he had made a great fortune in the City and had huge influence in finance, but he wasn't anybody. And, what was more, everybody knew that he was nobody. Papa made no secret of it. I remember hearing old Lord Tweedlepip, our neighbour, in the drawing-room before dinner ask Papa who Sir John was and Papa said, 'As far as I know, he isn't anybody.' But in meeting with him Papa was courtesy itself: indeed he often explained to us children that even though prominent people – writers, painters, sculptors, for instance – were often nobody, we sould treat them in society as if they were like ourselves.

It was such a large party that I can hardly remember all the people, especially as it was my first real dinner party: I was out, but hadn't yet been presented. But there was one man there I especially noticed, although he was not only nobody but was an American. He was the first I think I ever saw, though now of course you meet them anywhere, and many of them such cultivated people that you can hardly tell them. But this man, the first American I saw, seemed different from the men around him, more hard and dangerous, and yet pleasant enough, but no manners.

I couldn't even be sure of his name because Papa and Sir John, who both seemed to know him well, kept calling him different things like 'Old Fortyfour Calibre,' and 'Old Ten-spot.' His family seat was called Colorado and I gathered that he owned gold mines. I gathered all this because I happened to be near the library door, a little before dinner when Papa and Sir John and Mr Derringer – that perhaps was his real name – were all talking together. Mr Derringer wanted to give Papa an enormous part of a gold mine and then Papa was to pass it on to Sir John and the new bank was to pass it over to the public. It all seemed very generous. I heard Mr Derringer say to Papa, laughing, 'Gloops, if we had you in the States you would be sent to Sing-Sing in six months.' Sing-Sing it seems was a new place they had just started in America. It corresponds, Mama said, to our House of Commons. Mr Derringer laughed when he said that Papa could get in, but I am sure he meant it.

But I am leaving out, in a feminine way, I fear, the great thing of the evening which was that it was dear Alfred, my later husband, who took me in to dinner. So wonderful he looked, over six feet high and as straight as a piece of wood, with beautiful brown hair and those handsome high side whiskers, the French call them *côtelette de mouton*, which were worn then. I had never seen him before and all that I knew of him was that his name was the Hon. Alfred Cyril Nancie Slopover, eldest son of the tenth Marquis of Slopover and Bath, and that his people were West Country people, but very old and very good. His mother was a Dudd, which made her a first cousin of Lord Havengotteny.

Alfred, I say, took me in. We hardly spoke at dinner, because I think I was shy, and at any rate at our end of the table Mr Derringer was telling Mama wonderful stories about hunting the wild papooses in Colorado, which must be fascinating, and how the Cactus Indians pursue the buffalo with affidavits, and we were all listening. But Alfred, though he never talked much, had that firm incisive way of saying things, just in a word, that sounds so final. For instance, after dinner when the men came into the drawing room for tea, I said to Alfred, 'Shall we go into the conservatory?' And he said, 'Let's.' And I said, 'Shall we sit among the begonias?' and he said, 'Rather!' and after a time I said, 'Shall we go back to the drawing-room?' and he said, 'Ah!' When we got back to the drawing-room, Mr Derringer was still telling Mama of his wonderful adventures – indeed they were all listening.

It made me realize what a vast country America is. In fact I have always felt, and still feel, that some day it will have a great future. But that evening I could hardly listen to Mr Derringer because my heart was beating so with happiness, as I felt certain that Alfred had fallen in love with me. He looked so noble, sitting there listening to Mr Derringer, with his mouth half open, seeming to drink it all in. Now and again he would make such intelligent comments as when Mr Derringer told about the easy social life in the West, and the lynching parties, and of how they invite even the negroes to them. And Alfred said, 'Do they really!' He seemed that evening, in fact he always has seemed, so typically British, so willing to be informed.

Everybody was so loud in praise of Alfred next day. Tiptoeing round the house, because I did not think it dishonourable, I was able to hear such a lot of complimentary things about him. Mr Derringer, who used a lot of those fascinating American expressions, taken from their machinery, called him a 'complete nut', and Lord John, who is so brusque and quick himself that he admires Alfred's dreamy, poetical nature, said he seemed 'only half there'. But think of my delight when a day or two later Alfred sent Mama a beautiful bouquet of roses from Slops, his father's seat, and then a basket of hothouse grapes, and then, for Papa, a large fish, a salmon. Two weeks after that he wrote and definitely proposed to Papa, and Papa went up to London and saw the solicitors and accepted Alfred. It all seemed so romantic and wonderful, and then Alfred came over for a blissful week at Gloops as my betrothed, which meant that we could walk in the grounds together by ourselves, and that even in the drawing-room Mama would sit at the other end of the room and pretend not to see us.

Of course Love always has its ups and downs and never runs smooth: I remember that there was a dreadful quarrel with my sister Lucy who said that Alfred was ignorant and didn't *know* anything: and I said why should he? What did a man like Alfred need to know? It seemed so silly. I remember I often thought of it later on when Lucy made her own unhappy marriage.

Then for a little while there was a little trouble about my dowry, or jointure. Papa at first offered five thousand pounds and Alfred refused it flat. He said he ought to have at least ten thousand. It seemed so romantic to be quarrelled over like that, as a sort of gage of battle. Alfred was so firm: even when Papa raised from pounds to guineas he held out. So at last Papa gave way completely, and not only gave way, but went generously further and gave Alfred twelve thousand pounds, all to be paid in shares in Mr Derringer's gold mine. Papa explained that they were called 'preferred' shares, which made them very desirable. He said that if Alfred and I kept them long enough there was no telling what they would be worth. So Alfred was delighted at his victory over Papa, especially as Sir John always said that Papa could have been a financier and Mr Derringer had said he could have got into Sing-Sing.

I remember that Papa, in the same generous fit, gave away a lot of the same gold shares, practically all he had, to various people, to Alfred's father, Lord Slopover, to old Lord Tweedlepip, our neighbour, and others, for next to nothing or at least nothing like their real value.

Then came the happy day when Alfred and I were married in the little church at Gloops, by old Dr Glowworm. Everybody was there, and all the tenantry and cottagers in a long line outside the church, for Alfred and me to walk through; and Papa gave a grand fête for the tenantry on the lawn with beer to drink our health in and an orange and bun for each of the children, and work-box for each grown-up girl, a work-basket each for the old women, and for each young boy a book called *Work*. I think the working people were far happier then than now. They often strike me now as restless. I think they need more work.

After our marriage we went to live in London because the Prime Minister wanted Alfred to go into the House, as he said that England needed men like Alfred. Alfred accepted the seat, but on the firm condition that he needn't speak, or work, or attend, or have anything to do with the voters. The Prime Minister said yes at once: he didn't want Alfred to see the voters at all.

Naturally, of course, our earlier married life had its ups and downs as it does with all people. When we first went to London we were quite poor, I mean not at all well off, and it was difficult for us to afford enough servants to manage our house properly: on the other hand, without a house that size it would have been hard to use all our servants. Even as it was Alfred would himself often fetch up his own shaving water, and more than once I have seen him light his own fire, touch the match to it himself, sooner than ring up a servant. But we both agreed that these little discomforts only make life all the more worthy.

But after a little while Papa's influence got for Alfred a Court appointment as Gentleman Equerry of the Bloodhounds, which made our position much easier. Alfred, of course, didn't have to take the bloodhounds out himself, as that was done by the Yeoman Equerry; but he had to countersign all the warrants for what they ate, which often kept him busy.

Then on top of little hardships at home came the terrible trouble of my poor sister Lucy's marriage. Lucy had always, I think, been a little wanting in making proper social distinctions. I remember that even as a girl she would often speak with cottagers in what seemed quite a wrong way, as if she were their equal. So in a way it was not surprising when she married absolutely beneath her. Papa and Mama were utterly consternated when they heard of it, and Mama decided to do the only brave thing about it and not speak to Lucy any more. She had married a man who not only had no family – I mean in the literal sense absolutely none

– but who worked as a journalist on a newspaper. I know that, of course, nowadays things are different and a journalist can be received anywhere, I mean if he is properly born. But it was not so then, and Lucy's husband, whose name was Mr Smith, was even worse than that, as he had tried to write books as well: indeed he had one published, a book about flowers and botany. The whole thing was, of course, a great pity to us – I mean, Lucy's living like that, until at last Papa, who naturally had great influence, got the Colonial Office to pay Mr Smith's expenses, with Lucy and the children – there were three already – to go out to British Borneo to study flowers: as he couldn't afford to get back, they all stayed there and it was all right. Papa had a letter later from one of the boys from Sarawak, and Papa said he seemed promising and might grow up to be a Dacoit.

But much more serious were the financial troubles which once or twice threatened to overwhelm us. The first was when Papa's bank broke and Sir John and the directors went to jail, because in those days the law was very strict and fair and the bank directors went to jail like anybody else – except, of course, Papa. In his case, as the Lord Chief Justice explained, it had to be understood that he acted in utter ignorance, in fact that he knew nothing, being a nobleman. Indeed Lord Argue, after sentencing the directors, complimented Papa very highly: he said it was men like Papa who make embezzlement possible – which we all thought very handsome. But after all it was a great relief when it was over, especially as it turned out that by a lucky chance Papa had sold all his own shares in the bank the very day before it broke.

But to us, Alfred and me, a much more direct blow was the failure of Mr Derringer's gold mine. We never knew just what happened. It seemed that the mine had not exactly failed but it had never been there. Alfred heard in the City that Mr Derringer had 'salted' the mine, but Alfred couldn't see how he could do that, as it would take such a lot. At any rate it was all in the American papers, and poor Mr Derringer's trial, and he was sent to prison for ten years and was there for weeks and weeks before he could get out. Papa's name came into it all, of course, as a first director, but he was out of it since, though there might have been a sort of scandal except that the American judge spoke very handsomely of Papa's ignorance of it all. Indeed he said that what Papa didn't know would fill a book, and that it was men like Papa who gave England the name it had.

So it all blew over, but presently Alfred and I found that after that the dividends from the mine stopped, which we couldn't understand as they were preferred. Alfred would have been very cool with Papa over it, but as Papa was getting old it seemed wrong to get cool with him. If anything happened to Papa while Alfred was cool, it might make a difference. Indeed it was just at that time that dear Papa got a stroke, his first stroke. It didn't really incapacitate him at first but we thought best to call in a consultant opinion, and then he got a second stroke, and so, in real alarm, we sent for a great Harley Street specialist and Papa got a third stroke. With the third stroke he passed out.

* * *

I will not carry these Memoirs down any further than the day of Papa's funeral which seems a good place to stop. Such a wonderful day, one of those bright crisp autumn days when it just feels good to be alive! Gloops looked so wonderful in the bright sunlight and everywhere the late autumn flowers. And such wonderful messages of sympathy! One from the House of Lords, official, to say that the House had learned with satisfaction that Lord Gloops was to be buried; and one from the Home Secretary expressing his personal appreciation of Papa's burial; and one from the Secretary in Waiting at Windsor Castle that the whole Court was ordered to go into half mourning for a quarter of an hour. And then the funeral service in our dear little church at Gloops. Old Dr Glowworm, though he must have been nearly a hundred at the time, preached the funeral sermon. It was just a little hard to hear him, except the text which was, 'where has he gone?' – we all thought it so beautifully apt – but we couldn't quite follow Dr Glowworm's answer. Then as the crowning thing in the day came the reading of Papa's will, by Papa's own solicitor, Mr Rust, who came from London to Gloops on purpose. Of course we knew that everything would be all right, but of course couldn't help feeling a little nervous. Poor Papa had always been a little uncertain and when we remembered about Papa's bank and the mine, we couldn't feel quite sure what would happen to Gloops. The title, of course, would go to my cousin, the present Marquis of Gloops, but the entail had been cut long ago and Papa was free to do as he liked. I remember how dear Alfred sat so bolt upright, trying so hard to understand every word, though of course that was impossible as most of the will was in law terms. But the meaning came out clear enough. Dear Papa had done everything just as it should be, according to the fine old traditions of the time. Mama was given the Dower House for life, with the full right to use her own money in maintaining it. All the old servants were remembered – Papa gave them each a suit of mourning and quite a substantial sum, I forget what, but I think at least ten pounds, which meant a great deal to people in their class. For my sister Lucy, Papa could not, of course, in view of what had happened, do very much: but even in her case he left her something to remember him by, a beautiful set of books from his library – sermons bound in old leather – and a purse for each of her children – there were only five at that time – with half a sovereign in it, and a prayer book each. Alfred and I got Gloops and all the residuum – that was the word Mr Rust used – residuum of the estate – which was only fair as we should need it to keep the estate up: on the other hand we could hardly have used the residuum if we hadn't had the estate itself. Mr Rust explained it all very clearly.

After it was all over Alfred said, 'Well, it's all over.'

Overworking the Alphabet

I admit that this is the age of brevity. Our rapid life demands condensed speech. We have not enough leisure to talk like Daniel Webster. Even our words must be cut to the shortest limits. We have no time to say *telephone* and *debutante* and *cinematograph* and *automobile*. Not at all: we *phone* an invitation to the *cinema*, and our *debs* ride in *cars* and *planes*.

But when it comes to cutting out words altogether and falling back on letters, it is time to ask where we are 'at.' I mean is it really O.K. to talk about the C.I.O.? And if the C.I.O. joins with the A.F.L. does the mixture become the C.A.I.F.O.L. or the A.C.F.I.L.O.? Similarly, is a man a D.F. if he finds that he can't remember what the O.G.P.U. is, and whether it is in Spain or Russia?

Our grandfathers with their pioneer thoroughness knew nothing of this haste. If they founded a farmers' society they were willing to call it the Oro Township Agricultural Autumn Fair and Flower Show Association, and let it go at that. The more often they said it the better they liked it.

But nowadays three or more people no sooner get together in anything than they fuse themselves with the alphabet. A ladies' sewing circle formed overnight appears as L.S.C. in the morning. If the Junior Pygmies of equatorial Africa ever get organized, the Press will call them J.P.E.A. next morning.

I think the Great War started it. Before the War came we made use of alphabet abbreviations but they were kept fairly within reason. We spoke of the U.S.A. and the Y.M.C.A. and with an effort of brain power we could understand what the Y.W.C.A. ought to mean.

Before the War, business used the letters of the alphabet, but not too much. People signed I.O.U.s or had to pay C.O.D., and business men sent things F.O.B., though no one else knew what it meant. Before the War, teachers in the schools used to make use of A, B and C to work arithmetic, and long ago, 200 years before Christ (B.J.C.), Euclid used to sign his theorems Q.E.D. to mean that that was the end. But the letters were only used to give a touch of finality, just as on a tombstone they put R.I.P., to mean that the man was dead and there was no need to waste words on him.

In fiction, too, especially detective and comic fiction, letters were used to give a touch of mystery, to indicate the unsolvable. I mean, a passage would run something like this:

My friend X had taken the early train to ⟨.⟩ where he met Miss M. on the platform accompanied by her uncle, the Bishop of Asterisk, waiting, apparently to take the down train to H–.

All this excited in the reader's mind a queer suspicion that perhaps X was not the man's name and that the bishop was not going to H –.

But beyond such usages the Alphabetical Contractions never extended till the Great War came and flooded us with them. I think I can see how the War started it. In wartime at the front if a man took full time to say 'General Headquarters' he might get shot before he finished it, whereas if he said 'G.H.Q.' he still had a chance for his life. So when the soldiers came back we heard them all talking in the new alphabetical jargon about the G.H.Q. and the C.O. and who gave the D.S.O. to a V.A.D.

Naturally, we started to imitate them and the thing spread till the alphabet invaded all our Government and civil administration, then overwhelmed all corporate business and labour organization, and now threatens to submerge private life. The United States began it with the N.R.A. (even before F.D.), and when we had learned that, lengthened it to the N.R.A.A. and then hurried us on to the P.W.A. and its fellows. The only trouble is to remember what they all do for everybody. In an emergency, people can fall back on the F.E.R.A.; or enjoy a cosy sense of security under the S.S.B. There's a peculiar protection against want in F.S.C.C., and a man who wants to break up his home can do it under the F.H.I.B.B.

But many of us now find that we are losing our grip on what these things mean, and when we hear that the Supreme Court has set aside the P.D.Q. we don't know whether to get mad about it or not. The spread of the same thing across the field of labour has given us the A.F.L. – not difficult if you remember F for federation – and the C.I.O. (not to be confused with the one that means the high explosive).

If things are difficult at home on our own continent, think what they must seem abroad. Tell a foreigner that the allegiance of the United

States Navy is undermined by the Y.W.C.A. and he'll believe it. Offer to give to Hitler the order of a D.F. in the W.C.T.U. and he'll accept it. The use of the overworked alphabet is creating a sort of new language. We are getting so accustomed to it that things written out in full look needlessly prolix. If we want to keep our history alive, it will have to be rewritten. A new outline of history (O. of H.) will contain an account of the American Revolution (the A.R.) as follows:

SIGNING OF THE D.O.I. AND THE BIRTH OF THE U.S.A.

The excitement over the S.A. and the B.T. (it means the Stamp Act and the Boston Tea Party) soon led to open resistance (O.R.) The battle of B.H., outside of Boston, was followed by the appointment of G.W. as C.I.C. of the C.A., and a congress of delegates (F.O.B. Philadelphia) signed on July 4, 1776, the famous D.O.I. written by T.J. The stubborn K.O.E. – G.3 – refused all conciliation, looking upon G.W. as P.E. No.1 of his Empire. The war ended in a C.V. (complete victory) at Yorktown, presently followed by the drawing up of the T.O.V. in which G.3 recognized the I.O.U.S.A. G.W. became the first P.U.S., and was recognized in history as the F.O.H.C.

But I perceive, as I go on thinking about it, that it is not only our history but our English and American literature of the past that must be revised to make it properly alphabetical. Tennyson's *Charge of the Light Brigade* – renamed as the C.L.B. – will read:

> *Half a league, half a league,*
> *Half a league onward!*
> *Into the V.O.D. rode the S.H.*

Gray's immortal *Elegy in a Country Churchyard* – the E.C.C. – will explain how the 'Curfew tolls the K.P.D.,' while 'the ploughman homeward plods his W.W.'

It will reach its climax in the immortal stanza read aloud by General Wolfe to his officers as their boat stole up the St Lawrence in the dusk of an autumn evening – the evening before the battle of the P.O.A. The stanza, as revised, reads:

> *The B.O.H., the P.O.P.,*
> *And all that beauty, all that wealth e'er gave,*
> *Await alike the I.H.:*
> *The P.O.G. lead but to the capital G.*

But one last despairing stand must be made to keep the alphabet of private life. Don't call your stoker 'my S.,' or your dearest friend 'my

D.F.' Invite your guests to a week-end cocktail party but not to a W.E.C.P. As you grow old let people call you a venerable old gentleman but never a V.O.G., and when you die arrange for a private funeral, but not a P.F.

STEPHEN LEACOCK
Self-appointed Secretary Anti-
Alphabet Association (or better,
S.A.S.A.A.A.)

Sixteen
Fiction and Reality

A STUDY OF THE ART OF CHARLES DICKENS

It was in one of those literary circles into which I am sometimes permitted to enter that the talk fell not long ago upon the art of Charles Dickens and his place in the world's literature.

'Dickens, of course,' said a gentleman with a velvet jacket and long black hair, 'is not really to be taken seriously.'

'Is he not?' I said.

'Oh, no. One can't really call him a *novelist* in the true sense. His characters after all are not characters but merely caricatures.' The speaker put his hand up to his necktie and gave it a peculiar little hitch. I had seen him do it twenty times already that evening.

'Every one of the characters in Dickens,' he went on, 'has some peculiar little tag, something that he is always doing and that you know him by' (here he hitched his necktie again) – 'for example, Traddles in *David Copperfield* is always trying to flatten his hair, What's-his-name in *Bleak House* is always taking snuff, someone else, Uriah Heep, is it not? is perpetually rubbing his hands together, and so on. Now in real life,' continued the gentleman in the velvet jacket in a pitying tone, 'people don't do these things' – (here he hitched his necktie) – 'they simply don't do them, that's all.'

'Precisely,' joined in another person who was standing near us, by occupation a professor of literature and hence one who ought to know; 'there's no complexity in the characters, eh, what? Everything they say so stilted, eh? Take their way of speaking, eh, what? Always using some little phrase, something you can tell them by, a sort of formula, eh, what?'

'Do you think so?' I said musingly. I was counting the number of times the professor was saying 'eh', and I noted that he was up to four. I knew by experience that he could easily run up a hundred in five minutes.

'Take Mark Tapley,' he went on, 'you know – in *Martin Chuzzlewit*, eh? Dickens can't make him speak without having him say "jolly." It seems like an obsession, eh? Don't you think so, eh, what?'

270

Some others joined us and the conversation became general. It appeared from it that Dickens was after all but a poor cheap comedian, a sort of black-faced vaudeville artist, a ventriloquist with a box full of grotesque impossible dolls, each squawking out its little phrase amid the laughter of the uneducated. But as a writer in the real sense, he was, it seemed, nowhere. Put him beside – I forget who – and he shrinks to a pigmy. Compare his work to – somebody I have never heard of – and it withers into dead grass. Take a really *great* man, a *big* man like – I can't remember the name; he writes, I understand, a quarter of a column every third week in *The Saturday Supplement*: to do more would exhaust his vein – and where is Dickens? Or take a man with the penetration of – I can't recall whose penetration – but again, where is Dickens?

From hearing which, I went home sad. For I have been reading Dickens now for thirty-two years – ever since I first opened the pages of the *Pickwick Papers* and stepped into an enchanted world of English lanes, and stage coaches, and gabled inns and London streets, where I walked arm-in-arm with Micawber and Thomas Pinch and that great company of immortals, more real than life itself.

That evening, after I had come home and sat down beside my fire, I fell to thinking what Dickens would have said, or what his characters themselves would have thought of the accusations to which I had been listening. If one could only get them together and put it to them, what would they think about it?

So I sat before the fire, a volume of Dickens upon my knee, musing, till it grew late.

And then –

* * *

'If the company will now come to order,' said Mr Pickwick, rapping gently on the table and beaming through his spectacles with a kindliness that seemed to irradiate the whole of the assemblage before him, 'I will ask my good friend Mr Sergeant Buzfuz to read the indictment in the matter before us.'

There was an almost instant silence. Everybody present, from sagacious persons such as Mr Perker of Gray's Inn, or his unfathomable colleague Mr Tulkinghorn, to such simple souls as Mr Willett Senior, or Mr Dick, could not fail to perceive that there must be something quite unusual on foot when Mr Pickwick should speak of the learned Sergeant as his good friend, and should even appear to direct a glance of something like affectionate recognition towards Mr Dodson and Fogg who were seated in close proximity to the great legal luminary himself.

'Half a minute, Pickwick' – interrupted the cheery voice of a rather dilapidated but altogether brisk personage seated in one of the front rows of chairs, 'dry business – lawyer's speech – go on talking – won't stop – perish of thirst – better let someone brew us punch – eh, sir – only a minute.'

'Egad, Pickwick, Jingle's right,' cried out Mr Wardle, 'let the lawyers talk away if you like, but I'll be dashed, sir, if I'll sit here all evening with a dry throat listening to their palaver. Here Emily, Joe – where the dooce is that boy gone to –'

But long before the fat boy could be roused up from his slumbers in a remote corner of the hall where he lay enthroned upon a pile of rugs and wraps, among which the greatcoat of Mr Weller Senior and the shawl of Mrs Gamp were plainly discernible – another volunteer had stepped into the breach.

How and whence Mr Micawber was suddenly able to produce a bag of lemons, by what necromancy sugar was added to them (set into such fascinating little lumps that the soul of the sugar trust might well shrink with envy at the sight of them), by what artifice he was able to combine them in proportions known only to himself with a square bottle of extra gin, and to bedew the surface of the steaming mixture with nutmegs that must have come from the very groves of Lebanon itself – how all this was done, I say, passes the imagination to conceive. Necromancy it must have been indeed. For as the steaming bowl of punch sent its vapours thoughout the room, so transfigured and yet so strangely lifelike did the assembled company become as seen through its haze, that I vow it must have been brewed from the very lemons of reminiscence, mixed by that strange alchemy of affection that is wafted to us still from the pages to *The Unforgotten Master.*

* * *

'Excellent,' said Mr Pickwick, as he put down his glass, 'I don't know when I've tasted better punch.'

'Only once, perhaps,' chuckled Mr Wardle.

'Ah, well, yes, once, perhaps!' assented Mr Pickwick with perfect serenity. And then turning to old Mrs Wardle, who sat close on his left hand, attired in her very best cap, and who for this evening seemed to have laid aside every trace of deafness, he added – 'Your son will have his joke, madam: he is reminding me of an incident to which I fear perhaps already too much attention has been given by – by –'

Mr Pickwick seemed to hesitate for a phrase. He looked in a somewhat dubious way towards Mr Perker of Gray's Inn, and added:

'– by an undiscerning public.'

'Quite so,' nodded Mr Perker lustily – 'by an undiscerning public. You may say that, Mr Pickwick, with entire impunity. An undiscerning public. I take your meaning. Very good, sir; a glass of punch, sir?'

'With pleasure,' said Mr Pickwick. Whereupon there was such a hobnobbing of glasses and such an exchange of compliments, and such an affectionate reciprocity of sentiment in various parts of the hall that it seemed for a time as if the serious business of the evening were likely to be indefinitely suspended.

All good things, however, even the drinking of punch by Mr Micawber and his associates, must of necessity come to an end. Partly by sundry mild knockings on Mr Pickwick's table and partly by more violent disturbances on the floor created by Mr Bumble's staff a measure of quiet was restored.

'With your permission, then,' said the illustrious chairman, 'I will resume the course of my remarks. My intention had been to content myself with asking my good friend Mr Sergeant Buzfuz to state the whole matter which brings us together. But perhaps I shall not be trespassing upon my valued friend's prerogative if I say a word or two in introduction of his discourse.'

Loud cries of 'Hear! hear!' mingled perhaps with a sound not entirely unlike the crowing of a cock and which may have proceeded from the lungs of Mr Samuel Weller, indicated an ample assent.

'Very good,' said Mr Pickwick, evidently very much gratified. 'I shall try to be very brief and, as I dare not pretend to emulate the talent of my learned friend, I will endeavour to say what I mean in as few words as possible.'

Mr Pickwick paused for a moment, and then, with a look of something like constraint or even distress upon his usually unruffled countenance, he resumed:

'None of you, I fear, are altogether ignorant of the name of Mr Blotton of Aldgate.'

Loud groans, coupled with cries of 'Shame! Traitor! Snake in the grass!' gave ample evidence to Mr Pickwick (had he needed it) of the reputation which Mr Blotton of Aldgate enjoyed among his associates. Indeed it had so long been the practice to exclude that gentleman and all mention of him from every assemblage of this sort that the company were filled with wonder that Mr Pickwick himself should thus openly name his arch enemy and detractor.

'It is only with great reluctance,' continued the good gentleman, 'that I pronounce the name of this individual. His offence towards myself I readily pass over: but his want of respect towards that illustrious body which was good enough to honour me by designating itself after my name (I refer, more explicitly, to the Pickwick Club) is a matter which has, I think, already been condemned by the verdict of impartial history.'

Mr Pickwick looked about him. His audience, evidently impressed by the fervour of the Chairman's eloquence, were now completely silent. Some of them indeed, as Mr Weller Senior, were evidently so spellbound by Mr Pickwick's oratory that they leaned back in their seats with their eyes closed as in an ecstasy of enjoyment.

'Had Mr Blotton of Aldgate confined his malice to his disruption of the Pickwick Club, or even to the foul blow which he dealt to the noble science of Archaeology in his unwarranted attack on the authenticity of an inscription which I may say at least stands, in spite of his onslaughts, unique in the annals of literature – had his malice stopped here, despicable though it was, I for one should have been content to consign his memory to the ignominy which it has so richly deserved.

'But, gentlemen, it has not stopped here. It did not so stop. It has gone on. It is still with us.'

Here Mr Pickwick made another pause so dramatic and impressive that even those of his associates who were not yet aware of the purpose of the present gathering realised that it was no ordinary communication that Mr Pickwick was about to impart.

'It is now,' continued Mr Pickwick, 'some eighty years since the individual to whom I allude first gave evidence of the singularly malicious composition of his individuality. It might have been hoped that it would long since have passed into oblivion. Alas, it was not to be. Like everything that was touched by that master hand of which we all, my assembled friends, are the common product, Mr Blotton of Aldgate has proved immortal. More than that, he appears, like every character created by our great originator, to have been multiplied to infinity. I lament to say that in this later age every civilised country has its Aldgate, and every Aldgate, I grieve to state, is disfigured by its Blotton.

'One might have thought that our dead master's memory would have been left unassailed. Alas! every genius has its detractors. In every generous bosom a snake is warmed. And from this snake, from these snakes of whom I speak, from the cohort of snakes' – here Mr Pickwick spoke with the greatest animation, while his spectacles glittered with a just indignation that was reflected upon the listening faces before him – 'from these reptile Blottons of the Aldgates of all countries there has gone forth against our great originator, and hence, gentlemen, against each and every one of us, an accusation so foul, so despicable, that I know no other way to characterise it than to say that it could have only emanated from the mind of a Blotton of Aldgate. That accusation is –'

Here Mr Pickwick paused and looked about him while the assembled company remained breathless upon the very verge of expectancy.

'That accusation is,' repeated Mr Pickwick, 'that *we are not real, that we are caricatures*, that not one of us, and I beg the company to mark my words, not a single one of us, ever existed, or ever could exist; in short, my friends, that we are mere monstrous exaggerations, each of us drawn in a crude and comic fashion from a few imaginary characteristics!'

The mingled roar of indignation and contempt that burst from the throats of the auditors gave evidence at once to the power of Mr Pickwick's oratory, and to the unanimity of their contempt. The loud cries of 'Shame! Monstrous!' that broke from the lips of the indignant Wardle and the vociferous Boythorn were not unmingled with the sound of the crowing of cocks and the popping of corks, which gave evidence of the lively feelings of Mr Sam Weller, Alfred Jingle, Esqre., Mr Tapley, and others of the lighter spirits of the company, while the voice of Mr Micawber was heard above the din in loud enquiry as to whether this was still a British country or whether his own immediate return to his adoptive Australia was not necessitated by the lamentable but evident degeneration of the British Isles.

Mr Pickwick waited until a measure of quiet had been restored and then resumed:

'Under the circumstances, gentlemen, you will not be surprised to learn that after consulting with my valued friend, Mr Sergeant Buzfuz, we have decided to hold an enquiry, or inquisition – my learned friend will pardon me if the term is misapplied.'

'A halibi, governor, make it a halibi,' interrupted a deep warning voice, 'it's far safer. Halibi first and henquiry afterwards.'

'In any case,' said Mr Pickwick, 'what I desire to do, with your concurrence, is to place the whole case in the hands of our legal colleagues here present and to request our learned and distinguished friend, Sergeant Buzfuz, to conduct it for us.'

Mr Pickwick paused, turned with a courteous bow towards the long table at his right hand at which a phalanx of lawyers in full wigs and gowns were seated, and indicating with a wave of his hand the commanding figure of the illustrious Sergeant who sat at the head of the table, he resumed his seat.

Could any reader of the works of the Great Master have been present on this momentous occasion, it would have warmed his heart to have looked upon the solid array of legal talent at the long table over which Sergeant Buzfuz here presided. Nor could he, in the face of such an imposing panel, have felt the faintest apprehension that the base allegations of Mr Blotton of Aldgate, and of the numerous and loathsome progeny which have sprung from him, would not be scattered to the four winds of heaven.

Here sat in friendly colloquy with Buzfuz the equally illustrious Snubbins: beside them, among his piles of papers and his sacks of reference books, laboured the industrious Phunkey: near him the massive brow of the great Stryver, bound with a wet towel, was bent over a glass of still steaming punch as if seeking a final inspiration: the nimble Perker of Gray's Inn was side by side with the inscrutable Tulkinghorn of Lincoln's; here sat Wakefield, his wasted face imprinted with the dumb pathos of his broken mind, clasping his daughter's hand for comfort: here even the ghastly Vholes and the unregenerate Heep and the obsequious Dodson and Fogg mingled their false plaudits with the approbation of the crowd; and here at the further end, with head back-tilted on the chair, with eyes that sought the ceiling, and with pale lips that still murmured the threnody of the guillotine, the immortal figure of Carton, lit with a softer light as of the dead among the living.

So sat they, the unreal lawyers of the unreal books of the Master, and as they sat, betokened by their very presence a greater power of life and truth than life itself.

* * *

Sergeant Buzfuz rose. We wish it were within our power to present to our readers a full report of the magnificent oration delivered by that learned man. The introduction alone, in which the Sergeant, with the aid of books and documents, handed to him by Mr Stryver, rapidly reviewed the history of literature from Plato to Chesterton, was of such singular merit that Mr Solomon Pell was heard to remark, that not even his intimate friend the Lord Chancellor could have made a better presentation. They had before them, said the learned Sergeant, not merely a question of art, but a question of reality, and of the relation between the two. Of the nature of reality he would not leave them long in doubt. Witnesses would be called (witnesses of unimpeachable character) who should establish the nature of reality to an iota. Nor should they long remain in doubt as to the nature and meaning of art. He would, if need be, call to the witness-box a gentleman of unexcelled antiquarian learning who should establish to their satisfaction the fact of the existence of art among the Romans (here all eyes were turned for a moment towards Dr Blimber). He would, if it were necessary, further establish the point from the lips of the consort of that distinguished scholar who would testify that there were distinct traces of art even in the writings of Cicero. He would have the word itself examined, searched and impounded by one of the greatest lexicographers of the age (here the Sergeant bowed politely in the direction of Dr Strong) – a lexicographer, he would add, whose labours had now long since overpassed the question of Art, and all other questions beginning with the noble letter A and were now rapidly traversing the letter D.

'But, gentlemen,' continued the Sergeant, and at this point we are able to reproduce his words verbatim, 'we need here something more than mere definitions. It is ours to enquire how far ART – which in this instance is represented by FICTION – is at one with reality: how far the picture of life presented must correspond lineament for lineament with the literal aspect of the thing itself. The accusation has been made in the affidavits of Mr Blotton of Aldgate that the art of the Great Master is false: that it shows life and character not as they are but distorted into a series of caricatures. The fatal word "exaggeration" has been launched upon an unsuspecting world. Charles Dickens' – here the Sergeant for the first time, and with an intense majesty of bearing and expression, uttered that noble name before the company – 'CHARLES DICKENS EXAGGERATES. That is the charge of which he stands accused. That is the foul calumny by which his fair name is rapidly being overcast. He has made each of us here present represent and typify (so runs the allegation) merely a single characteristic, and that, too, distorted and magnified beyond its natural shape. I, myself, gentlemen, as presented in the laudable, though I admit somewhat too impartial pages of the *Pickwick Papers*, represent (so it is said) a mere abstraction of forensic eloquence (I believe the word "bombast" is used in the allegation before us) –'

The Sergeant paused for the fraction of a second, and something like an expression of doubt, of uncertainty was seen to rest upon his features. But it passed as rapidly as it had come and he resumed:

'My good friend, Mr Pickwick, is mere benevolence, sheer insipid benevolence, nothing else –'

At this point, somewhat to the distraction of the speaker, the genial countenance of the Chairman, from his spectacles to his double chin, was seen to beam with an expression of such utter and complete benevolence that the Sergeant thought it well to leave that item of his argument incomplete.

'Our friend, William Sikes (he is not in this gathering, but I understand that he is at present engaged in crawling about the roof of this building) – our worthy colleague, Mr Carker, our esteemed ally, Mr Jonas Chuzzlewit, these are said to impersonate sheer malice of disposition and nothing else – nay, even my good friend, Mr Pecksniff, whom I believe I see at the end of the hall warming his back at the fire in a manner I think familiar to all, is said to stand for sheer hypocrisy and for no other conceivable characteristic.'

At this point Mr Pecksniff, for he indeed it was, was seen to lift a deprecating hand and those who stood or sat nearest to him were able to hear him enjoin his daughter Mercy in an audible whisper that she should remind him that night to make explicit mention of all literary critics in his prayers.

'Or to come down to mere particulars and idiosyncrasies,' went on Sergeant Buzfuz, 'it is said that our good friend, Mr Uriah Heep, is always "rubbing his hands".' ('I admit,' said the Sergeant, glancing with a slight frown at the lawyers' table where Uriah sat, 'that he is doing so – happens to be doing so – at this particular moment.') 'But the allegation runs that he is always and perpetually doing so beyond the verge of human credence. It is similarly charged that Mr Micawber is always and perpetually brewing punch.' (Mr Micawber's guilty hand was seen to retreat noiselessly from the punch bowl as the Sergeant's eye turned to him.) 'That he also is always waiting for something to turn up, that Mr Mark Tapley is always "jolly", that my honoured friend Mr Wardle owns and conducts a country house where it is always and perpetually Christmas, that Mr Jingle only speaks in monosyllables and broken phrases and has never been known to make a sentence in his life –'

'Stop, there' – interrupted the voice of the dilapidated Alfred Jingle, 'damn lie – sentence once – Fleet Street sentence – never forget – noble conduct – everlasting gratitude –'

'Tut, tut,' interrupted the Chairman, 'I am sure there are lots of things that we all had better agree to forget.'

The Sergeant's unhappy introduction of the word 'sentence' seemed to occasion so peculiar a feeling of discomfort in a number of the auditors (the lively agitation of Mr Heep, Mr Micawber and others was especially noticeable) that the speaker with the instinctive feeling of the orator realised that it was impossible to resume his suspended period.

'But, gentlemen,' he continued, 'the hour waxes already late. I will no longer expatiate upon the nature of the charge before us. I will proceed at once in its rebuttal.'

Here the Sergeant consulted for a moment a list of names that was handed to him by Mr Phunkey.

'Call Sarah Gamp,' he cried.

There was a sudden stir in a distant part of the hall, as of a heavy body being set in motion, and to the evident satisfaction of everybody the familiar form of Mrs Gamp, who had apparently resumed her shawl and her pattens, was seen to approach the table. She presently brought up alongside it with as much majesty of movement as that of a full-rigged coal barge coming to anchor beside the Embankment.

The Sergeant now turned to the lawyers' table and addressed one of the members of the panel whose rusted black attire, whose pale, indeed ghastly face and whose uncertain eyes and ambiguous expression left no doubt of his identity.

'Mr Vholes,' he said, 'I understand from the Chairman that it is the general desire of the assemblage that you should act, as it were, as the *advocatus diaboli*, in other words, should have the privilege of appearing for the prosecution. You are at liberty to question the witness.

Mr Vholes arose. Accustomed as he was to the more leisurely procedure and the congenial delays of the Court of Chancery, he may well have felt somewhat ill at ease in the summary methods of investigation here adopted by the Sergeant. But his courage was fortified by the presence of sundry volumes of literary criticism that lay heaped before him, written in various languages, mostly other than English, on which he relied to establish his case.

'Your name,' he said, 'is Sarah Gamp?'

'Widge I scorn to deny it,' answered that lady.

'Your profession, I understand, is that of a nurse.'

'Widge it is,' said Mrs Gamp, 'and as I was saying only yesterday to Mrs Harris, which I don't see here tonight owing to the fact of her being unable to come, and it being the third time, poor soul, in as many years –'

Mr Pickwick coughed.

'I must beg you, Mrs Gamp,' he said, 'to realise that in the lapse of eighty years a certain change in public taste has dictated – a – has prescribed certain forms of reticence –'

'Retigence!' said Mrs Gamp, bridling, 'don't talk to me of retigence as if I was a Betsy Prigg that couldn't be trusted within a sight of a brandy bottle. Widge I abhor,' she added, 'except it might be for a chill and being overtired after sitting up with a demise –'

'Very good, Mrs Gamp,' broke in Mr Vholes, delighted to find his witness developing immediately and without guidance the very characteristics and no others which he wished to elucidate – 'now tell us, please, Mrs Gamp, and remember that you are virtually under oath – Are you real?'

'Am I widge?' said Mrs Gamp.

'Are you real?' said the rusty lawyer. 'Do you mean to tell this court – this assembly – that there ever have been or could be women like you; are you willing to assert that you are anything more than an abstraction? Have you, in the eighty years of retrospect laid open to us, ever really lived?'

Mrs Gamp might have answered. We say advisedly 'might have', in the course of time, although to all intent and purpose she seemed suddenly to be rooted immovable, her mouth half open, her features fixed in a stare of mingled surprise and contempt at her interlocutor. But her answer was not needed. For at this moment a very singular thing happened. Whether it was due to the necromancy of Mr Micawber's punch, or to the lateness of the hour, or to the growing absorption of the assembled auditors, we cannot say. But the truth is that as they sat gazing fixedly at the witness a strange and wonderful phenomenon made itself felt. The face and form of Mrs Gamp were multiplied before their eyes into not one but a thousand forms. It was as if the bounds of space and time were pushed aside and the eye could see through the long vista of the years, and through the broad expanse of space from country to country, not one but a thousand – a hundred thousand Gamps. Here were Gamps in London garrets tending dying fires beside the already dead – Gamps moving to and fro in area kitchens, their mysterious pattens clicking on the stone floor – Gamps with monstrous umbrellas staggering in the rain – Gamps tending market stalls in the London fog – nay, it was as if Mr Vholes' words had acted like a talisman to call forth a legion of Gamps to prove the existence of a single one. Nor were the Sarah Gamps confined to a single time or country: there were mid-Victorian Gamps and Gamps of the closing century, Australian Gamps vigorously washing clothes beneath the gum trees, Canadian Gamps scrubbing stone steps regardless of the thermometer, French Gamps busily checking umbrellas in the theatres, American Gamps superin-tending ladies' withdrawing rooms in railroad stations, nay, I will swear it – Gamps that in form and fashion were negro, negroid or mulatto, but still evidently and indisputably Sarah Gamp. Strangest of all, no two of the figures in the vision seemed quite alike: the red shawl might or might not be present, the brandy bottle might or might not be there, the clicking of the pattens might or might not be heard – and yet indisputably and undeniably each of the figures was the same illustrious, undying, ever repeating Sarah Gamp.

Mr Vholes, aghast at the vision that he had summoned, sank into his seat.

'I think, Mrs Gamp,' said Mr Pickwick, 'that we need not question you further. You, at least exist.'

* * *

Sergeant Buzfuz rose again to his feet.

'Call Mr Pecksniff,' he said.

That gentleman, who was carefully attired in his customary long black coat and irreproachable white tie and who had by this time warmed his back until it had attained to that comfortable sensation demanded by his altruistic feelings, drew near to the lawyers' table.

'Perhaps, Mr Fogg,' continued the Sergeant, 'as our friend Mr Vholes appears to be incapacitated for further effort, you will yourself be good enough to examine this witness.'

Mr Fogg rose in his place, bowed to the Sergeant and the Chairman, and directed his attention to Mr Pecksniff.

'Your name, I believe,' he said, 'is Mr Pecksniff?'

The latter gentleman bowed.

'Will you kindly tell the assembled company,' went on Mr Fogg, looking about him with a great assumption of sharpness, 'what is the nature of your profession?'

'I am,' said Mr Pecksniff, 'in my humble capacity an architect.'

'And will you please tell us,' pursued Mr Fogg, 'what principal buildings you have designed?'

'Certainly,' said Mr Pecksniff with great urbanity, 'none at all.'

'None at all!' repeated Mr Fogg surprised.

'None at all,' reiterated Mr Pecksniff. 'To be quite frank and candid,' he continued, 'as we are speaking here purely among friends and I presume under the seal of confidence, I may say that the buildings which I am supposed to have designed were all the work of other people.'

'Do you see any of them here?' queried the lawyer.

'One or two,' said Mr Pecksniff unabashed. 'I think I see my young friend Thomas Pinch, whose talent was for many years invaluable to me, and, I believe, Mr Martin Chuzzlewit, whose design for a grammar school has always been considered one of my most successful inspirations.'

'In other words, sir,' said Mr Fogg, with great severity, 'you are an arrant hypocrite.'

'I am,' said Mr Pecksniff, with a bow.

'And a fraud, sir.'

'At your service,' said Mr Pecksniff.

'You pocket money that you never earned.'

'I do,' assented Mr Pecksniff.

'And you cover it up with a cloak of religion and family affection.'

'Precisely,' said Mr Pecksniff, smiling urbanely and placing his hands beneath his coat tails with his familiar gesture of self-satisfaction, 'that is exactly my policy.'

'And do you mean, sir,' said Mr Fogg, swelling visibly with the importance of his enquiry, 'do you mean to tell this sensible, this sagacious company that in face of these facts – of your carrying on business in this fashion, that you are a real person? Have you the assurance, sir, to state in the face of this damning evidence that there are real people such as you in actual business in actual life?'

Mr Fogg, to judge by the way in which he here drew himself up, apparently expected that the result of his enquiry would be so to crush and annihilate both the witness and the auditors as to explode the very existence of Mr Pecksniff into the thinnest nothingness of the most impossible fiction. If so his expectation was doomed to disappointment. For he had no sooner propounded his question as to whether real business by real people was carried on in this fashion than the entire audience broke into loud and uncontrolled laughter. It may have been that the seventy years that have elapsed since the first earthly incarnation of Mr Pecksniff have accentuated the character of modern business. But certain it is that the notion that the existence of Mr Pecksniff and his methods was a thing unheard of in the present business world convulsed the assembly with spontaneous merriment. We will not say that the same strange phenomenon repeated itself as in the case of Mrs Gamp. But it is undoubted that before the minds of the auditors there might well have arisen the vision of an unending, undying series of Pecksniffs – English, American, and Continental – Pecksniffs of the old world and Pecksniffs of the new – Pecksniffs in little white ties sitting at board meetings of corporations, Pecksniffs in long black coats presiding at funerals, Pecksniffs interviewing delegations of working-men and refusing with deep reluctance all suggestions of increases of wages, Pecksniffs presiding over colleges, Pecksniffs elected into senates, Pecksniffs in city councils – till from the very length and extension of the series it appeared as if Mr Pecksniff expressed within himself the whole spirit and essence of modern business and modern politics. Indeed it appeared not merely as if Mr Pecksniff were extremely real and actually existed, but as if there existed more of him than of any other human being.

Small wonder then that when Mr Fogg resumed his seat and Mr Pecksniff complacently returned to his place in front of the fire there was a general feeling that the reality of at least his character had been more than vindicated.

We could only wish that the limits of space before us would allow of an extended description of the examination of the succeeding witnesses. We could wish that we might convey to our readers some notion of the genial warmth with which Mr Wardle met the accusation that his house at Dingley Dell was an impossible place such as could only have existed in the grossest and most exaggerated fiction: of how he took his oath, with perhaps unnecessary emphasis, that it was just the kind of house that might be found by those who had the eyes to see it, especially at Christmas time, throughout the length and breadth of England: of how he met the accusation that it was always Christmas time at his house by the simple but convincing statement that it always was: of how he met the charge that his young medical friends, Mr Bob Sawyer and Mr Benjamin Allen, were not possible or actual people by offering to turn any two dozen distinguished modern doctors inside out and find a Bob Sawyer and a Ben Allen coiled up in the composition of any one of them:

and of how he presently retired triumphant from the witness stand amid the uproarious applause of Mr Weller, Mr Tapley and even the excitable Mr Sawyer himself.

Equally fain should we be to describe the examination of Mr Weller Senior, and how he refused to be drawn into any generalisation as to whether actual London bus-drivers and hackney coachmen might be said to resemble himself: or how his solicitor and friend, Mr Pell (an intimate acquaintance of the Lord Chancellor), saved the day by producing no less than fifty sworn and authenticated photographs of London busmen and cabmen of the year of grace 1916, every one of which we conceived in the very spirit and likeness of Mr Tony Weller. Equally regrettable it is that we cannot linger to describe the triumphant exoneration of Mr Micawber, of Mr Wackford Squeers, of Captain Cuttle and others whose characters had been made the subject of unjust aspersions. In every case it was shown with the greatest ease that these gentlemen not only had actually lived but were still living, and that too in every habitable country of the Christian globe. Only one incident of a slightly discordant nature occurred to mar the symmetry of the occasion. At the very height of the general enthusiasm a number of females – conspicuous among whom were Mrs Annie Strong and Little Nell – forced their way to the front and burst into such floods of tears that for the time being they threatened to wash away the entire assembly in the flood-tide of their grief. Mrs Strong, indeed, kneeling at the feet of each of the lawyers in turn and offering to make an ample atonement to each one of them for the errors of her past life, may be said to have pushed the bounds of reality to the breaking point. Indeed for a moment when the loud sobs of Ham Peggotty, John Perrybingle, and others of the men were conjoined with those of the women, it seemed as if the meeting might end in disaster.

But at the critical moment the voice of Sergeant Buzfuz, who declared that the evidence was now all complete and that under the rules of the court evidence given through tears could not be admitted, saved the situation. And when a moment later the Sergeant called upon Dr Blimber to summarise the general conclusions of the assembly, it was felt that a great cause had been saved.

Of the final discourse of Dr Blimber we fear that we can only give the briefest outline. Whether from the lateness of the hour or from the majestic roll of the doctor's periods, our eyes were closed in such an exquisite appreciation of his eloquence that the details of it escaped our apprehension. But we understood him to say that the truth was that from the time of the Romans onward Art had of necessity proceeded by the method of selected particulars and conspicuous qualities: that this was the nature and meaning of art itself: that exaggeration (meaning the heightening of the colour to be conveyed) was the very life of it: that herein lay the difference between the photographer (we believe the doctor said the daguerreotype) and the portrait: that by this means and by this means alone could the real truth – the reality greater than life be conveyed.

All this and more we truly believe the doctor to have said.

But as he continued speaking his voice to our ears seemed to grow fainter and fainter, the pictured company around grew dim before the eye, a gentle haze gradually enshrouded the benevolent face of Mr Pickwick as he sat with closed eyes and head sunk forward, intent upon the doctor's every word – fainter to the ear and dimmer to the eye – until somehow, as with the soft vanishing of a cherished vision, the picture drifted from our sight – and we sat alone awake beside the smouldering fire, the open book of the Great Master across our knee, musing over the profundity of its God-given message.

Seventeen
The New Education

'So you're going back to college in a fortnight,' I said to the Bright Young Thing on the veranda of the summer hotel. 'Aren't you sorry?'

'In a way I am,' she said, 'but in another sense I'm glad to go back. One can't loaf all the time.'

She looked up from her rocking-chair over her Red Cross knitting with great earnestness.

How full of purpose these modern students are, I thought to myself. In my time we used to go back to college as to a treadmill.

'I know that,' I said, 'but what I mean is that college, after all, is a pretty hard grind. Things like mathematics and Greek are no joke, are they? In my day, as I remember it, we used to think spherical trigonometry about the hardest stuff of the lot.'

She looked dubious. 'I didn't *elect* mathematics,' she said.

'Oh,' I said, 'I see. So you don't have to take it. And what *have* you elected?'

'For this coming half semester – that's six weeks, you know – I've elected Social Endeavour.'

'Ah,' I said, 'that's since my day; what is it?'

'Oh, it's *awfully* interesting. It's the study of conditions.'

'What kind of conditions?' I asked.

'All conditions. Perhaps I can't explain it properly. But I have the prospectus of it indoors if you'd like to see it. We take up Society.'

'And what do you do with it?'

'Analyse it,' she said.

'But it must mean reading a tremendous lot of books.'

'No,' she answered. 'We don't use books in this course. It's all Laboratory Work.'

'Now I *am* mystified,' I said. 'What *do* you mean by Laboratory Work?'

'Well,' answered the girl student with a thoughtful look upon her face, 'you see, we are supposed to break Society up into its elements.'

'In six weeks?'

'Some of the girls do it in six weeks. Some put in a whole semester and take twelve weeks at it.'

285

'So as to break it up pretty thoroughly?' I said.

'Yes,' she assented. 'But most of the girls think six weeks is enough.'

'That ought to pulverize it pretty completely. But how do you go at it?'

'Well,' the girl said, 'it's all done with Laboratory Work. We take, for instance, department stores. I think that is the first thing we do, we take up the department store.'

'And what do you do with it?'

'We study it as a Social Germ.'

'Ah,' I said, 'as a Social Germ.'

'Yes,' said the girl, delighted to see that I was beginning to understand, 'as a Germ. All the work is done in the concrete. The class goes down with the professor to the department store itself –'

'And then –'

'Then they walk all through it, observing.'

'But have none of them ever been in a departmental store before?'

'Oh, of course, but, you see, we go as Observers.'

'Ah, now I understand. You mean you don't buy anything and so you are able to watch everything?'

'No,' she said, 'it's not that. We do buy things. That's part of it. Most of the girls like to buy little knick-knacks, and anyway it gives them a good chance to do their shopping while they're there. But while they *are* there they are observing. Then afterwards they make charts.'

'Charts of what?' I asked.

'Charts of the employés; they're used to show the brain movement involved.'

'Do you find much?'

'Well,' she said hesitatingly, 'the idea is to reduce all the employés to a Curve.'

'To a Curve?' I exclaimed, 'An In or an Out?'

'No, no, not exactly that. Didn't you use Curves when you were at college?'

'Never,' I said.

'Oh, well, nowadays nearly everything, you know, is done into a Curve. We put them on the board.'

'And what is this particular Curve of the employé used for?' I asked.

'Why,' said the student, 'the idea is that from the Curve we can get the Norm of the employé.'

'Get his Norm?' I asked.

'Yes, get the Norm. That stands for the Root Form of the employé as a social factor.'

'And what can you do with that?'

'Oh, when we have that we can tell what the employé would do under any and every circumstance. At least that's the idea – though I'm really only quoting,' she added, breaking off in a diffident way, 'from what Miss Thinker, the Professor of Social Endeavour, says. She's really fine. She's making a general chart of the female employés of one of the biggest stores to show what percentage in case of fire would jump out of the window and what percentage would run to the fire escape.'

'It's a wonderful course,' I said. 'We had nothing like it when I went to college. And does it only take in departmental stores?'

'No,' said the girl, 'the laboratory work includes for this semester ice-cream parlours as well.'

'What do you do with *them*?'

'We take them up as Social Cells – Nuclei, I think the professor calls them.'

'And how do you go at them?' I asked.

'Why, the girls go to them in little laboratory groups and study them.'

'They eat ice-cream in them?'

'They *have* to,' she said, 'to make it concrete. But while they are doing it they are considering the ice-cream parlour merely as a section of social protoplasm.'

'Does the professor go?' I asked.

'Oh, yes, she heads each group. Professor Thinker never spares herself from work.'

'Dear me,' I said, 'you must be kept very busy. And is Social Endeavour all that you are going to do?'

'No,' she answered, 'I'm electing a half-course in Nature Work as well.'

'Nature Work? Well! Well! That, I suppose, means cramming up a lot of biology and zoology, does it not?'

'No,' said the girl, 'it's not exactly done with *books*. I believe it is all done by Field Work.'

'Field Work?'

'Yes, Field Work four times a week and an Excursion every Saturday.'

'And what do you do in the Field Work?'

'The girls,' she answered, 'go out in groups anywhere out of doors, and make a Nature Study of anything they see.'

'How do they do that?' I asked.

'Why, they look at it. Suppose, for example, they come to a stream or a pond or anything –'

'Yes –'

'Well, they *look* at it.'

'Had they never done that before?' I asked.

'Ah, but they look at it as a Nature Unit. Each girl must take forty units in the course. I think we only do one unit each day we go out.'

'It must,' I said, 'be pretty fatiguing work, and what about the Excursion?'

'That's every Saturday. We go out with Miss Stalk, the Professor of Ambulation.'

'And where do you go?'

'Oh, anywhere. One day we go perhaps for a trip on a steamer and another Saturday somewhere in motors, and so on.'

'Doing what?' I asked.

'Field Work. The aim of the course – I'm afraid I'm quoting Miss Stalk but I don't mind, she's really fine – is to break nature into its elements –'

'I see –'

'So as to view it as the external structure of Society and make deductions from it.'

'Have you made any?' I asked.

'Oh, no' – she laughed – 'I'm only starting the work this term. But, of course, I shall have to. Each girl makes at least one deduction at the end of the course. Some of the seniors make two or three. But you have to make *one*.'

'It's a great course,' I said. 'No wonder you are going to be busy; and, as you say, how much better than loafing round here doing nothing.'

'Isn't it?' said the girl student with enthusiasm in her eyes. 'It gives one such a sense of purpose, such a feeling of doing something.'

'It must,' I answered.

'Oh, goodness,' she exclaimed, 'there's the lunch bell. I must skip and get ready.'

She was just vanishing from my side when the Burly Male Student, who was also staying in the hotel, came puffing up after his five-mile run. He was getting himself into trim for enlistment, so he told me. He noted the retreating form of the college girl as he sat down.

'I've just been talking to her,' I said, 'about her college work. She seems to be studying a queer lot of stuff – Social Endeavour and all that!'

'Awful piffle,' said the young man. 'But the girls naturally run to all that sort of rot, you know.'

'Now, your work,' I went on, 'is no doubt very different. I mean what you were taking before the war came along. I suppose you fellows have an awful dose of mathematics and philology and so on just as I did in my college days?'

Something like a blush came across the face of the handsome youth.

'Well, no,' he said, 'I didn't co-opt mathematics. At our college, you know, we co-opt two majors and two minors.'

'I see,' I said, 'and what were you co-opting?'

'I co-opted Turkish, Music, and Religion,' he answered.

'Oh, yes,' I said with a sort of reverential respect, 'fitting yourself for a position of choir-master in a Turkish cathedral, no doubt.'

'No, no,' he said, 'I'm going into insurance; but, you see, those subjects fitted in better than anything else.'

'Fitted in?'

'Yes. Turkish comes at nine, music at ten and religion at eleven. So they make a good combination; they leave a man free to –'

'To develop his mind,' I said. 'We used to find in my college days that lectures interfered with it badly. But now, Turkish, that must be an interesting language, eh?'

'Search me!' said the student. 'All you have to do is answer the roll and go out. Forty roll-calls, give you one Turkish unit – but, say, I must get on, I've got to change. So long.'

I could not help reflecting, as the young man left me, on the great changes that have come over our college education. It was a relief to me later in the day to talk with a quiet, sombre man, himself a graduate student in philosophy, on this topic. He agreed with me that the old strenuous studies seem to be very largely abandoned.

I looked at the sombre man with respect.

'Now your work,' I said, 'is very different from what these young people are doing – hard, solid, definite effort. What a relief it must be to you to get a brief vacation up here. I couldn't help thinking today, as I watched you moving round doing nothing, how fine it must feel for you to come up here after your hard work and put in a month of out-and-out loafing.'

'Loafing!' he said indignantly. 'I'm not loafing. I'm putting in a half summer course in Introspection. That's why I'm here. I get credit for two majors for my time here.'

'Ah,' I said, as gently as I could, 'you get credit here.'

He left me. I am still pondering over our new education. Meantime I think I shall enter my little boy's name on the books of Tuskegee College where the education is still old-fashioned.

Eighteen
Bass Fishing on Lake Simcoe

WITH JAKE GAUDAUR

(It ought to be the privilege of an author to reserve some part of his book as his own, and to put into it whatever he likes. Especially in the present volume of which the earlier part contains so much that is controversial and might arouse anger and disagreement, is it fitting to end with a discourse on fishing where no anger is and where disagreement is only on the surface – which in fishing is of no account. – S.L.)

Among the pleasant memories of my life is the recollection of my fishing days on Ontario's Lake Simcoe with Jake Gaudaur – little excursions that extended over twenty or twenty-five years. If you don't know the name of Jake Gaudaur it only means that you were born fifty years too late. Half a century ago Jake was for several years the champion oarsman of the world – a title won on the Thames at Henley. In those days, before motor cars and aeroplanes, rowing was one of the big interests of the nations, and Jake Gaudaur was a hero to millions who had never seen him. The fact that his name was pronounced exactly as Good-Oar helped to keep it easily in mind.

Jake was of mixed French and Indian descent but belonged in the Lake Simcoe country and English had always been his language – the kind we use up there, not the kind they use at Oxford. I can talk both, but the Lake Simcoe is easier and, for fishing, far better. It cuts out social distinction. Jake was a magnificent figure of a man: he stood nicely six feet in his stocking feet – the only way we ever measure people up there. He was broad in the shoulders, straight as a lath – and till the time when he died just short of eighty he could pick up the twenty-pound anchor of his motor-boat and throw it round like a tack-hammer. Jake – standing erect in the bow of his motor-boat and looking out to the horizon, his eyes shaded with his hand – might have stood for the figure of Oshkosh, war chief of the Wisconsin Indians.

When Jake's championship days were over he came back to Canada and 'kept hotel' in Sudbury. That was the thing for champions to do: in

290

the unregenerate days of the old bar, thousands of people spent five cents on a drink just to say they had talked with Jake Gaudaur. I wish that retired professors could open up a bar. It must be a great thing to be an ex-champion or a quintuplet, and never have to work.

So Jake made his modest pile and then came back to our part of the country, the Lake Simcoe district, and set up at 'the Narrows', at the top end of the lake, as a professional fisherman, taking out parties on the lake for bass fishing.

Now, who hasn't seen Lake Simcoe has never seen a lake at all. Lake Simcoe on a July morning – the water, ruffled in wavelets of a blue and green and silver, as clear as never was: the sky of the purest blue with great clouds white and woolly floating in it! Just the day for fishing – every day is, for the enthusiastic.

The lake is just right in size to be what a lake ought to be – twenty to thirty miles across in any direction – so that there's always a part of the horizon open where you can't see the land – the shore is all irregular with bays and 'points' and islands and shoals, so that any roads thereabouts are away back from the water, and the shore line of trees and sand and stone looks much as Champlain saw it three hundred years ago. Over it in the summer air of July there hovers an atmosphere of unbroken peace. When I think of it I cannot but contrast it with the curse that lies over Europe where mountain lakes are scarped and galleried for guns, and every church steeple on their shores a range and target. I wish I could take Hitler and Mussolini out bass fishing on Lake Simcoe. They'd come back better men – or they'd never come back.

* * *

So here we are at ten o'clock in the morning helping Jake load the stuff out of our car into his motor-boat! Notice that – ten o'clock. None of that fool stuff about starting off at daylight. You get over that by the time you're forty. The right time to start off bass fishing is when you're good and ready to. And when I say ten o'clock, I really mean about ten-thirty. We just call it ten o'clock and when you look at your watch after you're actually started, it's always ten-thirty, or not much past it. Anyway there's no finer time in the day on the water than ten-thirty, still all the freshness of the morning and all the day in front of you – half-way between windy and calm with little ruffled waves in the sunlight, and a cool breeze, partly made by the boat itself.

As for the bass, they bite as well at any one time as at any other. The idea that they bite at daylight and don't bite after lunch is just a myth. They bite when they're ready to – the only reason they don't bite after lunch is that the fishermen are asleep till three.

Jake's boat is no 'power' boat, to hit up twenty-five miles an hour.

That fool stuff came to our lakes later and is out of keeping with bass fishing. Jake's is a big, roomy open boat with a front part for Jake and big open part at the back where we sit: a broad stern seat with leather cushions and wicker armchairs on a linoleum floor. Solid comfort. No rough stuff for us: we're not sailors. And no cover to keep off the sun – who cares a darn about the sun when you're fishing? – and nothing to keep off the wind – let it come: and no protection against the rain. It *won't* rain. Any man who thinks it's going to rain shouldn't go fishing.

'Will it rain, Jake?'

'I don't think so, professor: not with that sky.'

We've gone through that little opening dialogue, I suppose, a hundred times. That's the beauty of bass fishing: always doing the same things in the same way, with the same old jokes and the same conversation.

'I was thinking we might go out and try the big rock at McCrae's point first, professor,' says Jake.

Seeing that we've never done anything else in twenty years it seems a likely thing to do.

This gives us two miles to go, down from the Narrows to the open lake and then sideways across to the first point. For me this is always the best part of the day – the cool fresh air, the anticipation better than reality, the settling into our wicker chairs and lighting up our pipes, with the stuff all properly stowed around us, the fishing gear, the lunch and the box with the soda on ice. Not that we take a drink at this time of the day. Oh, no! We're all agreed that you don't need a drink on a beautiful fine morning at ten-thirty – unless perhaps for the special reason today because it's such a damn fine day that you feel so good or the other – because you don't feel so good. So perhaps this morning, 'Eh, what?' 'Well, just a starter.' 'Jake, can I pass you along a horn?' 'Thanks, professor, I don't mind.'

There are four of us, mostly, apart from Jake, so it takes most of the time of the run to mix up and serve the drinks. I am thinking here especially of one party though really it was just like all the others. There was my brother George and George Rapley, the bank manager (a tear to his kind memory), and Charlie Janes, the railroad man of a Lake Simcoe town. George Rapley always came because he could fish, and Charlie Janes because he *couldn't*. You may have noticed that bank managers are always good fishermen; it's something in their profession, I think, a kind of courtesy, that gets the fish. And I am sure that everybody who goes bass fishing will agree that to make the party right you need one fellow who *can't* fish. In fact in any bass fishing party of friends who go out often together there is always one who is cast for the part of not knowing how to fish. No matter how often he's been out, he's not supposed to know anything about fishing and he good-naturedly accepts the role. If he loses a fish that's supposed to be because he didn't know how to land it, if we lose a fish that is supposed to be because it was *impossible* to land it. It's these little mutual understandings that fit life together.

*   *   *

So, almost before the 'horn' is finished here we are bearing down on the big rock off McCrae's point. It's nearly a quarter of a mile from shore and six feet under water, but Jake steers to it like a taxi to a hotel door. The anchor goes down with a splash, our swing on it timed to throw us right over the rock! There it is! See it – big as a wagon! – and in another minute down go the baited lines trailing to go under the edge of the great rock.

This is the great moment of fishing, the first minute with the lines down – tense, exhilarating. It's always the same way – either something big happens, or nothing, Perhaps – bing! the lines are no sooner down than a bass is hooked – by Charlie Janes, of course – just like the luck of the darned fool. And while he's still hauling on it – biff! there's another one – and Jake, it seems, has quietly landed a third one when the other two were plunging round. With which there's such a period of excitement and expectation that it's nearly three-quarters of an hour before you realize that those three fish are all there are – or rather *two* fish: George Rapley lost his – too bad! he was playing it so beautifully. Charlie Janes, the darned old fool, flung his over the side of the boat, right slap into the ice-box.

Or else – the other alternative – the lines go down and nothing happens.

In either case we fish on and on under the rock till excitement fades into dullness, and dullness into dead certainty. That's *all*. At last someone says, 'I guess they ain't biting here any more.' Notice. '*They're not biting*' – we never say, '*They're not here.*' Any man who says, as I have heard some of our old guests say, 'Oh, hell, there are no fish here,' is not fit to be brought again. The only theory on which bass fishing can be maintained as a rational pastime is that the bass are *everywhere* – all the time. But they won't bite. The wind may be wrong, or the air just too damp, or too dry, or too much sun, or not enough – it's amazing how little will start a bass not biting. But the cause must always be one that can change in five minutes, or with a move of five yards. These beliefs are to a fisherman what faith is to a Christian.

'We might try out past Strawberry Island,' says Jake. This means a change farther out, right out in the open water of the lake with the whole horizon of wind and wave and sun open for twenty miles all around to the south. This is not exactly a shoal. The bottom of the lake drops here from twelve feet to thirty feet of water – like the side of a hill. Jake explains it all fresh every time, and he makes each new spot seem so different and so likely that we go at each with new hope eternal. If we don't get any fish as each half-hour stop goes by, Jake tells the story of how he and I fished once and never had a bite till after sundown and then caught thirty-three bass in half an hour off McGinnis's reef. 'You mind that evening, professor?' he says (to 'mind' a thing is to remember it). 'It was thirty-three wasn't it?' 'Thirty-four, I think, Jake.' I answer, and he says, 'Well, mebbe it was.' We've brought those fish up a little every year.

Or else Jake tells the story of the young girl from Toledo who came up with her father and had never been fishing before and never even in a motor-boat and it was a caution how many she caught. This story, of course, conveys the idea that if inexperienced fishers, like the young lady from Toledo, can catch fish, experienced people like ourselves could hardly expect to.

*   *   *

Then all of a sudden, as it always seems, comes the idea of lunch – all of a sudden everybody hungry and ready for it. And does ever food taste better than out in the wind and sun in a motor-boat – salmon sandwiches, cold chicken in a salad, chunks of home-made bread, mustard pickles; all eaten partly off a plate and partly with your fingers and with bottled ale to wash it down.

People who go fishing but are not real fishermen land on shore for lunch, light a fire and, I believe, even cook the fish caught: some of them go so far as to have a game of poker or, in extreme cases of mental derangement, go for a swim. All of this to a proper fisherman is just deplorable, just lunacy. The true fisherman eats right in the boat with the lines still hanging in the water. There seems to be a sort of truce during lunch time: I never knew a bass to touch a hook till it's over. But lunch on the other hand isn't hurried. It's just eaten in the natural way. You put into your mouth all it will hold; then eat it; then start again. Eating in the open air knows no satiety, no indigestion.

The whole point is that the longest day is all too short for fishing, and no one who really loves bass fishing can bear the thought of knocking off from it even for an hour. As a matter of fact, we do take time off but we never admit it. For there always came in our fishing with Jake a drowsy part of the day when we took a sleep. Not that we ever called it that deliberately. The sleep was just a sort of accident. A little while after we'd eaten all the lunch we could hold Jake would say, 'I thought we might go and try for a spell down round the corner of that shoal, just off that way a piece. You mind we was there before?' 'Yes, sure, I remember it, Jake.'

The place is a sort of convenient little hook among the shoals – nothing showing on top of the water; we always reckoned as if the bottom were in sight – it had the advantage that the waves couldn't reach it because of the shallows, and it was always quiet, and no fish ever came there. Jake could anchor the boat where there were just enough waves to rock the boat gently and just enough light breeze to murmur a lullaby, and with the two o'clock sun to make you pull your straw panama away over your eyes, a man seated like that in a wicker chair, with two pounds of sandwiches and six ounces of whisky in him, is as drowsy as a flower nodding on its stem, and asleep in five minutes. The lines dangle in the water; there is no conversation, no sound but the breeze and the lapping of the little waves. Up in front we could see only Jake's broad back; but there was slumber in every line of it.

It didn't matter who woke first. After about an hour anybody could straighten up and say, 'By jove, I believe I was almost asleep, were you?' And the others would answer 'Darn near!' and then Jake would say, as if he'd never stopped talking, 'I was thinking we might go out and try the dry shoal.'

This rouses us to a new search for bass, hither and thither half a mile, a mile at a time. Even then we are only covering one corner of Lake Simcoe. The lake is just big enough to seem illimitable.

Bass fishing on Lake Simcoe is not like the bass fishing you can get a hundred miles north of it, on the rivers in the bush, out of easy reach. Up there it's no come-and-go business in a day; you must stay at least two nights. You catch one hundred bass in the first day and the next day you don't even keep them, you throw them back. The third day you hate the stinking things; a bass two days dead, with its skin discoloured, would sicken even a cannibal.

Not so Lake Simcoe. There are just not enough bass, just never too many – some dead, dull days without any – they're there, but they won't bite. But even on the deadest, dullest day, always the hope of a strike.

You might wonder, if you don't know the life, why the afternoon never gets dreary, what there can be to talk about – especially among men often and always out together on the same ground. That's just ignorance. In bass fishing there are vast unsettled problems to be discussed for ever. For, example, do you need to 'play' a bass? or is that just a piece of damn nonsense imitated out of salmon fishing? The school to which I belong holds that 'playing' a bass is just a way of losing it.

What you need is a steel rod with the last section taken out and an 'emergency tip' put in – making a short, firm rod about six feet long.

When the bass nibbles, *wait* – then wait some more – then strike – with such power as to drive the hook right through his head – then shorten the line – not with a reel; that's too slow – haul it in beside the reel with your left hand and hold it firm with your right – shove the rod close to the water, if need be *under* the water – by that means the bass *can't* jump out of the water, there isn't line enough – drag him against his will till someone else holds the net – and in he comes.

Contrast this with the artistic 'playing' of fish that *looks* so skilful – paying out line – the fish leaping the air thirty feet from the boat – and all that show stuff – only good for a picture-book!

Now can't you see that the discussion of that point alone can fill an afternoon?

Personally I am always an extremist for a short rod and rapid action – the bass right in the boat in twenty seconds. I think that in his heart Jake Gaudaur agreed with this. It's the way all Indians fish and always have. But Jake's calling demanded compromise. He favoured both sides. Rapley, like all bankers, played a fish as they play a customer with a loan, taking it in gradually.

* * *

We always knew that the afternoon was closing to evening when Jake said, 'Suppose we go out and try that big rock inside McGinnis's reef: you mind, professor, the place where you caught all them bass that night – thirty-four, wasn't it?' 'Yes, or thirty-five, Jake. I'm not sure: let's try it.'

This sunken rock is the triumph of Jake's navigation of the lake. It's mile from even the nearest point of land, and sunk six feet down. Beside it the big rock at McCrae's is child's play. That one you can find if you keep on looking for it. This one, never. It's all very well to say that you can do it with 'bearings': any amateur yachtsman that ever wore panama pants will tell you that. But try it. Try to get bearings that are good at all hours and all lights and shadows on the shores, good in rain and good in mist, and you soon see where you are – or are not.

Jake, erect at the bow as he steers, is as straight as Oshkosh, the boat gathers speed in a curve that picks up one of the bearings and then straight as a pencil line over the water for a mile – then a stop with a reversed engine without a turn or the bearings would be lost, and there we are – right over the rock. In a clear light it's as plain as day, but on a dull day you can just make it out, a great rock sunk in a wide basin of water for the bass to get in.

Here we try our final luck. We can't leave. If the bass are there (I mean if they are biting), it's too good to leave. If we don't get a bite, we just *can't* leave.

We haven't realized it but the afternoon has all gone. The sun is setting behind the hills on the west side of the lake.

Just before it goes its beams light up for a moment the windows of unseen farmhouses ten miles the other side of us – and then, before we know it, the sun is gone. But we can't leave. It's still broad daylight, nearly. 'There's two or three hours' good fishing yet, Jake, eh?' 'All of that, professor.' Somehow it seems as if the day were suddenly all gone. 'Have another horn, Jake?' Surely that'll hold the daylight a little, giving Jake a horn. Anyway we can't leave. The light is fading a little. A cold wind begins to move across the lake, the water seems to blacken under its touch as the boat swings to it. 'The wind's kind o'gone round,' says Jake. 'I thought it would.' It's not surprising: the wind has gone round, and the air turned chill after sundown, every evening of the sixty years I've known Lake Simcoe. But we can't leave. Charlie Janes has had a bite – or says he has – we never take Charlie's word, of course, as really good: he may have caught in a crack of rock. But Rapley thinks he had a nibble. That's better evidence. So we stay on, and on, till the dark has fallen, the shores all grown dim and then vanished and the north-west wind beginning to thump the waves on the bow of the anchored boat.

'I guess, gentlemen, it's about time to pull up,' says Jake. If we had caught fifteen or twenty bass he'd have said, 'Boys, I guess it's about time to quit.' But 'gentlemen' brings us back to the cold cruel reality.

So the anchor is up and the motor-boat at its full power set for home. It's quite rough on the water now: the boat slaps into the waves and sends the spray flying clear astern to where we have our chairs huddled together, back to the wind. It's dark, too, you have to use a flashlight to open the soda for the 'consolation drinks' that mark the end of the fishing. 'Have a horn, Jake?' 'Thanks, professor.' Jake, with his oil clothes on, can't leave the wheel now: he sits there all in the spray with one hand for steering and one for the drink.

* * *

It's amazing how a lake like Lake Simcoe can change – a few hours ago a halcyon paradise, still and calm – and now with the night the wind gathering over it – 'Oh, well, Jake knows the way,' and anyway it's only three miles till we'll be in shelter of the Narrows! – Whew! that was a corker, that wave! 'Here, put these newspapers behind your back, Charlie, they'll keep off the spray.'

Just enough of this to give one a slight feeling of night and mimic danger – and then in no great time, for the distance is short, we round into the shelter of the Narrows with just a mile of water, smoother and smoother, to run. All different it looks from the morning; what you see now is just lights – a perplexing galaxy of lights, white and green and red here and there on the unseen shore – and great flares of moving white light that must be the motors on the highway.

'What's the red light away up, Jake?'

'That's the one above the railway bridge.' We always ask Jake this and when he answers we know we are close in. The water suddenly is quite smooth, a current running with us – the summer cottages and docks come in sight, with 'young fellers' and girls in canoes and the sound of a radio somewhere discussing war in Europe.

We're back in the world again, landed at Jake's dock with a little crowd of loafers and boys standing round to see 'how many fish Jake got,' – not us, *Jake*. We unload the boat and take a look at the string of fish. 'Let's see that big one that Rapley caught, eh?' But where is it? Surely it can't be this small dirty-looking flabby thing – I'm afraid it is.

We divide the fish. Jake won't take any. We try to work them off on one another. Fishermen want *fishing*, never fish – and end by slinging them into the car all in one box. 'Well, we certainly had a fine day, good night, Jake.' And another fishing day has gone – now never to return.

I can only repeat, in tribute to a fine memory, 'Good night, Jake.'

Nineteen
The Boy I Left Behind Me

PART ONE

Some Chapters of Autobiography

CHAPTER I

There'll always be an England

I was born in Victorian England on December 30th in 1869, which is exactly the middle year of Queen Victoria's reign. If I were analysed by one of those scientific French biographers who take full account of the time, the place, the circumstance, or by the new school of psychologists who study 'behaviour', I imagine much could be made of this. As expressed in a plain sense, I am certain that I have never got over it.

I was born at Swanmore, which is a hamlet and parish on 'Waltham Chase' in Hampshire. They use names like that in Hampshire because it is so old: it doesn't say who chased whom: they may have forgotten. Anyway, it is a mile and a half from Bishop's Waltham, which is ten miles from Winchester and of which details may be had by consulting the Domesday Book, though of course there is earlier information also. One reason why one feels proud of being born in Hampshire is that it is all of such immemorial antiquity. The Norman Conquest there is just nothing. Porchester and Winchester and Chichester are all a thousand years older than that.

I fell into an error about my birthplace and put it into print a good many times during the several years it lasted, so that I came near to having the honour of a disputed birthplace like Homer and Mr Irvin Cobb. It was Irvin Cobb – was it not? – who said he had nearly got one but couldn't keep the dispute going. Mine arose quite innocently. I discovered that there is a Swanmore which is a suburb of Ryde in the Isle of Wight, and as I knew that my grandfather lived near Ryde I moved my birthplace into that suburb. Finding there was doubt, I wrote to a solicitor at Ryde who had conducted the family business of the Leacocks for generations and asked about it. He wrote that he thought it extremely unlikely that I was born in such a locality as Swanmore, Ryde. But I didn't know whether this was one on Swanmore or one on me, whether Swanmore was not fit for me to be born in, or whether I had not the required class for Swanmore. So it stands at that. In any case it was in 1869 and Swanmore may have picked up since.

But I was led by this to write to the Vicar of Bishop's Waltham and he sent me back a certificate of my birth and christening at Swanmore Parish Church, and he said that I was not only born in Swanmore but that Hampshire was proud of it. This gave me such a warm thrill of affection for Hampshire that I very nearly renewed my subscription (one guinea per annum) to the Hampshire Society: very nearly – not quite. I knew they'd take the guinea but I was not sure how they'd feel about it. People who come from celebrated places like Hampshire, known to all the world, and go away and don't see them again year after year, are apt to get warm rushes of sudden affection and pride towards the good old place. I've known people feel this way towards Texas or Newfoundland or in fact anywhere to which you can't get back.

In such a glow of feeling years ago I subscribed to the Hampshire Society (one guinea per annum) and it was certainly a delight at first to get the annual circular, with the names of the Lord-Lieutenant and a lot of people as fellow-members, and the receipts and disbursements, and the balance carried forward – excitements like that. So it went on that way year after year for years – a guinea, and a guinea, and a guinea – till one year all of a sudden I got an angry fit of economy (in the depression) and asked, What am I getting out of all this? – a guinea, and a guinea – that could go on for ever – and I wrote and cut out my membership. It's nothing against Hampshire. People do that to Texas and Newfoundland. And in any case it was in the same year and about the same time that I cut out my subscriptions to the Royal Society of Canada, and the Authors' Association – even to things that I didn't belong to. But it seemed a dirty trick to have dropped the Hampshire Society and to have fallen out of the Receipts and Disbursements and General Balance.

My family were Hampshire people on both sides, not of course the real thing going back to the Conquest, but not bad. The Leacocks lived on the Isle of Wight where my grandfather had a house called Oak Hill near Ryde, but I gather that he wanted the Island for himself and didn't want his sons to come crowding on to it. That's why they were sent out across the world wherever it was farthest. The Leacocks had made a lot of money out of plantations in Madeira and the Madeira wine trade, so much that my great-grandfather John Leacock had retired and bought the house at Oak Hill. After that nobody in the family did any work (any real work) for three generations, after which, in my generation, we were all broke and had to start work, and work in the low-down sense where you work by the hour – a thing that would disqualify anybody in Hampshire right off the bat. My brothers, I think, got 17 cents an hour. I got a cent a minute, but that was as a school-teacher. But I am anticipating and I turn back.

The Leacocks, I say, were in Madeira wine and the wine trade and some of my cousins are still there and still in it. The senior member of the family got out a few years ago a booklet about Madeira wines and the Leacock family and he put into it the fatal sentence – 'The first recorded Leacock was a London day-labourer, whose son was brought up at a charity school and went out as a ship's cabin-boy to Madeira!' Think of it! What can you do after that? It's no use going on to say what a wonderful fellow the ship's cabin-boy was, and how he built up great plantations and ownerships. That's no good. You can't get over that day-labourer stuff. The Lord-Lieutenant of Hampshire knows just where to class me.

My mother's family, the Butlers, were much better, though you couldn't really call them Hampshire people as they had not, at the time of which I speak, been in Hampshire for more than a hundred and fifty years. They lived, and do still, in a house called Bury Lodge which is on a hill overlooking the immemorial village of Hambledon, Hants, a village so old that they talk there of the Great Plague of 1666 when so many people were buried in the churchyard as an affliction of yesterday. Hambledon, Hants, is to all people who play cricket and love the game, as Mecca is to a Mohammedan. Here, more than anywhere else, began the sacred game, for there is no other adjective that can convey what cricket means to Englishmen than only the word 'sacred'. Here on the windswept open space of 'Broadhalfpenny Down' was bowled the first ball, the first rushing underhand ball where bowling began. Here men in tophats planned and named the game, designated by a flight of daring fancy the strip of ground between the wickets as the 'pitch', indicated the right side of the batter as the 'off' side and the left as the 'on' side – names taken from the English carriage driving – christened the brave man fielding thirty feet behind the batter's bat as 'squareleg' (he needed to be), invented the 'over' and the 'wide' and the 'no ball' and 'l.b.w.' – to be carried round the world later as the abiding bond of the British Empire.

The Butler family were intimately concerned with the beginnings of cricket and in the drawing-room of Bury Lodge are preserved (on blue foolscap paper, gummed on to the firescreens) some of the earliest scores at Broadhalfpenny Down. When I was lecturing in London in 1921 I mentioned to E. V. Lucas, the famous humorist (also one of the great authorities on cricket) this family connection and the old score sheets at Bury Lodge. I found that he at once regarded me with a sort of reverence. Nothing would do him but we must drive down to Hampshire to look at them. This we did, Lucas supplying the car while I felt that my presence with him was compensation enough. The house was shut up, as the Butlers were in London, but a housekeeper showed us the scores, and then we drove up to Broadhalfpenny Down and stood there in the wind, well, just as people stand on the ruins of Carthage. After that we went down into Hambledown village and to the 'pub', where I had all that peculiar gratification that goes with 'the return of the native'. There were several old men round and it was astonishing what they could remember over a pint of beer, and still more over a quart. I had been away from Hambledon for nearly fifty years, so it enabled one to play the part of Rip Van Winkle. I didn't mention that I had only been there once before, for ten minutes, as a child of six.

Generally the return of the native to his native town (for its old home week or for what not) is apt to be spoiled by the fact that after all he hasn't been away long enough, only ten or a dozen years at most. So when he says, 'What's become of the queer old cuss who used to keep the drugstore? When did he die?' they answer in chorus, 'He's not dead. He's right there still.' In such circumstances never say that you'd give ten dollars to see So-and-so again, or they'll go and bring him.

As I say, my grandfather needed all the Isle of Wight to himself and so when my father married my mother, whose name was Agnes Butler, daughter of the Reverend Stephen Butler, they were promptly sent out to South Africa. That was in 1866–7, long before the days of diamonds and gold created the South Africa of sorrows that came later. Those were the days of sailing ships, of infinite distances and of long farewells. They went 'up country' to Maritzburg in oxcarts and then out beyond it to settle. It was all as primitive then as we see it in the movies that deal with Dr Livingstone and Darkest Africa. I saw Maritzburg forty years later when its people seemed a mass of Asiatics, the immigrant wave from India that first awoke South Africa to the 'Asiatic peril'.

Maritzburg in 1867 no doubt appeared singularly quiet, but to those who lived there the whole place, as my mother has told me, was 'seething with the Colenso controversy'. I imagine few people of today remember the name of Colenso, the Bishop of Natal, the mathematician over whose *Arithmetic* and *Algebra* a generation of English schoolboys groaned and whose mild aspersions on the Pentateuch – I think it means the first five books of the Old Testament – opened the way, like a water leak in a dam, to heresies that swept away the literal interpretation of Scripture. Colenso became a sort of test case, in orthodoxy, and in the law as to the government of the Church of England in the colonies, and locally a test case in the fidelity of the congregation. Some people in Natal would allow their children to be baptized by the Bishop and some wouldn't and held them over for the Dean any time the Bishop was away. My eldest brother who was born in Natal got caught up in this controversy and torn backward and forward before he could be christened. But the South African climate proved impossible for my mother, and the locusts ate up their farm, and so the family came home again to Hampshire.

My grandfather then took another big think as to where he would send them to, and it was in this interregnum of thinking that my father was supposed to be 'learning farming' to fit him to be sent to America. There was at that time in England a prevalent myth that farming could be 'learned', especially by young men who couldn't learn anything else. So my father seems to have been moved round from one centre to another, drinking beer under the tutelage of Hampshire farmers who of course could drink more than he could, an agreeable life in which a young man was supposed to remain a gentleman even if he acted like a farmer. As those of us who have been brought up on farms know, you can't 'learn farming', at least not that way. We could in fact whisper to one another the way you learn it. First of all, as Course No. 1, or First Year Agronomics, you get on to a wagon-load of manure at six in the morning and drive up and down a seven-acre field throwing it in all directions, in fact seeing how far you can throw it. Then you go back for another load. Course No. 2, or Cultivation, involves driving two horses hitched to what is called a set of field harrows up and down a dry ploughed field so as to turn it into a cloud of dust and thistledown. During the driving you shout *Gee* and *Haw* at the horses. They don't know what it means, but they are used to hearing it and they know where to go, anyway. Courses like that carried on systematically over a period of years make a man a farmer.

Of course I don't deny that over this and above it are the real courses in Agriculture such as they teach at Ste. Anne's, P.Q., out near Montreal and at the Ontario Agricultural College at Guelph, both splendid places. Here a student goes at it all scientifically, learning the chemistry of the thing and the composition of soils and all that. Hence when he goes back on the farm he sees it all with a new eye. He still spends his days driving the manure wagon round a seven-acre field, and driving harrows in a cloud of dust. But it is all different. He now knows what manure *is*. Before that he thought it was just manure. And he now understands why dust floats and he knows what he is doing when he pulverizes the soil, instead of merely thinking that he is 'breaking it up good'.

During this period of interregnum my father and mother lived at different places – Swanmore and Shoreham (in Sussex) and then Porchester. Their large family (which ultimately reached eleven in England and Canada) were borne round in this way, only two in the same place of the six born in England. It was from Porchester that my father was sent out ahead of us by my grandfather to Kansas, a place of which my grandfather must have heard great things in the early seventies, though its first charm of the John Brown days was fading.

Porchester is the only place of my childhood days in England that I really remember. I lived there for two years (age 4½ to 6½) and in a sense it still means the England that is England to me. At the opening of the recent war when the inspiring song, *There'll Always be an England*, burst upon the world, I set forth this theme as centred for me round Porchester in a magazine publication which I reproduce here.

The England I Remember
There'll Always be an England.

I imagine that somebody first said that away back in Anglo-Saxon times. The people who heard him say it most likely remarked, 'Well, naturally!' and 'Poetic chap, eh?'

Yet when I first heard those words sung, they brought back to me a sudden remembrance of the England of my childhood and a poignant affection for it, more than I knew I had. This, I am sure, happened to many people . . .

ALWAYS BE AN ENGLAND

This, most certainly, is true of the immemorial village of Porchester in which I was brought up, for which the flight of time was meaningless. But my father's farm in South Africa, as I have said before, was eaten out by locusts and so he and my mother came home where I and other brothers were born. Meantime, my grandfather was consulting the map and picked on Kansas because at that time the railways only got that far. My father went first and we were placed in Porchester so that we couldn't get to the Isle of Wight too often. We were ready to go to America when word came that my father's farm in Kansas had been eaten by grasshoppers (they are the same as locusts). This meant delay while my grandfather looked for something farther still. So we waited on in Porchester, and I had altogether six years of an English childhood that I had no right to have under rules.

Porchester? Where is it? Right across the water from Portsmouth. What water? Ah, now, that I never knew – it's the water between

Portsmouth and Porchester. You could tell it then by the tall masts and yards of the men-of-war, and of the *Victory* swinging there at anchor . . . Up at the end of it was Paul's Grove, where St Paul preached to the ancient – ah, there you have me – but to a congregation probably very like my Uncle Charles's congregation in the little Porchester church . . . The church stood – or it did in 1876, and things can hardly have changed in so short a time – inside the precincts of Porchester Castle. You've seen the Castle perhaps, a vast quadrangle of towers and battlements, and a great space inside for cattle during sieges. The newer parts were built by the Normans but the original part by the Romans. The Normans built the church, but Good Queen Anne 'restored' it, with a lot of others, and so, on the wall, there was a great painted lettering in gilt and faded colours: BY THE BOUNTY OF QUEEN ANNE. You could spell it out from your tall pew by the sunlight falling on the wall through the dancing leaves, while Uncle Charles preached, quietly so as not to wake the Normans, and the people gently dozed.

. . . ALWAYS, AN ENGLAND.

Why, of course, to the people of Porchester. Time left no trace there; all the centuries were yesterday, St Paul, and the Castle, and Queen Elizabeth's bedroom, and Uncle Charles and Queen Anne.

. . . WHEREVER THERE'S A BUSY STREET . . .

Busy? Well, I suppose you could call it busy, the village street with the little 'common' breaking it in the middle. There was only one of everything: one public-house, one grocery, one rectory (Uncle Charles's), one windmill (Pyecroft's), one fly (Peacock's), and so on. There'd been no competition for years. The public-house, the Crown and Anchor, stood where it should, where the street came together at the 'common,' and looked as it should in *Father, Dear Father, Come Home with me Now* . . . with red curtains in the windows.

. . . WHEREVER THERE ARE TURNING WHEELS . . .

Pyecroft's mill looked just right, standing down on the water a little way from the Castle. The sails of Pyecroft's mill moved so slowly they seemed to soar and hover. Tennyson speaks of a 'tall mill that whistled on the waste.' He fell down there, eh, Pyecroft? Pyecroft looked the part admirably, all dust . . . and Peacock who had the fly matched it. All the people in Porchester looked like that, each fitted the part . . . Old

General Hurdle coming down the street, a frail, old, soldierly figure, so upright that he quivered on his stick. Take old Grubb, who had been in the navy in the 1914–18 War (what we called the Great War then), he sat catching periwinkles or whatever they caught, where the Castle moat drained into the sea. He looked it exactly, all tar . . .

All the people, as I say, looked the part, the kind of things despaired of by the movies. I never knew whether Gilbert and Sullivan copied England or England copied Gilbert and Sullivan.

. . . A MILLION MARCHING FEET . . .

I am afraid that would be a large order for Porchester in 1876 . . . a million, well, perhaps it seemed so to us children when swarms of people used to come to the Castle on holidays – I only half recall them – Whit-Monday, something Wednesday, Coronation Day – with Aunt Sally's ginger beer and swings and drunken sailors.

. . . RED, WHITE AND BLUE . . .

The blue, of course, was the sea. As for the 'drunken sailors,' why indeed shouldn't they be drunk? They were 'ashore,' weren't they? Those sailors were better drunk than sober . . . scattering pennies and full of fun. Now a soldier was different . . . a low sort of fellow, hanging around public-houses and getting poor girls into trouble . . . Why isn't he off in Ashantee or some place like that where soldiers belong?

. . . BRITONS, AWAKE . . .

Awake? Well, not too completely. I think of Uncle Charles preaching decorously, quietly, the congregation nodding. I wouldn't disturb that, it has been undisturbed too long. Uncle Charles, I have heard him say it, was singularly fortunate. In Porchester there was no outbreak of 'religion'. There was no chapel, no open-air preaching, no vulgar confession of sin. No people got sudden 'salvation' – they got it gradually, through eighty years of drowsy Sundays. When I was six it all came to an end. My grandfather found a place called Upper Canada, clean out of reach of a railway . . .

. . . WHAT DOES IT MEAN TO YOU? . . .

Then came the most vivid memory, saying good-bye to England as a child . . . We went on board a great ship at Liverpool, a ship with the towering masts and rigging of the grand old days . . . went on board from a hole in the side, it seemed. It was all very wonderful to us, though lots of people, like my mother, cried, because going to America in 1876 meant good-bye.

But for us, the children, it was different, it was all wonderful . . . the crew and all the passengers joined to haul up the anchor . . . And they sang the song of the departing English, *Cheer, boys, cheer, no more of idle sorrow*, that echoed down the decades. As the words died away on the ear . . . Farewell, England, much as we have loved thee, courage, true hearts, will bear us on our way! . . . the great ship was surging into the darkness under press of sail, heading to what we call 'America'.

. . . SHOUT IT LOUD: THE EMPIRE TOO . . .

It was all fun for us . . . the wind, the waves, the magnificence of the 'saloon' . . . And then the great sheets of ice until the ship stopped. On Sunday the clergyman prayed to have it taken away and it went.

Then came a morning when someone called down the companion-way . . . 'Come and see America.' . . . And there it was, a tall, hard coast of trees and rock, clear and bright in the sunshine, not a bit soft, like England.

. . . IF ENGLAND MEANS AS MUCH TO YOU . . .

It was the Gaspé Coast, and we were entering the St Lawrence. I understand that one of the members who represents this section in a legislature proposes to break away from England the three million people of English race and birth, to say nothing of the other three million British, who live in Canada. It would be to blot out, for some, the memories of childhood, and for all, the remembered talk of parents and old people . . . tear up the books that hold the elegies in country churchyards, and hush the sea songs of England on which Tom Bowling's name floats to us down the wind . . .

Speaking of Porchester I may say that after I had gone down to Hambledon with E. V. Lucas I was so fascinated with the role of the returned native that I found time to make a hurried trip to Porchester, to try it out again. When I got there I found my way from the station up (or down, you never know which they call it in England) the straggled street to the village common and to the Father-Dear-Father-Come-Home-With-Me-Now public house of which I spoke. I went into the Crown and Anchor and struck the proper attitude over a glass of beer at the bar. 'Nearly fifty years ago,' I said (feeling like the Silver King come home), 'I used to live in this village. Perhaps you can tell me something about the people I remember.'

The barmaid threw her head indignantly in the air, 'No, indeed, I couldn't,' she said, 'the idea!'

I saw that I was mistaken. 'Not you yourself,' I said, 'you weren't born and couldn't remember, but you may have heard of them from your – grandparents.'

'Well,' she said, mollified, 'grandfather's in behind now. You might come in and see him.'

I went 'in behind' and there was grandfather looking just right, as everything does in Porchester – seated in a chair, snow-white hair, a stick – age, say ninety.

'I thought, perhaps,' I said, 'you could tell me something of the people I remember here fifty years ago.'

'Eh,' he shouted.

'Could you tell me anything about my uncle, the Reverend Charles Butler, who used to be the rector here fifty years ago?'

'The Reverend Charles Butler,' he shouted bitterly, 'indeed I could! There was the meanest man that ever came to this village. He'd a' stopped every poor man's beer, he would, if he'd had his way. Don't talk to me of the Reverend Charles Butler.'

I decided not to.

So I went out and I managed to find the house where we lived when I was a child in Porchester. But what a poor, humble-looking place! I had no idea that it could have been as poor as that! A little 'hall' just wide enough to squeeze through, a room on the left of it, the size of a box – the 'drawing-room' I called it at once from memory – and another box behind it. I think my mother had the nerve to call it the 'breakfast-room'. I felt hurt and humiliated coming out. I hadn't realized how used I had become to being well off, to living in comfort and having everything. As I came out I saw that there were some men there, evidently a builder and his 'hands'. They told me they were going to knock down the house. I told them to go right ahead.

After that I had no heart to go on and see the castle. It might have turned out to be just nothing as beside, say, the Royal York Hotel in Toronto or the Château Frontenac in Quebec.

It is better not to go back to the place you came from. Leave your memory as it is. No reality will ever equal it.

It is from my Hampshire childhood that I draw my interest in the American frigate *Chesapeake*, of which noble old ship I have a 'chunk' on my library table.

Everyone recalls from his school history the immortal story of the great fight between the American frigate *Chesapeake* and the British frigate *Shannon* outside of Boston on 1 June 1813. It is not merely the victory of the *Shannon* that is remembered but the chivalrous nature of the conflict, the ships meeting after a courteous challenge from Captain Broke of the *Shannon* to Captain Lawrence of the *Chesapeake*. Broke generously offered to send any of his attendant vessels out of range of helping him. The ships were an even match – *Shannon*, 1,066 tons, broadside 544 pounds, crew 330; the *Chesapeake* 1,135 tons, broadside 570, crew (about) 400.

The result of the battle was a complete victory for the *Shannon* but with terrible loss on both sides. Lawrence was mortally wounded; Broke so desperately wounded as never to fully recover, though he lived to be an Admiral and only died in 1841.

Now, I have always had a certain personal interest in the *Chesapeake*. I have, as I say, on my library table a 'chunk' of very hard wood (teak or mahogany, I suppose) about 8 inches by 3 by 2½ inches, that was originally a piece of the *Chesapeake*. I have had it for nearly seventy years, the kind of thing you never lose if you pay no attention to it, and like the fidelity of an old friend.

When we were leaving England in 1876 to go to 'America' we were taken over to the Isle of Wight to see my grandfather, who was naturally delighted: so much so that he gave me from the drawing-room table at Oak Hill this bit of wood and said, 'That was a piece of the *Chesapeake*.' Written on it in his writing, but now faded beyond recognition, were the words: *A Piece of the American Frigate Chesapeake – captured 1813*.

I always wondered how my grandfather came to have a piece of the *Chesapeake*, and this gave me an interest in the fate of the vessel. But any printed account in the histories merely said that the *Chesapeake* was taken across the Atlantic to England – which is quite true – and was commissioned in the service of the Royal Navy – which is not so. But it has only been of late years when I have been concerned with writing Canadian History that I have been able to get full details of the fate of the old ship. I am indebted here very greatly to the library staff of the Boston Public Library.

* * *

The amazing thing is that the *Chesapeake* was taken over to England, and is still there – all the best timbers of the vessel, built in solid as they came out of the ship, went into the making of a mill and are still throbbing and quivering all day as the mill, a hundred and twenty-three years old, still hums in an English village, grinding corn.

The mill is at Wickham – and if you don't know where Wickham is, I may say it's near Fareham – and Fareham? well, close to Porchester – and Porchester? – well, that's where I lived in England. Anyway, all these places are in Hampshire, freely admitted to be (by all who live there) the noblest of the English counties.

So there's the mill, and nobody knows about it. The reason is that people who know all about the *Chesapeake* know nothing of Wickham, and people who live in Wickham know nothing about the *Chesapeake*, though of course they all know about the old mill. If you said, 'That mill was built out of the American ship *Chesapeake*, wasn't it?' they'd say, 'Ay, like as not!' – meaning that that would be just the kind of thing to build a Hampshire mill out of.

Here is the story, though lack of space forbids full citation of authorities.

After the battle of the 1st June the *Chesapeake* was sailed (or partly towed) to Halifax harbour – a voyage of five days. She entered the harbour in the wake of the *Shannon* on June 6, presenting a terrible contrast of glory and tragedy, pride and honour – gay strings of bright flags of victory flying above battered ports and broken bulwarks, patched up as might be after the havoc of the broadsides.

Judge Haliburton, the famous writer still remembered for *Sam Stick*, went on board. 'The *Chesapeake*,' he wrote, 'was like a charnel house . . . main deck filled with hammocks of the wounded, dead and dying . . . the deck had of necessity (heavy weather?) not been cleaned . . . steeped in gore as in a slaughter-house.' The body of Captain Lawrence, who had died on board, lay on the quarterdeck under the Stars and Stripes. He was buried, with many of his men, in Halifax.

The *Chesapeake*, refitted as might be, was sailed across to Portsmouth. There history loses her with the false lead that the Royal Navy recommissioned the ship. This is not so, nor can I find any definite authority to say that she ever sailed again. She was bought as she stood for £500 by a Mr Holmes. He broke up the vessel, sold several tons of copper from the sheeting, with all fittings and timber, and doubled his money. The main timbers were pitch pine, new and sound, and some of them were sold for house-building in Portsmouth, but the best of them were bought by a Mr John Prior for £200 to build a mill. This he duly erected (1820) in the hamlet of Wickham. The main timbers of the deck, built into the structure intact, were (and are) 32 feet long and 18 inches square. The purloins were used, just as they were, for joists.

With that the *Chesapeake* was forgotten and Wickham – it antedates the Norman Conquest – fell asleep again.

Forty years later a descendant, or relation (I cannot trace him), of Captain Broke of the *Shannon* got interested in gathering information. In a memoir which he wrote he quotes a letter from the Vicar of Fareham, date of 1864, with the information given above and the statement that the timbers of the *Chesapeake* (in fact the whole mill) seemed 'good for centuries yet'.

They talk in centuries in Hampshire.

Then comes another sleep.

Then a *Hampshire Gazetteer and Guide* of 1901 reports that the mill at Wickham made of the timbers of the *Chesapeake* is still intact and in active operation.

Then followed another sleep of the topic till in 1943 I woke it again by writing to the present Vicar of Fareham. I hadn't written sooner because, although I knew the *Chesapeake* was in a mill, I was looking for the mill to be on the Isle of Wight.

So I wrote to the Vicar of Fareham who referred me to Mr George Orwell, of Fareham, who has done a lot of antiquarian work, especially in things concerning the Navy and whose writings under the name of Histories are well known to all people who love British Antiquities (very fine people).

Mr Orwell wrote me to say that the mill is still (April 4, 1943) quite as it was, timbers and all, going strong and likely to see a long while yet.

What ought to be done about it? These timbers of the deck of the *Chesapeake* – rebuilt into their earlier semblance – should have something of the sacred memory of the deck of the *Victory*. Why not buy them and give them to the United States? They should be a gift to the Naval Academy at Annapolis. Those who know that place will recall its trophies – the proudest part of the establishment. There swings still afloat the schooner *America*, that won the cup in 1850 something, never recaptured; there is the old *Constitution* and the *Reina Mercedes* and there in the great hall is Perry's flag with his '*Don't give up the Ship*,' and much else.

The *Chesapeake* would build into a fine platform, the old deck reproduced, for Mr Churchill to lecture from.

When I look back on this mid-Victorian England into which I was born and which first stamped itself on my mind, it gives me many things to think about. How deeply set it was in the mould in which England was cast and in which to a great extent it still remains. Side by side with all that is splendid in history and in character is that everlasting division that separates people from one another with the heavy ridges and barriers of class distinction. Here are people born to be poor, and how poor they were. I can remember that when we had done with our tea-leaves old women (the place seemed full of them) would come and take them away to use over again. There were the poor and there were the half-poor, and there were the respectable people and the genteel people, and the gentry and above them the great people, all the way to the Queen. And they all knew their places.

There was an elementary school called a National School where the children of the poor and of the respectable went at a fee of one penny a week. I can see now that it must have been one of the schools set up under the new Act, as it was then, of 1870, the first statute that ever gave England general primary education. England had got afraid that an illiterate population might mean danger to the nation. They had had the object lesson of the armies of the Civil War in America. The loud laughter of the *London Times* and the haw! haw! of the professional British officers had been exchanged for silent admiration and deep respect when the same people realized what it meant to have an army of men every one of whom could read and write, of skilled mechanics who could interpret a printed diagram and private soldiers with the technical knowledge to repair a damaged locomotive and reset a dismantled telegraph line. It had become plain enough that England had to do what one of its statesmen of the moment called 'educate its masters', if only for the masters' sake.

That is seventy-five years ago. And strangely enough the wheel has turned a full circle and a similar discussion runs in the current journals of 1944. All through the present controversy over the schools and how to make the public schools public, runs the note of anxiety, are we really finding all the brains of the nation? All, we need them all! National brains are the first line of public safety for everybody. There must be no gifted children left too poor for their gifts to give service to the nation. Scholarships, endowments, anything! We must have them.

It is a wonderful change. Compare it with the sentiment of Gray's *Elegy* in which the poet sorrows for the lack of opportunity that kept people down to the level of the poor, and buried them in a country churchyard, but sorrows only for their own sakes.

> *Perhaps in this neglected spot is laid*
> *Some heart once pregnant with celestial fire;*
> *Hands, that the rod of Empire might have sway'd,*
> *Or waked to ecstasy the living lyre.*

With Gray the sentiment is as of a wishful luxurious pity, and has nothing to do with any keen, anxious fear that the nation needs these men and must not bury them unknown. His very phrases show it: 'waking the living lyre' is a thing that most of us could postpone for a while.

But, as I say, there was the National School functioning at a penny a week for the poor and the respectable. But for the genteel, no, not if they could reach a little higher, and of course not under any circumstances for the gentry. So two older brothers and I – aged 9 and 8 and 6 – went therefore to a Dame's School with which my academic education began in 1875, not to be completed till 1903 with a Chicago Ph.D. I recall but little of the Dame's School except the first lesson in geography in which the Dame held up a map and we children recited in chorus, 'the top of the map is always the north, the bottom south, the right-hand east, the left-hand west'!! I wanted to speak out and say, 'But it's only that way because you're holding it that way,' but I was afraid to. Cracks with a ruler were as easy to get in a Dame's School as scratches down on the Rio Grande.

So, as I say, it was an England all of class and caste, with everybody doing his duty in the state of life into which it had pleased God to call him. But of this later.

CHAPTER II

Life on the Old Farm

I enjoy the distinction, until very recently a sort of recognized title of nobility in Canada and the United States, of having been 'raised on the old farm'. Till recently, I say, this was the acknowledged path towards future greatness, the only way to begin. The biographies of virtually all her great men for three or four generations show them as coming from the farm. The location of the 'old home farm' was anywhere from Nova Scotia to out beyond Iowa, but in its essence and idea it was always the same place. I once described it in a book of verse which I wrote as a farewell to economics, which was so clever that no one could read it and which I may therefore quote with novelty now.

> The Homestead Farm, way back upon the Wabash,
>   Or on the Yockikenny,
> Or somewhere up near Albany – the Charm
> Was not confined to one, for there were many.
>
> There when the earliest Streak of Sunrise ran
> The Farmer dragged the Horses from their Dream
> With 'Get up, Daisy' and 'Gol darn yer, Fan,'
> Had scarcely snapped the Tugs and Britching then

> The furious Hayrack roared behind the team
>> All day the Hay
>> Was drawn that way
>> Hurled in the Mow
>> Up high – and how!
> Till when the ending Twilight came, the loaded Wain
> With its last, greatest Load turned Home again.
>> The Picture of it rises to his Eye
> Sitting beside his Father, near the Sky

I admit that within the last generation or so, in softer times of multiplying luxury, men of eminence have been raised in a sickly sort of way in the cities themselves, have got their strength from High School Athletics instead of at the woodpile and behind the harrows, and their mental culture by reading a hundred books once instead of one book a hundred times. But I am talking of an earlier day.

It was a condition of course that one must be raised on the old farm and then succeed in getting off it. Those who stayed on it turned into rustics, into 'hicks' and 'rubes', into those upstate characters which are the delight of the comic stage. You had your choice! Stay there and turn into a hick, get out and be a great man. But the strange thing is that they all come back. They leave the old farm as boys so gladly, so happy to get away from its dull routine, its meaningless sunrise and sunset, its empty fresh winds over its fields, the silence of the bush – to get away in to the clatter and effort of life, into the crowd. Then as the years go by they come to realize that at a city desk and in a city apartment they never see the sunrise and the sunset, have forgotten what the sky looks like at night and where the Great Dipper is, and find nothing in the angry gusts of wind or the stifling heat of the city streets that corresponds to the wind over the empty fields . . . so they go back, or they think they do, back to the old farm. Only they rebuild it, but not with an axe but with an architect. They make it a great country mansion with flagstoned piazzas, and festooned pergolas – and it isn't the old farm any more. You can't have it both ways.

But as I say, I had my qualifying share, six years of the old farm – after I came out as a child of six from England – in an isolation which in these days of radio and transport is unknown upon the globe.

As explained in the first chapter, I was brought out by my mother from England to Canada as the third of her six children in 1876 on the steamship *Samatian*, Liverpool to Montreal, to join my father who had gone ahead and taken up a farm. The *Samatian* was one, was practically the last one, of those grand old vessels of the Allan line which combined steam with the towering masts, the cloud of canvas, the maze of ropes and rigging of a full-rigged three-masted ship. She was in her day a Queen of the ocean, that last word which always runs on to another sentence. She had been built in 1871, had had the honour of serving the Queen as a troopship for the Ashanti war and the further honour of carrying the Queen's daughter to Canada as the wife of the Marquis of Lorne, the Governor-General. No wonder that in my recollection of her the *Samatian* seemed grand beyond belief and carried a wealth of memories of the voyage of which I have already spoken. For years I used to feel as if I would 'give anything' to see the *Samatian* again. 'Give anything' at that stage of my finance meant, say, anything up to five dollars, anyways a whole lot. And then it happened, years and years after when I had gone to Montreal to teach at McGill (it was in 1902) that I saw in the papers that the *Samatian* was in port; in fact I found that she still came in regularly all season and would be back again before navigation closed. So I never saw her. I meant to but I never did. When I read a little later that the old ship had been broken up I felt that I would have 'given anything' (ten dollars, then) to have seen her.

In those days most people still came up, as we did in 1876, by river steamer from Montreal to Toronto. At Kingston we saw the place all decked with flags and were told that it was 'The Twenty-fourth of May.' We asked what that meant, because in those days they didn't keep 'Queen's birthday' as a holiday in England. They kept *Coronation* Day with a great ringing of bells, but whether there was any more holiday to it than bell-ringing I don't remember. But as we were presently to learn, 'The Twenty-fourth' was at that time the great Upper Canada Summer Holiday of the year, Dominion Day was still too new to have got set. There wasn't any Labour Day, or any Civic Holiday.

From Toronto we took a train north to Newmarket, a funny train it seemed to us, all open and quite unlike the little English carriages, cut into compartments that set the fields spinning round when you looked out of the window. Newmarket in 1876 was a well-established country town, in fact, as they said, 'quite a place'. It still is. It was at that time the place from which people went by the country roads to the south side of Lake Simcoe, the township of Georgina, to which at that time there was no railway connection. From Newmarket my father and his hired man were to drive us the remaining thirty miles to reach the old farm. They had for it two wagons, a lumber wagon and a 'light' wagon. A light wagon was lighter than a lumber wagon, but that's all you could say about it – it is like those histories which professors call 'short' histories, they might have been longer. So away we went along the zigzag roads, sometimes along a good stretch that would allow the horses to break into a heavy attempt at a trot, at other times ploughing through sand, tugging uphill or hauling over corduroy roads of logs through thick swamps where the willow and alder bushes almost met overhead and where there was 'no room to pass'. On the lift of the hills we could see about us fine rolling country, all woods broken with farms and here and there in the distance, on the north horizon great flecks of water that were Lake Simcoe. And so on, at a pace of four or five miles an hour, till as the day closed in we went over a tumbled bridge with a roaring mill dam and beyond it a village, the village of Sutton – two mills, two churches and quite a main street, with three taverns. My father told us that this was our own village, a gift very lightly received by us children after memories of Porchester and Liverpool and the *Samatian*. My mother told me years afterwards that to her it was a heartbreak. Beyond the village, my father told us, we were on our home road, another dubious gift, for it was as heavy as ever, with a great cedar swamp a mile through in the centre, all corduroy and willows and marsh and water: beyond that up a great hill with more farmhouses, and so across some fields to a windswept hill space with a jumble of frame buildings and log barns and outhouses, and there we were at the old farm – on a six-year unbroken sentence.

The country round our farm was new in the sense that forty years before it was unbroken wilderness, and old in the sense that farm settlers when they began to come had come in quickly. Surveyors had marked out roads. The part of the bush that was easy to clear was cleared off in one generation, log houses built, and one or two frame ones, so that in that sense the country in its outline was just as it is now: only at that time it was more bush than farms, now more farms than the shrunken wastes of bush. And of course in 1876 a lot of old primeval trees, towering hemlocks and birch, were still standing. The last of the great bush fires that burned them out was in the summer when we came, the bush all burning, the big trees falling in masses of spark and flame, the sky all bright and the people gathered from all round to beat out the shower of sparks that fell in the stubble fields . . .

This country around Lake Simcoe (we were four miles to the south of it and out of the sight of it), beautiful and fertile as it is, had never settled in the old colonial days. The French set up missions there among the Hurons (north-west of the Lake) but they were wiped out in the great Iroquois massacre of 1644 in the martyrdom of the Fathers Lallement and Breboeuf. The tourist of today sees from his flying car the road signs of 'Martyr's Shrine' intermingled with the 'Hot Dogs' and 'Joe's Garage'. After the massacre the French never came back. The Iroquois danger kept the country empty as it did all Western Ontario. Nor did the United Empire Loyalists come here. They settled along the St Lawrence and the Bay of Quinte and Niagara and Lake Erie, but the Lake Simcoe country remained till that century closed, as empty as it is beauiful.

Settlement came after the 'Great War' ended with Waterloo and world peace, and a flock of British emigrants went out to the newer countries. Among them were many disbanded soldiers and sailors and officers with generous grants of land. These were what were called in England, 'good' people, meaning people of the 'better' class but not good enough to stay at home, which takes money. With them came adherents and servants and immigrants at large, but all good people in the decent sense of the word, as were all the people round our old farm, no matter how poor they were. The entry of these people to the Lake Simcoe country was made possible by Governor Simcoe's opening of Yonge Street, north from Toronto to the Holland River. It was at first just a horse track through the bush, presently a rough roadway connecting Toronto (York) with the Holland River and then by cutting the corner of Lake Simcoe with the Georgian Bay and thus westward to the Upper Lakes, a line of communication safe from American invasion. It was part of Governor Simcoe's preoccupation over the defence of Upper Canada which bore such good fruit in its unforseen results of new settlement.

So the settlers, once over the waters of Lake Simcoe, found their way along its shore, picked out the likely places, the fine high ground, the points overlooking the lake. Here within a generation arose comfortable lakeshore homes, built by people with a certain amount of money, aided by people with no money but glad to work for wages for a time, till they could do better. From the first the settlement was cast in an aristocratic mould such as had been Governor Simcoe's dream for all his infant colony. Simcoe was long since gone by this time. He left Canada in 1796 and died in England in 1806. But the mark that he set on Upper Canada only wore faint with time and is not yet obliterated. Simcoe planned a constitution and a colony to be an 'image and transcript' of England itself. An established church and an aristocracy must be the basis of it. To Simcoe a democrat was a dangerous Jacobin, and a dissenter a snivelling hypocrite. He despised people who would sit down to eat with their own servants, as even 'good' people began to do in Upper Canada; 'fellows of one table' he called them and he wanted nothing to do with them in his government. Others shared his views and hence that queer touch of make-believe, or real aristocracy, that was then characteristic of Simcoe's York (Toronto) and that helped to foster the Canadian rebellion of 1837.

So after the first 'aristocracy' houses were built on the Lakeshore of Georgina Township settlers began to move up to the higher ground behind it, better land and cheaper. For the lake, for being on the water, most of them cared nothing. They wanted to get away from it. The Lakeshore was cold. It is strange to think that now you can buy all of that farm land you want at about thirty or forty dollars an acre, but an acre down at the Lakeshore is worth say, a couple of thousand, and you can't get it, anyway.

Our own farm with its buildings was, I will say, the damnedest place I ever saw. The site was all right, for the slow slope of the hillside west and south gave a view over miles of country and a view of the sunset only appreciated when lost. But the house! Someone had built a cedar log-house and then covered it round with clap-board and then someone else had added three rooms stuck along the front with more clap-board, effectually keeping all the sunlight out. Even towards the sunset there were no windows, only the half-glass top of a side door. A cook-house and a wood-shed were stuck on behind. Across a grass yard were the stable, cedar logs plastered up, and the barns, cedar logs loose and open, and a cart-shed and a henhouse, and pigsties and all that goes with a farm. To me as a child the farm part just seemed one big stink. It does still: the phew! of the stable – not so bad as the rest, the unspeakable cowshed, sunk in the dark below a barn, beyond all question of light or ventilation, like a medieval *oubliette*: the henhouse, never cleaned and looking like a guano deposit island off the coast of Chile, in which the hens lived if they could and froze dead if they couldn't: the pigsties, on the simple Upper Canada fashion of a log pen and a shelter behind, about three feet high. Guano had nothing on them.

We presently completed our farmhouse to match the growing family by adding a new section on the far side of it, built of frame lumber only with lath and plaster and no logs, thin as cardboard and cold as a refrigerator. Everything froze when the thermometer did. We took for granted that the water would freeze in the pitchers every night and the window-panes cover up with frost, not that the old farm was not heated. It had had originally a big stone fireplace in the original log-house, but as with all the fireplaces built of stone out of the fields without firebrick. As the mortar began to dry out the fireplace would set the house on fire. That meant getting up on the roof (it wasn't far) with buckets and putting it out. My father and the hired man got so tired putting out the house on fire that we stopped using the fireplace and had only stoves, big stoves that burnt hemlock, red hot in ten minutes with the dampers open. You could be as warm as you liked according to distance, but the place was never the same two hours running. There were, I think, nine stoves in all; cutting wood was endless. I quote again from my forgotten book.

Winter stopped not the Work; it never could
Behold the Furious Farmer splitting wood.
The groaning Hemlock creaks at every Blow
'Hit her again Dad, she's just got to go.'
       And up he picks
       The Hemlock sticks
       Out of the snow.

For light we had three or four coal-oil lamps, but being just from England where they were unknown we were afraid of them. We used candles made on the farm from tallow poured into a mould, guttering damn things, to be snuffed all the time and apt to droop over in the middle. It is hardly credible to me now, but I know it is a fact that when my brother and I sat round a table doing our lessons, or drawing and painting pictures, all the light we had was one tallow candle in the middle of the table. It should have ruined our eyesight, but it didn't. I don't think any of us wore spectacles under fifty: just as the ill-cooked food of the farm, the heavy doughy bread, the awful pork and pickles, should have ruined our digestions but couldn't. Boys on the farm who go after the cattle at six in the morning are in the class of the iron dogs beside a city step.

My father's farm – a hundred acres, the standard pattern – was based on what is called mixed farming, that is, wheat, and other grains, hay, pasture, cattle, a few sheep and pigs and hens, roots for winter, garden for summer and wood to cut in the bush. The only thing to sell was wheat, the false hope of the Ontario farmer of the 70s, always lower in the yield than what one calculated (if you calculated low it went lower) and always (except once in a happy year) lower than what it had to be to make it pay. The other odd grains we had to sell was nothing much, nor the cattle, poor lean things of the pre-breeding days that survived their awful cowshed. My father knew nothing about farming and the hired man, 'Old Tommy', a Yorkshireman who had tried a bush farm of his own and failed, still less. My father alternated furious industry with idleness and drinking, and in spite of my mother having a small income of her own from England, the farm drifted on to the rocks and the family into debt. Presently there was a mortgage, the interest on which being like a chain around my father's neck, and later on mine. Indeed these years of the late 1870s were the hard times of Ontario farming with mortgages falling due like snowflakes.

Farming in Ontario in any case was then and still is an alternating series of mortgages and prosperity following on like the waves of the sea. Anyone of my experience could drive you through the present farm country and show you (except that it would bore you to sleep) the mark of the successive waves like geological strata. Here on our right is the remains of what was the original log-house of a settler: you can tell it from the remains of a barn because if you look close you can see that it had a top story, or part of one, like the loft where Abraham Lincoln slept. You will see, too, a section of its outline that was once a window. Elsewhere, perhaps on the same farm, but still standing, is an old frame house that was built by mortgaging the log-house. This one may perhaps be boarded up and out of use because it was discarded when wheat went to $2.50 a bushel in the Crimean War and the farmer, suddenly enriched, was able to add another mortgage and built a brick house – those real brick houses that give the motorist the impression that all farmers are rich. So they were – during the Crimean War. Later on and reflecting the boom years of the closing 90s and the opening century are the tall hip-roofed barns with stone and cement basements below for cattle and silos at the side, which give the impression that all farmers are scientists – only they aren't, it's just more mortgages.

Such has been the background of Ontario farming for a hundred years.

Our routine on the farm, as children, was to stay on it. We were too little to wander and even the nearest neighbours were half a mile away. So we went nowhere except now and then as a treat into Sutton village, and on Sunday to the church on the Lakeshore. Practically, except for school, we stayed at home all the time – years and years.

There was, a mile away, a school (School Section No. 3, Township of Georgina) of the familiar type of the 'little red schoolhouse' that has helped to make America. It was a plain frame building, decently lighted, with a yard and a pump and a woodpile, in fact all the accessories that went with the academic life of School Section No. 3. The boys and girls who went there were the children of decent people (there were no others in the township), poor, but not exactly aware of it. In summer the boys went barefoot. We didn't – a question of caste and thistles. You have to begin it at three years old to get the feel for it.

There were two teachers, a man teacher and a lady teacher, and it was all plain and decent and respectable, and the education first class, away ahead of the Dame's School stuff in England. All of the education was right to the point – reading, spelling, writing, arithmetic, geography – with no fancy, silly subjects such as disfigure our present education even at its beginning and run riot in the college at the top. Things about the school that were unsanitary were things then so customary that even we children from England found nothing wrong. We spat on our slates to clean them with the side of our hand. We all drank out of the same tin mug in the school yard. The boys and girls were together in classes, never outside.

* * *

The only weak spot in the system of the little red schoolhouse was that the teachers were not permanent, not men engaged in teaching making it their life work, like the Scottish 'dominie' who set his mark upon Scotland. You can never have a proper system of national education without teachers who make teaching their life work, take a pride in it as a chosen profession, and are so circumstanced as to be as good as anybody – I mean as anything around. In the lack of this lies the great fault in our Canadian secondary education, all the way up to college.

So it was with the country schools of 1876. The teachers were young men who came and went, themselves engaged in the long stern struggle of putting themselves through college for which their teaching was only a stepping stone. An arduous struggle it was. A schoolteacher (they were practically all men, the girl teachers were just appendages to the picture) got a salary of $300 to $400 a year. Call it $400. During his ten months a year of teaching he paid $10 a month for his board and washing. I don't suppose that his clothes cost him more than $50 a year and all his other extras of every kind certainly not more than another fifty. For in those days after necessaries were paid for there was nothing to spend money on. The teacher never drank. Not that he didn't want to, but every drink cost money, five cents, and he hadn't got it. If a teacher did begin to drink and did start to loaf around the taverns it undermined the sternness of his life's purpose as a slow leak undermines a dam. It became easier to drink than to save money: he felt rich instead of poor, and presently, as the years went by, he drank himself out of this purpose altogether, quit school teaching, went north – to the lumber shanties; or worked in a sawmill – living life downhill, marked out still by the wreck of his education as a man who had once been a teacher and still quoted poetry when he was tight.

But most, practically all, stuck right at it saving, say, $200 a year towards college. And this is what college cost, college being the University of Toronto. The fees were $40 a year (say $60 in medicine) and board and lodging in the mean drab houses of the side streets where the poorer students lived cost $3.00 a week and washing, I think 25 cents a week. They washed anything then for 5 cents, even a full dress shirt, and anyway the student hadn't got a full dress shirt. College books in those days cost about $10 a year. There were no college activities that cost money, nothing to join that wanted five dollars for joining it, no caféterias to spend money in, since a student ate three times a day at his boarding house and that was the end of it. There was no money to be spent on college girls because at that time there were no college girls to spend money on. Homer says that the beauty of Helen of Troy launched a thousand ships (meaning made that much trouble). The attraction of the college girl was to launch about a thousand dollars – added to college expenses.

But all that was far, far away in 1876, and a student's college budget
for the eight months of the session including his clothes, and his travel
expenses and such extras as even the humblest and sternest must incur,
would work out at about $300 for each college year. That meant that what
he could save in a year and a half of teaching would give him one year at
college. Added to this was the fact that in the vacation – the two months
of a teacher's vacation or the four months for a college vacation – he
could work on a farm for his board and $20 a month and save almost the
whole of the $20. I have known at least one teacher, later on a leader of
the medical profession of Alberta, who put in seven years of this life of
teaching to get his college course. But in most cases there would be some
extra source of supply, an uncle who owned a sawmill, and could lend
two or three hundred dollars, or an uncle over in the States, or an older
brother who came down from the 'shanties' in the spring with more
money than he knew what to do with. For what could he do with it,
except drink or go to college?

So in the end adversity was conquered, and the teachers passed through
college and into law or medicine, with perhaps politics and public life,
and added one more name to the roll of honour of men who 'began as
teachers'. Some failed on the last lap, graduated and then got married,
tired of waiting for life to begin and thus sank back again on teaching –
as a high school teacher – a better lot but still not good enough.

But the system was, and is, all wrong. Our teacher with his thirty
dollars a month didn't get as much as our old Tommy, the hired man, for
he and his wife had $20 a month and cottage with it and a garden, milk
and eggs and vegetables and meat to the extent of his end (I forget which)
of any pig that was killed. A teacher situated like that could be a married
man, as snug and respected as a Scottish dominie with his cottage and his
nailyard, his trout rod and his half-dozen Latin books bound in vellum
– 'as good as anybody' – which is one of the things that a man has got to
be in life if he is to live at all. The teachers weren't. I never was, and
never felt I was, in the ten years I was a teacher. That is why later on I
spent so many words in decrying school-teaching as a profession, not
seeing that school-teaching is all right for those who are all right for it.
The thing wrong is the setting we fail to give it.

Such was our school at School Section No. 3, Township of Georgina,
County of York. It had also its amenities as well as its work. Now and
again there were school 'entertainments'. I can't remember if the people
paid to come. I rather think not, because in that case they wouldn't
come. For an entertainment the school was lit with extra lamps. The
teacher was chairman. The trustees made speeches, or shook their heads
and didn't. The trustees were among the old people who had come out

from the 'old country' with some part of another environment, something of an older world, still clinging to them. Some, especially Scotsmen like old Archie Riddell, would rise to the occasion and made a speech with quite a ring and a thrill to it, all about Marmion and Bruce and footprints on the sands of time. Then the teachers would say that we'd hear from Mr Brown, and Mr Brown, sitting in a sunken lump in a half-light would be seen to shake his head, to assure us that we wouldn't. After which came violin music by local fiddlers announced grandiloquently by the Chairman as 'Messrs Park and Ego', although we knew that really they were just Henry Park and Angus Ego. Perhaps also some lawyer or such person from the village four miles away would drive up for the entertainment and give a reading or a recitation. It was under those circumstances that I first heard W. S. Gilbert's *Yarn of the Nancy Bell*. It seemed to me wonderful beyond words, and the Sutton lawyer, a man out of Wonderland.

But going to the country school just didn't work out. It was too far for us, and in rough weather and storm impossible, and it was out of the question for a younger section of the family (the ones in between the baby and ex-baby and the 'big boys'). Moreover, my mother was haunted with the idea that if we kept on at the school we might side-slip and cease to be gentlemen. Already we were losing our Hampshire accent, as heard in *Twinkle, Twinkle, Little Star* – not stah, and not star, but something in between. I can still catch it if I am dead-tired or delirious. We were beginning also to say, 'them there' and 'these here', and 'who all' and 'most always', in short phrases that no one can use and grow up a gentleman.

So my mother decided that she would teach us herself and with characteristic courage set herself at it, in the midst of all her other work with the baby and the little children and the kitchen and the servants and the house. Servants of course we always had, at least one maid – I beg pardon, I'm losing my language – I mean one 'hired girl' and a 'little girl' and generally an 'old woman'. Top wages were $8.00 a month, a little girl got $5.00. There was a certain queer gentility to it all. The hired man never sat down to eat with us, nor did the hired girl. Her status in fact, as I see it in retrospect, was as low and humble as even an English Earl could wish it. She just didn't count.

My mother had had in England a fine education of the Victorian finishing school type, and added to it a love and appreciation of literature that never left her all her life, not even at 90 years of age. So she got out a set of her old English school books that had come with us in a box from England. Colenso's *Arithmetic*, and Slater's *Chromology*, and Peter Parlay's *Greece and Rome* and Oldendorf's new method of French, and gathered us around her each morning for school, opened with prayers – and needing them. But it was no good, we wouldn't pay attention, we knew it was only mother. The books didn't work either – most of them were those English manuals of history and such specially designed for ladies' schools and for ladies who had to teach their own children out in the 'colonies'. They were designed to get a maximum of effect for a minimum of effort and hence they consisted mostly of questions and answers, the questions being what lawyers call leading questions, ones that suggest their own answer. Thus they reduce Roman History to something like this:

> Q. Did not Julius Caesar invade Britain?
> A. He did.
> Q. Was it not in the year 55 B.C.?
> A. It was.
> Q. Was he not later on assassinated in Rome?
> A. He was.
> Q. Did not his friend Brutus take a part in assassinating him?
> A. He did.

In this way one could take a bird-like flight over ancient history. I think we hit up about 200 years every morning and for ancient Egypt over 1,000 years. I had such a phenomenal memory that it was all right for me, as I remembered the question and answer both. But my elder brothers Dick and Jim were of heavier academic clay and so they just, as the politicians say, took it as read.

The *Arithmetic* of Bishop Colenso of Natal was heavier going. After multiplication and division it ran slapbang into the Rule of Three, and mother herself had never understood what the rule of three was, and if you went on beyond it all you found was Practice and *Aliquot Parts*. I know now that all this is rule-of-thumb arithmetic, meant for people who can't reason it out, and brought straight down from the Middle Ages to Colenso. The glory of the Unitary method whereby if one man needs ten cigarettes a day then two men need twenty, and so on for as many men and as many cigarettes and as long as you like, this had not dawned on the British mind. I think it was presently imported from America.

So my mother's unhappy lessons broke down and we were just about to be sent back to the red schoolhouse when by good luck we managed to secure a family tutor, from whom we received for the next three or four years teaching better than I have ever had since, and better than any I ever gave in ten years as a school-teacher. Our tutor was a young man off a nearby farm, stranded half-way through college by not having taught long enough and compelled to go back to teaching. So my grandfather from England put up the money (for fear of course that we might come back home on him) and there we were with a tutor and a school-room, ink wells, scribblers, slates, in fact a whole academic outfit. Our tutor was known as 'Harry Park' to his farm associates, but to us, at once and always, 'Mr Park' and he ranked with Aristotle in dignity and width of learning. Never have I known anyone who better dignified his office, made more of it, so that our little school-room was as formal as Plato in his Academy could have wished it. Mr Park rechristened my brother Jim as 'James' to give him class, and Dick reappeared as 'Arthur'. The hours were as regular as the clock itself, in fact more so, since Mr Park's watch soon took precedence over the kitchen clock, as the 'classes' (made up of us four boys and my little sister, just qualified) were as neatly divided as in a normal school. I had to be Class 1, but my brothers didn't care. They freely admitted that I was the 'cleverest' – as they looked on it as no great asset. For certain purposes, poetry and history, we were all together.

For us 'Mr Park' knew everything, and I rather think that he thought this himself. Ask him anything and we got the answer. 'Mr Park, what were the Egyptians like?' – he knew it and he told it, in measured formal language.

Under 'Mr Park's' teaching my brothers at least learned all that could be put into them and I personally went forward like an arrow. At eleven years of age I could spell practically anything, knew all there was to know of simple grammar (syntax, parsing, analysis) beyond which there is nothing worth while anyway, knew Collier's *British History*, and *History of Literature*, all the geography of all the countries including Canada (the provinces of Canada which had not been in mother's book) and in arithmetic had grasped the unity system and all that goes with it, and learned how to juggle with vulgar fractions even when piled up like a Chinese pagoda, and with decimals let them repeat as they would.

After Mr Park came to us as tutor and the little red schoolhouse of School Section No. 3, Township of Georgina, was cut out, our isolation was all the more complete. We practically stayed on the farm. But of course a part of the old farm to children of eight to twelve years old, newly out from England, was a land of adventure; all the main part of it as it sloped away to the south and west was clear fields of the seven-acre pattern with snake fences all round it, piles of stones that had been cleared off the field lying in the fence corners, raspberry bushes choking up the corners but here and there an old elm tree springing up in an angle of the fence as a survival of the cleared forests. Elm trees have the peculiarity that they can do well alone, as no storm can break them, whereas hemlocks isolated by themselves are doomed. Hence the odd elm trees scattered all through this part of Central Ontario as if someone had set them on purpose to serve as shade trees or landscape decoration. Heaven knows no one did. For the earlier settlers trees, to a great extent, were the enemy. The Upper Canada forest was slaughtered by the lumber companies without regard for the future, which in any case they could neither foresee nor control. In the early days the export of lumber was only in the form of square timber – great sticks of wood from 12 to 18 inches each way – not cut up into the boards and deals and staves of the later lumber trade. Hence the trees were squared as they fell in the falling forest and about one-third of the main tree and all its branches burned up as litter to get rid of it. That was the early settler's idea of the bush, get rid of it where he could, and where it lay too low, too sunken, too marshy to clear it. Then cut out the big trees and haul them out, leave the rest of the bushes there and let farm clearings and roads get round it as best they could. As to planting any new trees to conserve the old ones, the farmers would have thought it a madman's dream. The only trees planted were the straight, fast-growing Lombardy poplars still seen in their old age set out in single or in little rows in front of the early Ontario houses. These owe their origin to the legend or the fact that they act as lightning conductors, a part of Benjamin Franklin's legacy to North America, along with the box stove and much else.

I am saying then that our old farm at its north end fell slap away down a steep hillside at the foot of which began the bush that spread off sideways in both directions as far as one could see; and directly in front it rose again in a slope that blotted out all view of Lake Simcoe, four miles away. Along the fringes of it were still some of the giant hemlock that had escaped the full fury of the last bush fire, dead, charred and still standing, but falling one by one. The bush as one tried to penetrate it grew denser and denser, mostly underbrush with tangled roots and second growth sprung up after the fires. It was so dense that for us it was impenetrable, and we ventured our way farther and farther in, carrying hatchets and alert for wild cats which I am practically certain were not there, and for bears which had left years and years ago.

We had hardly any social life as we were prevented partly by 'class' and mainly by distance from going over to the other farms after dark. To one farm where lived a family of English children of something the same mixed antecedents as ourselves we sometimes went over for tea, and at times all the way to the village or to the Lakeshore Houses. But such treks meant staying overnight.

So mostly we stayed at home, and in the evenings we did our lessons if we had lessons to do and my mother read to us Walter Scott and carried us away to so deep an impression of the tournaments and battlefields of the Crusade and of the warring forests of Norman-Saxon England that any later 'moving picture' of such things is but a mere blur of the surface. We cannot have it both ways. Intensity of mental impression and frequency of mental impression cannot go together. Robinson Crusoe's discovery of Friday's footprints on the sand – read aloud thus by candlelight to wondering children – has a dramatic 'horror' to it (horror means making one's hair stand up) that no modern cinema or stage can emulate. Similarly I recall the reading aloud of *Tom Sawyer*, then of course still a new book, and the dramatic intensity of the disclosure that Indian Joe is sealed up in the great cave.

Our news from the outside world came solely in the form of the *Illustrated London News* sent out by my grandmother from England. In it we saw the pictures of the Zulu War and the (second) Afghan War and of Majuba Hill. With it we kept alive the British tradition that all Victorian children were brought up in, never doubting that of course the Zulus were wrong and the Afghans mistaken and the Boers entirely at fault. This, especially, as mother had lived in South Africa and said so.

On one point, however, of British Victorian orthodox faith I sideslipped at eight years old and have never entirely got back, and that too the greatest point in all British history. I refer to the question of George Washington and George the Third, and whether the Americans had the right to set up a republic. It so happened that there came to our farm for a winter visit an English cousin of my father's who had become (I do not know how, for it must have been a rare thing in the 70s) a female doctor in Boston. She used to tell me, while Jim and Dick were mucking out the chores in the barnyard, which was their high privilege, about the United States and the Revolution; and when she saw how interested I was she sent to Boston and got a copy of Col. Thomas Wentworth Higginson's *Young Folk's (or People's) History of the United States*. There it was, pictures and all – General Gage and the Boston Boys (very neat boys and a very neat General), Washington crossing the Delaware (hard going), Washington taking command at Cambridge. 'Cousin Sophy' used to read it out loud to us – a needed rest for Walter Scott – and we were all fascinated with it, Jim and Dick with the pictures and the soldiers but I chiefly from the new sense of the burning injustice of tyranny, a thing I had never got from history before.

Forthwith the theory of a republic, and the theory of equality, and the condemnation of hereditary rights seemed obvious and self-evident truths, as clear to me as they were to Thomas Jefferson. I stopped short at the Queen, partly I suppose because one touched there on Heaven and

Hell and the Church service and on ground which I didn't propose to
tread. But for me from then on a hereditary lord didn't have a leg to
stand on. In the sixty years (nearly seventy) since elapsed I have often
tried to stand up hereditary peers again (I mean as members of a
legislature) but they won't really stay up for me. I have studied it all, and
lectured on it all, and written about it all. I know all about the British
idea that if a thing has existed for a long time, and if most people like it
and if it seems to work well and if it brings no sharp edge of cruelty and
barbarity such as the world has learned again, then it is silly to break
away from established institution on the ground of a purely theoretical
fault. But I can't get by with the arguments. I broke with the House of
Lords, with its hereditary peers and its Bishops voting because they are
Bishops in 1879 – or whenever it was – and the breach has never been
really healed.

People from India have told me that no matter how scientific an
education you may smear over an Indian doctor or scientist, put him in
any emergency or danger and back he comes to his first beliefs: away
goes medicine in favour of incantation and charms, and science abandons
its instruments and its metric measurement and hooks back a thousand
years to astrology, and mysticism. I'm like that with my underlying
Jeffersonian republicanism: back I slip to such crazy ideas as that all men
are equal, and that hereditary rights (still leaving out the British
monarch) are hereditary wrongs.

Occasional treats broke the routine of our isolation on the farm, such
as going into Sutton village for the 'Twenty-Fourth' (of May) the great
annual holiday, or to see cricket matches between Sutton and other
places, such as Newmarket, within cricket reach. For up to that time
cricket still remained the game of the Upper Canada countryside, living
on strongly against the competition of Yankee baseball and dying hard.
At present cricket has shrunken in on Toronto and a few larger cities and
school centres. But in the 70s and 80s it was everywhere. The wonder is,
though, that it could survive at all – it makes such heavy demands – a
decent 'pitch' of prepared ground without which the game is worthless,
an outfield not too rough, and even for decent practice, a certain
minimum of players; while cricket 'at the nets' is poor stuff without a
good pitch and good bowling, especially if you haven't any nets. Nor can
you have a real 'match' at cricket without a real side of eleven or
something close to it. Baseball on the other hand is quick and easy and
universal. It can be played in a cow pasture or behind the barnyard or in
the village street: two people can 'knock out flies'. and three can play at
'rolling over the bat', and if you can't get nine for a game, a pitcher,
catcher and baseball will do – what's more, the game can be played out

in an afternoon, an hour, or a minute. The wonder is that the British settlers in Upper Canada kept doggedly on with their British cricket as against the facile Yankee baseball and the indigenous lacrosse. I am quite sure that in the township of Georgina no one had ever seen the latter game in 1880.

Rarest and most striking of all treats was to be taken on a trip to Toronto. The new railway which reached Lake Simcoe from the south by a branch line of the Toronto and Lake Nipissing Railway extended from Stouffville to Sutton and Jackson's Point Wharf (on the Lake). It was part of that variegated network of little railways, of varied gauges and plans, all crooked as country roads, all afraid of a hill and all trying to keep close to a steamer dock, each under different ownership, which represents the short-sighted railway building of Ontario. Short-sighted? – and yet I suppose it was hard to see ahead at all, in a community that stumbled and fell with every new onslaught of bad times, and fought stubbornly against its forests and its torrents, half-strangled in its own opportunity.

The completion of the railway and the arrival of the first train was a great event. Much ringing of bells and blowing of whistles – then the train itself arrived by the sash factory and the grist mill. It made a great difference too, with commodities such as coal and oranges seen in Sutton for the first time. But as with most town and village advances of that date, it just went so far and then stopped. Sutton fell asleep again and only woke to the sound of the motor horn and the advent of the tourist, in another world years later.

But for us children a trip on the train to Toronto, a treat that was accorded to each of us about twice in the next three years, was a trip into wonderland – England had grown dim. Toronto, even the Toronto I describe in the next chapter, was marvellous beyond all description.

But the most real of our standing treats and holidays came to us on contact with Lake Simcoe. This grew out of our going every Sunday in summer to the Lake Shore Church, four miles away. To our farm equipment there had been added a 'phaeton' for mother to drive and the kind of horse that is driven in a phaeton, that is born quiet, never grows old and lives on into eternity. The ease and comfort of a phaeton can be appreciated by riding once in a buck-board (just once is all you need), a vehicle that means a set of slats on axles with a seat on the slats. Its motion is similar to that of the new 'sea-sickness medicine'. A phaeton with steel springs, low entrance and two seats can carry a capacity load and attain a speed, on the level, of six miles an hour. Even at that we walked in turns.

The parish church of Georgina stood on the high bank dotted with cedar trees overlooking Lake Simcoe, and oh, what a paradise the view presented! I have often and often written of Lake Simcoe. I know, with a few odd miles left out here and there, its every stick and stone, its island and points; and I claim that there is in all the world no more beautiful body of water. Writing it up years ago in a Canadian *Geographical Journal* I said:

'The Islands of the Aegean Sea have been regarded for centuries as a scene of great beauty; I know, from having seen them, that the Mediterranean coast of France and the valleys of the Pyrenees are a charm to the enchanted country; and I believe that for those who like that kind of thing there is wild grandeur in the Highlands of Scotland, and a majestic solitude where the midnight sun flashes upon the ice peaks of Alaska. But to my thinking none of those will stand comparison with the smiling beauty of the waters, shores and bays of Lake Simcoe and its sister Lake Couchiching. Here the blue of the deeper water rivals that of the Aegean; the sunlight flashes back in lighter colour from the sandbar on the shoals; the passing clouds of summer throw moving shadows as over a ripening field, and the mimic gales that play over the surface send curling caps of foam as white as ever broke under the bow of the Aegean galley.

'The Aegean is old. Its islands carry the crumbling temples of Homer's times. But everywhere its vegetation has been cut and trimmed and gardened by the hand of man. Simcoe is far older. Its forest outline is still what Champlain saw, even then unchanged for uncounted centuries. Look down through the clear water at the sunken trees that lie in the bay south-east of Sibbald's Point. They sank, as others sank before them, a hundred years ago; no hand of man has ever moved or touched them. The unquarried ledges of Georgina Island stood as they stand now when the Greeks hewed stone from the Pentelicus to build the Parthenon.'

The whole point of our going to Church on the Lake Shore on summer mornings was that we were allowed, by a special dispensation from the awful Sunday rules we were brought up on, to go in for a swim and to stick around beside the Lake for an hour or so. The spot was one of great beauty. The earliest settlers had built a wooden church among the cedar trees and in the very years of which I speak it was being replaced by the Lake Shore Church of cut stone that is one of the notable landmarks of the scenery of the district. It was built by the members of the Sibbald family, one of the chief families of the district, whose sons had gone abroad for service in the British Army and Navy and in India; and returning (in our day) as old men enriched in fortune and experience built the stone church still standing as a memorial to their mother. A Latin motto (which outclassed me at nine years old) cut in a memorial stone on the face of the tower commemorates the fact. The church was built during two of our summers of church-going and swimming. The masons were not there on Sundays, but we could follow its progress every Sunday, in the stones new drilled for blasting, in the fresh-cut completed stones and then in the rising layers of the walls, the upsweep of the tall roof (one Sunday to the next), the glass, the slates and then, all of a sudden as it were, we were singing in it.

Better still was it when my mother a year or two later, 1880, was able to take a 'summer cottage' near the church for a holiday of a month or so. 'Summer cottage' is a courtesy title. It was an old log building built as a 'parsonage' which in time proved unfit for habitation even by the meekest parson. But for a summer habitation it did well enough, and with it went the glory of the Lake and of the return to the water, which we had lost since Porchester. We were like Viking children back to the sea! So will you find any British children, used to sight and sound of the sea, shut off from the water in some inland or prairie town, but exulting to get back to their age-long heritage. So were we with Lake Simcoe! – making rafts of logs and boards before we had a boat, blown out to sea on our rafts and rescued, and thus learning what an offshore wind means – a thing that even today few Lake Simcoe summer visitors understand. After rafts a flat-bottomed boat, liberally plugged up with hot pitch; then an attempt at making a sail and discovering that a flat-bottomed boat is no good – and so on – repeating the life of man on the ocean as the human race repeats in the individual its every stage of evolution.

In my case Lake Simcoe was a more interesting field of navigation then than now, more real. It is strange how our inland lakes have deteriorated from the navigation of reality to the navigation of luxury. What do you see now? Motor boats! Power boats! Sailing dinghies built like dishes and used for aquatic displays but having no connection with sailing in the real sense. And all this in any case only a fringe that fills the Lake Shore resorts, crowds round luxury hotels and leaves the open water of Simcoe and such lakes emptier than when La Salle crossed them.

Not so in the 1880s. Navigation filled the Lake. Far out on its waters a long ribbon of smoke indicated a tug with a tow of logs heading for the mills at Jackson's Point. Sailing vessels, lumpy, heavy and ungainly, and nearly as broad as long, carried quarry stone and heavy stuff from the top of Lake Couchiching to the railway pier at Belle Ewart. At that time the *Emily May* steamer circulated the Lake all day and all night (in her prime days) with double crew, half of it awake and half asleep – two captains, two mates, two stewardesses and two bartenders. The railways bit off her job point by point and place by place; the railway to Sutton and Jackson's Point being the last straw that broke her back. Yet for years after the passenger boats in the real sense had gone, the excursion lived on. *Ho! for Beaverton!* read its placards on the broadside fence; *Ho! for Jackson's Point*. And there it was on a summer morning carrying its sons of England, or its Knights of Ireland, its brass band, its improvised bar, its ladies' cabin as tight shut and as uncomfortable as being at home – all that went with Ho! for a day on the water in 1880. And so for years – then came the motorcar and killed all that was left of navigation.

And all this time, although we didn't know, for my mother kept it hidden from us, at intervals my father drank, drove away to the village in the evening to return drunk late at night after we were in bed. And the more he drank the more the farm slid sideways and downhill, and the more the cloud of debt, of unpaid bills, shadowed it over, and the deeper the shadow fell. My mother, I say, hid it all from us for years with a devotion that never faltered. My father as he drank more changed towards us from a superman and hero to a tyrant, from easy and kind to fits of brutality and cruel beatings for my elder brothers. I was small enough to escape from doing much of the farm chores and farm work. But I carry still the recollection of it, more no doubt than Jim or Dick ever did. In fact the sight and memory of what domestic tyranny in an isolated, lonely home, beyond human help, can mean, helped to set me all the more firmly in the doctrine of the rights of man, and Jefferson's liberty.

By the end of the year 1881 the 'old Farm' as a going concern had pretty well come to a full stop. Bad farming had filled the fields with weeds: wild oats, a new curse of Ontario farming spread by the threshing machines, broke out in patches in the grain: low price cut out all profit: apples rotted on the ground, potatoes hardly paid for digging. There was the interest on the mortgage of $250 a year, wages not paid, store bills paid – just a welter of debt and confusion. So my father was led to give it all up and go away to Manitoba, the new land of promise that all the people on the farms were beginning to talk about. The opening of the North-West by the Dominion taking it over had revealed the secret, so carefully guarded for two hundred years, that what had been thought of as a buffalo pasture and a fox range, a land for the trapper to share with the aurora borealis, was in reality a vast bed of deep alluvial soil, black mould two or three feet deep, the gift of the ages, the legacy of the grass and the flowers that had blossomed and withered unseen for centuries. You had but to scratch and throw in the wheat, and such crops would grow as older Canada had never seen! and with no clearing of the land to do, no stubborn fight against the stumps still all around us on the Ontario farms: empty country and land for the asking, 160 acres free under the new homestead law and more if you wanted it 'for a song'. No phrase ever appealed to the farmer's heart like that of getting land for a song! In the glory of the vision he forgets that he can't sing, and starts off looking for it.

To this was added the fact that there was rail connection now (1878) all the way to Manitoba by Chicago and St Paul and the Red River route, and that it was known that the new government – which carried the election of 1878 under John A. Macdonald – was pledged to build a Canadian Pacific Railway clear across the plains and over the Rockies to the Ocean. Thus was set up a sort of suction that began to draw people to Manitoba from all the Ontario farms, and presently beyond that from the old country itself, and in particular to Winnipeg, a place that had been a sort of straggled-out-settlement of the Hudson's Bay Company. Fort Garry now broke on the horizon as a town whose geographical site in the bottleneck entrance of the West marked it as a future metropolis. Hence the 'Winnipeg boom' and the noise of hammers and saws, and the shouts of the real estate agents, selling real estate all day and all night, and selling it so far out on the prairie that no one ever found it again.

My father was to go to Manitoba not on his own initiative – he hadn't any – but at the call of a younger brother who had gone on ahead and was already riding on the crest of the wave. This was 'My remarkable Uncle', to whose memory I have devoted many sketches and even the scenario of a moving picture which I hope will one day move. He had come out to Canada, to our farm in 1878, had captivated the countryside with his brilliant and unusual personality, taken a conspicuous part in the election of 1878 and passed on to a larger local notoriety in Toronto. He scented Winnipeg from afar, was one of the first in, and at the time of which I speak was piling up a fortune on paper, having been elected to the New Manitoba legislature and Heavens knows what.

In my sketches I referred to my father and uncle as going away together, which is an error in the record. My father and presently my brother Kim followed.

So we had a sale at the farm at which, as I have said elsewhere, the lean cattle and the broken machinery fetched only about enough in notes of hand (nobody had cash) to pay for the whisky consumed at the sale.

So my father left for the West, and my mother was left on the farm with the younger children and Old Tommy, and my elder brothers and I were sent away to school at Upper Canada College. That was for me practically the end of the old farm, though the rotten place hung round our family neck for years, unsaleable. For the time being it was rented to the neighbouring farmer for $250 a year, the same amount as my mother had to pay on the mortgage. The farmer didn't pay the rent and mother didn't pay the mortgage: all debts in those days dragged along like that.

But the year after that my mother moved into Toronto on the strength of a casual legacy from England that should have been hoarded as capital but was burnt up as income. Then my father came back (broke) from the North-West in 1886, and this meant another move back from Toronto to the old farm; but I was not in it, being a boarder at Upper Canada College. Things went worse than ever for my father on his return to the farm – a shadowed, tragic family life into which I need not enter. I always feel that it is out of place in an autobiography to go into such details. The situation ended by my father leaving home again in 1887. No doubt he meant to come back, but he never did. I never saw him again. My mother lived on at the old farm, because it was unsaleable, for four more years, with eight children to look after as best she could on about $80 a month and with Old Tommy and his wife as bodyguard. Tommy's wages had not been paid for so long that he couldn't leave, but anyway he didn't want to. In his old-fashioned Yorkshire mind wages due from the aristocracy were like shares in the National Debt. My elder brothers Jim and Dick had both left home for good, both to the West, Dick into the North-West Mounted Police and Jim in the wake of my remarkable uncle. That made me, my father being gone, the head of the family at seventeen. But since I was away at school and college and then teaching school, I was only at the farm in holidays and odd times. I at last got rid of the rotten old place on my mother's behalf simply by moving mother off it and letting it go to the devil, mortgages, creditors and all. I don't know who finally got it. But for me the old farm life ended with my going to Upper Canada College in the beginning of the year 1882.

CHAPTER III

My Education and What I Think of it Now

I came down to Toronto from our old farm and entered Upper Canada College as a boarder in February 1882. My two elder brothers, Jim and Dick, had been sent on ahead (I don't remember why) the November before. So from this time on, for seventeen years and a half, as a schoolboy (boarder or day), or as a student, or teacher, or as both college student and teacher together, Toronto was the city I lived in; and it has retained all the detail of remembrance and the peculiar charm of the past which goes with one's own city. Nor did I see any other, anyway, for about ten years.

Toronto was then just in its final stage of comfortable and completed growth as a prominent centre of life and industry, intercourse and arts, before the coming of the electrical age brought the rapid transit and communication that was to turn it into something ten times greater; to foster suburban growth, bring great industries to the fringe of the city itself, feed the country in part from the city as its base and turn all such provincial towns into metropolitan centres. Toronto today, we admit, is ten times the size it was then. Yet perhaps in a certain aspect the advantage is not all with the new as against the old. Individual life, now lost in the mass, perhaps felt larger.

I have written a description of the Toronto of those earlier days in a book of mine on *Canada* which was distributed as a private gift book and did not reach the hands of the public, and from which therefore I may fittingly quote in these pages:

'In Upper Canada, henceforth Ontario, Toronto was a commodious capital city of 60,000 inhabitants. Its streets were embowered in leaves above which rose the many spires of the churches. Its wooden slum district was herded into the centre and, like poverty itself, forgotten. Where the leaves ended a sort of park land began and in it stood the University of Toronto, secular and scientific, but housed in Norman architecture of beauty unsurpassed. To the west, more rural but less beautiful with earthly beauty, was Trinity College, founded in protest against the existence of secular Toronto. But down below, along the waterfront, was a business district, built like a bit of London, all of a skyline with cobblestones rattling with cabs. The new railways sliced off, as everywhere in Ontario, the shore line, vilified with ash-heaps and refuse. All over Canada between the vanishing beauty of nature and the later beauty of civic adornment, there extended this belt of tin cans and litter.

'Just above the railway lines rose the red-brick Parliament buildings, the red-brick Government House flew its flag, and over the way the red-brick Upper Canada College set itself to make scholars and gentlemen as good as real ones. Guarding the harbour entrance was the Old Fort, its frame barracks of the same old pattern and roof-slope that had already gone round the Empire, its ramparts crumbling, but its ponderous old guns in embrasures still looking feebly dangerous. The tone of society was English at the top, but the barber shops spoke American. There was profound peace and order and on Sunday all bells and Sunday-best. It seems, as most places do, a pleasant place in retrospect. At least it was cheap. The Chair at Toronto that Professor Huxley tried in vain to get, carried a salary of $400 and meant an ample living.

'From the business district the shops ran for half a mile up Yonge Street and, beyond that, Yonge Street ran thirty-five miles to Holland Landing where water communication began. It had a tavern to every mile and plenty of grain wagons to keep them busy. The main railway

ran through from Montreal to Sarnia-Chicago. But from the half-dozen
little railway stations of the Toronto of early Confederation days, there
radiated, like the fingers of a hand, half a dozen little railways with
various gauges, reaching out north to the lumber woods – Huntsville,
Coboconk, Haliburton – and north and west to the lake ports of Lake
Huron and the Georgian Bay. Along the stations of these railway lines
the horse and buggy and the lumber-wagon took up the traffic. General
stores, each a post-office with a near-by blacksmith shop, arose at the
cross-roads, and if there was also a river with a waterfall, there appeared
a sawmill and a gristmill, and presently, as the farms multiplied, a village.
Then the village became a little town, with not one but rival stores, a
drugstore, a local paper and a cricket club. In it were four churches and
three taverns. One church was of the Church of England, one Presbyterian, while the Roman Catholics, Methodists and Baptists divided the
other two. On the map of Ontario, Protestantism was everywhere, but
Roman Catholicism ran in zig-zags. The three taverns were one Grit,
and one Tory, and one neither. Many things in Ontario ran like that in
threes, with the post-office and the mail-stage alternating as the prize of
victory in elections. The cricket club is now just a memory, gone long
ago. Thus the little Ontario town grew till the maples planted in its
streets overtopped it and fell asleep and grew no more. It is strange this,
and peculiar to our country, the aspect of a town grown from infancy to
old age within a human lifetime.'

Upper Canada College, to describe it more narrowly, occupied all the
space lying along King Street and extending from Simcoe St to John St
and backward to Adelaide St. I have no idea how many acres this meant
but there seemed lots of it; room for spacious gardens and big chestnut
trees and such in front, the school building, a large square red-brick
structure of three stories with ample windows, occupying the centre and
flanked right and left with the masters' houses, square, separate,
comfortable houses, with one at the left end of the row of buildings more
commodious and with a large fenced-in garden beside it which constituted
the principal's residence. Some of the boys at that time were housed in
masters' houses, but the bulk of them were in a building that stood
farther still to the left: the Boarding House, red-brick, two stories high,
shaped like the letter T, but with much more cross-piece to the T than
the upright. One end of the cross-piece was the Old Wing made up of
rooms each holding four boys, the Nurseries they called them. The other
end, still called the New Wing and only about ten years old, was cut into
rooms holding two boys each. In the Old Wing there lived two resident
masters with the boys, one on each floor. Each had a comfortable sitting-
room and a bedroom and the services of a waiter to serve his evening

supper. These of course were junior unmarried masters, and their position was adequate and comfortable to that status. It had grown to be the custom that young men held this position after graduation in Arts, and studied Medicine while active as resident masters. A number of men who were later among the distinguished medical men of Ontario served this apprenticeship to aid them in their medical course.

The senior boys lived in the New Wing under the care of the Senior resident master who occupied a permanent position, had a suite of rooms, a waiter of his own and lived in what seemed to us, as schoolboys, magnificent luxury. This was the position held for a whole generation by 'Gentle' John Marland, MA, Oxon., famous in the history of the school. The upright of the T was filled with a large dining-room and over it a large night study. There was a smaller dining-room across the far end of the New Wing, but it was only used for midday dinner when a certain number of day-boys took their dinner at school and the space in the main dining-room was insufficient. All the boys from the 'Nurseries' went into night study from seven to nine (I think it was), but the senior boys studied in their rooms.

Boys were not allowed to leave the school grounds except on Saturday and Sunday, but there was a little 'tuck shop' called The Taffy on the street behind the school (Adelaide St) to which leave was given every afternoon. The boys went over on lists of half a dozen at a time for twenty minutes drawn up by the drill sergeant. One could do oneself very well with five cents a trip – three cents for pop drunk out of the bottle and two cents for two doughnuts or cakes.

The school at that time was at the height of its reputation and popularity. There were very few private schools of any size in the province except the once famous school of Dr Tassie in Galt, and the only 'rival' school in a real sense was Trinity College School, Port Hope. This had been founded in the interest of the Church of England with a special view of educating the sons of its clergy and the sons of members of the Church who distrusted the 'godlessness' that they saw spreading over education in Toronto. All who know the city will recall its long story of friction as between various degrees of godliness and godlessness. Governor Simcoe and his aristocratic settlement at Muddy York were all for the Church of England. But the members of the Church of Scotland and the Scottish Churches couldn't be ignored: nor presently the Methodists and the Baptists. Hence it was hard to find a way, even if one granted full freedom of worship, of reconciling the claims of the different Protestant sects and varieties. This applied especially to the division of the vast area of public land (one-eighth of it) originally set aside when the province was created (1791) for the support of the Protestant Clergy.

The difficulty applied also to all creation of public education, notably that of a university. Make it a part of the Church of England and half the province would be against it. Make it suit all the Protestants at once and you got it so broad that to the true Churchman it appeared flat – trampled to the ground. Thus it was that when the provincial university was at last put on a wide basis as the University of Toronto, a seceding body headed by the vigorous Bishop Strachan, heir to the Simcoe tradition, founded Trinity University. Upper Canada College all through its early years, in fact till 1891, was financially, and by its endowments, united with the University of Toronto. Hence came the formation of Trinity College School, Port Hope, to offset this connection with ungodliness. It was at the time the only rival. Ridley College (separating low-church godlessness from high-church godliness) came later, as did also St Andrews, separating I forget what from what except perhaps the crude ugliness of the Upper Canada College of 1891 from its own rural beauty – a school built by people who knew what a school was as compared with people who just took a guess, starting from a deaf-and-dumb asylum or a penitentiary.

So the school on King Street was, I say, at the height of its reputation and prosperity in 1882. There were about a hundred boarders and over a hundred day-boys, but of course the boarders were, and thought themselves, the school. They had never introduced the division of play hours and work hours specially adapted for Warden, as in British schools with playtime in the best of the afternoon and school and study time in the worst. School ended at three and all the day-boys went home and the boarders could play till tea-time. But this division was not specially made for the sake of the day-boys, but by the custom of the country. People forget, anyway, that darkness falls on autumn and winter play-grounds far earlier in Great Britain than in the more southerly latitude of Toronto.

The old school as I see it was a fine, decent place, with no great moral parade about it, no moral hypocrisy, but a fundamental background of decent tradition. I have elsewhere described what I have called the struggle of the school to make us gentlemen – or even Christian gentlemen – with the conclusion that it couldn't be done. We always looked on it as a false hope ourselves. I think it must have been Dr Arnold of Rugby who first said that it didn't matter whether the school was a school of a hundred boys or of one boy, but it must be a school of Christian gentlemen. Since then all headmasters of boarding-schools have made that announcement in the Assembly Hall, but they fail to put it over. Certainly it failed with us at Upper Canada: we knew it was well meant but outside the realm of practical life. But the moral tone was good. There was little, indeed none, of that hideous bullying which has been the curse of many English schools: nothing that I ever saw or knew about, of that brutal beating, flogging of boys by masters just one layer short of criminal insanity. There was none of the 'fagging' of little boys as servants for the seniors in which many British people seem to exult as a rare feature of school life, but which I personally have never been able to understand. Church and religious service there was, but not too much of it, and the little there was was formal and impersonal. We had Sunday school each Sunday morning, consisting (for Church of England boys) of reciting the collect for the day: but by the time the master had read an opening prayer and heard all the collects then, I think, Sunday was 'all' and he read a benediction. All boys went to church according to their parents' preferences. The Church of England boys, the majority, needed two churches, St George's nearby, up John Street, and the Cathedral along King Street. There was a master in charge, but they didn't go in a flock. Presbyterians went to St Andrew's and Methodists went somewhere else. Among all the wonders there were only three or four Roman Catholics.

But the morality of the school lay in the ideas that guided it, being of course the ideas of the decent families from which we came. We didn't lie – except in the sort of neutral zone where lying didn't count, such as in making up a list for leave to go to the Taffy (the tuck shop). There was no stealing and indeed very little to steal. Pocket money was recommended as 25 cents a week for junior boys, 50 cents for seniors. The era of 'new rich', of schoolboy luxury, of ostentatious parents, had not yet come.

It has been a singularly fortunate thing for Canada that the foundation of Upper Canada College and presently of other private schools on the same plan has never created any disturbing division of education but a cross-wise division of social classes such as vexes England now. As everybody knows, the problem of the 'public' schools (Eton, Harrow, Rugby and a hundred less-known others, apparently called public schools because that is the last word that any stretch of language could apply to them) rises on the horizon as one of the great post-war problems of England. Till yesterday, as it were, in spite of the successive advances of political rights, nominal political equality, England remained a country profoundly based on class, and accepting it. Landed property, hereditary rights, social class and the privileges and posts of government held in accordance with it, was the real basis of British Administration in spite of all the expansion of legal rights from the Reform Act of 1832 and onwards.

The public schools of England were a part of it, had grown up as a part of it, and can only be thought of in that light. Generations of people, not rich, but adhering to the class, gentlemen with a grip all the tighter for the forces tugging it away, clung to the idea of sending their boys to a public school, no matter what the sacrifice; a public school, the old school tie; and then off if need be for British Columbia and Matabeleland. There was often much in it that meant out of sight out of mind. Parents in an English rectory who said that 'Jack was doing well in Manitoba' would have felt less sure of it if they could have seen Jack sleeping in straw as the ostler of a livery stable. But for others a little higher up or more fortunately connected, the 'public schools' and the school tie presently meant the civil service, the Foreign Office, the vast administrative range reserved, not by law but by practice, for gentlemen.

All this is breaking up in England in the new world now shaping. All the wealth of the old hereditary classes available for endowed schools and pious foundations is just nothing as beside the national fund of public money available for buildings, apparatus and equipment, etc., of public schools in the real sense. The lean kine have eaten up the fat. The penny-a-week National School of my Porchester days has grown to the vast science college of today, based on the people's money and itself only a part, in co-operation and competition with the state education of America and the outside world.

What then are they to do? Just have one set of schools in England all maintained by the State? But if so, asks the country rector and the retired colonel, are you sure that you would turn out gentlemen? Leave it all alone to the open competition of pounds, shillings and pence, people paying for what they want different from a State school, or else going without it? But in that case few public schools could survive – Eton and Harrow and such, but the bulk, not. Certainly they could not survive if they tried to adapt their education to the new demands of practical science, engineering, aeronautics, without which any school is left behind mumbling Greek. The 'classics' held their place as the equipment for a ruling class. That is all over. No class can rule that can't understand the science that holds in its hands the life and death of the world.

Such is the English public school problem, a part of the problem of a classless society. Luckily for us the problem is not ours. Give our people money enough and they will take a chance on what class you put them in.

So, as we say, it was a good thing that the foundation of Upper Canada College and its fellow private schools did not create a line of class division running through the schools of the province, as between Upper Canada and England. In Upper Canada, from the days of the Loyalists onwards, all the sensible people were advocates of schools. Those who came from Massachusetts and New York knew what they had left behind, as did those who migrated from Scotland. Hence there grew up in the province an excellent system of public elementary and presently public high schools, and they got better and better as time went on. Then the high schools in the larger towns took on more equipment and bigger staff and turned into Collegiate Institutes. As against this in England there was no public elementary education worthy of the name till the Act of 1870, and even after that the system was still governed by the fact that in the eyes of most people a Board School was no place for a gentleman's son.

But in Canada, gentlemen or not, people, even well-to-do people, living in the big towns mostly saw no reason why they shouldn't send their sons to High School, where the teaching was excellent and the companionship corresponded pretty much to what they got themselves in their social life. The thing was true also the other way round. Many of the boys sent to Upper Canada were not sent there because they were specially rich or specially gentlemanly but because, as in the case of my brothers and myself, they lived in out-of-the-way places and there was nothing else to do with them.

All this got truer and truer as time went on, as education became less and less classical, as science made greater and greater demands on public money for premises and apparatus. Then came the Great War, and the splendid record of boys from High Schools and Colleges obliterated any surviving notion of the private schools as the home of an officer class. The case of the Royal Military College at Kingston, founded in 1876, stands by itself. It was, and is, a Technical School devoted single-mindedly to the profession, with an *esprit de corps* and a pride of its own that in no way interferes with other affiliations and affections.

So then there only remains the question, is a boarding-school any good anyway, except for boys whose homes are isolated from day-schools? Is there anything of value in the life and experience of a boarding-school that a boy cannot get in a day-school? It is a question that has been put to me hundreds of times. And I think that within proper limitations and understanding the answer is in favour of the boarding-school. I say limitations and understanding. For I would never agree with the British people of the older type who think a boarding-school (one made for gentlemen) so necessary that they would sooner send their sons to a bad one than to none at all. The harm of a bad boarding-school, an immoral place, outweighs a hundred times all the shortcomings (after all only negative) of a day-school. Parents should never send their boys to a boarding-school unless they are assured of it on the side of a decent moral life. A rotten school does harm that nothing can ever remedy. So also in a less vital sense does a snobbish school, one whose aim is to take in money (from those who can pay it in potsful) and turn out gentlemen – as far as boys can be made so by expensive clothes, expensive habits, premature luxury and exotic accents.

Leaving out the rotten schools and the snobbish schools, the decent boarding-school has certain disciplines in life to offer, salutary and useful, not to be got elsewhere. One is the value of the break from home, of being compelled for the first time to stand on one's own feet. It is in choking down the sobs of homesickness that we first learn how much home has meant, and how fond we are of it, and the humbler and more dilapidated the home the more suffocating is the sob of affection for it. With the break from home we learn a whole lot of new values, as for instance that of the friend in need, the decent fellow who shows the new boy where everything is and where to put things away: first thing you know you are talking to him about your home and how your mother had warned you not to pack your books the wrong way into your trunk; and he says that about half his stuff got bashed up coming on the train coming down, and so there you are two fellow adventurers, both smashed up by railway baggage men. How eagerly a new boy at school reaches out for such contacts of friendliness, like the shoots of a young plant on hard ground; how quickly he responds to a kind accent in a master's tone, to a hand upon his shoulder; with what penetration he sees that the old drill-sergeant, even if half tipsy, isn't half bad, and what encouragement he finds in a half-wink and a 'cheer up' from the jolly old janitor. Then as the days go by, and the weeks go by, and he begins to settle into the place and have his part in it, what a new life and pride! Something about him as it were that is his, that he has made, a new integument about him like the shell put on by a crab.

It is this new integument – call it if you like this new fellowship – that gives the peculiar meaning to boarding-school friendship, even as the years go by and it all turns into retrospect, to broadening companionship and acquaintance. It is a commonplace, as often repeated as it is true, that the friendships made at boarding-school are different in kind, deeper in meaning, than ordinary friendships. And how they last! I am not thinking here of the school friendships of men who were at school together and owing to the good luck of circumstances spent their life side by side. I am thinking rather of those who were boys together at school and for uncounted years, for long decades, never saw one another, life passing separately for each of them: yet bring them casually together after twenty years, after forty if you like, and the passage of the years is just as nothing, the call of the past bridges it in an instant.

Such has often been my experience, meetings with boys of the old school whom I had neither seen nor much thought about for half a lifetime. It was after one of my lectures in a great American city, a lecture to be followed by a reception, that they told me that there would be a Mr Lyon at the reception who said that he had been at Upper Canada College with me fifty years before. Did I remember him? Remember him? What a ridiculous question! Remember Eph. Lyon, three years senior to me, one of the stars of the First (Cricket) Eleven – a big, striking fellow, as a boy I put him at over six feet, say six and a half – in a cricket blazer, walking back from the wickets to the marquee scoring tent at the corner of the college cricket ground, amid the burst of applause that greeted his score of thirty not out? And I, a college junior, not even fit for the third eleven! Remember him? No, the only thing was the compliment that he remembered me.

So there he was sure enough in the crush of the reception, one of those stand-up-and-talk affairs where one lady was asking me what I thought of Galsworthy's *White Monkey* (I hadn't heard of it) and another telling me that I ought to have gone on lecturing another half-hour. But for me Lyon was the feature of the reception. I admit that fifty years had altered him. He had turned from a Canadian schoolboy into an American business man. He had lost about a foot in height and most of his width. He said the lecture was fine and that he never came to them, and then he asked me what became of Old Gentle, and I told him that all the old school buildings had been knocked down and the ground remade and rebuilt into great square blocks, and we stood there in the dust and memory of the falling school house, the wind from the chestnut trees of the college garden blowing in our faces. All about us was the babble of Galsworthy's *White Monkey* and literary discussion, but the call of the years had carried us beyond it.

Or, similarly, I recall how one day at my club a message came to me to say that a gentleman from Arizona was downstairs in the lower hall who said he had been at school with me fifty years ago. I went down and there he was, sure enough. Who would he be? Why, Jimmy Douglas, of course; who else could he be? We were in form 2A together and in the old boarding-house together in 1882. 'Well, Jimmy!' I said, as I asked him whether he remembered that he had said to me in 2A that he believed a fellow didn't need algebra. Evidently he hadn't needed it in Arizona, solid and prosperous, rugged and simple with it, and, as memory cleared away the haze from his features, unchanged since twelve years old.

Another time, in my club also, a man said, 'Let me introduce my cousin,' – and I exclaimed as I shook hands with what looked like a tall, very dignified and formal gentleman, but which I knew wasn't, but was just a schoolboy in disguise, 'Why! Hullo, Friday!' He laughed. It is amazing how quickly the barriers break down. 'Friday all right,' he said, 'but no one has called me that for forty years.' 'You remember,' I said, 'how you entered Upper Canada College alongside of a boy from Coburg called Crusoe, and after the master had written down Crusoe's name, he said to you, "I suppose you must be Friday"?' With that the scene rose before us, the typical master's joke, that goes such a long way with a class, the subservient laughter, and afterwards in the playground the nickname *Friday*, plastered on and there for keeps.

All that, I say, is apropos of the question, what is there in a boarding-school? – to which the answer is that there is a heap. Incidentally, though I forgot to mention it before, in my day a boarding-school still carried the advantage that it gave athletics, games and the life surrounding them. This exclusive aspect is gone in our present age, when athletics and sports are universal, and the new and wholesome worship of health, strength and fitness a dominant idea of the day. Yet even in athletics the bond of union for the boarding-school is always closer and more real.

For me my first initiation into boarding-school life and into the valley of tears of homesickness in February 1882 was brief enough. I entered at an awkward time scholastically though it fitted the financial quarters of the year, because all the subjects had been begun and for the moment I didn't fit in anywhere. The class in algebra had begun it at New Year and I hadn't had any, so the master in charge said to one of the boys, 'McKeown, take this boy to the back of the room and explain to him what Algebra is.' McKeown did so, and I don't believe that even the great Arabian scholar, Ibn Ben Swot, who invented Algebra and gave it its Arabic name, could have put it more exactly where it belonged, as mystery, than did McKeown of Form 2A in 1882. McKeown set out his Todhunter's *Algebra* and some bits of paper on a desk. He opened Todhunter at a page marked examples and all spotted with x, y and z, mixed with figures. I had never seen Algebra before. 'Now,' said McKeown, 'you take x,' and he wrote it down. 'We'll say it's 10.' 'Is it?' I said. 'Say it is,' said McKeown. 'Then you see $x + 1 = 11$.' 'But,' I persisted, 'how do you know x is 10?' 'I don't,' said McKeown, 'say it's 12 if you like.' 'No, no,' I said. 'I only meant how much *is* x?' 'Oh, I don't know,' said McKeown, and of course that is exactly what Ibn Ben Swot would have said, only McKeown felt ashamed of ignorance and Ibn Ben exulted in it. Indeed he would have explained that the whole point of Algebra is that it enables us to deal with unknown quantities, so much of this and so much that, and find out all sorts of results connected with it, without giving them any single fixed meaning.

I spent three or four days in such class exercises, and in standing up, utterly homesick, and chorusing out declensions and conjugations after the old-fashioned system of the day, and in living through clattering meals that I could hardly eat for homesickness, and in night study, and in the nursery bedroom with my two brothers, and then the fourth or fifth day brought it all suddenly to a close. I woke up in the morning with a headache and my stomach as red as a lobster, and that was scarlatina. So the Lady Matron of the boarding-house took me in charge, and packed up a bag of my things and said, 'And now come and see what a nice little house we have out behind the school!' It didn't look to me like a nice little house, in fact it looked just like a brick coal-shed converted into two rooms as a 'sanatorium', which is just what it was. This was before the days of isolation hospitals and trained nurses. So there I was established in the sanatorium under the care of an old dame, a kinder and a cleaner version of Mrs Gamp. My illness was nothing and was over in a day, and then the next day somehow my mother turned up and I didn't care how long I stayed isolated, drawing pictures and having her read out loud to me.

At the end of so many weeks I went back to the old farm, and in the intervals of convalescence went up and down to the red school twice a week, learning Latin. After Easter I went back to Upper Canada, but in less than no time it had all changed, all began to feel familiar and easy. The lessons were to me a mere nothing because they had shoved me a class down and I knew it all, and with that I began to make a few timid friendships, and to feel proud of walking with my friends down King St all in college cricket caps (dark blue and white) and hearing people say as they passed, 'Those are Upper Canada boys.' Oh, my! Eh what! I remember how my bygone friend, Chic Sale, that great artist of the comic, told me that the first time he heard someone say in a hotel rotunda, 'Look, that's Chic Sale!' he threw his head up so high with pride that he tripped his left foot behind his right and made a sort of stage fall into the air. Chic had it to perfection. That is exactly how my twelve-year-old associates and I felt when someone said 'Upper Canada boys!' Then came the springtime and the cricket season of May and June. The college grounds all beautiful, great days on Saturday afternoons, cricket matches and heroes, and receptions with great quantities of ice cream and cakes; and then, ecstatic beyond wonder, the close of the term, the school breaking up in a torrent of oratory exhorting us to be gentlemen, packing trunks and off to take the train to go home for the holidays. My brothers and I went down to the little old Toronto and Nipissing Station at the foot of Berkeley St two hours before the train was due to be made up, and 'fooled around' among the cinderhead beside the bay, waiting to start home, and there wasn't a dull minute in all the two hours.

We came back as boarders that autumn, and after that, as I said before, I stayed on at Upper Canada, passing all through the school as a boarder and as a day-boy and finally as a boarder again. My brother Jim dropped out to go to my remarkable Uncle in Winnipeg, and Dick presently grew so tall that they couldn't keep him there any longer. Dick couldn't learn anything by any known academic process. They promoted him out of the first form into the second on the ground that he was nearly six feet high, but they refused to carry him beyond six feet. So Dick dropped out and back to the old farm now occupied only by old Tommy, the hired man. Then presently there came the North-West Rebellion of 1885 which brought after it that autumn an outbreak of placards calling for recruits for the North-West Mounted Police. Dick ran true to form, made his way to Ottawa, was accepted and then went off to the Regina barracks. My younger brother Charlie filled in in his place at Upper Canada as a day-boy alongside of me.

I look back to the education I received in those years and I find in it plenty to think about. It was what is, or was, called a splendid classical education, as it was for a couple of hundred years in England and America looked on as the mainstay of national culture, the keystone in the arch of civilization; and before that in England it was the only kind of education, embedded deep in theology and so intimately connected with the Church that it was inseparable from it. Any form of education not connected with the Church was held to belong to the devil, as witness the education for which Oxford in its infant years imprisoned or secluded Roger Bacon for ten years. There was the Church's education and the devil's education. In the long run the devil's education has won out. Any nation whose leaders are not trained in it will no longer survive; any nation whose life is not based on it, whose people are not equipped with it, cannot last a generation. In other words the 'survival quality' that was attributed to the old classical education has passed away, or is visibly passing away with the generation of the present leaders.

People who admit they know nothing of the history of education among English-speaking peoples may tolerate a few words of explanation. All through the Middle Ages the only education (we are speaking broadly) was that of the Church. It was carried on in Latin. When the modern age began, say about A.D. 1500, and printing multiplied books, education widened and included a lot of what had been the education of the Greeks and Romans; such as the philosophy of Aristotle, which in no way contradicts the teaching of the Church and could be read side by side with it, and the great poems and plays of the Greeks, of Homer and the tragedians, and those of Rome, such as Virgil's account of how Aeneas escaped from the fall of Troy and founded the Roman nation, and the great histories, Thucydides' *History of Greece*, and the works of Livy and Tacitus and Julius Caesar in Latin, of Demosthenes and of Cicero. All this made such an imposing body of literature, especially when set off in the new glory of print on vellum, that there was in vernacular English, or indeed in any vernacular, nothing like it at all. It was so to speak the world's literature, containing all the wisdom of the world. Even when people in England such as Shakespeare began to write things that were better, no one knew it or admitted it. Many people still don't. A Greek professor, especially if growing old and apt to sit under a tree and fall asleep over Theocritus, will tell you, of course, that Greek literature is unsurpassed. Nor can you contradict him, since you don't know it, except by telling him that the Chinese classics are better still.

So here then was the education that went with the rising glory of England and the earliest beginnings of the United States. Oddly enough it carried with it a fringe, that kept growing and expanding, of Mathematics and Physics that had not been part of the education of the Greeks at large. The Greeks abhorred anything practical (just as Oxford a hundred years ago tried to ignore 'stinks', meaning chemistry) and they never had any decent system of calculation by numbers on paper, so that Greek mathematics was queer odd ingenious stuff, as if one worked out puzzles for puzzles' sake. It was complicated and difficult enough, as when they speculated on the kind of curves made by slicing through a cone (conic sections), an enquiry carried on 'just for fun' in their time. Only one part of their Greek mathematics, the art of field measurement, or geometry, was especially developed into a complete and rounded form, particularly in Egypt, in the great Greek centre of learning in Alexandria. This was because in Egypt with each annual flood of the Nile land measurement by sight lines had a special importance. Hence the treatise of Euclid came into our education intact and stayed there till into the present century.

To what the Greeks had of Mathematics the new English classical education as it got consolidated, after, say, A.D. 1500, added all that went with the wonderful system of calculating by giving figures a 'place value' (so that for example the figure two may mean two, or twenty, or two hundred). We are so accustomed to this that we take it for granted and no longer see how wonderful it is. The Greeks and Romans and all the ancient nations fooled round with it and got very close to it with the method of counting of beads on strings, etc., but they never learned how to put it on paper and so make the figures add and subtract and multiply in our present marvellous and simple method of columns and places. It was the Hindus who worked this out; but the Arabs put the cap on it by inventing the use of the figure zero, the round 0 for nothing that means everything.

Luckily for English education, mathematics developed side by side with classical education not as an equal partner but as an adjacent. This was partly due to the genius of the nation, which tends to produce men of exception as seen in Napier, who invented logarithms, Isaac Newton, who invented the Calculus and went in an effortless way beyond all known boundaries, and Halley, who invented Isaac Newton by keeping him at work. Nor could even Halley keep him at it for good. It is odd that Newton, who lived to a great old age, was all done with science relatively early in life, pursued no more discoveries, and felt proud to be in Royal Service as the Master of the Mint.

But what made mathematics for England was its connection with navigation. When the era of colonial expansion brought England on to the seven seas, navigation by means of mathematical astronomy became the peculiar privilege and pursuit of the British. The Portuguese and the Spanish had only known the beginnings of it. Columbus was really, in spite of some tall talk on his part, quite ignorant. He merely threw a chunk of wood overboard to see how fast the ship was going. The English forged ahead. The Elizabethans 'took the sun'. Isaac Newton himself explained that longitude at sea could be accurately known each day at noon as soon as someone could invent a clock to keep time at sea. Even so, the Admiralty prize of £10,000 went begging till late in the eighteenth century. But with the use of chronometers and sextants and the compilations of astronomical tables worked out on shore and applied at sea, and ingenious mathematical tables of logarithms to apply them with, British navigators led the world. It was the British government that sent out astronomers with captains to observe the transit of Venus in the South Pacific in 1769. After which the use of mathematics got mixed up with the glory of Old England and Britannia ruling the waves, and no scheme of English education was complete without. Not that English schools took to it gladly. We are told (in the Memoirs of General Lyttleton) that even at Eton the study of mathematics was tolerated rather than appreciated as late as the 60s of the last century.

In all this I am not wandering from the point. I am explaining where I got my Upper Canada College education. Well, that's where it came from, from the theologians and the classical scholars and Isaac Newton and the Nautical Almanac.

But the thing that especially consolidated the position of the Classical Education in England, as it presently did also in America, was the discovery, by experience, that it was a great training for leadership. This applied particularly to a nation which had grown not democratic, but parliamentary; a nation where oratory in the legistlature counted for more and more, and where forensic oratory in free and open courts was one of the great highways to success and political preferment.

To this was added presently the power of the Press, the value of the written word and the persuading paragraph, things for which the classical education had, and still retains when most else is gone, a commanding eminence.

Side by side with classical education, in a position that has slowly grown from the lowest to the highest, grew up medicine and medical education: from its earliest beginnings in black art and barbers' surgery with its red and white rags: out of the mists of astrology and the incantations of superstition: out of empirical remedies and old wives' tales, till with the age of science it began to build on definite organized truth, and on knowledge gathered from the facts of dissection and the observations of anatomy. But medicine was no part of the education of a cultivated man, and till far down the nineteenth century the social status of a doctor other than a court physician was dubious and humiliating.

Science remained for the few, for the investigators, for the Royal Society founded under Charles II, a factor in the national advance of England second only to the Royal Navy. The list of the great names in science, Priestley, Faraday, Lyell, Darwin, lies outside of the orbit of academic education.

Such was the classical education. It is my opinion that the world moved it on just in time, and that England especially was only saved in the nineteenth century from degenerating into intellectual stagnation by the fact that other forces in the nation, clear outside of its scholars and all that they stood for, pursued science for science's sake; promoted invention, applied it to industry and transport and presently – by the dead weight of circumstance and opinion – thrust it into the schools and colleges.

A chief trouble with the classical scholarship was its infernal conceit. The typical classical scholar developed under encouragement into a sort of pundit. He knew it all – not part of it, all of it. What he didn't know wasn't college. The phrase was used long after by Benjamin Jowett, Master of Balliol, but it might have been used by any of them from Dr Busby of Westminster, in the days of Charles II, down to their last octogenarian successors of yesterday. They knew it all. That is to say, they knew nothing whatever of medicine and would have roared with laughter over their own ignorance of it, with a neat Latin quotation to cap it. They knew nothing whatever of the geographical and geological globe about them, replacing it with an intimate knowledge of the Aegean

Sea as of 500 B.C. They knew nothing of modern languages, regarding them as a thing for couriers or dragomen. They knew nothing of the investigations of natural science, had no vision as to where it was leading, knew nothing of its application to industry, nothing of industry itself, nothing of finance; in fact, looked at in a proper focus, all that they did know was nothing as compared with the vast portentous knowledge that was rising on the horizon of a changing world.

Even for literature and the drama, all that goes with the republic of letters, their point of view was turning hopelessly astray by their persistent tradition that of course Latin and Greek literature was far superior to that of our own day. To say this in A.D. 1500 was to state a plain truth. To say it in A.D. 1900 was to talk pure unadulterated nonsense.

The old classical education had at least the advantage that it was hard and difficult, with no royal road. It was as hard as ever a teacher liked to make it. For witness, call in anyone who has studied Greek moods and tenses or tried to translate the Greek Dramatists into something intelligible. In all this it was miles above a great deal of the slush and mush which has in part replaced it, the effortless, pretentious study of things that can't be studied at all, the vague fermentations that tend to replace stern disciplinary work when education is all paid for and free for all and popular and universal, provided that it is not made difficult.

The classical curriculum had also the advantage, to be rightly or wrongly used, that it lent itself admirably to competitive study, to examinations, to marks, to prizes, to going up and down in class. It was from that aspect that I made my Upper Canada College education even less beneficial than it need have been, accentuating its faults by utilizing its weakness. We had at Upper Canada College the system whereby each day's class consisted mainly of questions and answers, that is, either questions on home work done the night before or on something done at sight in class. The boys sat all alone one side, or all across the front of the room. If the master asked a boy a question and he couldn't answer it was passed on, 'Next! Next!' till somebody did answer. The boy who thus answered correctly moved up above the ones who had failed to answer. Theoretically, but very rarely in practice, a question might be asked of a boy at the top of the class, and be passed on 'Next, Next' with increasing excitement all the way to the bottom boy of the class, who might answer correctly and 'go up ahead' in one swoop. Hence the system had in it a certain element of sport, something of the attraction of a horse-race. At least it kept the class from going to sleep and it made the class do the work and not the teacher. It always seems to me that in a lot of the revised education of today, which quite rightly undertook to modify the severities, the rigour, the physical punishment and the needless difficulties of the older teaching, the mistake is made in the contrary direction. Everything is made too easy. The teacher has to 'sell' the subject to the class, and in trying to make everything clear and simple it is forgotten that there are some things that can't be made clear and simple because they are by nature difficult and complex.

For me the old-fashioned system of going up and down, and trying to move up to the head of the class and stay there, proved altogether too congenial and attractive and helped to give a false bias to my education. In the junior form, the first and second, I took my studies easily, didn't bother whether I went up or down, and got a very good place without trying for it. But from the third form on I got more and more drawn into study and overstudy, till presently I filled all my time outside of school as well as in. After the third form, by this continuous industry, I ranked first in everything except mathematics; and after the fourth form first in everything, by learning by heart in mathematics every possible thing that would let itself be learned by heart.

Study by this pattern knocked all the reality out of certain subjects. History for me just turned into an underlined book of which I knew by heart all the underlined tags, headings and dates. I knew them then, and I still know all the clauses of the Treaty of Utrecht of 1713, and all sorts of dates and lists, and all kinds of headings. The reality of history gradually was lost from sight behind this apparatus of preparation for examinations.

The very thoroughness of the old classical system made it still worse suited for modern education.

CHAPTER IV

Teaching School

I spent ten and a half years of my life (February 1889 – July 1899) in teaching school, and I liked the last day of it as little as I liked the first. As a consequence I have spoken and written very often and very bitterly about school-teaching and the lot of the school-teacher. Looking back on it all I think I ought to retract about one half of all I said, for I think now that half of the fault was with me, and only half with the profession as such. Even at that it seems to me a shame that school-teaching cannot be organized as a profession which a person can enter as a life-work, and in which success should bring at least the main part of what success means in the other learned professions such as medicine, law and the church. As it is, school-teaching offers too much at the beginning, too little as the years go by. The initial salary is better than anyone could hope to gain in his opening years of law or medicine. The final salary is nowhere beside the great prizes the other professions offer. It is true that in the other professions they may fall by the way, lawyers without a case and medical men forced out of their profession by lack of opportunity and glad to earn a living in any other kind of way. In teaching very few fall by the way; very many rise out of it; but those who remain in it for a lifetime find as the years go on that it gives them less than what is fair, less than what is commensurate with other pursuits.

There are certain things without which the life of a person who has grown up in cultured surroundings and received a cultivated education is not properly complete, does not stand on a fair level with other lives and opportunities. Every career should look forward to marriage as a thing that can in due course and time be accepted with all that it brings in the way of children and a home, without the pinching and semi-poverty that reduces it to a status not good enough to rank with that of other professions. With marriage should go a sufficient command of money to allow for the amentities of life, to permit one to belong to a club, to buy, within reason, books, etc., furniture and house things, to enjoy art and the theatre, and such special holiday 'blow outs' as punctuate the monotony of life's routine. Most necessary of all is money enough to launch one's children in the world.

Any man who has that much need ask for no more. Granted that much of ease and affluence, the rest depends on himself, on what kind of mind and personality he has. The trouble with our school-teaching in Canada is that up to now it does not offer these things. Hence its characteristic features, too much at first, too little later. An in-and-out profession through which a series of bright young men pass on to something better, and in which a certain number of young men, too dull or too devoted, remain for ever. The running stream leaves its deposit as it flows on, but is the deposit gold or mud?

In my case I went into school-teaching with my eyes wide open, as into something temporary on the way to a real career. To go into teaching was a matter of sheer necessity. My education had fitted me for nothing except to pass it on to other people. And as I have explained, my mother's finances had come to a full stop with the final exertion of getting enough money to give me the one year of full undergraduate status at the University, for which my scholarship of $100 was quite inadequate. Meanwhile, as my father had vanished into space, my mother was still on the old farm with eight children younger than me to look after, and with an income of, I think, $80 a month to do it on. Of my two older brothers, Jim was in Winnipeg with some small job in the Court House but quite unable to send money home, and Dick in the North-West Mounted

Police had nothing to spare from his pay. How my mother managed in the ensuing years before any of us could help her I do not know. I imagine the answer is that she drifted into debt and stayed there. Even when we could presently give her money it was merely applied over the surface of the debt below, like a warm growth of Arctic flowers in the sun over cold frozen muskeg.

I found out by asking those who knew, that my college status as a third-year undergraduate, for I had taken the first and second years in one as already explained, would entitle me to teach in a High School or Collegiate Institute, provided I put in three months as a teacher in training. This new feature was still quite recent, as was the first instalment of that qualification in 'education' (so-called) superadded to the academic qualification of time spent and examinations passed at the University. From the modest three months of technical education as a qualification for teaching, the requirement has now been lengthened in Ontario, as it has in most similar jurisdictions in Canada and the United States, to one year. It thus represents as much as 25 per cent of the academic qualification itself. I have always thought, and still think, this is out of all proportion. I have always had a very low opinion of the educational qualification, too low I am sure, always looking upon it as about 10 per cent solid value and 90 per cent mixed humbug and wind. I have always felt that the only way to learn to teach is to go and do it, just as Mr Squeers, immortalized by Dickens, taught his pupils to spell *windows* by going and cleaning them. In so far as the educational qualification helps to close the profession and keep out superfluous numbers, I am convinced that the same time and money spent on an extra academic year would be more to the point.

* * *

I sent in my application and was duly assigned in September of 1888 to a group of half a dozen men and women teachers allotted for three months' training to the Strathroy Collegiate Institute, Strathroy being in Eastern Ontario, beyond London.

So in due course I got on the train and went to Strathroy. Apart from trips up and down to Sutton, it was my first railway journey. I had a wooden trunk tied with a clothes-line and something called a valise – I forget whether of imitation straw or of imitation something else. It is the kind of baggage I still use. I have never risen to the luxury of aristocratic baggage as a mark of status. For years I was too poor to buy it, and when I could I didn't any longer care for it. I think that Dr Johnson once said something like that in a letter to the Earl of Chesterfield, about having a literary position. I feel just as he did about having a pigskin valise: 'had it been early it had been kind, but now I am known and do not need it.'

If it is true that a man is known, as is indicated in romantic novels, by his baggage, then my valise places me every time.

So, as I say, I arrived at Strathroy. I left my trunk at the station and walked up the street and presently I saw a sign, *Rooms with Board*, and went in and took a room with board. I think the price was $3 a week. I went upstairs and unpacked my valise and wrote a letter home saying, 'Dear Mother, I arrived at Strathroy all right, but the boarding-house I am in looks a pretty rotten place, so I don't expect to stay long.' Then I went down to supper. After I had finished it I met the landlady coming downstairs and she said, 'If you find this boarding-house such a rotten place I guess you better not stay in it,' so I was on the street again, less 25 cents, moving on to the next sign *Rooms with Board*.

That was the beginning of my contact with boarding-houses, which spread intermittently over many years and from which presently I found much food for reflection. Some readers may recall my *Boarding-House Geometry*, in which was laid down the axiom that all *Boarding-Houses are the same Boarding-House*, and the postulate that a *beeline* may be made *from any one boarding-house to any other boarding-house*. No doubt the origin of those truths reaches back as far as Strathroy.

When I duly found a boarding-house (across the lapse of years I quite forget it and where it was) and had entered the Teachers' School next day I found it easy beyond words after the hard study to which I was habituated. The little group of teachers-in-training moved about the school, listened to sample lessons (in no wise different from the lessons and classes we had all taken for years) and presently were entitled to stand up and 'take the class' themselves under the supervision of the teacher.

In doing this I learned on the side a lesson on how not to be funny, or the misuse of a sense of humour, which lasted me all my life and echoed back to me in a strange way nearly thirty years later. The principal of the Strathroy Collegiate was Mr James Wetherell, the well-beloved 'Jimmy' Wetherell whose memory is still dear to the heart of a thousand pupils. He seemed to us old at the time, as all adult people do to the eyes of eighteen, but he must have been relatively young, for he lived on and on, still in harness when the Great War came, and died at a ripe age later. He was a fine scholar, his chief subject, at least the one he liked best to teach, being English. But he had acquired, as most scholars do if absorbed in their work and exulting in the exposition of it, little tricks of speech and manner all his own and all too easy to imitate. I had at that time a certain natural gift of mimicry, could easily hit off people's voices and instinctively reproduce their gestures. So when Jimmy Wetherell, half-way through a lesson in English, said to me most courteously, 'Now will you take the lesson over at that point and continue it.' I did so with a completeness and resemblance to Jimmy's voice and manner which of course delighted the class. Titters ran through the room. Encouraged as an artist I laid it on too thick. The kindly principal saw it himself and flushed pink. When I finished he said quietly, 'I am afraid I admire your brains more than your manners.' The words cut me to the quick, I felt them to be so true and yet so completely without malice. For I had no real 'nerve,' no real 'gall.' It was the art of imitation that appealed to me. I had not realized how it might affect the person concerned. I learned with it my first lesson in the need for human kindliness as an element in humour.

Now when this happened there was in the class somewhere on a back bench a boy of thirteen whose name was Arthur Currie, who had entered the school that autumn. He was destined to become one of the celebrated men of our Canadian Dominion, Arthur Currie, later on General Sir Arthur Currie, Commander-in-Chief of the Canadian Overseas forces of the Great War, the victor of Vimy Ridge, a really great man. I had occasion to know it, as I served under him for the thirteen years during which he was Principal of McGill. I used in those years in public speeches to refer to the parallel fact that Aristotle had taught Alexander the Great of Greece, and to say that in my opinion Aristotle had nothing on me. And since like all other speakers I prefer an old joke to a new, I worked this one overtime for thirteen years.

As a matter of fact I didn't know General Currie as a boy at Strathroy School, but, with his usual and phenomenal memory, he recalled me. When he came to McGill I went, as in duty bound, to pay my respects to him in his office and I said, for I had just been reading as had everybody his full biography in the newspapers, 'I think, General Currie, I must have had the honour of teaching you when I was a teacher in training at Strathroy in 1888.' He gave me a closer and more scrutinizing look. 'Why, yes,' he said. 'I recognize you now. You were the young man to whom Jimmy Wetherell, the principal, said that he admired your brains more than your manners.'

The work of the Teachers in Training Course was easy and agreeable and companionable. Hard it was certainly not, and it was useful provided that the quantity was kept down to the proportions then existing and not extended out of all reason, as I think it to be today. As examination work we had to study two or three books, one on school management with discussion of such things as ventilation, etc., and one on the outline of the history of education. This last was very interesting but a little of it went a long way. I should think that any trained student could get all that he needed of the history of education in a week of reading, I mean as far as its utility in actual teaching goes. Beyond that he could study it till he was grey with increasing interest to himself. The trouble with so many of our new curriculum subjects is that they confuse what is agreeable reading for old men with what is necessary reading for young ones. As I see it the whole of sociology lies in this field, a wonderful subject of reflection for riper years but hopelessly artificial as a class study for youth.

The training school ended with examinations, a school entertainment and good-bye and goodwill all round. I found myself a qualified Secondary School teacher of the province of Ontario and a specialist in Latin, Greek, French, German and English. I presume that I still am.

Being a specialist is one thing, getting a job is another. So I found myself back at the old farm with nothing to do but send in applications for such teaching jobs as I could hear of or find advertised in the papers. Among other things I had the honour of being an applicant for a job on the staff of the newly and not yet opened Bishop Ridley College, at St Catherine's, a school that has since traced a long and honourable record of over half a century. I doubt very much whether my application, to use an upstate expression, caused any headache to the trustees, seeing that my application for the position of modern language master went in alongside of that of H. J. Cody, the successful applicant, who had just taken his degree in Arts that year. Cody had had a phenomenal record, universally first in everything, so that in his year the lists in all the languages as in English and History began (1) H. J. Cody and should have added – and the rest nowhere. He began here that long and distinguished life of service to the Church and to education which sees him now President of the University of Toronto. I remember by the way when we, his college contemporaries, heard that Cody had gone into the Church, we looked on it as a case of a good man gone astray. We realized the success he was thus renouncing as a great criminal lawyer, or criminal politician, for his college eminence was so outstanding that he could easily have reached out for any of the great prizes of life. There was no other way for any college contemporary to escape competing against Cody except to take a dive clear into another faculty, and even at that he would be apt in medicine to come up alongside the similar record of Llewelyn F. Barker, later on the famous Dr Barker of Baltimore, who was always first in every class in each subject. I remember that years later I asked Barker if this was literally true and he told me that there had been an exception, that once he had been put into third class, and that in the very subject which he regarded as his best and on which he had written voluminous examination answers, all, he was certain, correct. Barker told me further that very soon after the occurence, when he had come to know the examiner in question as a fellow doctor and fellow examiner, he asked him if he recalled how and why the third class happened. 'Most certainly,' answered the examiner. 'I put you in third class because I wanted *answers*, not a whole damn book.' Those who know the vagaries of examiners will realize the truth of the story. Barker carried the bitterness of it throughout the years and never forgave the injustice. He was fond of telling the story, and at his death it appeared in many of the notices written of his career.

Meanwhile I was trying in vain in January 1889 to get a job in a school. Unexpectedly I got one at the beginning of February through the good offices of an old friend, the 'Mr Park' who had been for some years our tutor on the old farm. Park, after his tutorship ended in 1881, had gone back to college, finished his course in Arts and had gone into teaching. At this time he occupied the position of headmaster of Uxbridge High School. He wrote to me to say that a modern language teacher was needed at the school and if I applied for the post he didn't doubt that his recommendation would get it for me. This turned out to be true, and in due course I drove over to Uxbridge and found myself installed as teacher of modern languages in the bright new red-brick High School that had recently been added to the town's attractions.

Uxbridge was then a town of about 1,500 people, situated nowhere in particular on the high ground between Lake Ontario and Lake Simcoe: one of those agricultural centres that grew up around a grist-mill and sawmill when the settlers moved in, grew to a certain extent and then planted trees in the street to replace the shattered forests and fell asleep under the trees. Uxbridge, as its name shows and as the adjacent township of Brock indicates, belongs among the settlements that followed the Great War (once so called) when the Battle of Waterloo and Lord Uxbridge as a Waterloo hero and General Brock's heroic death at Queenstown Heights were memories of yesterday. Around the town were settled a fine class of British, and as beside my village of Sutton its main street with a flood of light from the shop windows looked quite metropolitan. It had the usual equipment of taverns and churches, but was a clean bright orderly little place, dull as ditchwater but quite unaware of the fact.

From the old farm to Uxbridge was a distance of eighteen miles. To-day, travelling in a motor-car over gravelled roads, there is hardly time to get well settled in the car before the trip is over. But in 1889 it was a real pilgrimage, not be done there-and-back in a day, up and down over one sandhill after another, in winter through hill cuttings blocked with snow, in spring among sunken roads covered with spring floods. Nowadays of course all such distances have shrunk to nothing; Toronto Sunday trippers run out to and beyond Uxbridge to fish in the streams, or drive through Uxbridge (apart from the Main Street) without noticing that it is there. Such as it was the town became my home for the next half-year, and I owe it all the gratitude that goes with the payment of a first salary.

I had no trouble with teaching from the very start, no difficulty in doing it, no question of discipline. There are certain people who from the moment they step into a classroom present themselves as easy marks to pupils inclined to disorder, who even provoke disorder among pupils inclined to silence and attention. I remember such among those who taught me at Upper Canada College, as does everyone else among those who taught him at his school. Very generally the recollection of such incompetents is among the fondest memories retained across the years. Pupils or students look back to the memory of 'old Billy', or whoever it was, who couldn't keep order, with a singular gratitude, with a laughing memory that is all attention. Such incompetents cannot be trained out of it. They are hopeless from the start. I remember (years later than Uxbridge) how General Currie at McGill undertook to explain the principles of class discipline to a young incompetent teacher attached to my department whose students were turning his classroom into a bear garden. 'Mr Smith,' said the general, 'you can't keep order. Now listen, you were a soldier in my army, weren't you?' 'Yes, sir.' 'In France, weren't you?' 'Yes, sir.' 'Well, then can't you take the first of these miserable young – (General Currie here used his own private vocabulary) who starts trouble in the class out on the campus and try to kill him?' 'Yes, sir,' said Mr Smith. Yet within another month or so the class had Mr Smith beaten to a standstill. He had to give up teaching and was out in a cruel world without resources. I have often wondered what would have happened if Mr Smith had murdered a McGill student on the campus. But no doubt General Currie was right. The mere intent to murder, the murderous look was all that was needed. Poor Smith couldn't command it.

At Uxbridge I didn't have to murder or threaten to murder any of my pupils. Instinctively I went at class order in the right way, and when you know how it is very simple. It is the beginning which counts. Face the class. Begin talking to them at once. Get to business, not with one of them but with all of them. Talk: don't mumble. Face them: don't turn your back. Start work: don't get fumbling about with a class list of names and a roll call, which you may pronounce correctly or may not. Leave all that till later. Start work, and once started they are lost as far as disorder goes. In fact they won't expect any. Above all, don't try to be funny; feeble teachers attempt a footing of fun as a means of getting together.

The real teacher only descends to fun when he has established a sufficient height to descend from.

So there I was with my class, all bright and easy with Pass Matriculation French out of Pass Matriculation French book rippling merrily round. As I was only just turned nineteen the senior pupils were nearly as old as I was, one or two perhaps quite as old, and one at least a good deal older. He was preparing for the ministry; and with my help he ultimately got there. The others in the senior class were preparing for Pass Matriculation into the University of Toronto, Arts, Science or Medicine. Of these, my first pupils, local pride in Uxbridge still honours the memory of Colonel Sharpe, who gave his life in the Great War.

The teaching of Matriculation French and German was easy to me because I had been trained in exactly that kind of stuff. In reality it belonged to that futile and worthless brand of teaching French in Ontario which has so long disfigured the otherwise high standard of the province. It was based purely and simply on the final goal of a worthless examination consisting of translating English into French and French into English. Observe the result. Pronunciation didn't matter. Whether I pronounced well or ill, and whether my class pronounced still worse or rather better, was of no consequence. There was no test in pronunciation, no requirement of reading out loud. Nor did it matter in the least whether they understood French when they heard it spoken. There was no test in dictation, no question and answer, nothing but written French – dead as a dead language. On the other hand, there was a regular egg-dance of ingenuity in translating verbal phrases and such back and forward – things like 'Give him some of it: do not give him any of it. Speak to me of them: do not speak to me of them' – and so on, endlessly. Anybody who has ever learned to translate in this way will never be able to speak or use French. The English words crowd into his mind. What he does is to think in English and translate into French. In German things are not so bad. The two idioms being so similar, translation, if one will let it do so, keeps tending to merge into actual use of language.

The whole fault with Ontario French arises in the Provincial examination and floods back to the source from that, like water checked by a dam. Once introduce dictation as a test of comprehension, and reading aloud as a test of pronunciation, and the whole thing would alter. As it is, Ontario French isn't in it with French learned out of a phrase book, one with pronunciation given by those who know it. In any case language for use can only be learned word by word and phrase by phrase. We learn to say *carte blanche* by saying *carte blanche*: learning off a list of feminines won't help.

But there is my class waiting. I must get back to them.

My salary was $700 a year and seemed a lot of money, $59.33 a month. In a way it was a lot of money. Board in Uxbridge in 1889 was $12.00 a month, washing about $2.00. All the clothes I would need in a year would represent about $100 or $8.00 a month, drinks (meaning, say, a couple of glasses of beer a day, at 5 cents a glass) about $2.50 a month, the bars being closed on Sunday. That was all the necessary expenses, and all the remaining money was extra. One hardly knew what to do with it. There were of course no moving pictures, no soda fountains, no motor-cars, no paid dances, no slot machines, none of the hundred and one odd expenses that make the life of young people today one continuous expenditure of money big or little. I forgot tobacco in my list above. Call it a plug of 'T and B' once a month at 25 cents.

I felt so rich on receipt of my first salary that I hired a 'livery rig' (charge $1.00 for the trip), a cutter, and drove over to the old farm, one afternoon to go there and back the next. I have always hated the care of horses from my early recollections of chores on the farm, but of course I could, like anybody else, drive a horse if I had to. I remember that a wild blizzard came on that evening with big snowdrifts, and that I turned into a farmhouse half-frozen to thaw out, or to thaw the horse out, I forget which. When I got home I gave $10 of my salary to my mother, the first instalment of relief to her finances, seeming like the first relief of Lucknow. It proved to be only the first of plenty, for as the years went by my brothers and I were able to give her help; and then, when two or three of us became well-off we were able to banish all her money perplexities and give her everything she needed. The long evening of her life, for she lived to be ninety, paid her back dividends on her past devotion. The cottage beside the river which my sister Rosamond built for her use at Sutton remains – a marvel of beauty of site and scene which even the passing motor tourist pauses a moment to admire. My mother lived there in a network of perpetual correspondence and casual visits from children and grandchildren, her house a sort of family centre, a No. 10 Downing St, reaching out across the continent. She was so habituated to being in debt that, manage as she would, mother always carried a little cloud of debt along with her. But it made no difference. We wiped it off the slate every now and then and let it go at that. Perhaps after all there is more in raising a large family, in spite of all that it entails, than many young women of today are inclined to think.

I worked away contentedly enough at Uxbridge. But of course the situation carried with it the drawback that, as I reckoned it, I was getting nowhere. I had dropped out of college and saw no way to get back and finish the two years towards my degree. To try to save money to do so on my High School Salary would have taken years and years. To settle down and try to make my life and get married and live on a High School salary was a thing I never thought of for a moment. I tried to do a little odd study at my college books but did not get very far, and in any case teaching every day from nine to four was sufficiently tiring to leave little energy for anything else. Teaching like anything else is immensely tiring to a novice, later on it gets less and less so in proportion to one's ability to teach. But it is never easy, except to people who can't teach at all or don't try to.

On such terms I finished out my first half-year at Uxbridge and went up to Lake Simcoe for those summer holidays beside the Lake which have played such a large part in my life for over half a century. My mother had again rented the old parsonage, the ancient tumbledown habitation of the first parson of Georgina of which I spoke before. I had also a sailboat acquired in Toronto a year or two before from a remnant of my mother's temporary affluence and my father's temporary gains of the Winnipeg boom. It was what was called a double lugger, but I put it into a higher class when I brought it to Lake Simcoe by getting a local farmer boat-builder to convert it into a single-masted sloop. Operations of this sort, which sound as if they ought to cost a couple of hundred dollars, then represented only about five dollars plus the price of a little paint. That was the first of a series of sailboats of varying sizes and rigs which I sailed on Lake Simcoe and its sister Lake Couchiching, from those days until now.

The marvellous thing about the good old summer time of those days was how little it all cost. I remember some years ago at my present country house in Orillia a medical man, a contemporary of mine, explaining to a group of people how he and another medical student used always to take a six weeks' holiday of summer camping and that all it cost them was twenty-five dollars each. The up-to-date auditors could scarcely believe it, but my medical friend was easily able to prove and over-prove it. He and his fellow-students owned between them a canoe and a tent and blankets. So there was their lodging for nothing. For food they had a certain amount of canned beef and canned salmon, which along with fish that cost nothing but the easy catching represented a meal bill of, say, ten cents a day each. For milk they went to farmhouses along the lake and got all they wanted at five cents a quart, and the farm people felt so mean at charging anything that they 'threw in' a lot of vegetables: or they bought vegetables and the farm people felt so mean that they threw in the milk: and if the campers came back a second day the farm people threw it all in. So there was their board. For light they had a coal-oil lantern at twenty-five cents a month. As to drinks, it is astonishing how little young people (not old soaks) drank before the days of prohibition:

an odd glass or two of beer when in reach of a bar, at five cents a drink, and a bottle of rye whisky at seventy-five cents a quart for first-class liquor, carried along in the canoe for a 'snifter' in the evening. Calculated this way one wonders how the two medical students could spend as much as twenty-five dollars each on their trip.

In the good old summer time of those days our chief diversions were boating, sailing, swimming and above all lawn tennis, newly introduced and all the go. Swimming never took the form of mixed bathing except for a few 'sissies' who might care for it. Girls in those days when they went into the water were equipped from top to toe with bathing caps, full bathing suits more voluminous than their ordinary dresses, and bathing stockings and bathing shoes. 'Swimming' for them just meant getting wet with their clothes on. Ordinary young men of wholesome minds looked on girls in the water as a damn nuisance. But for tennis they came into their own, since we all played so indifferently and had so little idea of the smashing game that tennis could turn into, that any girl who could stand up beside the net and prevent the ball from hitting her in the face did well enough for a partner. Here again was a cheap game. The grass court cost little trouble to make, no expert work and people made it for themselves. The net cost three dollars and lasted for ever, and the balls never got lost since we hunted them till after dark rather than lose them. As yet no one had ever heard of golf, not in that part of Canada, except as a sort of crazy game played in Scotland by knocking a ball around among sand-hills which forbid any other exercise.

But compare again the cost of our lawn tennis of the 90s and the cost of the golf of forty years later which drove it out. Golf meant a high cost to make the premises and build a clubhouse and fence, high annual dues; with that, suburban fares, green fees, caddy fees, tips, at least one meal at the clubhouse on account of the distance from home. In the pre-war days I knew of many people in Montreal who found that they had all that they could do to keep up their annual golf subscription without attempting to go out to the club and play. Yet in Scotland and in England, where golf links were clipped by grazing sheep, where the 'clubhouse' was just such a small building as might serve to drink Scotch whisky in, or smoke a pipe in a rainstorm, golf was carried on for years and years at an annual subscription in ordinary country places of five dollars (one guinea) a year. Many people have told me of cases of minor revolution when the subscription was moved up to two guineas. But very likely for all I know the game may have been over-swamped by wealth and by the pretence of being rich that has swamped out for us in America so much of the inexpensive amusement of the past.

The good old summer time of 1889 being ended, I went back with deep regret to my teaching job, with no particular prospect in front of me. And then unexpectedly things began to open up indeed, and in less than a month altered my whole outlook. It is possible that the market for teachers had taken a favourable turn, or it is possible that I had made a hit as a teacher and that this one or that one may have spoken of me to someone else, but at any rate, quite unexpectedly and unsolicited, I got an offer to come to Napanee High School at a salary of $900, an increase of $200 in pay. By all the ethics of the teaching profession the Uxbridge trustees should have let me go, or raised my salary. It is among the few redeeming points of the teaching profession that a school is not supposed to stand in a teacher's way: what is a temporary inconvenience to the school may mean a life advancement for the teachers.

The Uxbridge trustees didn't see it that way: they proposed to hold me to my contract. Looking back on it as I see it now, they felt that they had got a good article cheap and meant to hang on to it. They were, or most of them were, a poor lot. So they refused to let me go, and I had to accept it with the best grace I could and stick at my work.

Then right on the heels of this came a real offer, one that meant for me light out of darkness, salvation out of disaster. Upper Canada College needed a junior master at $700 a year and offered me the job if I was free to take it at once. This would mean of course that I could go on with my college course towards a B.A. degree. For the residence requirement in those days was not strict, involved no actual roll call of attendance and in any case, since the Upper Canada School day finished at three o'clock, I would take odd lectures that came at four or five. What it all meant to me I can find no words to describe.

But the Uxbridge trustees hardened their hearts and again they refused to let me go. No doubt they were more than ever impressed with what a fine cheap bargain they had picked up. But this time the refusal was too bitter for me to sit down under it. I asked leave to come and talk to the trustees in person. They consented, and I went down to an evening's meeting of the board of trustees and laid my case before them, with something, I imagine, like impassioned eloquence. I tried to show them how much it meant to my future. I took up no other aspect of it. I had no precedents to quote, no usage, no real argument, just how much it meant to me. It didn't seem to touch them. The Chairman explained the difficulty of getting a new teacher when the term was already three weeks old, and that seemed likely to be the end of it: when to my surprise an elderly trustee who hadn't spoken – his name was Britton and I am glad to honour it – hit the board table with his fist and said, 'Damn it, gentlemen' – or words to that effect – 'let that boy go. Do you think you can keep a boy of his ability in a place like Uxbridge?' With that the situation was saved: on a sudden inspiration I asked them to give me a week to find them a teacher and they consented.

The situation, I say, was saved. For it so happened that 'my remarkable Uncle,' E. P. Leacock, was on one of those visits to the East by which he eluded his creditors in the West, and I was able to enlist his services on my behalf. I have written elsewhere of my remarkable Uncle and of the phenomenal career that made him one of the notable figures of the spacious days of the Winnipeg boom. He amassed a great fortune, on paper, went up like a rocket and came down like a stick but with the more varied and graceful descent of a parachute. I wrote to him in Toronto and he set to work at once with characteristic energy, interviewed the Principal of Upper Canada and obtained a few days' delay, and in those days with the aid of the teachers' lists and flood of telegrams (there was as yet no general telephone) he unearthed a teacher, a modern language teacher. It is true that his candidate when produced looked far from modern and short on language, indeed I believe the good old man was hauled out of retirement, but he filled the bill and I was free.

PART TWO

A Last Miscellany

CHAPTER I

Are Witty Women Attractive to Men?

Slaves murmur to one another in their chains. They whisper what they think of their masters. In the same way the generality of men, being enslaved by women, whisper, when in safety, what they think. Slave No. 1 in his Club murmurs to Slave No. 2 that women have no sense of humour. Slave No. 2 agrees, and Slave No. 3, overhearing from his armchair, says quite boldly, 'They certainly have not.' After which quite a colloquy ensues among the slaves. But when the wife of Slave No. 1 asks at dinner what was the talk at the Club, he answers, 'Oh, nothing much.' Yet his inmost feeling is that women have no sense of humour, and if a woman is witty, she has somehow come by it wrongly. He daren't speak right out, but I will speak for him.

Having been asked to answer the question, 'Are witty women attractive to men?' I answer decidedly, 'No.' Having said this I dodge behind the Editor and explain it.

There are, of course, a lot of immediate qualifications to be made to it. In the first place, are witty people in general attractive to anybody?

Not as a rule. They get tiresome. It is terribly hard to be witty without getting conceited about it. I used to be very witty myself, till I learned to be careful about it. People don't like it. There are two things in ordinary conversation which ordinary people dislike – information and wit. Most people – most men at any rate – like to gather up information out of the *Digests*, which are the passion of the hour. But they won't take it from you. You're not a *Digest*. So, too, with wit. They've learned by experience that if they laugh at one thing, they'll have to go on . . . So if this applies to men with men, it applies all the more to men with women. Luckily women don't go in for information; or, if they give it, it is so incorrect as to be harmless.

In the next place, it goes without saying that some witty women are attractive to some men. This, by a happy disposition of providence, happens to all kinds of women, like attracting unlike. Hence witty women always have silent husbands. That's why they got married. There is a particularly decent type of man who finds it restful not to have to talk. When, in his youth, he meets a girl who talks all the time, that exactly suits him. He doesn't have to say anything. Ten years later you'll see them enter a drawing-room together. The host says to the man, 'Looks like an early winter,' and he answers, 'Certainly does!' The host says, 'Have a cocktail,' and he answers, 'Certainly will.' By that time his wife has started in on the conversation; he doesn't have to talk any more. People commonly call this type an adoring husband. He isn't. His wife is just a sort of firescreen. The real adoring husband over-talks his wife, over-dominates her, pays with unexpected presents for easy forgiveness of his ill temper, and never knows that he adored her till it is too late, because now she cannot hear it . . .

We will add another qualification, that one reason why some men don't care for the society of witty women is because of their own egotism. They want to be *it*. A wise woman sitting down to talk beside such a man will not try to be witty. She will say, 'I suppose you're just as busy as ever!'

All men, you see, have the idea that they are always busy, and if they are not, a woman can soon persuade them that they are. Just say, 'I don't see how you do it all,' without saying what all is.

Another very good opening for women sufficiently self-possessed is to say, 'Well, I hear you are to be congratulated again!' You see, there is always something; either the office staff gave him a stick last month, or the Rotary Club elected him an Elder Brother. He'll find something. If he doesn't, then say to him that if he hasn't heard of it yet, you are certainly not going to tell. Then don't see him for a month, till the

Firemen's Benevolent Union has elected him an Honorary Ash Can. He'll get something if you wait.

So you see there are ever so many ways for women to make a hit without trying to be witty.

Nor have women, themselves, any particular use for witty men. Instinctively they admire courage, though unhappily courage often goes with brutality and savagery. In the next degree they admire the courage of character of strong people on whom one can rely. But intellect comes last. Unhappily, women also have their superficial admirations, things they *fall for* – it's too bad, but they do. Women are apt to fall for a poet, for anything with long hair and a reputation. Round him they cluster, searching his thoughts. He probably hasn't got any. But wit, in all the procession, comes last, with only a cap and bells behind it.

Another thing is this. By this very restriction of their province of humour, women are saved from some of the silly stuff that affects the conversation of men. Take puns. They have pretty well died out now. The last of the punsters is probably dead, or in hiding. But many of us can still remember the social nuisance of the inveterate punster. This man followed conversation as a shark follows a ship, or, to shift the simile, he was like Jack Horner and stuck in his thumb to pull out a pun. Women never make puns; they think them silly. Perhaps they can't make them – I hope not.

Nor have women that unhappy passion for repeating funny stories in order to make a hit, which becomes a sort of mental obsession with many men. The 'funny story' is a queer thing in our American life. I think it must have begun on the porch of the Kentucky store where they whittled sticks all day. At any rate, it has become a kind of institution. It is now a convention that all speakers at banquets must begin with a funny story. I am quite sure that if the Archbishop of Canterbury were invited to address the Episcopal Church of America, the senior bishop would introduce him with a story about an old darky, and the Archbishop would rise to reply with a story about a commercial traveller. These stories run riot in our social life and often turn what might be a pleasant dinner into an agonized competition, punctuated with ruminating silence. Women keep away from this. They like talk about people, preferably about themselves, or else about their children, with their husband as a poor third, and Winston Churchill competing with Mrs Chiang Kai-shek for fourth place. It may not be funny but it's better than darkies and commercial travellers . . .

There is also the most obvious qualification to be made in regard to women's sense of humour in general and women's wit in particular, that of course individual exceptions, however conspicuous, do not set aside

the general rule. There is no doubt that at least one of the most brilliant
humorists of the hour in America is a woman. Many would say, *the* most
brilliant. Such a faculty for reproducing by simple transcription the
humour of social dialogue has, it seems to me, never been surpassed. But
one swallow doesn't make a summer, though one drop of ink may make
all humour kin.

The truth is that the ideal of ordinary men is not a witty woman, but
a sweet woman. I know how dangerous the term is, how easily derided.
Sweetness may easily cloy into sugariness, or evaporate into saintliness.
A saint with hair parted in the middle, with eyes uplifted, may be all
right for looking out from the golden bars of heaven, but not so good for
the cocktail bars below.

And yet, I don't know. A saint can kick in sideways anywhere.

It might easily be objected that all such opinions about sweetness in
women are just left-over Victorianism, half a century out of date. Witty
women, it will be said, may have seemed out of date in the stodgy days
of women's servitude, but not now. The men and women of today – or
call them the boys and girls – mix on an entirely different plane. All the
old hoodoos and taboos are gone. All the girls smoke. They use language
just as bad as any the men care to use. They drink cocktails and give the
weaker men the cherry. In other words, they can curse and swear and
drink – they're real comrades. In point of physique, they may not be
equal to the men, but after all they can drive a car and fly a 'plane and
telemark all over hell on skis – what more do you want?

So why shouldn't a girl of that type, the new girl who has conquered
the world, be witty if she wants to? What more charming than a witty
girl, half-stewed, as compared with a girl half-stewed and silent as a toad
full of gravel?

To all of which I answer, 'No, no, it's just an illusion!' There are no
new girls, no new women. Your grandmother was a devil of a clip half a
century before you were born. You telemark on skis; she cut ice in a
cutter. You only knew her when she was wrinkled and hobbling, reading
the Epistle to the Thessalonians in a lace cap and saying she didn't know
what the world was coming to. The young have always been young, and
the old always old . . . men and women don't change. It took thousands,
uncounted thousands, of years to make them what they are. The changes
that you think you see lie just on the surface. You could wash them away
with soap and hot water.

But now I'll tell you another thing. All this new era of ours of
emancipated women, and women in offices and women the same as men,
is just a passing phase, and the end of it is already in sight. A great social
disaster fell on the world. The industrial age built up great cities where

people lived, crowded into little boxes, where there was no room for children, where women's work vanished because they were dispossessed, where national population was kept going by additions from God knows where, and national safety was jeopardized by the increasing scarcity of our own people . . . We had a close shave of it.

Then came the war in the air . . . It has bombed the industrial city out of future existence. They know that already in England. The bomb is decentralizing industry, spreading the population out. They will never go back. This will mean different kinds of homes, homes half-town, half-country, with every man his acre . . . Everyone's dream for a little place in the country, a place to call one's own, will come true. Socialized up to the neck, the individual will have its own again under his feet.

And the children? There must be four or five for every marriage. It is the only path of national safety, safety by the strength and power of our kin and kind, bred in our common thought and speech and ideal. Without our own children, the wave of outside brutes from an unredeemed world will kill us all. Later, we can redeem the world, but we must save ourselves first . . . Everybody will know that. In re-organized society the nation's children will be the first need, the main expense of government. Women who see to that need see to nothing else . . . That will be done in the home, for there will be no paid domestic service except contract labour by the hour from the outside, labour as good as ladyship, wearing a gold wrist watch and a domestic college degree . . . But the main thing will be the home and behind it the long garden and trim grass and flower and vegetable beds, and father trying to plant a cherry tree from a book.

When England has been bombed into the country, America will follow. Our cities will go, too . . . No one will *live* in New York any more than miners live in a coal mine.

So the world will be all different. One little century will do it. Even half a century will show the full outline of it. Surviving on . . . surviving on into this altered world will be the queerest old set of left-over creatures, as queer as our left-over Victorians, only queerer. These old women will be happy and alert and self-assertive, but they will still not know how to fry an egg or repeat a nursery rhyme, for they only had three-quarters of a child each . . . The boys and girls of twenty will think them very funny . . . But my! Won't they be witty when they get together and cackle.

So that, you see, is why I don't think witty women are attractive to men. You don't see the connection? Well, perhaps you remember Molière's play called *The Doctor by Accident (Le Médecin Malgré Lui)* where the supposed doctor, called in to diagnose a case, gets off a vast rigmarole about nothing in particular and adds at the end, '. . . that this is why your daughter has lost her speech.' You see, he didn't know anything about it.

Possibly it was like that.

CHAPTER II

Living with Murder

I am a great reader of detective fiction. That is, I have been, up to now, but I see I shall have to give it up. It begins to affect one's daily life too much. I am always expecting something sudden, something sensational to happen, such as that a criminal will 'burst around the corner' on the run and I shall immediately have to 'time' his burst.

They always *time* everything in the stories so as to have it ready for the evidence.

That is why I now find myself perpetually 'timing' myself all day, so that I can swear to everything.

For instance, I went down to dine three or four days ago with my old friend Jimmy Douglas at his house. He lives alone. This by itself would make any reader of crime fiction *time* him. I paused a moment at the lighted doorway before ringing the bell and noted that my watch said 7:00 p.m. A street clock just visible down the street, however, marked 7:02 p.m. and a half. Allowing my watch was one minute slow I was thus able to place the time fairly accurately as at 7:01 and a quarter.

What did I do that for? Well, don't you see – what if I rang the bell, received no answer, and at length pushed the door open (it would yield quite easily) to find Jimmy Douglas lying prone in the doorway? That would settle the time, wouldn't it? – and, what if he were still warm (he would be, good fellow), that would settle just how warm he was.

So I rang the bell. The Chinese servant who answered the door showed me noiselessly into the lighted sitting-room and motioned me to sit down. The room was *apparently* empty. I say *apparently*, because in the stories you never know. If Douglas's body was lying hunched up in a corner (you know the way they hunch them up) my business was to take care to look up in the air, round the room, everywhere except in the right place to see him.

I did this and I had noticed that there was an ormolu clock on the mantel (there always is) and that it stood at 7.04 p.m., practically corroborating my previous estimate.

I was just checking it over when Douglas came in.

I noticed his manner at once and could only describe it as extremely normal, even quiet, certainly I would say free from an exhilaration.

Whether this was a first effect of arsenic poisoning, or just from seeing me, I am not prepared to state.

We had a cocktail. Douglas left two distinct fingerprints on the glass. I held mine by the rim.

We sat down to dinner at 7.30 p.m. Of this I am practically certain because I remember that Douglas said, 'Well, it's half-past,' and as he said it the ormolu clock chimed the half-hour. A further corroboration is that the Chinese servant entered at that moment and said, 'Half-past seven!' I gather therefore that the hour was either seven-thirty or possibly a little before or a little after it.

At any rate – not to make too much of details – we sat down to dinner. I noticed that at dinner Douglas took no soup. I attached no importance to this at the time, so as to keep it for afterwards. But I also took care on my part to take no fish. This of course in the event of arsenic poison would at least, by elimination, give a certain indication of how the poison had been administered. Up to this point the Chinese servant's manner was quite normal, in fact, Chinese.

I am not able to say whether Douglas took coffee after dinner: I slipped up there; I had got talking, I remember, of my views on Allied Strategy and for the time forgot not only to time him but to notice what he ate. This makes an unfortunate gap in the record.

Douglas, I noticed, however, seemed but little inclined to talk after dinner. I was still unfolding to him my views on Allied Strategy in the war but he seemed unable to listen without signs of drowsiness. This obviously might be due to arsenic poisoning.

I left at nine, having noticed that Douglas roused up with a slight start as the ormolu clock struck, and said, 'Nine! I thought, I thought it was ten.'

I drove home in a taxi; and can easily identify the taxi, even if abandoned in a stone quarry, by a mark I made in the leather. I can identify the taxi-man by a peculiar scar.

That, as I say, was three days ago. I open the newspaper every morning with a nervous hand, looking for the finding of Douglas's body. They don't seem to have found it yet. Of course I don't know that he lost it. But then it is never known that a body is lost until someone finds it.

One thing is certain, however. I am all ready if they do . . . If any news comes out I can act at once. I have the taxi-man, and the fingerprints and the ormolu clock – that's all you need usually.

CHAPTER III

What Can Izaak Walton Teach Us?

Everybody – or at least everybody who goes fishing, and the rest don't count – knows the name of Izaak Walton. Many of them would also remember that he was called the Father of Angling and that he wrote a book called *The Compleat Angler*. This is acknowledged to be one of the world's books. Only that the trouble is that the world doesn't read its books, it borrows a detective story instead.

So it may not be without interest to outdoor people, anglers, men of the bush and streams and such, to turn over again the pages of the old volume and see what Izaak Walton can teach us. This especially, if we can catch something of the leisurely procedure, the old-time courtesy and, so to speak, the charming tediousness of people with lots of time, now lost in our distracted world.

Izaak Walton, let us pretend to remember, was born in the reign of Queen Elizabeth (1593) but lived so long and so peacefully – old fishermen never die, they merely fade away – that he only passed away at the age of ninety at the end of the Stuart period. People reading *The Compleat Angler* would take him for a country gentleman. But he wasn't. Indeed in the phrase of the times he wasn't a gentleman at all. He came to London from the little town of Stafford and in London he kept an ironmonger's shop in the very heart of the town.

It was so small a place that there was hardly room to turn round in, certainly not with a fishing rod, for it was only six feet by seven feet six inches. But it must have been a grand little place from which to dream of the woods and meadows around Stafford and to let the noise of the city die on his ear till he could catch the murmur of the babbling streams . . . Thus you may see today, if you have the eye for it, many an imprisoned incomplete angler working at a desk with the sound of a waterfall in his ears, or selling across a sporting-goods counter the tackle that he never has the good fortune to use. Walton says that fishermen are the Lord's own people, and no doubt he's right. 'The primitive Christians,' he remarks, 'were, as most anglers are, quiet men and followers of peace.' He undertakes to prove it from the fact that four of the Apostles actually were fishermen, and these four taught all the others to fish. Thus worked Izaak Walton till he was over fifty years old.

But, oddly enough, he made money, and soon was able to move to larger quarters on Fleet Street. Iron-mongery was evidently all the thing in the days of the English Civil War. So when the great battles were over and there was peace, iron peace, under Oliver Cromwell, Izaak Walton gave up his London life, and bought himself the thing of which all anglers dream, a little place in the country, his own country, and all his dreams came true.

From then on, for some forty years, Izaak Walton spent a life of leisure, or of leisure broken with leisurely activity. At times he was on his own little place, at times he wandered about the country, a welcome and indefinite guest, an old man who never grew older, who had said good-bye to the world and its troubles and to whom Roundhead and Royalist were all one. Especially he sought, and was welcome in, the homes of the clergy. He had been greatly assisted in his London days by famous Dr John Donne, Vicar of St Dunstan's. Both his wives, for he married twice, were of clerical families; he seems to have borne married life easily as a basis (as with some among us now) from which to go fishing. For his last twenty years he wandered and fished alone. When he died he left his little place to the poor of the parish.

He wrote his *Compleat Angler*, so to speak, while angling. The first edition of it was mainly thought out in his Fleet Street days, the fruit of odd holidays and chance journeys. But later, with copious leisure and larger experience, he kept finding new things to put into the book, new verses, new jests and even new people.

As even casual readers remember, *The Compleat Angler* is built up on talks between various characters. They meet and go fishing together and they talk – or they can't go fishing, so they talk; or they come in from fishing, and they talk. Some of us do it still. And in among the talk they have so many pleasant cups of ale and draughts of the 'best barley wine', that it's a pleasure to be with them; plenty to smoke, also, from the long pipes of the period, for tobacco, in spite of King James I, had now come into its own. Indeed, the comfortable entertainment begins in Chapter I, page 1, paragraph 1, of the *Compleat Angler*. An angler, PISCATOR, accosts two travellers on the road with the words:

'You are well overtaken, Gentlemen! A good morning to you both. I have stretched my legs up Tottenham Hill to overtake you, hoping your business may occasion you towards Ware, whither I am going this fine, fresh, May morning.'

'Sir,' replies one of them, 'I, for my part, shall almost answer your hopes; for my purpose is to drink my morning's draught at the Thatched House in Hoddesden . . .'

So away they wander together, talking of fishing, so that the three miles to Hoddesden seems nothing, and there they are at the Thatched House, and must needs all enter together 'for a cup of drink and a little rest.'

What fisherman, then or now, could pass a Thatched House?

Thus it was with the freshness of the morning; but equally so with the pleasant weariness of the evening after a long day.

'Come, hostess, where are you? Is supper ready? Come, first give us drink and be as quick as you can, for we are all very hungry . . . Come, hostess, more ale . . . and when we have supped, let's have your song!'

The early people in these wayside talks were a fisherman, PISCATOR, and a traveller, VIATOR. But later on Izaak thought it a good idea to let the second man be a huntsman VENATOR and then he put in a third who was called AUCEPS which we understand to mean a falconer, a man who hunts birds with birds. Time has dropped him clean out. Today we have to make him an AIRMAN. That is probably exactly what Izaak Walton would have done, for he kept on putting in new things and new people till death made a final edition.

You ask perhaps, I hope not with impatience, what we can learn from Izaak Walton. Why, don't you see we've learned a lot already; that fishing is the Apostles' own calling; that fishing must be carried on in an atmosphere of good will and forbearance; that the longest story must never seem prosy; that a cup of ale beneath a tree is better than a civic banquet, and an old familiar song from a familiar singer outclasses grand opera.

And you can also learn, or learn over again, the peculiar and manifold charm of our English language. For what Izaak Walton writes is sufficiently like our own speech to be familiar, and sufficiently unlike to have a quaintness of its own. He has a chapter, for example, which he entitles, *How to fish for, and to dress, the Chavender, or Chub*. A witty English writer of to-day was so impressed by the conversion of the everyday chub, into the romantic chavender that he followed it up with a gallop of analogous synonyms:

> *There is a fine stuffed Chavender,*
> *A chavender, or chub,*
> *He decks the rural pavender,*
> *The pavender, or pub,*
> *Wherein I eat my gravender,*
> *My gravender, or grub.*

And so on, amazingly. But I must not further trespass on the good nature or the copyright of Mr St Leger, whose complete poem may be found in the fascinating little anthology, *The Comic Muse*.

All things you can learn from Izaak Walton. But if you ask what you can learn of the technique of fishing the answer is that you can't learn anything at all. The apparatus of the modern expert, the mechanisms of reels – all these have left good old Izaak two centuries and a half in the rear. All that he can teach is the *spirit*; yet the performance in the long run rests on that.

To take an example. Nowadays we always connect trout-fishing with the art of casting flies – an exquisite art indeed when at its highest. What more beautiful than a cast far across a wide stream to where the broken water round the end of a sunken log marks where a trout must lie? What more beautiful indeed except the ensuing leap of the foolish trout itself, a victim of its own delusion. It is an art that, personally, I can envy but not share; I can never catch anything that way except willow trees.

But at least I have the consolation that Izaak Walton is in my company. He knew very little about casting flies and that was not his ordinary method of catching fish, anyway. He caught them, as I do, and perhaps you, with anything they would eat, taken off anything they would eat it on.

This seems odd in view of the long discussion in the *Compleat Angler* on fly-fishing and how to do it and how to make flies. The discussion, moreover, has its setting in one of these charming sylvan scenes – under a sycamore tree with wine and a snack of food – which are the very inspiration of the book.

'It is now past five of the clock' says Piscator, meaning *five in the morning*, 'we will fish till nine; and then go to breakfast. Go you to yon sycamore tree and hide your bottle of drink under the hollow root of it; for about that time, and in that place, you will make a brave breakfast with a piece of powdered beef and radish or two that I have in my fish bag. We shall, I warrant you, make a good, honest, wholesome, hungry breakfast.' But as a matter of fact Izaak Walton did not himself write the discussion of the 'making and useing of flies' which follows. He knew that he ought to have something of the sort in his book so he got a fellow angler to write in it, thereby lifting his friend Mr Thomas Barker to an immortal seat beside himself. Mr Barker was by trade a cook and may have aided also in the hints of cooking fish ('dressing the chavender') that are freely inserted in the *Angler*. Mr Barker is also said to have been a 'humorist'; he may have helped with the jokes.

But all agree that when it comes to fishing with worms, grasshoppers and frogs, Izaak Walton was a past master. There is comfort here for those who suffer, as I do, from the insolent superiority of men who refuse to use 'bait'. Izaak used nothing else. Indeed many who knew very little about his book have heard the quotation from it about the use of a frog as bait – 'Use him as though you loved him, that is, harm him as little as you may possibly, that he may live the longer.' The implication of a slow death behind the apparently kindly words is one that might make the coldest-blooded frog boil with indignation.

But the point is that Izaak Walton was out to get the fish. In the same way he and his friends were fond of using little floats, tied to sticks or anchored in the stream. This with us is viewed among good sports as the last resort of ignoble minds. Indeed, the game laws forbid that kind of fishing to all except Indians on a reservation. But to Izaak and his friends it represented the very best of sport and the rarest of opportunity. They had only to choose a grassy sward beneath a spreading sycamore, among whose roots babbled the passing stream, to fix their floats, pour out a cup of ale, light a long pipe and open a discussion on the Gospel of St John or listen to Mr Barker tell in his own humorous way how to cook a carp – and there you were. Leave the rest to the frog.

Indeed, Izaak Walton is willing to go a little further with 'bait' than the stomachs of more degenerate anglers could tolerate. He specializes on worms, distinguishing earthworms from dug-worms, worms found in excrement and in dead flesh such as the maggot or gentle worm; to which are added lobworms, brandling worms for which we search in cow-dung, 'horse-dung being somewhat too hot and dry for that worm.' Beside which an artificial fly on a bit of cardboard seems singularly clean and attractive.

Such dainty considerations are nothing to Izaak. He is out for fish. Indeed, he'll go further if we let him. 'If you desire,' he says, 'to keep gentles, that is maggots, to fish with all the year, then get a dead cat and let it be fly-blown; and when the gentles begin to be alive and to stir, then bury it and them in soft moist earth but as free from frost as you can; and these you may dig up at any time you intend to use them.'

And there you are. But if you don't care to prepare the bait in this fashion, then Izaak explains to us a method of preparing the water, of any likely pond, so as to make it attractive. 'You are to throw into it,' he directs, 'either grains, or blood mixed with cow-dung or with bran; or any garbage as chicken guts or the like.'

If you are going to be an angler the thing is to be a complete one.

One might think that at least the discussions on cooking would be helpful, especially to us in war and post-war days when we want to make the most of all kinds of food, and turn even coarse fish into something edible. The carp itself, the very fish which the *Compleat Angler* helps us to turn into a dainty dish, is very commonly thrown away with us in Canada as worthless, or else – if I may say it without offence – exported to the United States. Izaak Walton, I say, shows how to turn it into a dainty dish, and no doubt succeeded in doing it. But his process is quite beyond us. Here is the recipe.

'Put the Carp in a kettle; take sweet marjoram, thyme and parsley, each a handful; a sprig of rosemary and another of savoury; put them

into two or three small bundles, and put them to your Carp with four or
five whole onions, twenty pickled oysters and three anchovies –'

So far that's only about three dollars' worth of stuff, and you could
gather it up in about a week but wait –

'. . . pour on your Carp enough claret as will cover him' (lucky carp)
'and season your Carp well with salt, cloves and mace, and rinds of
oranges and lemons –'

– we're up now to about ten dollars –

'– That done, cover your pot and set it on a quick fire till it be
sufficiently boiled. Then take out the Carp; and lay it, with the broth into
the dish – and pour upon it a quarter of a pound of the best fresh butter,
melted and beaten with half a dozen spoonfuls of the broth, the yokes of
two or three eggs and some of the herbs shred; garnish your dish with
lemons and so serve it up. And much good do you!'

I think so too.

Thus lived and wandered Izaak Walton from middle age to old age and
then on to immortality. Especially was he welcome, we are told, 'in the
families of the eminent clergy of England of whom he was much beloved.'
Their kindness was returned. It was Izaak Walton's secondary interest,
in the pauses of his leisure, to write biographies, or perhaps, eulogies to
his departed friends and benefactors, lay or cleric. Here belong Sir Henry
Wotton, Dr John Donne, Bishop Sanderson and others. Their names,
once known, now half-forgotten, still float down the stream of time with
the *Compleat Angler*.

CHAPTER IV

Andrew Macphail

I am not attempting to write here a biography of Andrew Macphail.
That must be left for other and worthier hands, inscribing a larger page.
I am not qualified for the task. I never knew him during the earlier and
more strenuous days in which his career was made; I never knew him in
his home on 'the Island,' the environment most congenial to his temper;
and I never had the honour of that war service which illustrated his
middle age and earned him his fitting knighthood. It will remain for
someone intimate with these phases of his career to write for us presently
a full and worthy biography of Sir Andrew Macphail, undoubtedly one
of the most outstanding and distinctive personalities that our country
has known.

But till such a task is undertaken it is fitting that those of use who enjoyed his long friendship and companionship should record our tributes to his memory.

I first knew Andrew Macphail nearly forty years ago when I came to McGill, as nothing and nobody in particular, in the unstable equilibrium of a 'sessional lecturer.' On the strength of a few random excursions into the kingdom of letters I was honourably admitted to membership in the old Pen and Pencil Club, and there I first knew Andrew. He was my senior by some five years, and already an established and recognized man, the first arduous period of his career gone by, his life enlarged and tempered by marriage and fatherhood, and shadowed already by the premature bereavement that lay large across it.

From the first Andrew Macphail seemed to me, as he still does, one of the most distinctive personalitites I have ever known. In his outward semblance he wore, then as always, an air of gloom and deliberation, carried not as a pose, but as the native expression of a mind always heavy with thought that did not of necessity break to the surface in voluble expression. It was as a shadowed pond with shifting shades but no ripples. What Andrew really thought of life in general I didn't know, and never knew, and I doubt if he did. He carried with him from his hereditary background and his upbringing, a stern, set frame of beliefs and traditions from which he was unwilling to depart: he always hated idle scoffing, cheap rationalism, one might almost say, reason and logic itself, and he always loved the sterner ideas of conduct that went with the illumination of older beliefs. If there had been no Westminster Catechism, Andrew would have invented it for himself.

The old Pen and Pencil Club of forty years ago, in which I first knew Andrew, used to meet every other Saturday night in Edouard Dyonnet's studio, under the Fraser Institute on Dorchester Street. It was made up as a sort of half and half of painters – who certainly could paint, as later recognition has shown – and of writers who were at least challenged to prove themselves by reading something they had written not less than once in six weeks. On the roll of the artists were such well-known names as those of Robert Harris, William Brymner, Maurice Cullen – to name only those now gone. The writers included dear old 'Uncle' George Murray, whose memory is still carried as a garland by generations of Montreal High Schools boys; Paul Lafleur, chivalrous as knighthood and touchy as a sensitive plant; Jack McCrae of 'Flanders Fields,' admitted just when I was, whose works being poetry, had the signal merit of brevity.

It was the routine of the Club that the artists should first show to us their latest work. We, of the 'pen' class, like George the Third with the British Constitution, admired where we couldn't understand, and took a more than equal vengeance by reading aloud our current writings. Our poets, Jack McCrae and John Logan (a tear to his rugged memory), made but a small demand. A very little poetry goes a long way. But Andrew and I were the chief sinners. I can still call up a vision of the kindly club, drawn up in a horseshoe of armchairs, the room darkened, and apparently getting darker all the time, listening to the measured tones of an essay-writer reading his essay, with the full consciousness that even when he had finished another essay-writer would pick up the torch. Somnolence gained them; they tied themselves in knots in their chairs; or broke from the ranks to dive behind the curtains where the whisky and soda was.

This fellowship in evil brought Andrew and me together. It was characteristic of him that the more the listeners suffered the better he liked it. His attitude was that no one should show him pictures without his striking back. He was fond of saying – he loved an epigram – that a really good essay always put people to sleep. Those who remember Andrew Macphail will bear me out as to how characteristic such a saying was. You couldn't tell whether Andrew really meant it, or just said it. I don't think he knew. He just coined these things out of his lower consciousness and palmed them off on his upper. Again and again I have heard Andrew get off such judgements to plain business men, to the man in the next seat at a dinner, or a casual visitor at the club – to the great perplexity of the listener.

Witness this example. Speaking of the latest sermon at his church, Andrew said (to a casual friend we were with): 'Edgar Hill gave us a great sermon on the poor this morning.' 'Is that so?' said the listener, making conversation, 'what did he say about them?' Andrew answered, 'He gave them hell!' – then uttered a deep sigh and no further information. I knew, but of course the man didn't, that underneath in Andrew's mind were deep thoughts about the merits and defects of the poor, which he didn't propose to bring to the surface. He let it go at that. He loved mystification. Most people, most writers, are terribly touchy if their meaning is mistaken. Not so Andrew. Much of his humour was of that ruly Scottish kind which is best when least shared.

This love of epigram, of shaded meaning, trained Andrew in the course of years to an exquisite exactness of words. He never wrote careless English. The last essay that I know of from his pen, his appreciation of the most recent Life of General Lee,[1] is fascinating, not as reflecting General Lee or his biographer, but as reflecting Andrew Macphail. You feel as you read it that it is the writer, not the topic, that fascinates. This literary interest he often brought to an intense focus in single sentences,

[1] *Queen's Quarterly*, Spring, 1938 (Ed.).

terse and final. Consider the opening of his essay on General Wilson. 'The Irish have always had a sure instinct in murder.' Who wouldn't go on, after reading that? The plain man feels like saying – 'An instinct in murder, eh? Have they really? – you don't say so! – tell me more about that.' Such sudden beams of illumination are among the best part of Andrew's literary work. There is neither space nor occasion here to catalogue the long and interesting list of all he wrote. Much of it was spent on topics of mere ephemeral interest, as the rise and fall of Conservatives and Liberals, or at best of an interest that time must soon dim, but all of it was illuminated with this peculiar quality of salient phrase and pointed epigram.

It is naturally in connection with the bygone *University Magazine* of 1907 onwards, that one chiefly recalls Macphail's literary career. Full justice has still be to done to the great service which he here performed for Canadian letters. The magazine was a transformed resurrection of an older college publication, that had died from sheer bulk, the kind of literary dropsy that attacks the writing of professors. It was proposed – no doubt Principal Peterson fostered the idea – to found a magazine as learned as its predecessor but more susceptible to common sense in the length of the topics and the 'availability' of its artices. The magazine was to be conducted by some sort of board – I think perhaps I was on it – I don't remember. But it didn't matter, for the 'board' was virtually swept aside by Andrew, as you brush away the chess pieces of a finished game. Historians recall to us the first meeting of General Bonaparte in 1799 while the Abbé Siéyès and the others who were to be the joint government of France under the new 'consulate.' As they came out the Abbé remarked to a colleague, 'Nous avons un maître' – and with that the 'joint-stuff' ended. So it was with Andrew. After a meeting or two, the magazine became and remained Andrew Macphail. Like all competent men who can do a job and who knew it, he had no use for co-operation. We, his colleagues, were invited occasionally to have Scotch whisky in Andrew's queer little library and then some more Scotch whisky with cold beef in his beautiful big dining-room. That was all the co-operation he wanted: and in this we met him (I am sure I did) more than half-way.

On this frail support, with a diligence such as only a man bred to hard work can maintain, with a taste found only in a scholar but mated to the discrimination of a journalist – thus, and with one hand even in his generous pocket, Andrew Macphail carried the *University Magazine* to a place second to nothing of its type. Only those of us who knew him well could tell what unremitting work this labour of love entailed.

But it was not only by his literary work that Andrew Macphail, in the fuller years of his career, obtained the high consideration which fell to his lot. He had his part and place, as much as he could ask, in everything that was social, public, or ceremonial. Andrew seemed so different from other men that his presence seemed to lift an occasion out of the commonplace. Introduced to strangers, he made an instant impression. Those of us who had to entertain, in public or in private, a visiting celebrity at once sent for Andrew: just as one sends for the doctor; and no celebrity could 'celebrity' him. He treated them as a man used to horses treats a new one. It always seemed amazing to me that he could handle them so easily. Rudyard Kipling came to Montreal. Andrew had him tamed in half an hour, took him over to his house and then put him upstairs to write a speech. 'Has Kipling come?' asked a next-entering visitor, in the awestruck tones we used for celebrities in the days before the Great War gave us our own. 'He's upstairs,' Andrew said. 'I told him he ought to *write* his speech for McGill; he's writing it.' From this beginning, incidentally, dated the long friendship, the mutual services and mutual esteem of these two men.

I am not qualified, as I have said, to talk of Andrew's boyhood in the country, his early years of school and farm life, in days when rural Canada offered little more than a pioneer life with few alleviations. The Canadian countryside in those days was dark and solitary, and life there had little converse and less amenity. Yet it bred, unconsciously, a love of the open air, of early hours, of the remembered stillness of the woods and the unceasing breaking of the sea. This, to people lucky enough to get out of it, as both Andrew and I had been, was coloured with the mellow hues of retrospect. Adversity that has long since gone by, leaves a sweet memory for luxury to linger on. And for people like Andrew and myself our country upbringing became a source of pride and a bond of sympathy and, as the years drew on, something of an affectation. It is hard in such cases to know where reality ends and attitude, or at least self-deception, begins. Andrew at any rate could push reality hard, much harder than I ever could. He could speak of buttermilk (over a glass of whisky and soda) with wistful relish, and talk of long drinks of maple sap out of its wooden trough – a beverage little better in reality than a solution of sawdust and dead flies. It became with Andrew a sort of whimsical make-believe that everything in the country was right, and everything in the city wrong. The only real boots were made by country cobblers: homespun clothes fitted better than the tailored product of the city: and so forth, till the thing verged on burlesque and Andrew himself would start to laugh at it. In all this, as in so much else, I am certain that he never quite knew what he believed and what he didn't; but underneath it was a deep-seated feeling that the real virtue of a nation is bred in the country, that the city is an unnatural product. From this point of view

Andrew, though frequenting the rich in his daily walk of life, was never quite satisfied of their right to be. Towards plutocrats, bankers, manu-facturers and such, he felt a little bit as a rough country dog feels towards a city cat. He didn't quite accept them. Andrew would have made a fine radical if he hadn't hated radicalism.

Andrew Macphail's death came to those of us who were his friends with a shock as of something that could not be. It had not seemed that he could die. Always he had kept his sorrows and his ailments to himself. In the thirty-seven years I knew him I never heard him once refer to what I know had been the greatest sorrow of his life. His damaged sight he faced with equanimity and dismissed with scorn. He never complained because he hated complaint. Those of us of weaker temper carried our troubles to Andrew but never were asked to share his. Few people knew of his removal from his Island to Montreal. To most of us the news of his death came, sudden and unbelievable, for the moment holding even sorrow numb. Even now it is hard to think that he is gone. As I write this page I recall how generous was his praise of things I wrote, how quick he was to send his scribbled lines of congratulation over this or that, and how much I valued them. And now this, these sentences of appreciation and affection that I would wish him most to see – this he cannot read.

There is a well-worn rubric of the Church that runs, 'while we have time . . .' Andrew's death makes me think of it – the pity that we cannot, while we have time, value one another better. We do not see till it is too late. The light has gone.

CHAPTER V

Gilbert's 'Bab' Ballads

It is a great change from the secluded woodland of *Wonderland* to the open scenes, the noise and the combat of the *Bab Ballads*. Here are the breezes of the sea, the thunder of guns, the clash of swords and the thud of the executioner's axe. In Alice's *Wonderland*, the characters just fade away and disappear. In the *'Bab' Ballads*, they are thrown into the sea, knocked on the head, or cut clean in two with scimitars of exquisite sharpness and their remains fed to sharks or boiled up by enthusiastic cannibals. In the most 'popular' of the ballads, meaning the one that the plain people have liked best, *The Yarn of the 'Nancy Bell'*, one character eats all the others, one by one. 'Mr Gilbert,' says a penetrating critic of today, 'shows a sort of cruelty . . . In fact, he cared little about the feelings of others.' Very little, one would think, if he boiled them alive and chopped them up, as one famous ballad puts it, 'particularly small'.

The same critic, however, adds that Gilbert was a 'full-blooded, impatient Englishman,' which explains the whole thing.

But there are other differences between *Wonderland* and the *Ballad-land*: The people in *Wonderland* have no names. They are all generalizations – the Mad Hatter, the Red Queen, or fictions like Humpty Dumpty and Tweedledee. But in the *Ballads* they are all real people, with names and rank. Here are Captain Reece, R.N., and Captain Parklebury Todd; here is the Reverend Simon Magus – people you might meet in London any day. The scholarly world is represented by Gregory Parable, LL.D., and here is little Annie Profterie who kept a small post office in the neighbourhood of Bow – just what she would naturally do. Anyone guesses at once, as Gilbert admitted in advance, that Macphairson Clonglocketty Angus McClan was a Scotchman. The whole setting is intended to show that we are dealing with real life, simply presented. Even the outsiders, not English, are equally convincing. Alum Bey is a proper Turk. The name of King Borria Bungalee Boo certainly indicates him as a 'man-eating African swell'. Yet in spite of all these features of normality, these home touches, so to speak, the world of Gilbert's *'Bab' Ballads* is just as topsy-turvy as the world of Alice's *Wonderland*.

Let us see how it originated.

The name of W.S. Gilbert is known to most people to-day only as the larger half of Gilbert and Sullivan, a combination now as familiar as Damon and Pythias or Lea and Perrins. But, in reality, Gilbert had already achieved quite a celebrity in London before the resounding and prolonged triumph of the Savoy Operas.

W.S. Gilbert (1836–1911) was born a gentleman – a matter that must have been a permanent satisfaction to him. His father was a surgeon in the Royal Navy and later a novelist, a fiery, peppery old gentleman who went around trying to give editors a thrashing and offering to throw people out of the window – in short, right out of the *'Bab' Ballads* alongside of Captain Parklebury Todd who 'couldn't walk into a room without ejaculating, "Boom!" ' Gilbert went to the kind of private school called, in England, a public school, and was to have been sent up, or down, whichever it is, to Oxford. But the outbreak of the Crimean War led him to take a quicker training at King's College, London, in order to get a commission in the army. Just as he finished it, the war ended. So Gilbert got neither Oxford nor war and turned off sideways to the bar. At the bar he acquired that wealth of legal phrases which adorned all his works and broke into song again and again in the operas – 'When I went to the bar-as-a-very-young-man, said I to myself, said I.'

Gilbert had, in all, twenty clients in five years. One, a Frenchman, acquitted, threw his arms around Gilbert's neck in court and kissed him.

Another, a woman pickpocket, convicted, threw her book at him in disgust. Another, an Irishman, prosecuted by him, kept shouting, 'Sit down, ye devil, sit down!'

So Gilbert gave up the law and turned to art and humour and was an immediate success. His mock-heroic ballads and the drawings he made for them became the leading feature of *Fun*, the new comic journal that was running *Punch* hard in the 'sixties. They were signed *Bab*, which had been a childish nickname for Gilbert himself, and so when published as a book, they appeared as the *'Bab' Ballads* – first in 1869, and then enlarged, and reprinted, and recollected and so around the world.

Hence W.S. Gilbert was already quite a celebrity in London long before the Gilbert and Sullivan operas turned celebrity to glory. But in a way it was not altogether an enviable celebrity. Gilbert from all accounts was a singularly disagreeable man, self-important and domineering, rating everybody else as poor trash. By good rights, great humorists ought to be gentle, agreeable people to meet, with a breadth of view and a kindly tolerance of trifles – such as they show in print. Mostly they are not. Charles Dickens, in spite of a boundless energy and exuberance of fun, was an intolerable egotist who had to be 'it' all the time, who supplied sob-words and slow music for the fathers of broken homes and smashed his own with an axe. Mark Twain, though good, easy company when young, became, so some people tell us, intolerably boring in old age. Lewis Carroll was a sissy, and Gilbert was a bully, over-conscious of his own talent.

Thus Gilbert used his, this singular talent, to point the barbs of his retorts and jokes. Very funny to read, they are, these retorts and repartee. But some of them must have cut people to the heart.

'What did you think of my Hamlet?' asked an actor friend in the first flush of his pride in his new part . . . 'Excellent,' said Gilbert, 'funny all through, but never vulgar.'

A barber cutting Gilbert's hair once bent over his ear to murmur, 'When are we to expect anything further, Mr Gilbert, from your fluent pen?'

'What do you mean, sir, by fluent pen?' snapped Gilbert. 'There is no such thing as a fluent pen. A pen is an insensible object. And, at any rate, I don't presume to enquire into your private affairs; you will please observe the same reticence in regard to mine.'

Anyone who could thus snub a barber out of his one privilege, would strike a child . . . though, as a matter of fact, Gilbert wouldn't. He was friendly and companionable with children, just as he was an excellent host and a generous supporter of charitable things. He kept his quarrels for his own world, and for the law courts, where he lived in litigation . . .

'The judge,' he said, in writing of one of his lost actions, 'summed up like a drunken monkey. He's in the last stage of senile decay.' After Sir Edward Carson won a case against him, Gilbert made a point of cutting him dead.

As a result, Gilbert's life was filled with bitter quarrels. There were some people he wouldn't speak to for ten years; others were on the twenty-year list. As his old age drew on, a strange repentance seized him, especially as the former friends, put on the silent list, began to pass into a silence longer still. As each died, Gilbert was all contrition, with flowers sent to hospitals, looking for old ties to rebind, the egotism all paled out of him. He could have made a wonderful *Ballad* out of it – *The Contrite Playwright*.

But all that was far away at the time of which we speak.

But to understand the *'Bab' Ballads* we need not only to understand Gilbert himself but to see in its proper perspective the period in which he wrote.

This was the period of the Great Peace, after 1815, that was going to last for ever; everybody knew it, and the Crystal Palace proved it. There might be wars as a matter of distant adventure, like the Crimean War; or wars in suitable out-of-the-way places like Ashanti; and among crazy European revolutionists. But, for England, war had been removed for ever by Trafalgar and Waterloo. There sat the right little, tight little island, snug behind the waves, and you couldn't get at it. 'The English,' wrote a very witty person of the time in referring to the new misty German philosophy, 'are supreme on the sea, the French on the land, and the Germans hold the supremacy of the air.' How strange it sounds now.

In the safeness and snugness, with outside protection and internal order and personal liberty guaranteed, all values shifted. The things that seemed so vital before – religion that people burned for, liberty that people hanged for, defence that people died for – began to be taken for granted. They were all embodied in the policeman, the magistrate, the M.P. and the justices of the peace. With the sole proviso of keeping the poor in the proper place, if need be by shooting them, the government had nothing to do. Hence the whole apparatus of government, British constitution and all, began to seem amazingly funny, especially because of all its forms and its feathers and its fuss, its Beef-eaters and Yeoman of the Guard.

In fact, to clever men like young Dickens and young Gilbert, it was really a huge joke, just a scream. Take the Royal Family, with its multiplying household and its German regularity and parsimony.

The Queen she kept high festival in Windsor's lofty hall.
And round her sat her gartered knights and ermined nobles all.
There drank the valiant Wellington, there fed the Wary Peel
While at the bottom of the board Prince Albert carved the veal.

Carved the veal! Pretty funny, eh? And, of course, the statesmen and the cabinet, chasing one another in and out of office, were just as funny – what was it Dickens called them? Coodle, and Doodle and Foodle! . . . and the Members of Parliament always making speeches and laying their hands on their heart! . . . and the army, now there *is* something to laugh at! all drooping plumes and dangling swords! What did they think they were out to kill, anyway? And the House of Lords, all in robes doing nothing, and the clergy all in gaiters doing less. Let's have a song about the House of Lords which, throughout the War, did nothing in particular and did it rather well! And let's make up comic verses about the Bishop of Rum-ti-Foo.

All these things seemed out of date! We can see it all better now. A generation that has seen the world swept back into barbarism by two world wars can see reality again. Why, these mean the things – this funny Parliament, this comic magistrate, even Coodle and Doodle – the things that people die for.

But not being able to see it, the world seemed all topsy-turvy.

We left out the navy above. Was it comic or real? They weren't quite sure. The sea lies close to the British heart. Even Gilbert was an amateur Yo-ho yachtsman of the coast. Hence the England of this epoch never knew whether to admire the navy, or to laugh at it like the army. And the government never knew whether to improve its lot and feed and warm it decently or whether to 'give it every day at least six dozen lashes,' as Gilbert gave to Joe Golightly.

So Gilbert took the navy both ways. Here belongs the famous ballad of *Captain Reece*, Commander of *The Mantelpiece* that turned later on into the opera *Pinafore*. Captain Reece represents that fatal pelting of the seamen under the new philanthropy in which the real old bluewater school saw the approaching downfall of England, the scuttling of the ship.

CAPTAIN REECE

Of all the ships upon the blue,
No ship contained a better crew
Than that of worthy Captain Reece,
Commanding of *The Mantelpiece*.

He was adored by all his men,
For worthy Captain Reece, R.N.,
Did all that lay within him to
Promote the comfort of his crew.

If ever they were dull or sad,
Their captain danced to them like mad,
Or told, to make the time pass by,
Droll legends of his infancy.

A feather bed had every man,
Warm slippers and hot-water can,
Brown windsor from the captain's store,
A valet, too, to every four.

Did they with thirst in summer burn?
Lo, seltzogenes at every turn,
And on all very sultry days
Cream ices handed round on trays.

Kind-hearted Captain Reece, R.N.,
Was quite devoted to his men;
In point of fact, good Captain Reece,
Beatified *The Mantelpiece*.

This idyllic situation culminated in the happy idea of marrying all the crew to Captain Reece's sisters, cousins and aunts. Even the captain was not forgotten:

The boatswain of *The Mantelpiece*,
He blushed and spoke to Captain Reece:
'I beg your honour's leave,' he said,
'If you would wish to go and wed,

'I have a widowed mother who
Would be the very thing for you –
She long has loved you from afar,
She washes for you, Captain R.'

And the curtain falls on a happy and united family crew. Such a picture must have another side. The navy was not all human kindliness and new philanthropy. There was still the same old brutality to denounce where some ferocious martinet got his evil way, flogging his crew into submission. Tennyson denounced this in his own medodramatic way; Gilbert showed how topsy-turvy it was; in fact, turned it into fun. Which helped more to abolish it?

Tennyson begins:

> He that only rules by terror
> Doth a grievous wrong,
> Deep as hell I count his error.
> Let him hear my song.

and goes on to tell of a brutal ship's captain whose men took vengeance on him in a naval engagement by curling up and dying on the deck without fighting. It sounds a little bit like the Chinese system of getting even with an enemy by committing suicide on his doorstep.

Now let us see how Gilbert does it. The Admiralty have heard about *The Mantelpiece* and are horrified at Reece's leniency. A new commander, Sir Berkely, a martinet, is sent to take over:

> Sir Berkely was a martinet –
>   A Stern, unyielding soul –
> Who ruled his ship by dint of whip
>   And horrible black-hole.
>
> When first Sir Berkely came aboard
>   He read a speech to all,
> And told them how he's made a vow
>   To act on duty's call.
>
> Then William Lee, he up and said
>   (The Captain's coxswain he):
> 'We've heard the speech your honour's made.
>   And werry pleased we be.
>
> 'We don't pretend, my lad, as how
>   We're glad to lose our Reece;
> Urbane, polite, he suited quite
>   The saucy *Mantelpiece*.
>
> 'But if your honour gives your mind
>   To study all our ways,
> With dance and song we'll jog along
>   As in those happy days.
>
> 'I like your honour's looks, and feel
>   You're worthy of your sword.
> Your hand, my lad – I'm doosid glad
>   To welcome you aboard!'

Sir Berkely looked amazed, as though
   He didn't understand.
'Don't shake your head,' good William said,
   'It is an honest hand.

'It's grasped a better hand than yourn –
   Come, gov'nor, I insist!'
The Captain stared – the coxswain glared –
   The hand became a fist!

'Down, upstart!' said the hardy salt;
   But Berkely dodged his aim,
And made him go in chains below:
   The seamen murmured 'Shame!'

A sailor who was overcome
   From having freely dined,
And chanced to reel when at the wheel,
   He instantly confined!

And tars who, when an action raged,
   Appeared alarmed or scared,
And those below who wished to go,
   He very seldom spared.

E'en he who smote his officer
   For punishment was booked,
And mutinies upon the seas
   He rarely overlooked.

In short, the happy *Mantelpiece*
   Where all had gone so well,
Beneath that fool Sir Berkely's rule
   Became a floating hell.

This intolerable situation very naturally led the crew to shoot Sir Berkely. The Admiralty on hearing the news of his death realized the wrong that had been done and restored the noble Reece to his command.

But Gilbert's topsy-turvy navy would, of course, not be complete without a picture of the life and sorrows of the common seaman. This is given to us in the pathetic story of Joe Golightly, who had fallen hopelessly in love at a distance, an immeasurable social distance, with the daughter of the First Lord of the Admiralty. Having no other way to voice his love, Joe sang it on board his ship to the mournful thrumming of a guitar:

The moon is on the sea,
     Willow!
The wind blows towards the lee,
     Willow!
But though I sigh and sob and cry,
No Lady Jane for me,
     Willow!
She says, ''Twere folly quite,
     Willow!
For me to wed a wight,
     Willow!
Whose lot is cast before the mast';
And possibly she's right,
     Willow!

His skipper (Captain Joyce)
   He gave him many a rating,
And almost lost his voice
   From thus expostulating:

'Lay out, you lubber, do!
   What's come to that young man, Joe?
Belay! – 'vast heaving! you!
   Do kindly stop that banjo!

'I wish, I do – oh, Lor'! –
   You'd shipped aboard a trader:
Are you a sailor, or
   A negro serenader?'

But still the stricken cad
   Aloft or on his pillow,
Howled forth in accents sad
   His aggravating 'Willow!'

Stern love of duty had
   Been Joyce's chiefest beauty:
Says he, 'I love that lad,
   But duty, damme! duty!

'Twelve years' black-hole, I say,
   Where daylight never flashes:
And always twice a day
   Five hundred thousand lashes!'

But Joseph had a mate,
   A sailor stout and lusty,
A man of low estate,
   But singularly trusty.

Says he, 'Cheer hup, young Joe,
   I'll tell you what I'm arter.
To that Fust Lord I'll go
   And ax him for his darter.

'To that Fust Lord I'll go
   And say you love her dearly.'
And Joe said (weeping low),
   'I wish you would, sincerely!'

That sailor to that Lord
   Went, soon as he had landed,
And of his own accord
   An interview demanded.

Says he, with seaman's roll,
   'My Captain (wot's a Tartar)
Guv Joe twelve years' black-hole,
   For lovering your darter.

'He loves Miss Lady Jane
   (I own she is his betters).
But if you'll jine them twain,
   They'll free him from his fetters.

'And if so be as how
   You'll let her come aboard ship,
I'll take her with me now.' –
   'Get out!' remarked his Lordship.

That honest tar repaired
   To Joe, upon the billow,
And told him how he'd fared:
   Joe only whispered, 'Willow!'

And for that dreadful crime
   (Young sailors, learn to shun it)
He's working out his time:
   In ten years he'll have done it.

The most celebrated of all the nautical ballads is the one mentioned above, *The Yarn of the 'Nancy Bell'*. It is a ballad of shipwrecked sailors, as sung by the solitary survivor. They had been driven to cannibalism and had eaten one another, one by one, till only this man is left, but he, as he himself says, embodies all the others. The topic is certainly gruesome, yet it was thought roaring fun for half a century. It became a standing literary reproach against Mark Lemon, the editor of *Punch*, that when Gilbert wrote *The Yarn of the 'Nancy Bell'*, he wouldn't accept it. The joke was supposed to be that the editor of *Punch*, of all papers,

didn't know humour when he saw it. Looking back on it, we don't feel
so sure. Gruesome things, if they are to be humorous, must never show
actual detail. We remember Lear's comic pictures in which people are
cut neatly into halves, but of course with no trace of blood, and no sign
of emotion except surprise. We recall out of *Alice in Wonderland* how in
the Jabberwocky poem:

> One, two! One, two! And through and through
> The vorpal blade went snicker-snack!
> He left it dead, and with its head
> He went galumphing back.

But Gilbert in the *Nancy Bell* not only puts in details that won't bear
actual visualization, but seems so to speak, to 'feature' them; this is
especially true of the climax of the poem; only two survivors are left –
the cook, naturally kept as long as possible by acclamation, and one
seaman. The cook prepares the boiling pot.

> . . . He boils the water, and takes the salt
> And the pepper in portions true
> (Which he never forgot), and some chopped shalot,
> And some sage and parsley too

That's all right. We can stand for them because it isn't real. It's as
harmless as Mark Twain's *Cannibalism in the Cars*. But notice what
follows. The surviving sailor steals a march on the cook and tips him into
the pot.

> And he stirred it round and round and round,
>   And he sniffed at the foaming froth;
> When I ups with his heels, and smothers his squeals
>   In the scum of the boiling broth.
>
> And I ate that cook in a week or less,
>   And – as I eating be
> The last of his chops, why, I almost drops,
>   For a vessel in sight I see.

The survivor is saved, but at the price of an internal burden that weighs
him down for ever.

The poem, I say, seemed great fun to a whole generation and more. I
remember hearing it read aloud at a country schoolchildren's entertainment in darkest Ontario in 1878. It called forth rounds of laughter. The
more they ate one another the better we liked it. Not so now. I think the
Great War killed the *Nancy Bell* – the new actuality of the horrors and

sufferings of the sea, of the agonies of wounded men thirsting or starving in open boats – no, the topic is off.

Very different is Mark Twain's *Cannibalism in the Cars*, as accomplished by a group of western congressmen, snowed in by a mountain blizzard – but done with the scrupulous regard for legislature procedure that robs it of all offence.

After the navy came the Church. Mr Gilbert's cruel tendency to make fun of bishops and curates had broken out long before Lewis Carroll complained of the *Pale Young Curate* in the *Sorcerer*. The *'Bab' Ballads* are filled with clerical characters. Nevertheless, there were clear limitations as to how far fun could go in this direction. In Gilbert's England, even when made topsy-turvy, you must not ridicule the doctrines of the Church; funny verses about the Resurrection or the Holy Communion wouldn't go. But you might laugh all you liked at queer clerical characters and satirize odd clerical usages.

And here a very peculiar distinction had grown up in the current humour of that day. It was not 'the thing' to make fun of the Church of England or to ridicule its doctines. But it was all right to ridicule the doctrines of the Roman Catholic Church. It was all right to laugh at relics and indulgences and pardons because these things were really funny, being superstitions. It was all wrong to laugh at the Holy Communion of the Church of England because this was a sacred mystery. Indeed, at a certain point, such ridicule became blasphemy and the law would deal with it. Even for people who didn't believe much, it was 'bad form' to make fun of the Church. But you could have all the jokes you liked about fat friars and drunken abbots and juggling priests and hocus-pocus. Take this for example. It comes in the description of a dinner given in a monastery by the Abbot to the Devil, who had wickedly assumed the deceptive form of a pretty lady visitor:

> She pledged him once and she pledged him twice
> And she drank as lady ought not to drink;
> And he pressed her hand 'neath the table thrice
> And he winked as Abbot ought not to wink.
>
> And Peter the Prior and Francis the Friar
> Sat each with a napkin under his chin;
> But Roger the monk got excessively drunk
> So they put him to bed and they tucked him in.

Roaringly funny, isn't it? I am sure that Lewis Carroll, who found it very wicked of Mr Gilbert to make fun of bishops and curates of the real Church, would have doubled up with laughter over Roger the monk getting excessively drunk. But how would it be if the Archbishop of Canterbury gave the dinner and the Bishop of Ripon was as full as a pippin and the Bishop of Bath was more than half? No, that wouldn't be amusing at all because it would be making fun of men whose sacred calling removes them from all humour. Such was the peculiar way in which the Anglican pot laughed at the Catholic kettle. Indeed, the author of the above verses was himself a clergyman, the Reverend Richard Harris Barham (1788–1845), a man much respected for his piety, his kindly life and his antiquarian knowledge. But when he picked up the pen as Thomas Ingoldsby and wrote the *Ingoldsby Legends*, a book of mingled humorous verse and droll legend, that was very different. He, it was, who wrote the still surviving *Jackdaw of Rheims*, the story of the unhappy bird which stole the cardinal's ring and so encountered the full explosive blast of a curse of the Church of Rome, which knocked all its feathers sideways.

This queer attitude towards 'Romanism' was, like the other things, a survival. The days had gone when people died in the flames at Smithfield for Protestantism; or when Roman Catholic priests were hunted down as criminals, and witches burned with universal approval. But the smouldering ashes were there still, deep down, still are. Hence, even with active persecution gone and practical rights granted by the Catholic Emancipation Act of 1829, it was quite in order to make jokes on Roman Catholic idolatry. It was like kicking a dead dog that might not be quite dead.

With which we can open our '*Bab' Ballads* again and see where we are in regard to the Church of England itself. Here is the Bishop of Rum-ti-Foo, a very merry character, hailing evidently from what were, in Gilbert's day, the Cannibal Isles, but, in ours, sunk far below that. The Bishop amuses his curé of dark souls with conjuring tricks. That was all right and very funny, being only in the Colonies. The Bishop had left his flock and made a visit to London. On his return he was horrified to find that during his absence rough sailors had landed on Rum-ti-Foo and taught the natives all sorts of dreadful profanity such as 'bother!' and 'blow!' They had reverted to their native Pacific Island dress, or lack of dress:

> Except a shell – a bangle rare –
> A feather here – a feather there –

The Bishop, of course, is greatly concerned and devotes himself with true missionary zeal and self-sacrifice to the redemption of his flock.

The Bishop's eyes with water fill,
Quite overjoyed to find them still
Obedient to his sovereign will,
        And said, 'Good Rum-ti-Foo!
Half-way I'll meet you, I declare:
I'll dress myself in cowries rare,
And fasten feathers in my hair,
        And dance the "Cutch-chi-boo!" '

And to conciliate his see
He married Piccadillillee,
The youngest of his twenty-three,
        Tall – neither fat nor thin.
(And though the dress he made her don
Looks awkwardly a girl upon,
It was a great improvement on
        The one he found her in.)

The Bishop in his gay canoe
(His wife, of course, went with him too)
To some adjacent island flew,
        To spend his honeymoon.
Some day in sunny Rum-ti-Foo
A little Peter'll be on view;
And that (if people tell me true)
        Is like to happen soon.

So much for the labours of the Bishop of Rum-ti-Foo. One doubts if it
was calculated to advance the cause of missionary enterprise. One may
compare it with Dickens' Mrs Jellyby (in *Bleak House*) and her labours
for the natives of Borrioboola-Gha. One may compare it, too, with the
grim picture of Somerset Maugham's *Rain* that has gone around the
world as story, play, and picture. I rather think I prefer the Bishop of
Rum-ti-Foo to anything we have now.

Equally merry on the surface but deeply satirical below is another
church picture, *The Reverend Simon Magus*. Here the satire is directed
only against the usages, not against the doctrines, of the Established
Church. It begins:

A rich advowson high prized,
    For private sale was advertised;
And many a parson made a bid;
    The Reverend Simon Magus did.

We must pause a moment to explain what an advowson is, or rather was,
in Gilbert's time, for the right it carries has been greatly modified by
later statutes. It meant the right of 'Presentation to a vacant ecclesiastical

benefice'; that is, the right, in plainer language, to name (practically to appoint) a clergyman to a particular position fallen vacant. This was a form of property. It originated centuries ago out of various gifts given to the Church which carried a *quid pro quo* or, shall we say, a string on them. The right could be bought or sold, even at auction, and in the case of a rich benefice it carried a high price. It is only fair to admit that the right could not be exercised by a lunatic or a Roman Catholic; still less by a Roman Catholic lunatic. Here the universities of Oxford and Cambridge stepped in and took the place of the lunatic. It is fair, also, to admit that the bishop of the diocese might object to the person presented as not fit to be a clerk in holy orders. In which case the owner of the advowson could come back at him with a writ of *quare inpedit* (why is he stopping me?) and the proposed clerk could join in with a *duplex querela* – that means a side kick – and the whole matter drift slowly sideways towards the Court of Chancery. We don't have fun like that in newer countries.

So now one can understand Gilbert's delight in Simon Magnus' dickering with an agent for the advowson . . .

> A rich advowson, highly prized,
> For private sale was advertised;
> And many a parson made a bid;
> The Reverend Simon Magus did.

> He sought the agent's: 'Agent, I
> Have come prepared at once to buy
> (If your demand is not too big)
> The Curé of Otium-cum-Digge.'

> 'Ah!' said the agent, *'there's* a berth –
> The snuggest vicarage on earth;
> No sort of duty (so I hear),
> And fifteen hundred pounds a year!

> 'If on the price we should agree,
> The living soon will vacant be;
> The good incumbent's ninety-five
> And cannot very long survive.

> 'See – here's his photograph – you see,
> He's in his dotage,' 'Ah, dear me!
> Poor Soul!' said Simon. 'His decease
> Would be a merciful release!'

> The agent laughed – the agent blinked –
> The agent blew his nose and winked –
> And poked the parson's ribs in play –
> It was that agent's vulgar way.

The Reverend Simon frowned: 'I grieve
This light demeanour to perceive;
It's scarcely *comme il faut*, I think:
Now – pray oblige me – do not wink.

'Don't dig my waistcoat into holes –
Your mission is to sell the souls
Of human sheep and human kids
To that divine who highest bids.

'Do well in this, and on your head
Unnumbered honours will be shed.'
The agent said, 'Well, truth to tell,
I *have* been doing very well.'

'You should,' said Simon, 'at your age;
But now about the parsonage.
How many rooms does it contain?
Show me the photograph again.

'A poor apostle's humble house
Must not be too luxurious;
No stately halls with oaken floor –
It should be decent and no more.

'No billiard-rooms – no stately trees –
No croquet-grounds or pineries.'
'Ah!' sighed the agent, 'very true:
This property won't do for you.

'All these about the house you'll find' –
'Well,' said the parson, 'never mind;
I'll manage to submit to these
Luxurious superfluities.

'A clergyman who does not shirk
The various calls of Christian work
Will have no leisure to employ
These "common forms" of worldly joy.

'To preach three times on Sabbath days –
To wean the lost from wicked ways –
The sick to soothe – the sane to wed –
The poor to feed with meat and bread;

'These are the various wholesome ways
In which I'll spend my nights and days;
My zeal will have no time to cool
At croquet, archery, or pool.'

The agent said, 'From what I hear,
This living will not suit, I fear –
There are no poor, no sick at all;
For services there is no call.'

The reverend gent looked grave. 'Dear me!
Then there is *no* "society"? –
I mean, of course, no sinners there
Whose souls will be my special care?'

The cunning agent shook his head,
'No, none – except' – (the agent said) –
'The Duke of A., the Earl of B.,
The Marquis C., and Viscount D.

'But you will not be quite alone,
For, though they've chaplains of their own,
Of course this noble well-bred clan
Receive the parish clergyman.'

'Oh, silence, sir!' said Simon M.,
'Dukes – earls! What should I care for them?
These worldly ranks I scorn and flout,
Of course.' The agent said, 'No doubt.'

'Yet I might show these men of birth
The hollowness of rank on earth.'
The agent answered, 'Very true –
But I should not, if I were you.'

'Who sells this rich advowson, pray?'
The agent winked – it was his way –
'His name is Hart; twixt me and you,
He is, I'm grieved to say, a Jew!'

'A Jew?' said Simon, 'happy find!
I purchase this advowson, mind.
My life shall be devoted to
Converting that unhappy Jew.'

But observe how different is the treatment of the Roman Catholic Church. All of its doctrines, except where they are identical with those of the Established Church of England, are a fair mark for ridicule. Nothing is too sacred, not even the confessional and the forgiveness of sins. Take as evidence the Ballad of *Gentle Alice Brown*, in which Gentle Alice confesses her sins to Father Paul and receives an easy absolution.

It was a robber's daughter, and her name was Alice Brown,
Her father was the terror of a small Italian town;
Her mother was a foolish, weak, but amiable old thing;
But it isn't of her parents that I'm going for to sing.

As Alice was a sitting at her window-sill one day,
A beautiful young gentleman he chanced to pass that way;
She cast her eyes upon him, and he looked so good and true,
That she thought, 'I could be happy with a gentleman like you!'

And every morning passed her house that cream of gentlemen,
She knew she might expect him at a quarter unto ten;
A sorter in the Custom-house, it was his daily road
(The Custom-house was fifteen minutes' walk from her abode).

But Alice was a pious girl, who knew it wasn't wise
To look at strange young sorters with expressive purple eyes;
So she sought the village priest to whom her family confessed,
The priest by whom their little sins were carefully assessed.

'Oh, holy father,' Alice said, ''twould grieve you, would it not,
To discover that I was a most disreputable lot?
Of all unhappy sinners I'm the most unhappy one!'
The padre said, 'Whatever have you been and gone and done?'

'I have helped mama to steal a little kiddy from its dad,
I've assisted dear papa in cutting up a little lad,
I've planned a little burglary and forged a little cheque,
And slain a little baby for the coral on its neck!'

The worthy pastor heaved a sigh, and dropped a silent tear,
And said, 'You mustn't judge yourself too heavily, my dear:
It's wrong to murder babies, little corals for to fleece;
But sins like these one expiates at half-a-crown apiece.

'Girls will be girls – you're very young, and flighty in your mind;
Old heads upon young shoulders we must not expect to find,
We mustn't be too hard upon these little girlish tricks.
Let's see – five crimes at half-a-crown – exactly twelve and six.'

But Alice now confesses to her improper conduct in connection with the young sorter. Father Paul is, of course, horrified at the idea of the robber's daughter falling in love outside of the bandit class into respectable society. That kind of thing would mean the end of crime and confessional fees. However, it all ends happily. Father Paul communicates at once with Robber Brown who goes after the young sorter without delay.

He traced that gallant sorter to a still suburban square;
He watched his opportunity and seized him unaware;
He took a life-preserver and he hit him on the head,
And Mrs Brown dissected him before she went to bed.

Observe the last line.

Mrs Brown dissected him before she went to bed.

This is another example of that apparently open 'brutality' which offended Mark Lemon when the *Nancy Bell's* cook was tipped into the pot, boiled and eaten! Here we have Mrs Brown, sitting quietly at her dissection, carefully separating the *os femoris* from the *patella*, and laying aside the articular cartilege for later disposal. This sounds very horrible if you really think of it. But the point is you don't think about it. We have a sort of compartment in our minds, evoluted for our protection, to keep actuality and fun apart. I admit that if you push too hard on the partition it will give way. The boiling of the cook is at too high pressure for most of us. I remember, also, the story of a funeral of a locomotive engineer who had been scalded to death. The clergyman spoke of him to the mourners as 'our steemed friend'. That, I always found a little bit thick – with steam.

But good Mrs Brown and her dissection may pass for another reason; namely, the excellence of the phrase, 'before she went to bed'. The *'Bab' Ballads* and the Gilbert and Sullivan operas are filled with those happy phrases which people loved to quote, though probably few people could explain just exactly why. The point here is the beautiful domesticity of the phrase. It belongs in family life. It suggests one of those domestic tasks which no good housewife likes to leave undone overnight. She always gets all her dishes washed and her kitchen tidy every night. And so good Mrs Brown felt that she must get her dissecting done 'before she went to bed'.

Probably many people will agree that the most sustained effort, the most finished satire and the most exquisite flow of verse in the *'Bab' Ballads* is found in the poem *Etiquette*. This was not one of the original ballads of *Fun*. It was written years later for a Christmas number of the *Graphic*. But Gilbert himself gathered it into the large volume of early ballads and later songs which he collected in 1897 as the *'Bab' Ballads, etc*.

I was about to say that here at any rate, we have a poem with none of those disfiguring details of horror of which we have just spoken. But I notice on looking again that the poem starts off with the wholesale drowning of an entire ship's company, including the owners. Still that's nothing. It's not the point of the poem and, as Gilbert himself says, they were all insured.

The underlying satire of the poem turns on the aloofness of English manners, the impossibility of knowing anybody that you don't know. But its great merit lies in the smooth perfection of its lines, which seem so effortless and so inevitable, the last word in comic verse.

CHAPTER VI

Common Sense and the Universe

I

Speaking last December at the annual convention of the American Association for the Advancement of Science, and speaking, as it were, in the name of the great 100-inch telescope under his control, Professor Edwin Hubble, of the Mount Wilson Observatory, California, made the glad announcement that the universe is not expanding. This was good news indeed, if not to the general public, who had no reason to suspect that it was expanding, at least to those of us who humbly attempt to 'follow science'. For some twenty-five years past, indeed ever since the promulgation of this terrific idea in a paper published by Professor W. de Sitter in 1917, we had lived as best we could in an expanding universe, one in which everything, at terrific speed, kept getting farther away from everything else. It suggested to us the disappointed lover in the romance who leaped on his horse and rode madly off in all directions. The idea was majestic in its sheer size, but it somehow gave an uncomfortable sensation.

Yet we had to believe it. Thus, for example, we had it on the authority of Dr Spencer Jones, the British Astronomer Royal, in his new and fascinating book of 1940, *Life on Other Worlds*, that 'a distant universe in the constellation of Bootes has been found to be receding with a velocity of 24,300 miles a second. We can infer that this nebula is at a distance of 230,000,000 light years.' I may perhaps remind my fellow followers of science that a light year means the distance travelled in one year by light, moving at 186,000 miles a second. In other words, this 'distant universe' is now 1,049,970,980,000,000,000,000 miles away!

Some distance! as Mr Churchill would say.

But now it appears that that distant universe has *not* been receding at all; in fact, it isn't away out there. Heaven knows where it is. Bring it back. Yet not only did the astronomers assert the expansion but they proved it, from the behaviour of the red band in the spectrum, which blushed a deeper red at the revelation of it, like the conscious water that 'saw its God and blushed' at Cana in Galilee long ago. One of the most distinguished and intelligible of our astronomers, Sir Arthur Eddington, had written a book about it, *The Expanding Universe*, to bring it down to our level. Astronomers at large accepted this universe expansion in all directions as calmly as they once accepted the universal fall of gravitation, or the universal death in the cold under Carnot's Second Law of Thermodynamics.

But the relief brought by Professor Hubble is tempered on reflection by certain doubts and afterthoughts. It is not that I venture any disbelief or disrespect towards science, for that it as atrocious in our day as disbelief in the Trinity in the days of Isaac Newton. But we begin to doubt whether science can quite keep on believing in and respecting itself. If we expand today and contract tomorrow; if we undergo all the doubled-up agonies of the curvature of space only to have the kind called off, as it has been; if we get reconciled to dying a martyr's death at one general, distributed temperature of 459 degrees below zero, the same for all, only to find that the world is perhaps unexpectedly warming up again – then we ask, where are we? To which, of course, Einstein answers 'Nowhere,' since there is no place to be. So we must pick up our little book again, follow science, and wait for the next astronomical convention.

Let us take this case of the famous Second Law of Thermodynamics, that inexorable scroll of fate which condemned the universe – or at least all life in it – to die of cold. I look back now with regret to the needless tears I have wasted over that, the generous sympathy for the last little band of survivors, dying at 459 degrees below our zero (ms273 degrees Centigrade), the absolute zero of cold when the molecules cease to move and heat ends. No stove will light at that, for the wood is as cold as the stove, and the match is as cold as both, and the dead fingers motionless.

I remember meeting this inexorable law for the first time in reading, as a little boy, a piece of 'popular science' entitled *Our Great Timepiece Running Down*. It was by Richard Proctor, whose science-bogeys were as terrifying as Mrs Crow's *Night Thoughts*, only slower in action. The sun, it appeared, was cooling; soon it would be all over. Lord Kelvin presently ratified this. Being Scotch, he didn't mind damnation and he gave the sun and the whole solar system only ninety million years more to live.

This famous law was first clearly enunciated in 1824 by the great French physicist, Nicolas Carnot. It showed that all bodies in the universe kept exchanging their temperature – hot things heated cold, and cold things chilled hot. Thus they pooled their temperature. Like the division of a rich estate among a flock of poor relations, it meant poverty for all. We must all share ultimately the cold of absolute space.

It is true that a gleam of hope came when Ernest Rutherford and others, working on radioactivity, discovered that there might be a contrary process of 'stoking up'. Atoms exploding into radioactivity would keep the home fires burning in the sun for a long time. This glad news meant that the sun was both much older and much younger than Lord Kelvin had ever thought it was. But even at that it was only a respite. The best they could offer was 1,500,000,000 years. After that we freeze.

And now what do you think! Here comes the new physics of the Quantum Theory and shatters the Second Law of Thermodynamics into gas – a word that is Dutch for chaos. The world may go on for ever. All of this because of the final promulgation of the Law of the *Quantum* – or, shall we say, the Law of Just So Much – of which we shall presently speak. These physical people do not handle their Latin with the neat touch of those of us who knew our declensions as they know their dimensions. Of course they mean *Tantum* – but let it go at that. *Quantum* is drugstore Latin, *quantum sufficit*. *Tantum* is the real thing – *Virgilium vidi tantum* ('I saw something of Virgil').

At this point I may perhaps pause to explain that the purpose of this article is not to make fun of science, nor to express disbelief in it, but only to suggest its limits. What I want to say is that when the scientist steps out from recording phenomena and offers a general statement of the nature of what is called 'reality', the ultimate nature of space, of time, of the beginning of things, of life, of a universe, then he stands exactly where you and I do, and the three of us stand where Plato did – and long before him Rodin's primitive thinker.

Consider this. Professor Hubble, like Joshua, has called upon the universe to be still. All is quiet. The universe rests, motionless, in the night sky. The mad rush is over. Every star in every galaxy, every island universe, is at least right where it is. But the old difficulty remains: Does it go for ever, this world in the sky, or does it stop? Such an alternative has posed itself as a problem for every one of us, somewhere about the age of twelve. We cannot imagine that the stars go on for ever. It's unthinkable. But we equally cannot imagine that they come to a stop and that beyond them is nothing and then more nothing. Unending nothing is as incomprehensible as unending something. This alternative I cannot fathom, nor can Professor Hubble, nor can anyone ever hope to.

Let me turn back in order to make my point of view a little clearer. I propose to traverse again the path along which modern science has dragged those who have tried to follow it for about a century past. It was at first a path singularly easy to tread, provided that one could throw aside the inherited burden of superstition, false belief, and prejudice. For the direction seemed verified and assured all along by the corroboration of science by actual physical results. Who could doubt electricity after the telegraph? Or doubt the theory of light after photography? Or the theory of electricity when read under electric light? At every turn, each new advance of science unveiled new power, new mechanism of life

– and of death. To 'doubt science' was to be like the farmer at the circus who doubted the giraffe. Science, of course, had somehow to tuck into the same bed as Theology, but it was the theologian who protested. Science just said, 'Lie over.'

Let us follow then this path.

II

When the medieval superstition was replaced by the new learning, mathematics, astronomy, and physics were the first sciences to get organized and definite. By the opening of the nineteenth century they were well set; the solar system was humming away so drowsily that Laplace was able to assure Napoleon that he didn't need God to watch over it. Gravitation worked like clockwork and clockwork worked like gravitation. Chemistry, which, like electricity, was nothing but a set of experiments in Benjamin Franklin's time, turned into a science after Lavoisier had discovered that fire was not a thing but a process, something happening to things – an idea so far above the common thought that they guillotined him for it in 1794. Dalton followed and showed that all things could be broken up into a set of very, very small atoms, grouped into molecules all acting according to plan. With Faraday and Maxwell, electricity, which turned out to be the same as magnetism, or interchangeable with it, fell into its place in the new order of science.

By about 1880 it seemed as if the world of science was fairly well explained. Metaphysics still talked in its sleep. Theology still preached sermons. It took issue with much of the new science, especially with geology and the new evolutionary science of life that went with the new physical world. But science paid little attention.

For the whole thing was so amazingly simple. There you had your space and time, two things too obvious to explain. Here you had your matter, made up of solid little atoms, infinitely small but really just like birdseed. All this was set going by and with the Law of Gravitation. Once started, the nebulous world condensed into suns, the suns threw off planets, the planets cooled, life resulted and presently became conscious, conscious life got higher up and higher up till you had apes, then Bishop Wilberforce, and then Professor Huxley.

A few little mysteries remained, such as the question of what space and matter and time and life and consciousness really were. But all this was conveniently called by Herbert Spencer the *Unknowable*, and then locked in a cupboard and left there.

Everything was thus reduced to a sort of Dead Certainty. Just one awkward skeleton remained in the cupboard. And that was the peculiar, mysterious aspect of electricity, which was not exactly a thing and yet more than an idea. There was also, and electricity only helped to make it worse, the old puzzle about 'action at a distance'. How does gravitation pull all the way from here to the sun? And if there is *nothing* in space, how does light get across from the sun in eight minutes, and even all the way from Sirius in eight years?

Even the invention of 'ether' as a sort of universal jelly that could have ripples shaken across it proved a little unconvincing.

Then, just at the turn of the century, the whole structure began to crumble.

The first note of warning that something was going wrong came with the discovery of X-rays. Sir William Crookes, accidentally leaving round tubes of rarefied gas, stumbled on 'radiant matter', or 'matter in the fourth state', as accidentally as Columbus discovered America. The British Government knighted him at once (1897) but it was too late. The thing had started. Then came Guglielmo Marconi with the revelation of more waves, and universal at that. Light, the world had learned to accept, because we can see it, but this was fun in the dark.

There followed the researches of the radioactivity school, and above all, those of Ernest Rutherford which revolutionized the theory of matter. I knew Rutherford well as we were colleagues at McGill for seven years. I am quite sure that he had no original intention of upsetting the foundations of the universe. Yet that is what he did and he was in due course very properly raised to the peerage for it.

When Rutherford was done with the atom all the solidity was pretty well knocked out of it.

Till these researches began, people commonly thought of atoms as something like birdseed, little round solid particles, ever so little, billions to an inch. They were small. But they were there. You could weigh them. You could apply to them all the laws of Isaac Newton about weight and velocity and mass and gravitation – in other words, the whole of first-year physics.

Let us try to show what Rutherford did to the atom. Imagine to yourself an Irishman whirling a shillelagh round his head with the rapidity and dexterity known only in Tipperary or Donegal. If you come anywhere near you'll get hit with the shillelagh. Now make it go faster; faster still; get it going so fast that you can't tell which is Irishman and which is shillelagh. The whole combination has turned into a green blur. If you shoot a bullet at it, it will probably go through, as there is mostly nothing there. Yet if you go up against it, it won't hit you now, because the shillelagh is going so fast that you will seem to come against a solid surface. Now make the Irishman smaller and the shillelagh longer. In fact you don't need the Irishman at all; just his force, his Irish determination, so to speak. Just keep that, the *disturbance*. And you don't need the shillelagh either, just the *field of force* that it sweeps. There! Now put in two Irishmen and two shillelaghs and reduce them in the same way to one solid body – at least it seems solid but you can shoot bullets through it anywhere now. What you have now is a hydrogen atom – one proton and one electron flying round as a *disturbance* in space. Put in more Irishmen and more shillelaghs – or, rather, more protons and electrons – and you get other kinds of atoms. Put in a whole lot – eleven protons, eleven electrons; that is a sodium atom. Bunch the atoms together into combinations called molecules, themselves flying round – and there you are! That's solid matter, and nothing in it at all except disturbance. You're standing on it right now: the molecules are beating against your feet. But there is nothing there, and nothing in your feet. This may help you to understand how 'waves', ripples of disturbance – for instance, the disturbance you call radio, – go right through all matter, indeed right through *you*, as if you weren't there. You see, you aren't.

The peculiar thing about this atomic theory was that whatever the atoms were, birdseed or disturbance, it made no difference to the way they acted. They followed all the laws of mechanics and motion, or they seemed to. There was no need to change any idea of space or time because of them. Matter was their 'fort', like wax figures with Artemus Ward.

One must not confuse Rutherford's work on atoms with Einstein's theories of space and time. Rutherford worked all his life without reference to Einstein. Even in his later days at the Cavendish Laboratory at Cambridge when he began, ungratefully, to smash up the atom that had made him, he needed nothing from Einstein. I once asked Rutherford – it was at the height of the popular interest in Einstein, in 1923 – what he thought of Einstein's relativity. 'Oh, that stuff!' he said. 'We never bother with that in our work!' His admirable biographer, Professor A. S. Eve, tells us that when the German physicist Wien told Rutherford that no Anglo-Saxon could understand relativity Rutherford answered, 'No, they have too much sense.'

But it was Einstein who made the real trouble. He announced in 1905 that there was no such thing as absolute rest. After that there never was. But it was not till just after the Great War that the reading public caught on to Einstein and little books on 'Relativity' covered the bookstalls.

Einstein knocked out space and time as Rutherford knocked out matter. The general viewpoint of relativity towards space is very simple. Einstein explains that there is no such place as *here*. 'But,' you answer, 'I'm here; here is where I am right now.' But you're moving, you're spinning round as the earth spins; and you and the earth are both spinning round the sun, and the sun is rushing through space towards a distant galaxy, and the galaxy itself is beating it away at 26,000 miles a second. Now where is that spot that is here! How did you mark it? You remember the story of the two idiots who were out fishing, and one said, 'We should have marked that place where we got all the fish,' and the other said, 'I did, I marked it on the boat.' Well, that's it. That's *here*.

You can see it better still if you imagine the universe swept absolutely empty: nothing in it, not even *you*. Now put a *point* in it, just one point. Where is it? Why, obviously it's nowhere. If you say it's right there, where do you mean by there? In which direction is there? In *that* direction? Oh! hold on, you're sticking yourself in to make a direction. It's in *no* direction; there aren't any directions. Now put in another point. Which is which? You can't tell. They *both* are. One is on the right, you say, and one on the left. You keep out of that space! There's no right and no left. Join the points with a line. Now you think you've got something, and I admit this is the nearest you have come to it. But is the line long or short? How long is it? Length soon vanishes into a purely relative term. One thing is longer than another: that's all.

There's no harm in all this, so far. To many people it's as obvious as it is harmless. But that's only the beginning. Leave space alone for a moment and take on time and then things begin to thicken. If there is no such place as there, a similar line of thought will show that there's no such time as now – not absolutely now. Empty the universe again as you did before, with not a speck in it, and now ask, what time is it – God bless me, how peculiar. It isn't any time. It can't be, there's nothing to tell the time by. You say you can feel it go; oh, but you're not there. There will be no *time* until you put something into space with dimensions to it – and then there'll be time, but only as connected somehow – no knowing how – with things in space. But just as there is no such thing as absolute top or bottom in space, so there is a similar difficulty as to time backward and time forward –

The relativity theory undertakes to explain both space and time by putting them together, since they are meaningless without one another, into a compound called 'space-time continuum'. Time thus becomes, they say, the fourth dimension of space. Until just recently it was claimed further that to fit these relationships together, to harmonize space and time, space must have a curve, or curvature. This was put over to the common mind by comparing what happens in space with what happens to a fly walking on a sphere (a globe). The fly walks and walks and never gets to the end. It's curved. The joke is on the fly. So was the joke long ago on the medieval people who thought the world flat. 'What happened to the theory of the earth,' writes Eddington, 'has happened also to the world of space and time.'

The idea was made plainer for us by comparing space-time to an onion skin, or rather to an infinite number of onion skins. If you have enough you can fill all space. The universe is your onion, as it was Shakespeare's oyster.

The discovery by Einstein of this curvature of space was greeted by the physicists with the burst of applause that greets a winning home-run at baseball. That brilliant writer just mentioned, Sir Arthur Eddington, who can handle space and time with the imagery of a poet, and even infiltrate humour into gravitation, as when he says that a man in an elevator falling twenty stories has an ideal opportunity to study gravitation – Sir Arthur Eddington is loud in his acclaim. Without this curve, it appears, things won't fit into their place. The fly on the globe, as long as he thinks it flat (like Mercator's map), finds things shifted as by some unaccountable demon to all sorts of wrong distances. Once he gets the idea of a sphere everything comes straight. So with our space. The mystery of gravitation puzzles us, except those who have the luck to fall in an elevator, and even for them knowledge comes too late. They weren't falling at all: just curving. 'Admit a curvature of the world,' wrote Eddington in his Gifford Lectures of 1927, 'and the mysterious agency disappears. Einstein has exorcized this demon.'

But it appears now, fourteen years later, that Einstein doesn't care if space is curved or not. He can take it either way. A prominent physicist of today, head of the department in one of the greatest universities of the world, wrote me on this point: 'Einstein had stronger hopes that a general theory which involved the assumption of a property of space, akin to what is ordinarily called curvature, would be more useful than he now believes to be the case.' Plain talk for a professor. Most people just say Einstein has given up curved space. It's as if Sir Isaac Newton years after had said, with a yawn, 'Oh, about that apple – perhaps it wasn't falling.'

Now with the curve knocked out of it, the space-time continuum with these so-called four dimensions becomes really a very simple matter, in fact only a very pretentious name for a very obvious fact. It just means that information about an occurrence is not complete unless we know both where it happened and when it happened. It is no use telling me that Diogenes is dead if I didn't know that he was alive.

Obviously 'time-when' or 'place-where' are bound together and coexist with one another. If there were no space – just emptiness – there could be no time: It wouldn't count itself. And if no time, no space; start it and it would flicker out again in no time: Like an electric bulb on a whobble-

plug. Space-time continuum is just a pretentious name for this consequence of consciousness. We can't get behind it. We begin life with it as
the chicken out of the egg begins with its cell memory. All the
mathematics based on 'space-time continuum' get no farther, as far as
concerns the search for reality. It gets no farther than the child's
arithmetic book that says, 'If John walks 2 miles every day for 10 days,'
etc. etc. The child hooks space and time with a continuum as easily as the
chicken picks up gravel.

III

But unhappily we can't get away from the new physics quite as simply as
that. Even if we beat them out on space and time, there is far worse to
come. That's only the start of it, for now, as the fat boy in *Pickwick* said,
'I'm going to make your flesh creep.' The next thing to go is cause and
effect. You may think that one thing causes another. It appears that it
doesn't. And of course, when cause and effect go, the bottom is out of
the universe, since you can't tell, literally can't, what's going to happen
next. This is the consequence of the famous Quantum Theory, first
hinted at by Professor Max Planck about forty years ago and since then
scrambled for by the physicists like dogs after a bone. It changes so fast
that when Sir Arthur Eddington gave the Gifford Lectures referred to,
he said to his students that it might not be the same when they met next
autumn.

But we cannot understand the full impact of the Quantum Theory, in
shattering the world we lived in, without turning back again to discuss
time in a new relation, namely, the forward-and-backwardness of it, and
to connect it up again with the Second Law of Thermodynamics – the
law, it will be recalled, that condemns us to die of cold. Only we will now
call it by its true name, which we had avoided before, as the Law of
Entropy. All physicists sooner or later say, 'Let us call it Entropy,' just
as a man says, when you get to know him, 'Call me Charlie.'

So we make a new start.

I recall, as some other people still may, a thrilling melodrama called
The Silver King. In this the hero, who thinks he has committed a murder
(of course, he hasn't really), falls on his knees and cries, 'Oh, God, turn
back the universe and give me yesterday.' The supposed reaction of the
audience was 'Alas, you *can't* turn back the universe!'

But nowadays it would be very different. At the call the Spirit of Time
would appear – not Father Time, who is all wrong, being made old, but
a young, radiant spirit in a silver frock made the same back and front.
'Look,' says the Spirit, 'I'm going to turn back the universe. You see this

wheel turning round. Presto! It's going the other way! You see this elastic ball falling to the floor. Presto! It's bouncing back. You see out of the window that star moving west. Presto! It's going east. Hence, accordingly,' continues the Spirit, now speaking like a professor, so that the Silver King looks up in apprehension, 'time as evidenced by any primary motion is entirely reversible so that we cannot distinguish between future time and past time: indeed if they move in a circle both are one.'

The Silver King leaps up, shouts 'Innocent! Innocent!' and dashes off, thus anticipating Act V and spoiling the whole play. The musing Spirit, musing of course backwards, says, 'Poor fellow, I hadn't the heart to tell him that this only applies to primary motion and not to Entropy. And murder of couse is a plain case of Entropy.'

And now let us try to explain. Entropy means the introduction into things that happen of a random element, as opposed to things that happen and 'unhappen', like a turning wheel, good either way, or a ball falling and bouncing as high as it falls, or the earth going around the sun. These primary motions are 'reversible'. As far as they are concerned, time could just as well go back as forward. But now introduce the element of random chance. You remember how Humpty Dumpty fell off the wall. All the king's horses and all the king's men couldn't put Humpty together again. Of course not. It was a straight case of 'entropy'. But now consider a pack of cards fresh from the maker, all in suits, all in order again? They might, but they won't. Entropy. Take this case. You show a motion picture of a wheel spinning: you run it backwards: it spins the other way. That's time, the time of primary motion, both ways alike. Now show a motion picture of a waiter with a tray of teacups: he drops them: they roll in a hundred fragments. Now run it backwards: you see all the fragments leap up in the air, join neatly into cups, and rest on the tray. Don't think that the waiter smiles with relief: he doesn't: he can't smile backwards: he just relaxes horror to calm.

Here then is Entropy, the smashing down of our world by random forces that don't reverse. The heat and cold of Carnot's Second Law are just one case of it. This is the only way by which we can distinguish which of two events came first. It's our only clue as to which way time is going. If procrastination is the thief of time, Entropy is the detective.

The Quantum Theory begins with the idea that the quantities of disturbance in the atom, of which we spoke, are done up, at least they act that way, in little fixed quantities (each a Quantum – no more, no less), as if sugar only existed by the pound. The smallness of the Quantum is beyond comprehension. A Quantum is also peculiar. A Quantum in an atom flies round in an orbit. This orbit may be a smaller ring or a bigger ring. But when the Quantum shifts from orbit to orbit it does not pass or drift or move *from one to the other*. No, sir. First, it's here and then it's there. Believe it or not, it has just shifted. Its change of place is random, and *not because of anything*. Now the things that we think of as matter and movements and events (things happening) are all based, infinitely far down, on this random dance of Quantums. Hence, since you can't ever tell what a Quantum will do, you can't ever say what will happen next. Cause and effect are all gone.

But as usual in this bright, new world of the new physics, the statement is no sooner made than it is taken back again. There are such a lot of Quantums that we can feel sure that one at least will turn up in the right place – by chance, not by cause.

The only difficulty about the Quantum Theory has been that to make the atomic 'orbits' operate properly, and to put the Quantum *into two places at once*, it is necessary to have 'more dimensions' in space. If they are not in one they are in another. You ask next door. What this means I have no idea.

Nor does it tell us any ultimate truth about the real nature of things to keep on making equations about them. Suppose I wish to take a holiday trip and am selecting a place to go. I ask, How far is it? – how long does it take?– what does it cost? These things all come into it. If I like I can call them 'dimensions'. It does no harm. If I like I can add other dimensions – how hot it is, how much gold it has, and what sort of women. I can say, if I wish, that the women are therefore found out to be the seventh dimension of locality. But I doubt if I can find anything sillier to say than the physicists' talk of ten and twelve dimensions added to space.

Let it be realized, I say, that making equations and functions about a thing does not tell us anything about its real nature. Suppose that I sometimes wonder just what sort of man Chipman, my fellow club member, is. While I am wondering another fellow member, a mathematician, comes in. 'Wondering about Chipman, were you?' he says. 'Well, I can tell you all about him as I have computed his dimensions. I have here the statistics of the number of times he comes (t), the number of steps he takes before he sits down (s), his orbit in moving round (o), aberrations as affected by other bodies (ab), velocity (v), specific gravity (sp), and his saturation (S). He is therefore a function of these things, or shall we say quite simply:

$$F \int \frac{s.v.o.sp.S'}{t.ab}$$

Now this would be mathematically useful. With it I can calculate the likelihood of my friend being at the club at any particular time, and whether available for billiards. In other words, I've got him in what is called a 'frame' in spacetime. But just as all this tells me nothing of ultimate reality, neither do the super-dimensions of the new physics.

People who know nothing about the subject, or just less than I do, will tell you that science and philosphy and theology have nowadays all come together. So they have, in a sense. But the statement, like those above, is just a 'statistical' one. They have come together as three people may come together in a picture theatre, or three people happen to take apartments in the same building, or, to apply the metaphor that really fits, as three people come together at a funeral. The funeral is that of Dead Certainty. The interment is over and the three turn away together.

'Incomprehensible,' murmurs Theology reverently.

'What was that word?' asks Science.

'Incomprehensible; I often use it in my litanies.'

'Ah yes,' murmurs Science, with almost equal reverence, 'incomprehensible!'

'The comprehensibility of comprehension,' begins Philosophy, staring straight in front of him.

'Poor fellow,' says Theology, 'he's wandering again; better lead him home.'

'I haven't the least idea where he lives,' says Science.

'Just below me,' says Theology. 'We're both above you.'

CHAPTER VII

A Plea for Geographical Science

I will begin by saying in a word what I mean to elaborate in an essay. This is a plea for the restoration of geography to the place it once had in school study, from which it was ousted by the mechanization of matriculation. With this aim, I wish with the same stone to hit another bird, or, rather, a small flock of them, the natural science subjects akin to geography – astronomy, geology, biology, the theory of evolution and such. These subjects occupy an odd place, or lack of place, in our college study. They are things of which every educated graduate should know something, of which no one but a specialist can know much and of which many present graduates know nothing. They seem too advanced, for the schools and the colleges can't find time for them, the college curriculum being older (academically) than they are. The best the college can offer to the Arts student is a choice of a half-portion selected among them, as if a little of geology would make up for a complete lack of biology – like the choice of roast meat or fish in a table d'hôte dinner.

What I propose to do is to gather all these various 'knowledges of the Earth' up into one combined Geographical Science and turn it into an A1 matriculation subject so that it covers four years in a high school and that even then the pupils don't know it. I'd like to call it *Geosophy* but that sounds stuffed at the start.

The situation is really an historic one. Our college curriculum in Canada, and especially our formal matriculation, comes down from a hundred years ago – with the extinction of King's College and the formation of the University of Toronto, and others. At that time 'learning' meant overwhelmingly Latin and Greek, either taken with athletics and brandy and water as for the Oxford Pass degreee, or with the intense and prolonged industry that produced the portentous figure of the Classical Scholar, knowing nothing but classics and not needing to. Classical Scholars knew everything, like Molière's 'people of quality', without learning anything. The new discoveries in natural science from Priestley to Darwin, from Boyle to Faraday, meant nothing to them. Speak of Evolution and they quoted impressively Homer, Book VI, line 175, on the fall of the leaves. Talk of atoms and they were back at once to Democritus – *Panta Rei* – 'everything is on the move'. So there you were, and the other people took their cue from them. Smart people like Mr Disraeli joked about being 'on the side of the angels'; and dull people like Bishop Wilberforce called Mr Huxley a monkey.

That was why, when the new science knocked at the doors of our colleges it got a very grudging reception. It only squeezed in; part of it is still caught in the door.

That, then, is one side of the subject before us, the unsatisfactory place given to the rudiments of natural science in institutions where no one enters without the rudiments of Latin and mathematics. Beside this, as the other half of the topic that dovetails where the edges join, is the mean place now accorded to geography, once a favoured subject of the schools.

It has been said that everything has the defects of its merits. That was the expression used by the Frenchman who first said it, one of those 'witty Frenchmen', who thought of everything first. The plain English for it is that there are two sides to everything. Our progress in education in a hundred years has been no doubt unparalleled, especially in sheer bulk, numbers and cost. In a way, what went before seems twilight. Yet even progress in its forward movement scrapes off and loses something of its quality. There are things also seen better in the twilight than in a glare. Our education in these hundred years has of necessity – from its extent and its use as a legal qualification for something else – become mechanized, systematized, all reduced to a standard, and a provable standard at that. Hence a lot of subjects not capable of that kind of credit measurement got left behind. The older school education laid great stress on such things as reading aloud, and with it the cultivation of the voice, and the learning of poetry, and reciting it, and on such useful queerities as mental arithmetic and dictation in foreign languages and, in a general way, character and the fear of God. In other words there was about the older education a certain reality which gets lost, in part at least, when education becomes mechanized.

I remember that grand enthusiast, Professor A. B. Macullum, of McGill and Toronto (he died young), once talking to me of what was, seventy or eighty years ago from now, the realities, the meaning, of Scottish Canadian education. 'My brother,' he said, 'had never been to college, only school, but he had a wonderful education. I've seen him jump down off the load in the harvest field and recite a whole Canto of Walter Scott, with the men standing round him, spellbound.' Cynicism might object that men paid by the hour would easily spellbind – perhaps even for a Canto of my *Elements of Political Science* – but the meaning, and the attraction, of the scene is obvious.

So when formal matriculation began, exercises like learning and reciting poetry went overboard, and bad voices that wouldn't do in a harvest field were good enough for college. Yet even when it slowly dawned on the teachers that these things didn't count, they died hard. But die they must. What good was reading out loud if you didn't have to read at matriculation? Of what use is a cultivated voice to the ear of the examiner who never hears it? As to the fear of God, that was needed only for divinity, not for pass matriculation in Arts.

Some things, I say, died hard. Take the case of Latin Verse – turning English verse into Latin. In the big days when Classical scholarship was in flower, or in the pod, Latin Verse was a compulsory acquirement. So it was at Toronto when the University began, a compulsory matriculation subject. After a while they dropped it as a compulsory subject but it still hung around the old gateway for years and years like a faithful old dog, wagging its tail to attract a few students. I happen to be the last living student who ever took it at matriculation, to wit in 1887, the examination paper being still there in the records to prove it. The verse that I and my fellow-students wrote sounded, I admit, like coupling up freight cars. But we did it for its own sake as we were only just learning that round a college you must only take things which 'count', things for which you are 'liable'. In my McGill teaching days I have noted students ask whether they were 'liable' to the French Revolution or rejoice that they were 'not responsible' for Chaucer. What I want to do in this article is to make them liable to sedimentary rocks and responsible for the origin of species.

Let me quote a concrete example to show the odd historical changes of our school and college studies. Here on the one hand is the matriculation requirement of the University of Toronto in 1851, and on the other the programme of the Sixth Form studies of Upper Canada College – that is, of the boys who were going to matriculate.

Matriculation into the Faculty of Arts at Toronto, from the report of the 'Caput' – (a piece of gratuitous scholarship) – as printed in Appendix I.I.I. to the journals of the legislative Assembly of Canada, 1851. Homer, *Iliad*, Books I, VI; Lucan, *Charon, Vita* and *Simon*; Virgil, *Aeneid*, Book II and VI; Horace, *Odes*, Book V; Sallust, *Catilina*; Ovid, *Fasti*. Translation into Latin Verse and Prose. Mathematics, Algebra, Elementary Rules to Quadratic Equations; Euclid, Books I, II, III, IV: Definitions of Book V, Book VI.

That's it and that's the whole of it. One observes with amazement the attitude of mind involved. These are the things that the matriculant *must know*. There was no harm in his knowing something of history or English or French – or even of the fear of God – it wouldn't hurt him. But this was the qualification for matriculation, this unadulterated mass of Latin and Greek and the mathematics that neither scholarship, nor stupidity, nor divinity had ever been able to kill . . . To some of us it looks like a bag of sawdust.

Here on the other hand is the new programme of Upper Canada College, the grand old school on King St that Sir John Colborne founded in 1829 as the successor to the old 'grammar school' on Church St. He took its original programme of studies from the old Elizabethan school (1563) to 'Sarnia' – not our Sarnia of today but the island with that Latin name, the Channel Island distorted into Guernsey. Colborne had been Governor of Guernsey before he came to Canada and the naming of Sarnia was a compliment to him.

That was the original programme. But now in 1851 they drew up a new one, for the moment it was singularly auspicious. Upper Canada College had now just been broken away (Act of 1849) from the old 'King's College' (once in Queen's Park; too religious to survive) which had controlled its studies. A committee of the Principal and some enthusiastic 'old pupils' (they didn't call them 'old boys' then; they weren't old enough for that) worked out the new programme and laid it, a labour of love, before the Legislative Assembly to be duly preserved in Appendix I.I.I. (In those simple days they called the first Appendix, or sessional paper as now known, A, and the next B, and on to Z; then they began again with AA, BB, . . . to ZZ.; then if there was any more to say it was AAA, BBB, etc. It's a good plan; done like that (statistics never need stop).

Here is the programme, and – as that man in the States says – believe it or not.

Proposed Course of Education in Upper Canada College, Aug. 6, 1851. Sixth Form. Scripture; Map of Palestine – Greek Testament – Arithmetic, same as Fifth Form, with Allegation and Simple and Double Position – Mental Arithmetic – Euclid, Books IV and VI with Definitions of V – Shakespeare – Burke on the Sublime and English Composition – Algebra – Homer, *Iliad*, Book IV, and *Odyssey*, Book IX – Lucian (life) – Xenophon, *Anabasis* with retranslation – Cicero, *Oratio in Catilinam* and retranslation – Horace, *Odes*, III – Livy – Geometrical Drawing – Latin Grammar, kept up – Greek Grammar to end of ¾ of Book – French, same as Fifth Form with Henriade and ½ History of France – Dictation – Anthon's *Latin Versification* – Arnold's *Latin Prose Composition* (pp. 163–260), Arnold's *Greek Prose Composition*, second ⅓ of the Book – Light and Optics (Comstock's *Philosophy* (pp. 209–72) – Elocution Reader, Vaudenhoff – Modern Geography (America and Africa) – Physical Geography, Somerville, pp. 158–254 – Ancient Geography and History (Putey, pp. 1–96) – Greek Versification – Smith's Antiquities (Third ¼ of the Book) – Music – Singing – Ornamental Drawing.

It looks unbelievable, doesn't it? You wouldn't think anybody could know all that; neither would I, except that I learnt it all in 1886–7. The programme was a little changed by then; some of it never 'got by'; some gradually got left off. What happened was that if the university tacked on a subject to compulsory matriculation the school kept it. If not, do what you might, it faded out. When I was at Upper Canada music and ornamental drawing were gone – at least were snuffy, optional subjects. Scripture was pretty dead; the First Form had it but the Sixth weren't responsible for it; Anthon and his verse were out. But we had taken on a new cargo of English History (till 1815 only), Trigonometry and German.

The big change was geography – clean gone from its high place; moving downwards form by form, the heart all out of it. It was still needed for High School Entrance, but no one was 'liable to geography' after that. As a consequence the subject had dwindled from its glorious meaning in the days of the Strabos; and the Ptolemys; and Martin Behaim cartographers of the New World. It just meant a map with a list of names, and a master half asleep, or thinking of something else, saying, 'Now then, first boy, name the capes of Europe – Second boy, name the capes of Africa' . . . Funny world we lived in – all colours and capes.

Thus died geography. And now come people and tell us that it isn't dead after all but only asleep a hundred years. It's like the beautiful sleeping princess behind the wood of thorns. And enthusiasts like Professor Griffith Taylor of Toronto are already hacking away at the thorn bushes to get her out; for proof of which I invite any reader to turn to the stimulating pages of some of his papers on the subject: *Structure and Settlement in Canada, The Geographical Approach to European History,* and to his book of 1937, *Environment, Race and Migration.* But finish this article first, because when Professor Taylor and his fellow-workers have rescued the geographical princess, I want to marry her to Darwin, or Lyell, or some of her own contemporaries; I must not say, the First Electric Spark.

I hope that no one will here interrupt, or shall I say, wake up, to tell me that I am proposing to do something that has already been done. I am well acquainted with many of the new books, on both sides of the Atlantic, which expand Geography into something far beyond the old list of capes – which make it as it were a description, illustrated and detailed, of all the world and its people. There has been indeed a notable development of geography as general literature. There is no more fascinating reading than the books dealing with mankind in relation to physical environment, and the animated and detailed description of the uttermost parts of the earth that go with them. One thinks here of the work of Professor Elsworth Huntington, . . . E. C. Semple, and H. Jeffreys, the author of *The Earth, its Original and Physical History.*

I freely admit, however, that I find it hard to accept, difficult to swallow, the new term 'ecology' which has come to us with these books. It sounds a little too much like being sick. But this literature at its highest reach is not part of a school or college curriculum but something that comes after it, something which a proper college education should enable one to read. In its lower reach, it appears in works obviously meant as educational. Some of these new books are, I admit excellent: *World Geography for Canadian Schools* (Denton and Lord, 1942), the nearest approach, I know, to what I have in mind but still without enough segregated science; or again the widely used *Canadian School Geography* of Professor Cornish (1922). These books are miles ahead of the old Atlas Geographies out of which we used to learn the projecting capes and the coloured counties.

But the difficulty with all such books, admirable though they are, is that they do not attain the goal that might be reached because they lack a full appreciation of what it is. Thus for want of a better conscious purpose they are driven towards expanding Geography into cumulated description of what countries are like, and then more description of other countries. It is like the three wishes accorded to the sailor who had saved a fairy's life, and registered as – rum, and then more rum, and as the final wish, after reflection – some more rum. Many geographers never get beyond that, especially when the facile aid of illustration can make a book like a picture film; here, Laplanders in the Snow, there Arabs in the Sun, Pygmies in the equatorial forest, Canadian Lumbermen walking on ten acres of saw-logs, and Constantinople without a saw-log in sight.

Another most plausible expansion is coaxed off into what is called Commercial Geography. This is like letting cattle out into a big pasture; they're off, Heaven knows where – past pictures of the Bank of England, past columns of statistics, lists of exports, description of frozen-meat steamers from Argentine – a mass of stuff which is certainly *information* but doesn't somehow seem to be study.

Here again is '*Human Geography*', the fortunate phrase by good old Jean Brunhes, while still young, so fortunate that he lived on it for the rest of his life. It is marvellous what a good title does; it turns otherwise indifferent people into peasants at a peep show. I am sure that if Dr Cudmore of Ottawa would label his admirable *Year Book*, '*The Pageant of Arithmetic*', it would be a bestseller. So with Jean Brunhes. The appeal of his phrase is so instantaneous that no one stops to ask if there is anything in it. '*Human Geography*' – it sounds as if there must be. But it means too much or too little – mankind on earth? where do you stop? It's like Bob Benchley's remark on India – 'India, what does the name *not* suggest?' To which Benchley himself gives the answer – 'a hell of a lot of things.' But whatever 'Human Geography' and its counterpart 'Ecology' suggest they are certainly not studies for an academic curriculum, least of all to a school.

The proposal I have to make is that of an ordered system of study, what used to be called a *Schema*, as follows:

Geographical Science

I. Astro-Physical Science – The Earth and the Universe.

II. Geology – The Physical Evolution of the Earth.

III. Biology – The Evolution of Life and Man . . . (including Anthropology and Races).

IV. Physical Geography – The surface of the Globe (Climate, Resources, Power).

V, VI, VII, VIII, IX. – Political Geography by Continents (or subdivided some other way).

Looking at these divisions at large one sees the attempt is made to cover a vast ground in a small compass, a thing condemned by certain minds as doomed to failure from the start. My own opinion is exactly to the contrary. I admit that in the actual development of a child's mind from infancy, details come first, generalization later. No child can start with a broad general view of its parents, or a working outline of its nurse. Even when lessons begin it can't start with a preliminary theory of the alphabet but must take it letter by letter. But this stage passes. Later on this process is reversed. The true way to learn history is to begin with the general history of the world – all on one page, learned in an hour; then to pass to an advanced History of the World – ten pages spread over a week, and so on. For all the above subjects the broad view of the total is more interesting, more profitable, more lasting than to begin on one end of a string of details like a goat eating a rope. With some subjects, I admit, it is not possible to begin with a broad view. With Arithmetic most people live and die without ever getting it – indeed are glad to – since it only comes away near the back of the book as the Theory of Numbers.

Nor let it be said that under such a Schema as mine the pupils (we are at school, you note, not college) learn so little of a subject that what they learn is practically useless. This is exactly wrong; it is taken from old adages of the classical scholarship days – 'a little learning is a dangerous thing' – 'learning maketh a full man.' Inspired by such precepts pupils in Latin learned all five declensions and all four conjugations and all the deponent verbs before they learned to say *How d'ye do*? In fact they never said it. The malicious word 'smattering' was invented to warn off amateurs and outsiders from the field of knowledge. As a matter of fact there is nothing like a good smattering of as many things as you can smatter. Any student of living languages knows what a lot you can thus get from a little. Only one subject I admit to be an exception – Chemistry. A little smattering of chemistry might help to blow you up or poison you, that's all. It doesn't help you to live. Chemistry we leave alone. Where chemistry meets life, it joins hands with physics, anyway. As to physics, the working parts of it are, or should be, parts of mathematics. You can work out Galileo's falling stones and Kepler's Areas as mathematics. When we get further on, to the constitution of matter, then Maxwell's Equations, and Plack's Constant and Niel Bohr's hop-skip-and-jump electron are so utterly beyond your reach and mine that we can only take them as read, and ask the ultimate physicist where we are to get off at.

That is what I mean by division I. The structure of the universe – leaving out of it as calmly, as Herbert Spencer left out the Unknowable – the question of how the universe began, and when it's going to stop, and what it is really made of – this structure, I say, can be presented in intelligible useful form – ought to be so presented as part of a decent education. Most geography books do present it, or attempt to, but perhaps in too 'earthly' a fashion, too many tides, too much moon, not enough outer universe. I admit that some books are very good. All of them of necessity run into the difficulty of who made the universe and when? To which the answer seems to be, regretfully, 'Hush – ' or as Amos and Andy say, 'Why bring that up?' Nor will we bring it up here; how to reconcile scientific phenomena with dogmatic interpretation is a problem solved so far only in Tennessee.

But the value of this elementary astro-physical knowledge, and the instinctive recognition of its value, is shown by the increasing popular demand for popular science of the universe. Such titles as the *Mysterious Universe, The Stars in Their Course, An Outline of the Universe, Life on Other Worlds,* run round the English-speaking world. The same uneasy taboo as hushes the teaching of astro-physics warns and whispers in the background of the Divisions of Geology and Biology, and with the same difficulty of solution. But a compromise seems to have been reached whereby if the teachers hurry past 'ultimate beginnings' – as past a graveyard in the dark – they may walk where they will in the daylight beyond. Nor should there be any need to expatiate here on the value of an outline of such studies.

Physical Geography needs no advocacy since it is in the books now. It needs only trimming into form, to fit in with the knowledge already imparted. Political Geography speaks for itself. It is the original geography of kingdoms and republics, their configuration and boundaries, even the *capes*. It deals with the names on the map.

One other division I had planned, but scarcely venture to include – a division of Economic and Social Organization. I deeply distrust it. One would have to be as careful with it as with putting a sleeping draft into a pudding. Political Economy has, quite obviously, turned out to be the Idiot Boy of the Scientific Family; all the more pitiful, as having been so bright at first; put up on a chair to recite by old Dr Adam Smith and Mr Ricardo – and then somehow went wrong; never really grew up though utterly overgrown in the physical sense; sits there and mutters, poor boy, about 'marginal consumption', and 'consumers' increment', and if you don't watch him will try to steal mathematics, actually take a formula and hide it under his chair . . . As to Sociology – there's another disappointment. My Heavens! The girl never stops talking. What about? About anything! She'll start any topic, or you'll start it, and she'll break out into that silly laugh and exclaim, 'Say! that's Sociology, isn't it? Say! I'm going to make a whole book on that. What did you say it was? The influence of the Moon on Digestion! Isn't that bully!'

The only bother is that these two afflicted creatures are sitting on some really good things – such as Transport and Communications, and Mechanical Invention. We'll have to coax them off somehow. We might hunt up some of those big sawdust dolls, empty the classics out and let them fill them with their stuff . . .

However, as Mr Joe Macdougall has said in his *Goblin* poem about the Professor, 'That will be all for today.'

CHAPTER VIII

An Apology for the British Empire

It is related of George III that a learned divine once presented to the King his new volume, *An Apology for the Bible*. 'I did not know,' said the simple monarch, 'that the Bible needed an apology.' It was explained to him that the word *apology* was used in its Greek meaning of a defence. It is in this sense that I want to offer an apology for the British Empire, a humble apology, as coming from a person without rank or honour, neither a statesman nor a general, but just a subject of the King, and glad to be one. Such qualifications as I have to voice the apology rest upon an English childhood, a lifetime mostly spent in Canada but with much knowledge at first hand of the other Dominions, as of the United States.

There has been of late some queer talk and odd misunderstanding about the British Empire. Mr Churchill has found it necessary to explain that we are not liquidating the Empire after the war. Others, on the contrary, have suggested that the parts of the Empire unable to look after themselves should be put under 'international control'. This is a status, a strait-jacket, entirely fitted for blood-crazy Germans and treacherous 'wops', but scarcely for the people living in peace in the open freedom of the Empire.

Nor do we want to be internationalized, any of us, in the Empire; I don't and the Canadians don't, and the Nigerian boys don't, nor the Cingalese, nor the Bahamians nor the shepherds that watch their flocks on the windswept Falkland Islands – none of us. How would you like international control for the United States? – or even for Chicago?

* * *

Such a notion can only come from a very feeble understanding of what the Empire is and does.

The British Empire covers about one-quarter of the globe (13,353,000 square miles) and includes about one-quarter (525,000,000) of its inhabitants. It's a pity it's not bigger. It is made up of a group of six Associated Commonwealths and about fifty, more or less, dependent areas.

Constitutionally the Empire is supposed to be held together by the

Statute of Westminster, a British imperial statute of 1931. But that's just a suppose. In reality it is just held together by a vast gentlemen's agreement, and in the case of Ireland it isn't even gentlemanly.

The Statute of Westminster indeed is just a myth, a sort of idealization of unity or reality otherwise created. We keep it just as the Nigerian savages keep a wooden God with big glass eyes in the half-dark of a grass bungalow. People shake when they go in. So do our lawyers. But in plain logic the Statute won't stand overhauling. It was passed by the British Parliament in 1931, after advice from an Imperial Conference, and then sent on to the Dominions. So far it has never been accepted, not on its face value. Australia never ratified it; meant to and never has yet. There seemed something fishy about it, some trick in it. So in twelve years they haven't touched it. South Africa ratified it, yes indeed, they ratified the life out of it, with a local statute that ripped it to pieces. Canada didn't formally ratify it, but accepted it, took it as read, till they found that if it went into force it would tie up Canada hand and foot with no supreme public authority left. We can only amend our Constitution by an imperial statute, in other words, by calling the Westminster Statute off. Newfoundland, shivering and starving with the depression, accepted the Statute and then gave up Dominion Status (1935) and crawled back into its little old colonial cot where it had slept since 1583. Ireland, call it Eire, if you know how, never even looked at the Statute of Westminster. They made a Constitutional Amendment Act of their own (1936). By this the British King is King of Ireland, but not King of Ireland in Ireland, only outside of it. To find the solution turn to the back of the book.

That's the sole connection of Ireland with the Empire, except its language. Even as to that, they're working hard to restore the old Gaelic. If they're not careful, they'll learn to speak it and then they'll be sorry.

I forgot – one Dominion ratified the Statute, New Zealand. But any British person, knowing New Zealand, would take that for granted. Down there they ratify anything as soon as they see the British trade mark. New Zealand is New Britain, about 150 per cent. British. Same size of islands (110,000 sq. miles), upside down in the Pacific instead of right side up in the Atlantic. Same people exactly, English and Scots, with enough Irish to make an Irish vote, a thing you have to have in any British country, like pepper in a soup. In a population of 1,600,000 we may leave out the 80,000 native Maoris – great fellows, all admit, a big asset in any trouble. *A! Kia! Kia!* Come on, boys! Climate just the same as 'at home', plenty of rough snow for the Scots down south, rain for the Irish and for the English, meadow-land beside willows, and cricket and the bells of the Church of England . . .

So that's the way the major parts of the Empire, the Associated

Commonwealth, hang together – associated under the same King. In reality, not quite even that, for they have to accept him separately. As a matter of fact King George VI didn't begin to reign in England till he had been reigning for a day already in South Africa and in Ireland he didn't reign for another day after that.

The Crown is the imperial link. Legally there is no other except, oddly enough, that Canada keeps up the appeal from its own law courts to the final decision of the British Privy Council in London. We get better justice. It must be better because it costs ten times as much, as our lawyers assure us on their return from pleading.

Associated also under the British Crown are all kinds of areas – islands, colonies, naval and military stations, protectorates, all round the globe. It's hard to count them: some are half in the Empire and half out. But they number about sixty units of government. At first sight they seem to defy classification, but when you look close they seem to represent a beautiful symmetry of structure according to how much, how little, or how not at all, they govern themselves. Canada governs itself. So does Southern Rhodesia – almost– the Governor, the Ministerial Cabinet and everything, look like real, but in reality certain ground is 'reserved.' Nearly as much, not quite, the Bahamas (West Indies, class I, Partly White) – a parliament, but the cabinet not exactly a cabinet. Vote granted to all who have a very small property qualification. Most haven't.

And so you pass on down through the grades and degrees till you come to the great protectorates of the tropics, the places where white men cannot live.

Take one as a sample . . .

Here is Nigeria. It is a vast tropical river country sunk in the hollow side of West Africa, a huge place, with low coasts all surf and foam, swamps, jungles, fever and the sleeping-sickness, then dense equatorial forests, then wide plains of grass, on into the heart of Africa to die in the desert. Nigeria covers half a million square miles – more than the whole Atlantic seaboard of the United States. There is a native population of 25,000,000 people. The climate never varies, each day awful. White people cannot *live* there; those who survive go home. This was the famous Bight of Benin where 'for one that comes out there were ten who went in.'

And how many white people do you suppose 'hold down' this vast protectorate of 25,000,000 people? About two or three hundred. There are in all 5,000 whites but a large proportion of these are missionaries, nurses and teachers, holding down a job, not a country, along with the clerks and traders of the steamship companies and the Staff of Government House. The whole Nigerian national defence (pre-war) consisted of three guns (3½ inches each), four battalions of infantry, one mortar and a signal-school class. But even at that the whole army is black, anyway, except the officers and those who have to use signals in the dark. That's how Nigeria is 'held down' by imperialism. In other words the people of Nigeria could rise up and kill all the whites in one day. But why should they? So could the people of Omaha Nebraska, rise up and kill all the commercial travellers. But I doubt if they would care to.

How was this vast undisturbed rule brought about? It was like this. The British are terribly lazy about fighting. They like to get it over and done with and then get up a game of cricket. In the tropics cricket is played on coconut matting. Well, Nigeria grows one-half of the world's coconuts. So there you are! What with playing cricket and learning how to mix a gin fizz and to tie on one-piece, two-leg cotton pants, the place was civilized in no time. Not quite, of course. The British took away all the brutalities of savagery – the hideous human sacrifices of Ashanti – and left only its pleasant sides, such as polygamy. Cannibalism went right out as soon as the American canned food came in.

The Government! – yes, there's a real Government House at Lagos with all the forms that go with it, but mostly the Nigerians, those inland, govern themselves under their own chiefs, Emirs and such. All the revenue raised in taxes wouldn't keep Chicago going for six months. As to religion it's entirely free, but Mohammedanism beats Christianity to a standstill. Yet the few Christian converts are full of zeal, expecting the day of judgement any time, and all set for it with music.

Some natives, it must be admitted, want a change. They have had enough education to look around and compare other countries. They want to be like Canada: you can hardly blame them. So they talk in a vague way of a great Gold Coast Nation under the British flag – by taking in all the other odd lots between the Congo and Senegal. It may come some day, or something like it, but meantime this is not a political scheme, just a forlorn African fancy, like the Golden Gates and the Year of Jubilo! Longfellow's dreaming slave came from the Gold Coast.

Now, can any sane person think of setting up a European International Committee – of Dagos, Wops and Slats – to look after Nigeria! And if 'International' means British, we've got it already. If it means American and British, that's all right if they promise not to introduce baseball – after all, we saw them first.

Nigeria is just one of ever so many such areas, great and small. It is the biggest of them next to India but the pattern is the same all the globe round.

India is of course the Empire's problem. By all means give it self-government. But how do you do it? You can't start self-government with a civil war. In the United States there was a century between the Stamp Act and the Civil War. But imagine the situation if the North and the South had been all ready to start the Civil War as soon as Independence was granted. That's India. There is no such thing as the Indian nation. There are in India over 200 nations, as distinguished by distinct languages. The great mass of the Moslem races cannot tolerate the Hindu races, nor the Hindus the Moslems. The Hindus think the Moslems rough and uncultivated, people of physical force and not of the spirit. The Moslems think the Hindus a set of flabby intellectuals, not men at all. It's the difference between football players and divinity students. We have it in all the colleges. The football teams would liquidate the divinity students, only they're not allowed to. That's India. While the British stay, liquidation can't start.

An American lawyer would say, Federate India. You can't. It won't. Inside the Moslems the Sikhs refuse any rule but British. No 'pakistan' for them. All through Hindu India are the cast-out people, the 'untouchables,' the 60,000,000 people that the rest won't eat with, from whose hands they will not even take water. Are they to be slaves? You can't talk freedom to men who treat 60,000,000 others as dogs.

There is no union in India but the British Raj and the English language and the imported British transport and industrialism. India is a misfit. It was old when England began, full when England was empty, and fallen asleep over dead books when England learned to read with Shakespeare and think with Newton.

Except to Great Britain India has no meaning for the Empire, no cohesion nor even any commercial interest. To us in Canada it is utterly alien. We would never dream of letting in Indians, touchable or untouchable. We forbid their immigration, not by law but a lawyer's trick. In Australia they forbid it flat out. South Africa let them in till they began to swamp Natal, then shut the door. In all goodwill there can be no co-operation between India and the Dominions except by and through and because of Britain. Cut that out and it's all gone.

What can be done about India? International Control by a Committee? They have 222 nations already. Anyway, they'd only send Mr Gandhi in a loincloth to lie down and die on the committee's door-step – it's called Swa-raj, or Swa-slush, or something. There's no answer. We always pick Gandhi up – and feed him.

There is nothing to be done but wait. If and when the people in India agree, all of them, or most of them, on what they want, and cut out the hideous untouchable stuff – then, I am sure, they can have Dominion Government tomorrow.

So India must for the present stay as it is. You can't have a free, united state till you have first a free, united people. At present the Indians in India won't let one another be that.

India must stay and the Empire must stay. You can't mark it out with rule and compass as we mark out on the flat ground of empty prairie an Oklahoma or an Alberta before it is there. Such places can begin with a ready-made constitution put up over them like a circus tent – you can't do that with older places. The Empire is a long produce of history. It began as a mixed result of national defence and plundering the Spanish Main. It was hard to tell a patriot from a pirate. Some were both. Then it shifted into adventure and commerce and refugee settlement. Puritans sang in the wilderness, till they were too busy with business and stopped singing. Empire wars with France and Spain came and went, accepted like rounds in a prize-fight. Then came the Independence of America. We are just getting over it after 100 years. That started Australia and New Zealand.

The first Great War of 1793–1815 brought in more colonies than they could use. They gave back some, like Argentina. Then followed the wonderful era of free trade with all men brothers, too good to be true – there weren't enough brothers. Then the scramble to partition Africa and Asia and everything left over. That's when many people first learned the word imperialism and learned to hate it. But that is half a century ago, as long ago and as far away as Rudyard Kipling's Mandalay.

That's not the Empire today. We know better now. The Empire to-day means co-operation of hundreds of millions of people not on equal terms, but on decent terms. What would have been a hundred discordant states, each a powerless prey for rapacity to destroy, has turned to the united buttresses that held alone a while the falling walls of a broken world.

We prefer to keep all this going under a set of medieval forms and observances, offices and dignities that sound as the very converse of popular liberty and equality. We pretend that the King is an absolute sovereign, and to make him look like it we surround him with Beefeaters, Lords of the Buckhounds, Norroy Kings-at-Arms, a Poursuivant Unicorn, Red Dragon and an officer of the Black Rod. These are all actual offices, but in reality these people are as harmless as a pack of cards, ranking somewhere below a full house. And with that we have Dukes and Earls who pay feudal homages, giving the King dead birds once a year, other offices all gone except the salary, and salaries all gone except the office, and an official list of precedence – it is a fact – that distinguishes seventy-one classes of British subjects before it even lets in Gentlemen. The point of it all is that it works. People like a bit of humbug. If a reader of this book heard that the King had appointed him Keeper of the Swans, he'd be all over town with it in a minute.

That's the way we run the Empire. Now send us along that International Committee and we'll invite them to a cricket match, and let them see all Australia beat half England, have a gin-fizz with the Archbishop of Canterbury and go home.

CHAPTER IX

Britain and Canada

Old Phases and New

Many of us are wishing now that we had learned more while we were still at school about the British Empire and how it is made up and how it works. Our recollection of the old school geography doesn't help us much. We recall a picture of the solar system in full swing, with a huge earth sweeping around an insignificant sun, and after that the names of the counties of Ontario and the capes of North America. But indeed the whole vast system which we call the British Empire presents in its structure such a mass of oddities and inconsistencies that not even the lawyers can understand it. Is it one solid unit, or just a collection of units, 'freely associating' while they care to, and off somewhere else when they are ready to? There is supposed to be at the centre of it a body called the Privy Council, or more properly the Judicial Committee of the Privy Council, to decide all cases that arise in regard to the laws and constitutions of the Empire. This is a very pleasant thing for the lawyers, as they have to take long trips at someone else's expense (lawyers never travel on their own) from various parts of the Empire to see what the Privy Council thinks of some contested case. As a matter of fact, the Privy Council, made of wise, experienced men, far too wise to think on their own account, merely whisper to the visiting lawyers, 'What do they think about the matter over in your country?' and they say, 'Well, that's what we think too . . .' As a matter of fact, some parts of the Empire, namely Eire (don't call it Ireland) and South Africa, no longer consent to appeal to the Privy Council – which is a pity as they lose a lot of goodwill and friendly intercourse.

But, in reality, the British Empire doesn't hang together by any set of hard and fast statutes, such as the Statute of Westminster (1931) that everybody talks about and nobody understands. This statute was passed by the British parliament and declares, practically in the same breath, that the Empire is permanent and that it can be dissolved at will. Nor need the Americans laugh at this, since it is practically what their Constitution said from 1789 till 1865 about the relation of the States to the Federal Government. It took a whole Civil War to find out what it did mean.

We've learned, with the help of this American experience, a better system of dealing with our imperial constitution. We don't ask what it *means*; we just take it as a sort of gentlemen's agreement. There are certain things which it is 'the thing' to do, and others that you simply 'don't do' because it's not 'the thing' to do them. It's like cricket – which many of you Canadians have now seen as played in England. When we play it in my home town of Orillia, or yours of Sussex, New Brunswick, or Red Deer, Alberta, there's lots of fighting and disputes in it, almost as good as American baseball, with argument and tumult around the umpire, so that you can't see which one he is till they carry him off the field. But in England cricket is cricket; you mustn't dispute or argue. It's not 'the thing'. If you're fielding at square leg (ask the nearest Englishman where that is) and you get a paste with the ball in the pit of the stomach, you mustn't complain; you must just say, 'Sorry, old man.' That's addressed to the bowler. Ask the Englishman why you say you're sorry for his sake; it wasn't his stomach.

What I am really trying to say is that all government rests, not on codes and laws (those are for criminals), but on decency, kindly feeling and a proper idea of the merits and rights and the good sides of others. This is especially true of our British Empire. We couldn't live a day without it. You should carry the idea up to the verge of truth, and for the sake of good fellowship, even a little beyond. I've had the good luck to see a great many parts of the British Empire and I make it a rule to praise it all. If a man says he comes from Jamaica, I say, 'And, now there's an island! . . . if you like . . .' So it is; it's an island. And if a man tells me he's from Western Australia, I say, 'My! my! What country, especially up island past Calgourlie! How fertile! I've seen a cabbage growing there in the open without support . . .' And for Prince Albert, Saskatchewan, 'Ah, now there's a climate for you! Never cold; that is, never *severely* cold; never far below zero – in summer . . .'

Nor do I say this to try to be funny. I mean it in earnest. And when you've done with your fellow Britisher, use it on an American and tell him that Nevada is your idea of a summer resort.

But just now we're to talk only of Britain and Canada and to illustrate various imperial phases through them. You may notice at once the difficulty, as all throughout the Empire, of finding suitable names. Britain. Where's that? When I was young, there was no such place outside of a poetry book. We always used to say 'England' – to mean in a general sense – well, whatever 'Britain' means now. A poet of the Crimean War days could write, 'One more gone for England's sake, where so many go,' though perhaps the man fallen in the snow was a Scotchman; and a learned professor could write a whole book called *The Expansion of England*, as if Ireland and Scotland hadn't swelled up, too.

Presently the other parts of – well, of what they are all parts of – got touchy about it. They wouldn't be called 'England' any more. The Channel Islands were especially bitter. They considered that they had conquered England under their own Duke in 1066 and that England was therefore an annex of the Channel Islands. Believe it or not, this fiction was actually kept up till 1914; the British parliament didn't legislate for the Islands and had no power there except through the King – but not as King – as ex-Duke of Normandy. This fairyland fell under the shadow of the 1914–18 War Income Tax.

But what name could be used? 'Great Britain' leaves out Ireland. 'British Isles' won't fit in ordinary sentences. The 'United Kingdom' is a law term. So now we say 'Britain'; when we get settled to it; we shall talk of taking a trip to 'Britain,' which in my youth would have sounded like going to 'Caledonia' or running over to 'Erin'.

The name 'Canada' used to be just as bad but is now pretty well straightened out. Nobody knows where it came from. When Jacques Cartier came up the St Lawrence in 1535 on his way to McGill University (then called Hochelaga), he came to the great river that we call Saguenay – in fact, the Indians told him that up this and beyond it, farther west, was the kingdom of Saguenay, full of gold and diamonds; they were right in a way. Savage legend always has a background. They meant the Hollinger mine, and God's Lake and FlinFlon, the legend of gold and silver beyond the divide, which later turned out to be true. But they told Cartier, also, that if he went on up the river he would come to 'Canada', and when he got to where Quebec is they said, 'This is Canada and beyond it is Hochelaga' (corner of McGill College Avenue and Burnside) . . . What did the name mean? We don't know. Some said it was Algonquin *Kanata* – the narrows; some said it was Algonquin *Kanada* – a collection of wigwams. Later someone made a joke, 'It's Spanish *Aca-Nada*' – meaning 'nothing there.' That joke got into the schoolbooks of my youth as dead earnest (the education department in Ontario was Scotch) and stayed there. So we don't know. The French called the country *New France* – a name that was, so to speak, spilt on the American coast (1524) by Verrazano (he never landed north of New Hampshire), and then picked up again by Chaplain. It was the official name of the country till the Conquest, but by about the year 1700 people commonly used 'Canada' and even put it in official correspondence.

After the cession of 1763, the British government adopted the name '*Quebec*' for its new possession, the reason being that General Amherst and General Murray both declared that they couldn't find out just how much territory the French meant by Canada. So Quebec it was, on a small scale, till 1774, and then it was the huge Quebec of the Quebec Act of that year, which reached from the Gulf of St Lawrence to the Mississippi, and took in Chicago, what there was of it to take – mudflats, reeds and an Indian Portage – and perhaps a Rotary Club.

The schoolbooks may have led you to think that France and England fought for the possession of Canada (1754–63). They didn't. They weren't thinking of it. They were fighting, so to speak, for the United States, for the marvellous Ohio territory just being revealed in all its park-land fertility. After the war the English didn't want Canada particularly, to which fact we owe a great deal of the freedom of our present institutions and especially the privileges of church and speech and nationality extended to French Canada, which alone made possible our Confederation.

A lot of the silly nonsense talked about Canada as a land of desolation began right then and has kept up till today. Voltaire's sneer about 'the snow' passed down in history, and people forgot the last, wistful phrase of the departing Governor Vaudreuil, 'a vast and beautiful country . . .'

But I was talking of the name. 'Canada' never got on the map till England decided to keep it and use it, after the loyalists came in, to name Upper and Lower Canada (now Ontario and Quebec) in 1791, and after that, in 1841, when they united the two together as the Province of Canada. That lasted till 1867 when the name 'Canada' was used to cover all British North America – yes, all, because New Newfoundland was invited in. But even long after that, forty years after that, people in the Maritimes used the term 'Canada' to mean a separate place; within my own recollection – and mind you, I'm not even eighty – I've heard Nova Scotia people say they had never been in 'Canada' . . . That's changed now. So, too, with the North-West. 'Canada' meant another country from their own till after 1869 . . . And with British Columbia till 1871 . . . The name triumphs now; it reaches from the forty-ninth parallel to the North Pole, in a long sort of wedge like a slice of orange peel. We own more of the North Pole than any other nation, except the Russians.

Even these casual references to history show something about where we got our relationships with Britain. Pretty thin they were at first. We 'owned' the Maritimes (the huge Nova Scotia that reached to what was called Massachusetts) as far back as 1713. But what there was of them was all French. Then as the shadow of a new war fell, things began to happen. The British government deliberately founded Halifax so as to have a real footing in Nova Scotia, founded it mostly with old soldiers, all pipeclay and mitred helmets (see Mr Jefferys' picture of the Foundation), but so unhandy on the land they couldn't even grow cabbages. So for that the government of England sent out a set of distressed Germans and located them at Lunenburg in Nova Scotia. There were always 'distressed Germans' in those days, ready to be sent out to America. I forget what they were distressed about; something pretty tough, I hope.

Every mother and every mother country has a favourite child. Now Halifax, all hearty British as compared with the West Indies, all black, and with the American plantations, fractious and bothersome, was the favourite child of the mother country. And so the law officers of the Crown decided (that is, somebody whispered it to them) that the settlers had an inherent British right to an elected assembly. They got it in 1758 and that became, and is, one of the great precedents of the British imperial system . . .

The dark side of this picture, the reverse of this bright medal, was the forcible moving out, the expulsion of the Arcadian French of Nova Scotia, some 6,000 of them, shipped away, some here, some there, with no compensation for their land or their stock. It makes bad reading. The British government tried to plead that the imminence of a new war made these people a danger, as they might fight on the side of France. One hopes they would have. But tears have fallen for nearly a century over the pages of Longfellow's *Evangeline* which chronicles their fate.

That much there was of British . . . and out in the West the wide sovereignty of the Hudson's Bay Company, under their Charter of 1670, covered all the watershed of Hudson Bay, and, by extension, all the Pacific coast, over two million square miles . . . It was all called Rupert's Land then (after the wonderful Prince Rupert who founded the Company). The name lasted officially till 1869. It only survives now in the name of the Province of Rupert's Land. But the North-West – the common name for it – was far more Scotish than English. The Company's vessels sailed from London around Scotland to the Bay. Most of their men on the ships and at the forts were Scots – islanders at that. The canoemen and servants were French, or French half-breed Métis. The language of the West was French and Indian Cree, with Scottish for the parlour . . . The West was empty till 1870. The Roman poet Virgil said that to found the Roman Empire was *tanta molis* – Latin for 'a hell of a business.' But he'd never seen Canada.

Through this maze of history, where did our government come in? Where did we get those privileges, presently rights, that gradually removed us from the control of Great Britain? As usual with British people, much of it was accident, much of it was done by the Turkish system óf doing nothing, and much of it, most of it, a result of that inherent 'decency' towards other people and towards those who can't hit back, that is the characteristic of the free government that grew up under British and American democracy. This democracy has not been the result of theory but of instinct and temperament; the fact came first and the theory afterwards. It is always thus; professors of theory merely hold postmortems.

With us in Canada the sequence of development in our relations with Britain ran like this: The grant of freedom of religion to the Roman Catholic French in Canada (1763) gave it, of necessity, to all Roman Catholics. In England they didn't have it till the emancipation of 1829. When the Loyalists came in (1784 and on), they had to have representative assemblies by virtue of the Halifax precedent and by what they had left at home. Here began Upper Canada's first government under Governor Simcoe. We may admit that Simcoe made it as aristocratic as he could; his little parliament at Niagara was all feathers, forms, uniforms, salutes of guns and speeches from the throne – in fact, just like 'home'. From him and from his senior, Lord Dorchester, we carried down a lot of those queer formalities of government that mean so little to the cynic, so much to the Philosopher. But aristocracy wouldn't work in Upper and Lower Canada (1791–1841). It broke down under the Rebellion of 1837, after which the British government hanged the rebels and adopted their programme. That gave the united province of Canada (1841–67) responsible government with a cabinet of its own, so that it controlled everything except foreign policy trade and navigation, etc. – all local things. Old-fashioned Tories, like the Duke of Wellington, were reported 'thunderstruck' when they heard of giving a colony its own government. But old-fashioned Tories always are thunderstruck. That's how they live; indignation keeps them warm. Cabinet government for the Province of Canada gave it automatically to the Maritimes.

Cabinet government failed to work in the province of Canada, because the parties simply couldn't get a majority that was a majority in each section (Canada East and West) and of each race, and also of the whole.

Hence the plan of a wide union of all British North America. Everybody had talked of this for years as an ideal. But ideals never come true till something else happens. It was the American Civil War, that and the naughty Fenians who grew out of it, that chased all the scattered British North American Colonies into Confederation like chickens into a coop. Great Britain was the mother hen herding them in, with a peck here and a push there – a railway for Nova Scotia, a railway for B.C. –

and free leave for them all to divide up the Hudson's Bay Company's land . . . In they came, and they couldn't get out.

Confederation in 1867, however, was on a different footing from our present relations. The British soldiers were still here till 1871; the British Navy at Halifax and Esquimalt till 1903. All foreign policy was managed from Downing Street – no Canadian ambassadors or ministers – treaties all made for us, though a Canadian might be invited to 'sit in' and see it done, as Sir John A. Macdonald at the Washington Treaty of 1871. We couldn't even hang our own criminals at first (not till 1878), as the fountain of mercy only flowed from Downing Street through the Governor-General. But now the Minister of Justice runs the fountain from his own tap of tears.

So it was with all of it. Bit by bit the special reservations, treaty powers, etc., all wore away. The Red River Rebellion of 1869 was put down (frightened away) by mingled imperial regulars and Canadian militia. The Rebellion of 1885 was put down with all-Canadian forces, with only an imperial general running up and down to show them how – or how not, I forget which . . . A string of Imperial Conferences presently turned the chief colonies into Dominions, and by the Great War of 1914 they were practically as free as Great Britain itself.

But the real thing was that Canada outgrew the idea of its own inferiority to Britain that had vexed its earlier years. No doubt the mingling of population in the great immigration (1900–13) helped a lot by welding into the structure of the Dominion the temper of American and Scandinavian people – some newcomers, we may admit, didn't help much and in some spots the thing was overdone, but in the main it helped to make a greater Canadian self-reliance. Other things helped also, other aspects of culture. British scholarship and learning; Latin and Greek, the seniority and sneeriority of Oxford, the dead weight of the classical tradition, sat heavy on the chest of Canadian academic aspiration. Ask any of us who spent years and years of study to get a B.A. degree at Toronto or Queens in the early 'nineties, only to find that a better B.A. (in the world's eyes) could be got at Oxford in less time on brandy and soda. They had other degrees, too, I admit. This burden sat until presently it got heaved off by the rise of the great practical science schools in Canada, McGill and others, with all the water-power of a continent thundering in their ears, with mines and mountains for geologists to rifle . . . schools, beside which the practical science schools of England were nursery games. Soon after 1900, hundreds of British students came over to 'get science' in Canada as humbly as Canadian students went to pick up crumbs of Greek under the Oxford table . . .

But at this point, with a lot still to say about British and Canadian culture, I must close. As the professors say to their classes, 'that will be all for today,' expecting a deep sigh.

CHAPTER X

This Business of Prophecy

I used to go in a great deal for prophecy. I found it safer and easier than fact, and more impressive. During my long years of lecturing at McGill I used to say to my classes, 'Mark my words, gentlemen, in another fifty years you will see –' so and so; or, 'Mark me, gentlemen, in another half-century you will see the end of' – of pretty well everything. The students were tremendously impressed. They didn't see how I could see it all coming. They just lived on the hope of it.

The only mistake was that I made the prophecies too short. They'll soon fall due. I began in 1901 and the first of the prophecies will come round in 1951. It is true that a great many of the older students have dropped out. Even those left begin to look pretty shaky. So I guess it will be all right. Yet it was timed too close. I wouldn't do it again.

But in any case, I have gone out of the prophecy business. Too many people are crowding into it, people without experience. And it is a thing that demands long preparation. Look at those prophets of the Old Testament. They were mature men, five to six hundred years old, with a bombing range of three thousand years.

But now everybody's in it. Why, only yesterday at my club a man told me to mark him that the world would be an absolutely different place after the war. I marked him right away (with a piece of billiard chalk) but I doubt if I can find him again – after the war.

That's it, all the time – after the war. They're prophesying and planning all the big things that are going to be done after the war. It seems that the whole framework of society has got to be reconstructed – from top to bottom, or from bottom to top. Some will begin one end, some the other. Fascinating, isn't it? In fact some of us can hardly wait till the war is over, and would end it right now so as to get at this post-war stuff. It seems that we've been living in the wrong ideology – I think that's it. Anyway, it's all got to change.

Naturally the biggest thing of all is the question of the future of Europe. We have simply got to consider what that is to be. In fact it is a thing that should have been attended to long ago. Only last week I heard two men discussing quite eagerly, indeed almost angrily, whether Europe after the war is to be a federation, or just a loose conglomerate under a guarantee of conglomeration. It is a thing you have to face. These two men were going to a meeting (I was so sorry I couldn't go) where they were to thresh this out. They said that after the discussion the future of Europe would probably be thown open to the audience. That was nice, wasn't it? I forgot to look in the paper to see what happened; often so much war stuff gets into the papers that you miss the news.

But anyway what is needed here is one of those big general polls of public opinion that show exactly what is going to be, or rather, the percentage of everything that is going to be. A lot of us would like to see the future of Europe put to a poll that way, along the lines (1) Future, (2) No future, (3) Any damn future. I'll bet you it would show Europe 62 per cent, or say 63, conglomerated. That's what I'd do with it. Of course there would be the usual 17 per cent 'indifferent'. Those fellows should keep out of the poll. If they don't care, why do they vote? In fact, the real trouble with these polls is that the very people whose opinions we don't want in the poll are the kind of people who give their opinions, and those we do, don't, if you see what I mean. If we could get the solid thought of the country to think it would be better.

* * *

But there are big things to plan for at home, too. Take education, one of the biggest. They are saying that after the war education will have to be reconstructed from top to bottom. They say it won't be recognizable. You won't be able to tell whether a man is educated or not. It seems there are a lot of committees, some of the biggest educationalists in the country, sitting on it already. One committee is sitting on arithmetic, and working on the multiplication table. They're up to nine times nine, already. They may scrap the rest. Another is working on long division; it's too long for them.

But of course the biggest post-war thing of all is the reconstruction of the cities. I imagine that that question has come up everywhere. I know that with us in my city it is the most acute problem of all and there's no use ending the war till we solve it. There's no doubt our city has got to go; it's no darned use; the streets all run the wrong way and cross one another. Indeed the only thing to do with it is to knock it all down, and shovel it away. When I look at my own house I just want to take a spade and knock it down flat. The thing is worthless; the upstairs ought to be downstairs. Anybody can see that now. And it's the same way with all the apartment buildings. That's the fascination of city planning. You see it all so clearly when you see it. You see, in practically all the apartments, the bottom floor should be the top one – to get proper light.

Anyway, in our city we all see eye to eye about it, though in different directions. I see my own house best. However, we've got a committee of experts working on it and they are beginning right at the beginning, at the very foundation, of reconstruction – drainage. Are we draining properly? And after that leakage, and then seepage and then garbage. We had a big man here a week or two back tackling garbage. He was certainly right up in it. He's been invited to talk elsewhere. That's the way with these experts; they know their stuff.

But of course it all takes time and spade-work. One of our speakers put it pretty neatly the other day, by saying you can't rebuild without spade-work. That seems to put in a nutshell or at any rate in a steam shovel.

The only trouble is the time. It would never do to have the war end on us and the city still right here.

Then there's post-war finance, I suppose the nation's greatest problem of the lot. But here the biggest experts, on the biggest salaries, seem to be pretty well agreed; after the war we must keep right on with big expenditure and high salaries for fear of a collapse. It seems that quite apart from the other allies, the United States and Great Britain and Canada are spending 365 billion dollars a year. That means a billion dollars a day and, spread out among the 200 million of us it means five dollars a day each. I just can't think now how I'll spend mine. How about a trip to Japan?

So you see with all these fascinating post-war problems to think about, you can't blame people if the war news sometimes seems a little dull. There is so much to plan and so little time. I hope those who are fighting won't stop till we get our ideology ready.

Twenty
My Remarkable Uncle

The most remarkable man I have ever known in my life was my uncle, Edward Philip Leacock – known to ever so many people in Winnipeg fifty or sixty years ago as E.P. His character was so exceptional that it needs nothing but plain narration. It was so exaggerated already that you couldn't exaggerate it.

When I was a boy of six, my father brought us, a family flock – to settle on an Ontario farm. We lived in an isolation unknown, in these days of radio, anywhere in the world. We were thirty-five miles from a railway. There were no newspapers. Nobody came and went. There was nowhere to come and go. In the solitude of the dark winter nights the stillness was that of eternity.

Into this isolation there broke, two years later, my dynamic Uncle Edward, my father's younger brother. He had just come from a year's travel around the Mediterranean. He must have been about twenty-eight, but seemed a more than adult man, bronzed and self-confident, with a square beard like a Plantagenet King. His talk was of Algiers, of the African slave market, of the Golden Horn and the Pyramids. To us it sounded like the Arabian Nights. When we asked, 'Uncle Edward, do you know the Prince of Wales?' he answered, 'Quite intimately,' with no further explanation. It was an impressive trick he had.

In that year, 1878, there was a general election in Canada. E.P. was in it up to the neck in less than no time. He picked up the history and politics of Upper Canada in a day, and in a week knew everybody in the countryside. He spoke at every meeting, but his strong point was the personal contact of electioneering, of bar-room treats. This gave full scope for his marvellous talent for flattery and make-believe. 'Why, let me see,' he would say to some tattered country specimen beside him, glass in hand, 'surely, if your name is Framley, you must be a relation of my dear friend General Sir Charles Framley of the Horse Artillery?' 'Mebbe,' the flattered specimen would answer. 'I guess, mebbe; I ain't kept track very good of my folks in the old country.' 'Dear me! I *must* tell Sir Charles that I've seen you. He'll be so pleased . . .' In this way, in a fortnight E.P. had conferred honours and distinctions on half the township of Georgina. They lived in a recaptured atmosphere of generals, admirals and earls. Vote? How else could they vote than conservative, men of family like them!

It goes without saying that in politics, then and always, E.P. was on the conservative, the *aristocratic* side, but along with that was hail-fellow-well-met with the humblest. This was instinct. A democrat can't condescend. He's down already. But when a conservative stoops, he conquers.

The election, of course, was a walk-over. E.P. might have stayed to reap the fruits. But he knew better. Ontario at that day was too small a horizon. For these were the days of the hard times of Ontario farming, when mortgages fell like snowflakes, and farmers were sold up, or sold out, or went 'to the States', or faded humbly underground.

But all the talk was of Manitoba now opening up. Nothing would do E.P. but that he and my father must go West. So we had a sale of our farm with refreshments, old-time fashion, for the buyers. The poor, lean cattle and the broken machines fetched less than the price of the whisky. But E.P. laughed it all off, quoted that the star of the Empire glittered in the West, and off to the West they went, leaving us children behind at school.

They hit Winnipeg just at the rise of the boom, and E.P. came at once into his own and rode on the crest of the wave. There is something of magic appeal in the rush and movement of a 'boom' town – a Winnipeg of the '80s, a Carson City of the '60s . . . Life comes to a focus; it is all here and now, all *present*, no past and no outside – just a clatter of hammers and saws, rounds of drinks and rolls of money. In such an atmosphere every man seems a remarkable fellow, a man of exception; individuality separates out and character blossoms like a rose.

E.P. came into his own. In less than no time he was in everything and knew everybody, conferring titles and honours up and down Portage Avenue. In six months he had a great fortune, on paper; took a trip east and brought back a charming wife from Toronto; built a large house beside the river; filled it with pictures that he said were his ancestors, and carried on in it a roaring hospitality that never stopped.

His activities were wide. He was president of a bank (that never opened), head of a brewery (for brewing the Red River) and, above all, secretary-treasurer of the Winnipeg, Hudson Bay and Arctic Ocean Railway that had a charter authorizing it to build a road to the Arctic Ocean, when it got ready. They had no track, but they printed stationery and passes, and in return E.P. received passes over all North America.

But naturally his main hold was politics. He was elected right away into the Manitoba Legislature. They would have made him prime minister but for the existence of the grand old man of the province, John

Norquay. But even at that, in a very short time Norquay ate out of E.P.'s hand, and E.P. led him on a string. I remember how they came down to Toronto, when I was a schoolboy, with an adherent group of 'westerners,' all in heavy Buffalo coats and bearded like Assyrians. E.P. paraded them on King Street like a returned explorer with savages.

Naturally, E.P.'s politics remained conservative. But he pitched the note higher. Even the ancestors weren't good enough. He invented a Portuguese dukedom (someone of our family once worked in Portugal), and he conferred it, by some kind of reversion, on my elder brother Jim, who had gone to Winnipeg to work in E.P.'s office. This enabled him to say to visitors in his big house, after looking at the ancestors, in a half-whisper behind his hand, 'Strange to think that two deaths would make that boy a Portuguese Duke.' But Jim never knew which two Portuguese to kill.

To aristocracy E.P. also added a touch of peculiar prestige by always being apparently just about to be called away, imperially. If someone said, 'Will you be in Winnipeg all winter, Mr Leacock?' he answered, 'It will depend a good deal on what happens in West Africa.' Just that; West Africa beat them.

Then came the crash of the Manitoba boom. Simple people, like my father, were wiped out in a day. Not so E.P. The crash just gave him a lift as the smash of a big wave lifts a strong swimmer. He just went right on. I believe that in reality he was left utterly bankrupt. But it made no difference. He used credit instead of cash. He still had his imaginary bank, and his railway to the Arctic Ocean. Hospitality still roared and the tradesmen still paid for it. Anyone who called about a bill was told that E.P.'s movements were uncertain and would depend a good deal on what happened in Johannesburg. That held them another six months.

It was during this period that I used to see him when he made his periodic trips 'East', to impress his creditors in the West. He floated, at first very easily, on hotel credit, borrowed loans and unpaid bills. A banker, especially a country banker, was his natural mark and victim. He would tremble as E.P. came in, like a stock-dove that sees a hawk. E.P.'s method was so simple; it was like showing a farmer peas under thimbles. As he entered the banker's side-office he would say, 'I say! Do you fish? Surely that's a greenheart casting-rod on the wall?' (E.P. knew the names of everything.) In a few minutes the banker, flushed and pleased, was exhibiting the rod, and showing flies in a box out of a drawer. When E.P. went out he carried a hundred dollars with him. There was no security. The transaction was all over.

He dealt similarly with credit, with hotels, livery stables and bills in shops. They all fell for his method. He bought with lavish generosity, never asking a price. He never suggested pay till just as an afterthought, just as he was going out. And then, 'By the way, please let me have the account promptly; I may be going away,' and, in an aside to me, as if not meant for the shop, 'Sir Henry Loch has cabled again from West Africa.' And so out; they had never seen him before; nor since.

The proceeding with a hotel was different. A country hotel was, of course, easy, in fact too easy. E.P. would sometimes pay such a bill in cash, just as a sportsman won't shoot a sitting partridge. But a large hotel was another thing. E.P., on leaving, that is, when all ready to leave – coat, bag and all – would call for his bill at the desk. At the sight of it he would break out into enthusiasm at the reasonableness of it. 'Just think!' he would say in his 'aside' to me, 'compare that with the Hotel Crillon in Paris!' The hotel proprietor has no way of doing this; he just felt that he ran a cheap hotel. Then another 'aside', 'Do remind me to mention to Sir John how admirably we've been treated; he's coming here next week.' 'Sir John' was our prime minister and the hotel-keeper hadn't known he was coming – and he wasn't . . . Then came the final touch, 'Now, let me see . . . seventy-six dollars . . . seventy-six . . . You – give – me' – and E.P. fixed his eye firmly on the hotel man – 'give me twenty-four dollars, and then I can remember to send an even hundred.' The man's hand trembled. But he gave it.

This does not mean that E.P. was in any sense a crook, in any degree dishonest. His bills to him were just 'deferred pay', like the British debts to the United States. He never did, never contemplated, a crooked deal in his life. All his grand schemes were as open as sunlight; and as empty.

In all his interviews E.P. could fashion his talk to his audience. On one of his appearances I introduced him to a group of college friends, young men near to degrees, to whom degrees mean everything. In casual conversation E.P. turned to me and said, 'Oh, by the way, you'll be glad to know that I've just received my honorary degree from the Vatican – at last!' The 'at last' was a knock-out – a degree from the Pope, and overdue at that!

Of course it could not last. Gradually credit crumbles. Faith weakens, Creditors grow hard, and friends turn their faces away. Gradually E.P. sank down. The death of his wife had left him a widower, a shuffling, half-shabby figure, familiar on the street, that would have been pathetic but for his indomitable self-belief, the illumination of his mind. Even at that, times grew hard with him. At length even the simple credit of the bar-rooms broke under him. I have been told by my brother Jim – the Portuguese Duke – of E.P. being put out of a Winnipeg bar by an angry bartender who at last broke the mesmerism. E.P. had brought in a little group, spread up the fingers of one hand and said 'Mr Leacock, five! . . .'

The bartender broke into oaths. E.P. hooked a friend by the arm. 'Come away,' he said, 'I'm afraid the poor fellow's crazy! But I hate to report him.'

Presently his power to travel came to an end. The railways found out at last that there wasn't any Arctic Ocean, and anyway the printer wouldn't print.

Just once again he managed to 'come East.' It was in June 1891. I met him forging along King Street in Toronto – a trifle shabby but with a plug hat with a big band of crape round it. 'Poor Sir John,' he said, 'I felt I simply *must* come down for his funeral.' Then I remembered that the prime minister was dead, and realized that kindly sentiment had meant free transportation.

That was the last I ever saw of E.P. A little after that someone paid his fare back to England. He received, from some family trust, a little income of perhaps two pounds a week. On that he lived, with such dignity as might be, in a lost village in Worcestershire. He told the people of the village – so I learned later – that his stay was uncertain; it would depend a good deal on what happened in China. But nothing happened in China; there he stayed, years and years. There he might have finished out, but for a strange chance of fortune, a sort of poetic justice, that gave to E.P. an evening in the sunset.

It happened that in the part of England where our family belonged there was an ancient religious brotherhood, with a monastery and dilapidated estates that went back for centuries. E.P. descended on them, the brothers seeming to him an easy mark, as brothers indeed are. In the course of his pious 'retreat' E.P. took a look into the brothers' finances, and his quick intelligence discovered an old claim against the British Government, large in amount and valid beyond a doubt.

In less than no time E.P. was at Westminster, representing the brothers. He knew exactly how to handle British officials; they were easier even than Ontario hotel-keepers. All that is needed is a hint of marvellous investment overseas. They never go there but they remember how they just missed Johannesburg or were just late on Persian oil. All E.P. needed was his Arctic Railway. 'When you come out, I must take you over our railway . . . I really think that as soon as we reach the Coppermine River we must put the shares on here; it's too big for New York . . .'

So E.P. got what he wanted. The British Government are so used to old claims that it would as soon pay as not. There are plenty left.

The brothers got a whole lot of money. In gratitude they invited E.P. to be their permanent manager. So there he was, lifted into ease and affluence. The years went easily by, among gardens, orchards and fish-ponds old as the Crusades.

When I was lecturing in London in 1921 he wrote to me. 'Do come down; I am too old now to travel; but any day you like I will send a chauffeur with a car and two lay-brothers to bring you down.' I thought the 'lay-brothers' a fine touch; just like E.P.

I couldn't go. I never saw him again. He ended out his days at the monastery, no cable calling him to West Africa. Years ago I used to think of E.P. as a sort of humbug, a source of humour. Looking back now I realize better the unbeatable quality of his spirit, the mark, we like to think just now, of the British race.

If there is a paradise, I am sure he will get in. He will say at the gate, 'Peter? Then surely you must be a relation of Lord Peter of Tichfield?'

But if he fails, then, as the Spaniards say so fittingly, 'may the earth lie light upon him.'

Twenty-one
Three Score and Ten

THE BUSINESS OF GROWING OLD

Old age is the 'Front Line' of life, moving into No Man's Land. No Man's Land is covered with mist. Beyond it is Eternity. As we have moved forward, the tumult that now lies behind us has died down. The sounds grow less and less. It is almost silence. There is an increasing feeling of isolation, of being alone. We seem so far apart. Here and there one falls, silently, and lies a little bundle on the ground that the rolling mist is burying. Can we not keep nearer? It's hard to see one another. Can you hear me? Call to me. I am alone. This must be near the end.

I have been asked how old age feels, how it feels to have passed seventy, and I answer in metaphor, as above, 'not so good.'

Now let us turn it round and try to laugh it off in prose. It can't be so bad as that, eh, what? Didn't Cicero write a book on old age to make it all right? But you say he was only just past sixty when he wrote it, was he? That's a tough one. Well, what about Rabbi ben Ezra, you remember – 'Grow old along with me.' Oh, he was eighty-one, eh? No, thanks, I'll stay right here around seventy. He can have all his fun for himself at eighty-one.

I was born in Swanmoor, a suburb of Ryde in the Isle of Wight, on December 30, 1869. That was in Victorian England at its most Victorian, far away now, dated by the French Empire, still glittering, and Mr Dickens writing his latest book on the edge of the grave while I thought out my first on the edge of my cradle and, in America, dated by people driving golden spikes on Pacific railroads.

It was a vast, illimitable world, far superior to this – whole continents unknown. Africa just an outline, oceans never sailed, ships lost over the horizon – as large and open as life itself.

Put beside such a world this present shrunken earth, its every corner known, its old-time mystery gone with the magic of the sea, to make place for this new demoniac confine, loud with voices out of emptiness and tense with the universal threat of death. This is not mystery but horror. The waves of the magic sea called out in the sunlight: 'There must be a God.' The demoniac radio answers in the dark: 'There can't be.' Belief was so easy then; it has grown so hard now; and life, the individual life, that for an awakening child was so boundless, has it drawn into this – this alley-way between tall cypresses that must join somewhere in the mist? But stop, we are getting near No Man's Land again. Turn back.

Moving pictures love to give us nowadays 'cavalcades' of events, to mark the flight of time. Each of us carries his own. Mine shows, as its opening, the sea beaches of the Isle of Wight . . . Then turn on Portchester village and its Roman castle . . . Queen Victoria going past in a train, in the dark, putting her head out of the window (her eight heads out of eight windows) . . . Now shift to an Atlantic sailing steamer (type of 1876) with people emigrating to Canada . . . Then a Canadian farm in a lost corner of Ontario up near Lake Simcoe for six years . . . Put in bears, though there weren't any . . . boarding-school, scenes at Upper Canada College – the real old rough stuff . . . University, cap and gown days, old style; put a long beard on the president; show fourteen boarding-houses at $4.50 a week . . . School teaching – ten years – (run it fast – I want to forget it) . . .

Then make the film Chicago University with its saloons of forty years ago, a raw place, nowhere to smoke . . . And then settle the film down to McGill University, and run it round and round as slowly as you like for thirty-six sessions – college calling in the Autumn, students and co-eds and Rah! Rah! all starting afresh, year after year . . . College in the snow, the February classroom; hush! don't wake them, it's a lecture in archaeology . . . All of it again and again . . . College years, one after the other . . . Throw in, as interludes, journeys to England, a lecture trip around the Empire . . . Put in Colombo, Ceylon, for atmosphere . . . Then more college years . . .

Then loud music and the Great War with the college campus all at drill, the boys of yesterday turned to men . . . Then the war over, lecture trips to the U.S. . . . Pictures of Iowa State University . . . Ladies' Fortnightly Club – about forty of them . . . Then back to the McGill campus . . . Retirement . . . An honorary degree ('this venerable scholar') . . . And then unexpectedly the war again and the Black Watch back on the McGill campus.

Such is my picture, the cavalcade all the way down from the clouds of the morning to the mists of the evening.

As the cavalcade passes down the years it is odd how gradually and imperceptibly the change of outlook comes, from the eyes of wonder to those of disillusionment – or is it to those of truth? A child's world is full of celebrated people, wonderful people like the giants and magicians of the picture books. Later in life the celebrated people are all gone. There aren't any – or not made of what it once meant.

I recall from over half a century ago a prize-day speaker at Upper Canada College telling us that he saw before him the future statesmen, the poets, the generals and the leaders of the nation. I thought the man a nut to say that. What he saw was just us. Yet he turned out to be correct; only in a sense he wasn't; it was still only us after all. It is the atmosphere of illusion that cannot last.

Yet some people, I know, are luckier in this than I am. They're born in a world of glamour and live in it. For them there are great people everywhere, and the illusion seems to feed itself. One such I recall out of the years, with a capacity for admiration all his own.

'I sat next to Professor Buchan at the dinner last night,' he once told me. 'He certainly is a great scholar, a marvellous philologian!'

'Is he?' I said.

'Yes,' my friend continued. 'I asked him if he thought the Indian word *snabe* was the same as the German word *knabe*.'

'And what did he say?'

'He said he didn't know.'

And with that my friend sat back in quiet appreciation of such accurate scholarship and of the privilege of being near it. There are many people like that, decent fellows to be with. Their illusions keep their life warm.

But for most of us they fade out, and life itself as we begin to look back on it appears less and less. Has it all faded to this? There comes to me the story of an old Carolina negro who found himself, after years of expectancy, privileged to cast a vote. After putting the ballot paper in the box he stood, still expectant, waiting for what was to happen, to come next. And then, in disillusionment: 'Is that all there is, boss? Is that all there is to it?'

'That's all,' said the presiding officer.

So it is with life. The child says 'when I am a big boy' – but what is that? The boy says 'when I grow up' – and then, grown up, 'when I get married.' But to be married, once done and over, what is that again? The man says 'when I can retire' – and then when retirement comes he looks back over the path traversed, a cold wind sweeps over the fading landscape and he feels somehow that he has missed it all. For the reality of life, we learn too late, is in the living tissue of it from day to day, not in the expectation of better, nor in the fear of worse. Those two things, to be always looking ahead and to worry over things that haven't yet happened and very likely won't happen – those take the very essence out of life.

If one could only live each moment to the full, in a present, intense with its own absorption, even if as transitory and evanescent as Einstein's 'here' and 'now'. It is strange how we cry out in our collective human mind against this restless thinking and clamour for time to stand still – longing for a land where it is always afternoon, or for a book of verses underneath a bough where we may let the world pass.

But perhaps it is this worry, this restlessness, that keeps us on our necessary path of effort and endeavour. Most of us who look back from old age have at least a comfortable feeling that we have 'got away with it'. At least we kept out of jail, out of the asylum and out of the poor house. Yet one still needs to be careful. Even 'grand old men' get fooled sometimes. But at any rate we don't want to start over; no, thank you, it's too hard. When I look back at long evenings of study in boarding-house bedrooms, night after night, one's head sinking at times over the dictionary – I wonder how I did it.

And school days – at Upper Canada College anno Domini 1882 – could I stand that now? If some one asked me to eat 'supper' at six and then go and study next day's lessons, in silence in the long study from seven to nine-thirty – how would that be? A school waiter brought round glasses of water on a tray at half-past eight, and if I asked for a whisky and soda could I have had it? I could not. Yet I admit there was the fun of putting a bent pin – you know how, two turns in it – on the seat where the study master sat. And if I were to try that now at convocation they wouldn't understand it. Youth is youth, and age is age.

So many things, I say, that one went through seem hopelessly difficult now. Yet other things, over which youth boggles and hesitates and palpitates, seem so easy and so simple to old age. Take the case of women, I mean girls. Young men in love go snooping around, hoping, fearing, wondering, lifted up at a word, cast down by an eyebrow. But if he only knew enough, any young man – as old men see it – could have any girl he wanted. All he need do is to step up to her and say, 'Miss Smith, I don't know you, but your overwhelming beauty forces me to speak; can you marry me at, say, three-thirty this afternoon?'

I mean that kind of thing in that province of life would save years of trepidation. It's just as well, though, that they don't know it or away goes all the pretty world of feathers and flounces, of flowers and dances that love throws like a gossamer tissue across the path of life.

On such a world of youth, old age can only gaze with admiration. As people grow old all youth looks beautiful to them. The plainest girls are pretty with nature's charms. The dullest duds are at least young. But age cannot share it. Age must sit alone.

The very respect that young people feel for the old – or at least for the established, the respectable, by reason of those illusions of which I spoke

– makes social unity impossible. An old man may think himself a 'hell of a feller' inside, but his outside won't justify it. He must keep to his corner or go 'ga-ga,' despised of youth and age alike . . .

In any case, to put it mildly, old men are tiresome company. They can't listen. I notice this around my club. We founded it thirty years ago and the survivors are all there, thirty years older than they were thirty years ago, and some even more, much more. Can they listen? No, not even to me. And when they start to tell a story they ramble on and on, and you know the story anyway because it's the one you told them yesterday. Young people when they talk have to be snappy and must butt in and out of conversation as they get a chance. But once old men are given rope, you have to pay it out to them like a cable. To my mind the only tolerable old men are the ones – you notice lots of them when you look for them – who have had a stroke – not a tragic one; that would sound cruel – but just one good flap of warning. If I want to tell a story, I look round for one of these.

The path through life I have outlined from youth to age, you may trace for yourself by the varying way in which strangers address you. You begin as 'little man' and then 'little boy', because a little man is littler than a little boy; then 'sonny' and then 'my boy' and after that 'young man' and presently the interlocutor is younger than yourself and says, 'Say, mister.' I can still recall the thrill of pride I felt when a Pullman porter first called me 'doctor' and when another one raised me up to 'judge', and the terrible shock it was when a taxi man swung open his door and said, 'Step right in, dad.'

It was hard to bear when a newspaper reporter spoke of me as the 'old gentleman', and said I was very simply dressed. He was a liar; those were my best things. It was a worse shock when a newspaper first called me a septuagenarian, another cowardly lie, as I was only sixty-nine and seven-twelfths. Presently I shall be introduced as 'this venerable old gentleman' and the axe will fall when they raise me to the degree of 'grand old man'. That means on our continent any one with snow-white hair who has kept out of jail till eighty. That's the last and worst they can do to you.

Yet there is something to be said even here for the mentality of age. Old people grow kinder in their judgement of others. They are able to comprehend, even if not to pardon, the sins and faults of others. If I hear of a man robbing a cash register of the shop where he works, I think I get the idea. He wanted the cash. If I read of a man burning down his store to get the insurance, I see that what he wanted was the insurance. He had nothing against the store. Yet somehow just when I am reflecting on my own kindliness I find myself getting furious with a waiter for forgetting the Worcester sauce.

This is the summary of the matter that as for old age there's nothing to it, for the individual looked at by himself. It can only be reconciled with our view of life in so far as it has something to pass on, the new life of children and of grandchildren, or if not that, at least some recollection of good deeds, or of something done that may give one the hope to say, *non omnis moriar* (I shall not altogether die).

Give me my stick. I'm going out on to No Man's Land. I'll face it.